Introducing Semantics

Semantics is the study of meaning in language. This clear and comprehensive textbook is the most up-to-date introduction to the subject available for undergraduate students. It not only equips students with the concepts they need in order to understand the main aspects of semantics, it also introduces the styles of reasoning and argument which characterize the field. It contains more than 200 exercises and discussion questions designed to test and deepen readers' understanding. More inclusive than other textbooks, it clearly explains and contrasts different theoretical approaches, summarizes current debates, and provides helpful suggestions for further reading. Examples are drawn both from major world languages, such as Mandarin Chinese, Japanese, Arabic, Spanish and English, and from minority ones. The book also highlights the connections between semantics and the wider study of human language in psychology, anthropology and linguistics itself.

NICK RIEMER is a Senior Lecturer in the English and Linguistics departments at the University of Sydney. His recent publications include *The Semantics of Polysemy: Reading Meaning in English and Warlpiri* (2005).

Cambridge Introductions to Language and Linguistics

This new textbook series provides students and their teachers with accessible introductions to the major subjects encountered within the study of language and linguistics. Assuming no prior knowledge of the subject, each book is written and designed for ease of use in the classroom or seminar, and is ideal for adoption on a modular course as the core recommended textbook. Each book offers the ideal introductory material for each subject, presenting students with an overview of the main topics encountered in their course, and features a glossary of useful terms, chapter previews and summaries, suggestions for further reading, and helpful exercises. Each book is accompanied by a supporting website.

Books published in the series:
Introducing Phonology David Odden
Introducing Speech and Language Processing John Coleman
Introducing Phonetic Science Michael Ashby and John Maidment
Introducing Second Language Acquisition Muriel Saville-Troike
Introducing English Linguistics Charles F. Meyer
Introducing Morphology Rochelle Lieber

Forthcoming:
Introducing Psycholinguistics Paul Warren

Introducing Semantics

NICK RIEMER

CAMBRIDGE
UNIVERSITY PRESS

CAMBRIDGE
UNIVERSITY PRESS

University Printing House, Cambridge CB2 8BS, United Kingdom

Cambridge University Press is part of the University of Cambridge.

It furthers the University's mission by disseminating knowledge in the pursuit of education, learning and research at the highest international levels of excellence.

www.cambridge.org
Information on this title: www.cambridge.org/9780521617413

First published 2010
8th printing 2018

Printed in the United States of America by Sheridan Books, Inc.

A catalogue record for this publication is available from the British Library.

ISBN 978-0-521-85192-3 Hardback
ISBN 978-0-521-61741-3 Paperback

to

P, P, T, F, G

you know who you are

Contents

Note to the reader

This introduction is intended for anyone coming to linguistic semantics for the first time, whether as part of a linguistics degree or independently. The best way to approach the contents is to work through the chapters in the order in which they appear. This is not the only way, however: after the first chapter, the rest of the book has a modular structure and can be read in whatever sequence the reader prefers. Chapter 1 lays out the framework for what follows and explains some important preliminary ideas; once the reader has familiarized themselves with these, they have all they need in order to begin reading anywhere else. For someone adopting this approach to the book, the glossary explains the most important recurrent terms, and can be consulted whenever an unfamiliar concept is encountered. The exercises interspersed throughout the text and at the end of each chapter are designed to deepen the reader's engagement with the material, and contain a mixture of questions of different lengths and degrees of concreteness and difficulty.

A few comments about the spirit in which the book has been written may be useful. Semantics is surely distinctive among the staple components of the introductory linguistics curriculum in the lack of disciplinary agreement over the basic theoretical questions at its centre. Langacker's (1987: 32) complaint about 'the striking lack of consensus about the proper characterization of even the simplest or most fundamental linguistic phenomena' applies in questions of meaning even more than elsewhere in the discipline, and theoretical proliferation in the years that separate us from 1987 has only increased the diversity of approaches available. This diversity is, I believe, a major source of semantics' vitality and interest, but it creates a problem for the writer who wants to present a comprehensive and balanced introduction to the field. Such basic theoretical

questions as the relation between meaning and use, the relevance of referential and truth conditional factors to linguistic meaning, the nature of presupposition, the usefulness of theta-roles in the explanation of argument structure, the relative merits of definitional and non-definitional approaches to semantic content, the semantics of aspectual categories or parts of speech, and the implications of prototype effects for semantic modelling, among many others, are all the focus of continuing debate. In this situation, questions of the way the field is presented to beginners, and of the representation given to differing theoretical perspectives, become central.

Any introduction to a discipline calls for a certain degree of simplification with respect to the various messy and unclear currents of ongoing inquiry that constitute it. But the danger is that beginning students may, through an arbitrary selectivity of theoretical perspective, be misled into believing that complex matters of genuine and legitimate controversy are in fact the objects of settled consensus. This would be a serious misrepresentation of the state of the discipline, which an introduction has the obligation to avoid. As Chomsky has noted (1995: 50), 'to make very clear the limits of understanding is a serious responsibility in a culture in which alleged expertise is given often unwarranted prestige'. There is, needless to say, nothing to be gained from a stipulative approach to basic questions, whose only result would be to perpetuate the theoretical fragmentation which is already such a striking feature of contemporary semantic investigations.

Accordingly, this introduction is intended to represent as much as is possible of the variety of ways in which meaning is currently studied in linguistics, without any one approach being privileged. Thus, although the reader will find an exposition of the bases of, among other topics, formal, cognitive, definitional, typological, structural, speech act and computational approaches, the book is not written from the unique point of view of any. No textbook, however, can fail to reflect the author's own conception of their field. But I have always tried to indicate the range of theoretical perspectives that inform linguistic semantic research, and to fairly and undogmatically indicate the attractions and disadvantages of each. In the same spirit, I have also included some discussion of recent important topics in the discipline, like semantic typology, computational semantics and corpus semantics, which are not always reflected in introductory contexts. Far from complicating things, the admission of alternative perspectives seems to me to be pedagogically desirable: beginning students find it useful to discover that the possibilities, questions and reservations which inevitably occur to them during their initial exposure to the field are often reflected in the range of differing theoretical approaches to the phenomena in question.

I have also tried not simply to present these various ideas, but to show where they come from and how they are relevant. This has been done by situating the ideas historically, by drawing out their connections with other questions confronting the empirical study of language in linguistics and elsewhere, or, simply, by making clear how they relate to each other. The aim in this has been to avoid the apparently arbitrary quality of the particular selection of topics which readers find in an introduction like this. The current state of a discipline like semantics does not reflect a unidirectional or homogeneous development, but is shaped in both outline and detail by many contingencies of different sorts. Where relevant, I have tried to comment on these, so that the reader can have some sense of the unfolding dynamics of semantic research. The further reading sections at the end of each chapter try to give some possible leads to follow in further exploration of the field.

An important part of the role of any introductory linguistics textbook, it seems to me, is to allow readers to appreciate the sheer variety of human language. The shock of confrontation with languages radically different from one's own remains as one of the most valuable consequences of my own initial exposure to linguistics, and has an important role to play within the general goals of a liberal education. As a result, I have often included examples from minority indigenous languages, as well as from major world languages like Arabic, Japanese, Chinese or English. The languages of small indigenous communities are in the process of being squeezed off the map by the forces of globalization; a linguistics textbook has an obligation not to allow them to be lost from the view of the discipline, and this needs to happen from students' first exposure to the subject. Little known languages are identified genetically and geographically on their first occurrence; the language's family is given first, at the most informative level of genetic classification, followed by its general geographical location. Citations from the unpublished Warlpiri dictionary database are marked 'WlpD'; I am grateful to the Warlpiri lexicography group for making it available to me. I am also grateful to Georgetown University Press (www.press.georgetown.edu) for permission to reprint Figure 7.1.

In writing this book I have accumulated many debts to people who read parts or all of the manuscript, supplied language data, made unpublished material available, or advised me on any number of points of detail. I never fail to be struck by the willingness and generosity with which people have answered my many requests for help, and I could not have written the book without them. It is therefore a pleasure to thank Eran Asoulin, Brett Baker, Marika Benedek, Antonio Castillo, Peter Dobrovic, Nick Evans, Marie Fellbaum, Iain Giblin, Amitavo Islam, Mark Johnston, Alex Jones, Ed McDonald, David Nash, Andrew Riemer, Craig Ronalds, Pieter Seuren, Peter Slezak, Lesley Stirling and Lawrence Warner, who all patiently and generously responded to the litany of queries I presented to them. A special thanks must go to my colleagues in linguistics at the Universities of Sydney and New South Wales, Bill Foley, Michael Walsh, Mengistu Amberber and Debra Aarons; I have appreciated their advice and encouragement enormously. In particular, I should single out Jane Simpson at the University of Sydney, who first taught me semantics, and who has been an unfailing source of wisdom ever since; several versions of the manuscript were trialled in undergraduate classes taught with her, and I am extremely grateful for her comments. Alan de Zwaan, Kristen Elliot, Olivia Rosenman, Birgit Raabe, Judith Kessel and Erin O'Brien, who were enrolled in various classes in which the book has been used, kindly gave me feedback from the reader's point of view. David Scarratt and Avery Andrews read and provided minute advice on Chapter 6, saving me from a number of embarrassing mistakes. Benjamin Schultz gave me the benefit of his wisdom on Chapters 3 and 4. James McElvenny and Nina Riemer read the finished manuscript in its entirety and suggested invaluable improvements; I am very obliged to both of them. I am also most grateful for the help in doing the research for this book provided by Winnie Chor, who not only supplied Chinese data, but also ably undertook many of the tedious and demanding tasks which the preparation of a manuscript like this entails. Helen Young also helped assemble the references and Ariel Spigelman the index. I am particularly indebted to Andrew Winnard at Cambridge University Press for his courtesy and understanding during the long gestation period of the manuscript, and to the numerous anonymous CUP referees, whose reactions and suggestions have led to many improvements. Finally, I could not have written any of this without the unique contribution of Briony Neilson, to whom the book would have been dedicated, if I did not feel that she deserves better.

1 Meaning in the empirical study of language

CHAPTER PREVIEW

In this chapter we will introduce some important concepts for the study of semantics. In 1.1 we place the notion of linguistic meaning in the wider context of human communication and behaviour. Section 1.2 then examines some of the vocabulary that English and other languages use for ordinary talk about meaning in language and related phenomena. A consideration of how this everyday non-technical vocabulary varies cross-linguistically can show some of the important different aspects of linguistic meaning. In section 1.3 the **semiotic triangle** of mind, world and language is discussed, followed in 1.4 by an introduction to five fundamental concepts:

◆ lexemes;
◆ sense and reference;
◆ denotation and connotation;
◆ compositionality; and
◆ levels of meaning.

Next (1.5), we introduce the concepts of **object language** and **metalanguage**, and distinguish a number of different possible relations between the language *in which* meanings are described (the 'metalanguage') and the language *whose* meanings are described (the 'object language'). We will then consider three different identifications of meaning: meanings as objects in the world (referents: 1.6.1), as objects in the mind (concepts: 1.6.2), and as brain states (1.6.3). An alternative identification is the notion of meanings as uses, discussed in 1.6.4. To end the chapter, we consider a view of meaning on which meanings are unobservable, hypothetical constructs posited to explain facts about language use (1.7).

1.0 What is semantics?

Any attempt to understand the nature of language must try to describe and explain the ways in which linguistic expressions have meaning. This book introduces some of the aspects of meaning studied in linguistic semantics, the branch of linguistics which, along with pragmatics, has responsibility for this task. Semantics is one of the richest and most fascinating parts of linguistics. Among the kinds of questions semanticists ask are the following:

- What are meanings — definitions? ideas in our heads? sets of objects in the world?
- Can all meanings be precisely defined?
- What explains relations between meanings, like synonymy, antonymy (oppositeness), and so on?
- How do the meanings of words combine to create the meanings of sentences?
- What is the difference between literal and non-literal meaning?
- How do meanings relate to the minds of language users, and to the things words refer to?
- What is the connection between what a word means, and the contexts in which it is used?
- How do the meanings of words interact with syntactic rules and principles?
- Do all languages express the same meanings?
- How do meanings change?

Clearly, semantics is a vast subject, and in this book we will only be able to introduce the most important parts of it. 'Meaning', however, is a very vague term. In ordinary English, the word 'meaning' is used to refer to such different things as the *idea* or *intention* lying behind a piece of language, as in (1), the *thing referred to* by a piece of language (2), and the translations of words between languages (3).

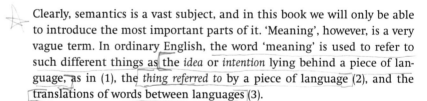

(1) '*I don't quite understand what you're getting at by saying "meat is murder": do you mean that everyone should be a vegetarian?*'

(2) '*I meant the second street on the left, not the first one.*'

(3) 'Seiketsu *means "clean" in Japanese.*'

As we will see, an important initial task of linguistic semantics is to distinguish between these different types of meaning, and to make it clear exactly what place each of them has within a principled theory of language (see Sections 1.4 and 1.6).

Each of the chapters of this book introduces some essential concepts for understanding the ways in which meaning can be analysed in linguistics. This first chapter is an introduction to the issues and concepts studied in linguistic semantics. In Chapter 2 we consider the relation between meanings and definitions. When we think about word meanings, definitions in dictionaries quickly come to mind: we know that, if uncertain about a word's meaning, we can look it up in a dictionary. This means that it is important to be clear about the similarities and differences between the aspects of meaning that interest linguists, on the one hand, and lexicographers (dictionary-writers) on the other. In Chapters 3 and 4 we discuss the relation between word meaning and word use: how do we distinguish between what a word actually means, and the way in which it happens to be used on a given occasion? Chapter 5 looks at attempts to analyse the meanings of words into sets of basic components, and discusses the problem of determining just how many meanings a given word has. In Chapter 6 we introduce some concepts from formal logic which have been fruitfully applied to the analysis of natural language meanings, and in Chapters 7 and 8 we look at the ways research inspired by psychology has been used to illuminate linguistic semantic questions, and how the results of this research can be modelled on computers. Chapter 9 explores the semantics of the parts of speech and of tense and aspect. Chapter 10 discusses the relationship between semantics and syntax, a subject which raises many important questions. Chapter 11 emphasizes a somewhat different aspect of meaning, its changeability. Meaning is always changing, both synchronically (i.e. between different speakers at the same time) and diachronically (over time). No comprehensive study of meaning can neglect this variation and change.

QUESTION How closely does the subject matter of semantics seem to correspond with what you would have thought are the main questions to ask about meaning in language?

1.1 Meaning, communication and significance

Informally, it is easy to agree that meaning is the heart of language. Meaning, we might say, is what language is *for*: to have a language without meaning would be like having lungs without air. Only when sequences of sounds or letters have (or are judged capable of having) a meaning do they qualify as language: infants' babbling and bird song, for example, use the same medium as human language – sound – but since they do not, and cannot, express meaning (except, perhaps, to the infants or the birds) we do not consider them as examples of language in the full sense of the word. Meaning is also central to the *experience* of using language, as anyone knows who has ever listened to people talking in an unknown language. Not only does such a language fail to express any meaning; it is also often hard to catch hold of individual words: without knowing the meaning of an utterance, it is hard to identify the separate words which constitute it.

Without a capacity to express meaning, then, language loses one of its essential aspects. We practically always speak or write in order to express a meaning of one kind or another. This is most obviously true for pieces of language which convey information: if someone suddenly says (4), then a meaning has been conveyed, and you are in possession of some information – whether true or false – which you may not have previously known.

(4)   *Engels was two and a half years younger than Marx.*

But not only sentences have meanings. Even the shortest, most everyday words, which we would not normally consider as containing information, like *the, not, of,* or even *ouch!,* contribute something specific to the meanings of utterances in which they occur and can thus be legitimately considered as having meanings in their own right. (For some scholars, the study of the meanings of words like these belongs as much to pragmatics and syntax as it does to semantics; we will discuss the difference between semantics and pragmatics in 1.4.4.)

QUESTION   Two apparent exceptions to the meaningfulness of language are T-shirts worn in Japan and elsewhere with 'nonsensical' English sentences on them, and people speaking in tongues at certain religious meetings. Are there other examples of this kind? Are instances of language use like this really non-meaningful? If so, what are some possible implications for semantics? If not, why not?

Although the study of meaning is extremely ancient, the name *semantics* was only coined in the late nineteenth century by the French linguist Michel Bréal. Like many other names of branches of linguistics, the word *semantics* reflects the origins of the Western tradition of linguistic analysis in the writings of Greek thinkers from the fifth century BC onwards. *Semantics* comes from the ancient Greek word *semantikos*, an adjective meaning 'relating to signs', based on the noun *sēmeion* 'sign'. In Ancient Greek, one of the original uses of *sēmeion* was as a medical term for the symptoms that were the *signs* of underlying diseases. This derivation highlights the close relation between the study of linguistic signs – words, phrases, sentences and utterances – and the study of signs in general: both artificial, conventional signs like road signs, clock faces, the symbols used in computer programs, or the 'signals' communicated by different choices of clothes; and natural signs like symptoms of disease, the level of the sun in the sky (a sign of the time of day) or tracks on the ground (the sign that an animal has passed). The study of signs in general is known as **semiotics** or **semiology** (both Greek words also deriving from *sēmeion*). In the twentieth century, the general study of signs became particularly important and the new discipline of semiotics was created, especially as the result of the work of the American philosopher Charles Sanders Peirce (pronounced 'purse'; 1839–1914) and of Bréal's student, the Swiss linguist Ferdinand de Saussure (1857–1913), often considered as the founder of modern linguistics.

   The meanings we can express through language are infinitely more numerous, detailed and precise than those expressible through other semiotic media. Yet the type of meaning found in language can be seen as a subset of two broader categories of meaningfulness: the significance of human behaviour in general, and the meaningfulness of communication specifically. There are many meaningful ways of behaving which do *not* involve language. These are not limited to those types of behaviour involving structured sets of conventional, accepted symbols like the left-right indicator lights on cars, the use of flags at sea to convey various specific messages, or the many types of symbol involving body parts (bowing, waving, nodding and shaking the head, the thumbs up/thumbs down signals, the hand signs used in baseball, etc.). Many types of intentional human behaviour can be seen as having a significance, or a meaning, in the (broad) sense of the word, since they both express, and allow observers to draw conclusions about, the nature and intentions of the participants. Someone who has just got up from their seat on the bus is probably intending to get off. Someone who suddenly stops walking down the street to search frantically through their pockets may just have realized that they have forgotten their keys. Unlike the use of language, these types of behaviour do not involve any structured set of symbols or, necessarily, any **communicative intention** and are therefore non-semiotic. The person getting up from their seat is not wishing to communicate anything to anyone, and is not making use of any structured communicative symbols: they simply want to get off. The use of fully articulated language, which does involve a communicative intention, is thus only the fullest and most explicit way in which we derive information about our environment: as a result, the meaningfulness of language can be seen as a subset of the meaningfulness of human behaviour.

QUESTION   We have just given a number of examples of conventional symbols. What are some others?

Even when an intention to communicate does exist, however, the use of language is only one of a number of ways in which the intention can be fulfilled. Take the example of someone at the dinner table suddenly choking on some food. They start to gasp, they go red in the face, their eyes water, and all they can do is make a muffled, indistinct cry. To the other people at the table, this communicates something: they realize that there is something wrong and that help is needed. As a result, they could quickly help the sufferer by giving them a glass of water or a slap on the back. This, then, is an example of some information being made known without the help of language: the person choking has just cried out, perhaps involuntarily, and this is enough to attract the attention of others, to tell them something about the current state of that person, and to stimulate them to bring the required help. Now imagine that the person choking, instead of simply crying out, articulates three quick syllables consisting simply of three choking-sounding vowels, with the middle syllable louder than the others: '*-*-*'. In this case, the other people at the table might conclude that the three cries were substitutes for the three syllables of the sentence 'I'm CHOking!', and would act on the basis of this (correct) assumption. Here, even though the speaker can only manage to articulate the syllable pattern of the intended phrase, communication

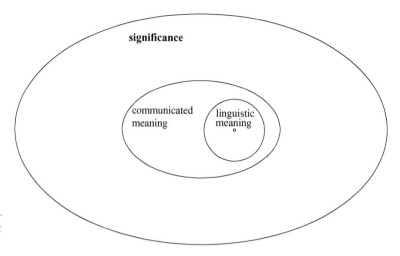

FIGURE 1.1
Significance, communicated meaning and linguistic meaning.

successfully takes place. Of course, if they had enough breath left, they could simply cry out 'I'm choking', and there would be no ambiguity. These cases show that a fully articulated sentence is not always necessary to communicate an intended meaning: the same meaning can be suggested in a variety of different ways, all of which rely on implicit conventions. The sentence expresses the intended meaning more precisely and unambiguously than the others: both the single cry and its three syllable variant are open to many interpretations, and are therefore much less reliable than the fully explicit sentence. But we can nevertheless remove the language from a communicative situation and retain much of the meaning. Situations are inherently meaningful. Meaning, we might say, is already there in the world: all we have to do is draw attention to it, and language is the most specific and unambiguous way of doing so. The different types of meaningfulness we have been discussing so far could be diagrammed as in Figure 1.1.

1.2 Talking about meaning in English and other languages

Semantics, then, is the study of meaning. But what actually *is* meaning? In Section 1.6 we will discuss some specific answers to this question. For the moment, we will make a start by looking at what place the notion of meaning has in our ordinary talk about language. The way we use the concept of meaning in ordinary language is important because it provides us with a *pretheoretical* starting point for theoretical semantic analysis, and gives us the initial vocabulary with which we can begin to identify and describe the phenomena which strike us. Informal talk about what pieces of language mean is a very common part of everyday life: we explain new words, give paraphrases of what people mean by a certain phrase or expression, sometimes translate words from one language to another in order to show their meaning. But even though we *use* the notion of meaning naturally and unproblematically, it is quite another thing to develop an explicit, rigorous *explanation* of it. In just the same way, it is one thing to talk about the movements of celestial bodies like the moon and stars – we do so, informally, all the time – but a different one entirely to have a scientific understanding of them. And since meanings cannot be seen, there is the initial question of how to pin down exactly what we are and are not supposed to be investigating. It will help us to accomplish this task if we examine the everyday vocabulary used to talk about meaning in English and other languages. This vocabulary varies considerably cross-linguistically; examining it can show some of the important different aspects of linguistic meaning, and can allow us to see how different languages impose different starting distinctions on what we, in English, call 'meaning'.

1.2.1 'Meaning' in English

English uses the verb *to mean* to refer to a relationship involving at least one of three different types of thing: language, the world (including people, objects, and everything outside of ourselves) and our own minds or intentions. Here are five typical examples of *mean* in English which exemplify some of these relationships:

(5)   *When I said 'Dublin has lots of attractions' I meant Dublin, Ireland, not Dublin, Virginia.*

(6)   *In Sydney, 'the bridge' means the Harbour Bridge.*

(7)   *'Stout' means 'short and fat'.*

(8)   *By turning off the music I didn't mean that you should go.*

(9)   *Trees mean water.*

Sentence (5) distinguishes two possible places that the speaker could have been referring to by the name 'Dublin', and specifies that only one of them was intended. This, then, is a three-way relation between a piece of language, a mind and the world: the world is represented by the two places called Dublin, language by the sentence 'Dublin has lots of attractions', and mind by the speaker's *intention* to refer to Dublin, Ireland. The second sentence is a relation between language and world, without any specific reference to people's intentions. It says that the expression 'the bridge' refers to one particular structure – the Sydney Harbour Bridge – rather than any of the other bridges in Sydney. Even though it is obviously only through the action of speakers' minds that *bridge* has this reference, there is no explicit mention of speakers' minds in (6). In (7), there is no explicit reference to either people's minds or to the world: the sentence reports an equivalence between two linguistic items, the word 'stout', according to (7), is simply equivalent in some way to the words 'short and fat'. Sentence (8) refers to a mind–world relation: it is thus like sentence (5), except that there is no language: the speaker denies that the action of turning the music off was the result of any *intention* for the guests to leave.

Sentence (9) names a world–world relationship: the presence of one type of object in the world (trees) reveals the presence of another (water).

The fact that the same verb is used in English for these non-linguistic situations as well as the linguistic ones is noteworthy if we consider the discussion in 1.1. Thus, while sentences (5)–(7) refer to linguistic meaning, sentence (8) refers to communicated meaning, and sentence (9) refers to what we have called significance. In sentence (8) (spoken, say, at a party where it has got late and there are only a few guests left), the act of turning off the music could be interpreted as a sign of the end of the party: sentence (8) is a way of saying that the speaker did not intend this. And to say that 'Trees mean water' is to say that the presence of trees allows us to conclude that there must be water nearby (compare the examples of significance in the previous section). This is a conclusion we reach simply by virtue of what we know about trees and water, and without there being any communication as such.

In ordinary English, then, we use the same verb to refer both to the meanings expressed by language and to those which are communicated non-linguistically, as well as to those which emerge, without any communication, as a result of the inherent significance of the world and human behaviour. In a number of these situations, the idea of the intention of the communicator seems to be an important part of what is being talked about through the use of the verb *mean*. But meaning is not the only way in which situations like those in (5)–(6) can be described in English: a number of other possible modes of description are also available. To see this, let's narrow the discussion down to one particular example of language – a piece which many people would think of as, simply, a mistake. Consider the following situation: Judy and Alastair are having a dinner party, and Alastair has gone out to buy a few extra plates and cups for the guests. Coming home, he says:

(10) *I've got some more cutlery for the party.*

For most speakers of English, this would count as a mistake, since 'cutlery' refers not to cups and plates, but to knives, forks and spoons. But the fact that this is a mistake in no way diminishes the need for a principled, linguistic account of it: like other branches of linguistics, semantics describes language as it is actually used and the use of a mistake as our example here will allow the relevant issues to emerge particularly clearly.

How then can we describe what is happening in (10)? In context, we can imagine three replies which Judy might make, each of which considers Alastair's 'mistake' from a different point of view:

(11) a. Judy: *Cutlery?! We've got lots of cutlery! You mean you got more* crockery!
          Alastair: *Oh yeah, crockery.*

   b. Judy: *Cutlery?! Why did you say* cutlery *instead of* crockery?
          Alastair: *Oh yeah, crockery.*

   c. Judy: *Cutlery?! You did not! You got more crockery!*
          Alastair: *Oh yeah, crockery.*

In (11a) Judy uses the category of meaning to describe Alastair's language, and says that Alastair did not actually *mean* 'cutlery': what he meant was 'crockery'. In (11b) she talks about what Alastair 'says'. Here, she could be described as talking not about language meaning, but language *use*: she notes that Alastair has used the term *cutlery* when the term *crockery* would be expected. In (11c), Judy simply denies what Alastair has said. In so doing, she can be described as applying the categories of truth and falsity to Alastair's utterance: according to her, it is simply not true that Alastair bought cutlery, a fact which Alastair then admits.

Ordinary English, then, makes available at least three different ways of talking about language: meaning, use and truth. Each of these three categories of ordinary language description highlights a particular aspect of the occurrence. Description in terms of truth places the emphasis on the objective facts of the situation by concentrating on the relation between language and reality: does the language used correspond to the actual state of affairs? Description in terms of use makes no explicit reference to the facts, but limits itself to a consideration of equivalences between the piece of language in question and an assumed norm: Alastair said *cutlery* when, in the same circumstances, most people would have said *crockery*. Lastly, description in terms of meaning places the emphasis on the speaker's intentions: for Judy to say that Alastair meant crockery is, in this context, the equivalent of saying that he *intended* to say *crockery*, and to note a discrepancy between this assumed intention and the actual words used.

As we will see in Section 1.6, each of these ordinary language modes of description has its own developed, theoretical analogue.

1.2.2 'Meaning' in Warlpiri

In English, then, the one verb 'mean' is used to describe reference, linguistic meaning, intention, and general significance. Given the frequency with which, in English, we use this verb to talk about the relations between language, intention and the world, it may be surprising to discover that there are languages which do not make use of any similar notion in order to talk about situations like those in (5)–(6) above. One such language is Warlpiri, a Pama-Nyungan language spoken in central Australia. In a sense, Warlpiri has no equivalent for the verb *mean*, and the links between reference, linguistic equivalence, intention, and general significance are quite differently constituted.

In Warlpiri, the most common way of asking about the 'meaning' of a word does not involve any verb. For example, to ask about the meaning of the word *karnta* ('woman'), one would simply say (12):

(12) *Nyiya*   *karnta-ju?*
     what   *karnta*-TOPIC
     'What is a *karnta*?'/'What does "*karnta*" mean?'

This could be translated as either 'what does *karnta* mean?' or as 'what is a *karnta*?'. And when the meaning of a word is explained or defined, once again no separate verb meaning 'mean' is involved. In the following example, for instance, the speaker is explaining the meaning of the word *ngalyarra*:

(13) *Ngalyarra   ngula-ju   yanjilypiri   panu.*
     Ngalyarra   that-TOPIC   stars   many
     'Ngalyarra – that is many stars'/'Ngalyarra means "many stars".'
     (WlpD: *ngalyarra*)

The absence of the specific verb 'mean' is characteristic of a wider set of contexts in Warlpiri; there is also very often no separate verb that would be the equivalent of 'is' in English, as the following examples show:

(14) *Ngamirliri,   ngula-ji   kirrirdipardu.*
     curlew   that-TOPIC   tall
     'The curlew is tall.' (WlpD: *ngamirliri*)

(15) *Jajirdi   kuyu   wita.*
     native cat   animal   small
     'The native cat is a small animal.' (WlpD: *jajirdi*)

The result of this is that Warlpiri makes less of a distinction than English between what a *word* means, and what its *referent* actually *is*. To say what a word means is simply to describe the object or situation it refers to. Language–world relations are described in the same way as world–world ones.

　Warlpiri does, however, have a way of explicitly mentioning the language-user, as can be seen in the following example:

(16) *Mirni-nya   karnalu   wurnturu ngarri-rni.   Kala mirnimpa,*
     mirni-FOCUS   1PL.SUBJ   far   call-NONPAST   but   mirnimpa
     ngula-ju   kutu-pardu   karnalu   ngarri-rni.
     that-TOPIC   close-rather   1PL.SUBJ   call-NONPAST
     'We use *mirni* to mean far, whereas by *mirnimpa* we mean rather close.' (WlpD: *mirnimpa*)

But the verb used here, *ngarri-rni*, which simply means 'call', does not make any reference to the speaker's intentions, an important component of the notion of 'meaning' in English. The literal meaning of (16) is something like 'we call far things *mirni*, whereas we call close things *mirnimpa*.' This is simply a fact about language use: *ngarrirni* 'call' makes no reference to any intention of the speaker, and the verb *manngi-nyanyi* 'think, intend', is not typically used to refer to the meaning of words.

1.2.3 'Meaning' in French

Whereas, in Warlpiri, the meanings of words are not discussed in the same terms as the intentions of speakers, in French there is a close link between these two domains. The most common way of expressing 'mean' in French is the expression 'vouloir dire', which literally means 'to want to say.' To ask 'what do you mean?' in French is to ask 'what do you want to say?' Talking about meaning in French, then, inherently involves talking about volition ('wanting'), as in the following expressions:

to want to say

(17) *Qu'est-ce   que   tu   veux   dire   par   cela?*
     what is it   that   you   want   to say   by   that?
     'What do you mean by that?'

(18) *Que   veut   dire   cette   phrase   latine?*
     what   wants   to say   this   phrase   latin
     'What does this Latin phrase mean?'

(19) *Que   veut   dire   ce   vacarme,   cette   agitation?*
     what   wants   to say   this   clamour   this   agitation
     'What does this clamour and agitation mean?'

(20) *Le baromètre a   baissé;   cela   veut   dire   qu'   il*
     the barometer has   gone down   that   wants   to say   that   it
     va   pleuvoir.
     is going   to rain
     'The barometer has gone down; that means it's going to rain.'

As (19) and (20) show, this is even the case when talking of what words, phrases and non-linguistic things mean: as in English, the same expression is used to refer both to the meaning of language, and the meaning of non-linguistic occurrences. *Vouloir dire* is not, of course, the *only* word available in French for the expression of ideas about meaning; the verb *signifier* (from the Latin *signum* 'sign' and *facere* 'to make') has a similar sense. Another contrast between French and English is that unlike in English, the French words that express the noun 'meaning' and the verb 'to mean' are not related. In French the noun 'meaning' is translated by the word *sens*, from which English gets the word 'sense', and which has a similar range of meanings: as well as referring to linguistic meaning, *sens* refers to the perceptual senses (sight, hearing, etc.), to a direct and intuitive grasp of something (e.g. a 'sense' of rhythm), as well as having the meaning expressed in English by saying that something 'makes sense'. Just like *vouloir dire*, then, *sens* classes linguistic meaning together with certain inner, subjective processes of human consciousness; not, however, as in the case of *vouloir dire*, volitional ones, but ones connected with the faculties of perception and judgement.

1.2.4 'Meaning' in Chinese

In Mandarin Chinese, there is no single word with the same range of meanings as English *mean* or *meaning*. The verb *zhi*, whose core meaning is 'point', can express all of the relations between mind, language and world discussed in the previous sections, except the world–world relation. Thus, we find *zhi* used for the mind–language–world relation, as in (21):

(21) *Dang*   *wo*   *shuo* 'Coles', *wo*   *shi*   *zhi*   *Central*   *de*
     when   I   say   'Coles' I   BE   point   Central   POSS
     'Coles',   *bu*   *shi*   *TownHall*   *de*   *'Coles'*.
     'Coles'   not   BE   TownHall   POSS   'Coles'
     'When I say "Coles", I mean the "Coles" in Central but not the
     "Coles" in Town Hall.'

As well, it can be used for the language–world relation:

(22) *Zao-can*   *shi* *zhi*   *zao-shang* *chi* *de*   *yi*   *can.*
     breakfast   BE   point   morning   eat   POSS   one   meal
     '"Breakfast" means the meal you have in the morning.'

Zhi may also be used to specify a word's translation:

(23) *'Linguistics'*   *shi* *zhi*   *yu-yan-xue.*
     'Linguistics'   BE   point   yu-yan-xue
     '"Linguistics" means *yu-yan-xue*.'

However, when a monolingual definition is given, the noun *yi-si* 'meaning' is typically used:

(24) *Miao-tiao*   *de*   *yi-si*   *shi*   *shou* *ji*   *xian-xi*
     'Miao-tiao' POSS meaning   BE   thin   and   delicate
     '"*Miao-tiao*" means thin and delicate.'

Yi-si is also used in a way that parallels the English use of *meaning* to express the language–mind relation:

(25) *Wo*   *ming-bai*   *ne*   *de*   *yi-si.*
     I   understand   you   POSS   meaning
     'I understand what you mean.'

A native speaker explains *yi-si* here in the following way: 'the speaker is conveying the message that he can reveal what's in the hearer's mind and the intention behind it. It is actually similar to saying "I understand what you are thinking about"' (W. Chor, p.c.). But *yi-si* cannot be used for the world–world relation:

(26) *Jin-qian de   *ji-si*   *shi quan-li.*
     money-POSS   meaning   BE power
     'Money means power.'

To express this, *deng-yu* 'equal' may be used:

(27) *Jin-qian* *deng-yu*   *quan-li.*
     money   equal   power
     'Money means power.'

We thus find that, taken together, the translations of *mean/meaning* in Mandarin have a similar range of senses to their English equivalents, except that Mandarin has no equivalent to *money means power* or *clouds mean rain*. However, the fact that the verb meaning 'point' is the basic way of expressing the verbal notion brings in a connection between meaning and gesture which is not familiar from English.

1.3 The semiotic triangle: language, mind, world and meaning

We have seen in the previous section that a number of languages, including French and English, make an important connection in their standard vocabularies between language and the world of inner conscious processes like volition, perception and intention. Other languages, by contrast, like Warlpiri, seem to bypass this connection by talking about the meaning of language in the same terms used to talk about the identity of things in the world. All of these relations are important. To describe meaning fully, we seem to have to make reference to three principal terms: language, the world, and the human mind. Following Ogden and Richards (1949: 10), these three aspects of the meaning phenomenon are often symbolized as the 'semiotic triangle', as shown in Figure 1.2 below.

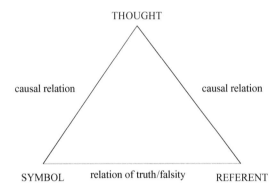

FIGURE 1.2
The semiotic triangle.

At the top of the triangle is what Ogden and Richards called 'thought'. This reflects the fact that language comes from human beings, and is therefore ultimately a product of processes in the mind or brain. But 'thought' can be a misleading label for these processes, for two reasons. First, these mental processes need not be conscious. Even though we sometimes do consciously think about what we are going to say, our speech is more often spontaneous, emerging without our being aware of any preliminary stage of mental preparation. Since it is the brain that produces language, we know that some such preliminary stage must have taken place, but since this stage is so often unconscious, the label 'thought' is not the most appropriate (see Chapter 11 for more discussion).

The second reason that 'thought' is an unfortunate label for the mental processes at the origin of speech is that it excludes the non-rational, emotional side of our inner life. The processes leading to speech should not be limited to what we would class simply as 'thinking', but extend to include our emotions and volition as well. This is most obviously true with exclamations: exclamations of pain, surprise or happiness often do not reflect anything we would describe as a 'thought', but rather reflect a particular feeling. The same is true for many other types of words, like diminutives, which may correspond to feelings of (roughly) affection; and imperatives, which may be accompanied by feelings of control, superiority, pride, etc. Evaluative words more generally, expressing the speaker's emotional attitude, often force us to recognize a strong emotional component. Thus, 'marvellous', 'wonderful', 'fantastic' and 'good'; and 'appalling', 'terrible', 'frightful' and 'bad' and their synonyms express more than the fact that the speaker approves or disapproves of whatever is being referred to: crucially, these adjectives are often associated with particular positive or negative *feelings* in the speaker. In order to remove the unwanted implication that the mental processes leading to speech are purely conscious and non-emotional, we can replace 'thought' in Ogden and Richards' diagram with the more neutral term 'psychology'.

QUESTION   Apart from emotion, what other aspects of psychology are relevant to the production and understanding of language? Which are of the most relevance to linguistic meaning?

The leftmost point of the triangle, the 'symbol', is the most straightforward. The symbol, in this terminology, is whatever perceptible token is chosen to express the speaker's intended meaning. In the case of spoken language, the symbols will be strings of speech sounds, in the case of written language, they will be marks on the page, and in the case of sign languages, they will be particular handsigns. Since in this book we are exclusively concerned with linguistic communication, we can replace the broader term 'symbol' with the simple 'language'.

The last apex of the triangle is the 'referent', or whatever things, events or situations in the world the language is *about*. Thus, the sentence *the dogs bark, the caravan goes by* has as its referent a particular situation: a situation in which certain dogs bark and a certain caravan goes by. Within that sentence, the expressions *the dogs* and *the caravan* also have referents: the actual dogs and caravan being spoken about. Note that someone who hears this sentence does not necessarily know what the exact referents of these nouns are; in the absence of any special knowledge about which dogs and caravans are being referred to, a hearer could only identify the dogs and caravan in question if the sentence was spoken when they were actually present (and even then they would have to assume that the hearer was talking about the dogs and caravan at hand, not some others).

This leads to the important point that we do not have any access to the world as it actually, objectively is. The only referents we can know are ones which are perceived by our senses or imagined in our minds: ones for which, in other words, we have **mental representations** (see 1.6.2 below). The dogs and caravan in question are only available and known to us insofar as they can be **represented**, that is perceived, remembered, or otherwise thought about by us. The world of referents, that is, must be considered not as a world of real external entities, but as a world of representations which are *projected* by the mind. Another way of putting this would be to say that the world of referents is *within* the domain of psychology. As humans with minds, we have no access to *the* world, with a definite cast of fixed, pre-established referents. All we can know, and all that can be relevant to our understanding of language, is the world as it is represented by our minds through perception, memory, imagination or other experience. And since we are all different, the ways in which we perceive, remember or imagine referents are also likely to differ in some ways.

QUESTION   What problems might the existence of differing representations of the same referent pose for understanding meaning?

We can now consider the relations between the three points of the triangle. First, note that psychology has a causal relation to both referent and symbol. On the side of the symbol, the causal relation to psychology is explained by the fact that, as already observed, it is our minds that create language by choosing and constructing the particular linguistic expressions used. It is in our psychology that the decision to speak is made, and the particular words used are chosen. In the case of the referent (which, as we have already seen, must itself already be considered as within the domain of psychology), the causal relation comes from the fact that in using language we intend our words to have a certain referent. For example, if I point to a car parked on the street and say 'that car has its lights on' I intend my words to refer only to the car in question, and not to any of the others that also happen to be present. I have, in other words, chosen this car, rather than another, as the referent of my words, and I expect the hearer of my words to do the same.

In contrast to the causal relations on the psychology-symbol and psychology-referent sides of the triangle, there is no causal relation between symbol and referent. Words have no direct relation to the things they stand for. There is no inherent relation between a string of sounds and a particular referent: this is the reason that different languages use entirely different words for the same thing. The only reason *dogs* refers to dogs and *caravan* refers to a caravan is that these are the referents which English speakers have learnt to associate with them, and this is a fact about people's psychology rather than an essential connection between the words and the objects to which they refer. Even **onomatopoeic** words like the names for animals' calls (e.g. 'cuckoo', 'moo', 'quack' and 'meow'), which might be thought to constitute an exception to this rule, since their sounds are similar to the calls they represent, are not in fact any different. Even though there is certainly a similarity between word and referent, this similarity is a conventional one which, just as for other words, has to be learned (that is why different languages represent these sounds differently: for example, 'quack' in French is *coin-coin*). The connection between onomatopoeic words and their referents is thus mediated by the psychology of language users.

In light of these remarks, we can redraw the semiotic triangle as in Figure 1.3:

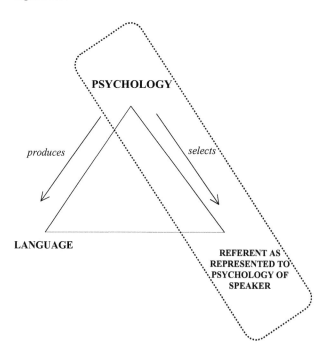

FIGURE 1.3
The semiotic triangle, re-labelled.

1.4 Some initial concepts

In this section we introduce some important concepts which we will need in the chapters that follow. The exposition here is only preliminary; each concept will receive a more detailed treatment later in the book.

1.4.1 Lexemes

To linguists and non-linguists alike, the *word* is the most basic and obvious unit of language. But in many languages, units which we would want to recognize as a single word can appear in many different morphological forms. Thus, in English, *go, goes, went, have gone* and *to go* are all forms of the verb *to go*. Other languages have many more morphological variants of a single word-form. In Ancient Greek, for example, a single verb, *tithēmi*, which means 'put', has several hundred different forms, which convey differences of person, number, tense and mood, such as *e-thē-ka* 'I put', *tithei-ētēn* 'you two might put', *thō-men* 'let us put', etc. But these different forms only alter some aspects of the meaning of the word. Both *go* and *tithēmi* share a large component of meaning between their different forms: *tithēmi* always has the sense 'put', and the forms of the verb *to go* always have the sense 'go', regardless of whether the sentence in question is 'I went' or 'you have gone'. For this reason, a semantic description does not need to treat all the variant morphological forms of a single word separately. The lexeme is the name of the abstract unit which unites all the morphological variants of a single word. Thus, we can say that *go, goes, went, have gone* and *to go* all are instantiations of the lexeme *to go*, and *e-thē-ka*, *tithei-ētēn* and *thō-men* are all instantiations of the lexeme *tithēmi*. We usually refer to the lexeme as a whole using one of the morphological variants, the **citation form**. This differs from language to language: for verbs, for example, English, French and German all use the infinitive as the citation form (*to go, aller, gehen*), whereas Warlpiri uses the non-past form of the verb (*paka-rni* 'hitting', *yi-nyi* 'giving').

Not all languages have a word for 'word'

Not all languages have a word corresponding to English 'word': Warlpiri, again, makes no distinction between 'word', 'utterance', 'language' and 'story', all of which are translated by the noun *yimi*. In Cup'ik (Yup'ik, Central Alaska), the word for 'word' also means 'sayings, message' and 'Bible' (Woodbury 2002: 81). Dhegihan (Siouan, North America) has a single word, *íe*, referring to words, sentences and messages (Rankin *et al.* 2002).

1.4.2 Sense/reference/denotation/connotation

As we have already seen, the English word 'meaning' is rather vague. One important distinction we can make within the general notion of a lexeme's meaning is between its **sense** and its **referent** (or **reference**). To simplify the introduction of these terms, we will confine our discussion to nouns; we will see in 1.6.1 how they apply to other lexical categories.

The sense of a lexeme may be defined as the *general meaning* or the *concept* underlying the word. As a first approximation, we can describe this as what we usually think of as contained in a dictionary entry for the word in question, although we will see later that this characterization needs significant modification. The notion of sense can be made more explicit through contrast with the category of referent. A word's **referent** is the object which it stands for on a specific occasion of use. For example, consider (28):

(28) *The queen has fallen off the table.*

If I am talking about a rowdy evening at Buckingham Palace in 2009, the referent of the word *queen* is Her Majesty, Elizabeth II, and the referent of the word *table* is a particular piece of English royal furniture. But if I am talking not about Elizabeth II but about Queen Margrethe of Denmark, the words *queen* and *table* have different referents: not Elizabeth II and the English piece of furniture, but Margrethe and the Danish one. On each of the occasions (28) is uttered, there is one and only one referent of each word.

A word's referent, then, is the particular thing, person, place, etc. which an expression stands for on a particular occasion of use, and it changes each time the word is applied to a different object or situation in the world. (As we will see in Chapter 3, not all uses of nouns are referring, but we will ignore this for the moment.) By contrast, a word's sense does not change every time the word takes on a new referent. Regardless of whether the referent of *queen* is Elizabeth II or Margrethe, its sense is something like 'female reigning monarch'. This is not to say, however, that 'female reigning monarch' is the *only* sense of the word *queen*. Another sense of *queen is* 'second highest ranking piece in a game of chess'. This would be the sense involved if I uttered (28) while talking about a game of chess in the café, where *queen* would refer to a particular chess piece. Yet another sense of the word *queen* is 'third highest card in a suit, behind ace and king': this would be the sense involved if I uttered (28) in reference to a game of bridge at the kitchen table. In these two cases, *queen* does not only have two new different referents, the particular chess piece and the particular card, but two new different senses as well: 'second highest ranking piece in a game of chess' and 'third highest card in a suit, behind ace and king'. In *all* the utterances of (28), by contrast, 'table' has the single sense 'piece of furniture with raised flat surface used for putting things on, eating at, etc.'. Obviously, words like *queen* and *table* stand for many different people and objects in the world: they have, in other words, many different referents. The referents change each time we talk about a different queen, or a different table. The entire class of objects, etc., to which an expression correctly refers is called the expression's **denotation**.

Words have the referents they have by virtue of a certain act on the part of the speaker, which we will call the act of **reference**. We will use this term to describe what the speaker does in applying a particular language expression to a particular referent in the world. In uttering (29), for example,

(29) *Dr Schreber suffered his first illness in the autumn of 1884.*

the speaker *makes reference* to a certain person, Dr Schreber, to a certain disease, his first illness, and to a certain time, the autumn of 1884. These individual objects are the referents of the words in (29), and it is only in virtue of an act of reference, undertaken by the speaker, that the words 'Dr Schreber', 'first illness', and 'the autumn of 1884', have the referents they do. Since reference is an act, it is subject to exactly the same problems as all other human ventures, and it may not be successful. Thus, if I suddenly say to you 'I saw that cat again', and you don't know what cat I mean, reference will not have been successful. Even though I, as speaker, have referred to a particular cat, you (the hearer) are not able to **recover the referent** intended, i.e. identify the cat in question.

Reference, referents and denotation

Some writers use the term **reference** and **denotation** interchangeably, but in this book we will distinguish the two. An expression's denotation is the class of possible objects, situations, etc. to which the word can refer. The term *reference*, by contrast, has two uses:

- as the name of the act by which a speaker refers to a referent;
- as a synonym of *referent*, i.e. as the term for the object(s) to which an expression refers on a particular instance of use.

In this book, we will not try to distinguish these two senses of *reference* with separate terminology. *Reference* sometimes means the act of referring, and sometimes means a referent. The context will remove any doubt about which sense is intended.

Sense, reference and denotation are three aspects of what is commonly conveyed by the loose term 'meaning'. A fourth, very important aspect of meaning is **connotation**. Connotation names those aspects of meaning which do not affect a word's sense, reference or denotation, but which have to do with secondary factors such as its emotional force, its level of formality, its character as a euphemism, etc. 'Police officer' and 'cop', for example, have very different connotations, but similar denotations, as do the following pairs:

(30) *brat* and *child*
 toilet and *rest room*
 country town and *regional centre*
 underprivileged area and *slum*
 mutt and *dog*
 doctor and *quack*
 incident and *accident*

We will consider connotation again in Chapter 11.

QUESTION Think of some other pairs of words in English or any other language you know which have different connotations. Would you also want to say that they have different senses?

1.4.3 Compositionality

All human languages have the property of **productivity**. This is simply the fact that the vocabulary of any given language can be used to construct a theoretically infinite number of sentences (not all of which will be meaningful), by varying the ways in which the words are combined. For example, given the words *the, a, has, eaten, seen, passing, contemporary, novelist* and *buffalo*, the following figure among the large number of meaningful sentences that can be constructed:

(31) *The novelist has seen the buffalo.*
    A novelist has eaten the buffalo.
    A contemporary novelist has seen a buffalo.
    The novelist has seen a passing buffalo.
    A buffalo has eaten a passing contemporary novelist

and so on. (We can also construct ungrammatical sentences like *A the novelist eaten passing has*, but since these are meaningless we will ignore them here.) Most people have probably never heard (32) before:

(32) *There are no remains of ancient Indian aircraft technology*

yet, as speakers of English, we understand immediately what it means. How does this ability arise? One answer is that meaning is **compositional**. This is to say that the meanings of sentences are made up, or **composed**, of the meanings of their constituent lexemes. We understand novel sentences because we understand the meanings of the words out of which they are constructed. Since we know the individual meanings of *there, are, no, remains, of, Indian,* and so on, we know the meaning of any grammatical sentence in which they are combined. On the contrary, if a novel sentence contains a word which we do not know, we do not know what the sentence means. Thus, if you are told that *the distribution of seats was aleatory*, and you do not know that *aleatory* means 'random', then the sentence, taken as a whole, will not be meaningful. It is important to note that not all combinations of words are necessarily compositional. One especially important category of non-compositional phrase is **idioms**. For example, if I say that so-and-so has *thrown in the towel*, most English speakers will recognize that I am not talking about anyone literally 'throwing' a 'towel', but that I simply mean that the person in question has given up on whatever venture is being spoken about. The phrase *throw in the towel*, then, is *not* compositional, since its overall meaning, 'to give up', does not derive from the meanings of its individual component lexemes.

QUESTION   In the following sentences, which of the highlighted expressions can be considered compositional, and which are idioms? Do any belong to some third category?

*If you **keep on** making that noise I'll **go through the roof.***
*He's just **kicked the bucket.***
*Stop **dragging the chain**: we'll never get there.*
*We've run out of time, so we'll have to **wrap things up**.*
*Can you **run off** twenty more copies?*
*After the delay the plane **took off** as normal.*
*I'll **take** twenty per cent **off** the price.*
*This is a **nice and hot** cup of tea.*
*My hands are **lovely and warm**.*
***Try and get** a better deal next time.*
Hello down there!

Based on the distinction between the meanings of words and the meanings of sentences, we can recognize two main divisions in the study of semantics: **lexical semantics** and **phrasal semantics**. Lexical semantics is the study of **word meaning**, whereas phrasal semantics is the study of the principles which govern the construction of the meaning of phrases and of **sentence meaning** out of compositional combinations of individual lexemes.

1.4.4 Levels of meaning

The distinction between word meaning and sentence meaning, then, defines a basic contrast between lexical and phrasal semantics. Another important contrast is the one between **sentence meaning** as just described and **utterance meaning**. We can define sentence meaning as the compositional meaning of the sentence as constructed out of the meanings of its individual component lexemes. But the meaning of a sentence as built up out of its component parts is often quite different from the meaning it actually has in a particular context. In everyday talk we regularly use words and expressions ironically, metaphorically, insincerely, and in other 'non-literal' ways. Whether there is any principled theoretical difference between these non-literal ways of talking and the literal ones, and, if so, what it is, is an important question which we will discuss in Chapter 7; for the moment, we can simply recognize that there are many uses in which words seem to acquire a strongly different meaning from the one they normally have. Suppose that while cooking Peter has just spilled a large quantity of spaghetti carbonara all over the kitchen floor. Hearing the commotion, Brenda comes into the kitchen, sees what has happened, and utters (33)

(33) *You're a very tidy cook, I see.*

It is clear that Brenda doesn't literally mean that Peter is a tidy cook, but that she is speaking ironically. What she actually means is the opposite of (33): Brenda is drawing attention to the fact that Peter has precisely *not* been a tidy cook. In cases like this, we say that there is a difference between sentence meaning and utterance meaning. The sentence meaning of (33) is the literal, compositional meaning as built up from the meanings of the individual words of the sentence. If we did not speak English, we could discover the sentence meaning of (33) by finding out what its translation was in our own language. The **utterance meaning**, by contrast, is the meaning which the words have on a particular occasion of use in the particular context in which they occur. (Utterance meaning is sometimes referred to in other books as **speaker meaning**. But since the role of the hearer is just as important as that of the speaker, the more neutral term **utterance meaning** is preferred here.) The utterance meaning is the one which is picked up in the conversation. In reply to (33), Peter might well say (34):

(34) *I'm sorry. I don't know how I could have been so clumsy.*

But if Brenda's comment in (33) was meant literally, the reply in (34) would be very strange: people do not usually have to apologise for being tidy. What (34) shows is that it is the utterance meaning, not the sentence meaning of (33) to which Peter is reacting: given the situation, Brenda is clearly not congratulating him on his tidiness as a cook, and it is the utterance meaning which forms the basis for the continuation of the conversation.

The distinction between sentence meaning and utterance meaning is also linked to the difference between **semantics** and **pragmatics**. For those linguists who accept such a division, semantics is taken to study sentence meaning, whereas pragmatics studies utterance meaning and other principles of language use. The job of semantics is to study the basic, literal meanings of words as considered principally as parts of a language system, whereas pragmatics concentrates on the ways in which these basic meanings are used in practice, including such topics as the ways in which different expressions are assigned referents in different contexts, and the differing (ironic, metaphorical, etc.) uses to which language is put. As we have already seen, a division between semantics and pragmatics is by no means universally accepted in linguistics. Many 'pragmatic' topics are of central importance to the study of meaning, and in this book we will not recognize any absolute distinction between the two domains.

1.5 Object language and metalanguage

Like any other branch of linguistics, semantics deals with the words, phrases and sentences with which we communicate. But for semantics the immediate objects of study are not these words, phrases and sentences themselves, in the sense of the sounds, sequences of letters or handsigns which we utter or perform and can then write down or record. As the study of meaning, semantics is interested in something which cannot be perceived directly through our senses, but which, in one way or another, we *experience* in using and thinking about language. We cannot see, hear or touch a word's meaning: meanings are things we understand. It is not meanings that go between speaker and hearer: the only things that are transferred from one speaker to the other are sound waves in the air. This means that in order to get started in semantics, we need a way of identifying meanings and bringing them to light in an unambiguous way so that we can begin to study them.

The main way in which we normally reveal the meanings of linguistic expressions is, quite simply, by describing them in language. But since it is language that we're interested in in the first place, we need to distinguish between the language *whose* meanings we want to describe and the language *in which* we couch the descriptions. The language whose meanings we are describing is called the **object language**. The language in which we describe these meanings is called the **metalanguage**.

When we propose a metalanguage description of the meaning of an object language expression, we are using one type of meaning (the meaning of the metalanguage expression) to explain another kind (the meaning of the object language expression). Let us take the example of English as the metalanguage for Dutch, as would be the case if we were explaining the meaning of the Dutch word *groot* to an English speaker. One possible metalanguage explanation, or **definition**, that we could give of *groot* in English would be the word 'tall', as in (35):

(35) *Dirk is groot, maar Lou is klein.*
    'Dirk is tall, but Lou is short.'

The object language expression *groot* is here defined by the metalanguage expression 'tall'. But note that not all aspects of the word 'tall' are relevant to this definition: it is completely irrelevant to the definition of *groot* that the metalanguage definition we have chosen, 'tall', has four letters, or is a monosyllable, or starts with the consonant /t/. All these phonetic and orthographic details are irrelevant to semantics, since the only thing that matters for the purpose of defining *groot* is what 'tall' *means*. To tell someone that *groot* means 'tall' is to make a statement about two meanings, and to say that these two meanings are the same. The particular phonetic and other characteristics of the metalanguage term are therefore irrelevant: as long as the person for whom the definition is intended understands the meaning of 'tall' in English, the definition is successful.

This confronts us with an interesting problem. For couldn't it be objected that, in one way, we haven't actually explained anything when we define *groot* as 'tall'? We have certainly given a definition of the word which will help an English speaker to understand the meaning of the Dutch sentence. But if we want to go beyond the problem of allowing people to translate from one language to another, hasn't our analysis left something crucial out? On hearing our explanation that the meaning of *groot* is 'tall', someone might easily object by pointing out that this explanation only shows an equivalence between two words in English and Dutch, and does nothing to explain what this meaning, which both *groot* and *tall* express, actually *is*. 'I know what *groot* means in English', they might say, 'but you haven't told me what it actually is for something to mean something.' And even though we could go on to give a more detailed explanation of 'tall', perhaps using terms like 'elevated in stature', 'not short', etc., for as long as we continue to explain the meaning of a word by using the meanings of other words, we will not have satisfied our objecter's curiosity.

For many linguists, this objection is rather forceful. As long as we go on defining meanings by other meanings, we leave out the essential task of explaining what meaning actually is. We can see this very clearly by considering the case of **circular definitions**. Consider someone who wants to find out the meaning of the English word 'humorous'. One possible definition of 'humorous' would be 'droll'. But this definition would only be effective if the meaning of 'droll' was already known. If it was not, it too would need to be explained: 'droll', perhaps, could be plausibly explained through the metalanguage definition 'amusing'. 'Amusing', in turn, could be defined as 'funny', as in (36).

(36) humorous ⇒ droll ⇒ amusing ⇒ funny.

Depending on the person for whom the definition was intended, this chain of definitions would sooner or later achieve its purpose: if the person knew the meaning of 'funny', we could stop the explanation at this point, so that 'humorous' would have been defined through 'droll', 'droll' through 'amusing', and 'amusing' through 'funny'. It is obvious, however, that this chain could not go on for ever. Sooner or later we would run out of new words: if the language learner did not know even what 'funny' meant, we can imagine giving up in frustration, and saying, simply, '*funny* just means "humorous"'. In this case, it's clear that our unfortunate language learner would be none the wiser, since 'humorous' was the word whose meaning was originally in question. Since 'humorous' has been used both as an object language term and a metalanguage term, the definition is **circular** and does not succeed in telling us anything new:

(37) humorous   ⇒   droll
       ⇑   ⇓
     funny   ⇐   amusing

Clearly, then, for as long as we remain within the circle of definitions by substituting one word or phrase as the definition of another, we remain confined within language. The lexical resources of any language are limited: at some point, the metalanguage definitions will *have* to include object language terms, and thereby introduce circularity. We can continue to refine our definitions and search out the most precise and explanatory ways of couching them, but in contenting ourselves with this task we will not have provided any account of what the meanings we are defining actually are, nor of how they relate to any of the three points of the semiotic triangle. In particular, we will have left it completely obscure what it is for a speaker to understand the meaning of a word. If I understand the meaning of 'droll', then the definitional chain can be stopped. But what does it mean to say that I understand the meaning of 'droll'? What is it that I actually understand? For many linguists, the fact that we cannot answer these questions about meaning by remaining inside the definitional circle means that we have to look outside language for answers. If linguistics is to play a part in explaining the way language can be actually used by real speakers, we need to find a point at which the circle can be broken in order to link meaning in with something non-linguistic. We will consider a few proposals about how this could be done in the next section.

1.6 Breaking the circle

As pointed out by Quine (1961: 47), until the development of 'a satisfactory explanation of the notion of meaning, linguists in semantic fields are in the situation of not knowing what they are talking about'. This is perhaps not such a dire situation as it sounds: after all, empirical investigation always aims to increase our knowledge of some unknown phenomenon, provisionally characterized using ordinary language. As the inquiry proceeds, we get a sharper idea of the nature of the thing being studied, and it may not matter that in early stages we have to rely on notions for which we cannot yet give any satisfactory explanation. Many fields of empirical inquiry begin with only hazy and imprecise conceptions of the real object of their investigation. The history of genetics is a case in point. Mendel, acknowledged by most historians as the founder of the field, discovered the principles of inheritance without any understanding of either chromosomes or DNA, both of which later became central parts of the theory of cell biology. The fact that his advances were thus made in ignorance of the fundamental nature of inheritance does not in any sense discredit them: Mendel might not have known exactly what his discoveries were ultimately about, or what the mechanisms were that implemented the facts he observed, but his rigorous investigations meant that he was able to reach valuable conclusions which would only be fully characterized later. The fact that he could not have precisely characterized the nature of the phenomenon he was observing was not an obstacle to progress (see Gribbin 2002: 536–541 for discussion).

Still, to say the least, it would obviously be *useful* if we had some initial idea about what meaning is best thought of as being – of how, in other words, we can break the definitional circle. This preliminary idea will help us to formulate the best set of specific questions to ask in our investigation. In this section, we will consider several suggestions about how the definitional circle might be broken and the notion of meaning explicated in a way which might satisfy objections like Quine's.

1.6.1 Meanings as referents/denotations

One way to break the definitional circle would be to stress the role of the referent or denotation as the main component of the meaning of a linguistic expression. Under this theory, metalanguage explanations of a meaning should be seen as names of the referents of the object language term. As we saw in Section 1.2.1, ordinary discourse about language in English often seems to make an implicit identification between an expression's meaning and its referent:

(38) *In Sydney, 'the bridge' means the Harbour Bridge.*

The 'meaning' of 'bridge', the speaker of (38) seems to be suggesting, is the actual harbour bridge itself. 'Bridge', we might say, *means* what it *refers to*; its meaning on any one occasion of use *is* its referent. Outside of the narrow context of (38), we could say that the meaning of *bridge* in general is just its denotation – the class of all bridges. This identification of meaning and referent/denotation succeeds in breaking the circle because it identifies meaning with non-linguistic objects in the world: the meaning of 'bridge' on a particular instance of use is the real bolts and metal structure. Given this interpretation of the meaning of 'bridge', it doesn't matter that we would eventually run out of new words with which to define it, since we can ultimately analyse its meaning **ostensively**, i.e. simply by pointing at the actual bridge itself.

As was pointed out in the discussion of the semiotic triangle (1.2.1), the referents of expressions must be taken not as actual objects in the world, but as representations in the world as projected by the speaker. This means that in order to understand reference we already have to invoke the realm of speakers' individual psychologies, the particular 'versions' of the world as projected by their psychology. The postulation of the world of projected representations allows us to avoid an objection which might otherwise count against referential theories of meaning. This is the objection that it is often the case that there simply is no referent for a given expression, as in (39a–c), or that the referent is unknown, as in (39d–f):

(39) a. *The German victory in World War II*
     b. *Robin Hood's private helicopter*
     c. *The water on the Moon*
     d. *The most distant point from Earth*
     e. *The first person ever to use language*
     f. *The fate of the environment*

A theory which identified meanings with *real world* referents would have to say that the expressions in (39a–c) simply have no meaning, since the things they refer to never actually existed, or are impossible; and it would have to say that the meaning (referent) of the expressions in (39d–f) was unknown, since although we can be confident that all of the things referred to by the expressions exist, we do not know what they are. But if referents are taken to be representations projected within the realm of people's psychology rather than real objects in the actual world, this problem disappears. Whether or not there is any object referred to by the words *Robin Hood's private helicopter*, we can easily think of situations in which a speaker might simply imagine, pretend or otherwise entertain the possibility that such a helicopter did exist. For the speaker of (39b), then, the referent of *Robin Hood's private helicopter* can be taken as the speaker's representation of the helicopter in their projected world. The reader will easily see that similar explanations can be constructed for the other examples in (39).

The identification between meaning and reference may be successful in breaking the definitional circle, but it leads to a very fragmented picture of the nature of language: on the reference theory of meaning, 'bridge' has as many different meanings as it has different referents. This variety clashes with our pretheoretical intuition that the meaning of *bridge* is actually something much more unitary: although there are many different individual bridges out there in the world, the meaning of the word *bridge*, or, we might say, the *concept* of a bridge is a unified, single entity.

The idea that an expression's meaning is its referent is at least easy to understand for nouns referring to discrete, concrete things. But it is much less clear what the referents of other lexical categories might be. What are the referents of abstract nouns like *scandal, generosity* or *impermanence*? Since there is no isolable object in the world to which these nouns apply, the notion of a referent is rather hard to invoke. And what about adjectives like *sweet, polished* or *ineffectual*, or verbs like *to have, to allow* or *to go*? In the case of 'grammatical' words the problem is even greater: what is the denotation of *of*, or of *the*? These cases all pose problems for the referential theory of meaning: because the words have no referents/denotations, they are left without any specifiable meaning. Yet it is obviously the case that these words *do* have meanings, which we can paraphrase metalinguistically and explain to others. We will consider this question further in Chapter 6.

A second problem with the theory of meaning as reference is the fact that a single referent may often be referred to by a variety of different expressions. Thus, the expressions in the two halves of (40a–d) each pick out just a single individual:

(40) a. *The first country to adopt a law requiring parental leave; the home country of IKEA*
   b. *The most frequently handed in, and the least frequently claimed, object on the Tokyo subway; portable device with handle used for protection against rain*
   c. *The inventor of Chupa Chups; friend of Salvador Dali and husband of Nuria Serra*
   d. *Institution for lending money; institution for depositing money*

In (40a) we have alternative ways of referring to Sweden, in (40b) of umbrellas, in (40c) of the Spanish confectionery king Enric Bernat Fontlladosa, and in (40d) of the word *bank*. Yet we surely do not want to say that the meanings of these expressions are the same. While the objects referred to by the expressions 'institution for lending money' and 'institution for depositing money' have the same denotation – banks – they clearly don't have the same sense. We could imagine a bank which suddenly stopped lending money even though it continued to accept deposits: something like this, indeed, happened during the Argentinian financial crisis of 2002 and the global one of 2008. If meaning simply *is* reference/denotation, then examples like this should not be possible. The fact that linguistic expressions can be identical in reference but different in meaning leaves us no choice but to conclude that there is more to meaning than reference/denotation.

1.6.2 Meanings as concepts/mental representations

The referential/denotational theory of meaning broke the definitional circle by emphasizing the referent side of the sense/referent pair. Another way out of the circle is to identify meanings with **concepts**: the metalanguage definitions of an object language meaning, in this theory, are the names of the concepts associated with the object language term. The use of the term 'concept' in linguistics derives from philosophy, where it has a very long history of discussion and controversy. For our purposes, concepts can be seen as a way of talking about the basic constituents of thought. In the words of Prinz (2002: 1) '[w]ithout concepts, there would be no thoughts. Concepts are the basic timber of our mental lives.' As we will see later, many investigators think it is necessary to distinguish between **primitive** concepts and others. On this view, our stock of concepts is built up from a stock of primitive concepts, which cannot themselves be broken down into any constituent parts. This level of primitive concepts is the bedrock of the whole conceptual system; all other concepts can be analysed into combinations of these simpler primitives, just as all molecules can be analysed down into their basic component atoms. For the moment, we will not distinguish between primitive and non-primitive concepts; we discuss the distinction in detail in Chapters 2 and 8.

If we imagine the process of thinking as a sort of internal conversation with ourselves, then concepts are the individual words and expressions of which this conversation consists. Concepts are implicated in practically every aspect of our mental lives. It is on the basis of concepts that we determine things' identity: if I want to know whether some animal is a mammal or a marsupial, for example, I subconsciously compare its properties against the properties of the concepts MAMMAL and of MARSUPIAL. Concepts are also needed to explain how we recognize objects in the world as themselves: if I know, when looking at a golf ball, that it is a golf ball, it is because the visual image accords with my concept GOLF BALL. Similarly, it is because of the involvement of concepts that our thought has continuity: if I am studying semantics, for example, I am progressively refining concepts like MEANING and REFERENCE with which I understand the functioning of language, and it is the same concepts MEANING and REFERENCE which are developed over the entire time I am studying. We have concepts corresponding to abstract words like *democracy*, *possession* or *time*, but equally for everyday ones like *hand*, *red*, *go*, *hungry*, *anticlockwise* and *up*.

One very common way of describing language in the Western tradition, going back to Aristotle, is to see language as *communicating ideas*: on this understanding, we choose the particular words we use in order to achieve the closest fit with the particular ideas we have. And, indeed, as pointed out by Reddy (1993), we often talk, in English and many other European languages, as though language was a receptacle into which we put ideas in order to transfer them to the hearer, as in (41):

(41) *There are a lot of ideas in that sentence.*
    You can get the same meaning across in different ways.
    I can put the same idea in different words.

Language, then, is often spoken about as though it was the 'conduit' for ideas. A natural extension of this common understanding of language is that what words actually mean are ideas or concepts. Thus, the meaning of the word 'tolerant' is our concept TOLERANCE: when we say 'Oliver is tolerant', we are attributing to Oliver certain properties which together define our concept TOLERANCE, like patience, kindness, respect for the opinions of others, and so on. These properties can be thought of as combined together into the concept TOLERANCE, rather like the different components of a definition of *tolerance* in a dictionary.

The hypothesis that meanings are concepts has considerable attraction. First, it answers to the intuition that language is intimately connected with the rest of our mental lives. It does seem precisely to be *because of* the thoughts and concepts we have that we use the words we use. If I say 'horse-drawn carriages are old-fashioned', then this will often be because this is exactly what I think: I am reporting a link between the concepts HORSE-DRAWN CARRIAGE and the concept OLD-FASHIONED. Language and thought are very hard to tease apart: whether or not we always think 'in language', we often need to use language to externalize the results of our thought, to bring these results into the public domain for the purposes of communication, and it seems to be in language that most of our ideas can be given their most precise form. Since there is this clear causal connection between language and thought, the idea that the meanings expressed through language correspond to concepts is a neat way of effecting the link between the world of public, external communication and our private, mental lives.

Second, the conceptual theory of meaning has often been taken to explain compositionality and relations between meaning. The concept HORSE-DRAWN CARRIAGE can be seen as built up from the concepts HORSE and the concept CARRIAGE, as well as some third element corresponding to the word 'drawn'. Similarly, the meaning of the linguistic expression *horse-drawn carriage* has these very three elements (at least), and they can be individually changed to create different expressions with different meanings. In such cases, we can explain the changed meanings as corresponding to changed concepts. Thus, instead of a horse-drawn carriage, we can imagine an *ox-drawn carriage* or a *horse-drawn plough*: in these cases, we have substituted the concepts OX and PLOUGH for HORSE and CARRIAGE, and these substitutions explain the altered meaning of the expressions. The conceptual hypothesis also explains certain other links between the words 'horse drawn carriage' and other words. For example, a little reflection will reveal that HORSE-DRAWN CARRIAGE is a member of the more inclusive concept MEANS OF TRANSPORT, and is linked, by association, with such concepts as COACHMAN, PASSENGER, REINS, WHEEL, etc. It is these conceptual links which ultimately explain the comprehensibility of sentences like (42a) and (43a), and of how they are different from those of (42b) and (43b):

(42) a. *A horse-drawn carriage is an old-fashioned means of transport.*
    b. *A horse-drawn carriage is an old-fashioned cheese.*

(43) a. *The coachman jumped down from the horse-drawn carriage.*
    b. *The sunrise jumped down from the horse-drawn carriage.*

The meaning of (42a) and (43a) is clear and easily understood because the words all express related concepts. But since the concepts expressed as the meanings of the words in (42b) and (43b) are not inherently connected, the meaning of these sentences is much harder to interpret.

Meaning relations like **synonymy** (sameness of meaning) are also easily explained by the conceptual hypothesis. Two words are synonyms if they have the same meaning. And 'having the same meaning' means 'instantiating the same concept'. Thus, 'Islamic' and 'Muslim' might be said to be synonyms, because the corresponding concept, which we can either refer to as MUSLIM or ISLAMIC, is identical.

Third, the hypothesis that meanings are concepts guarantees the genuineness of communication. Because meanings of words are concepts, two people who talk, agree or disagree about something are doing more than 'playing with words'; they are talking, agreeing or disagreeing about certain concepts, which are being compared and progressively reconciled with each other during the exchange. And as the concepts are complicated, easy, familiar or unfamiliar, so are the meanings. It is therefore the level of concepts that guarantees that genuine communication between people can actually take place.

What form do concepts take psychologically? This is an extremely controversial question. An answer favoured by many linguists, adopted from philosophy and cognitive science, is that concepts have the form of symbolic **mental representations**. Mental representations are the fixed mental symbols – the 'language of thought' – which are instantiated in our minds in some stable, finite medium, and which our thought consists in. On the view of concepts as mental representations, thinking and expressing meaning are both to be understood as the manipulation of mental symbols, in much the same way that using language is the manipulation of a fixed series of linguistic symbols in the medium of air, paper or hand-signs. Communication, then, involves using the conventional names for individual mental representations. Since these individual mental representations belong to a language-like format in which the contents of mental events are expressed or recorded in the mind, their 'translation' into the words of natural language follows readily.

There are, however, a number of reasons we should be cautious in the claim that meanings correspond to concepts. We will mention only three now. First, some words seem more naturally compatible than others with an interpretation of their meanings as concepts. Thus, while it seems quite plausible to say that the meanings of *democracy, punctuation, panorama,* or *love* are concepts, this move is less obvious for words like *ouch!, me, you* or *this,* or so-called 'function' words, like *if, not, like* or *very.* Words like these do not seem to be able to call up the rich range of associations and inherent connections which characterize *democracy, love,* etc. The point here is not to rule out the possibility that the meaning of all these words may in fact correspond to concepts, but simply to suggest that the initial intuitive plausibility of this is not as great.

QUESTION　Can you propose any 'conceptual' content for the above words? What about words like *brown, zig-zag* or *bitter*? If so, what is it? If not, why not?

Second, just like meanings, concepts cannot be seen or otherwise identified unambiguously. This means that their postulation is not immediately
controllable by objective, empirical means. Psychologists and psycholin-
guists have certainly developed experiments in which the properties of
particular hypothetical concepts can be experimentally tested, but this
has only been done for a fraction of words, largely from well-known languages, and, like any experimental result, the conclusions are open to a
variety of interpretations. It is therefore unclear, given the present state of
research, whether the postulation of concepts is scientifically justifiable,
or whether it is simply a term we have adopted from our untutored, pretheoretical views about the nature of our mental lives. There is, of course,
no *in principle* problem with postulating unobserved entities in semantics –
any science works by postulating the existence of unobserved (and sometimes unobserv*able*) factors which are hypothesized to explain the
observed facts. It is simply that, in linguistics, the detailed experimental
work is only starting to be done that would put these unobserved entities
on a more solid empirical footing.

Third, even if an expression's meaning can partly be identified with
the concept it evokes, there must be more to it than that. For example,
if I say the words *Wallace Stevens was a poet and an insurance broker*, I do not
mean that my *concept* of Wallace Stevens was a poet and an insurance
broker: I mean that a certain real person, Wallace Stevens himself, was.
Part of what I mean, then, is the actual, real-world person that my words
refer to. And this real-world person could prove to have quite different
properties from the ones reflected in my concept of him. For example, I
might mistakenly believe that Wallace Stevens is the author of *Death of a
Salesman*: that fact, then, forms part of my concept of Wallace Stevens.
But this doesn't mean that when I say *Wallace Stevens was a poet and an
insurance broker* I am saying something false, even though it isn't true
that the author of *Death of a Salesman* was a poet and an insurance broker. What makes my words true does not depend on the concept I have
of Wallace Stevens, but on who this expression refers to. This isn't just
the case with proper names. Imagine that I'm confused about the difference between lyrebirds and bowerbirds. I can tell the two apart, but I
wrongly believe that lyrebirds are the birds that decorate their nests,
and that bowerbirds are the birds that are incredibly good mimics.
When I tell someone that *the bowerbird has just come back*, my meaning
isn't just that 'the bird that is an incredibly good mimic' has just come
back; it's that *that particular bird* (whatever it's actually called) has just
come back. So while we might want to say that words express certain
concepts, there does seem to be an important referential component to
meaning which goes beyond concepts.

The hypothesis that meanings correspond to concepts has been very
popular in linguistics. For many semanticists, this hypothesis is not, as it
might appear, an alternative to an identification of meaning with reference or denotation, but is rather complementary to it. This is because
under the conceptual theory of meaning the semanticist's task is not
simply over once the referents and denotations have been identified for

the words under investigation. Concepts can be identified with senses, the general meanings of words as considered separately from their specific reference on any given occasion of use. Thus, once we have identified the referents and so the denotation of the noun *fire*, we can go on to explore the features of our *concept* FIRE which may be relevant to language. These features go beyond the mere identification of the objects denoted by the word. For example, we will discover that there is a close link between our concept FIRE and such other concepts as HOT, FLICKERING, DANGEROUS, BURN, RED etc. These conceptual links are useful for three reasons. First, they explain the compatibility between the word *fire* and words like *hot*, *flickering*, *dangerous* and *burn*, in just the same way as for examples (42a) and (43a) above, and account for the fact that these words will often occur in similar contexts in actual language. Second, the conceptual theory can explain certain *extended meanings*, such as that some hot things like intense summer weather or spicy food may also be described with the adjective 'fiery': presumably this has something to do with the close conceptual link between our concepts HOT and FIRE. Last, and most important, the postulation of the concept FIRE as the meaning of *fire* explains why *fire* has the referents it has. Thus, to the question 'why are these things, and not different ones, called *fires*?', the conceptual theory of meaning gives the reply 'because only these objects, and not others, accord with the concept FIRE which the word *fire* expresses'. Clearly, these are extremely informal explanations. Nevertheless, the only reason that even this low level of explanatory depth is possible is the presumed link between language and concepts. If we could analyse the meaning of *fire* no further than by itemizing a list of its referents, none of these commonsense observations about the relation of *fire* to other words would be justified. The conceptual theory of meaning thus provides a convenient rationale for a fruitful investigative practice, and justifies many commonsense observations about meaning.

QUESTION   How might concepts provide an answer to some of the problems of the referential/denotational theory of meaning?

1.6.3 Meanings as brain states

A natural thought about meaning is to identify it with brain states: understanding or intending a certain meaning, on this identification, would just be having the neurons of one's brain in a particular configuration. From one point of view, this identification seems very plausible. After all, isn't language ultimately a product of our brain? If we understood how the brain works, wouldn't we understand all the details of language, semantic ones included? Isn't it only the rudimentary state of our current understanding of brain processes that prevents us from giving the details of this identification? According to this line of thinking, semantics, along with the rest of linguistics, will one day be **reduced** to, or unified with, brain science, in the same way that the classical theory of genetics can be reduced to or unified with that of molecular biology. In other words, once brain science has progressed, we will no longer need the technical vocabulary of semantics, but will be able to talk wholly in terms of synaptic connections, neurotransmitters, proteins and so on. In just the same way, the modern language of molecular biology, involving chromosomes, nucleotides and DNA sequences, has at least partly replaced the older one of genes as the best way of describing the details of inheritance.

This is an attractive position in many ways: brain states must ultimately cause all behaviour, including language. But it is going too fast to conclude from this that we will eventually be able to *identify* meanings with brain states and reduce semantics to brain science. The first obstacle is that it's hard to see how brain states could have the properties that meanings have. Meanings, the way we normally think of them, have mutual connections to each other – of synonymy, antonymy, class inclusion and so on. For example, the meaning 'cat' has the following relations with other meanings:

- it is an instance of a broader class of meanings, 'mammals', 'domestic animals', 'four-legged animals' and so on;
- it is, in some sense, the 'opposite' of the meaning 'dog';
- it can be synonymous with the meaning 'feline'.

These are facts about the meaning of *cat* that we will presumably want a theory of semantics to reflect. It is not clear, though, how this could happen in a theory which identified meanings and brain states. How can one brain state be the opposite of, or synonymous with, another? The brain is just physical matter; it makes as little sense to say that a state of brain matter is the opposite of, or synonymous with, another as it does to say the same of the state of the electrons in my computer at any one time. It therefore seems that meanings have a property which prevents them from being completely identified with brain states.

This problem is just one instance of the broader problem of **intentionality**. Intentionality is the term philosophers use to describe the essential *aboutness* or *contentful nature* of language. A word like *cat* has a certain psychological content: it refers to (is about) a certain class of creatures, cats. The same is true of a verb like *sit*: this refers to, or is about, a certain class of actions, the actions of sitting. Many philosophers think there is something deeply special about intentionality, in that it is a property that is distinctively mental: purely physical things like my brain or my computer, which consist of configurations of electrons, just aren't the types of thing which can possess intentionality. Electrons, whether in my brain or in my computer, aren't about anything; they're just *there*. As a result, any attempt to simply identify something intentional like language with something non-intentional like a brain state cannot be successful.

How do we square this with the obvious truth that it is the brain that is ultimately responsible for linguistic production and understanding? If meaning is one of the factors to be taken into account in the production of utterances, and if brain processes will ultimately explain the *whole* production of utterances, then surely they must explain meaning too! It would just be illogical to say that everything that happens in language is determined by brain processes, and in the same breath to exclude meaning. Here we need to invoke the concept of **levels of explanation** or **levels of description**, an important notion in cognitive science discussed by Marr (1982). Attending to the notion of levels of explanation/description will show us that there is room for *both* intentional meanings *and* non-intentional brain states in our explanations of language.

Consider a computer chess program. There seem to be several levels on which we can describe and explain what the program is doing. The first is the informal level, on which we describe the computer as simply following the rules of chess with the aim of beating its opponent. A particular move might be described as 'castling to protect the king', for example, or 'taking a pawn', or 'sacrificing the bishop'. This mode of description uses ordinary, everyday vocabulary of the sort we could also use for explaining people's behaviour. It makes reference to beliefs, intentions, and desires: the computer's belief that its king could be threatened, its desire to protect it, and its intention to castle in order to achieve this. In one way, the computer doesn't really have beliefs, desires or intentions, of course, but we talk as though it does, since this is a useful way of describing and understanding what is happening. Let's call this the **intentional** level of explanation.

A second, lower level of explanation is more detailed: this level consists in specifying the different steps of the program that the computer is running. This explanation wouldn't use the ordinary terms of everyday intentional, psychological explanation, but would lay out the sequence of individual input and outputs that the computer processes. The computer has some way of representing the input positions (the position of the pieces after each move), and a set of algorithms for turning inputs into outputs in a way that makes it likely to win. Let's call this the **algorithmic** level of explanation. Understanding this level will give us a detailed way of predicting what the computer is going to do next: if we have access to the specific program it is running, we can work out its next move in advance. Notice that there are several different ways in which the intentionally described actions the computer performs could be realized algorithmically. There's more than one possible chess program that a computer could run, yet all of them produce behaviour which is open to a single type of intentional explanation: the difference between different chess programs disappears at the intentional level of explanation where, whatever program the computer is actually running, we can still always describe it as 'castling to protect the king', 'taking a pawn', 'sacrificing the bishop' and so on. The details of the program become invisible as we move to the higher level.

Finally, there's the lowest level, the level of **implementation**: this is the level of description/explanation which concerns the specific way in which the algorithm is instantiated physically in the particular machine involved. Just as a single fact on the topmost intentional level can correspond to several different states on the lower algorithmic level, so a single algorithm can be implemented in multiple ways in an actual physical machine. This is most obvious if we think about the difference between the most up-to-date type of computer, which runs on a solid-state drive, a conventional one using a spinning hard disk, and an old-fashioned one using magnetic tape or punch cards. All these machines can run the same algorithms, but the physical details of how they do so are completely different.

Clearly, all three levels of explanation are necessary to understand what is going on when the computer plays chess. Since there is a variety of possible physical realizations of the program on the implementational level, the next highest level, the algorithmic one, gives us a powerful way of abstracting from the details of the actual physical system that is performing the operations and describing the inputs and outputs of the program. But it is the intentional level that is the most relevant when we ask *why* the computer is behaving as it is. The intentional level, which consists of explanations like 'protecting the king', 'taking a pawn', 'sacrificing the bishop', makes sense of the computer's actions as a chess-player, not just as a machine. The algorithms and their physical instantiations are just a meaningless sequence of actions if we can't place them in the context that allows them to make sense, and it is only the intentional level that does this. Marr (1982) draws an analogy with trying to understand bird flight: we can't understand bird flight by limiting ourselves to feathers, the implementational level. We have to go beyond this to look at the wider place of feathers within a complex of notions like lift, air pressure, energy, gravity, weight and so on. Studying the physical constitution of the feathers in the absence of these other considerations will be fruitless.

Language is arguably the same way. Studying brain states will only tell us how language is implemented. It will tell us nothing about the higher-level relations that tie this implementation in with the rest of our psychology. As a result, meanings are unavoidable as part of the explanation of utterances. If I tell you that *my head is killing me*, then part of the explanation for my utterance involves my belief that my head hurts, my desire to communicate this fact to you, and the fact that those words convey that idea *as their meaning*. I could have expressed the same belief in a number of different ways, for example by saying *I've got a migraine*, or *my headache's come back*, or by clutching my head and saying *the usual problem again* in a long-suffering tone of voice. Since each of these utterances is expressed differently, they would correspond to different brain states. But we can concisely capture what they have in common by appealing to the level of their meaning: even though the brain states that produce them are different, they are united by the similarities of the meanings they convey. Just talking about brain states makes this elementary generalization impossible.

Especially at the current rudimentary stage of our knowledge of the brain, then, we have no choice but to continue to appeal to meanings in our explanations of language. Brain states are too complicated and too variable (both within and between individuals) to allow us to capture the straightforward generalizations we can capture using the intentional vocabulary of meaning. Meanings are the thread that guides us through the variety and confusion of brain states and input–output sequences; only by invoking meanings can we relate language to human behaviour and psychology in general. Understanding brain states will be important for understanding language, but not at the expense of meaning. Studying brain states will tell us *how* the brain does what it does. Studying meaning as part of an intentional level study of human psychology and behaviour will tell us *what* it is doing and *why* it is doing it. It is thus a confusion of explanatory levels to claim that meaning can be reduced to brain state.

1.6.4 Meaning and use

An alternative to the three previous theories is the view that a word's meaning consists simply in the way it is used. This is the **use theory of meaning**, and it has been advanced, in different forms, by behaviourist psychologists such as Skinner (1957), and linguists such as Bloomfield (1933). (A rather different, non-behaviourist use theory was advanced by Wittgenstein 1953.) Behaviourist proponents of the use theory typically reject the very notion that words have hidden, unobservable properties called meanings: since meanings are inherently unobservable, it is, they would claim, unscientific to use them in explanations. (This argument would no longer be accepted by philosophers of science: scientific explanation *usually* involves unobservables.) Use theorists have claimed that the only objective, scientific way to explain language is to avoid postulating unobservable objects called meanings, and to attend only to what may actually be observed, the particular sequences of words and expressions that occur in actual examples of language use, and to describe the relation between these linguistic forms and the situations in which they are used. According to these investigators, the explanatory task of semantics is to provide not an abstract characterization of meanings, whether interpreted as concepts or denotations, but a causal, predictive account of the way a given language is actually used. In the words of Skinner (1957: 5), 'What happens when a man speaks or responds to speech is clearly a question about human behavior', and the only correct way to answer it is to proffer a precise account of what linguistic behaviour is likely to be produced in different situations.

Thus, for Bloomfield (1933: 139), the only *meaning* a linguistic form has is 'the situation in which the speaker utters it and the response which it calls forth in the hearer'. To take a particularly simple example, one of the 'meanings' of 'sorry' in English might be described as a situation where the speaker apologises; the hearer's typical response will be to treat the utterance as an apology and behave accordingly (e.g. by letting the incident drop, by not accusing the speaker of rudeness, by themselves saying sorry, etc.). We can describe this situation without having to make any reference to a 'meaning' of *sorry*: external analysis of the situation is all that is needed.

QUESTION   Can the meanings of the following words be described in terms of situations? *Hi, please, you, apple, thanks, this*

The project of specifying the uses of linguistic units is not as remote as it might seem from the traditional semantic project of describing denotations or senses. Indeed, the traditional notion of meaning itself is ultimately aimed at explaining language-use, since it is the meaning of individual linguistic expressions that is taken to explain the way they are used: words are used *in accordance with* their meanings. For proponents of the use theory of meaning, we should directly describe the actual situations themselves in which language is spoken or written, rather than doing this via the intermediary notion of meaning. When we have developed a full theory of the way in which speakers actually use language, then the goal of semantics will have been fulfilled.

The main objection against use theories of meaning is simply the mind-boggling variety of the situations in which linguistic forms may be used. As Bloomfield acknowledges, the number of different situations in which language is used is infinite. There are very few, if any, linguistic expressions which are automatically called up by a specifiable external situation. If the meaning of a linguistic form is the situation of the speaker's utterance and the hearer's response, there will be very few words for which a description like the one just given for *sorry* would even *seem* plausible. It would not seem to be a feasible project to specify the situations in which most of the words in the previous paragraph are used, since they are not highly context bound and can be used in practically any situation. Think of some of the possible situations in which the noun *way*, for example, might be used. To catalogue these, we would need to know the individual circumstances of a representative number of speaker/hearer pairs in whatever linguistic community we were investigating, including what was referred to by *way* on each occurrence of use, the situation which prompted the speaker to utter it, and the response given by the hearer. For even straightforward, unremarkable instances of *way* like *I don't know the way* or *which way is quicker?* this will already involve a huge variety of different specific situations. But if we add instances where *way* is used sarcastically, metaphorically, dishonestly, or simply by mistake, it will be clear that the use theory is massively complicated, and that the extraction of any regularities or generalizations about language use will be extremely complicated (Chomsky 1959 has classic objections against this kind of use theory of language).

The prospects for a use theory might be better if the focus changes from the individual word to higher-level linguistic units. It does seem to be the case that there are many phrases and sentences which have a more predictable relationship to their situations than the individual words of which they are composed. Thus, conversational routines like greetings, invitations, asking for the time, congratulating, wishing luck and many others involve highly stereotyped instances of language such as those in (44), which are to some extent predictable from the situations in which they occur.

(44) *how are you?*
    do you have the time?
    good luck
    congratulations!
    have a nice weekend.

Yet in spite of the perhaps greater possibilities at the phrase level, the problem for the use theory of meaning remains the enormous variety of sentences which make up any individual's linguistic behaviour. Even if there are some very stereotypical phrases which crop up more or less predictably in given situations, this does not detract from the huge number of phrases and sentences uttered by a language user which are novel. The use theory of meaning, in other words, seems to ignore the compositionality of language. It is *because* the meanings of sentences are built up out of the meanings of words that we can put words into different combinations to suit new communicative needs, including in situations which we have never previously encountered. The situations in which language is used are constantly changing, yet we do not mysteriously lose our ability to communicate. A theory of meaning must be able to explain how it is that we can use old words to convey *new* meanings which have never been previously conveyed, in situations in which we have never previously been placed.

QUESTION   Do obsolete, old-fashioned or archaic words pose a problem for the use theory? If so, why? If not, why not? Do the conceptual and referential/denotational theories fare any better?

1.7 Meaning and explanation

We've now considered four proposals about the nature of meaning: meaning as reference/denotation, meaning as concepts, meaning as brain states and meaning as use. What conclusions can we draw? One particular conclusion concerns the status of the term 'meaning' itself. Even though the notion of a word's meaning can be used to facilitate many tasks on the level of practical language use (explanation of new words, translation from one language to another, prescriptive regulation of disputes over usage, etc.), and seems indispensable on the intentional level of explanation discussed in 1.6.3, we should consider the possibility that 'meaning' is essentially a *pretheoretical*, informal notion which will not have any precise equivalent in a detailed account of linguistic behaviour on the other two levels.

QUESTION   What are some other everyday, pretheoretical notions about language which have to be abandoned for the purposes of 'scientific' linguistics?

Perhaps, then, we do not need to choose between the different theories of meaning discussed in the previous section. As suggested in 1.2, 'meaning' can be seen as a shorthand way of talking about a whole variety of separate phenomena which are all individually important in our talk about language, especially on the intentional level of explanation, but which do not necessarily correspond to any single entity that will be revealed by careful empirical study. The English language category 'meaning', in other words, which in any case only has approximate equivalents in other languages, might have no precise role in a full understanding of language.

By contrast, the various aspects of meaning that we have distinguished in this chapter – reference, conceptual content, connotation, and so on – are all factors for which linguistic semantics *does* owe a principled explanation, and for which it should try to find theoretical analogues. There is no single way of breaking the definitional circle: 'meaning' is many different things, none of which should be ruled out as irrelevant to the eventual explanation of language.

In this context, we can specify an important condition that any principled theory of language must meet. This condition is linked to the idea that the ultimate goal of research into language must be to contribute to the *causal explanation* of people's utterances. To achieve a thorough understanding of our linguistic ability, we will eventually need to be able to specify the detailed causal mechanisms which lead up to the production of utterances by speakers in real time. In order to achieve this, we will need a precise account of what the various phonological, semantic, morphosyntactic and semantic properties of different linguistic forms are, and of the ways in which these properties are combined in actual discourse sequences in different contexts of use. This goal is exactly the same as the one aimed at in other sciences: chemistry, for example, specifies the various properties of different molecules, in virtue of which they enter into sequences of causal interaction with each other, and embryology aims at understanding the properties of fertilized cells, in virtue of which a step-by-step understanding of their development into full organisms can be achieved. In the case of linguistics, the detailed nitty-gritty of a causal account is a long way off. What is more, the fine detail of an account of linguistic behaviour on the implementational level will have to be provided by neurolinguists and other brain scientists who will be able to isolate the physiological underpinnings of linguistic phenomena. The semanticist's role is an earlier one, which consists in isolating the important properties of the linguistic system, on the intentional and perhaps algorithmic levels, for which these experimental scientists will need to find the physical mechanisms.

The distant goal of a causal account of language behaviour, however, suggests a possible role for the notion of meaning in semantics. From this perspective, we can suggest that to talk about a word's meaning is a shorthand way of talking about *whatever property of a word could enter into causal explanations of its use*. In our ordinary talk about language, one of the main functions of the category of meaning is to explain word use: we use the words we use because of the meanings they have. But in order to go beyond this pretheoretical level and explain a word's use in a rigorous way, which might be ideally compatible with a causal account of language, a word's meaning may include many different explanatory properties and necessitate consideration of referents *and* concepts *and* situations of use.

As a result, we do not need any single, categorical answer to the question of whether meaning is denotation *or* concepts *or* uses. To phrase the question as a set of exclusive choices like this is counterproductive, since it may well turn out that *all* of these categories will need to be invoked in order to explain the use of different words. Thus, as we noted at (44), there is a subclass of words and phrases in any language whose use seems particularly closely linked to certain recurrent and specifiable situations; the most obvious way of explaining the use of these words is to associate them with the particular contexts and situations in which they occur, and the use theory of meaning will be the most relevant. Other words, however, seem best explained by the particular conceptual associations they call up; for these, attention to the link between words and concepts will be the most relevant. If I say, for example, *The holidays were a nightmare*, then the words *holidays* and *nightmare* call up a whole variety of specific connotations and associations (see the question below) for which the conceptual theory of meaning will be most appropriate. In still other cases, such as proper names and 'deictics' like *here*, it seems to be a word's referent which is the most important factor in accounting for the word's use on a given occasion: if I say *that man just fell over*, the 'meaning' of *that man* is best described as the actual person to whom I am referring. This is not to say that concepts are irrelevant for expressions like *that man* or for words like those in (44), or that referents and denotations are irrelevant for words like *holiday* or *nightmare*. In most cases, indeed, we will need to attend to all three aspects of a word's 'meaning', in considering how its relations with referents/denotations, associated concepts and uses *mutually* combine to account for its presence in a particular linguistic context. It is just to say that in all these cases attention to the explanatory purpose of talk about meaning will direct us towards whichever conception of meaning seems to provide the best explanation of the particular semantic phenomenon at hand.

QUESTION   Describe the concepts HOLIDAY and NIGHTMARE in as much detail as possible. How much of this detail is relevant to explaining linguistic behaviour?

Summary

The meaningfulness of language is an instance of the meaningfulness of behaviour
The meaningfulness of language can be seen as just one instance of the meaningfulness of human behaviour and communication in general, and is one of the systems of structured meaningfulness studied in semiotics.

'Meaning' is a very vague term
'Meaning' is a very vague term: in English it refers to a variety of different relations between the world, language and speakers. Most languages do not have precise equivalents for the English term 'meaning', and some use a very different stock of lexical resources to talk about meaning-like phenomena.

The semiotic triangle
For the purposes of linguistics, we can isolate three particularly important factors relevant to the study of meaning: the **psychology** of

speakers, which creates and interprets language, the **referent** of the language expression as projected by the language user's psychology, and the **linguistic expression** itself: these three points constitute the **semiotic triangle**.

Lexemes

In providing a semantic description of a language, we do not need to treat all the variant morphological forms of a single word separately. Instead, we describe the meanings of a language's **lexemes**, or the abstract units which unite all the morphological variants of a single word.

Sense, reference, denotation and connotation

There are several different aspects of the meaning of a lexeme: its **referent** on any one occasion of use, its **denotation**, which is the set of all its referents, and its **sense**, or the abstract, general meaning which can be translated from one language to another, paraphrased, or defined in a dictionary. **Connotation** names those aspects of meaning which do not affect a word's sense, reference or denotation, but which have to do with secondary factors such as its emotional force, its level of formality, its character as a euphemism, etc.

Compositionality

Meaning is often **compositional**, which means that the meanings of sentences are made up, or **composed**, of the meanings of their constituent lexemes.

Sentence and utterance meaning

Sentence meaning is the compositional meaning of the sentence as constructed out of the meanings of its individual component lexemes. **Utterance meaning** is the meaning which the words have on a particular occasion of use in the particular context in which they occur. **Semantics** studies sentence meaning, whereas **pragmatics** studies utterance meaning and other aspects of language use.

Object language and metalanguage

In analysing meaning we distinguish the **object language**, or the language *whose* meanings are being described, from the **metalanguage**, the language *in which* we describe these meanings.

Explanations of meaning in terms of meanings are circular

When we propose a definition in a metalanguage as an analysis of the meaning of an object language term, the more basic questions, 'what is meaning?' and 'what is it to understand a meaning?' are left unanswered. All definitions of meaning in language, therefore, are ultimately **circular** because they use one kind of meaning to explain another.

Four ways of breaking the circle

There are four important answers to the question 'what is meaning?': the **referential/denotational theory** of meaning, the **conceptual theory** of meaning, the **brain states theory** and the **use theory**. We do not have to categorically choose between these theories. Instead, recognizing that the notion of meaning in linguistics is a way of talking about *the factors which explain language use*, we can see referents, concepts, brain states and uses as all relevant to this task.

Further reading

Saussure (1983) is essential reading for semantics, as for linguistics generally. For useful introductions to semiotics, see Sebeok (1994), Cobley (2001) and Hawkes (1983). Lyons (1977: Chapter 7) provides a thorough introduction to the concepts of sense and reference; see also Chapter 3 of this book and the references mentioned there. Levinson (1983) and Mey (2001) are standard introductions to utterance meaning and pragmatics. Martin (1987), Frawley (1992) and Chapter 2 of Allan (1986) are good introductions to different theories of meaning. On the role of concepts in semantics see Jackendoff (1983) and (1989) and on concepts more generally, the opening chapters of Prinz (2002). Cummins (1989) is an introduction to meaning and mental representation, and Murphy (2002) is a compendium of psychological research on concepts, including their relation to word meaning. Lakoff (1987) explores a specific conceptual theory of meaning. Lyons (1977: Chapter 5) is a detailed account of the use theory of meaning. Jung-Beeman (2005) gives a glimpse into research on meaning in cognitive neuroscience. On the history of modern European and American semantics, see Gordon (1982). For information on non-European semantic traditions and a discussion of the Greek origins of Western semantics, see van Bekkum *et al*. (1997). Ullmann (1972) and Ogden and Richards (1949) are classic works in the history of semantics which still have many insights. On the contrast between theoretical and pretheoretical perspectives in linguistics, see Chomsky (2000).

Exercises

Questions for discussion

1. In Section 1.1 we discussed the relation between meaning, communication and significance. Consider the cases of pure, wordless music and 'nonsense' language. Can either of these be said to be meaningful? If so, how is this meaningfulness different from that of language? Would you consider it as communication? If so, what is communicated? If not, why not?

2. In 1.2 we considered the words available for the representation of meaning-phenomena in English, French, Warlpiri and Chinese. Choose a language you know and describe what words are available to talk about meaning, and their similarities and differences with the languages discussed.

3. In ancient philosophy, the study of the meanings of words was not usually recognized as a distinct subject. Instead, language and meaning were mainly discussed for what they revealed about the nature of the world, logic and our ideas. What do you think the most important links are between the study of linguistic semantics and other branches of enquiry?

4. We saw in 1.6.1 that some linguistic expressions have a sense but do not have a reference/denotation. Do you think there could be any linguistic expressions with reference/denotation but no senses? If so, what are they? If not, why not?

5. For each word in the following sentences, assume a particular occasion of utterance, and try to specify a sense, referent and denotation. Is this possible for all the words? Could it make sense to talk about the referents of words which are not nouns? Do any words have particular connotations?

   (a) The standard incubation period of Mad Cow Disease is between three and five years.
   (b) You are squabbling about the question whether the buttons of the National Guard should be white or yellow.
   (c) Brazilian officials, like those from India to China, describe their steadily expanding space effort as a commercial and strategic necessity, as well as a matter of national prestige.
   (d) You gave that one to me then.

6. The phrase *Australian passport* is clearly compositional, since its meaning consists of the meaning of *passport* and the meaning of *Australian*: an *Australian passport* is a passport that is Australian. But consider the phrase *a false passport.* A false passport is not a passport that is false, since a false passport is not a (real) passport at all. There is thus a way in which the meaning of the phrase *false passport* does not contain the meaning of the word *passport*. Is this a problem or not for the idea of compositionality? Are the following phrases also problematic? If so, state why. If not, why not?

   This is **fake caviar.**
   My **old baby-sitter** was only eleven.
   A flea is less than a **millimetre high**.
   I am going **partly bald**.

7. Like other branches of linguistics, semantics is a *descriptive*, not a *prescriptive* enterprise, and aims to describe the meanings of words as they are actually used by speakers, and not as they 'should' be used. Give examples of, and describe the meanings of the following words, and comment on any discrepancies between this description and a prescriptive view of their meaning: *disinterested, infer, fulsome, inflammable, champagne, monkey, insane, golden.*

8. Consider the following quotation:

   We must not allow our words to change their meanings, but must make sure that we use them in their correct senses. For if we are careless with meanings, we will lose them, and there will be many ideas which we will no longer be able to express. For 'disinterested' does not mean the same as 'uninterested', 'fulsome' does not mean the same as 'full', 'infer' does not mean the same as 'imply'. If we lose these differences of meaning, we will lose the differences in the concepts they express.

   Do you agree with these statements? What assumptions about language do they contain?

9. Some dictionaries use pictures in order to escape the problem of circular definitions. What are the advantages and limitations of this strategy? Consider how easily the meaning of the following words could be conveyed pictorially: *oak, to punch, black, happy, microscope, water, underneath, arch, machine, sensitivity, internet, thin, popular, to sleep, horrendous.*

10. The Internet contains a number of automatic translation programmes. What problems do you think are posed by the project of translating meanings from one language to another automatically? Why are human beings so much better at translation than computers? Consider the role of context, background knowledge, intuition, memory and any others which you think are relevant.

11. We often talk about seeing or putting meanings into things which do not have them. Astrologers, for example, see 'meanings' in the stars. Other people claim to understand meanings in tea leaves. How are these 'meanings' different from the ones communicated in language?

12. Words are not the only linguistic units that communicate meaning. Discuss whether each of the following categories can communicate meaning, and, if so, what sorts: intonation, speech volume, speech speed, length of sentence, choice of language, and (for type-written language) choice of typeface.

13. Does it make sense to speak of a lexeme's reference?

14. Consider the following words: *squabble, fight, argue, bicker, dispute, disagree, debate, contend, spat*. Describe how they differ in sense and connotation.

15. Review the examples in (40). Now try to devise alternative descriptions of the denotations of the following nouns: *hand, baseball, breakfast, nine, red, stranger, person, heart disease*.

16. You are sent out to learn, and write a dictionary and grammar of a previously unrecorded language. While in the field, you notice that whenever a plane passes overhead the speakers look up and utter the word *paabo*. How many different possibilities can you think of for the meaning of this word? What problems can you imagine in trying to work out which is the right one? Are there any general consequences for the study of meaning?

2 Meaning and definition

This chapter considers the role of definition in the description of meaning, through four main questions:

◆ What units need to receive definition?
◆ What forms should the definitions take?
◆ Can definitions be grounded in a set of semantic primitives?
◆ What is the place of definition in semantics generally?

We begin by contrasting the types of definition that might appear in dictionaries from the types that interest a theoretical semantic analysis (2.1). Before any definition can begin, we have to confront an initial question: what are the meaning-bearing units of the language for which definitions are required? We explore this question by looking at meaning on, above and below the word level in 2.2, paying particular attention to certain problematic cases. The next section distinguishes definition of things (**real definition**) from definition of meanings (**nominal definition**), and **cognitive** from **extensional** definitions, and discusses some differences of opinion in linguistics as to what the proper objects of linguistic definition are (2.3.1). We then distinguish different possible definitional strategies, including

◆ definition by **ostension** (2.3.2)
◆ definition by **synonymy** (2.3.3)
◆ definition by **context and typical exemplar** (2.3.4)
◆ definition by **genus and differentia** (2.3.5).

The test of **truth preserving substitutability** is introduced as a standard criterion of definitional adequacy (2.4), and we discuss the problem of definitional **circularity** and the question of **semantic primitives** (2.5).

We then exemplify the extreme difficulty involved in couching successful definitions of words (2.6), before finally devoting some discussion to the relationship between definition and understanding (2.7).

2.1 Meaning and the dictionary

The concept of a word's meaning is closely linked to the concept of **definition**, which was first made explicit in Greek philosophy by Aristotle. Definitions have been particularly important for conceptual theories of meaning (1.6.2), which traditionally assumed a close link between concepts and definitions: knowing the concept HORSE, for example, is simply the ability to use the word *horse* in a way that accords with or fits its definition. If I have the concept HORSE, I will be prepared to utter, or assent to, a large number of propositions, including the following, which depend on the definition of horse as 'a large, four-footed mammal with hooves and a mane':

(1) a. If X is a horse, X is an animal.
     b. If X is a horse, it has a mane.
     c. X is a rooster, so X is not a horse.
     d. If X is a horse, it is a large four-footed mammal with hooves and a mane.

As a result, an understanding of definition is necessary for any attempt to develop a conceptual theory of word meaning. Furthermore, when people think of a word's meaning, they are inclined to think of something like its definition in a dictionary. Since about the sixteenth century, dictionaries have played an extremely important role in the way we think about and use our own language, and their existence and popularity can be related to a complex of pretheoretical ideas about the nature and role of language: a whole **linguistic ideology**. As a result, it is important to clarify the similarities and differences between the definitions that might be proposed in theoretical linguistic semantics, and the types that can be found in dictionaries.

2.1.1 Semantics and lexicography

Dictionary-writing, or lexicography, is, in the words of Landau (1984: 121), 'a craft, a way of doing something useful. It is not a theoretical exercise to increase the sum of human knowledge but practical work to put together a book that people can understand.' Linguistic semantics, by contrast, while also interested in the meanings of words, *is* exactly the sort of theoretical exercise with which Landau is drawing a contrast. Nevertheless, the model of the dictionary or 'lexicon' (an older term for the same thing) has been decisive in the way that many linguists conceive of the nature of language:

Language exists in the form of a sum of impressions deposited in the brain of each member of a community, rather like a dictionary of which identical copies have been distributed to each individual. It is, thus, something that is in each of them, while at the same time common to all and existing independently of the will of any of its possessors.

(Saussure 1967: 38)

According to a common assumption, our brains holds a 'store of words in long term memory from which the grammar constructs phrases and sentences' (Jackendoff 2002: 130). This stock of words and associated meanings is usually referred to as the **mental lexicon**. On this view, the primary task of linguistic semantics would be the specification of the stored meaning representation – the 'entry' – associated with each lexeme in the mental lexicon:

For the speaker/writer, accessing 'words' is a matter of mapping ideas onto those stored meaning representations in the mental lexicon that are associated with stable word forms, which can then be used to implement a spoken or written output. For the listener/reader, the major task is to map portions of the linguistic signal onto the stored neurosensory traces in the mental lexicon; once activated, these will in turn stimulate their associated meaning representations.

(Garman 1990: 240–241)

The process of matching a meaning with a word is analogous to that involved in consulting a dictionary. Just as a language-learner discovers the meaning of an unknown word by looking it up in a dictionary, the production and understanding of ordinary speech is conceived of as a process of matching between stored word-forms and the stored meaning representations associated with them in long-term memory. Like dictionary definitions, these meaning representations are imagined as discrete and relatively fixed. And just as dictionaries aim for a maximum degree of concision, it has been assumed that the mental lexicon also seeks the most efficient, least redundant listing of lexemes' meanings.

In order to serve the purposes of serious linguistic description, the entries in the mental lexicon must be much more detailed than is usual in ordinary dictionaries. As well as containing information about words' meanings, they must also specify their grammatical properties, and contain a representation of their phonological structure. Consider for example the *Concise Oxford Dictionary* entry for the verb *pour*:

v. 1 *intr. & tr.* (usu. foll. by *down, out, over,* etc) flow or cause to flow esp. downwards in a stream or shower 2 *tr.* dispense (a drink, e.g. tea) by pouring. 3 *intr.* (of rain, or prec. by *it* as subject) fall heavily. 4 *intr.* (usu. foll. by *in, out,* etc.) come or go in profusion or rapid succession (*the crowd poured out; letters poured in; poems poured from her fertile mind*). 5 *tr.* discharge or send freely (*poured forth arrows*). 6 *tr.* (often foll. by *out*) utter at length or in a rush (*poured out their story*).

This entry presents, at first sight, a rather comprehensive description of the verb. But there are a number of aspects of *pour*'s meaning and use which the definition does not cover. First, constructions like (2) correspond to sense number two, 'dispense by pouring', but are intransitive, contrary to the dictionary's specification.

(2) *Shall I pour?*

Furthermore, the dictionary is silent about the conditions under which *pour* in sense one is 'usually' followed by a preposition or prepositional phrase. Whereas (3a) and (3b) are quite acceptable without any following prepositional phrase, (4a) and (4b) seem more questionable, whereas (5a) and (5b) are perfectly acceptable:

(3) a. *I was pouring the tea when the phone rang.*
     b. *They were pouring the concrete when the phone rang.*

(4) a. *?I was pouring the rainwater when the phone rang.*
     b. *?I was pouring the mud when the phone rang.*

(5) a. *I was pouring the rainwater over the ground when the phone rang.*
     b. *I was pouring the mud down the hole when the phone rang.*

Clearly, then, the dictionary's statement that *pour* in this sense is 'usually' followed by *down, out, over* etc., needs significant fleshing-out. Similarly, the Concise Oxford does not tell us the limits on the prepositional and subject combinations with which *pour* is acceptable: why are the (a) examples in (6) and (7) clearly acceptable, but the others less so?

(6) a. *The crowd poured down the hill.*
     b. *?The firemen poured down the pole.*

(7) a. *The tourists poured into the museum.*
     b. *?The surfers poured into the ocean.*
     c. *?The passengers poured into the bus.*
     d. *?Fifty workers poured into the lift.*

Extended or metaphorical uses of the verb raise a host of similar questions. What is it that determines the acceptability of (8), the unacceptability of (10), and the 'punning' quality of (9)?

(8) *The government are pouring money into healthcare.*

(9) *?With its funding of a new dam, the government is pouring water into the driest parts of the country.*

(10) *??The government are pouring money out of education.*

These and other questions all need to be answered in a comprehensive description of the mental lexicon entry for the verb *pour*.

QUESTION   Can you refine the description of the meaning of *pour* in order to explain the facts in (2)–(10)? What other aspects of the meaning and use of *pour* are not made explicit by the quoted definition?

The history of the dictionary

Dictionaries are extremely popular tools. This has not always been the case, however: monolingual dictionaries did not exist in the West until about the sixteenth century (Matoré 1968). Different sorts of 'proto-lexicographical' document existed in Antiquity and the Middle Ages, such as the glossaries or word lists used to keep a record of words which had fallen out of use in everyday language, but which continued to be used in specialized speech genres like poetry. In China, Japan and India, similar documents are also known from an early date: the earliest Chinese proto-lexicographical work, for instance, the *Erya* (a title which means 'approaching what is elegant and correct usage'), which is not a dictionary in the modern sense but simply a collection of semantic glosses on classical Chinese texts, probably dates from the third century BC (Malmqvist 1994: 5–6). More surprising, perhaps, than the historical recency of the modern dictionary, is the fact that the monolingual dictionary is a later invention than the bilingual one: the direct precursor of the modern monolingual dictionary is the bilingual Latin-vernacular dictionary or 'lexicon' which became popular in Europe between the end of the fourteenth and the end of the fifteenth centuries (Auroux 1994: 119). As noted by Auroux (1994), the novelty of the modern monolingual dictionary lay in the fact that it was intended not for people who wanted to acquire a language which they did not yet command, as had been the case for the earlier bilingual dictionaries, but for people who wanted guidance in the use of a language which they already spoke. So completely has the monolingual dictionary eclipsed the bilingual one as the lexicographical standard that, as pointed out by Rey (1990: 19), we now largely think of definitions as exclusively monolingual: whereas a bilingual dictionary contains *equivalents* or *translations*, only a monolingual one contains *definitions*.

Word-based and meaning-based approaches to definition

The definitions found in dictionaries are the result of a word-based, or **semasiological** approach to meaning. This sort of approach starts with a language's individual lexemes, and tries to specify the meaning of each one. This is not the only possibility, however, for the analysis of meaning in linguistics. The other approach, the **onomasiological** one, has the opposite logic: start with a particular meaning, and list the various forms available in the language for its expression. Thus, whereas a semasiological analysis would start with a list of verbs, say *scare, frighten, terrify, startle, spook,* and *panic,* and specify a slightly different meaning for each (*startle,* for instance, referring to a considerably weaker form of alarm than *panic*), an ono-masiological analysis would start with a general concept, FRIGHTEN, and list *all* of these verbs as its possible realizations. The difference between the two approaches corresponds to the difference between a dictionary and a thesaurus. As a semasiological tool, a dictionary is a list of words, and one accesses meanings through words. A thesaurus, on the other hand, is a list of concepts: for a particular concept, the thesaurus gives access to the different words through which the concept could be expressed.

Semasiological and onomasiological analysis are in no way exclusive: the semasiological approach emphasizes differences between lexemes, the onomasiological one similarities. Furthermore, both are necessary to a full description of the processes underlying communication. A complete description of linguistic performance will show how a speaker achieves the mapping between the concept or meaning she wishes to express and the word forms actually chosen: given the need to express the concept or meaning FRIGHTEN, for example, what are the onomasiological principles according to which one of the possible verbs listed above is chosen? For the hearer, however, a semasiological approach is called for. Hearing or reading the word *frighten* in a particular context, what is the meaning which the hearer will assign to this verb?

2.2 The units of meaning

Any attempt to associate meanings and forms needs to ask what the minimal meaning-bearing units of language are. Individual lexemes like *spider*, *crazy* or *elongate*, are, quite clearly, the best examples of units with individually describable meanings. But as we will see, we need to recognize meanings both above and below the word level, and ambiguities about the level of grammatical structure to which meaning is correctly attributed are not infrequent.

2.2.1 Words and morphemes

How can we determine what counts as a lexeme (word) in a language? Without a secure criterion of wordhood, it will be hard to decide – especially in unfamiliar languages – what units we should be trying to attribute meanings to. For European languages with a well-established tradition of literacy, this question usually does not arise: words are the units surrounded by spaces in standard orthography. This definition of 'word' will not take us very far, however, for two reasons. The first is that languages which have only recently been written down often have a very fluid practice of word-division. A meaning-bearing unit considered by one speaker as only *part* of a word will not infrequently be written as a separate word by another speaker (see Dixon and Aikhenvald 2002: 7–9 for details). Speakers of Northern Sotho (Niger-Congo; South Africa), for instance, show two ways of writing the sentence meaning 'we shall skin it with his knife' (Dixon & Aikhenvald 2002: 8, quoting Van Wyk 1967). The first is to put spaces between each *morpheme*:

(11) *re*   *tlo*   *e*   *bua*   *ka*   *thipa*   *ya*   *gagwe.*
     1PLS   FUT   3SGO skin INST knife   9   his

The second is to recognize three distinct orthographic words:

(12) *retloebua kathipa yagagwe.*

These differing practices may sometimes become conventionalized in such a way that closely related, typologically similar languages may adopt differing orthographic conventions. For example, Northern Sotho's relations, Southern Sotho (Niger-Congo, South Africa) and Tswana (Niger-Congo, Botswana) are usually written according to the convention in (11), while Zulu (Niger-Congo, South Africa) and Xhosa (Niger-Congo, South Africa), whose morphological structure is entirely equivalent to that of the other group, typically follow the convention in (12).

The second reason to be suspicious of writing as an indicator of word-hood is that orthographic practice itself is not even stable within long-standing traditions of literacy. An unbroken tradition of literacy links Modern and Ancient Greek. Yet Ancient Greek was written without any word-division, whereas modern Greek observes the norms familiar from languages like English. We would obviously not want to say, however, that Ancient Greek did not have words. Similarly, the reform of German spelling rules made standard (for a trial period) in German schools since 1998 resulted in strikingly different word divisions, as can be seen from the following list:

(13) Old (pre-1998) spelling   Current spelling

Old (pre-1998) spelling	Current spelling	
eislaufen	*Eis laufen*	'skate'
aufsein	*auf sein*	'to be up'
gefangenhalten	*gefangen halten*	'keep prisoner'
wieviel	*wie viel*	'how much'

Linguists have advanced many criteria for the demarcation of the word as an isolable linguistic unit. One common criterion is that of 'potential pause': words are units before and/or after which pauses can be found in spoken language. For languages like Chinese, which lack complex morphology, this criterion may be workable. But for languages which show even a small degree of morphological complexity, like English, it is clearly unsatisfactory. Thus, Dixon and Aikhenvald (2002: 11) point out that one may well pause at morpheme boundaries within a single word, for example *'it's very un-* <pause, perhaps including *um*> *suitable.'* (Similarly, expletives in English can be inserted within what we normally consider a single word: *abso-bloody-lutely.*) Bloomfield's famous definition of 'word' (1933: 178), as 'a *minimum free form*', i.e. the minimal unit which may appear on its own without any additional grammatical material, is clearly insufficient: many canonical words like *the, of* or *my* do not usually appear alone, but must presumably be considered as fully fledged words.

In order to introduce some clarity into the confusion over wordhood, it seems necessary to distinguish two different levels on which words may be defined. The first is the phonological level. Here, divisions between words are determined according to the domain of application of phonological rules and processes. In Dagbani (Gur, Northern Ghana), for instance, the clearest description of stress can be given by assuming the existence of a unit – the **phonological word** – each example of which bears only one main stress, normally on the penultimate syllable (Olawsky 2002: 206). In order, therefore, to determine whether a given phonetic string is a phonological word in Dagbani, one need only count the number of main stresses: if the unit in question has more than one main stress, then it is more than one phonological word. Furthermore, the fact that the penultimate syllable is typically the tonic (accent-bearing syllable) allows us to determine *where* the word boundaries lie. Many languages are like Dagbani in calculating stress on the basis of phonological words: as a result, stress is typically a useful indicator of the phonological word. Other indicators are also found, however. Like Dagbani, Bare (Northern Arawak, Brazil) shows penultimate stress (Aikhenvald 1996: 494). But this language possesses an additional marker of phonological wordhood: aspirated consonants can only be found in word-initial position (Aikhenvald 1996: 494): as a result, given a string with *n* aspirated consonants, one is guaranteed of the presence of at least *n* phonological words.

The phonological level alone will often not be enough to demarcate word-boundaries. Thus, stress in Dagbani and Bare is only *mostly* on the penultimate syllable: exceptions are possible, and this can lead to ambiguity in word division. As a result, the *grammatical level* of wordhood must also be considered. Dixon and Aikhenvald (2002: 19) propose three criteria for the recognition of those linguistic units which are independent **grammatical words**: *cohesiveness, fixed order* and *conventionalized coherence and meaning*. The last criterion 'indicates that the speakers of a language think of a word as having its own coherence and meaning. That is, they may talk about a word (but are unlikely to talk about a morpheme)' (Dixon and Aikhenvald 2002: 20).

QUESTION How reliable a criterion of grammatical wordhood is this? Do speakers ever talk about the meaning of morphemes?

What about the first two criteria, cohesiveness and fixed order? Ancient Greek (Indo-European, Eastern Mediterranean) provides a clear illustration of both. Ancient Greek verbs were obligatorily multi-morphemic, consisting of at least the elements root + inflection, as in the verb meaning 'cure', *therapeu-ō*:

(14) *therapeu-ō*   'I am curing'
     cure-1SG.PRES.INDIC
     therapeu-ete   'You (pl.) are curing'
     cure-2PL.PRES.INDIC
     therapeu-ousi   'They are curing'
     cure-3PL.PRES.INDIC

These elements must co-occur: the verb root *therapeu-* cannot occur without an inflectional suffix, and the suffix cannot occur without a verb root. The combination of verb root and inflectional affix thus constitutes a word on the criterion of cohesiveness. These forms also illustrate fixed order, in that one cannot invert the order root-suffix: the inflectional markers are suffixes, not prefixes. As a result, the combination verb root + inflection constitutes an unambiguous grammatical word in Ancient Greek.

Mismatches between grammatical and phonological words

The criteria of grammatical and phonological word do not necessarily coincide, as can be shown by compound nouns in Georgian (Kartvelian, Georgia). Consider for example the following compound, constructed from the noun roots *t'ól* 'person of the same age group' and *amxánag* 'comrade':

(15) *t'ól-amxánag-i*
person.of.same.age.group-comrade-NOM
'comrades of the same age'

Based on considerations of cohesiveness and fixed order, this is a single grammatical word. Neither *t'ól* nor the suffix *-i* may occur on its own. Thus, the suffix *-i* is obligatorily an affix, and the root *t'ól* requires its own inflectional suffixes when it appears independently as a fully fledged noun. Similarly, the order of the elements of the word is fixed: the meaning 'comrades of the same age' is expressed by the form *t'ól-amxánag-i*, not (for example) **i-t'ól-amxánag* or **t'ól-i-amxánag*. *T'ól-amxánag-i* thus conforms to the criteria of cohesiveness and fixed order and constitutes a grammatical word. From the point of view of stress-assignment, however, (15) is *two* phonological words: Georgian phonological words take just a single primary stress per word (Harris 2002: 232–233), whereas *t'ól-amxánag-i* has preserved the stress of both of its original noun elements. Such mismatches between grammatical and phonological words are by no means the norm in the languages of the world. Nevertheless, their existence illustrates the problematic nature of the category 'word', which seems at first glance to be an entirely intuitive and straightforward concept.

If words are the clearest type of meaning-bearing unit in a language, they are certainly not the only ones: the domain of meaningfulness extends both above and below the threshold of the individual word. Below word level, morphemes, by definition, have meanings. Given the definition of a morpheme as the 'minimal meaning-bearing unit' of language, it is clearly impossible to conceive of a morpheme without a meaning – even if it is often hard to specify exactly what this meaning is. Quite often in linguistic analysis, it proves surprisingly difficult to come up with a settled analysis of the meaning of a given morpheme. This is the case, for instance, with the meanings of the possessive suffix -*s* and of many morphemes involved in the verbal tense/aspect system in English (see 9.2): semanticists agree that these morphemes *have* meanings, but disagree about exactly what they are.

Above the level of the individual word, phrasal verbs and compounds are two clear cases where a single meaning is associated with a combination of lexemes. Phrasal verbs consist of one or sometimes two 'full' verbs followed by one or more particles, as in (16):

(16) *dispose of, touch down, play around, call off, set up, break down, put up with, get on with, look down on, make do with…*

Compounds are most clearly illustrated by noun compounds, which consist of two or more nouns conjoined into a single conventionalized semantic unit:

(17) *tree house, tennis match, instruction book, computer problem, space age, ink jet printer, car insurance contract, pedestrian underpass, junk food, garbage collection, zebra crossing, box office, hit man, getaway car, bullet train, knuckle sandwich…*

QUESTION Noun compounding is an extremely frequent means of word-formation in English, and shows many different types of meaning relation between the compounded elements: *a tree house* is a type of house in a tree, but a *lighthouse* is a type of 'house' which contains a light, and a *poorhouse* was an institution for the accommodation of the poor. A *computer problem* is a problem *with* a computer, and a *zebra crossing* is a crossing that is striped *like* a zebra. Find twenty examples of noun compounds from a newspaper, and describe the semantic relationships between the constituent parts. Can you discern any regularities?

Idioms, discussed in 1.4.3 in relation to *throw in the towel*, also demonstrate the existence of units of meaning associated with several words simultaneously, and we will consider the question of the meaning of grammatical constructions in a later chapter (10.3). Thus, although we most often think of meaning as something belonging to individual words, we must actually recognize that words are only the most obvious of a number of meaning-bearing units.

2.2.2 Meanings below the morpheme: sound symbolism

The question of what level of grammatical structure a meaning should be attributed to may often be problematic, and boundary cases, where meanings seem to straddle several different grammatical units, occur quite frequently. One such boundary case is **sound symbolism**, (also known as **ideophony** or **onomatopoeia**). This is the existence of semi-systematic correspondences between certain sounds and certain meanings, usually within the domain of the individual morpheme, such as English *clash*, *clang, clatter,* etc. Such associations may sometimes have a clear imitative basis, as with English *click, thwack, meow,* etc. Sound symbolism is by no means limited to English, of course. In Ilocano (Cordilleran, Philippines), for instance, a high front vowel is often used in words denoting high pitched sounds, as in (18):

(18) *singgit* 'high pitched voice'; *sing-i* 'sobbing (of a child)'; *sultip* 'whistle'; *riri* 'whimper' (Rubino 2001: 304).

Here the choice of vowel imitates the characteristic timbre of the sound referred to. Similarly, the alveolar fricative is often found in words representing rustling sounds or the sound of water:

(19) *karasakas* 'rustling sound of leaves'; *karasikis* 'rustling sound of bamboo'; *kiras* 'sound of slippers'; *saraisi* 'sound of rippling water'; *barasábas* 'sound of heavy rain, downpour'; *barasíbis* 'sound of light drizzle, drizzle'; *dissuor* 'waves breaking' (Rubino 2001: 305)

A possible connection might be discerned here between the acoustic quality of the fricative and the irregular, 'perturbed' sound of the referent. But the imitative basis of such associations is often less obvious, at least to English speakers. Egbokhare (2001: 90–91), for example, documents the fact that many words indicating 'smallness' contain *kp* in Emai (Niger-Congo, Nigeria):

(20) *kpúkú* 'pointed/protruding'; small, compact and round, short
    kpútú 'stumpy'; small, compact and round, disproportional
    kpúshú 'stubby'; small, compact and round, rough
    kpódó 'round'; small, circular and supple, proportional
    kpúdú 'pellet-like'; small, compact and round, proportional
    kpédé 'proportionate'; small-sized, firm, proportional
    kpéké 'petit'; small, thin, short.

In all these cases we have a sound-meaning correspondence which exists *below* the level of the individual morpheme. Neither the high front vowel nor the alveolar fricative in Ilocano, nor *kp* in Emai can, formally, be considered as individual morphemes, since one cannot remove them from the ideophonic words in (19)–(20) and retain possible roots to which other morphemes could attach. Yet the correspondence is widespread: although not every *s* in Ilocano is used in words referring to rustling sounds (cf. *sarotsot* 'quick succession', Rubino 2001: 315), the correspondence is systematic enough to allow a hearer who is unfamiliar with *karasakas*, for instance, to infer that the word probably refers to some sort of sound. Reference to a rustling sound can therefore be considered as, in some way, a semi-predictable part of the meaning of a unit which is neither a word nor a morpheme. Yet it is only in the words in which they occur that this meaning exists: in describing sound symbolism in Emai, it is necessary to specify that there are many words containing *kp* which do *not* refer to small objects (e.g. *úkpun* 'cloth'; *ókpósó* 'woman'; Schaefer 2001: 344). Sound symbolism can therefore be considered simultaneously as a property of a word and of the relevant submorphemic unit, and the description of sound symbolism in these languages must invoke both lexical and submorphemic units: the reference to sound is conveyed by a particular segment or sequence of segments, but only in certain words.

2.2.3 Meanings above the word level: idioms

Idioms constitute another boundary case where it is not clear what the correct level is for the characterization of meaning. We defined idioms in 1.4.3 as non-compositional phrases – phrases like *throw in the towel* whose overall meaning is not the same as the combined meaning of the individual parts. However, it is often possible to advance an interpretation of the individual words of an idiom which removes its idiomatic or non-compositional character. For example, the English idiom *to scoop the pool*, which means something like 'to win or gain everything', seems on the face of it to lack any connection whatsoever with either pools or scooping: a speaker simply associates the meaning 'win or gain everything' with the entire unit *scoop the pool*, without trying to break the phrase down further. Nevertheless, if we imagine *scoop* as having a meaning like 'quickly gather up a large quantity of something in a single movement', and *pool* as meaning 'the entire set of available items' (cf. *car-pool*, *pool of credits*, etc.), then the arbitrariness and non-compositionality of the expression is reduced, and the interpretation 'win or gain everything' can follow unproblematically from the combined meanings of the expression's elements. For an empirical inquiry, everything hangs on the question of whether speakers *do in fact* interpret *scoop the pool* compositionally or non-compositionally, and there is doubtless no single answer to this question. Thus, some English speakers will analyse it completely into its constituent parts in the way just mentioned, others will interpret it as a single, non-compositional idiom, and still others will interpret it as partly compositional: the 'quickly gather up' interpretation of *scoop*, for instance, might be 'active' for some English-speakers, while *pool* will not receive any compositional interpretation. The fact that a *variety* of possible interpretations is available for each component of the idiom, with consequent differences in the overall interpretation of the expression, only adds to the ambiguity. Thus, other speakers of English might associate *scoop* with a *scoop* in journalism (a news story obtained exclusively by a single journalist), while others might analyse *pool* as in some way referring to a body of water.

As we have been using the term, an idiom is a non-compositional combination of *words*. But if we define an idiom as a non-compositional combination of *morphemes*, then idioms can also exist on the sublexical level. The English suffix *-able* is a case in point. Usually this suffix has its historical meaning, 'able to be V-ed': *fillable* 'able to be filled', *emailable* 'able to be emailed', *movable* 'able to be moved'. In words like *considerable* and *fashionable*, however, this meaning is not present, and the entire word needs to be given a different analysis. Sublexical idioms are often found in many American languages, which are characterized by a large degree of noun-incorporation, a process in which independent noun stems may be compounded with a verb stem in order to produce a larger, derived verb. In the following example from Lakota (Siouan, Mississippi Valley; Rankin *et al.* 2002: 181–182), a noun stem meaning 'heart' is compounded with the verb stem meaning 'be good'; the meaning of the resulting compound, 'I made him/her angry', is in no way simply the combination of the individual meanings of its component morphemes:

(21) *blučhą́lwaxtešni*

    Ø-   b-   yu-   *čhą́t-waxte=šni*

    3OBJ- 1ACTR-BY.HAND heart-be.good=NEG

    'I made him/her angry'

Not all noun-incorporation is as semantically opaque or idiomatic as this, but there are many less extreme examples. An interesting one comes from another American language, Comanche (Uto-Aztecan, Oklahoma). Thus, the composed meaning of the noun-verb compound in (22) is something like 'throw paper by force'. This verb can only be used, however, to refer to the type of paper-throwing that one does when playing cards: the meaning of the incorporated noun *wana* is 'paper', but in the verb in question it only designates playing cards. As a result, the compound means 'to gamble' (Mithun 1984: 855):

(22) *wana-roh-peti-*

    paper-by.force-throw

    'to gamble'

2.2.4 Contextual modulation of meaning

The examples of noun-incorporation we have just seen show the meaning of words and other morphemes varying according to their **collocation**, the immediate linguistic context in which they occur. This sort of variation is found throughout language. We can see a similar phenomenon in English, where the meanings of verbs seem to vary slightly depending on the noun which they govern. If I *cut my foot*, for example, I am doing something that is rather different from what I am doing when I *cut the grass*, or when I *cut a cake, cut someone's hair, cut the wood, cut a diamond, cut a deck of cards, cut a disc* or *cut a notch*. The nature of the event, the means by which it is accomplished, its typical object, and the extent to which it is deliberate may all vary in these different uses. Despite this variation, we have the strong sense that essentially the 'same' meaning of *cut* is involved in all those cases (in other words, we do not usually think of this verb as polysemous; see 5.3). Cruse (1986: 52) refers to this phenomenon as the **contextual modulation** of meaning. The degree of semantic 'distance' gets even greater if we consider more 'extended' meanings, like *cut a deal, cut corners, cut a paragraph* or *cut prices*.

    This type of phenomenon poses an interesting descriptive and theoretical problem: do the differences in meaning of the different collocations arise compositionally or not? Are the meanings of the collocations just the results of the combinations of the meanings of their parts, or are the whole collocations themselves the meaning bearing units? In other words, which of the following two possibilities gives the best semantic description of English:

- one which lists the meanings of *cut, foot, grass, cake, hair*, etc., and sees the specific meanings of the collocations *cut one's foot, cut the grass, cut a cake*, etc., as derived compositionally from the meanings of the parts; or
- one which just lists all the different collocations in which *cut* appears, and specifies a different meaning for the entire collocation?

We will examine each possibility in turn.

2.2.4.1 First possibility: compositionality

The first possibility is that the meanings of *cut one's foot, cut the grass, cut a cake*, etc., result compositionally from the meaning of the verb *cut* and the meanings of its noun objects. The meaning of *cut the grass* just *is* the meaning of *cut* combined with the meaning of *grass*. This might work in one of two ways.

- The general meaning hypothesis: *Cut* might have the same **vague** or general meaning in all its different collocations: it refers to some act of accomplishing a material breach in a surface, with the particular details of each type of breach being inferred by the listener, rather than being built into the meaning of the verb itself.

Alternatively,

- The multiple meaning hypothesis: *Cut* might have a separate meaning in each collocation: the *cut* in *cut one's foot* has its own entry in the mental lexicon ('breach surface of, usually accidentally'), as does the *cut* of *cut the grass* ('sever one part of surface from another, usually deliberately').

Problems with the general meaning hypothesis   The problem with the first option is that describing this common core of general meaning supposedly present in all cases of *cut* is not necessarily an easy matter (see section 2.6): the *Concise Oxford* 2004 edition gives 'make an opening, incision, or wound with a sharp tool or object' as its definition, but this is not involved when someone *cuts butter*, for example, nor when a whip *cuts* someone's flesh: the cutting object in these situations need not be sharp. Perhaps, then, we need to dismiss these uses as in some way special or extended and therefore absolve them from the scope of the vague definition: perhaps 'make an opening, incision, or wound with a sharp tool or object' will work for all the others. Even if it does, though, we still have a problem: the definition does not adequately distinguish *cut* from *chop, slit, stab* or *unpick*: to *chop a sausage, slit a letter, stab someone's side* or *unpick a seam* is equally to 'make an opening, incision, or wound with a sharp tool or object', but we could not also describe these actions as *cutting*. In our effort to formulate the most general definition possible, we have drawn the net too wide and failed to distinguish *cut* from various non-synonymous verbs in the same semantic field.

QUESTION   Can you formulate a general definition of *cut* which avoids these problems? Consider other possible cutting objects, like cheese-cutting wire.

QUESTION   Another example of a similar problem would be the verb *crush* in contexts like *crush petals in the hand, crush paper, crush sugar* and *crush a car under concrete*: in spite of the presence of the same verb, the action involved, and the resulting state of the object, differ considerably with each collocation. Can you formulate an adequate general definition which distinguishes *crush* from related verbs like *bend, crease, fold* and *squash*?

The prototype-based models of meaning discussed in Chapter 7 constitute a possible response to problems of this sort.

Problems with the multiple meaning hypothesis   The second option is to propose multiple meanings for *cut*, a separate one for each collocation. In *cut one's foot*, for example, *cut* could be described as meaning something like 'partially breach a surface with a sharp instrument, typically accidentally': when one *cuts one's foot*, one typically does not detach one's foot from the rest of the body (this would be *cutting it off*). In *cut the grass*, and *cut someone's hair*, on the other hand, the verb conveys the meaning of more than just a partial breach in the surface of the object: the meaning of these collocations is that one part of the object is completely detached from the rest. Now consider *cut a notch*: here the object is *brought into being* by the action of the verb: if I *cut a notch* into a stick, the notch did not exist before I created it. As a result, the meaning of *cut* in *cut a notch* could be paraphrased as 'create by breaching with a sharp instrument', an entirely different meaning from that found in the other collocations, which all presuppose the prior existence of the object being cut. Again, when we talk of a whip *cutting* someone's skin, we have the meaning of breach to a surface, as in *cutting one's foot*, but without the usual element of 'sharp object': being made of leather, whips are not normally considered as sharp.

We have, then, a list of different meanings of *cut*:

- 'partially breach surface with a sharp instrument, typically accidentally',
- 'create by partially breaching the surface with a sharp instrument',
- 'detach one part of object from another with one's hands',
- 'detach one part of object from another with a sharp instrument', etc.

These will all have highly specific collocational restrictions: the meaning 'partially breach surface with a sharp instrument, typically accidentally', for example, will be a very likely sense of *cut* in collocation with *foot*, but not with *cake*: *cutting a cake* is usually an entirely deliberate action. And the meaning 'create by partially breaching a surface with a sharp instrument' is quasi-obligatory in *cut a notch*, but excluded in *cut wood*, which does not, as we have seen, involve any creation.

This second option has two problems. The first is the sheer number of the different senses to be attributed to *cut*. Since the action of cutting in each of the examples in question is slightly different, we seem to need a very large range of different senses. While it is clearly impossible to define the meaning of *cut* in just a single paraphrase – extended meanings like *cut text*, *cut a disc*, etc., seem to demand a distinct set of definitions – the recognition of a different sense of *cut* in each of the collocations seems to fail to do justice to the fact that it is the *same* verb in all collocations: as a result, we have some reason to think that it is also the same meaning that is involved in all of them. Furthermore, given the assumptions about the organization of the 'mental lexicon' mentioned above (2.1.1), the attribution of a separate meaning to *cut* in each collocation has struck many linguists as inefficient and inelegant, given the explosion it entails in the number of separate verb entries: we no more want to propose separate 'mental lexicon' entries for the *cut* of *cut a cake* and *cut one's foot* than we would expect to find separate entries in a dictionary.

The second problem is related: given this variety of different possible meanings of *cut,* how does the correct specific meaning get chosen in a given case? How does a hearer know that the appropriate interpretation of *cut* in *cut a deck of cards* is 'detach one part of object from another with one's hands' and not 'create by partially breaching the integrity of a surface with a sharp instrument'? The second option would clearly be wrong, and our theory of the meaning of the expressions needs some way to exclude it. Yet the description of the process of **word sense disambiguation** is highly problematic, the best current computational models significantly failing to match human ability (see 8.2.2 for details).

We can now recap the discussion up to this point. We have been considering the possibility that the meaning of collocations like *cut one's foot, cut the grass* etc. are derived compositionally from the meanings of their elements. We looked at two options for the details of this. The first is that the meaning of *cut* is general or vague in each collocation. This creates the problem of adequately defining this general or vague meaning in a way which distinguished *cut* from other non-synonymous verbs. The second option is that *cut* has a separate meaning in each collocation. But if we adopt this solution we find that the number of definitions of *cut* explodes. Confronted with this vast array of different meanings, how do speakers know which one to choose in any given case?

The compositional solution therefore seems quite problematic. This is not to say that we should reject it, just that it involves us in complex questions. Let us now look at the non-compositional solution.

2.2.4.2 Second possibility: non-compositionality

A number of the problems of the first solution are avoided if each collocation *as a whole* is seen as the relevant definition-bearing unit. On this approach, the meaning of the collocation is not constructed composition-ally; we learn one definition for the unit *cut the grass*, another for *cut one's foot*, and a third for *cut a CD*. Thus, the fact that in *cutting the grass*, a mower or a scythe is the instrument of the action, and that in *cutting a disc* it is a CD-burner, is not part of the meaning of *cut* itself, but is a property of the collocation as a whole. This avoids several of the problems of the compositional solution:

- we do not have to advance a general definition of *cut* that will work in every context, as we do in the general-meaning version of the compositional solution
- we do not have the problem of word-sense disambiguation, since each collocation carries its own definition.

Here is another consideration in favour of non-compositionality. It is not just *cut* whose meaning is determined by its collocational environment: the collocation also determines what reading is operative for *cut*'s *object*. Thus, English speakers know that *cutting the grass* refers to the grown grass blades, whereas *planting the grass* refers to grass seeds or shoots, and *smoking grass* refers to the leaves of a completely different plant. They also know that it is the physical CD that is involved in *cutting a disc*, but the 'acoustic' object in *listening to a disc*. Because both verb and object have different meanings in different collocations, it seems reasonable to think that the basic meaning-bearing unit is the collocation as a whole, not the individual words.

Unfortunately, this solution is just as problematic as the compositional one. It seems precisely to ignore our intuition of the compositionality of the meanings of the collocations: the reason that *cut the grass* has the interpretation it does is, surely, something about the combination of the meanings of *cut* and the meaning of *grass*. It is not an arbitrary fact that *cut the grass* means what it does: instead, the meaning of the phrase is dependent on the meaning of its components, and this is the reason that this meaning is not conveyed by some other sequence of different elements like *plant the tree*. And if one takes the analogy of the 'mental lexicon' seriously, this option also involves the threat of an explosion in the number of entries. Analysing each collocation involving *cut* as having a separately specified meaning would lead to an enormous amount of repetition and redundancy in the mental lexicon, and would fail to extract the generalization that the meaning of *cut* in each such collocation is significantly similar to its meaning in other collocations.

We can summarize the choices here in Figure 2.1:

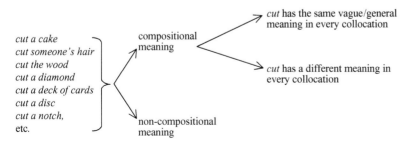

cut a cake
cut someone's hair
cut the wood
cut a diamond
cut a deck of cards
cut a disc
cut a notch,
etc.

compositional meaning

cut has the same vague/general meaning in every collocation

cut has a different meaning in every collocation

non-compositional meaning

FIGURE 2.1
Options for analysing collocations.

These arguments are obviously shaped by many assumptions about the nature and limits of linguistic competence. In the absence of a clear understanding of how the brain *actually does* process and store language, linguists have assumed that their description of assumed linguistic competence should reflect the same criteria of economy and non-redundancy that operate in real paper dictionaries. Thus, much linguistic research has assumed that the mental lexicon does not contain a huge number of independently listed entries, but that it extracts the maximum number of generalizations about the meaning of a verb like *cut* across all its collocational contexts, in order to present the most economical, least redundant entry. As a result, it has been the topmost solution in Figure 2.1 that has traditionally been considered preferable. We will see in later chapters how this assumption has been challenged in more recent theories of language. One of these, in particular, known as **cognitive linguistics**, specifically rejects the dichotomous reasoning we see embodied in the claim that *either* the separate listing *or* the compositional approach should be adopted to the question of the mental representation of the meaning of collocations like these. According to linguists in the line of Langacker (1987), this sort of thinking is an example of the **exclusionary fallacy**, the idea that 'one analysis, motivation, categorization, cause, function or explanation for a linguistic phenomenon necessarily precludes another' (Langacker 1987: 28). Langacker continues:

> From a broad, pretheoretical perspective, this assumption is gratuitous and in fact rather dubious, in view of what we know about the multiplicity of interacting synchronic and diachronic factors that determine the shape and import of linguistic expressions. (ibid)

Thus, even though it might seem inelegant to list all the different collocations of *cut* separately in the lexicon, this option should obviously not be rejected if it somehow turns out (for example, through neuroscientific experimentation) that this is, in fact, what speakers (unconsciously) do. And this discovery would not of itself invalidate the idea that speakers also *simultaneously* represent *cut* as having an independent meaning or set of meanings which enter into composition each time the verb gains a new set of arguments.

2.3 Different ways of defining meanings

So much, then, for the question of which units should be attributed definitions. In this section we will discuss a number of different ways in which a word's meaning can be defined.

2.3.1 Real and nominal definition

As already noted, the concept of definition goes back to Aristotle, who discussed it at a number of points in his voluminous works. One of the most important Aristotelian treatments of definition is to be found in the

Posterior Analytics, a treatise devoted to the explanation of the structure of scientific knowledge. As discussed there, a definition (*horismos*) has two quite different interpretations: 'in defining,' says Aristotle, 'one exhibits either what the object is or what its name means' (Tredennick 1960: II.7.92b). A definition can therefore be considered either as a sort of summation of the essence or inherent nature of a thing (**real definition**; Latin *res* 'thing'), or as a description of the meaning of the *word* which denotes this thing (**nominal definition**; Latin *nomen* 'name, noun'). Since Aristotle is interested in providing a basis for an understanding of nature, it is the first interpretation which he adopts: a definition of thunder, for example, is not a description of the meaning of the word *thunder*, but expresses thunder's essential nature (for Aristotle, the noise of fire being extinguished in the sky).

Some people have considered that definitions of the underlying nature of objects are the only type of definitions which can be of interest. Diderot, for example, stated that 'definitions of words differ in no way from definitions of things' (quoted in Meschonic 1991: 102). And since it is scientific research which is taken to reveal this underlying nature, these definitions will be formulated by scientific disciplines. The influential American linguist Leonard Bloomfield stated in a well-known passage that

The situations which prompt people to utter speech, include every object and happening in their universe. In order to give a scientifically accurate definition of meaning for every form of a language, we should have to have a scientifically accurate knowledge of everything in the speakers' world. The actual extent of human knowledge is very small, compared to this. We can define the meaning of a speech-form accurately when this meaning has to do with some matter of which we possess scientific knowledge. We can define the names of minerals, for example, in terms of chemistry and mineralogy, as when we say that the ordinary meaning of the English word salt is 'sodium chloride (NaCl)'...

Bloomfield (1933: 139)

On the other hand, according to Bloomfield, 'we have no precise way of defining words like *love* and *hate*' (ibid.). On this understanding, therefore, linguistics should appeal to technical scientific disciplines in formulating definitions; the true meaning of a natural language word, according to Bloomfield, is to be identified with the scientific 'definition' – or best possible theory – of its denotation. As a result, whenever a scientifically established definition of a denotation is missing, there is, simply, nothing that linguistics can say with any certainty about the word's meaning. (One problem with this is that scientific conceptions of the nature of objects are continually changing: just think of the current best theory of space, mass, light, or matter in the world view of modern physics, compared to the same notions just a hundred and fifty years ago, before the advent of relativity and quantum mechanics. These scientific developments radically changed our picture of space, mass and so on, but surely didn't have any effect on our everyday meanings.)

Bloomfield's view is a serious obstacle to a comprehensive account of meaning, for it is not just 'abstract' nouns like *love* and *hate* which lack a scientific definition, but the vast majority of the vocabulary of any natural language. There are two reasons for this. The first is that, as we saw in Chapter 1, words like *unicorn*, *time machine* and *light sabre* lack any denotation in the real world but nevertheless have a meaning. Secondly, most of the vocabulary of a language has only a small amount of overlap with terms of the sort which interest empirical science: most of the vocabulary consists of words for a huge variety of objects, processes, relations and states which have no simple analogue in the scientific picture of reality (think of *reportage*, *postpone*, *ready*).

There is another reason, however, to reject Bloomfield's approach to definition: even in the case of terms like *salt* which *can* be associated with a scientific definition, we do not want to say that the scientific definition ('NaCl') has anything to do with most speakers' understanding or use of the word. While this definition might perhaps be satisfactory as a real definition of actual salt, it is certainly unsatisfactory as a psychologically realistic one. Thus, people use and understand the word *salt* even without specialized scientific knowledge; indeed, English speakers' first exposure to this word will come at an age when the technical scientific knowledge that supposedly defines it is entirely inaccessible. Speakers with training in chemistry may eventually *come* to understand *salt* in this way; but this can only happen after they have already acquired the everyday, nontechnical meaning of the word. For these reasons, we will reject Bloomfield's approach to definition: linguistic semantics aims to define the meaning(s) of a word, not the underlying essence of the object it refers to. It is thus concerned with nominal, not real definition.

Before proceeding further, we need to distinguish two different functions which a nominal definition may fulfil: fixing the meaning of a word so that there can be no ambiguity about its denotation, and bringing about an *understanding* of the meaning of a word in someone who does not already understand it, typically in order to enable the word to be correctly used. Many actual definitions aspire to fulfil both these functions simultaneously. The two functions are, however, rather different, and they should be kept apart. In order to differentiate between them, let us call the first type of definition **extensional definition**, and the second type **cognitive definition** (Figure 2.2). Thus, the definition 'featherless biped' is an extensional definition of the noun *human*, since it accurately identifies all and only the members of the class of humans.

FIGURE 2.2
Types of definition.

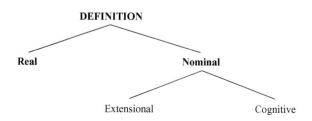

It is not, however, necessarily a very good cognitive definition, since *human* is not typically conceived of in terms of bipedality or absence of feathers: when we reflect on our concept HUMAN, we are likely to think of many different characteristics – a certain physical form and range of behaviours – before these ones.

2.3.2 Definition by ostension

As we saw in Chapter 1, the most obvious way to define many words is, simply, by ostension, or by pointing out the objects which they denote. In spite of the apparent obviousness of this method, it is beset by difficulties. Firstly, as we saw in Chapter 1, verbs, adjectives and prepositions are not open to this definitional method, to name only the lexical categories most familiar from English: if you point at a black cat running along a wall, you are pointing at a cat, not at 'black', 'running' or 'along'. Secondly, even in the case of objects, ostensive definition is extremely problematic. To illustrate this, imagine the following situation. You are in an optometrist's shop in France, trying to buy a new pair of sunglasses. You speak a little French, but are confused by the fact that the shop assistant continually refers to something called a [vɛʀ]. You ask what this word means, and in reply, the shop assistant taps several times with his index finger on the lens of the pair of sunglasses he is holding. This is a canonical instance of ostensive definition: the meaning of a word has been defined by indicating the object to which it refers. But exactly what part of the pair of glasses is being indicated? Is it the whole thing? In that case [vɛʀ] must mean 'glasses'. Or is it just the lens as distinct from the frame, in which case [vɛʀ] will mean 'lens'? If so, does it mean 'glasses lens' *and* 'camera lens' *and* 'contact lens', or only the first? But perhaps [vɛʀ] only refers to the *particular type of tinted, nonreflective sunglasses lens* which the shop assistant is holding: perhaps other lenses, with different shapes, compositions or functions, have different names. Or does [vɛʀ] refer to neither the lens nor the frame proper, but simply to the front, most visible part of the glasses, the lenses and those parts of the frame which are in contact with the front of the face?

QUESTION   Would it be possible to eliminate these uncertainties purely ostensively? If so, how? If not, why not?

None of these questions can, in fact, be settled by ostensive definition: every attempt to make the definition more precise ostensively would give rise to a new set of questions. Although it is an appealing idea that meanings can be defined simply by pointing at objects in the world, in practice this definitional method would seem to give rise to too many ambiguities to be viable.

The only way to overcome the problems of ostensive definition would seem to be to use language itself as the medium in which definitions can be phrased: only this way, apparently, can we get the level of definitional precision we need. There are several ways in which this can be done. We will discuss **definition by synonymy**, by **context** and **typical exemplar**, and **by genus and differentia**.

2.3.3 Definition by synonymy

We might try, for example, to define words by providing synonyms, in either the same language as the word being defined or in a different one. Thus, one could give *mad* and *furious* as English definitions of *angry*, and *kulu* as a Warlpiri one. The problem with this strategy is that it is usually possible to challenge the identity between the **definiens** (the metalanguage word proposed as the definition; Latin 'defin*ing*') and the **definiendum** (the object language word for which a definition is required; Latin 'needing *to be defined*'). Thus, one could object that neither *mad* nor *furious* is really synonymous with *angry*, since *mad* also means 'insane', which *angry* does not, and since *furious* actually means something like '*very* angry' (similar problems arise for other proposed synonyms, such as *cross*, *livid*, *irate*, *enraged*, etc.). Similarly, although Warlpiri *kulu* does often translate English *angry*, it has a whole range of other meanings, including 'mean' and 'fight', which do not correspond to those of *angry*:

(23) *Wati-lpa*   **kulu**-*wita-wangu*   *nyina-ja.*
     man-then   mean-excessively   be-PST
     There was a man who was very **mean**. (WlpD: *kulu*)

(24) *Kalaka-rna*   *nyampu-ju ngawu nyina* **kulu**-*jangka paka-rninja-warnu.*
     AUX.ADMON-1S this-1O   sick   be   fight-EL   hit-INF-ASSOC
     I might be sick like this from being hit in a **fight**. (WlpD: *langa nyiinpurupuru*)

And as (24) exemplifies, Warlpiri does not share the same system of lexical categories as English, having a single category 'nominal' which contains words translated into English as both nouns and adjectives. Consequently, many instances of *kulu* will be translated into English as nouns: as a result, the synonymy with the adjective *angry* is destroyed. Thus, the provision of synonymy fails both as an extensional and as a cognitive definitional strategy. We will return to the question of synonymy in Section 5.1.5.

QUESTION   What types of words are most easily defined through synonymy? For what words is synonymy least satisfactory as a definitional method?

2.3.4 Definition by context or typical exemplar

Another way to define a word is to situate it in a system of wider relations through which the specificity of the definiendum can be seen. This definitional strategy differs from the synonymy strategy in simply showing the position of a definiendum with respect to other related notions which are not themselves identical to it, as alleged synonyms are. A possible definition of the verb *scratch*, for example, would be 'the type of thing you do when you are itchy'. This is an example of **definition by context**: the definition identifies the event of scratching by placing it in relation to another event, being itchy, whose meaning is assumed to be already known, and which is taken as a typical context for the definiendum. This definition only works if the definition's addressee correctly infers the intended meaning on the basis of the cue given. Thus, if, when itchy, I am in the habit of lightly striking my head against the wall, and if I believe that others do the same, then the definition will not be effective. **Definition by typical exemplar** is another example of this relational strategy: here, the definition is a list of typical examples or instances of the definiendum. If, given the German definiendum *Vogel*, I supply a list like 'swans, robins, geese, hens, magpies, etc.' and add that bats, butterflies and aeroplanes are excluded, you could correctly conclude that *Vogel* means 'bird'. And if I give jars and conserve pots as examples of the French noun *bocal*, and exclude wine bottles, you will be in a good position to infer that it means something like 'wide-necked glass container'.

QUESTION   Can definition by context or typical example be applied to lexical categories other than nouns?

QUESTION   Definition by context or by typical example are both subject to similar difficulties. What might these be?

2.3.5 Definition by genus and differentia

The two preceding types of definition are essentially relational, defining a word's meaning through its connections with other words. They may often be workable as cognitive definitional strategies, but they are unlikely to be successful as extensional definitions. This is because they leave the essential nature of the definiendum's meaning to be worked out by the definition's addressee, and as a result carry the risk that the wrong meaning may be inferred: in the case of *bocal*, for example, what is it that jars and conserve pots have in common, that makes them a *bocal*? Smallness? A wide opening? Function? The only way to convey this essential nature, apparently, is the strategy of **definition by genus and differentia**, henceforth **GD definition**, the theory of which was developed by Aristotle in the *Posterior Analytics* (Tredennick 1960: XIII.96a ff.). According to Aristotle, definition involves specifying the broader class to which the definiendum belongs (often called the definiendum's **genus**), and then showing the distinguishing feature of the definiendum (the **differentia**) which distinguishes it from the other members of this broader class. A classic example of GD definition is the definition of *man* (in the sense of 'human being') as 'rational animal'. This definition names the broader class of entities to which man belongs – animals – and specifies the distinguishing feature which picks man out from the other members of the class of animals – rationality. Needless to say, many aspects of this definition might well be contested. Nevertheless, its status as an example of definition by genus and differentia should be clear.

For many definienda, GD definition seems to be almost inevitable. Inherent in the idea of saying what something *is* seems to be the idea of saying what sort of thing it is, and what makes it different from other examples of the same sort. Often, GD definition is a useful strategy of cognitive definition.

Thus, many definitions in dictionaries explicitly or implicitly exemplify this strategy. An example is the *Concise Oxford*'s (2004) definition of the noun *keg* as 'small barrel': the definition shows the larger class to which the definiendum belongs (barrel), and specifies that it is distinguished from other members of this class by the quality of smallness. Similarly, the definition of the verb *pay* as 'give a person what is due for services done' contains the information that *paying* is a type of transfer ('give'), with the specification that it is transfer of something that 'is due for services done'.

QUESTION   Which of the following definitions contain an implicit or explicit genus-differentia structure? For those which do not, would it be possible to formulate one?

eerie: gloomy and strange; weird, frightening
balance: bring into or keep in equilibrium
shirty: angry, annoyed
shine: emit or reflect light; be bright; glow
round: shaped like or approximately like a circle, sphere, or cylinder;
   having a convex or circular outline or surface; curved, not angular
under: in or to a position lower than; below; beneath
wet: soaked, covered, or dampened with water or other liquid
when: at the or any time that; as soon as

There are many problem cases, however, where GD definition may be either ineffective or, simply, impossible. This is particularly so if the GD definition is intended as a cognitive definition. The reason for this is as follows. GD definition presupposes a system of categories or genera according to which definienda can be classed: defining *man* as 'rational animal' presupposes that the addressee already knows the meanings of those two terms. But there is not a large number of genera and differentiae to work with: for many words, the relevant genus will not be familiar to the definition's addressee, and hence GD definition won't be an effective strategy for a cognitive definition. Consider for example a definition of *give* as 'transfer the possession of freely' (*Concise Oxford*). The category of *transfer*, arguably, is too abstract and ambiguous to serve as an illuminating genus for *give*, and, as a result, its use in a definition of *give* may not be cognitively successful. For what is it to transfer something? One possible answer is that transferring something is *sending* it: if I transfer some money to you, I send you some money. Thus, if the definition's addressee interprets the idea of *transfer* as 'sending', then *give* will be defined as 'send the possession of freely', a formulation which does not necessarily make any sense. On the other hand, *transfer* might be interpreted as 'moving': if I transfer books from one room to another, I am moving them. On this interpretation, *give* will mean something like 'move the possession of freely', a definition which is also unsatisfactory.

These problems are less serious for extensional GD definitions, which are not concerned with ease of understandability. Consider, for example, the following definition of *feather*:

one of the light horny epidermal outgrowths that form the external covering of the body of birds and that consist of a shaft bearing on each side a series of barbs which bear barbules which in turn bear barbicels commonly ending in hooked hamuli and interlocking with the barbules of an adjacent barb to link the barbs in a continuous vane (*Webster's Ninth New Collegiate Dictionary: feather*; quoted in Landau 1984: 134–135)

This situates feather within the larger class of *horny epidermal outgrowth*, but the terms in which this and the differentiae are couched makes them inaccessible to anyone who lacks specialist ornithological knowledge: given this definition, it is not at all obvious that an English speaker would realize that *feather* is the word being defined.

A different kind of problem affects cognitive and extensional GD definitions equally, in those cases where it is not clear that the definiendum *does* belong to any broader class. *Self* and *time* are two possible examples.

QUESTION   Try and formulate a GD definition of these words. How do you define the genera you have used?

QUESTION   Can you think of other words for which a GD definition seems difficult? What causes the difficulty?

2.4 Definition and substitutability

How can the accuracy of a definition be checked? For most semantic theories, a minimum requirement on a term's definition is the following:

- **substitution of the definiens for the definiendum should be truth preserving in all contexts.**

For example, 'keep in equilibrium' can be accepted as the definition of *balance* if it is possible to substitute this phrase for *balance* in all the contexts in which *balance* occurs without rendering any of them false. All the sentences in (25), for example, remain true if 'keep in equilibrium' is substituted:

(25) *I balanced the plank on my head.*
    She balanced the ball on the end of the bat.
    Now, children, you have to balance the egg on the spoon.
    I've never managed to balance the demands of work and play.

Substituting 'keep in equilibrium' into these sentences will change their register, and the resulting utterances will often sound considerably less idiomatic and more technical (e.g. *Now, children, you have to keep the egg in equilibrium on the spoon*). Nevertheless, the fact that the sentences remain true is taken to be a sign of the adequacy of the definition. The rationale of this requirement is the principle of **identity under substitution** articulated by the seventeenth-century German philosopher Leibniz: *eadem sunt, quae* *sibi mutuo substitui possunt, salva veritate* (Latin for 'things are the same which can be substituted one for the other with truth intact'). If a definiens can be substituted for a definiendum *salva veritate*, i.e. with the sentence in which the terms occur remaining true, then the definiendum and the definiens should be considered identical in meaning.

Preservation of truth is not the only possible criterion for the regulation of definitions. Instead, the criterion of preservation of meaning (in an informal sense of this term) is also conceivable. On this view, a definition is accepted if it can be substituted for the definiendum 'with sense intact' (*salvo sensu*): if, that is, it involves neither addition nor loss of meaning with respect to the meaning of the definiendum. This suggestion raises an important problem, however: since it is the definition itself that is supposed to reveal an expression's meaning, the best way to determine that two words have the same meaning is to compare their definitions. Preservation of meaning as a criterion of definitional adequacy is therefore circular.

2.5 Semantic primitives

Considered as a cognitive definition, the definition of *balance* as 'keep in equilibrium' poses an obvious problem: if someone does not know the meaning of *balance*, they are unlikely to know the meaning of *equilibrium*. And the most obvious way to define *equilibrium* would seem, in fact, to be by way of the term *balance*: to keep something in equilibrium is, quite simply, to *balance* it. Defining *keep in equilibrium* by *balance*, and *balance* by *keep in equilibrium* is a simple example of definitional circularity, which was introduced in Chapter 1. As discussed there, it is impossible to give a definition of *every* word in a language using other words of the same language: at some point the chain of definition must come to an end. Since the vocabulary of any language is limited, the metalanguage will eventually have to include object language definienda, thereby leaving some of the latter without independent definition. This is a problem for any attempt, such as that made in linguistic semantic theories, to specify the meaning of *every* lexeme in a language. Leibniz likened this problem to the situation of someone who is promised money and continually strung along from one alleged payer to the next, without ever actually receiving anything:

I give you a hundred crowns, to be received from Titus; Titus will send you to Caius, Caius to Maevius; but if you are perpetually sent on in this way you will never be said to have received anything.

(Parkinson (ed.) 1973: 1–2)

In the same way, a metalanguage which incorporates elements of the object language can also be said to 'defer full payment'. Only a metalanguage which is completely independent of the object language is in a position to offer a complete, non-circular explanation in which every definiendum receives its own semantic analysis independently of the analysis of the others. Without such a metalanguage, there will always be a residue of unexplained terms which escape definition.

In Chapter 1 we saw some proposals about how to escape from this chain of definitional circularity by grounding the study of meaning in various extra-linguistic realities. One of these was the conceptual theory of meaning, which identified meanings with concepts. Given such an identification, we can imagine several different possibilities for the relation between lexemes and concepts. One is that each lexeme corresponds to an entirely different concept. Thus, the English lexemes *cup* and *mug* would each correspond to the separate concepts CUP and MUG, each of which is unitary and undecomposable. The fact that *cup* and *mug* seem to share certain properties – they both refer to drinking vessels usually reserved for hot liquids – is not reflected on the conceptual level by any shared conceptual content. The two concepts are, that is, **semantic primitives**: in spite of appearances, they cannot be completely broken down into anything conceptually simpler. Something approaching this view has been advocated by Fodor, who argues for a lexicon where each lexical item is a semantic primitive or atom with no internal definitional structure:

… I take semantic facts with full ontological seriousness, and I can't think of a better way to say what 'keep' means than to say that it means *keep*. If, as I suppose, the concept KEEP is an atom, it's hardly surprising that there's no better way to say what 'keep' means than to say it means *keep*.

I know of no reason, empirical or a priori, to suppose that the expressive power of English can be captured in a language whose stock of morphologically primitive expressions is interestingly smaller than the lexicon of English.

(Fodor 1998: 55)

Typically, however, proponents of the conceptual theory of meaning in linguistics believe that most word meanings are not themselves primitive, but are composites of a finite stock of primitive concepts. These semantic primitives are the basic building blocks of meaning out of which all other meanings can be constructed (see Chapter 8).

The belief that responsible semantic analysis must be grounded in a level of elementary, primitive units is implicitly or explicitly held by many semanticists (Fillmore 1971, Jackendoff 1983, Allan 2001: 281; for some criticisms of primitives see Aitchison 1994). The most thorough-going example of a theory of semantic primitives in modern linguistics is the Natural Semantic Metalanguage (NSM) theory of Wierzbicka and Goddard. Painstaking cross-linguistic research in this framework has led to the development of the following list of semantic primitives which the NSM approach uses for the definition of meaning:

I, you, someone, people, something/thing, body; this, the same, other; one, two, some, all, much/many; good, bad; big, small; think, know, want, feel, see, hear; say, words, true; do, happen, move; there is, have; live, die; when/time, now, before, after a long time, a short time, for some time; where/place, here, above, below, far, near, side, inside; not, maybe, can, because, if; very, more; kind of, part of; like.

(Goddard 2002: 14)

These 58 elements represent the 'atoms of meaning' which are claimed to be impossible to define in a non-circular manner, and which can be used to fashion definitions for a large range of words.

A definition in NSM is a **reductive paraphrase** of the definiendum's meaning. Reductive, in that it reduces this meaning into a set of primitive components, and a paraphrase in that it consists of a *textual* explanation of the meaning, which is not simply a list of synonyms or a GD definition (although it may contain this structure) but a collection of natural language sentences in which the meaning is expressed. Among the many definitions proposed in NSM are those of *sun* and *watch*:

> *sun*
> something
> people can often see this something in the sky
> when this something is in the sky
> people can see other things because of this
> when this something is in the sky
> people often feel something because of this (Wierzbicka 1996: 220)

> X was *watching* Y =
> for some time X was doing something
> because X thought:
>   when something happens in this place
>   I want to see it
> because X was doing this, X could see Y during this time. (Goddard
>   2002: 7; cf Wierzbicka 1996: 251)

(Note that *sky* is not a semantic primitive, but a 'semantic molecule' which can be independently defined with the 58 primitives, perhaps as 'a place above all other places', and which is used here as shorthand for pure space-saving reasons.)

QUESTION   Are these definitions accurate? What is their structure?

But while the semantic primitives can be used to define other members of the vocabulary of a language, the primitives themselves are impossible to define in terms of anything simpler.

Semantic analysis in NSM thus consists in explaining a definiendum in simpler and more comprehensible terms than the definiendum itself. The 58 semantic primitives are supposed to represent the simplest possible explanatory terms, which cannot themselves be explained by anything simpler. It is not, for NSM, simply a matter of chance that it is these particular terms, and not some others, that represent the simplest metalinguistic definientia. NSM theory claims that the indefinable nature of its primitives derives from their status as *conceptual* primitives: the primitives are hypothesized, in other words, to express the set of 'fundamental human concepts' (Wierzbicka 1996: 13), considered to be both innate and universal. What this means is that every natural language possesses an identical semantic core of primitive concepts from which all the other lexicalized concepts of the language can be built up. Since this common core is absolutely universal, it can be stated in any language, and NSM scholars have devoted considerable energy to testing the list of primitives reproduced above in order to confirm that every language does, indeed, have an 'exponent' of each suggested primitive.

This commitment to the universality of the metalanguage has involved NSM theory in more cross-linguistic investigation than is common in many semantic theories, which still largely focus on familiar Indo-European languages as the empirical base for the assessment of theoretical semantic adequacy. This rigorous cross-linguistic orientation is one of the main advantages of the NSM approach to meaning. Not least among its benefits is NSM's utility as a practical tool. Because only defining terms have been chosen for which well-established cross-linguistic equivalents exist, the NSM set of primitives provides a convenient tool for cross-linguistic explanation, and NSM scholars have been able to define a surprising range of vocabulary, including words from domains in which strikingly delicate and culture-dependent information is contained. An example would be Wierzbicka's preliminary definition of the Japanese emotion term *amae*:

amae

(a) X thinks something like this:
(b) when Y thinks about me, Y feels something good
(c) Y wants to do good things for me
(d) Y can do good things for me
(e) when I am near Y nothing bad can happen to me
(f) I don't have to do anything because of this
(g) I want to be near Y
(h) X feels something good because of this (Wierzbicka 1996: 239)

The reader of this definition is arguably in a better position to appreciate the intricacies of the concept *amae* than is the reader of any of the numerous other English explanations of this term which have been proposed in the literature, and which include 'lean on a person's goodwill', 'depend on another's affection', 'act lovingly towards (as a much fondled child towards its parents)', 'to presume upon', 'to take advantage of', 'be coquettish', 'coax', 'take advantage of', and 'play baby'! As a cognitive definition, in other words, the NSM paraphrase may be an attractive way of conveying the meaning of definienda.

In spite of the fact that some linguists find NSM a useful tool for the analysis and representation of certain aspects of meaning, the method's theoretical soundness, as opposed to its practical utility, has been the subject of considerable criticism (Riemer 2006). As for other definitional theories of semantics, many of these critiques bear on the alleged inadequacy of NSM's proposed definitions: we will look at this type of criticism more generally in 2.6.

Aside from these more general problems, we may distinguish two particular challenges faced by NSM, each of which tells us a lot about the problems of cross-linguistic definition. The first concerns the universality of the NSM primitives. Some languages simply lack some of the allegedly universal primitive terms. As discussed by Bohnemeyer (1998, 2002, 2003), Yukatek Maya (Mayan, Mexico) lacks lexical exponents of the primitives 'after' and 'before': the expression of these temporal relations is achieved primarily through particular combinations of aspectual and/or modal information (Bohnemeyer 2003: 216). Another particularly common case is where languages *merge* putative primitives, as when Japanese *ba* translates both the primitives 'if' and 'when' (Goddard 1998: 138), or when Pitjantjatjara (Pama-Nyungan, Australia) *kulini* has the meanings 'think' and 'hear' (Goddard 1996: 44). If each primitive represents a genuinely distinct semantic atom, these mergers should not be possible.

Even if a language does have unproblematic equivalents for all the NSM primes, it is not necessarily the case that the types of paraphrase that can be written in English using these primes will also be possible in other languages. Diller (1994), for example, discusses some of the problems raised by the attempt to write NSM definitions using a set of possible Thai (Tai, Thailand) exponents of the primitives. Thai typically omits overt pronominal reference forms – the equivalents of the primitives 'I' and 'you' – unless speakers want to achieve specific communicative goals. When explicit equivalents of the pronouns are present, Thai offers a number of possible translations of 'I' and 'You', which differ in the sociolinguistic roles (gender, politeness, formality, deference, urbanity) which they impute to speaker and addressee, as the following list shows:

(26) 'I'/'You'   sociolinguistic register

   ku:/mu'ng   non-deferential, speaker either sex, considered rude or insulting in educated urban speech; common in rural speech

   khǎ:/e:ng   non-deferential, speaker either sex, considered rustic or coarse in urban speech; common in rural speech

   chǎn/thoe: non-deferential, speaker either sex

   kan/kae: non-deferential, intimate, mainly male interlocutors

   dichǎn/khun   non-intimate, non-deferential, female speaker

   phǒm/khun   deferential, male speaker;

   krphǒm/thân   very deferential; male speaker

   khǎphacǎw/thǎn impersonal, formal, speaker either sex

   úa/lú: non-deferential (Chinese associations). (Diller 1994: 167)

To illustrate the effect of these differing dynamics, consider a possible Thai translation of the sentence 'I want to go with you', which only uses primitives:

(27) *chǎn   yà:k   pay   kàp   thoe:*
    1SG   want   go   with   2
    'I want to go with you.' (Diller 1994: 168)

From a sociolinguistic point of view, English 'I want to go with you' is relatively neutral, able to be uttered by a large range of speakers of differing genders, habitual politeness relations and social statuses. The Thai equivalent in (27), however, is much more restricted: it is the type of sentence which a mother might say to her daughter, but which a daughter would never say to her mother. None of the possible translations into Thai of 'I' and 'You', in fact, is sociolinguistically neutral, but carries with it suggestions about the identities of the speakers and the relationships between them. As a result, a semantic explication which uses any of them will have nothing of the neutral force of the English NSM paraphrases quoted above, but will carry with it all sorts of subtle indications about sociolinguistic register – indications which could be misleading if they are meant to embody entirely abstract, general statements about the meanings of words throughout an entire language community.

An NSM supporter might reply that this is just a fact about the way these forms are *used*, and not a fact about what they *mean*: we will discuss this distinction in the next two chapters. But even if we decide that this type of issue is not relevant to the analysis of the *meaning* of the forms, the bias introduced by the particular meanings of the Thai pronouns looks like a significant obstacle to the efficacy of NSM as a real tool of semantic analysis. NSM was designed not primarily as a method of extensional definition, but as a tool of cognitive definition. It is intended to make hard to understand concepts in one language comprehensible by translating them into primitive, allegedly universally understood terms. To the extent that the sociolinguistic values of the Thai forms confuse this task, NSM's claim to furnish cognitive definitions must be considered as compromised.

The second problem with NSM is the fact that many – perhaps all – of the English exponents of the NSM primes have several senses, with only one of these senses being identified as universal. (This is not just a problem with the English exponents of the primitives; the same problem would exist regardless of the language in which the primitives were expressed.) For example, in testing for the presence of an exponent of a primitive meaning in some language, it is not enough simply to ask whether the language in question has words for 'I, you, someone, etc.'; instead, we have to distinguish the sense claimed as universal from the others: is the primitive TRUE, for instance, better represented by the meaning present in (28) or (29)?

(28) *If you read it in a book it must be true.*

(29) *You must be true to yourself.*

The most obvious way to distinguish the intended sense would be simply to *define* it verbally. But since, *ex hypothesi*, the semantic primitives are indefinable, this option is unavailable. As a result, the project of testing the primitives cross-linguistically is seriously compromised, since you can never be sure that a claimed exponent of a primitive in a given language does in fact correspond to the required primitive meaning. (See Goddard (2002) for some suggested solutions to this problem.)

These problems disappear if NSM's claim to universality is abandoned, since only *universal* theories of semantic primitives are open to the sorts of criticism just advanced. If your theory only commits you to the existence of indefinable primitives within a single language, problems about cross-linguistic equivalence do not arise. This is the approach of, for example, Apresjan (2000: 228), for whom '[s]emantic primitiveness is determined ... by the structure of the lexicon of the language being described: lexeme L is considered a primitive if the given language has no $L_1, L_2 ... L_n$ via which it might be explicated'. In the next section, however, we will see that even this type of practice is threatened by quite general problems with the notion of definition.

2.6 Problems with definitions

So far we have been assuming that it is actually possible to formulate successful definitions for words in a significant number of cases. We should not take this for granted, however. One of the most frequent criticisms of definitional theories of semantics (as opposed, for example, to referential/denotational ones: see 1.6.1) is that no satisfying definition of a word has ever actually been formulated. The scepticism about the existence of definitions is so widespread, in fact, that many researchers in disciplines closely related to linguistics, such as cognitive science and artificial intelligence, have completely abandoned the idea that definitions even exist (see Fodor 1998 for details): the emphasis on definition in linguistics strikes many from these other disciplines as misguided. The overall rejection of definition outside linguistics as a defensible mode of meaning analysis has various motivations. Many of them derive from the problems involved in a psychologistic interpretation of definitions as concepts, in which the structure of a definition reflects the structure of the underlying concept (so that, for example, the concept BACHELOR could be said to be the combination of the concepts UNMARRIED and MAN in just the same way as the *definition* of *bachelor* might be thought to be 'unmarried man').

Linguistics, however, is not necessarily committed to a conceptualist interpretation of definitions. As our initial typology of definition suggested, a definition can serve many purposes, of which revealing the putative underlying conceptual structure of a unit of language is only one. Nevertheless, the extreme difficulty of phrasing accurate definitions should be an embarrassment to any theory in which definitions are a privileged mode of semantic analysis.

A classic case of definitional inadequacy is the proposed 'definition' we have just mentioned of *bachelor* as 'unmarried man'; this is the type of definition found in many popular dictionaries. One problem here is that there are many types of unmarried male, such as widowers, the Pope and Tarzan, whom we would not describe as bachelors. As a result, 'unmarried male' is not substitutable for bachelor *salva veritate*, and the definition therefore fails. There are many other examples like this. Even though we typically think of many words as having concise definitions, and that these definitions accurately convey the word's meaning, more detailed investigation reveals that our intuitions on this are in fact mistaken: when these definitions are subjected to scrutiny, it readily emerges that they are not, in fact, successful (for more examples, see 7.1.2).

A possible response here would be to claim that it is only the extreme brevity of the definition of *bachelor* which accounts for its inadequacy. If a definer tries hard enough, satisfactory definitions can be achieved: it is just that no one has yet taken the time to do so. This is exactly the point made by Wierzbicka (1996). According to her, the true definitions of most ordinary words are significantly longer than the brief statements we are used to reading in dictionaries. Here, for example, is her 'imperfect first approximation' definition of *paint*:

X painted Y with Z. =

(a) X did something to Y
(b) like people do
(c) when they want something to look good
(d) when X did it
(e) X put some stuff Z on all parts of Y that one could see
(f) if someone looked at Z at that time
(g) this person could say what colour Z was
(h) at the same time, this person could think that part of Z was water
(i) X wanted Z to be like part of Y
(j) after X did it, Z was like part of Y. (Wierzbicka 1996: 254–255)

As Wierzbicka points out, this definition is both longer, and structurally different from the types of definition familiar from dictionaries. It is essentially a definition by context, specifying 'a fairly complex scenario, with a number of temporal and causal links between the components' (Wierzbicka 1996: 255). Even in this complex, detailed form, however, the definition's accuracy can be challenged. If I have painted a car with red car enamel, there are many visible parts of the car which are not painted – the glass, the bumper bar, the headlights, the number plate, etc. Similar remarks apply to the sentence *She painted her face with rouge.* This invalidates component (e) of the definition. Components (i) and (j) are also problematic: if I *painted a box with red paint,* do we really want to say that I *wanted the red paint to be like part of the box* and that when I had finished *the red paint was like part of the box?* Maybe we do, maybe we don't: in any case, it doesn't seem clear enough to warrant inclusion in a definition. Similarly, the whole definition is equally appropriate as a definition of the word *spray,* as in the sentences *I sprayed my arm with insect repellant* or *I sprayed the flower with water.* I did this in order for my arm/the flower to look good (in the case of the arm, so that it would not be covered with ugly bites (component (c)), anyone looking at the repellant or the spray at that time, as at any other, could say what colour it was (component (g) – white, or transparent), the spray is clearly water-like (h) and I wanted the spray to become like part of the arm/the flower (components (i) and (j)). But since *spray* and *paint* are intuitively not synonyms, the definition of *paint* should exclude *spray.* (Note that *spraying* is also not *a kind of* painting; we cannot define *spray* simply by adding some extra components to the definition of *paint*.) This objection is possible because of the definition's description of the physical action of painting as *putting* stuff on the visible parts of the object. There are several ways of putting stuff on the visible parts of an object which observe all the conditions in (a) to (j) but which are not painting: as well as spraying, the process of dipping comes to mind. Apparently, then, increasing the length and detail of a definition does not necessarily increase its accuracy. (See Geeraerts 1993 for more discussion.)

One typical response to criticisms of definitions has been to claim that the definition captures the *core*, *central*, or *prototypical part* of the definiendum's meaning, and that the respects in which the definition fails all involve special or peripheral aspects (for a discussion of the notion of prototype, see Chapter 7). Thus, Wierzbicka introduces components (b) and (c) into the definition of *paint* in order to take account of cases like painting something with a special solution in order to protect it against rust: this is not strictly done in order to make something look good, but it is *like* other acts of painting which do have this goal. Similarly, one could respond to the above criticism of component (e) by saying that the *usual case* when painting something is that the thing being painted be completely covered, and that other cases are somehow derived from this one. And to return to our earlier examples, a linguist could claim that 'unmarried male' is still a legitimate definition of *bachelor* in spite of the counterexamples of widowers, etc., because it captures the core sense of *bachelor*.

These sorts of response are reasonable insofar as it does seem to be true that many words have a central set of typical applications, and a set of less typical ones. *Bachelor*, for instance, does indeed very often refer to unmarried males, even if not all unmarried males can be described as bachelors. We will consider this type of view of word meaning in Chapter 7. But without a principled way of delimiting what does and does not count as a core meaning or a prototypical instance of a word, it is too easy for the definer to simply dismiss *any* counterexample to a definition as simply relating to a 'non-core' aspect of the definiendum's meaning. Fodor puts this option with characteristic bluntness:

'Core meaning' and the like are not, however, notions for which much precise explication gets provided in the lexical semantics literature. The upshot, often enough, is that the definitions that are put on offer are isolated, simply by stipulation, from prima facie counterexamples.

This strikes me as a mug's game, and not one that I'm tempted to play. I take the proper ground rule to be that one expression defines another only if the two expressions are synonymous; and I take it to be a necessary condition for their synonymy that whatever one expression applies to, the other does too. (1998: 48)

Under this view, a definition has to be substitutable for the definiendum in every single context. As we will see in the next chapter, given the infinite variety of language use, it would seem that any word can be used in *any* context (to see this, think of errors, joke contexts and fantasy): as a result, a comprehensive definition would seem unattainable.

Many linguists, however, would reject the argument that the heterogeneity of uses renders comprehensive definition impossible. For them, the fact that any word can be used in any context is only true in a trivial sense: there are clear differences between core and non-core uses, and definitions are possible for the former.

2.7 Definition, understanding and use

What is the point of defining meaning? In some domains of human activity, definitions function as the guarantors of the consistency of language. This is particularly so in science and technology. If metallurgists, for example, did not have any fixed working definition of terms like *iron* or *copper*, it would be impossible to check that two metallurgists talking about *iron*, for example, were in fact talking about the same substance. Needless to say, this need for checking does not usually arise in a domain like metallurgy, where the definitions of terms are well established; in any cases of doubt, however, it is precisely the existence of the definition that provides the ultimate guarantee that language is being used in a consistent way. The law is another obvious domain in which the role of definition is central. Juridical terms like *murder*, *contract* or *fraud* require clear definitions which fix their denotation by designating exactly what does and does not count as an example of each. The provision of these definitions is a time-consuming and unending process, and there is often little agreement as to what the 'true' definition of such terms actually is. But whenever a legal argument is mounted about the appropriateness of a certain legal term to a certain situation, it is, in effect, that term's definition in that domain which is in question.

The case of ordinary uses of natural language is both similar and different. Mostly, conversation and other examples of language proceed without the need for explicit definition: this is only ever required to resolve confusions. And when we do ask for clarification about the correct use of a word, nominal definitions of words' meanings are not usually either solicited or provided. Thus, if I am unsure about the meaning of the word *dupe*, I am more likely to ask the question 'what's a dupe?' rather than the question 'what does *dupe* mean?' Furthermore, the answer I receive will usually not, as noted by Riegel (1990: 97–98), be of the form 'the word *dupe* means/signifies/designates a gullible person', but rather of the form, 'a dupe is a gullible person'. Even when a genuine nominal definition is offered, the gap between a cognitive and an extensional definition is very great. Thus, I can define the meaning of *water* extensionally as H_2O, but if the addressee of the definition has no knowledge of chemistry this definition will not be effective in bringing about an understanding of the word's meaning.

But definitions do take on a central role in language use if we take concepts to be essentially definitional in nature, and assume that concepts are or enter into the meanings of words. If concepts correspond to word meanings, and word meanings can be captured in definitions, then it is the definition which is in some sense activated during language use. To claim that definitions are involved in language use in this way is not to claim that they are so involved *consciously*. We may be quite able to use a word appropriately, without being able to phrase a satisfactory definition of it: the knowledge enabling correct use of the word is unconscious, and in no way implies an ability to produce an *explicit* definition. To say, then, that concepts are or function as definitions is certainly not to say that we consciously carry around a dictionary-like list in our heads.

Summary

Meaning, definition and the mental lexicon
The concept of a word's meaning is closely linked to the concept of definition. Many linguists identify the task of linguistic semantics with the task of describing the entries stored in the **mental lexicon**, a stock of words and meanings stored in long-term memory: the definition of a word is part of its entry in the mental lexicon, and the process of matching a meaning with a word-form is assumed to be analogous to that involved in consulting a dictionary. In order to serve the purposes of serious linguistic description, the definitions in the lexicon must be much more detailed than is usual in ordinary dictionaries.

What units need to receive definition?
Any attempt to analyse the meanings of language must specify what the meaning-bearing units are. Individual lexemes are the central examples of units with individually describable meanings. Morphemes also have meanings, as do phrasal verbs and compounds.

Ambiguities about the level of grammatical structure to which meaning is correctly attributed are not infrequent: sound symbolism and idioms exemplify cases where the correct level for the analysis of a meaning may not be clear.

Real and nominal definition
We can distinguish two types of definition:

- definition of the essence of a thing (**real definition**), or
- definition of the meaning of a word (**nominal definition**).

Most linguists take nominal definition to be the type that is of interest to linguistic semantic research.

Cognitive and extensional definition
A nominal definition may be of two types:

- **cognitive** (aimed to inculcate an understanding of the word's correct use), or
- **extensional** (aimed at delimiting the denotation of the word).

Modes of definition

Cognitive nominal definition can take a number of forms. It may be

- definition by ostension,
- definition by synonymy,
- definition by context or typical exemplar, or
- definition by genus and differentia.

Often, definitions combine these means.

Definitions are typically required to be truth-preserving under substitution for their definiendum.

Semantic primitives

Certain theories of semantics try to restrict the language of definitions to a set of universal or language-specific semantic primitives, but these attempts are faced with many difficulties. Not least of these is the extreme difficulty in accurately defining words: whether based on semantic primitives or not, no fully accurate definition of a word has ever been advanced in linguistics.

Mostly, conversation and other instances of language use proceed without the need for explicit definition: this is only ever required to resolve confusions. From this point of view, explicit definition plays a rather insignificant role in language. But definitions take on a central role in language use if we take concepts to be essentially definitional in nature, and assume that concepts are or enter into the meanings of words.

Further reading

On dictionaries and their histories, see Landau (1984), and, for readers of French, Collinot and Mazière (1997) and Matoré (1968). Dixon and Aikhenvald (2002) is an up-to-date discussion of the problem of wordhood in the languages of the world. On onomasiology and semasiology, see Baldinger (1980). Voeltz and Kilian-Hatz (2001) is a volume of articles on sound symbolism. On English compounds, see Bauer (1998). On theoretical lexicography, see Apresjan (2000). On contextual modulation, see Murphy (2002: 415–422). Robinson (1950) and Chapter 6 of Ogden and Richards (1949) are accessible (if somewhat old-fashioned) introductions to issues in definition quite generally; Chaurand and Mazière (1990) is a useful collection (in French) of short articles on historical and theoretical aspects of definition. For an influential discussion of synonymy see Mates (1950). On semantic primitives, see Katz and Fodor (1963). Wierzbicka (1996) is a comprehensive introduction to NSM. For discussion and criticism of the theory, see the special volume of *Theoretical Linguistics* 29 (2003). Fodor (1998) contains a detailed critique of definitional attempts in linguistic semantics. The *International Journal of Lexicography* publishes articles relevant to many of the themes of this chapter.

Exercises

Analytical questions

1. Use the internet to find as many examples as possible of sentences containing one of the following words: *hold, fluffy, horse, keep, early, finish, problem* and *pernicious.* Aim for at least fifty examples of each word from as wide a range of contexts as possible, and formulate definitions of them which fit all the examples.

2. Consult a German dictionary and try to find possible examples of sound symbolism. Is it always clear whether a form should be considered ideophonic? How might one decide? (Some suggestions: *Glanz* 'gleam, shine, sparkle', *gleißen* 'gleam, glisten', *glimmen* 'glow', *glitzern* 'glitter', *glühen* 'glow', *Glut* 'embers', 'glow', *glitschen* 'slip', *glitschig* 'slippery', *glatt* 'smooth', *Glatze* 'bald head', *gleiten* 'glide, slide, skid'.)

3. How compositional or idiomatic are the following verbs/verb phrases: *take pride in, cut short, see fit, put paid to, catch sight of, lose touch, lose hope, make allowance for, pride oneself on, pay attention to, put up with, look down on, break even, make do with, get rid of, get going, play around, take off, touch down, bring up (children), turn on (a light)*?

4. *Webster's* dictionary and the *Concise Oxford* relate the meaning of *green* in *green with envy* to the 'pale, sick, wan' sense of *green* (e.g. *She looks quite green when she is seasick*). COBUILD, however, lists it as a separate sense, and OALD lists it as an idiom. What are the pros and cons of these different arrangements? Is there any evidence one could bring to bear to determine the best description?

Questions for discussion

5. Consider the following comment of Bloomfield's: 'In language teaching the difficulty of describing meanings makes a great deal of trouble. By tradition we assign a meaning, in the shape of a brief English definition, to each foreign word; then, whenever the foreign language does not agree with our grammatical rules and definitions, we say that it has an "idiom"' (Quoted in Hockett 1970: 404). Bloomfield implies that the category of idiom is only a result of the inadequacy of definition: given adequate definitions, idioms disappear. Is this a reasonable view of the status of idioms in the lexicon?

6. Consider the English form written *'ll* (as in *tomorrow I'll be skiing*). Semantically, this form has the same meaning as the auxiliary verb *will*, but its syntactic properties are very different: unlike *will*, *'ll* may not occur independently in English, but must always be suffixed to a preceding Noun Phrase (typically a pronoun). This is because *'ll* violates **phonological minimality** in English. What this means is that *'ll* not only *is* not, but *cannot* be an independent word in English, since every independent English word must have at least one vowel (a 'pure' vowel or a diphthong). Thus, while a fully fledged word like *I* [aɪ] or *owe* [əʊ] does not have any other segments than a single diphthong, anything lacking a diphthong or vowel does not have word status in English. *'ll* is not thus a phonological word in English. Is it a grammatical word?

7. In 2.1.1 we discussed the *Concise Oxford's* definition of *pour.* Compare the definitions from the other dictionaries below, and describe them with respect

to their definitional technique (GD, synonymy, context, typical example). What are the virtues and disadvantages of each? How accurate are they?

Webster's Unabridged 2nd edn. (2001)

v.t. 1. to send (a liquid, fluid, or anything in loose particles) flowing or falling, as from one container to another, or into, over, or on something: *to pour a glass of milk; to pour water on a plant.* 2. to emit or propel, esp. continuously or rapidly: *The hunter poured bullets into the moving object.* 3. to produce or utter in or as in a stream or flood (often fol. by *out*): *to pour out one's troubles to a friend.* – v.i. 4. to issue, move or proceed in great quantity or number: *Crowds poured from the stadium after the game.* 5. to flow forth or along; stream: *Floodwaters poured over the embankments.* 6. to rain heavily (often used impersonally with *it* as subject): *It was pouring, but fortunately we had umbrellas.*

Oxford Advanced Learner's Dictionary 6th edn. (2000)

1. [VN] [usually + *adv./prep.*] to make a liquid or other substance flow from a container in a continuous stream, especially by holding the container at an angle: *Pour the sauce over the pasta. Although I poured it carefully, I still managed to spill some.*
2. [V + *adv./prep.*] (of liquid, smoke, light, etc.) to flow quickly in a continuous stream. *Tears poured down his cheeks. Thick black smoke was pouring out the roof.*
3. (**sth**) (**out**) to serve a drink by letting it flow from a container into a glass or cup: [VN] *Will you pour the coffee? I was in the kitchen, pouring out drinks.* [VN, VNN] *I've poured a cup of tea for you. I've poured you a cup of tea. Shall I pour?*
4. [V] when rain **pours** down or when it's **pouring with rain**, rain is falling heavily: *The rain continued to pour down. It's pouring outside. It's pouring with rain.*
5. [V + adv./prep.] to come or go somewhere continuously in large numbers. *Letters of complaint continue to pour in. Commuters came pouring out of the station.*

PHR V **pour sth into sth** to provide a large amount of money for sth: *The government has poured millions into the education system.* **pour out** when feelings or someone's words **pour out**, they are expressed, usually after they have been kept hidden for some time: *Wave after wave of pent up emotion poured out. The whole story then came pouring out.*

COBUILD English Learner's Dictionary (1989)

1. If you **pour** a liquid or other substance, you make it flow steadily out of a container by holding the container at an angle. Eg *The waiter poured the wine into her glass… …a machine that poured grain into sacks.* = decant
2. If you **pour** someone a drink, you fill a cup or glass with the drink so that they can drink it. Eg *He poured Ellen a glass of wine… …Lally poured herself another cup of tea… She poured a drink for herself.*
3. When a liquid or other substance **pours** somewhere, for example through a hole, it flows there quickly and in large quantities. Eg *The rain poured through a hole in the roof… The sweat began to pour down his face.* = stream

4. When it rains very heavily, you can say that it **is pouring**. Eg *In London it poured all the time… It was absolutely pouring with rain.* = bucket

5. If people or animals **pour** into or out of a place, they go there quickly and in large numbers. Eg *Refugees are now pouring into this country.* = stream

6. If information **pours** into or out of a place, a lot of it is obtained or given. Eg *Messages of encouragement poured in from people of all kinds… … the lies that poured from headquarters.* = flood, stream

7. If you **pour** money or energy into an activity or organization, you use a lot of money or energy in order to do the activity or help the organization. Eg *The state is pouring money into further education… They poured their energies into religious reform.* = pump,

pour out

1. If you **pour out** a drink, you fill a cup or glass with it. Eg *Castle poured out two glasses of whisky.* 2. If you **pour out** your thoughts, feelings or experiences, you tell someone all about them. Eg *I was on the verge of pouring out all my feelings… He poured out a horrifying story.* = reveal

8. Answer the same questions for the following definitions of *ram:*

OALD 6th edn. 2000.

vb. '1 [VN] (of a vehicle, ship, etc.) to drive into or hit another vehicle, ship, etc. with force, sometimes deliberately: *Two passengers were injured when their taxi was rammed from behind by a bus.* 2 [VN + adv./prep.] to push smth with force: *She rammed the key into the lock.* (figurative) *The spending cuts had been rammed through Congress.* IDM *ram sth home (especially BrE)* to emphasize an idea argument, etc. very strongly to make sure people listen to it. PHR V *ram into sth, ram sth into sth* to hit against sth or to make sth hit against sth *He rammed his truck into the back of the one in front.*

Concise Oxford 9th edn. 1995

v.tr. 1 force or squeeze into place by pressure. 2 (usu. foll. by *down, in, into*) beat down or drive in by heavy blows. 3 (of a ship, vehicle, etc) strike violently, crash against 4 (foll. by *against, at, on, into*) dash or violently impel. ● ram home, stress forcefully (an argument, lesson, etc.)

Webster's 2nd edn. 2001

v.t 10 [entry numbers continuous with noun entries] to drive or force by heavy blows. 11. to strike with great force, dash violently against: *The car went out of control and rammed the truck.* 12. to cram; stuff: *They rammed the gag in his mouth.* 13. To push firmly: *to ram a bill through the Senate.*

9. The Warlpiri verb *pakarni* has a multitude of possible English translations; just some are 'hit', 'strike', 'bump', 'crash into', 'slap', 'kick', 'knock', 'whip', 'run into', 'beat', 'thrash', 'thresh', 'thresh out of', 'get by hitting', 'get by threshing', 'hunt', 'hunt and kill', 'chop', 'cut', 'fashion into', 'chop (into)', 'chop out of', 'pierce', 'dig in(to)', 'thrust into', 'stick into', 'paint', 'put on', 'apply to', 'smear with', 'fill oneself with', 'stuff oneself with', 'have one's fill of', 'gorge oneself', 'try to catch up with', 'dance', 'perform', 'initiate', and 'circumcise'.

The main Warlpiri dictionary arranges these glosses into the following seven meaning groups (ERG stands for ergative case; the 'double dative' is a particular syntactic construction):

1. xERG produce concussion on surface of y, by some entity coming into contact with y

   hit, strike, bump, crash into, slap, kick, knock, whip, run into, beat, thrash, thresh
   Where *y* is a game animal:
   hunt, hunt and kill.
   xERG cause some entity to move towards yDAT [Double Dative], in order to hit *(pakarni)* y
   take a swing at, hit at, strike (out) at

2. xERG produce separation in y, by causing sharp edged instrument (typically axe) to come into contact with y, by forcefully manipulating said instrument

   chop, cut

3. xERG produce indentation in y (typically ground), by causing some sharp pointed entity to come into contact with y, by forcefully manipulating said entity

   pierce, dig into, thrust into, stick into

4. xERG paint y

   paint, put on, apply to, smear with

5. Idiom: xERG cause self to be excessively satiated, by ingesting large quantity of food or drink

   fill oneself with, stuff oneself with, have one's fill of, gorge oneself

6. Idiom: xERG move along path towards y [Double Dative], in order to be at same place as y

   try to catch up with, try to reach

7. Idiom: xERG (typically man) performs y (= ceremony), by moving along a path in a stylized manner usually involving a high stepping movement of legs and forceful lowering of feet to the ground

   dance, perform corroboree

8. Idiom: xERG (= initiated man) perform ceremonial actions for the benefit of y (= male human previously uninitiated) at circumcision ceremony

   initiate, circumcise, make man

9. xERG (= head cold/influenza) produce characteristic effect on y (= being)

   have a cold, have the flu, have pneumonia, have bronchitis

   Based simply on the meanings of the English glosses, what other arrangements are conceivable? Can you see other ways of grouping the glosses into broader definitional categories? What would one need to know about Warlpiri in order to decide what the best arrangement is?

10. Words like *good/bad* and *right/wrong* seem particularly hard to define. Why? Do they present any special problems for the belief that all words have definitions?

3 The scope of meaning I: external context

CHAPTER PREVIEW

Linguistic expressions can only occur in particular contexts; as a result, working out what role context plays in the determination of meaning is an important part of semantic analysis. This chapter considers one essential type of context: the **external** or **real-world** context to which linguistic expressions refer.

We begin by discussing an important distinction: the distinction between what a word inherently means, and what it can be *used* to mean in a particular context, showing that this distinction is often not self-evident. We then distinguish the different types of task a hearer must perform to correctly understand a linguistic expression in its context (3.1).

In 3.2 we begin the treatment of external context by considering the relation between **sense** and **reference**, discussing

◆ the origins of this distinction in Frege;

◆ its applications in linguistics; and

◆ the nature of **deictic expressions**, which can be seen as a bridge between language and its surrounding external context.

In 3.3. we discuss, and reject, a possible distinction between knowledge of a word's inherent, linguistic meaning (**dictionary knowledge**) and knowledge of facts about the word's external context (**encyclopaedic knowledge**).

3.1 Meaning and context

For the purposes of deciding what a piece of language means, no utterance can be considered as a self-standing whole: words only exist within particular contexts, and we will not be able to achieve an adequate description of meaning if we don't take these contexts into account. Indeed, one of the main questions which any theory of meaning has to answer concerns the *scope* of an expression's meaning: how much of the total effect of an expression is to be attributed to its meaning, and how much to the context in which it occurs? For example, consider the meaning of the English possessive morpheme (-s) in (1a) and (1b):

(1) a. *Denise's teacher got burnt.*
     b. *Denise's brioche got burnt.*

The possessive morpheme expresses two quite different relationships in each sentence: in (1a) it denotes a relationship like that of the verb *teach* to its object: (1a) means 'the person who teaches Denise got burnt'. In (1b), on the other hand, it denotes a relation of ownership or possession: *Denise's brioche got burnt* means 'the brioche belonging to Denise got burnt'. But does this difference result from a difference in the *meaning* of the possessive case, or is it a product of the context in which it is used? To many linguists, it would seem wrong to claim that the English possessive morpheme -*s* has two different *meanings* in (1a) and (1b). Instead, these linguists would claim, we should analyse its meaning in abstract terms, as denoting a quite general *relation of dependence* between two nouns, and leave the details of this relation in a given context to be supplied through the application of our real-world knowledge about the things being referred to. We know that people's relationships with teachers are different from their relationships with food. As a result, the possessive case in the context of a word like *teacher* receives a quite different interpretation from the one it has in the context of a word like *brioche*, even though the general, abstract meaning of the possessive – marking an (unspecified) dependence between the two nouns – is the same in each case. The fact that the exact details of this general, unspecified meaning may be vague, and in any case are open to various interpretations, does not detract from the intuition that it is the *same* meaning present in both cases.

In this chapter, we will consider the **external** or **real-world** context *to* which linguistic expressions refer. Our understanding of expressions' meaning is often closely related to our knowledge of this context. The next chapter discusses the **interpersonal** context of linguistic action *in which* any utterance is placed. In order to interpret an expression correctly, it would seem that a hearer must perform a number of related tasks which involve these two different types of context. For example, consider someone interested in learning to play golf, who receives the advice *All golfers need to find some good clubs.* In order to understand what the speaker means, the hearer must:

1. **Disambiguate** the noun *club*, which can mean both 'implement used to hit golf ball' and 'association in charge of a golf course'. Given the context, which interpretation is intended?
2. **Assign referents** to the noun phrases *all golfers* and *good clubs*: who does the speaker mean by *golfers*? What, for them, is a *good club*?
3. Determine the quantity referred to by *some*: roughly how *many* clubs does the speaker count as *some*, as opposed to *lots*?
4. Realize that the expression is intended as part of the context of advice, and is an *instruction* to find good clubs, not an assertion about a universal obligation falling on all golfers: this realization concerns the **illocutionary force** of the utterance.
5. As a result of (4), **extract the implication** that since all golfers need to find some good clubs, the hearer must also try to find some.

QUESTION Is there anything else which the hearer must realize in order to interpret the statement properly? How separate are the tasks in (1)–(5)?

In cases like this, the hearer makes the important interpretative decisions quite automatically. In fact, it is rather artificial even to differentiate the five different elements above: all that is required, you might think, is for the hearer to realize how, holistically, to take the instruction. Nevertheless, each item of the list expresses aspects of utterance interpretation which can be observed separately. The question of the interrelations between these different types of interpretative task will be important throughout this and the next chapter.

QUESTION Describe the decisions the hearer has to make about the interpretation of the following utterances in order to understand the speaker's likely meaning:

> *Customers are informed that the shop will be closing in fifteen minutes.*
> *Could you pass the chilli sauce?*
> *No one's going to the bar tonight.*
> *I'm sorry to bother you.*
> *What are you doing here?*
> *Will you ever grow up?*
> *I can't believe you called me that.*

Semantics is not the only field interested in phenomena like these: the subdiscipline of linguistics called **pragmatics** (Greek *praxis*, 'action'), which concerns the use of language in real contexts, also studies them. Semantics and pragmatics are closely related. Pragmatics cannot study language use without a prior conception of meaning: without knowing what words mean, one cannot decide how speakers modify and manipulate these meanings in actual situations of language use. Similarly, semantics cannot arrive at any description of what words mean without looking at the ways they are used in different contexts. This interrelation between meaning and use means that pragmatics and semantics exist in a close symbiosis.

3.2 External context: sense and reference

Perhaps the most basic type of context is the extralinguistic context of **reference**, which concerns the entities which an expression is *about*. (Following the Austrian philosopher Franz Brentano (1838–1917), the property, shared by thoughts and meanings, of being about things other than themselves – objects in the world, possible states of affairs, etc. – is known as their **intentionality**.)

As discussed in Chapter 1, reference is one of the fundamental concepts of the study of meaning. However, for a long time the distinction was not explicitly drawn between an expression's referent (the object to which it refers) and its sense (its general meaning, abstracted from its use to refer). It was the German logician and philosopher of mathematics Gottlob Frege (1848–1925) who first saw the significance of this distinction. Frege's primary concerns had little to do with language; for much of his career, his main goal was to clarify the logical bases of arithmetic. Between about 1891 and 1906, however, he became interested in questions of meaning, and elaborated the distinction between sense (*Sinn*) and reference (*Bedeutung*) that subsequent philosophy and linguistics have inherited.

3.2.1 The Fregean distinction

Frege had no single term for 'meaning', in the sense of the knowledge needed to understand a word (Dummett 2001: 12). Instead, he distinguished three aspects of a word's total semantic effect:

- its 'force', which covered whether it was a statement or a question (he seems not to have considered other categories like commands);
- its 'tone' or 'colouring', which refers to differences of register and connotation (such as the difference between the verbs *die, be deceased,* and *pass away*: Dummett 2001);
- and its sense.

The notions of force and tone are reasonably self-explanatory. But what is sense? In his famous 1892 essay 'On sense and reference' (sometimes translated 'sense and nominatum'), Frege introduced the distinction between sense and reference in order to explain a puzzle about statements of identity like those in the (a) and (b) pairs of (2)–(7) below:

(2) a. *The morning star is the morning star.*
    b. *The morning star is the evening star.*

(3) a. *Abou Ammar is Abou Ammar.*
    b. *Abou Ammar is Yasser Arafat.*

(4) a. *Amber is amber.*
    b. *Amber is fossilized tree resin.*

(5)　a. *The president of the World Chess Federation is the President of the World Chess Federation.*
　　b. *The president of the World Chess Federation is the president of the Republic of Kalmykia.*

(6)　a. *The founder of the FBI is the founder of the FBI.*
　　b. *The founder of the FBI is the grandson of the King of Westphalia.*

(7)　a. *The Feast of Saint Sylvester is The Feast of Saint Sylvester.*
　　b. *The Feast of Saint Sylvester is New Year's Eve.*

If all there is to meaning is simply reference, there should be no difference between each pair of sentences (we are ignoring tone and force, which are not relevant in these examples). This is because in each case both noun phrases have the same referent: the planet Venus in (2), the former president of the Palestinian Authority in (3), amber in (4), the Kalmykian president Kirsan Nikolayevich Ilyumzhinov in (5), Charles Joseph Bonaparte in (6), and December 31 in (7). There is, however, a clear difference: while the (a) sentences are tautologies and uninformative – they don't give us any information – the (b) sentences clearly do tell us something. But if a term's reference is all there is to its meaning, how can this be explained? If meaning is no more than what a term refers to, the two pairs of sentences should not differ at all in their cognitive effect.

Frege's solution to this puzzle was that an expression's reference is not, after all, the only part of its meaning: there is something else, which he called its **sense.** An expression's sense is the way in which we grasp or understand its referent. It is sense which gives an expression its cognitive value or significance. One way of thinking of an expression's sense is as the *mode of presentation* of its referent: the way in which the referent is presented to our understanding. It is precisely because the noun phrases in the (b) sentences above have different ways of presenting their referents that the phrases are informative. The sense of 'morning star', which must be something like 'star visible in the morning', is clearly apparent from the elements of the expression itself; this is a different mode of presentation of the term's referent, Venus, from the one we see in the 'evening star'.

In other cases, the exact nature of an expression's sense – its mode of presentation to our understanding – may be less obvious: what, for example, is the sense of a proper name like Yasser Arafat or Abou Ammar? The nature of sense is one of the central topics of the philosophy of language. Philosophers like Frege and Bertrand Russell (1872–1970) thought that the sense of a proper name is some information which uniquely distinguishes the referent. The other main theory about the reference of proper names is a causal-historical one, according to which names are linked to their referents by a chain of actual naming events: in the first instance, a referent is given a name, and the name is passed down through the speech community: see Donnellan (1972) and Kripke (1980).

Sense and reference are not on an equal footing in Frege's theory of meaning. For him, sense determines reference. It is the sense of an expression which allows us to know what it refers to. For example, if I know what the word *amber* can refer to, this is because I have a conception of its sense which allows me to pick out real examples of amber when I am confronted with them. If the sense of amber is 'fossilized tree resin', then whenever I encounter a piece of fossilized tree resin, I can identify it as a referent of the word *amber* and accordingly call it *amber*. Alternatively, if the sense of amber is 'golden-yellow semiprecious stone', then every time I come across a golden-yellow precious stone I can also identify it as amber. Thus, for Frege it is not just an arbitrary fact that words have the denotations (classes of referent) they do. A word only refers in virtue of its sense. Senses, not referents, form parts of our thoughts. The only access we have to actual referents is via the senses of the words which refer to them, and these senses are the forms (modes of presentation) in which they come before our understanding. Actual amber obviously cannot be embodied physically in our thoughts; instead, in order for us to think about it, it must be presented to our minds in some particular way, and this particular 'mode of presentation' is the sense of the word *amber*. It is consistent with this picture of the relation between sense and reference that some expressions (*square circle*, *six-foot high midget*, etc.) clearly have sense, but lack reference: sense, not reference, is the essential part of meaning (see Chapter 1 for discussion).

It is not just individual expressions which have sense and reference, according to Frege: entire sentences do as well. Sentences, for Frege, are the expressions of thoughts, so the sense of a sentence is the thought it expresses. This is reasonably straightforward. On the other hand, Frege's ideas about a sentence's reference are at first sight fairly surprising: Frege said that the reference of a sentence is the sentence's status as true or false: its **truth-value**. Thus, a true sentence refers to Truth, and a false sentence refers to Falsity in the same way as proper names like *Tom* refer to particular individuals.

The Fregean doctrine of the reference of sentences is likely to cause considerable bewilderment. Naively, one might have thought either that the notion of reference was simply not relevant to sentences, or that the referent of a sentence would be some sort of situation (for a development of this line of thinking, see Barwise and Perry 1983). In any case, it is not easy to see how a sentence – or, for that matter, anything else – can be said to refer to Truth. There is not enough space here to go into Frege's motivation for his position (see Dummett 2001: 13–14). What it shows, though, is the central place occupied for him by the notion of truth. Truth is the basic notion in Frege's semantic theory, through which both sense and reference are to be explained. To know the sense of a sentence, or to have the thought expressed by the sentence is, for Frege, to know how the sentence could be assigned a value as true or false: to know what the *conditions* are that would make it true or false. These conditions are known as the sentence's **truth conditions**. If I know the meaning of the sentence *Satie subsequently collapsed into a state of extreme introspection and alcoholism*, I know what state the referents of the sentence would have to be in for this

sentence to be true – I know, in other words, the statement's truth conditions, i.e. what the world would be *like* if this statement were true. And
knowing what the world would be like were the statement true then
allows me to determine, by looking at the words' referents, whether the
world actually is this way, and whether or not the sentence is therefore
true. To take another example, knowing the sense of the sentence *Your
father wants to recite a poem* involves knowing what the conditions are that
would make this sentence true: thus, if you were told that *Your father would
like to recite a poem* you would be able to determine whether this was true
by finding your father and seeing whether he wanted to recite a poem. It
is the fact that you know how to go about determining the truth of a statement that therefore constitutes your knowledge of the statement's sense.

Why did Frege give truth such a central place in his conception of
semantics? Kamp and Reyle justify the centrality of truth as follows:

…truth is of the utmost importance to us. This is especially so in the context of *practical reasoning*. When I reason my way towards a plan of action,
and then act according to that plan, my action will be prone to fail, or
even to lead to disaster, if the factual beliefs underlying my deliberation
are false – even if my deliberation cannot be faulted in any other way.

…

Since truth and falsity are of such paramount importance, and since it
is in virtue of their meaning that thoughts and utterances can be distinguished into those that are true and those that are false, it is natural
to see the world-directed, truth-value determining aspect of meaning as
central; and, consequently, to see it as one of the central obligations of a
theory of meaning to explain how meaning manifests itself in the determination of truth and falsity.

(Kamp and Reyle 1993: 11)

However, as pointed out by Lyons, there are many occasions in which it is
not the truth of a linguistic expression which seems to be the most important factor governing its use:

…successful reference does not depend upon the truth of the description contained in the referring expression. The speaker (and perhaps also
the hearer) may mistakenly believe that some person is the postman,
when he is in fact the professor of linguistics, and incorrectly, though
successfully, refer to him by means of the expression 'the postman'. It is
not even necessary that the speaker should believe that the description
is true of the referent. He may be ironically employing a description he
knows to be false, or diplomatically accepting as correct a false description which his hearer believes to be true of the referent; and there are
yet other possibilities.

(Lyons 1977: 181–182)

As we will see at various points in what follows, many linguists reject the
elevation of truth as the central notion in semantic analysis (for other
limits to the relevance of truth in semantics, see 4.3.1).

Sense and psychology

Before leaving Frege, it is important to emphasize the theoretical status of the concept of sense. Sense should not be identified simply with the pretheoretical term *meaning*; rather, it is a quite specific way of thinking about the cognitive effect of words, which contrasts strongly in a number of ways with the term *meaning*. One aspect of Fregean sense in particular may appear somewhat surprising for people who, like most linguists, are accustomed to thinking about meanings psychologically – as, in other words, private mental entities. One of the cornerstones of Frege's whole approach to philosophy was the rejection of the interpretation of the meaning of a linguistic expression as a private psychological entity of any sort whatsoever. In his philosophy of mathematics, he similarly rejected any attempt to reduce the meaning of mathematical terms to mental entities. Fregean sense is thus not to be confused with the subjective, individual ideas or mental images which an earlier philosophical tradition derived from Aristotle and Locke, and many people today, think of as constituting the meanings of lexical items. Even though senses are things which we grasp mentally, they are not private ideas or mental images. The sense of an expression is a part of a thought; and thoughts, for Frege, are not subjective entities which vary from one individual to another. Instead, thoughts are *objective but intangible* entities, and it is this objective character which guarantees that people may talk about the same thing. Thus, while we often informally say that two people have different concepts of something (honesty, a good time, etc.), and are inclined to extend this way of thinking to word-meanings, this sort of move is incompatible with the Fregean theory of sense. Senses – objective, shared, non-private modes of presentation – do not differ from one person to another.

3.2.2 The sense/reference distinction and linguistic description

For the purposes of linguistic description, the Fregean theory of sense and reference needs considerable development. There is not room here to discuss anywhere near the full range of questions necessarily raised in any thorough exploration of the place of reference in language. Instead, we can only indicate some of the most important.

3.2.2.1 Reference, speakers and hearers

Sense seems clearly to be a property of linguistic expressions: it is words and sentences which have senses. Even though we grasp senses with our minds, the question of what sense a given expression possesses is not, for Frege, under the speaker's control (see text box). Reference, however, is quite different. Unlike sense, reference *is* under the speaker's control. It is not words which refer, but speakers. Searle (1969: 82) gives the following two necessary conditions for accomplishing an act of reference:

1. There must exist one and only one object to which the speaker's utterance of the expression applies.
2. The hearer must be given sufficient means to identify the object from
   the speaker's utterance of the expression.

Clearly, since the hearer can be given any number of means to identify the
intended object, the reference of a term in a particular context depends
on the speaker (and also of course, if it is successful, on the hearer), not
on the term itself. Codes are perhaps the most obvious example of the fact
that it is the speaker, not the expression itself, which refers. A code is a
speech-style in which speaker and hearer have agreed to reassign conventional referents (and senses). There are many others, however. In Warlpiri,
for example, a particular style of speech called Jiliwirri, used by men during initiation ceremonies, replaces the conventional referents of words
with their antonyms (opposites) (Hale 1971). For example, to express the
idea 'I am sitting on the ground' in Jiliwirri, the Warlpiri sentence
'Someone else is standing in the sky' is used; similarly, the sentence 'I am
short' conveys in Jiliwirri the idea 'you are tall':

(8) *kari*   *ka*   *nguru-ngka*   *kari-mi*
     other   AUX   sky-LOC   stand-NONPAST
     'Someone else is standing in the sky' (ordinary Warlpiri)
     'I am sitting on the ground' (Jiliwirri) (Hale 1971: 473 [reglossed])

(9) *ngaju-rna*   *rdangkarlpa*
     I-1S   short
     'I am short' (ordinary Warlpiri)
     'You are tall' (Jiliwirri) (Hale 1971: 473 [reglossed])

One might, of course, say that in this sort of situation it is also the words'
senses which have changed. Under that description, Jiliwirri would constitute a separate language with its own repertoire of senses: a language
which happened to have a very close relation to standard Warlpiri in phonology, morpho syntax and in much of the vocabulary, but in which certain crucial semantic differences existed. Another example of the variability of reference may often be found in people's kitchens. Imagine a
kitchen in which rubbish was placed in a plastic bag hanging on hooks
behind the door of a cupboard under the sink. We can easily imagine that
this might be referred to as *the bin*, even though the *sense* of the noun *bin*
is in no way simply that of a plastic bag. (Of course, if the sense of *bin* is
'receptacle *of any kind* for rubbish', then *bin* will be being used here in a
way compatible with its sense.)

The variability of reference is even more deep-seated in language than
these examples suggest. If we reflect on real discourse, which along with
'literal' uses of languages also contains metaphors, ironical statements,
exaggerations and many other types of non-standard reference, to say nothing of simple mistakes, it will soon become obvious that the referential
scope of words is extremely large – that, given the right conditions, any
word can be used to refer to *any* referent. This poses a considerable challenge

to the theory of sense. For if a word's reference is determined by its sense, then the range of reference that any word may have is extremely wide – in fact, indefinite. As a result, the characterization of sense will have to be broad enough to accommodate all the referential possibilities.

If a given word can refer to any referent, we need to distinguish its typical, expected referents from its atypical, unexpected ones. We take this problem up in Chapter 7. More importantly, we need to distinguish between **successful** and **correct** acts of reference. If an act of reference is successful, it succeeds in identifying the referent to the hearer. If it is correct, it refers to the referent in a way which conforms to an assumed standard. Thus, to take up the example of the bin, if I say *the bin is under the sink*, then I may well successfully refer to the rubbish-bag in which I expect the hearer to put their rubbish; but I do not correctly refer to it, on our usual understanding of the sense of the word *bin*.

3.2.2.2 The limits of sense and reference

A linguistic expression refers if it picks out an entity or set of entities in some world – either the real world, or some possible or imagined world. It will be obvious from this description that whether or not a linguistic expression refers will depend on the context in which it is used. For example, consider the sentence *Marion is a professional harpist.* The first noun phrase, the name *Marion*, identifies a particular individual as the entity about whom the information *is a professional harpist* is given. The second noun phrase, however, *a professional harpist*, would usually be said not to refer in this context. This is because it does not pick out a particular entity or set of entities as its object in the same way as expressions like *Marion*. Instead, *a professional harpist* has a **predicative** function: it is part of the *information given about* Marion. Similarly, the phrases *high in fibre, low in fat* and *cholesterol free* in (10) are predicative and thus non-referring:

(10) *Like all dried fruit, apricots are high in fibre, low in fat and cholesterol free.*

Apricots, by contrast, refers (to the class of apricots), and *all dried fruit* refers to the class of *dried fruit*.

Many lexical categories are typically non-referential. Verbs, for example, are typically predicative: the inherent role of a verb is to give information about some already identified entity, rather than to refer to that entity directly. Nevertheless, it will often be useful to think of verbs as referring to actions, and of sentences as referring to situations, and this is a usage we will often adopt in this book.

It is also important to note that reference is usually accomplished at the phrasal, not the lexical, level. Thus, in English, it is noun phrases which refer and not the individual nouns which make them up. In the sentence *An heir to a Danish steel fortune must leave behind his quiet life in Stockholm* it is the noun phrases – *An heir to a Danish steel fortune, a Danish steel fortune, his quiet life in Stockholm*, and *Stockholm* – which accomplish the identification of particular entities in the world. Since *Stockholm*, as a proper noun, is analysed as a noun phrase in its own right, it is the only noun in the sentence which does uniquely pick out or refer to a particular entity (the capital of Sweden) – but it only does this as a noun phrase, not as an individual noun. None of the other individual nouns in the sentence constitutes a noun phrase, and as a result, none of them refers: *heir, fortune,* and *life* do not in themselves identify any single entities about which information could be given. However, in other contexts, they can certainly refer. For example, *life* in the sentence *life is uneventful* is part of a noun phrase referring to an entity, life.

QUESTION   Which of the following noun phrases are used referentially? What problems are there in deciding?

> *The winner will receive this set of plastic-coated barbecue forks.*
> *A woman came into the room.*
> *No one wants a hole in the head.*
> *Any novelist would want to win the Booker.*
> *Some woman came into the room.*
> *Every novelist would want to win the Booker.*
> *Boeing is planning to build a new passenger jet.*
> *Santa Claus was invented by the Coca Cola company; he doesn't really exist.*
> *The kangaroo is most active at night.*
> *If you hear some news, let me know.*
> *Is there any such thing as time travel?*
> *There is no life in a fluorescent tube.*
> *Make me a ham sandwich, would you?*
> *The only thing left is broken.*
> *The only thing to do is cancel.*
> *Smith's murderer is insane.*
> *The ability to pour patterns into drinks will let your customers and friends*
>   *know that you are serious about espresso.*

The importance of predication shows that reference is not always a relevant aspect of the meaning of a linguistic term. Furthermore, the difference between referring and non-referring uses of lexemes is often not marked by any overt grammatical means: languages, in other words, often don't seem to care whether an expression refers or not. As a result, the question of whether a given noun phrase refers may sometimes be ambiguous. While some expressions clearly refer and others clearly don't, there is a range of intermediate cases in which an expression may or may not be referring. These possibilities are reflected in the following sentences, from Givón (1984: 389):

(11) a. *If you see **the man** with the green hat, tell him…*
      b. *If you see **a man** with a green hat, tell him …*
          (i) *Referential*: I have such a man in mind, and if you see **him**
          (ii) *Non-referential*: I don't have any particular man in mind, so if you see **one**…
      c. *If you see someone with a green hat there, tell **him/them** …*
      d. *If you see anybody with a green hat there, tell **them** …*

(11a) is clearly referential, (11b) may or may not be, (11c) is probably non-referential, but still might be intended to pick out a specific individual, whereas (11d) is least likely to refer to a specific person.

QUESTION What factors apart from the existence or non-existence of a specific referent might determine the speaker's choice between (11) a–d?

3.2.3 Deixis

Certain types of expression, called **deictic** or **indexical expressions** (or simply **deictics** or **indexicals**), are defined as those which make reference to some aspect of the context of utterance as an essential part of their meaning. Examples would be the English words *here* and *there* and their equivalents in other languages, such as Chinese *zhe* and *na*, or Hungarian *ez* and *az* ('this', 'that'). Deictic expressions have the peculiarity that their reference is relative to the situation in which they are used. They lack any independently paraphraseable sense: what they mean cannot be given any general description other than describing a procedure for isolating the intended referent. The meaning of *this* in (12), for example, cannot be described except by saying that it refers to some entity in the speaker's context of utterance – probably a person, but also perhaps an electronic chess board, a computer, or an introductory book about chess:

(12) *This is my old chess coach.*

The speaker of (12) might well accompany their utterance with a gesture pointing to, or otherwise indicating, the object they have in mind. In the absence of such a gesture, the listener has to infer what the intended referent is. This they will partly be able to do as a result of the **deictic system** available in the language. The hearer of (12), for instance, would be justified in assuming that the speaker is referring to something nearby: if this were not the case, the deictic *that* would have been used instead (for example if the speaker and hearer had passed someone on the street and a few moments later, when they had disappeared from sight, the speaker exclaimed *That was my old chess coach!*). The meaning or sense of *this*, therefore, could be described as an instruction to the hearer to identify some likely referent in their near proximity, and the meaning of *that* as the instruction to identify some likely referent further away.

There is not nearly enough space here for a full discussion of the semantics of deictics in the languages of the world. Different sorts of deixis, or reference to elements of the context, have been observed cross-linguistically. These include the following:

- person deixis, by which speaker (*I*), hearer (*you*) and other entities relevant to the discourse (*he/she/it/they*) are referred to;
- temporal deixis (*now, then, tomorrow*); and
- discourse deixis, which refers to other elements of the discourse in which the deictic expression occurs (*A: You stole the cash. B: That's a lie*).

Here, we will confine ourselves to a discussion, closely based on Diessel (1999), of spatial deixis as it is manifested in **demonstratives**, of which English *this* and *that* are cardinal examples.

All languages have at least two deictically contrastive demonstratives: the *this* demonstrative is usually called a **proximal**, the *that* demonstrative is called a **distal**. Sometimes these demonstratives are uninflected particles; in other languages, demonstratives are marked for gender, number and/or case and may combine with derivational affixes or with other free forms (Diessel 1999: 13). The demonstrative systems of some languages may be dizzyingly complex: Inuktitut (Eskimo-Aleut, Canada), for example, shows 686 forms in the demonstrative system (Denny 1982: 372).

Deictic systems which, unlike English, involve more than two deictic terms are of two basic sorts: distance-oriented systems, where the **deictic centre** (usually but not necessarily the speaker) is the only point of reference for the location of the referent, and person-oriented systems, where the hearer serves as another reference point (Diessel 1999: 50). Yimas (Sepik-Ramu, Papua New Guinea; Diessel 1999: 39) is an example of a distance-oriented deictic system, with the singular deictics *p-k* 'proximal', *m-n* 'medial', *p-n* 'distal'. The proximal and distal forms could be translated as 'this here' and 'that over there' respectively; the medial term means something like 'that just over there'. Pangasinan (Austronesian, Philippines; Diessel 1999: 39) is an example of a person-oriented system, with the singular forms *(i)yá* 'this near the speaker', *(i)tán* 'that near the hearer' and *(i)mán* 'that away from both speaker and hearer'.

Distance is not the only feature expressed by demonstratives: they may also indicate such variables as whether the referent is in or out of sight, at a higher or lower elevation, up- or downstream, moving towards or away from the deictic centre, and others (Diessel 1999: 50). The deictic system of Khasi (Mon-Khmer, India; Diessel 1999: 42) combines a number of these categories, indicating, as well as the gender or plurality of the referent, its distance with respect to speaker and hearer, its elevation, or its visibility (see Table 3.1):

Table 3.1. Khasi demonstratives (Diessel 1999: 42).

	MASC.SG.	FEM.SG.	PL
PROXIMAL	*u-ne*	*ka-ne*	*ki-ne*
MEDIAL (NEAR H)	*u-to*	*ka-to*	*ki-to*
DISTAL	*u-tay*	*ka-tay*	*ki-tay*
UP	*u-tey*	*ka-tey*	*ki-tey*
DOWN	*u-thie*	*ka-thire*	*ki-thie*
INVISIBLE	*u-ta*	*ka-ta*	*ki-ta*

Demonstratives usually also provide some qualitative information about the referent: 'they may indicate whether the referent is a location, object or person, whether it is animate or inanimate, human or non-human, female or male, a single entity or a set, or conceptualized as a restricted or extended entity' (Diessel 1999: 50). In Apalai (Carib, Brazil), for instance, there are two deictic series, one for animate, the other for inanimate referents, and each series distinguishes collective from non-collective referents:

Table 3.2. Apalai demonstratives (Diessel 1999: 48).	ANIMATE		INANIMATE	
	NON-COLL	COLL	NON-COLL	COLL
PROXIMAL	*mose*	*moxiamo*	*seny*	*senohne*
MEDIAL	*mokyro*	*mokaro*	*moro*	*morohne*
DISTAL	*moky*	*mokamo*	*mony*	*monohne*

3.3 Dictionary and encyclopaedia

Since reference is an important part of the meaning of many words, many linguists have wanted to distinguish knowledge we have of a word's meaning (sense) from knowledge we might have about its denotation – the set of things it refers to. Some sort of distinction like this seems to be required for a number of reasons. The most powerful is that it is firmly present in our pretheoretical intuitions. For example, all of us know many things about frogs, but something seems wrong about regarding all this information as part of the *meaning* of *frog*. Examples of information about frogs that it would seem absurd to claim as part of the *meaning* of *frog* include the facts that there is a famous fairy story in which a frog is an enchanted prince waiting to be released by the kiss of a princess, that frogs are often (and somewhat offensively) associated by English speakers with French people, or that the Australian water-holding frog burrows underground and surrounds itself in a transparent cocoon made of its own shed skin. There are many English speakers who do not know these things about frogs, but who can correctly refer to frogs. This contrasts with speakers of other languages, or with learners of English who have not yet learned the word *frog*, who may know these things about frogs, but do not yet know what the English word *frog* means. It would seem, then, that there is a firm line between knowledge of a word's meaning and knowledge of factual information about the word's denotation.

3.3.1 Knowledge of meaning and knowledge of facts

In Chapter 2 we mentioned the contrast between dictionary and thesaurus models of semantic organization (see the text box in 2.1.1). The sort of considerations we have just mentioned give rise to another contrast, that between **dictionary** and **encyclopaedia** aspects of meaning. This is the distinction between knowledge of a word's meaning (**dictionary knowledge**), which would be conceived of as something fairly concise, perhaps like a dictionary definition, and **encyclopaedic knowledge** of facts about the objects to which the word refers. Dictionary knowledge is knowledge of the essential meaning of a word that all speakers must possess, and which dictionaries must accurately represent in order to allow the meaning to be acquired for the first time. Encyclopaedic knowledge, by contrast, is not essential to the meaning of the word and will vary significantly from speaker to speaker. Encyclopaedic knowledge is *not linguistic in nature*: that is, it does not determine any of a word's linguistic behaviour. The question of which elements of the encyclopaedic information associated with a given word are relevant in any one situation is decided by general pragmatic principles, which have been described in a number of different ways (see Chapter 4).

The motivation for the distinction between dictionary and encyclopaedia is the fact that encyclopaedic knowledge seems to be quite independent of dictionary knowledge: thus, I need not know anything about fairy tales or the Australian water-holding frog in order to be able to use the word *frog*. Furthermore, it has been assumed that some such distinction must be psychologically realistic. If all of the encyclopaedic information associated with a word were part of its meaning, this would surely be too much for the brain to process. If, on the other hand, all that language-processing involves is the retrieval of the concise dictionary-style representation associated with each word, then it appears as a much more streamlined and efficient process, much easier for the brain to accomplish – and much easier also for the computers on which we try to model the brain-processes involved in language (see Chapter 8).

The distinction between dictionary and encyclopaedia is not limited to referring expressions like *frog*. It also applies to predicating ones, like English verbs and adjectives. If we accept the distinction, it becomes important to be able to say exactly which pieces of information about a lexeme belong to the dictionary and which to the encyclopaedia. This is a particularly acute problem where it is necessary for practical reasons (for example lexicographical ones) to arrive at some precise description of a lexeme's semantic content. In order to appreciate the descriptive issues involved here, we can consider the Warlpiri verb *pinyi*, usually glossed 'hit', which is often ambiguous between the meanings 'hit' and 'kill':

(13) *yapa   kapu-rna   pinyi.*
    person   AUX.FUT-1S   hit/kill
    'I'll hit that person'/'I'll kill that person'.

There are at least two possible ways of analysing this ambiguity. The first is that *pinyi* has two meanings, 'hit' and 'kill', which, in certain contexts, may be simultaneously present. The second is that there is one single, **underspecified** meaning, which we can only describe in English as 'hit/kill'. On this theory, it is the context which determines whether *pinyi* describes an act of hitting or of killing, just as context determined the reading of the English possessive morpheme in (1) above. This second solution would be favoured by many scholars. Whenever we are faced, says Levinson (2000: 20), 'with a linguistic expression that is apparently systematically ambiguous, we should entertain the possibility that the correct analysis is in fact a simple, univocal, semantically broad sense with a defeasible set of generalized pragmatic restrictions'. (*Defeasible* means that the restrictions can be overcome by adding elements to the sentence which enforce one reading at the expense of the other. In (13), we could add an expression meaning 'dead' to the sentence which would eliminate the ambiguity.)

What would the details of this underspecified solution be? How does context contribute to the contextual interpretation of *pinyi*? The English translations usually offered of sentences like (14) and (15) suggest that typically domestic animals like dogs usually provoke the 'hit' interpretation of *pinyi*, whereas typically wild, edible ones like kangaroos are associated with 'kill':

(14) *maliki*   *pi-nyi*
    dog   hit/kill-NPST
    'hitting the dog'

(15) *marlu*   *pi-nyi*
    roo   hit/kill-NPST
    'killing the kangaroo'

In contexts like (15), the 'kill' reading is quite strongly entrenched: as noted by the exclamation mark, the following statements appear bizarre to Warlpiri speakers:

(16) ¡*wati-ngki*   *marlu*   *pu-ngu*   *kala*   *kula*   *marlu-ju*
    man-ERG   roo   hit/kill-PST   but   NEG   roo-TOP
    pali-ja.
    die-PST
    'The man *pinyi* the kangaroo but the kangaroo did not die.'

(17) ¡*wati-ngki*   *ka*   *marlu*   *pi-nyi*   *marlu-ju*
    man-ERG   AUX   roo   hit/kill-NPST   roo-TOP
    wankaru   *juku.*
    alive   still
    'The man *pinyi* the kangaroo but the kangaroo is still alive.'

On an underspecified view of the meaning of *pinyi*, it is the encyclopaedic knowledge which Warlpiri speakers have about their world which allows them to correctly understand what is meant in the sentences above. In contexts such as (13), where the object is equally likely to be hit or killed, there is no way of telling which interpretation is appropriate without further specification: the underspecification of the verb leaves no way of deciding. Further support for the underspecified solution comes from sentence (18):

(18) *cat*   *pi-nyi*
    cat   hit/kill-NPST
    'hit a cat'/'kill a cat'

Cats are neither traditional domestic nor wild animals for Warlpiri people; as a result (18) constitutes a 'neutral' context without established encyclopaedic expectations, where the verb may convey either sense. But once the verb is inserted into a grammatical context which specifies the object, encyclopaedic facts come into play to determine the intended reading.

Distinguishing between lexical dictionary knowledge and factual encyclopaedic knowledge thus enables an economical description of meaning. The lexical entry for *pinyi* does not need to detail the different contexts in which the two readings occur: this is not part of our knowledge of the *meaning* of the verb. Instead, the lexical entry simply contains the meaning 'hit/kill', and the choice of reading in any one context is reached on encyclopaedic grounds. The details of Warlpiri speakers' representation of their encyclopaedic knowledge, and its interaction with linguistic structures, can then be legitimately neglected by linguists, as part of the explanatory job of psychology.

3.3.2 Problems with the dictionary–encyclopaedia distinction

In spite of its obvious labour-saving advantages in semantic description, the dictionary–encyclopaedia distinction is not accepted by many linguists. This is largely because the boundary between the two seems to be highly permeable, even non-existent. As any comparison of dictionaries will reveal, it is very hard to determine where information stops being part of a word's dictionary meaning and becomes part of the encyclopaedic knowledge we have of its denotation. Which of the following pieces of information, for example, should be considered dictionary information about the meaning of the word *cow*, and which as facts about cows which form part of the encyclopaedic knowledge we have about them?

- they are mammals
- they moo
- they eat grass
- they are four-legged
- they have large eyes
- they live in fields and dairies
- they sometimes wear cow-bells
- they are often farmed for their milk
- they have several stomachs
- their young are called *calves* in English
- they incubate Mad Cow Disease for three to five years if infected
- they chew their food slowly

The difficulty of resolving this kind of question stems from the fact that, depending on the context, it would seem that any part of the supposedly encyclopaedic information associated with a word may become linguistically significant (see Katz and Fodor 1963: 178–179 for discussion). To return to the example of *frog*, note that I can use this in contexts where the dictionary meaning is not even present, and two pieces of encyclopaedic information are invoked. In the context of a discussion about a French person who is unlucky in love, for example, I might utter (19):

(19) *He may be a Frog, but no princess is kissing him.*

Someone would be able to understand this sentence without ever learning the dictionary meaning of the word *frog*, as long as they could make the connections with 'French person' and 'enchanted prince'.

It might be argued that this sort of context simply shows that 'Frenchman' and 'sleeping prince' are, in fact, part of the dictionary entry for *frog* after all, and not just encyclopaedic facts about frogs. But this acknowledgment undermines the very reasons for drawing the dictionary–encyclopaedia distinction in the first place. If we simply reassign a piece of previously encyclopaedic knowledge to the dictionary every time it becomes relevant to the linguistic behaviour of a word, the dictionary starts getting a lot bigger, and looking more and more like an encyclopaedia. The supposed processing benefits of concision in lexical representation thus disappear. Furthermore, we can assign an innovative piece of encyclopaedic knowledge to a word, which can then usurp the word's former dictionary meaning. For example, some people do not know that tomatoes are, strictly speaking, fruit and not vegetables. This allows someone who has just been made aware of this to pedantically use sentences like (20):

(20) *Get me some tomatoes and other fruit.*

Here, a newly acquired piece of encyclopaedic knowledge has affected the co-occurrence possibilities of a lexical item: whereas *tomato* would typically be categorized as a *vegetable*, here it belongs to the incompatible category *fruit*. This sort of phenomenon suggests that there is no possible boundary between knowledge of the meaning of a word, and knowledge about the objects the word denotes. We know a variety of things about words and their denotation, and the greater the likelihood that a particular piece of this knowledge is shared between speaker and hearer, the greater the likelihood that it will determine the word's linguistic properties. Sentence (20), for example, would be perfectly natural in the mouth of a botany student who was about to do an experiment on seeded fruit.

Langacker (1987: 159) sums up the case for the abandonment of any strict division between the dictionary and the encyclopaedia:

I do not specifically claim that all facets of our knowledge of an entity have equal status, linguistically or otherwise – quite the contrary. The multitude of specifications that figure in our encyclopedic conception of an entity clearly form a gradation in terms of their **centrality**. Some are so central that they can hardly be omitted from even the sketchiest characterization, whereas others are so peripheral that they hold little significance even for the most exhaustive description. Distinctions of this kind can perfectly well be made within the encyclopaedic approach. The thrust of this view is simply that no specific point along the gradation of centrality can be chosen nonarbitrarily to serve as a demarcation, such that all specifications on one side can uniformly be attributed linguistic significance and all those on the other side are linguistically irrelevant.

This sort of position has some significant methodological and theoretical consequences. Most importantly, it problematizes the notion of *the* meaning of a word. Since any fact known about a referent may become linguistically significant, the traditional linguistic semantic project of describing the lexical entry associated with each lexeme becomes an unending task, each lexical entry being, in principle, infinite.

QUESTION   Consider the Arrernte (Pama-Nyungan, Central Australia) verb *lyelye-ipeme*, whose meaning is described as follows by Henderson and Dobson (1994: *lyelye-ipeme*): 'push a stick or crowbar into creek sand, moving it around to make the hole bigger so as to force the stick further down. This is done to see if there is enough water there to dig out into a soakage.' How might one go about deciding which parts of this definition were dictionary knowledge, and which were encyclopaedic? Are there any general criteria for deciding this question?

Summary

The basic question: meaning and context

One of the main questions to be answered by any theory of meaning concerns the *scope* of an expression's meaning: how much of the total effect of an expression is to be attributed to its meaning, and how much to the context in which it occurs?

We can distinguish two essential types of context:

- the **external** or real-world context *to* which linguistic expressions refer, and
- the **interpersonal** context of linguistic action *in* which any utterance is placed.

External context: sense and reference

Frege distinguished an expression's **reference**, which concerns the entities which the expression is *about*, from its **sense**, which is the way in which we grasp or understand its referent. In the Fregean view, two crucial features of sense are as follows:

- sense is what our minds 'grasp' when we understand the meaning of a word;
- sense *determines* reference; words' referents are identified through their senses.

Truth has a central place in Frege's semantics. To know the sense of a sentence is, for Frege, to know how the sentence could be assigned a value as true or false: to know what the *conditions* are that would make it true or false. Knowledge of a sentence's truth conditions allows us to determine, by looking at the sentence's referents, whether the world actually is the way the sentence represents it, and thus whether or not the sentence is therefore true.

Predication and deixis

As well as referring, linguistic expressions can often be used to **predicate** (attribute properties). Verbs, for example, are characteristically limited to this function. **Deictic** expressions (otherwise known as deictics or indexicals) are defined as those which make reference to some aspect of the context of utterance as an essential part of their meaning. Examples of deictics in English include the words *I, you and here*. The languages of the world show a large variety of deictic systems.

Knowledge of meaning and knowledge of facts

Since reference is an important part of the meaning of many words, many linguists have wanted to distinguish knowledge we have of a word's meaning (sense) from knowledge we might have about its referent. This is the distinction between **lexical ('dictionary') knowledge** and **factual ('encyclopaedic') knowledge**.

The distinction enables an economical description of word meanings, but is often criticized: the boundary between dictionary and encyclopaedia seems to be so highly permeable as to be non-existent.

Further reading

In twentieth-century linguistics, the importance of context has been particularly stressed in the philosophical (Bar-Hillel 1954, Austin 1962, Searle 1969) and social-functional (Halliday 1978, Halliday and Hasan 1985) traditions. For an introduction to approaches to sense and reference in the philosophy of language, see the second part of Devitt and Sterelny (1999). On reference specifically, see Allan (1986: 142–160) and Lyons (1977: 174–196). Lambrecht (1994) looks at reference in discourse. Kripke (1980) and Donnellan (1972), both of which presuppose a certain philosophical literacy, promote an alternative philosophical treatment of sense and reference, opposed to Frege. Readers of French will find short descriptions of numerous deictic systems in Morel and Danon-Boileau (1992). On the dictionary/encyclopaedia distinction see Haiman (1980), Langacker (1987:154–166) and Jackendoff (2002: 281–293).

Exercises

Questions for discussion

1. Illustrate and discuss the following quotation (Haiman 1980: 347):

   'Obviously, the classical idea of *meaningfulness, like that of grammaticality,* makes a silent appeal to the idea of "normal circumstances".'
   How does it relate to the question of the distinction between dictionary and encyclopaedia in semantics?

2. Characterize the non-truth-conditional differences between the following statements:

   Well, there wasn't a fight on Saturday.
   Still, there wasn't a fight on Saturday.
   After all, there wasn't a fight on Saturday.
   Therefore, there wasn't a fight on Saturday.
   Alas, there wasn't a fight on Saturday.

1. Read Section 2.2.4 of the previous chapter. Can the contextual modulation of the meanings of *cut* be described in terms of a dictionary/encyclopaedia distinction? How?

4 The scope of meaning II: interpersonal context

CHAPTER PREVIEW

Following the treatment of external context in the previous chapter, this chapter considers the **interpersonal** context of linguistic action in which any utterance is placed.

Section 4.1 introduces the notion of **illocutionary force**, which refers to the different interpersonal functions or **speech acts** which a linguistic expression may be made to perform (stating, questioning, ordering, requesting, advising, warning, promising, etc.).

Section 4.2 considers the role of **speaker's intention** and **hearer's inference** in meaning: in general, the meaning of an expression can often be described as whatever it was that the speaker intended the hearer to understand in using the expression; the hearer's task, on this picture, is to make inferences about what this intention was.

In 4.3 we discuss the Gricean theory of **implicature**, which is the theory of how meanings may be implied rather than explicitly stated. In 4.4 and 4.5 we turn to an exploration of the principles which have been proposed as governing the operation of implicature in conversation. Section 4.6 considers an important alternative tradition in the analysis of interpersonal context, **Relevance Theory**, and 4.7 discusses, in general terms, the interrelation between semantics and **pragmatics**, the branch of linguistics in which the relations between language and context are specifically studied.

4.1 Interpersonal context: illocutionary force and speech acts

The relations between language and context are not limited to those in which a linguistic expression simply names or describes an already existing referent or state of affairs. The assertion of facts about the world is just one of the acts which we can use language to perform: we also ask questions, issue orders, and make requests, to mention only the three most obvious types of other act for which language is used. For much of the history of reflection on language (principally in philosophy), it was the asserting function that was seen as the most basic and important. Language was seen essentially as a means of describing (asserting facts about) reality, and its importance as an instrument which could perform a whole variety of different functions was not fully appreciated.

As it happens, there is good reason to see description or fact-assertion as a particularly basic function of language. As noted by Givón (1984: 248), the fundamental role of assertion in language can be seen as a consequence of four large-scale features of human social organization and the types of talk-exchange it engenders:

- communicative topics are often outside the immediate, perceptually available range;
- much pertinent information is not held in common by the participants in the communicative exchange;
- the rapidity of change in the human environment necessitates periodic updating of the body of shared background knowledge;
- the participants are often strangers.

Givón continues (1984: 248):

> Under such conditions, even granted that the ultimate purpose of the communicative transaction is indeed to manipulate the other toward some target action, the interlocutors must first – and in fact constantly – create, recreate and repair the body of shared knowledge which is the absolute prerequisite for the ultimate communicative transaction.

Nevertheless, assertion is not the *only* kind of function which language may be used to perform. We do not just use language to talk about or describe the world; we *do* things with language in order to manipulate and induce transformations in it. One way to think about how we use language to provoke transformations in the external world is in terms of the idea of **force**. As we saw in 3.2.1, Frege had already distinguished the force of a linguistic expression from its sense. The conception of force in Frege is still rather sketchy: the only types of force he considers seem to be statements and questions. In a famous series of lectures delivered in the early 1950s, the British philosopher John L. Austin, one of Frege's translators, extended the Fregean notion of force. Austin's pupil, John R. Searle, developed these ideas into a comprehensive philosophy of language, the theory of **speech acts**. We will explore this tradition in the present section.

4.1.1 Locutionary, illocutionary and perlocutionary acts

In his investigation of the force of linguistic expressions, Austin distinguished between three types of act present in every utterance, the **locutionary**, **illocutionary** and **perlocutionary** acts. He defined them as follows:

- locutionary act: the act *of* saying something;
- illocutionary act: the act performed *in* saying something; and
- perlocutionary act: the act performed *by* saying something.

What do these definitions mean? The locutionary act – the act *of* saying something – is the act of expressing the basic, literal meanings of the words chosen. For example, in uttering the words *You will get your hands blown off*, a speaker performs the locutionary act of stating that the hearer will get their hands blown off. The illocutionary act is the act that the speaker performs *in* saying something. In many contexts, utterance of the statement *You will get your hands blown off* is intended, and understood, as an act of warning: the utterance thus has the **illocutionary force** of a warning. Thanking, congratulating, and advising are all acts which differ in their illocutionary force; in all of them, the speaker does more than describe or assert facts about some situation. As Austin puts it, the speaker of this type of act does not simply *say something*, instead, (s)he *does something* (thank, congratulate, or advise) by engaging in a certain conventionalized form of verbal behaviour. Illocutionary acts are also referred to as **speech acts**. Lastly, the **perlocutionary** act is the act of producing an effect in the hearer by means of the utterance. Depending on the circumstances, the perlocutionary act involved in saying *You will get your hands blown off* might be to *dissuade* the hearer from playing with a lighter and a stick of dynamite, to *frighten* the hearer, to *encourage* them to go on provocatively waving a naked flame in front of a bag of fireworks, etc.

The linguistic expressions which figure in illocutionary acts do not simply have the function of describing or stating facts about a situation (this Austin called the **constative** function). When we say something like *You will get your hands blown off*, we are not only stating something: we are also performing an action, the action of warning. If it was not obvious that the words *You will get your hands blown off* were intended to constitute a warning, the speaker could explicitly say *I'm warning you, you'll get your hands blown off*. In using the verb *warn*, the speaker makes the force of their utterance as a warning explicit; there is, indeed, no other way to explicitly warn someone other than to use the words 'I'm warning you', 'I warn you that', or synonymous constructions. Austin called this type of utterance an **explicit performative** utterance: when I say *I warn you that* ... I am not describing or stating the existence of any independent fact; I am, instead, performing an act (the act of warning) which cannot be explicitly performed in any other way. (By contrast, the basic utterance *you will get your hands blown off* may well have the illocutionary force of a warning, but it is not an explicit performative; we will call it an **implicit performative**.)

It would be impossible to provide a full catalogue of all the illocutionary (or speech) acts which may be performed in English. As well as asserting, questioning and ordering, a very modest list would include promising, thanking, requesting, congratulating, greeting, advising, naming, swearing, scolding, apologizing, guaranteeing and warning. All these are particular conventionalized ways of using language which we recognize as associated with a particular repertoire of conditions and responses. In order for a speaker S to request a hearer H to perform an act A, for example, a particular set of social conditions needs to be fulfilled. Searle's summary of these conditions appears in (1):

(1)   (i) A must be in the future, not in the past;
      (ii) H must be capable of A;
      (iii) it must be obvious to S and H that H will not do A anyway, in the normal course of events,
      (iv) S must want H to do A, etc. (see Searle 1969: 57–61).

QUESTION Consider the following sentences, and label them as always performative (P), possibly performative (PP), or never performative (NP). For the first two categories, state whether they are explicitly performative or not:

I resign.
I'm resigning.
A poet is chairman of the Australian Tax Research Foundation.
Bali is not the same place as Mali.
I resigned ten minutes ago.
I'm telling you not to try sour herring.
You're not allowed to smoke here.
We had a lovely time.
The storeroom is out of bounds.
There's nothing more I can do to help you.
I don't accept that argument.
Bingo!
The audience are asked to turn off their mobile phones.
I believe it's important to be ethical.
I believe in Hinduism.
I guarantee you're going to love this!
Can I help you?
For an introduction to Relevance Theory, Blakemore (1992) can be recommended.

QUESTION Consider the following sentences. What illocutionary acts could they realize?

I'm glad you're here. Take your time. I'm allergic to milk. Was that the doorbell? Don't worry about putting out the rubbish.

4.1.2 Consequences of the illocutionary perspective

Focusing on the illocutionary aspects of utterances has two important consequences for linguistic theory. The first concerns the centrality of truth and falsity to meaning. We saw in 3.2.1 that Frege had made truth the central notion of his semantic theory. However, considerations of truth and falsity are simply irrelevant for many types of illocutionary act. This is particularly so for performatives, such as the sentences in (2):

(2) *I apologize for the mess I've made.*
     I bet you as much as you like that it'll rain for the party.
     I forbid you to touch that diamond.
     I promise that I'll never give you such a fright again.

As Austin points out, it does not make sense to ask whether it is *true* that 'I apologize for the mess I've made': the very act of saying the words *I apologize* constitutes the apology. Instead of being assessed as true or false, the sentences in (2) must conform to certain conditions, just like the conditions governing the act of requesting described above. Austin called these conditions **felicity conditions**.

QUESTION   What might the felicity conditions be for each of the speech acts mentioned above? What problems are there in deciding?

The second break with traditional theories of language brought about by a focus on speech acts concerns the question of the basic object of semantic analysis. Austin was struck by the fact that it seems impossible to specify any list of criteria which might distinguish expressions which can function as performatives from those which cannot. *Any* expression, for Austin, can carry *any* illocutionary force. There is no single way, in any language, of performing a given illocutionary act: the illocutionary force of an utterance is in principle unpredictable from its overt syntactic or lexical form. Speakers often perform speech acts whose communicative purpose (utterance meaning) does not correspond to their obvious sentence meaning. For instance, to get someone to close the door, I may well *not* choose an imperatival construction (*close the door, please*), but may opt instead for either a question (*could I get you to close the door?*) or a statement (*it's suddenly got draughty in here*). Speech acts like this, whose illocutionary force does not correspond to the most obvious illocutionary force of their sentence type, are known as **indirect speech acts**.

   Because of the frequency of indirect speech acts, any proposed convention linking a given communicative purpose with a given illocutionary form will thus have to reckon with the fact that the same form may also be used to achieve quite different purposes. French, for example, uses a variety of linguistic mechanisms to express commands. As well as the expected imperative form (*tais-toi* 'be quiet'), these include verbs in the infinitive mood (*ne pas ouvrir* 'do not open'), and in the indicative (*vous dresserez une liste des consonnes sourdes*, 'write a list of voiceless consonants') – even, in some conventional cases, noun phrases (*ta gueule* 'shut up!', literally 'your mouth'). Furthermore, even explicit performative expressions may be used in ways which do not correspond to their conventional meanings. The phrase 'I guarantee there are no slackers in this company', for example, has the apparent illocutionary force of a guarantee, but could function as a warning, a threat, a promise, and so on. As Davidson (1979: 73) says, the fact that a single linguistic structure may serve an unlimited number of contextual communicative ends points up a fundamental feature of human language that he calls the *autonomy* of linguistic meaning:

> Once a feature of language has been given conventional expression, it can be used to serve many extra-linguistic ends; symbolic representation necessarily breaks any close tie with extra-linguistic purpose. Applied to the present case, this means that there cannot be a form of speech which, solely by dint of its conventional meaning, can only be used for a given purpose, such as making an assertion or asking a question.

The impossibility of discerning fixed characteristics of illocutionary force bearing expressions imposes a major reorientation on one's perspective on meaning. If, given the right context, any expression can be used to create any contextual effect, then

> [t]he unit of linguistic communication is not, as has generally been supposed, the symbol, word or sentence, or even the token of the symbol, word or sentence, but rather the production or issuance of the symbol or word or sentence in the performance of the speech act.
>
> (Searle 1969: 16)

Under this perspective, the meaningful nature of human communication cannot simply be attributed to the semantic properties of words: meaningfulness is not a property of language on its own, but of language use as part of an **interpersonal context**, as part of a network of shared social practices. This insight extends even to the assertive, referential use of language. As noted by Recanati (1987: 128), 'It is not the *sentence* "It will rain," but rather *the fact of its being uttered by Jules*, that "expresses" or conveys pragmatically Jules' belief that it will rain.' As Austin himself pointed out, the use of language to describe aspects of reality needs itself to be seen as just one other speech act among many – it is, in other words, an activity subject to a set of conventions entirely equivalent to the conventions governing obvious speech acts like promising, thanking or congratulating.

The conventions governing constative utterances (statements) – let us say the statement *that p* – include the following (Searle 1969: 66; cf. Austin 1962: 136–147):

(3) i. S has evidence for the truth of p
     ii. It is not obvious to both S and H that H knows (does not need to be reminded of, etc.) p
     iii. S believes p

QUESTION   Do all statements conform to these conventions? If not, can you reformulate them to remove the problems?

The utterance of a statement, just like the performance of an illocutionary act like promising, thus involves both speaker and hearer in a network of commitments and consequences which imply certain things about their current states and beliefs, and commit them to certain future actions. If, for example, I utter the words *Rat soup and leather belts were eaten on the Long March*, then, in many types of situation, I will be understood to have made a factual statement which I have some evidence or justification for making, and to which I can be expected to be held. The uttering of this statement commits me, as a matter of convention, to certain other propositions, the statement's **entailments** and **presuppositions** (see Chapter 6), such as the proposition that the Long March took place, that leather belts were available, and that there were rats in China at the time. If I subsequently denied any one of these propositions, or the original statement itself, I could incur sanctions from the other members of the exchange: I could be accused, for example, of inconsistency. These sorts of conditions and commitments can be seen as essentially of the same order as those involved in other types of utterance, such as promises. Just as the act of making a statement suggests I have evidence or justification for what I say, the act of making a promise suggests I have the intention to fulfil what I say I will do. And just as the statement commits me to assent to its entailments and presuppositions, a promise commits me to follow through on the promised act. In both cases, then, the utterance of a linguistic expression can be seen as occupying a place in a structure of past and future actions and mental states, maintained and enforced by social convention.

The use of language is thus not the disembodied exercise of human reason asserting neutral facts about the world. It is a situated, contextual act in a network of social roles and responsibilities. This is always the case, regardless of whether the utterance in question seems essentially constative (factual) or performative. As Austin says (1962: 145–147), the difference between constatives and performatives can be seen principally as one of emphasis. Thus, constative utterances (statements, descriptions) abstract away from the illocutionary aspects of the utterance act in order to focus on its locutionary aspects, and the extent to which the utterance corresponds with facts. Performative utterances, contrastingly, focus on the illocutionary aspects, abstracting away from the locutionary dimension.

4.2 Interpersonal context: speaker's intention and hearer's inference

As we have seen, Austin did not believe that illocutionary acts were accompanied by any predictable grammatical or lexical markers. Both he and Searle did, however, believe that the making and understanding of speech acts is governed by social conventions like the ones for statements and requests discussed above. However, the idea that conventions underlie the illocutionary force of utterances has been much criticized. The central problem with such a theory is that it proves to be exceedingly difficult to state what the convention behind any given speech act might be. Thus, the conventions governing statements mentioned above seem inadequate: we often state things for which we do not have evidence (e.g. *You're not going to go bald*), which it is obvious that the hearer knows already (*You have lost a bit of hair, though*), and which we do not believe anyway (*But it's nothing to worry about*). Similarly, the putative conventions governing the making of requests may also be violated, without detracting from the nature of the utterance as a request. For example, imagine that S feels obliged to invite H to dinner, but does not want her to come. S may thus invite H to come at a time at which they know H is unavailable. In a case like this, the request *Do come and have dinner with us tomorrow* is made with S not wanting H to come (condition (iv) in (1) above), and knowing that H is unable to do so (condition (ii)). The utterance is none the less, however, a request (see Strawson 1971: 153–154 for further examples).

The general problem with convention-based approaches to illocutionary force is that they ignore the role of the appreciation of speakers' **intentions** in our understanding of meaning. The importance of intention in meaning was first emphasized by the British philosopher H. P. Grice, a collaborator of Austin's in the 1940s and 1950s. For Grice, 'the meaning (in general) of a sign needs to be explained in terms of what the users of the sign do (or should) mean by it on particular occasions' (1989: 217). If I understand that a certain utterance is a statement, a request, or a warning, on Grice's theory, it is because I attribute to the speaker a certain type of intention: the intention to state, to request, or to warn. It is because I attribute these intentions to the speaker that I am able to interpret the utterance in the right way; if I had credited the speaker with a different intention, I would have taken the utterance differently.

The importance of speaker's intention applies to both the illocutionary and the locutionary aspects of utterances. On the illocutionary side, the hearer's interpretation of the speech act performed by the speaker will depend, as we have just seen, on their interpretation of S's intentions. S's utterance of the words *It's easy to fall over in the dark* may function as a request for H to turn on the lights, a warning to H to be careful, or a metaphorical observation about the dangers of ignorance, uttered without the intention of provoking any particular immediate action on the part of H. In reacting to the utterance, H has to **infer** which of these possibilities was the one S intended. This is not to say, of course, that S intended only a single one of them: it is quite possible that S had several intentions in uttering those words. Perhaps, indeed, S didn't even know what their intention was; they just uttered the words. Nevertheless the hearer is obliged to make inferences about S's overall intentions in order to respond appropriately.

On the locutionary side, it is by making inferences about the speaker's intentions that the hearer selects the relevant aspects of the encyclopaedic knowledge called up by a linguistic expression: the encyclopaedic information relevant to the interpretation of an utterance is the information which the speaker *intended* to convey, and the hearer must decide which of the potentially infinite elements of encyclopaedic knowledge the speaker had in mind. Thus, if I use the word *frog* in reference to a French person in the phrase *He may be a Frog, but no princess is kissing him* (see (19) in the previous chapter), it is because I am considering certain facts and not others as relevant in this context: the fact that there is a fairy story in which a princess kisses a frog, and the fact that French people may be referred to as frogs. In order to understand (19) correctly, any hearer will have to appreciate my intent to convey this information. But the role of intentions is not limited to the selection of the appropriate encyclopaedic facts about a word. We also need to understand the speaker's intention in order to disambiguate words and assign referents, both basic aspects of the determination of the locutionary act of what is actually *said*. If I hear the sentence *There was a mouse here this morning*, my choice between the interpretations *there was a small rodent in the house this morning* and *there was a computer accessory on this table this morning* will be made on the basis of my beliefs about the speaker's intentions: did the speaker intend me to understand her to be making a comment about the presence of wildlife somewhere in the house or about a computer part that should have been on the table?

So inferring the speaker's intention is, on this view, a fundamental aspect of the process of meaning-creation and understanding in language. Linguistic communication is an **intentional-inferential** process, in which hearers try to infer speakers' intentions on the basis of the 'clues' provided by language. It is, as described by Sperber and Wilson (2002: 3), 'essentially an exercise in *metapsychology*, in which the hearer infers the speaker's intended meaning from evidence she has provided for this purpose'. The viability of an analysis of meaning in terms of intentions has not infrequently been called into question by philosophers of language, and it does indeed seem, for reasons that there is not space to go into here, as though the details of this analysis are rather problematic (see e.g. Schiffer 1987: 242–249). Nevertheless, Grice's programme of intentional-inferential semantics is assumed by many linguists and has proven to be a fruitful way of understanding language use.

Grice called the type of intention-dependent meaning characteristic of human language **non-natural meaning (meaning_{NN})**. The label 'non-natural' is intended to contrast with natural types of meaningfulness which are not mediated by a speaker's intentions, such as when we say *those spots mean measles*: here, the link between the spots and their 'meaning' (measles) is causal, direct and independent of any human agency, whereas the meaning of an utterance in human language depends on the intention of the utterer. In general, for Grice, the notion of what a *word* means is only explicable in terms of what *speakers* mean by using the word. What is important in communicating is thus what speakers *intend* by their use of language, what speakers *use* words to mean, and it is only derivatively, in light of these intentions, that we may speak of words themselves meaning anything (Grice 1989: 214–221).

QUESTION   Consider involuntary exclamations of pain like *ouch* or *ow*. Are these instances of meaning_{NN}? If so, why? If not, why not?

4.3 Interpersonal context: implicature

We observed at the start of the discussion of meaning and context in the previous chapter (3.1) that one of the crucial tasks of a semantic theory must be to characterize the *scope* of an expression's meaning. Given that all utterances occur in some context, it is necessary to separate off those aspects of an utterance's effect which may be due to its use in a particular context from those created by the meanings of its constituent elements. So far, we have distinguished two particular ways in which context may be manifested linguistically: reference, discussed in the previous chapter, and illocutionary force. Both, we have claimed, need to be distinguished from linguistic meaning (sense): neither the object to which an expression refers, nor the speech act of which it is a part, need necessarily to be considered to constitute part of that expression's meaning (sense).

Within the intentional-inferential framework initiated by Grice, one of the principal ways of thinking of the interrelations between meaning and context has been in terms of the notion of **conversational implicature**. The theory of conversational implicature was developed by Grice in a famous series of lectures delivered in 1967, and has been extremely influential in subsequent philosophy, linguistics and cognitive science. Grice's primary interest was in precisely the question of the scope of meaning: how can the boundary between what an expression means and the use it is given in a particular context be satisfactorily drawn (1989: 4)? How, in other words, does **sentence meaning** relate to **utterance meaning** (see 1.4.4)? In particular, his project was to develop a way of thinking about language which insulates our conception of an expression's meaning from the purely accidental facts about the ways in which it happens to be used. Not all of the features of an utterance in a particular context, Grice claimed, are directly dependent on the meanings of its constituents. Meaning does not determine use directly, and the apparent features of the overall effect of an expression in a certain context may be due not to the expression's meaning as such, but to the interrelation between that inherent meaning and the way in which the expression is *being used* in that context: in a different context, the same expression, with the same inherent meanings, could have quite different features.

4.3.1 Discrepancies between truth-functional meaning and utterance meaning

Grice was committed to a **truth-conditional** or **truth-functional** view of meaning, which can be described as the view that knowing the meaning of an expression consists in knowing the conditions under which it is true (see 3.2.1 for discussion). It was from this point of view that he was struck by a disparity between the (truth-conditionally conceived) sentence meaning of certain fundamental linguistic expressions and the utterance meanings they seem to have in actual language use. Grice's main example is provided by logical operators like *and*. Grice takes the sense of *and* to be the function it has in logic, where it simply denotes the *union* of two entities or propositions – apples *and* oranges, seeing *and* believing, Toni *and* Amitavo (see Chapter 6 for explanation). It may not at first sight be obvious why one should take the logical function of *and* to be primary in natural language. The essential reason is that, for many philosophers, the principles of logic are universal and underlie the operation of all human conceptual activity, including language: to study logic is thus to study the fundamental bases of rational human thought. As a result, words like *and, or* and *not*, which have analogues in the 'language' of logic, are naturally thought of as basically expressing the same ideas as their strict logical counterparts. In light of this basic function of *and*, consider (4):

(4)   *He got into bed and took off his shoes.*

Grice notes the obvious fact that it would not be appropriate to utter (4) about someone who *first* took off his shoes and *then* got into bed. One might claim, therefore, that there is an element of temporal succession to the meaning of *and* which is not reflected in its logical, truth-functional meaning. Grice does not want to say, however, that the *meaning* of *and* in (4) is any different from its basic meaning as a logical connective. This is for two reasons. Firstly, he is committed to a truth-functional approach to meaning in which the sense of logical operators like *and* simply *is* their role as a logical connector. This means that he needs a way of dealing with instances like (4) which seem to show that ordinary language does not obey truth-functional principles. Second, he believes that most people would say that although (4) is a *misleading* description of the situation in question, it is nevertheless *true*: strictly speaking, there is nothing *false* in (4) as a description of the situation in which someone took off his shoes and then got into bed, although it is an unusual and confusing way to describe this situation.

   Another example of a discrepancy between truth-conditional (logical) and conventional meaning would be the meaning of *some* in the following sentence:

(5)   *Tuptim has finished some of her homework.*

Under normal circumstances, the speaker of (5) would be taken to mean that Tuptim hasn't finished all her homework. From a strictly logical point of view, however, (5) is just as true if Tuptim has finished all her homework as it is if she has just finished some of it: if she has finished all her homework (say her history, geometry and German homework), it follows logically that she has also finished some of it (say her history and geometry homework). This would, however, be a misleading way of describing the situation, since in real conversation *some* typically gives rise to the interpretation 'not all': if I say that I have read *some* of the book, I imply that I have not read *all* of it. (This is called a **scalar implicature**; see Horn 1984.)

   A final example of the same sort is the conjunction *but*. Strictly, *but* has exactly the same truth-conditions as *and*: there is no logical distinction between them (see 6.2). As a result, the following pairs of sentences have identical truth-conditional meanings:

(6) a. *He's rich and he's unhappy.*
     b. *Hilda took a cab and Dirk took the bus.*

(7) a. *He's rich but he's unhappy.*
     b. *Hilda took a cab but Dirk took the bus.*

From the truth-conditional point of view, there is no difference between the sentences in (6) and (7): they are true in exactly the same conditions. There is, however, a clear *non*-truth-conditional difference between (6) and (7): (7) has an implication of contrast entirely missing in (6).

4.3.2 Conventional and conversational implicature

How should we think about these discrepancies between logical and conventional meaning? Grice introduced the term **implicature** in order to talk about these different facets of what we might call (informally) the meaning of an expression. The introduction of this term is a way of generalizing over the different types of communicative intention which hearers attribute to speakers: the implicatures of an utterance are what it is necessary to believe the speaker is thinking, and intending the hearer to think, in order to account for what they are saying. Some of these implicatures, like the implicature of contrast carried by *but*, are **conventional implicatures**: they are part of the typical force of the word, whether or not they conform to its strict, truth-conditional (logically defined) meaning. Conventional implicatures are what we might otherwise refer to as the standard or typical meanings of linguistic expressions. Other implicatures are **conversational**. Conversational implicatures are those that arise in particular contexts of use, without forming part of the word's characteristic or conventional force: the choice of the term 'conversational' is explained by the fact that Grice's examples are mostly taken from imagined conversations.

Here are some examples of exchanges involving conversational implicatures; in all of them, the sentence meaning of B's reply has no direct connection to A's question: it is the implicated utterance meaning which contains the answer:

(8) A: *Have you read Sebald?*
     B: *I haven't read the back of the cereal packet.*

(9) A: *Do you know how to get to rue du Pasteur Wagner?*
     B: *I've got a map in my bag.*

(10) A: *Do you like anchovies?*
     B: *Does a hippo like mud?*

In (8) B implicates that he hasn't read anything by Sebald, since he hasn't even read the back of the cereal packet. In (9) B implicates that he does not know how to get to the rue du Pasteur Wagner, but that he is prepared to consult his map for directions. In (10) B implicates that since the answer to his question is 'yes', then the answer to A's question is also 'yes' and that, as a result, he does indeed like anchovies. In all these cases, what is implied goes beyond the conventional meanings of the words used. The sentence *I haven't read the back of the cereal packet* is not usually able to convey the information 'I haven't read Sebald'; in the context of this conversation, however, this is precisely the information which it does convey. In order to understand the use of language in real communicative exchanges, therefore, it is essential to develop some analysis of the ways in which implicatures like these arise.

4.4 Gricean maxims and the Cooperative Principle

Within an inferential-intentional approach to meaning, Grice claimed that implicatures like those in (8)–(10) arise as the result of the infringement of certain principles or 'maxims' of rational conversational behaviour which, he claimed, govern speech exchanges. Grice claimed that conversation is (and should be) governed by the **Cooperative Principle**, a general condition on the way rational conversation is conducted. The Cooperative Principle is essentially the principle that the participants in a conversation work together in order to 'manage' their speech exchange in the most efficient way possible:

> Our talk exchanges do not normally consist of a succession of disconnected remarks, and would not be rational if they did. They are characteristically, to some degree at least, cooperative efforts; and each participant recognizes in them, to some extent, a common purpose or set of purposes, or at least a mutually accepted direction.
>
> (Grice 1989: 26)

This direction, Grice noted, may well change continually in the course of the conversation.

> But at each stage, *some* possible conversational moves would be excluded as conversationally unsuitable. We might then formulate a rough general principle which participants will be expected (ceteris paribus) to observe, namely: Make your conversational contribution such as is required, at the stage at which it occurs, by the accepted purpose or direction of the talk exchange in which you are engaged. One might label this the Cooperative Principle.
>
> (Grice 1989: 26)

Grice distinguished four general **maxims**, itemized below, which he claimed that speakers mainly observe, and expect others to observe, in conversation:

> *The maxim of Quality*
> Try to make your contribution one that is true, specifically:
> (i) do not say what you believe to be false
> (ii) do not say that for which you lack adequate evidence
> *The maxim of Quantity*
> (i) make your contribution as informative as is required for the current purposes of the exchange
> (ii) do not make your contribution more informative than is required

The maxim of Relevance
Make your contributions relevant
The maxim of Manner
Be perspicuous, and specifically:
  avoid obscurity
  avoid ambiguity
  be brief
  be orderly

(Grice 1989: 26–27)

Not all the maxims have equal importance (Grice 1989: 27). The brevity clause of the Manner maxim, for example, is frequently disobeyed. Furthermore, Grice notes (1989: 28) that there are also 'all sorts of other maxims (aesthetic, social, or moral in character), such as "Be polite," that are also normally observed by participants in talk exchanges'; the ones he has identified, however, have a special connection with what he takes to be the primary purpose of conversation: a maximally effective exchange of information (Grice 1989). He acknowledges, however, that conversation serves many other purposes and that, as a result, the maxims will need to be modified in order to take account of these other purposes.

QUESTION   What other purposes than the exchange of information does conversation serve? Is it possible to formulate different maxims in order to reflect the nature of these other types of purpose?

4.4.1 Infringing the maxims

Obviously, these maxims are frequently not observed. Grice considers four ways in which a speaker may fail to observe a maxim. First, a maxim may be *violated*, as for example when one deliberately sets out to mislead (in violation of the first maxim of Quality), to confuse or to bore (violation of various Manner maxims). Second, one may simply *opt out* of the Cooperative Principle, for example by saying 'I can't say more, my lips are sealed', in order to avoid divulging a secret. Thirdly, one may be faced by a *clash*, for example if it was impossible to fulfil the informativity maxim without infringing the evidentiary one (see (11) below).

   The last, and most important category of non-observance of the maxims is maxim-**flouting**. This is where the speaker exploits an obvious infringement of one of the maxims in order to generate an implicature. Flouting is the origin of the implicated meanings conveyed in (8)–(10) above. In all these sentences, the maxim of Relevance is obviously flouted to varying degrees: most flagrantly in (8) and (10); less so in (9). These infringements of the maxim are meaningful: it is by assuming that the speaker is still adhering to the Cooperative Principle on a higher level in (8)–(10) that the hearer is able to extract the implications intended by the speaker. For example, B's reply in (8) concerns a completely different topic to that of A's question. In replying with information about reading cereal packets, B seems clearly to be disobeying the maxim of Relevance. How does A interpret this? Grice articulates A's dilemma as follows:

On the assumption that the speaker is able to fulfill the maxim and to do so without violating another maxim (because of a clash), is not opting out, and is not, in view of the blatancy of his performance, trying to mislead, the hearer is faced with a minor problem: How can his saying what he did say be reconciled with the Cooperative Principle?

(Grice 1989: 30)

The solution to this 'minor problem' is to assume that B is **implying** the answer to the question rather than saying it outright. Assuming that he is still adhering to the Cooperative Principle, A can make B's remark relevant by inferring the answer to the question from it by appeal to general principles of world-knowledge: if B hasn't even read the back of the cereal packet, it is hardly likely that he would have read Sebald; therefore, B may reasonably be taken to be implicating that the answer to the question is 'no'. B is therefore exploiting the maxim of Relevance in order to generate the implication which answers A's question.

QUESTION   Sentences (9) and (10) also involve infringements of the maxim of Relevance. Describe the steps A could apply in reasoning in order to extract the correct implication.

Another case of maxim-flouting is the following (Grice 1989: 154–155). A is planning a trip with B to southern France. Both know that A wants to see his friend C, as long as doing so wouldn't involve too great a detour from their original itinerary. This is the context for the following exchange:

(11) A: *Where does C live?*
      B: *Somewhere in the South of France.*

Grice glosses this (ibid.) by noting that there is no reason to suppose that B is opting out of the conversation: the Cooperative Principle, in other words, should still be assumed to be active. However, his answer is, as he well knows, less informative than A needs. The first maxim of Quantity ('make your contribution as informative as is required for the current purposes of the exchange') has therefore been infringed. But A can explain this infringement by supposing that B is simply avoiding an infringement of a different maxim, the second maxim of Quality, 'do not say that for which you lack adequate evidence'. In this situation, B has chosen the reply which gives the most information of which he is capable, and A can extract the implication that B is unaware of C's exact address.

QUESTION   Consider each of the Gricean maxims, and describe ways in which their infringement could generate implicatures. Are some maxims more likely to be infringed meaningfully than others?

4.4.2 Questions about implicatures

According to Grice, much of the contextual force of an utterance is derived by the hearer through a rational process of inference based on general assumptions in the framework of a cooperative speech exchange – and not, as for Austin or Searle, through the observance of any specific conventions governing different speech acts. For scholars sympathetic to the Gricean approach, this is a theoretically significant discovery about the nature of meaning in general (see Levinson 2000 for a development of Grice's ideas). Three observations, however, are relevant. The first is that whole conversations can often proceed without any implicatures of the sort Grice discusses: we often talk in a much more literal way than Grice's treatment suggests. The second is that not all language occurs in the context of cooperative talk exchanges. Instances of language use do, certainly, often presuppose an addressee (cf. Bakhtin 1986), but this is not the same as being part of a *cooperative exchange*. Sometimes our conversational contributions are quite the opposite of cooperative: our remarks may be disjointed or contradictory; we often make assertions for which we lack evidence, which we know not to be true, and which, in fact, we do not even *expect* to be understood. Language use is, in short, often not the streamlined, collaborative, rational enterprise which Grice suggests.

QUESTION   Give other examples of language use which do not seem to presuppose a cooperative background like the one Grice assumes. A Gricean might defend the validity of the Cooperative Principle by saying that even where a speaker's intention is to mislead, confuse, etc., this intention can only be accomplished if the hearer succeeds in understanding the meaning of the speaker's words – and for this to happen, there must be a principle of cooperation at work on some level. Would this defence be justified?

The third point about Grice's examples is that the analysis always depends on it being possible to say (i) that an implicature is clearly being conveyed, and (ii) more or less what this implicature is. But how realistic is this? Sometimes (often?) it is entirely unclear *whether* the speaker is implying anything beyond what they are saying, and, if so, what. And in cases where the presence of an implicature is possible, it is not the case that a hearer will proceed (at least consciously) in a linear Gricean manner, in which an infringement of one of the maxims is noted, and the appropriate implication computed on the basis of rational considerations of what the speaker could be intending. The course of real conversations, in other words, often seems much more chaotic and irrational than Grice's analysis suggests.

4.5 Are the maxims universal?

If it is accepted that maxims like those formulated by Grice underlie many types of conversation in English, it is obviously an important question whether the same is true for other languages. The universality of the Gricean maxims has been strongly questioned by Keenan (1976). Keenan says that we can readily imagine situations even in our own society which do not observe the first maxim of Quantity, which stipulates that hearers are to make their contributions 'as informative as is required for the current purposes of the exchange'. As she points out, there are many situations where it would be indiscreet, impolite or unethical to be informative.

Situations of professional confidence like those involving lawyers, doctors, spokespeople, accountants, etc. are only the most obvious examples where 'be discreet' seems a more appropriate description of the maxims governing conversation than 'be informative'.

Having demonstrated the lack of applicability of Quantity (i) in certain types of familiar Western context, Keenan goes on to claim that societies exist where, in general, the maxim 'be informative' does not hold at all. One such society, Keenan claims, is Madagascar, where 'the expectation that speakers will satisfy informational needs is not a basic norm' (Keenan 1976: 218). Information in traditional Malagasy society is, according to Keenan, characteristically withheld – especially if the information in question is important. Keenan derives this tendency not to inform from certain large-scale features of traditional Malagasy social organization:

New information is a rare commodity. Villages are composed of groups of kinsmen whose genealogical backgrounds and family lives are public knowledge. Their day-to-day activities are shaped to a large extent by the yearly agricultural cycle. Almost every activity of a personal nature (bathing, play, courtship, etc.) takes place under public gaze. Information that is not already available to the public is highly sought after. If one gains access to new information, one is reluctant to reveal it. As long as it is known that one has that information and others do not, one has some prestige over them.

(Keenan 1976: 218)

Keenan claims that this unwillingness to inform fits into a wider pattern in Madagascar, which includes a general reluctance both to identify individuals explicitly, and to make explicit statements about either present or future. 'It would be misleading', she continues, 'to conclude that the maxim "Be informative" does not operate at all in a Malagasy community':

We would not be justified in proposing the contrary maxim 'Be uninformative' as a local axiom. Members of this speech community do not regularly expect that interlocutors will withhold necessary information. Rather, it is simply that they do not have the contrary expectation that in general interlocutors will satisfy one another's informational needs.

(Keenan 1976: 224)

The Gricean maxims must not, therefore, be seen as universal principles governing the entire range of human conversational behaviour: conversational maxims seem to vary situationally and cross-culturally, and the set of maxims operative in any given culture is a matter for empirical investigation.

Many scholars working in the tradition of Gricean analysis are committed to the universality of the maxims and therefore need to reply to this attempted relativization of them. Kasher (1982), for example, has claimed that Keenan's observation of apparent violations of the Quantity maxim isn't a violation at all: Keenan has not, according to Kasher, taken into account the role of *cost* in the Malagasy speaker's avoidance of informativeness. In developments of Gricean theory, Kasher states, a rational speaker opts for a speech act which not only attains his purpose most effectively but also does so at least cost, *ceteris paribus*. Now, it is up to the speaker himself to determine what counts as a cost and what may be disregarded... For Malagasy speakers, commitments should be spared...

(Kasher 1982: 207)

For Kasher, then, Keenan's apparent counter-example is nothing of the sort. Malagasy speakers attach high value to the possession of information which their interlocutors do not have. Given these values, the social cost of disclosing information counteracts the maxim of informativeness, and there is no reason to doubt that 'Be informative' really is a maxim adhered to – according to their own broader conventions – by Malagasy people.

Keenan might well reply, however, that the reformulation of the maxim in order to take cost into account means that the maxim can never, in fact, be infringed. Grice's definition of the maxim – 'make your contribution as informative as is required for the current purposes of the exchange' and 'do not make your contribution more informative than is required' – allows any possible counter-example like Keenan's to be dismissed by varying the parameter of the requirements of the exchange. Thus, if we include as one of the 'requirements of the exchange' the speaker's desire to avoid cost by not releasing information, the maxim survives intact. Whatever the rights and wrongs of the Keenan/Kasher debate, the issues involved illustrate the difficulty of applying Gricean insights, which are derived from idealized reflection on conversation, to real linguistic description.

QUESTION   Are Keenan's Malagasy examples conclusive evidence that the maxims are not universal, or is Kasher's defence justified? Discuss the issues involved.

4.6 Relevance theory

Relevance is a crucial notion in the Gricean programme, and Grice had called (1989: 86) for it to be clarified. Working in a tradition inspired by Grice, Sperber and Wilson (1987, 1995, 2002) have developed an important theory of pragmatics in which a notion of relevance supplants all the other factors Grice considered. We noted in 4.2 that Grice's theory depends on an intentional-inferential view of communication. For Sperber and Wilson, in contrast, language-use is an **ostensive-inferential** process: the speaker ostensively provides the hearer with evidence of their meaning in the form of words and, combined with the context, this linguistic evidence enables the hearer to infer the speaker's meaning. But the hearer does not do this by entertaining assumptions about the speaker's intentions and using them to explain infringements of a set of conversational maxims, as in Gricean approaches. Sperber and Wilson argue against any account of utterance interpretation which assumes that hearers decide what meaning or implication the speaker could have intended their words to have and assume that it was this meaning that the speaker intended to achieve. The range of possible meanings that a speaker may intend to convey is, they say, far too great to make this sort of procedure possible (2002: 10–11): the speaker could conceivably have been intending to communicate *anything*. Furthermore, they complain that Grice's conversational maxims do not sufficiently narrow down the range of possible interpretations a hearer may reach for an utterance:

> There may be a whole variety of interpretations that would meet whatever standards of truthfulness, informativeness, relevance and clarity that have been proposed or envisaged so far. The theory needs improving at a fundamental level before it can be fruitfully applied to particular cases.
>
> (Sperber and Wilson 1995: 37)

Rather, Sperber and Wilson claim that there is a single overarching cognitive principle, the **Principle of Relevance**, which determines the way in which hearers interpret – and speakers intend – utterances.

Relevance, in Sperber and Wilson's definition (see e.g. 2002: 14), is a potential property of utterances and other phenomena (external events, thoughts, memories) which provide input to cognitive processes:

> The relevance of an input for an individual at a given time is a positive function of the cognitive benefits he would gain from processing it, and a negative function of the processing effort needed to achieve these benefits.
>
> (Sperber and Wilson 2002: 14)

We can think of relevance as a kind of 'cognitive nutrition' (Breheny 2002: 181): a maximally relevant utterance is one that provides the desired information (for instance by answering a question, confirming a hypothesis, or correcting a mistake: Sperber and Noveck 2004: 5), and which does this in the way easiest to understand. Thus, if you ask me what my first name is and I reply 'Nick', my answer is maximally relevant: there is no other way I could have conveyed this information more efficiently. If, on the other hand, I reply 'My first name is an abbreviation of the name derived from the Greek expression "victory of the people"', then my answer will be considerably less relevant (though still true) because it will cost you considerable effort to interpret.

Every utterance, for Sperber and Wilson, 'communicates a presumption of its own optimal relevance' (1995: 158). This is the communicative **principle of relevance**. What it means is that a speaker implies the relevance of their words by the very act of speaking: in saying something to a hearer, a speaker implies that the utterance is the most relevant that they could have produced under the circumstances, and that it is *at least relevant enough* to warrant the hearer's attention. Sperber and Wilson posit that there is a universal cognitive tendency to maximize relevance: human beings seek information from which they will benefit, and this tendency makes it possible, at least to some extent, to predict and manipulate the mental states of others, including those that result in the production of utterances. Thus, speakers will try to produce optimally relevant utterances, in the knowledge that this is what will be most useful for hearers, and hearers assume that the speaker's utterance is the most relevant possible, given the speaker's circumstances.

The principles which govern hearers' interpretations of utterances are described by a two step **comprehension procedure** (Sperber and Wilson 2002: 18):

(a) Follow a path of least effort in computing cognitive effects. In particular, test interpretative hypotheses (disambiguations, reference resolutions, implicatures, etc.) in order of accessibility.
(b) Stop when your expectations of relevance are satisfied.

The most relevant utterance is the easiest to understand. Since the speaker is expected to make her utterance as relevant as possible, the hearer is justified in following the path of least effort by considering the most accessible (obvious) interpretation of the speaker's words first. 'The hearer is also justified', Sperber and Wilson continue, 'in stopping at the first interpretation that satisfies his expectations of relevance because, if the speaker has succeeded in producing an utterance that satisfies the presumption of relevance it conveys, there should never be more than one such interpretation' (Sperber and Wilson 2002: 19). Let's see an example of how the comprehension procedure accounts for the contextual interpretation of an utterance. Consider the following dialogue (taken from Sperber and Wilson 2002: 19):

(12) Peter: *Can we trust John to do as we tell him and defend the interests*
        of the Linguistics Department in the University Council?
    Mary: *John is a soldier!*

Sperber and Wilson's explanation of the processing steps involved here is worth quoting in full:

Peter's mentally represented concept of a soldier includes many attributes (e.g. patriotism, sense of duty, discipline) which are all activated to some extent by Mary's use of the word 'soldier'. However, they are not all activated to the same degree. Certain attributes also receive some activation from the context (and in particular from Peter's immediately preceding allusions to trust, doing as one is told, and defending interests), and these become the most accessible ones. These differences in the accessibility of the various attributes of 'soldier' create corresponding differences in the accessibility of various possible implications of Mary's utterance, as shown in (4):

(4)   a. John is devoted to his duty.
      b. John willingly follows orders.
      c. John does not question authority.
      d. John identifies with the goals of his team.
      e. John is a patriot.
      f. John earns a soldier's pay.
      g. John is a member of the military.

Following the relevance-theoretic comprehension procedure, Peter considers these implications in order of accessibility, arrives at an interpretation which satisfies his expectations of relevance at (4d), and stops there. He does not even consider further possible implications such as (4e)–(4g), let alone evaluate and reject them.

(Sperber and Wilson 2002: 19–20)

Whereas on a Gricean account – as for many other pragmatic accounts – recognition of the literal meaning of the utterance is the basis of its subsequent interpretation, for Sperber and Wilson this literal meaning is not even considered: Peter simply considers what are, for him at the time, the most relevant possible meanings of Mary's statement, among which the literal one does not even figure. It is the Principle of Relevance which therefore allows the appropriate piece of factual (encyclopaedic) information about the concept SOLDIER to be selected as the relevant meaning of *soldier* in this instance.

Note that Sperber and Wilson's argument depends on the implications of *John is a soldier* being ranked in the way shown in (4). Their justification for this ranking is that (4a)–(4d) are more accessible than (4e)–(4g) since they are already activated by the preceding context. They acknowledge, however, that the question of which implications are more accessible in a given context is an empirical one, and that their account must be tested experimentally. As they put it (1995: 138–139), 'it is not enough to point out that information may be carried over from one conceptual process to the next; one would like to know which information is kept in a short-term memory store, which is transferred to encyclopaedic memory, which is simply erased', adding that '[h]ere we have neither formal arguments nor empirical evidence for any particular set of hypotheses'. On a traditional picture of linguistic meaning, the literal meaning is *always* the basis of interpretation: soldier *means* (something like) 'member of the military', and any account of its actual use must take this original meaning into account. We might, for example, see this as an example of a **metaphor**: the utterance of *soldier* immediately evokes the literal meaning 'member of the military', and the real-world knowledge that members of the military are associated with patriotism, team spirit, sense of duty and discipline is what allows Peter to recover Mary's metaphorically intended meaning. The confirmation of the relevance theory account therefore depends on an independently confirmed ranking of the accessibility of the different pieces of information associated with an expression.

There is, however, some experimental evidence consistent with Sperber and Wilson's claim that the 'literal' meaning of *soldier* may not be operative here: Gibbs (2002), for example, surveys a certain amount of evidence in favour of the 'direct access' view of interpretation. On this view, speakers go directly to the intended meaning without the literal meaning functioning as a preliminary step (for more discussion and supporting conclusions, see Glucksberg 2004). This evidence has considerable implications for our whole view of literal and non-literal meanings. For the moment, we can simply summarize Sperber and Wilson's theory by observing that the postulation of a single cognitive principle – Relevance – as the central consideration in utterance interpretation is simultaneously a more comprehensive and a less verifiable theory of communicative behaviour than the Gricean approach which it is intended to supersede. As we have seen, Grice's rather detailed list of maxims allows for the possibility of specific empirical disconfirmation of individual maxims (barring methodological problems like those discussed in 4.5 above). But Sperber and Wilson's single generalized principle of relevance is much harder to pin down in the details of the empirical description of language use, whether cross-linguistic or psycho-linguistic. If relevance is assessed against considerations of cognitive effort and gain, how can we measure these without some specific insight into the details of cognitive functioning? How, equally, can we rank the possible interpretations of an utterance with respect to their abstract accessibility without direct investigation of the psychology of the speaker concerned?

Sperber and Wilson are far from the only theorists whose work raises this kind of question, and the newly emerging field of Experimental Pragmatics (Noveck and Sperber 2004) promises to supply at least some answers. In particular, experiments reported in Van der Henst and Sperber (2004) lend support to the idea that principles of relevance are, in fact, operative in certain domains of psychology. There is still a long way to go, however. As Van der Henst and Sperber themselves put it (2004: 169), 'it would take many more successful experiments involving a variety of aspects of cognition and communication to come anywhere near a compelling experimental corroboration of relevance theory itself'.

On a more general level, the basic presuppositions of theories of meaning like those discussed in this chapter have been the subject of considerable critique. Mey, for example, criticizes Relevance Theory for its treatment of speaker and hearer as 'spontaneous individual[s] consciously working on unique problems, rather than…social agent[s] working within preexisting conventions with resources available to [them] of which [they] cannot be aware' (1988: 294). This criticism could equally well be advanced against any of the approaches to communication in the tradition of Grice. In their focus on rational interactions between autonomous individuals, such theories can be charged with ignoring both the subconscious and the social determinants of linguistic behaviour. These traditions largely ignore the ways in which what we say and what we take others to mean are constrained by a whole range of factors well beyond the horizon of our individual conscious intentions, including social expectations and unconscious motivations, to name only the two most important. Do we, in fact, always speak with an intention? Could we always say what it is? Do we always react to others' utterances by trying to determine either their intention, or the specific proposition that is most relevant? On the conscious level, the answer to these questions is clearly 'no'. On the subconscious one, the answer is much less clear. Many linguists, however, would feel that in spite of these concerns, the inferential picture of communication is the best approach we currently have to the question of the relation between meaning and use. In spite of the problems confronting Gricean and related approaches, something like their view is assumed by most investigators of natural language.

4.7 Semantics and pragmatics

The study of pragmatics has only arisen fairly recently in linguistics. Investigation of meaning, by contrast, without which the study of grammar is impossible, has always been considered as a central part of the study of language, even before its constitution as a separate subdiscipline round the time of Bréal (see Chapter 1). The focus in pragmatics on language as it is actually used in context poses a significant challenge to linguistic semantics. If, as an empirical discipline with 'scientific' aspirations, linguistics doesn't set out to study language as it is actually used, then what is it supposed to study? If semantics focuses on the abstracted, idealized, context-free meanings of linguistic expressions, what genuine evidence is there for these meanings other than the ways words are used in actual discourse? And if the very hypothesis of meaning is supposed to explain how words are used, couldn't the kind of gaps between meaning and use studied in pragmatics suggest that there's something wrong with the very postulation of abstracted, idealized, context-free meanings in the first place?

Considerations like these lead many pragmatists to see pragmatic questions, not semantic ones, as the central ones in any study of meaning. One of the first to realize the importance of pragmatic questions was the philosopher Rudolph Carnap. For Carnap, pragmatic facts are especially central since they are discovered before any possible semantic ones in empirical investigation of unknown languages:

> Suppose we wish to study the semantical and syntactical properties of a certain Eskimo language not previously investigated. Obviously, there is no other way than first to observe the speaking habits of the people who use it. Only after finding by observation the pragmatical fact that those people have the habit of using the word 'igloo' when they intend to refer to a house are we in a position to make the semantical statement '"igloo" means (designates) house' and the syntactical statement '"igloo" is a predicate.' In this way all knowledge in the field of descriptive semantics and descriptive syntax is based upon previous knowledge in pragmatics.... *pragmatics is the basis for all of linguistics.*
>
> (Carnap 1942: 21; italics original)

As we have observed at several points, pragmatic considerations like reference assignment, scope interpretation and implicatures like the temporal subsequency reading of *and* may enter into the truth-conditions of an utterance. Even on the strictest truth-conditional approach to meaning, then, the boundary between semantics and pragmatics is porous: acts considered as prototypically part of the domain of pragmatics are necessary to the very calculation of truth-conditional meaning. The interpenetration of semantics and pragmatics also applies in the domain of speech acts. As noted by Strawson (1971: 150), in performative utterances like *I apologize*, meaning and illocutionary force are co-extensive: the *meaning* of *I apologize* is that the speaker is performing the speech act of apologizing. In lexical semantics, also, rejection of the dictionary-encyclopaedia distinction amounts to a rejection of any split between semantics and pragmatics. If any piece of encyclopaedic knowledge may become linguistically relevant, there would seem to be little reason to view some as part of dictionary knowledge of meaning, governed by semantic processes, and others as part of encyclopaedic knowledge, governed by pragmatic ones.

This interpenetration between semantics and pragmatics has led some scholars, such as Sperber and Wilson, to reconceive of the nature of linguistic communication in general. On the traditional view, language consists in the communication of a definite content: a certain proposition either is or is not communicated by a given utterance; other propositions, in turn, may or may not be implied by it, but, if they are implied by it, this means that they are not specifically communicated. Grice had already questioned this view: it is probably not possible, according to him, to

> devise a decisive test to settle the question whether a conversational implicature is present or not – a test, that is to say, to decide whether a given proposition *p*, which is normally part of the total signification of the utterance of a certain sentence, is on such occasions a conversational (or more generally a nonconventional) implicatum of that utterance or is, rather, an element in the conventional meaning of the sentence in question.
>
> (Grice 1989: 42–43)

While we seem to be able to react to implications in the course of normal discourse, it does not seem to be possible for us to formulate any absolute test to distinguish between what an expression means and what it merely implicates: the boundary between semantics and pragmatics, therefore, is entirely fluid.

Sperber and Wilson share Grice's view. For them, communication is a matter of degree. Each utterance draws a certain set of propositions to the attention of the hearer, weakly activating a vast number of pieces of encyclopaedic knowledge, and the hearer will apply the comprehension procedure in order to determine which is the one the speaker probably intends. It does not make sense, on this picture, to speak of a single proposition which is uniquely conveyed by an utterance: an utterance's meaning is always the product of a choice from among a set of options, and the factors leading to the choice of one interpretation can only be understood against the background of the other interpretations which the hearer considered and rejected. Adopting this picture allows us to avoid the fallacy that communication is always what Sperber and Wilson call *strong communication* (Sperber and Wilson 1995: 58–60): communication, that is, in which a single, definite content is uniquely conveyed. There is much more vagueness and indeterminacy in real language than this idealized picture suggests, and to suggest otherwise is to endow communication with spurious precision.

Summary

Interpersonal context

The relations between language and context are not limited to those in which a linguistic expression describes a preexisting world. The assertion of facts about the world is just one of the acts which we can use language to perform: we also ask questions, issue orders and make requests. In these types of speech act, truth is not a relevant parameter in the appreciation of meaning.

Austin and Searle on speech acts

Austin's theory of **speech acts** distinguished three types of act we perform in any utterance:

- the **locutionary** act is the act *of* saying something, i.e. the act of expressing the basic, literal meanings of the words chosen
- the **illocutionary** act is the act performed *in* saying something, i.e. the act of using words to achieve such goals as warning, promising, guaranteeing, etc.
- the **perlocutionary** act is the act performed *by* saying something, i.e. the act of producing an effect in the hearer by means of the utterance.

Considerations of truth and falsity are simply irrelevant for many types of illocutionary act. Austin distinguished **constative** utterances like *snow is white*, which have the illocutionary force of simply stating something, from **performative** utterances like *I apologize*, which themselves bring about the state of affairs they mention. Fregean truth conditions are relevant to constatives but not to performatives. Instead of truth conditions, performative utterances have **felicity conditions**. Typical felicity conditions for many types of constative and performative utterance were described by Searle.

Grice on implicature

Grice recast the study of the relations between language and context by highlighting the central role of **intention** to meaning, and developed a theory of implicature and conversational maxims which described the relation between sentence and utterance (speaker) meaning. Grice's main contribution is the four conversational **maxims** of **Quality**, **Quantity**, **Manner** and **Relevance**. Many implied meanings result from speakers' deliberate infringement of these maxims.

Relevance theory

Relevance Theory, finally, represents a third tradition which challenges some of the central presuppositions of the study of meaning. According to Relevance Theorists, the production and understanding of utterances is explained as the result of a universal **comprehension**

> **procedure** which consists in selecting the most relevant aspects of a word's meaning in a given situation. There is no distinction between literal and non-literal meaning, and what meanings are activated by a word is highly dependent on the particular context in which it is uttered.

Further reading

Tsohatzidis (1994) contains discussion of various aspects of speech-act theory; for an ethnographically based critique, see Rosaldo (1980), discussed in Duranti (1997: chapter 7). Levinson (2000) and Horn (1984) are good examples of modern pragmatic work in a neo-Gricean tradition. For a clear introduction to Relevance Theory, Blakemore (1992) can be recommended; see May (1988) and Mey and Talbot (1988) for a critique of the theory. Noveck and Sperber (2004) reports on more recent experimental work. Kasher (1998) is a comprehensive anthology of key writings in pragmatics; Levinson (1983), Verschueren (1999) and Mey (2001) are standard introductions to the field. Ariel (2008) is a recent introduction to pragmatics and grammar. For discussion of current issues in pragmatics, start with the journals *Journal of Pragmatics* and *Pragmatics and Cognition*.

Exercises

Questions for discussion

1. Give some examples, from English and other languages you know, of indirect speech acts, i.e. situations where a particular grammatical structure (question, command, statement, etc.) is used with an illocutionary force different from the one it is typically assumed to express. What considerations might lie behind a speaker's choice of an indirect speech act to achieve their intended illocutionary effects?

2. As pointed out by Carston (1988), there are in fact cases where a temporal subsequency reading of *and does* form part of the utterance's truth-conditions. The following sentences thus all depend on a reading of *and* in which the conjunct (the phrase after the *and*) is interpreted as later in time:

   He didn't steal some money and go to the bank; he went to the bank and stole some money.
      It's better to meet the love of your life and get married than to get married and meet the love of your life.
      Either she became an alcoholic and her husband left her or he left her and she became an alcoholic; I'm not sure which.

   Is this a problem for Grice's theory?

3. Relevance theory assumes that speakers, as well as hearers, maximize relevance. When asked to give answers involving times, people often give rounded answers. For example, when asked for the time, a speaker is more likely to give an answer of the form 3.30, not 3.32. Can this be accounted for in terms of relevance theory? How would the speaker's circumstances (e.g. whether they were wearing a watch, if so, whether it was digital or analogue, etc.) affect their calculation of relevance? How

would considerations of relevance differ if the question was 'My watch isn't working properly. Do you have the time please?' or 'Do you know the time of the next train to X'?

4. Choose a sixty-line excerpt from one of the conversations in the Saarland corpus of spoken English, viewable online at www.uni-saarland.de/fak4/norrick/scose.html. For each conversational turn, describe:

    (i) What, if any, speech act it exemplifies;
    (ii) If it does not obviously exemplify a speech act, what its role in the conversation is;
    (iii) Whether the contribution observes or infringes any of the Gricean maxims;
    (iv) Whether there are any implicatures and, if so, how these arise.

    In general, how useful are (a) Gricean and (b) Searlian categories in the analysis of the excerpt?

5. As we discussed, one of the classic problems of speech act theory is the problem of indirect speech acts: the problem of why speakers often fail to choose the standard grammatical form for their obvious communicative purpose (e.g. uttering the statement *it's cold in here* in order to request someone to open the door). Mey (2002: 116) comments on this as follows:

    A possible solution to the problem capitalizes on the observation that these so-called 'indirect' speech acts derive their force not so much from their lexico-semantic build-up, as from the situation in which they are appropriately uttered. It is the situation which makes the speech act possible, and intelligible to the hearer.

    But he then says (2002: 117) that if this is true for some speech acts, it's true for all of them – not just indirect ones.

    In such a 'radically pragmatic view'…, the indirect speech act dilemma is resolved by moving the focus of attention from the words being said to the things being done in the situation. Since all speech acting, for its meaning, depends *on* the situation, while the indirectness of a speech act derives *from* the situation, no speech act, in and by itself, makes sense; alternatively, every speech act is to some degree indirect. Consequently there are, strictly speaking, no such 'things' as speech acts, but only what I will call the language users' situated acts, or *pragmatic acts*. (italics original)

    He continues (2002: 117):

    But if there are no objects called 'speech acts', then it is a mistake to believe (as most philosophers and linguists do) that one can isolate, and explain, our use of words by referring to certain individual speech acts, having well-defined properties (such as illocutionary force), to be assigned strictly in accordance with philosophical and linguistic criteria (semantic, syntactic, perhaps even phonological). It further implies that all efforts by the linguists to break out of this linguistic and philosophical straightjacket… in the end must be frustrated, since no single theory of language or of the mind will ever be able to explain the activities of the human language user *in the concrete situation of use*. Such a situation depends neither on the mind nor on language exclusively, hence cannot be expressed in terms intended to specifically operate within, and describe, the mental or linguistic.

Discuss these claims. Are they justified? What are their implications for the investigation of language?

6. As described by Grice, the examples of implicature like those in (8)–(10) in 4.3.2 are all cases in which sentence and utterance meaning do not correspond. Why should speakers opt for such a lack of correspondence?

7. Consider the following observation: if I say *X went into a house yesterday and found a tortoise inside the front door*, the implication is that the house is not my own; the same implication arises for analogous sentences involving the expressions *a garden, a car, a college*, and so on. Sometimes, however, there normally would be no such implicature (*I have been sitting in a car all morning*), and sometimes the opposite one (*I broke a finger yesterday*). Account for these facts in terms of encyclopaedic knowledge and Gricean principles.

8. Grice notes the following paradox in the investigation of implicatures:

If nonconventional implicature is built on what is said, if what is said is closely related to the conventional force of the words used, and if the presence of the implicature depends on the intentions of the speaker, or at least on his assumptions, with regard to the possibility of the nature of the implicature being worked out, then it would appear that the speaker must (in some sense or other of the word *know*) know what is the conventional force of the words which he is using. This indeed seems to lead to a sort of paradox: If we, as speakers, have the requisite knowledge of the conventional meaning of sentences we employ to implicate, when uttering them, something the implication of which depends on the conventional meaning in question, how can we, as theorists, have difficulty with respect to just those cases in deciding where conventional meaning ends and implicature begins?

Grice (1989: 49)

Can you suggest any answers?

5 Analysing and distinguishing meanings

CHAPTER PREVIEW

The different sections of this chapter follow three logical steps in meaning analysis. In 5.1, some of the different possible **semantic relations** among words are exemplified and discussed. We concentrate on those relations which are of most use for semantic description:

- **antonymy** (oppositeness; 5.1.1),
- **meronymy** (*part of*-ness; 5.1.2),
- the class-inclusion relations of **hyponymy** and **taxonomy** (*kind of*-ness; 5.1.3–4) and
- **synonymy** (5.1.5).

These meaning relations can be seen as reflecting the presence of various isolable components in the meanings of the related words; accordingly, Section 5.2 introduces the possibility of analysing senses as composed of bundles of **semantic components**, and considers the wider applicability of **componential analysis** as well as the problems it faces. The third section (5.3) discusses the necessity for a theory of meaning to specify the number of senses associated with a lexeme in a rigorous way. In 5.3.1 we distinguish the case where a single lexeme possesses several related meanings (**polysemy**) from two other cases: the case where it possesses only a single meaning (**monosemy**) and the case where it possesses two unrelated meanings (**homonymy**). Section 5.3.2 then shows that any attempt to make these definitions rigorous confronts serious problems, the implications of which are discussed in 5.3.3.

5.1 Lexical relations

Knowing an expression's meaning does not simply involve knowing its definition or inherent semantic content. As well as knowing a word's definitional meaning, a competent speaker knows how it relates to other words of the language: which words are synonyms? Which are antonyms? Which are meronyms, linked by the relation of a part to a whole? And which are hyponyms, linked by the relation *kind of*? Describing and accounting for these relationships has often been taken as one of the principal tasks of lexical semantics. Relationships like synonymy, antonymy, meronymy and so on all concern the **paradigmatic** relations of an expression: the relations which determine the choice of one lexical item over another. In the construction of any utterance, the speaker is typically confronted with a choice between various lexical items. Thus, the highlighted expressions of (1a) stand in various types of paradigmatic relation to those of (1b): *kitchen* is a meronym of *restaurant*; *often* is the antonym of *rarely*, *many* is (in this context) a synonym of *numerous*, and *sushi* is a hyponym of *Japanese food*.

(1)   a. *The **restaurants often** have a sort of pan-Asian flair and there are **many** sushi bars.*
       b. *The **kitchens rarely** have any sort of pan-Asian flair and there are **numerous** Japanese food bars.*

The choices between different antonyms, meronyms and hyponyms will be made on the basis of the different meanings which they convey: if the speaker utters (1b) instead of (1a), it is because the different paradigmatic choices result in different propositions being expressed. (The choice of one synonym over another cannot be made on the basis of meaning, synonyms being words which have the same meaning: we will consider some of the factors behind synonym choice in 5.1.5.) Antonyms, meronyms, hyponyms and synonyms are only the most important of the lexical relations it is possible to identify within the vocabulary of a language. Their study is important since, as noted by Nyckees (1998: 178), they play a determining role in linguistic intercomprehension:

It would seem that the members of a linguistic community must be able to construct relations between different expressions in order to understand each other. Being genuinely able to speak a language involves understanding the equivalence or the differences between different phrases, in other words, mastering the relations of synonymy and paraphrase; it involves the ability to draw out the consequences of a given utterance, and the ability to sequence utterances in a reasonably coherent, intelligible way; the ability to reformulate one's own messages in different ways, make one's expression tighter or looser according to the demands of the situation . . .

We will exemplify the four most important types of semantic relation in 5.1.1–5.1.5.

5.1.1 Antonymy

Speakers of English can readily agree that words like *good-bad, love-hate* and *in-out* are opposites or **antonyms**. The notion of oppositeness involved here seems to cover several different types of relation; in general, however, antonymy may be characterized as a relationship of incompatibility between two terms with respect to some given dimension of contrast. Some words seem to have more than one antonym, depending on the dimension of contrast involved (*girl* has both *boy* and *woman*, depending on whether the dimension of contrast is sex or age; *sweet* has both *bitter* and *sour*: see Murphy 2003: 173).

Not every word has an obvious antonym: *library, of,* and *corresponding* are three cases for which there is no obvious relevant dimension of contrast and for which antonyms are consequently hard to identify. And even where an obvious dimension of contrast does exist, antonyms are not always available: *angry*, for instance, does not have any obvious antonym in English even though we can easily conceive of the scale of arousal and calmness to which it belongs.

QUESTION   Name ten other lexical items which do not seem to have obvious antonyms. Can you construct contexts in which antonyms become available?

Nevertheless, antonymy is an important relation within the vocabulary of a language. We discuss in Chapter 3 how Warlpiri specifically exploits antonymy in the special Jiliwirri speech style (3.2.2.1). Another mark of the significance of antonymy is the fact that many languages can create antonyms morphologically. English does this productively with the prefix *un-*. In Ancient Greek, antonyms were created through the addition of the prefix *a(n)-*, as in *an-eleutheros* 'unfree' (*eleutheros* 'free'), *an-omoios* 'unlike' (*omoios* 'like') and *an-artios* 'uneven' (*artios* 'even').

When discussing antonymy, the principal distinction we have to make is between **gradable** and **non-gradable** antonyms. Non-gradable antonyms are antonyms which do not admit a midpoint, such as *male-female* or *pass-fail*. Assertion of one of these typically entails the denial of the other. Thus, if someone is female, they are necessarily not male, and someone who has failed an exam has necessarily not passed it. Gradable antonyms, however, like *hot-cold* or *good-bad*, seem to be more common than non-gradable ones. A gradable pair of antonyms names points on a scale which contains a midpoint: thus, *hot* and *cold* are two points towards different ends of a scale which has a midpoint, lexicalized by adjectives like *tepid*, which is used to refer to the temperature of liquids which are neither hot nor cold, but somewhere in between. A consequence of the fact that gradable antonyms occur on a scale is the fact that they are open to **comparison**. Thus, we may say that one drink is *hotter* than another, or that some water is *less cold* than another.

QUESTION   List fifteen gradable and fifteen non-gradable antonym pairs.

Gradable antonyms have a number of subtle characteristics. For example, one of the members of an adjectival antonym pair often behaves 'neutrally' in questions and comparative constructions, in that it simply serves to invoke the dimension of contrast as a whole, without attributing either of the opposed properties to the object it qualifies. In the pair of gradable antonyms *good* and *bad*, for instance, *good* is the neutral or **uncommitted** member. Thus, (2) and (3) do not imply that the film is actually *good* (it might just be average, or even bad):

(2)   *How good is that film?*

(3)   *The film is better than the TV series.*

The fact that *good* does not commit the speaker here is shown by the following examples:

(2′)   A: *How good is that film?*
       B: *Really bad.*

(3′)   *The film is better than the TV series, but it's still really bad.*

Contrastingly, *bad* and its comparative *worse* do commit the speaker to the badness of the film, as shown by B's denial of this implication in (4), and the oddness of (5)

(4)   A: *How bad is that film?*
      B: *It's not bad, it's good!*

(5)   *?The film is worse than the TV series, but they're both really good.*

Not all gradable antonyms show these imbalances, however. Some antonyms, like those in (6), are **equipollent**, in other words symmetrical in their distribution and interpretation, with neither member of the pair having an uncommitted ('neutral') use. Thus, both members of the following pair imply an assertion of the mentioned property:

(6)   a. *How hot is the saucepan?* [implies that it is hot]
      b. *How cold is the saucepan?* [implies that it is cold]

However, such properties seem quite context-dependent. In (7), for example, *hot* functions as the uncommitted member of the pair:

(7)   a. *How hot was it last summer?* [doesn't imply that it was necessarily hot]
      b. *How cold was it last summer?* [implies that it was cold]

Uncommitted antonym pairs, which are in the minority in English, typically name objectively measurable qualities like size, age and weight (Lehrer 2002: 498). Very little research has been conducted into committedness cross-linguistically. Cruse (1992) investigated antonyms meaning *long-short*, *good-bad* and *hot-cold* in English, French, Turkish (Altaic, Turkey), Macedonian (Indo-European, Macedonia), Arabic and Chinese. For the adjectives meaning 'longer', 'shorter' and 'better' all languages allow an impartial or uncommitted use, suggesting that antonym behaviour may show some cross-linguistic uniformity. Phenomena like (7), however, suggest that such cross-linguistic findings should be approached with caution. Indeed, one of the main results which cross-linguistic research into antonymy could bring is an appreciation of just how context-dependent committedness is cross-linguistically.

Languages with many adjectives are the most likely to have gradable antonyms. However, languages without adjectives can convey similar contrasts. In Chinese, for example, the same gradable contrasts are represented through static verbs such as *gāo* 'be tall' and *hǎo* 'be good' (Murphy 2003: 190). Similarly, the English verbs *love-hate* show comparable behaviour to many gradable adjectives (Murphy 2003: 190). Thus, they establish points on a scale which admit differing degrees (8a, b), and assertion of one necessitates the denial of the other:

(8)   a. *I love/hate him a lot.*
      b. *I love/hate him more than you do.*
      c. *I love him* entails *I don't hate him*

QUESTION   Consider the noun pairs *hero/coward, genius/dolt, giant/shrimp*. Are these gradable antonyms?

A certain number of words in English which have more than one meaning can be given descriptions which make them seem **autoantonymous**, i.e. their own opposites (Murphy 2003: 173). Thus, *temper* means both 'to harden' and 'to soften'; *cleave* means both 'stick together' and 'force apart' and *sanction* means both 'to approve' and 'to censure'. Furthermore, there are many denominal verbs for putting in or taking out things which show similar autoantonymy, (e.g. *to string a bean* vs. *to string a violin*, Clark and Clark 1979). Murphy points out (2003: 173) that contextual factors limit the risk of confusion in many of these cases: if you *temper your comments* you are softening them, not making them harder, whereas *tempering metal* can only refer to hardening it.

There are many other types of relation which are commonly thought of as exemplifying antonymy. Examples include what Lyons (1977) calls *converse opposition*, exemplified by relations like *parent-child, buy-sell, give-receive, above-below*; *directional opposition* such as *north-south*, and *come-go*; and *reversive opposition* like *do-undo, colour-bleach, build-demolish*. Still other pairs which could be described as antonyms, but do not fall under any of these categories, are *nut-bolt* and *hand-glove* (Murphy 2003: 199). Our initial description of antonymy as incompatibility with respect to a given dimension will cover these examples. Thus, a nut and a bolt are complementary tools which do not fulfil the same function and are therefore incompatible (a nut cannot be used instead of a bolt), and hand and glove show similar complementarity: the visible end of an arm is either a (gloveless) hand or a glove.

A general problem with subtypes of antonymy is that of determining their boundaries. Is *sell-refund* a converse, a reversive, or neither? Cruse

(2002b: 507) defines reversives as a class of verb opposites which 'denote either changes in opposite directions between two terminal states . . . or the causation of such changes'. He notes that 'a test which permits the delimitation (for English) of a fairly coherent set of reversible verbs (that is, verbs which are potential members of reversive oppositions) is the *again*-test. This depends on the possibility of using unstressed *again* without the process denoted by the verb having happened before.' Thus, the following sentences are taken as evidence that *enter* and *leave* are a reversive pair:

(9)   a. *The spacecraft left the earth's atmosphere.*
       b. *Five days later, the spacecraft entered the atmosphere again.*
       c. *The alien spacecraft entered the earth's atmosphere.*
       d. *Five days later, the spacecraft left the atmosphere again.*

QUESTION   Which of the following verbs is unstressed *again* possible with: *screw-unscrew, do-undo, colour-bleach, build-demolish, fill-empty, clean-dirty, fold-unfold, stand up-sit down, rehearse-perform, plant-harvest*? Can you think of any similar tests for conversives and directionals?

As pointed out by Murphy (2003: 10), the amount of certainty we have in acknowledging a pair of words as antonyms seems to have an important cultural component. Some antonyms, like *hot-cold* or *big-small*, seem well established culturally, whereas others, like *sweltering-frigid* or *gigantic-tiny*, which seem to convey equally 'opposite' notions, have less of an antonymic ring. This leads Murphy to conclude that a speaker's knowledge of the relation of antonymy (as, in fact, of all lexical relations) is **metalexical**; the fact that two words are antonyms (synonyms, etc.) is not, in other words, part of our dictionary knowledge *of* the word's meaning, but part of our encyclopaedic knowledge *about* the word's meaning.

5.1.2 Meronymy

Meronymy (Greek *meros*: 'part') is the relation of part to whole: *hand* is a meronym of *arm*, *seed* is a meronym of *fruit*, *blade* is a meronym of *knife* (conversely, *arm* is the **holonym** of *hand*, *fruit* is the holonym of *seed*, etc.). Surprisingly, not all languages seem to have an unambiguous means of translating the phrase 'part of' (Brown 2002: 482; Wierzbicka 1994: 488–492 disagrees), but meronymy is nevertheless often at the origin of various **polysemy** patterns (where a single word has more than one meaning; see 5.3 below), and an important lexical relation for that reason. Thus, according to the figures given by Brown and Witkowski, roughly one in five of the world's languages use the same term to designate the eye (meronym) and the face (holonym) (Brown and Witkowski 1983). Similarly, slightly fewer than half of the world's languages polysemously relate 'hand' and 'arm' as separate meanings of the same word, and 39 per cent 'foot' and 'leg' (Witkowski and Brown 1985). These figures are only estimations, but polysemy patterns based on meronymy are certainly frequent cross-linguistically. (See 11.4.1 on the semantics of body-parts in the world's languages.)

The definition of meronymy as based on the 'part of' relation is not without problems. Typically, meronymy is taken to be **transitive**: if A is a meronym of B, and B is a meronym of C, then A is also a meronym of C. This follows what seems to be the logical structure of the part-whole relation: if A is a part of B, which is in turn a part of C, then it seems to be necessarily true that A is also part of C. The use of *part of* in English is often consistent with the transitivity of the meronymic relation. Thus, sequences of embedded parts and wholes, such as *seed-fruit-plant*, yield perfectly natural-sounding sentences highlighting the *part of* relation:

(10) a. *A seed is part of a fruit.*
      b. *A fruit is part of a plant.*
      c. *A seed is part of a plant.*

The transitivity of meronymy also applies for the triple *cuff-sleeve-coat*: a *cuff* is part of a *sleeve*, a *sleeve* is part of a *coat*, and a *cuff* is also part of a *coat*.

But the use of *part of* in natural language does not always respect the logically transitive nature of meronymy. Consider the relation *handle-door-house*. While clearly we can naturally say *a handle is part of a door* and *a door is part of a house*, it seems unnatural to say that *a handle is part of a house*. The chain of meronymies in (11), moreover, is not only unnatural, but also false:

(11) a. *Simpson's finger is part of Simpson.*
      b. *Simpson is part of the Philosophy Department.*
      c. **Simpson's finger is part of the Philosophy Department.* (Winston, Chaffin and Herrmann 1987: 431)

These facts suggest that the linguistic category *part of* does not have the same properties as its logical counterpart. Lyons (1977: 312) suggested that there are in fact several different types of meronymy in language. Acting on this suggestion, Iris, Litowitz and Evens (1988) isolate four different types of meronymy in English: the relation of the functional component to its whole, such as the relation between *heart* and *body* or *engine* and *car*; the relation of a segment to a preexisting whole (*slice-cake*); the relation of a member to a collection or an element to a set (*sheep-flock*); and the relation they call subset-set (*fruit-food*; this would normally be considered an example of hyponymy, which we discuss below). Transitivity holds for the subset and segmented wholes types of meronymy, but not for the functional part or collection-element types.

For their part, Winston, Chaffin and Herrmann (1987) propose a six-way typology, according to which *part of* has six possible different meanings: component-integral object meronymy (*pedal-bike*), member-collection (*ship-fleet*), portion-mass (*slice-pie*), stuff-object (*steel-car*), feature-activity (*paying-shopping*) and place-area (*Everglades-Florida*). They claim that meronymy is transitive when the same type of meronymic relation is involved in all parts of the chain, as in (12), which contains the component-object type of meronymy:

(12) *Simpson's finger is part of Simpson's hand.*
    Simpson's hand is part of Simpson's body.
    Simpson's finger is part of Simpson's body.
    (Winston, Chaffin and Herrmann 1987: 431)

Contrastingly, (11) above involves component-object meronymy in (a) and member-collection meronymy in (b); hence, transitivity fails.

5.1.3 Hyponymy

Hyponymy (Greek *hypo*- 'under') is the lexical relation described in English by the phrase *kind/type/sort of.* A chain of hyponyms defines a hierarchy of elements: *sports car* is a hyponym of *car* since a sports car is a kind of car, and *car*, in turn, is a hyponym of *vehicle* since a car is a kind of vehicle. Other examples of hyponym hierarchies include

- *blues – jazz – music,*
- *ski-parka – parka – jacket,*
- *commando – soldier – member of armed forces,*
- *martini – cocktail – drink* and
- *paperback – book.*

A standard identification procedure for hyponymy is based on the notion of class-inclusion: A is a hyponym of B if every A is necessarily a B, but not every B is necessarily an A. For example, every car is a vehicle, but not every vehicle is a car, since there are also buses, motorbikes and trucks. Hence, *car* is a hyponym of *vehicle*. Furthermore, hyponymy is usually taken to be transitive: if A is a hyponym of B, and B of C, then A is a (more remote) hyponym of C.

As we will see, hyponymy is a major semantic relation in the grammar of many languages. Furthermore, a particular type of hyponymy, taxonomy, discussed in the next section, is an important aspect of the way we talk about the natural world.

Hyponymy also has a crucial communicative function. It often happens that we are unable to retrieve the most accurate, precise term for the referent we have in mind. At other times, mention of the most precise term would be needlessly informative and thus violate one of the pragmatic constraints which often seem to be operative in communication (see 4.4). In cases like these, the existence of a term (referred to as a **hyperonym**) further up the hyponymic hierarchy allows reference to be accomplished. Thus, wanting to mention the fact that my brother has started learning to play the sackbut, but momentarily unsure of the name of this instrument (or worried that my interlocutor will not know what I'm talking about), I can simply say *my brother is learning a weird musical instrument*, using the hyperonym *musical instrument* to refer to its hyponym *sackbut*. The possibility of referring at a number of different hierarchical levels is also crucial for cross-cultural communication. At specific levels of categorization, languages often lack exactly corresponding terms: Japanese *wasabi*, for example, isn't accurately translated into English by any of the choices *mustard, chutney, vinaigrette,* etc. But in order to explain what it is, a combination of modifier and hyperonym can always be found: thus, wasabi can be referred to as a *horseradish condiment.* Similarly, the names of the various female outer garments often worn in Muslim countries lack precise English equivalents. But by adding modifying adjectives to appropriate superordinate terms, translations can be given: *khimar* 'long veil', *chador* 'full-body cloak'.

The concept of hyponymy can be made intuitively clear on the basis of examples like those given above, and hyponyms in other languages are often easy to identify: in Tzeltal (Mayan, Mexico), for example, *chenek'* 'beans', *ixim* 'corn', *ti'bal* 'meat' and *wale'* 'sugarcane' are among the obvious hyponyms of *we'lil uch'balil* 'food' (Berlin 1992: 186). But as soon as one tries to make the notion of hyponymy explicit various problems are encountered. The definition of hyponymy as class-inclusion, for example, seems to be too powerful, since there are many cases which fit the class-inclusion definition which could not be described with the formula *kind/ type/sort* (Cruse 1986). For example, as noted by Wierzbicka (1984), every (male) policeman is necessarily someone's son, and not every member of the category 'someone's son' is a policeman, but this doesn't mean that a male policeman is a 'kind of son', and we would not want to describe the relation between *male policeman* and *someone's son* as an example of hyponymy.

Even the linguistic definition of hyponymy as the *kind/sort/type* relation admits instances which seem remote from the standard exemplars of hyponymy because they do not define a hierarchy. In English, for instance, one might very well utter the sentences in (13), for example in the context of an explanation to someone unfamiliar with the word involved:

(13) *A zebra is a kind of horse*
A DVD is a kind of video
A hang-glider is a kind of kite
A koala is a kind of bear
Writing is a kind of drawing
A watch is a kind of clock

In none of these cases, however, would we wish to claim that the nouns related by the phrase *a kind of* are hyponyms. *Kind of,* in other words, seems to have a variety of values in English, not all of which correspond to the strict class-inclusion model: in (13), *kind of* serves to establish a comparison between two terms without introducing any claim of class-inclusion of the sort which could define a hierarchy. This isn't such a problem for determining hyponymy in our native language, but it poses a particular challenge when the lexical structure of an unfamiliar language is under investigation. If English *kind of* seems ambiguous between a 'strict hyponymy' reading and a looser, comparison reading, how can we decide whether the equivalent of *kind of* in an unfamiliar language is being used in a strict or a loose sense? In Tok Pisin (English-based Creole; Papua New

Guinea), for example, we find the translation equivalent of *kind of*, *kain*, used in the following definitions:

(14) a. *haus kunai*

wanpela kain haus ol i wokim long kunai antap long ruf bilong en na bai i stap 4 yia samting. 'A kind of house which has been made with a grass roof and which will last about four years.'

b. *haus pisin*

wanpela liklik kain haus ol pisin i wokimm long diwai stik o lip samting. 'A small kind of house which is built by birds out of sticks or leaves.'

c. *haus sel*

wanpela kain haus ol i putim na rausim kwiktaim long wokim long laplap samting. 'A kind of house which can be put up or taken down quickly which is made of canvas-like material.' <www.sil. org/silewp/1998/002/SILEWP1998–002.html#Greenberg1963>

Judging from the translated definitions, the words concerned are the Tok Pisin translations of 'grass hut', 'nest' and 'tent'. Are they, however, hyponyms of TP *haus*? Without an appreciation of the range of uses of *kain* in TP, we are unable to tell. (The mere fact that the TP definienda *contain* the word *haus* is no evidence: in English, a *publishing house*, a *doll's house* and a *Royal house* are not kinds of *houses*: the first is a kind of company, the second a kind of toy, the third a kind of family.)

Hyponymy is often exploited by languages with classifier systems (Allan 1977; Aikhenvald 2000). In noun-classifying languages, the noun phrase obligatorily contains a morphological element (the classifier) whose choice is determined by semantic features of the referent of the head noun. Often, the semantic basis of this classification is implicitly hyponymic, with a given classifier naming a superordinate class of which the head noun is a particular kind. Thus, noun phrases in Jacaltec (Mayan; central America: Aikhenvald 2000: 285) contain a classifier morpheme which assimilates the noun to a broader set of superordinate kinds or classes. For instance, the person 'John' and the animal 'snake' are implicitly represented in (15) as hyponyms of the classes 'person' and 'animal' through the use of the classifiers *naj*, which classifies the noun as a human, and *no7*, which classifies it as an animal (Aikhenvald 2000: 82):

(15) *xil*   *naj*   *xuwan*   *no7*   *lab'a*
saw   CL:MAN John   CL:ANIMAL snake
'(man) John saw the (animal) snake.'

The number of classifiers may often be quite high: a non-human noun, for example, will be accompanied by one of the eleven following classifiers (Aikhenvald 2000: 285), depending on the semantic kind of which it is a hyponym:

(16) *no7*   animal
    metx' dog

te7	plant
ixim	corn
tx'al	thread
tx'añ	twine
k'ap	cloth
tx'otx'	soil/dirt
ch'en	rock
atz'am	salt
ha7	water
k'a7	fire

In Burmese (Tibeto-Burman, Myanmar), classifiers are based on the function which the noun fulfils:

(17) *hte*   clothing for the body (not headgear or footwear)
    sin   cutting tools
    si   vehicles
    saun   written materials
    le'   hand implements (also eyeglasses)
    koun   loop-shaped objects that are worn: garlands, necklaces
    hsaun   houses, monasteries, royal buildings (Aikhenvald 2000: 291)

Sometimes it is the verb which takes the classifier. This is the case in Ojibway and Cree (Algonquian, Canada), for instance, where verb classifiers categorize the referent of the verbal argument in terms of its shape, rigidity, size, structure, position and animacy, as in (18):

(18) a. *kinw-a:pe:k-an*
      long-one.dimensional.and.flexible-it.is
      'it is long' (e.g. rope)

    b. *kinw-e:k-an*
      long-two.dimensional-it.is
      'it is long' (e.g. cloth)

    c. *napak-a:pi:k-at*
      flat-one.dimensional.and.flexible.-it.is
      'it is flat' (e.g. ribbon)

    d. *napak-(i)minak-isi*
      flat-three.dimensional-it.is
      'it is a flat "roundish" thing'

    e. *w:awi:-(y)e:k-an*
      round-two.dimensional-it.is
      'it is round' (e.g. cloth) (Aikhenvald 2000: 297)

This classification relies on implicit hierarchies of long, one-dimensional and flexible things, flat and round things, etc. Implicit hyponymic structure is therefore an important principle in the grammatical structure of classifier languages. Elsewhere, however, it may be the case that hyponymic structure is minimal or even absent for certain lexemes. As Jackendoff (2002: 345) points out, the hierarchical connections of *junk* and *puddle* would not seem to be an important part of their meaning.

5.1.4 Taxonomy

As we saw in the last section, one of the problems in making the notion of hyponymy explicit derives from the equivocal nature of the predicate *kind of*. This seems to denote both the 'strict' hierarchy-defining, class-inclusion relation of the kind *sports car–car–vehicle*, and the 'looser' comparison relation of the sort exemplified in (13). The 'strict' reading of *kind of* is best demonstrated by **taxonomies**, hyponymic hierarchies of names for plants and animals. An English example of a taxonomy, accompanied by various labels discussed below, appears as Figure 5.1.

This taxonomy shows five ranks, each of which includes all those below it: all *swamp white oaks* are *white oaks*, all *white oaks* are *oaks*, all *oaks* are *trees*, and all *trees* are *plants*. Each rank in the hierarchy is thus one particular *kind of* the rank above it. A comparison with the examples in (13) will immediately reveal that the notion of *kind of* found here is clearly different from the one involved in phrases like *a koala is a kind of bear*. Even though we might utter sentences like these for comparative or explanatory purposes, to modern Westerners familiar with scientific classification there is an obvious sense in which a koala is not a kind of bear: a koala is a kind of marsupial. The strict notion of *kind of* operative in taxonomies and the class-inclusion categories it defines seem particularly stable: it is in general hard for us to revise the taxonomies of natural kinds which we have learnt as part of the process of acquiring our native language. We will not, in general, be able to reclassify an oak as a pine, or a lizard as a mammal: the categories in our natural-kind taxonomies are quite rigid and distinct. The arrangement of a language's natural kind terms into taxonomies like this allows speakers to draw important inferences about the distribution of the properties which characterize different features of the natural world. Consider for example the partial taxonomy *animal – mammal – cow*. 'Learning that one cow is susceptible to mad cow disease, one might reasonably infer that all cows may be susceptible to the disease but not that all mammals or animals are' (Atran 1999: 121).

How are taxonomies distinguished from non-taxonomic hyponymies? In non-taxonomic hyponymies, a hyponym (e.g. *mare*) can be replaced by a complex label consisting of a superordinate term and a modifier (e.g.

Unique beginner		*plant*	Level 0
Life-form	*tree*	(other life-forms)	Level 1
Generic	*oak*	(other generics)	Level 2
Specific	*white oak*	(other specifics)	Level 3
Varietal	*swamp white oak*	(other varietals)	Level 4

FIGURE 5.1
Five-level taxonomy
(Brown 1986: 2).

female horse; see Cruse 1986: 137–145). Similarly, *gelding*, another non-taxonomic hyponym of *horse*, can be replaced, without any loss of meaning, by *neutered horse*. This possibility does not exist throughout a taxonomy. There are no modifiers that can be added to the superordinate *bird* in order to distinguish the subordinates *robin, eagle* or *hawk*. Similarly, the non-taxonomic nature of the category *weed* is revealed by its paraphrase as *unwanted plant*, and that of *vegetable* by *edible plant*.

QUESTION   Can you think of any exceptions to this generalization? When you have thought about this, go on to read about the distinction between primary and secondary lexemes a few paragraphs below (after example (19)).

The cross-linguistic construction of taxonomies has been extensively investigated, especially by anthropologists working in the tradition of Berlin (Berlin 1972, 1992; Berlin, Breedlove and Raven 1973). Berlin proposed, mainly on the basis of name-elicitation interviews and grouping tasks with native-speaker informants, that there is a universal taxonomic structure of a maximum of five basic ranks, as shown, arranged into levels, in Figure 5.1. This structure is common to all ethnobiological classifications, and is assumed to reflect universal cognitive patterns. For any given plant or animal in a language, the ranks of the taxonomy to which it belongs need not all necessarily have distinct names; the structure shown in Figure 5.1 illustrates the basic template on which plant and animal taxonomies seem to be patterned cross-linguistically. The most inclusive level of the taxonomy is the *unique beginner* or *kingdom* rank, of which the English categories *plant* and *animal* are examples. This rank is numbered as level 0 in Berlin's system since it is commonly not lexicalized in taxonomies: many languages do not have general words corresponding to English *animal* and *plant*. In Itza (Mayan, Northern Guatemala), for example, there is no single word for *plant*: however, the cognitive reality of this level is suggested by the fact that the numeral classifier -*teek* is used with all and only plants (Atran 1999).

The next level, level 1, is the level of *life-forms*, e.g. categories like *tree, grass, vine* or *bird, fish, snake* in English. The number of different categories recognized at this level tends to be fairly small. In Hanunóo (Austronesian; Philippines), for example, plants are categorized as *kayu* 'wood', *ʔilamnun* 'herb' or *wakat* 'vine'. The first category includes all plants with typically woody stems, the second all non-woody or very small plants, the third all plants with twining, vinelike stems (Conklin 1954: 92–93, quoted in Berlin 1992: 164). Tobelo people (West Papuan, Indonesia) recognize five animal life-forms: *o totaleo* 'bird', *o dodihna* 'snake', *o nawoko* 'fish', *o bianga* 'mollusc' and a fifth unnamed category including all other animals (Berlin 1992: 165). In Itzaj (Mayan, Guatemala; Atran 1999: 123), plants generally fall under one of four mutually exclusive life forms: *che'* (trees), *pok~che'* (herbs, shrubs, undergrowth), *ak'* (vines), and *su'uk* (grasses). The animal life-forms of Rofaifo (Papua New Guinea) number five; their membership may be surprising to someone used to standard Western classifications:

(19) *hefa*   eel, cassowary, larger species of monotreme, marsupial
                     and rodent plus pig, dog, and the larger mammalian spe-
                     cies introduced by Europeans
     hunembe   smaller species of marsupial and rodent
     nema   bats and all birds except cassowaries
     hoifa   lizards, snakes, fish other than eels, molluscs, earth-
                     worms, leeches, planaria, centipedes, millipedes . . .
     hera   frogs other than those of the genera *Asterophrys,*
                     Xenobatrachus, and *Barygenys.* (Dwyer 1984: 323, quoted in
                     Berlin 1992: 166)

Below the life-form level is the *generic* level (Level 2): as well as *oak,* English
has *elm, gum, maple, poplar,* and many others. Generics may or may not
have further levels below them: for some taxonomies this is the last level.
The unique beginner, life form and generic level lexemes are usually
labelled by what Brown (2002: 474) calls *primary lexemes,* i.e. 'simple unitary words such as *plant, tree, oak, bird* and *robin'.* On lower levels of the
taxonomy, one typically finds *secondary lexemes,* which consist of the term
for the immediately superordinate class, accompanied by a modifier (e.g.
white oak, a kind of *oak* (Level 3) and *swamp white oak* (Level 4)). Secondary
lexemes are also known as *binomial labels.* Level 4, varietal classes, are rare
cross-linguistically, most taxonomies only extending to the third level.
Intensively studied systems of ethnobiological classification usually also
reveal an *intermediate* rank, located between the life-forms of Level 1 and
the generics of Level 2. An English intermediate rank would be *evergreen*
(tree), which includes generic classes like *pine, fir* and *cedar,* and is included
in the life-form category *tree.* Intermediate ranks distinguishing different
categories of the life-form *bird* have been noted in Kalam (Trans-New Guinea,
Papua New Guinea), Wayampi (Tupi, Brazil) and Huambisa (Jivaroan, Peru).
Thus, the Kalam life-form category *yakt* 'birds and flying things' is superordinate to an intermediate category *pow,* grouping together two types of
nightjar (Berlin 1992: 139–140).

It would appear that taxonomy-*like* structures exist in all of the world's
languages. Like Berlin, Atran (1990) argues that multi-level taxonomic
structuring like that shown in Figure 5.1 is universal, and he grounds this
claim in certain alleged features of human cognition. Human beings, he
claims, are cognitively predisposed to believe that each type of living
thing has a particular inner nature or essence. For people raised in
English-speaking cultures, for example, the oak is inherently seen as having an essence or nature which places it in the class of trees and distinguishes it from the pine; this belief in the inherent essences of living
things allows their insertion into taxonomic hierarchies on the basis of
their inherent properties. Taxonomic organization like that exemplified
in Figure 5.1 is thus an innate mental pattern shared by all human
beings:

Meaning for living-kind terms can thus be analyzed in a fundamentally
distinct way from the semantics of other object domains, such as the

domain of artifacts and perhaps that of chemical and physical substances as well. All and only living kinds are conceived as physical sorts whose intrinsic 'natures' are presumed, even if unknown.

(Atran 1990: 6)

Speculations like those of Berlin and Atran on the universal principles of taxonomic structure, however, have been extensively criticized by those who see the naming practices of different languages as arising out of practical, culture-specific forces, rather than putatively universal structuring principles of human cognition (Hunn 1982, Ellen 1993). Researchers working in the tradition of Berlin have been accused of 'attempting to impose a form of taxonomic rigidity on a cultural apparatus the general characteristics of which are quite antithetical: namely fluidity, flexibility and elasticity' (Ellen 1993: 220). The universality – and hence the cognitive basis – of the taxonomic structure shown in Figure 5.1 has frequently been called into question: Malapandaram classifications, for example (Dravidian, India; Ellen 1979: 19), appear highly individualistic, limited in scope, and relatively unconcerned with systematization, and the Malapandaram seem to lack any 'systematic knowledge of their natural environment clearly expressed in formal taxonomies' (Ellen 1979: 19). Discussing Bunaq (Trans-New Guinea, East Timor) classification, Friedberg (1979: 85) states that 'plants appear to be organized more according to a complex web of resemblances and affinities in which individual plants can belong to several categories, rather than according to a tree-like system of hierarchical categories' like the one assumed in Berlin's model.

This controversy over the universality of taxonomic principles is exemplary of the issues and questions raised by any exploration of cross-linguistic semantic universals (see Chapter 11). The fact that, like 'part of', the basic hyponymic/taxonomic notion 'kind of' does not seem to have reliable equivalents in all languages may be a problem for proponents of the universal structure of taxonomies. Ellen (1993: 61), for example, notes that there is no exact term in Nuaulu (Austronesian; Indonesia) for 'kind of'. Furthermore, many of the facts about Nuaulu ethno-classification suggest that neat taxonomies of the sort illustrated in Figure 5.1 are simply irrelevant to the way Nuaulu people actually think and talk about the biological world.

For example, . . . the question 'what is **asu** (dog, *Canis familiaris*) a kind of?' is culturally inappropriate because it is never, ordinarily, thought of as a 'kind of' anything, except perhaps 'animal'. Yet again, the question 'what is **asuwan** (cassowary, *Casuarius casuarius*) a kind of?' can generate a whole range of possible answers, no one of which is more 'correct' than any other . . . Similarly, to ask an informant how many types of an animal there are is likely to invite an answer where (in a strict taxonomic sense) none is possible. An informant, out of simple courtesy, because the situation demands it and through the creative use of dualism as a linguistic feature, may provide the name of the most closely related animals he or she can think of, and in this circumstance *relationship* can be described in morphological or ecological terms. In one elicitory context a monitor lizard might appear as 'a type of crocodile', and an earthworm 'a type of snake'.

Ellen (1993: 25–26)

Where class-inclusion arrangements can be discerned, these not infrequently violate taxonomic principles. On Berlin's original approach, for instance, categories of the same taxonomic rank must be mutually exclusive and contrasting: a given tree, for example, must either be an *oak, elm, ash, pine, gum,* etc., but may not be more than one of these; without this constraint, the very notion of a taxonomy breaks down (Berlin 1992: 15). Ellen (1993: 86) found, however, that category boundaries in Nuaulu are not discrete in this way. Thus, the same animal might be classed as either an *imanoma* ('rat') or as a *mnaha* ('mouse') depending on the context, even though these two are recognized as separate categories. According to Ellen (1993: 123), this is because Nuaulu actually has no permanent classificatory principles: animals are simply classified 'according to criteria that seem relevant at the time'. Similarly, ethnobiological terminology often seems to straddle hierarchical levels in a way which runs counter to the presuppositions of Berlin's model. In Yurok (Algic, USA; Bright and Bright 1965, discussed in Berlin 1992: 39–40), for example, the one term *tepo:* means both 'fir tree' (generic level), and 'tree' (life-form level), a circumstance which would seem to provide evidence against Berlin's observation (1992: 31) that the ranks are 'mutually exclusive'.

It would not be appropriate here to talk of either the Ellen or the Berlin approach being proven or disproven by this sort of evidence. Berlin can always make specific adjustments to his model to incorporate phenomena which seem to run against it. It is rather a question of which model seems to square *more* with the facts, and the answer to this will vary from one researcher to another. For many linguists and anthropologists, however, the concentration on putative cognitive universals of taxonomic structure is a distraction from the real business of cross-linguistic research, which should concentrate on the details of how animal and plant terms are actually used, rather than construct abstract taxonomies using formal methods designed to contribute to 'comparative and evolutionary speculation about general mental principles of classification or cognition' (Ellen 1993: 3). We take up the question of cross-linguistic semantic typology again in 11.4.

QUESTION   Could artificial objects like *clarinet, beanbag* or *wheelchair* be considered to belong to taxonomies like those of natural kinds? Read Atran (1990: 475–476) when you have thought about the answer.

5.1.5 Synonymy

In discussing synonymy, the relation of meaning identity, an initial distinction needs to be drawn between lexical synonymy (synonymy between individual lexemes) and **phrasal synonymy** (synonymy between expressions consisting of more than one lexeme). We will only be concerned here with lexical synonymy, assuming that phrasal synonymy can mostly be derived from the synonymy of the phrases' component lexemes (considered in their associated grammatical structures).

Meaning identity (synonymy) is a part of the metalinguistic stock-in-trade of ordinary speakers of English: we often refer to words as 'having the same meaning'. However, we usually restrict our statement of the synonymy of two words (or phrases) to the utterance level:

When questions of sameness of meaning arise for unsophisticated speakers, no appeal is made to an abstract entity of 'meaning': a given word or phrase is accepted as having the same meaning as another word or phrase if its substitution for the other in the given context yields an utterance which they will accept as having the same meaning as the first utterance.

(Lyons 1968: 75)

Speakers do not, that is, characteristically seem to base their judgements of synonymy on a 'bottom-up' analysis of the meaning of each of the words involved, concluding that words are synonymous if their separately established meanings are identical. Instead, a top-down procedure often seems to be at work: the fact that two expressions have the same contextual effect is what justifies labelling the substituted words as synonyms in that context.

Lexical synonymy has been variously defined in the semantics literature. The general definition of 'identity of meaning' is mostly accepted (Cruse 2002a: 486 however defines it as 'identity/similarity' of meaning), and it is the one we adopt here. Within this definition, however, there are a number of different terminological conventions. Of course, what is important in such cases is not to decide which of the different possible uses of a technical term like 'synonym' is better (or, even less, correct), but simply to define what is meant by the label in question and to use it consistently and without ambiguity.

For some authors synonymy is a context-bound phenomenon, two words being synonyms in a certain given context, whereas for others it is context-free: if two words are synonymous they are identical in meaning in all contexts. The question of synonymy and grammatical context is another on which disagreements exist. Thus, two words are synonymous for some authors if, like *likely* and *probable* in (20), they have the same meaning, even if they show a different set of grammatical cooccurrence possibilities – here, the possibility of raising the subject of the complement clause in (20a) to the subject of the main clause in (20b), which exists for *likely* but not for *probable*:

(20) a. *It's likely/probable that he'll be late.*
    b. *He is likely/*probable to be late.*

For other authors, however, both identity of meaning *and* identity of grammatical properties are required (see Hudson *et al.* 1996 for many other examples).

Another important distinction is between synonymy of words and synonymy of senses. Sense-synonymy is the synonymy of some, but not all, the senses of a word. Thus, *pupil* is arguably synonymous with *student* with respect to one of its senses ('person being instructed by a teacher'); but with respect to the sense 'centre of the eye' the two words are, of course, non-synonymous. *Pupil* and *student* are thus not lexical synonyms, but they are synonymous with respect to one of their senses. Similarly, Murphy (2003: 30) demonstrates that the pair *baggage/luggage* are synonymous with respect to the sense 'bags' but not with respect to the metaphorical sense 'emotional encumbrances':

(21) a. *Check your baggage/luggage with the gate agent.*
     b. *I won't date guys with baggage/*luggage from their divorces.*

Recognizing sense-synonymy as a category implies viewing meaning identity not as a binary property of two words, but as a **graded** one: the more senses two words share, the more synonymous they are.

     The limiting case of sense-synonymy is word-synonymy, which is the situation in which two words share *all* their senses. Typically, lexical synonyms are taken to be mutually intersubstitutable in every environment, with each synonym being equally normal in each environment (Cruse 2002a: 488; see box). The clearest examples of word synonymy are trivial ones, where there are alternative pronunciations for what is, in fact, intuitively a single lexeme, such as *(n)either* (pronounced ['(n)iːðə] or ['(n)aɪðə]) and *economics* (pronounced [iːkə'nɒmɪks] or [ɛkə'nɒmɪks]). In both these cases the same meaning is indisputably involved, but it is not clear that two words should be recognized. Some more interesting possible examples would be the pairs *Islamic* and *Muslim*, *Peking* and *Beijing* or *Bombay* and *Mumbai*.

QUESTION   Do these examples survive the test of mutual intersubstitutability?

Ullmann (1972: 141–142) points out that one of the few places where full word synonymy seems reasonably common is technical vocabulary, giving as example the fact that in medicine inflammation of the blind gut can be synonymously referred to as either *caecitis* or *typhlitis*.

     However, as Ullmann also notes (1972: 142), word-synonymy 'runs counter to our whole way of looking at language. When we see different words we instinctively assume that there must also be some difference in meaning.' Consistently with Ullmann's point, genuine lexical synonyms which are not, unlike the examples just given, proper nouns or adjectives prove extremely hard to find. Once their combinatorial environments have been fully explored, proposed lexical synonyms often prove not to be such. For example, Bolinger (1976, discussed by Murphy 2003: 164) showed that *everybody* and *everyone* are not lexical synonyms since they are not mutually substitutable in every context:

(22) a. *She vowed that it was a delightful ball; that there was everybody that everyone knew . . .*
     b. *¡She vowed that it was a delightful ball; that there was everyone that everybody knew . . .*

Similarly, *almost* and *nearly* fail the test, as demonstrated by (23):

(23) *I very nearly/*almost forgot my appointment* (Hudson, Rosta, Holmes and Gisborne 1996: 444).

QUESTION Can you find any lexical synonyms in any language you know? Are they really substitutable for each other in every environment?

Very often, the difference between lexical synonyms is not one of denotation but of connotation: the associations and emotional values of a word (see 1.4.2). Thus, the lexemes *doctor* and *quack* both arguably share the definition 'medical practitioner', and would be substitutable in every context but for the fact that they differ in the neutral and pejorative connotations attaching to each respectively. Other examples would be *lunch* and *luncheon* and *fag* and *cigarette*.

QUESTION Consider the pairs of nouns *prize/award*, *couch/sofa*, and *coronary/heart-attack*. Are any of these synonyms? If so, what kind?

Synonymy and 'opaque' contexts

We noted above that lexical synonyms are usually taken to be mutually intersubstitutable in every environment, with each synonym being equally normal in each environment. Note that this does not extend to so-called *opaque* or *de dicto* (Latin: 'concerning what is said') contexts, i.e. contexts which refer to the content of a proposition (which may be the object of a belief, thought or utterance), rather than simply directly referring to their referent. Thus, *Mumbai* is not necessarily a synonym of *Bombay* in the opaque context 'John thinks the biggest city in India is Bombay', since John may not know that Mumbai and Bombay are the same place. If we took opaque contexts into account in testing for synonymy, there would be no true lexical synonyms.

So far, we have concentrated on the place of synonymy within the paradigmatic language system and largely ignored its place in language use. An initial observation on this subject is that, at least in many varieties of educated English written discourse, it is considered good style to avoid the repetition of identical words in nearby contexts. As a result, near-synonyms are often enlisted as equivalents, without any semantic difference between the equivalent terms being intended. The surrounding context thus endows the equivalent words with the temporary status of synonyms, a status which is in no way permanent, and which may be subsequently revoked so that the formerly equivalent terms can be brought into a relation of contrast. Lyons (1968: 80) generalizes this conclusion to *all* lexical relations: 'any meaning relations that are established are established for particular contexts or sets of contexts, and not for the totality of the language'. Thus, *red* has different possible antonyms depending on whether the context is wine (where the antonym is *white*), traffic lights (*green*), or accounts (*black*).

Second, and lastly, we'll turn to a particularly interesting case of absolute lexical synonymy which has been observed widely in the Aboriginal societies of Australia (Alpher and Nash 1999). In most of these societies, an individual's name would not be used after their death. Furthermore, in many of them, words which sounded similar to that individual's name were also prohibited. This practice would clearly present many inconveniences if there were not some way of replacing the banned vocabulary. The usual practice, resting on the widespread multilingualism that was a standard feature of traditional Aboriginal society in Australia, was to adopt the translational equivalent of the prohibited word from a neighbouring language, and to use it until the old word became reusable (an interval of time which differed according to a number of variables). This process of temporary lexical replacement has resulted in Aboriginal languages possessing a wide range of absolute lexical synonyms. In Warlpiri, for example, a particularly well studied Australian language for which a large corpus of citations exists, facilitating semantic and lexical study, we could give perhaps hundreds of examples of absolute synonyms which appear to be completely equivalent and interchangeable in all contexts. The noun *karnta* 'woman', for instance, has at least the nouns *mardukuja* and *rduju* as absolute synonyms; 'dog' is translated synonymously by *jarntu* and *maliki*; *waku* 'arm' has the absolute synonym *nginyanyka*; and *marlu* 'red kangaroo' has *jurrkapanji*, *wawirri* and *yawarrangi*. Not all of these cases of synonymy are necessarily due to bereavement-induced borrowing: there may be a higher general tolerance of synonyms in Warlpiri than in familiar European languages. While it is possible that the synonymy of some of these examples may not survive the scrutiny of deeper lexicographical investigation, the number of candidates for synonymy in Warlpiri constitutes a striking exception to the pattern observed widely in European languages, which is that a loan-word synonym of an indigenous expression typically develops some semantic difference from the native word. This was the case with the words *beef*, *veal* and *mutton*, all borrowed into English from French, originally synonyms of *cow*, *calf* and *sheep*, but subsequently specialized to refer simply to the edible flesh of these animals.

QUESTION English has many pairs of near synonyms consisting of a native (Germanic) form and later Latin one. The verbs *begin-commence* and *end-terminate* are good examples. How many more can you find? How synonymous are they?

5.2 Componential analysis

The fact that semantic relations reveal aspects of meaning is one of the motivations for a **componential** approach to semantic analysis. Consider a series of hyponyms like *piece of furniture* – *chair* – *armchair*. It is easy to see that each successive level in such a hyponymy simply adds a further semantic specification (or component) to the previous one. Thus, the level

Table 5.1. Componential analysis of English furniture terms.

	with back	with legs	for a single person	for sitting	with arms	rigid
chair	+	+	+	+	−	+
armchair	+	+	+	+	+	+
stool	−	+	+	+	−	+
sofa	+	+	−	+	+	+
beanbag	−	−	+	+	−	−

chair adds a specification which we could describe as 'for one person to sit on' to *piece of furniture*, and *armchair* adds 'with arms' to *chair*. Similarly, we could describe the difference between *chair* and *sofa* through a contrast between the feature 'for one person to sit on' (*chair*) and 'for more than one person to sit on' (*sofa*). Continuing in this way, we could envisage an entire description of the semantic field of words for furniture items based on the presence or absence of a finite number of features, conceived as the 'conceptual units out of which the meanings of linguistic utterances are built' (Goodenough 1956: 196). This is illustrated in Table 5.1.

The information contained in componential analyses like this is essentially similar to the information contained in a definition; in principle, anything that can form part of a definition can also be rephrased in terms of semantic components. Its embodiment in binary features (i.e. features with only two possible values, + or −) represents a translation into semantics of the principles of structuralist phonological analysis, which used binary phonological features like [± voiced], [± labial] [± nasal], etc. to differentiate the phonemes of a language. The use of a restricted number of binary features was one of the most successful innovations of the structuralist programme of linguistic analysis developed in the wake of Saussure by early Prague Schools phonologists like Trubetzkoy and Jakobson, and continued in America in the generative tradition by Chomsky and Halle. The componential analysis of meaning like the one sketched in Table 5.1 is precisely analogous to the feature specifications of phonemes advanced in the structuralist tradition. Thus, just as *sofa* can be described through the use of binary semantic components like [+ with back], [+ with legs], [− for a single person], [+ for sitting], [+ with arms], [+ rigid], so the phoneme /d/ of English would be described (in the system of Chomsky and Halle 1968) as a constellation of the following distinctive features:

(24) /d/ [+ consonantal, − nasal, − sonorant, + anterior, + coronal, + voiced . . .]

These distinctive features serve to differentiate /d/ from the other phonemes of the English consonant inventory; /t/, for instance, shares all the feature specifications of /d/, except that it is [− voiced]:

(25) /t/ [+ consonantal, − nasal, − sonorant, + anterior, + coronal, − voiced . . .]

The use of distinctive binary features as an instrument of phonological analysis proved extremely fruitful and permitted a degree of formalization that many linguists took as a model of successful linguistic theorizing, and it was soon extended to the analysis of morphology (see Lounsbury 1956: 159–162 for details). From this, application of features to semantics was a natural development.

Whereas a standard dictionary represents the contrast between *chair* and *sofa* through differing definitions, as in (26), the componential analysis represents the same difference in meaning simply through the presence or absence of a single feature, [for a single person], an analysis which struck many linguists as superior in terms of its concision.

(26) *chair* 'a separate seat for one person, of various forms, usually
       having a back and four legs'
     sofa 'a long upholstered seat with a back and arms for two or more
       people' (Concise Oxford 1995)

Some componential analyses went beyond strict feature binarity to include a third value, 0, which indicated that a word was unspecified for a particular feature. Thus, in the analysis of German nouns for sounds given in Table 5.2 (Baldinger 1984: 85–87), a certain word may neither possess nor lack a certain feature, but may simply be unspecified for it. For instance, the superordinate term *Schall* 'sound' neither possesses nor lacks the feature 'self-produced': sometimes the sound referred to by *Schall* is self-produced (in the case of someone shouting, for instance), sometimes it is not (as in the sound of bells). 'Self-produced' is thus irrelevant to *Schall*; describing it as unspecified with respect to this feature allows it to be analysed using the same features as the other terms.

The description in Table 5.2 may 'certainly seem debatable from the point of view of contemporary German' (Coseriu 1971: 181). What is important for our purpose is not whether the analysis is accurate, but the conceptual framework to which it belongs.

Componential analysis was not simply an innovation with respect to preceding modes of semantic analysis. It also crystallized a number of the implicit characteristics of ordinary lexicographical description, particularly the idea (typical of a diverse range of thinkers like Leibniz or the

Table 5.2. Componential analysis of German sound terms.

	audible	self-produced	propagated	echoing	homogeneous
Schall	+	0	0	0	0
Laut	+	+	0	0	0
Hall	+	–	+	0	0
Widerhall	+	–	+	+	0
Klang	+	–	–	0	+
Geräusch	+	–	–	0	–

Port-Royal grammarians in France) that the definitional metalanguage used to describe meanings should ideally be constituted by a fixed number of elementary terms which, in order to avoid circularity, would not themselves be open to further analysis. It is only a small step from such a conception of definition to the formalizations of componential analyses with their fixed repertoire of features, taken to represent the elementary building blocks of meaning.

Despite the popularity it enjoyed for a time, especially in structuralist circles, componential analysis is confronted with a number of serious problems. One important problem is the rigidity of the binary feature system, according to which the only possible value of a specified semantic feature is + or − (or unspecified). This aspect of the analysis came to be seen as increasingly unsatisfactory from the 1970s onward, largely in light of psychological evidence about human categorization which we will discuss in Chapter 7. This was not the only problem, however. Another serious problem was the fact that it seemed simply not to apply to many areas of the vocabulary. Componential analysis is particularly suited to restricted semantic fields from which intuitively obvious semantic distinctions can easily be abstracted. The most obvious types of lexeme to which it can be applied are nouns with obvious properties available for conversion into features ('with legs', 'to sit on', 'for one person', etc.). Elsewhere, however, the utility of features is much less clear. Thus, whereas componential analyses were advanced of words for furniture (Pottier 1964, 1965), of dimension words like *tall, short, long, thick* (Greimas 2002) and, especially, of kinship terms (an area where the binarity of features such as [± female] [± same generation] is particularly justifiable; cf. Goodenough 1956, Lounsbury 1956), not many other areas of the vocabulary proved open to convincing analysis in this method. As a species of definitional analysis, componential analysis inherited the failings of traditional definitions, and words which are hard to produce definitions for are also hard to analyse componentially. The domain of colour terminology is exemplary in this respect, since it does not seem possible to distinguish any inherent components within the meanings of the different colour adjectives, any more than it is to propose definitions of them. What features, for example, could we plausibly advance in order to distinguish *yellow* from *red*? We could always advance the features [± red] and [± yellow], but this sort of move was not considered legitimate: the features were supposed to *analyse* the meanings concerned, not simply treat them as unitary elements (see 2.5 for discussion). Certainly these words do not have any obviously available *conceptual* components of the sort we could discern in the tables above.

Furthermore, many relational ideas which *can* easily be expressed in the propositional format of ordinary language definitions are hard to couch in sets of plausible-sounding binary features. The meanings of the verbs *buy, swap, sell, steal,* for example, do not seem to easily submit to description in terms of any distinctive features – or not, at least, to any distinctive features that would be significantly different from a definition. One could always, of course, develop a description through features like [± exchange] [± price]

Table 5.3. Componential analysis of English transfer verbs.

	transfer of possession	voluntary transfer	exchange	price	subject receives
buy	+	+	+	+	+
sell	+	+	+	+	−
steal	+	−	−	−	+
give	+	+	−	−	−
swap	+	+	+	−	+

Note that these features are meant to apply to transitive, active forms of the verbs: otherwise, the feature [subject receives] will not be an accurate description of the difference between the verbs.

[± transfer of possession] and similar, but the resulting feature decompositions, sketched in Table 5.3, do not seem to gain any explanatory advantage over verbal definitions – in fact, they seem rather less effective in their inability to incorporate the relational ideas which sentential definitions can easily accommodate. For example, the feature [subject receives] seems a clumsy way of capturing the difference between *buy* and *sell*, a distinction which emerges quite naturally from the definitions 'exchange for goods or services', and 'exchange goods or services for money'.

QUESTION Can you formulate a better set of features to describe the meaning of these verbs? What, if any, extra features need to be added in order to account for the verbs *transfer*, *take*, *barter*, *lend* and *hire*?

Another problem with componential analysis as a semantic method can be illustrated by a comparison with phonology, the domain in which the technique was first developed. In phonology, features like [± voice], [± coronal], etc. generally have clear physical definitions: a segment is [+ voice] if the vocal folds are vibrating during its production, and [− voice] otherwise. Whether a segment should be classified as [+ voice] or as [− voice] can therefore, at least in principle, be reasonably unambiguously established. In contrast, the definition of semantic features is much less clear. Consider as an example the case of [+ with legs] in the analysis of the noun *chair*. Many modern types of chair are supported by continuous metal runners which fulfil the same function as traditional legs. Does this type of chair count as [+ with legs] or not? We could, of course, simply stipulate, as a matter of definition, that the feature [+ with legs] applies to this type of chair as well, but if this type of stipulation is necessary too often there is a risk that the features used become arbitrary. Since there are no clear physical or psychological correlates of the semantic features, as there are for the phonological ones, which we could determine experimentally, it is often not obvious how a principled decision is to be reached: we cannot, after all, open up our heads and look inside in order to discover the 'real' nature of the concept involved, in the same way that we can determine observationally whether the vocal folds are usually in operation in utterances of a given segment.

In spite of these problems, the use of distinctive features in componential analysis had some subtle consequences for many linguists' conception of semantics, by making meaning seem something much more concrete and uniform than it had appeared in traditional dictionary definitions. If the definition of *chair* as 'a separate seat for one person, of various forms, usually having a back and four legs' provides an intuitively clear pointer to the word's denotation, it is still thoroughly informal, and open to a large number of different, and equally effective, phrasings. This did not seem to be the case with a componential analysis in terms of features like [+ with back], [+ with legs], [+ for a single person], [+ for sitting], [− with arms], [+ rigid], which brought two important innovations. The first was to suggest that semantic features, like phonological ones, have a higher degree of abstraction and technicality than informal dictionary definitions. Phonological features like [± nasal] or [± coronal] refer to postulated abstract properties of segments which do not have any independent existence: the feature [± nasal], for instance, never exists on its own, but is only found together with other features such as [+ consonant], and is abstracted as the common element from a whole range of sounds like [m], [n] and [ŋ]. Similarly, the adoption of componential analysis encouraged a view of semantic components as abstract, underlying elements of meaning. Given widespread conceptualist assumptions about meanings, it was easy to identify these abstract elements with the conceptual constituents of language (see Lounsbury 1956: 163).

Second, in spite of the fairly small number of words for which successful componential analyses were proposed, componential analysis encouraged the assumption that the same distinctive semantic features would recur again and again in the analysis of a vocabulary; assuming, for example, a feature [± edible] that distinguishes the nouns *beef* and *cow*, one could then use the same feature to distinguish *plant* and *vegetable*. As a result, the underlying semantic content of language was made to seem highly uniform, with word meanings all cut from the same cloth, and it became possible to identify the underlying conceptual content of a language's vocabulary with the finite list of distinctive semantic features required for its componential analysis, in the same way that the set of phonological distinctive features constituted the raw material out of which individual languages constructed their phonemic systems. And just as, in phonology, this repertoire of distinctive features was assumed to be universal, it was easy to assume that all human languages shared the same set of underlying semantic features – even though this was strenuously denied by certain proponents of the method (Coseriu 2001: 360–361).

QUESTION   Propose a componential analysis of nouns indicating means of transport (some suggestions: *bike, car, train, pram, skateboard, roller-blades, plane, helicopter, boat, dinghy, ferry, truck*). What are the advantages and disadvantages of this type of analysis?

QUESTION   As noted above, certain words do not seem obviously amenable to analysis in terms of semantic components. Can you advance componential analyses of *special, fluffy, few* and *Russian*? For each word, what other words can be analysed using the same features?

5.3 Polysemy and meaning division

A number of the analyses presented so far in this chapter necessitate the associated claim that the word under analysis is **polysemous** (Greek 'many meanings'), i.e. that it possesses several distinct senses (as discussed in 10.3, constructions, as well as words, can be polysemous, but we will not pursue this possibility here). To give just one out of several possible examples, the componential analysis of the English furniture terms in Table 5.1 can only be considered valid if certain additional senses of words like *chair* are first excluded from consideration. For example, as well as the meaning in which it refers to an item of furniture, *chair* may also mean 'professorship' and 'head of a committee', meanings to which features like [+ for sitting on] clearly do not apply. A similar point could be made about the description of the transfer verbs *buy* and *give*. These verbs show a constellation of 'metaphorical' uses like those in (27) which contradict the feature assignments in Table 5.3, since there is no price involved in (27a), and no change of possession in (27b):

(27) a. *It's a crazy theory, but I'll buy it.*
    b. *He gave them one last chance.*

These discrepancies are naturally explained by the contention that *chair, buy* and *give* have several distinct polysemous senses, and that the componential analysis does not apply to all of them.

QUESTION   Do any other analyses in the preceding parts of this chapter implicitly require the postulation of polysemy? Which?

This example of the necessity to postulate polysemy is quite typical of semantic analysis. In fact, for many semanticists it is a basic requirement on semantic theory to show how many senses are polysemously associated with a single lexeme: if a lexeme is thought of as the union of a particular phonological form with a particular meaning or meanings, then it is clearly essential for the analysis to specify, for any given word, what it is for a word to have one meaning, and what it is to have several meanings. If a theory of semantics cannot do this, it will be open to the charge that its conception of one of its basic terms is intolerably vague. As Kilgarriff (1993: 379) puts it, 'without identity conditions for word senses the concept remains hazardously ill-defined'.

    But polysemy is not required simply for the purposes of technical linguistic theorizing. The informal description of meaning in ordinary language would also be impossible without the recognition of separate senses within the same word. Consider for example the French noun *pièce*. This has at least five separate senses, as illustrated in (28):

(28) a. 'piece, bit': *les pièces d'un jeu d'échecs* 'the pieces of a chess set'
    b. 'coin': *pièce de deux euros* 'two euro coin'
    c. 'document': *pièce d'identité* 'identity document'
    d. 'play': *pièce en trois actes* 'three act play'
    e. 'room': *appartement de deux pièces* 'two room flat'

It would seem impossible to give any accurate definition of *pièce* that did not separate out these five meanings. This is because any definition which tried to cover all the meanings simultaneously would be excessively broad, and would apply to many referents for which *pièce* itself is not used. Virtually the only definition that will embrace the notions of a piece, a coin, a document, a play and a room is 'thing', but this definition will admit many referents to which *pièce* itself will not ordinarily apply, such as aircraft, stationery items and meals, to name only three out of the infinite number of possibilities. This excessive breadth disqualifies 'thing' as a possible definition of *pièce*, and imposes its division into a number of different senses, each of which can then receive a separate definition.

5.3.1 Polysemy, monosemy and homonymy

The different senses of *pièce* are not unrelated, as an examination of the word's history shows. *Pièce* comes from Mediaeval Latin *petia*, and the meaning shown in (28a) is the oldest sense from which the others are derived (Rey 1998: *pièce*). The other four meanings developed subsequently through ordinary processes of semantic extension which we will discuss in Chapter 11. The semantic links between many of these senses can still be easily imagined: the meaning 'coin', for example, is derived from the collocation *pièce de monnaie* 'piece of money', while 'play' is derived from *pièce de théâtre* 'piece of theatre'.

QUESTION Can you suggest how some of the other senses might be related? What problems are there in deciding?

The term polysemy is usually reserved for words like *pièce* which show a collection of *semantically related* senses. We can thus define polysemy as the possession by a single phonological form of several conceptually related meanings. We will return to this definition in a moment. The opposite of polysemy is **monosemy** (Greek 'single meaning'): a word is monosemous if it contains only a single meaning. Many technical terms are monosemous: *orrery*, for example, has no other recorded meaning in English than 'clockwork model of the solar system', and *appendectomy* (or *appendicectomy*) means only 'excision of the appendix'. Monosemous words may often be **general** over a variety of distinct readings. The English noun *cousin*, for example, is general over the readings 'son of father's sister', 'daughter of mother's brother', 'son of father's brother', etc., but is usually considered as having only the single meaning 'offspring of parent's sibling'.

Polysemy also contrasts with **homonymy** (Greek 'same name'), the situation where a single phonological form possesses unrelated meanings. A good example of a homonym is provided by the English verb pronounced [weɪv], and spelt *wave* or *waive*, depending on the meaning. The different spellings of this word are a clue to the fact that we are dealing with two historically different verbs whose pronunciations happen to have converged. Thus, *wave* derives from Old English *wafian*, whereas *waive* was borrowed into English, ultimately from Old French *gaiver*. These two words originally had different pronunciations, which intervening sound changes have removed. In a situation like this it would make no sense to talk of polysemy. We do not, in English, posit the existence of a single lexeme pronounced [weɪv], polysemous between the meanings 'make a sign with the hand' (*they waved goodbye*) and 'forgo' (*they waived the fee*). As well as the absence of any historical relation, the two meanings are unrelated: it is hard to imagine how they could plausibly be conceptually linked.

Not all homonyms are conveniently distinguished by spelling. The French verb *louer* 'hire', for example, is a homonym of *louer* 'praise', but these two meanings were originally expressed by historically unrelated verbs: 'hire' comes from Latin *locare*, 'praise' from Latin *laudare*. A second example is also a French word starting with *l*, *livre*, which means both 'pound' and 'book'. Again, these meanings are originally completely unconnected, 'pound' being derived from Latin *libra*, 'book' from Latin *liber*.

5.3.2 Tests for polysemy

The idea of 'conceptual relation' (or 'semantic relation') featuring in the definition of polysemy discussed above is notoriously unconstrained. If polysemy is defined as 'the possession of conceptually related senses by a single word', the fact that we can conceive of a conceptual relation between *any* two meanings means that we need never diagnose homonymy. The meanings 'pound' and 'book', for instance, might be conceptually related in that books were typically quite heavy objects, weighing several *pounds*. To give another example, the French noun *pic* means both 'woodpecker' and 'peak'. These are not, however, historically related: the 'woodpecker' sense comes from popular Latin **piccus*, the 'peak' meaning from Spanish *pico*, each of which took on the same pronunciation after it entered French (Rey 1998: *pic*). However, in order to motivate an analysis of *pic* as polysemous we could posit a conceptual link between the shape of a woodpecker's beak and a steep mountain-top: the only reason that modern French dictionaries do not do this is the separate origin of the two words. Even so, it might be objected, who is to say that contemporary French speakers do not relate the two meanings in just this way? Ordinary speakers have no access to the etymological history of their own language; when acquiring French, native speakers would have heard simply the single form [piːk], which they would have learnt to associate with two meanings. Might not they think about the two meanings as related by shape?

In languages whose histories are not well known, cases like this pose a considerable problem, and the uncertainty is aggravated when we have no clear sense of the plausibility of a conceptual relation between the meanings involved. In Warlpiri, for example, the verb *parntarni* means both 'hit on the head' and 'name, call'. Without a thorough appreciation of the cultural context, it is entirely unclear whether it would be possible to propose a plausible conceptual link between these two ideas. And even if we did have a detailed knowledge of the cultural context, it's not obvious what would constitute adequate evidence that the two meanings were 'conceptually related'. Clearly, then, the idea of 'conceptual relation' will not allow us to decide conclusively between cases of polysemy, monosemy and homonymy. What is needed is a more precise criterion which will discriminate the three cases unambiguously. Linguists have devised a number of **polysemy tests**, of which we will discuss the most important.

The oldest type of polysemy test, the **definitional test**, due originally to Aristotle (*Posterior Analytics* II.13; Geeraerts 1993: 230), identifies the number of senses of a word with the number of separate definitions needed to convey its meaning accurately. A word has more than one meaning if there is no single definition which can be applied to all of its uses, and it has no more meanings than the number of maximally general definitions necessary to define its complete denotation. This was the criterion we applied in (28) above in order to delimit the five separate senses of French *pièce*, and it corresponds to the common-sense idea that a word has as many senses as it requires separate semantic descriptions. Thus, the definitional criterion demonstrates the non-monosemy of the noun *quarry*, since there would seem to be no definition which could simultaneously cover the meanings 'site dedicated to the open-air excavation of stone' and 'object of a search or hunt'. Similarly, there seems to be no single definition capable of describing the meanings 'palace' and 'palate' of the French noun *palais*. (Note that the definitional criterion will not of itself distinguish polysemy and homonymy.)

Definitional tests for polysemy are widely rejected (Geeraerts 1993; Schütze 1997: 69; Fodor 1998; Dunbar 2001). The most significant problem with them is that, contrary to the beliefs of their proponents, they in fact presuppose that the number of meanings to be defined is already known (Geeraerts 1993: 236). Ironically, therefore, far from being a test of polysemy, they actually require that the question of the number of senses held by a lexical item is already resolved. To see this, let us once again take an example from French and consider the adjective *drôle*, which can be defined in two different ways, shown in (29) a and b.

(29) a. *drôle*: (1) amusing, humorous
           (2) peculiar

   b. *drôle*: (1) funny

Is *drôle* polysemous or not? The definitional criterion will not help us to decide, since two definitional strategies, each of which gives a different answer, are equally possible and there is not any obvious way to distinguish between them. On strategy (a), *drôle* has two distinct meanings and is therefore polysemous; on strategy (b) it is monosemous. It might be thought that (29b) is a rather unsatisfactory definition, only possible because of the convenient presence in English of a word which covers the same semantic territory as *drôle* in French; *funny* in English clearly covers two distinct notions which a definition should distinguish. We can, however, easily answer this objection by rephrasing (29b) as (30):

(30) *drôle*: provoking amusement or puzzlement

This definition combines the two cases in (29a) into a single **disjunctive** definition (one that contains two clauses linked by 'or'), thereby preserving the semantic analysis of *drôle* while abandoning its distinction into two meaning components. On purely formal grounds, there is nothing to distinguish these definitions of *drôle*: they are all equally accurate, in the sense that they may all be truthfully substituted for the definiendum (see 2.4). Yet they do not resolve the question of the monosemy or polysemy of the adjective.

Another serious problem with the definitional test is that the number of senses it diagnoses for the definiendum will vary according to the meta-language in which the definitions are couched. The Kukatja (Pama-Nyungan, Australia; Valiquette 1993) verb *yungkala* is defined in English as meaning either 'throw and pelt' or 'grind' (it also has other senses which do not concern us here). On the definitional criterion, therefore, it is shown to be polysemous. But if we change the defining metalanguage to Walmajarri (Pama-Nyungan, Australia), a related Australian language, we could simply propose the single definition *luwarnu*, a verb which is also defined in English as 'pelt, grind'. With Walmajarri as the defining meta-language, then, *yungkala* turns out to be monosemous. On the basis of this type of example, we can conclude that definitions should not be appealed to as evidence for the polysemy or monosemy of a lexical item.

Another frequently suggested test for polysemy is the **logical test** (first advanced by Quine 1960). A word (or phrase) is polysemous on this test if it can be simultaneously true and false of the same referent. The reasoning behind this test is that a word could only be simultaneously affirmed and denied if the affirmation and the denial applied to different meanings; otherwise, language would be self-contradictory. Examples of simultaneous affirmation and denial of the same word are given in (31), with the particular sense in question mentioned in brackets:

(31) a. *Bread is a staple* ('basic foodstuff'), *not a staple* ('stationery item').
   b. *This man is a minister* ('priest'), *not a minister* ('politician').
   c. *The exam paper was hard* ('difficult'), *not hard* ('firm to the touch').

The adoption of this test, however, would require us to diagnose polysemy (ambiguity) in many cases where we would not, in fact, want to recognize any more than a single meaning for the word in question:

(32) a. Said of a non-openable window:
       It's a window ('transparent glass fitting') *but it's not a window* ('openable transparent glass fitting').

   b. Said of someone making a half-hearted attempt:
       He's trying ('going through the motions') *but he's not trying* ('making a genuine effort').

   c. Said of a sixteen year old:
       He's an adult ('mature') *but not an adult* ('legally adult').

   d. Said of a lane:
       It's a street ('thoroughfare taking traffic') *but not a street* ('sizeable thoroughfare').

Instead of demonstrating polysemy, what seems to be happening in these utterances is that the speaker is simultaneously entertaining two different points of view, under only one of which the description applies. From one point of view, for example – that according to which windows can be opened – the referent of (32a) qualifies as a window; from the opposite point of view, it does not. To diagnose polysemy, however, in every lexical item that was amenable to this sort of perspectivization would leave virtually no monosemous words in the lexicon.

QUESTION   Devise some other examples like those in (32) involving the simultaneous affirmation and denial of different aspects of a word's meaning. In which cases would you want to say that the word was polysemous? What are your motivations?

A particularly common variety of test used to distinguish between polysemy (ambiguity) and monosemy (vagueness) are the so-called **linguistic tests**, which involve constructions which predicate the same information of two different subjects. In order not to sound bizarre, punning or just awkward, these constructions require that the same information be predicated of both subjects. For example, the *and so* construction in (33a) would not be appropriate if the quartet are playing a Schoenberg string quartet and Real Madrid (a football team) are playing sport; rather, it is only appropriate if the two types of playing are the same, as in (33b):

(33) a. *The quartet are playing, and so are Real Madrid.*
　　　b. *The quartet are playing, and so is the trio.*

Examples of constructions which, like (33a), are bizarre, punning or awkward, are referred to as **crossed** or **zeugmatic** (Greek *zeugma* 'yoke'), since they cross or 'yoke together' notions which do not belong together. As a result of the contrast between (33a) and (33b), some linguists (Lakoff 1970, Zwicky and Sadock 1975) have suggested that constructions like *and so* can be used to differentiate between polysemous and monosemous expressions. Thus, (33a) demonstrates that *play* is polysemous between the sense 'perform a musical piece' and 'engage in a sporting activity'. Similarly, the fact that (34) is not appropriate when intended with the bracketed senses testifies to the polysemy of *mad*:

(34) *Sarah is mad* ('insane'), *and so is Roger* ('angry').

Constructions using *and so* are far from being the only ones to require this sort of identity between the two parts of the predication. Thus, the pronoun *it* in (35) has to be understood as coreferential (anaphoric) with its antecedent, *time*. But since two different senses of *time* are intended in (35), the resulting sentence takes on a 'punning' quality, which has been taken as evidence of the polysemy of *time* with respect to the bracketed senses:

(35) *The drummer is doing time* ('penal servitude'), *but he can't beat it* ('rhythm') (anaphoric pronoun identity).

One major problem with the linguistic test is that whether or not a sentence seems punning, bizarre or awkward is open to significant variation between subjects. Indeed, even the reactions of a single subject to the same sentence may differ at different times. For the present author, for example, the following sentences (Riemer 2005: 141) have in the past seemed both awkward and normal:

(36) a. *The Michelin restaurant judges are eating, and so are the sausage dogs.*
 b. *He lacks taste and company.*
 c. *The fleet reached Samos and an end to the months of waiting.*

Because of this shifting status, the linguistic test would not seem to offer the stable results required for judgements of semantic structure.

Furthermore, as pointed out by Geeraerts (1993: 238), the linguistic test cannot be relied on to give correct results where the polysemy of the word in question is not in doubt. Consider for example (37):

(37) *The newspaper has decided to reduce its size.*

There is nothing awkward or peculiar about this sentence used in the context of a paper deciding to change its format from a broadsheet to a tabloid. Yet *newspaper* initially refers to the management in charge of publishing the physical newspaper, whereas *it*, which should be coreferential with this, refers to the physical object itself. Pretheoretically, we clearly recognize two distinct meanings of *newspaper*, the 'management/board of directors' sense and the 'material object' sense. Yet these different meanings do not show up on the linguistic test.

QUESTION   A possible response to this objection would be that our pretheoretical ideas about the polysemy of *newspaper* are simply wrong. Is this reasonable?

Another problem with the linguistic test is that it ignores the difference between the sense and reference of the lexemes in question. As pointed out by Tuggy (1993), the linguistic test is sensitive to the referents of the terms involved. For example, sentences on the pattern of (38) have been used to demonstrate polysemy, in this case polysemy of the verb *court*:

(38) *Hank is courting Tina and a disaster.*

The zeugmatic character of this sentence justifies the postulation of two separate meanings of the verb *court*: 'woo', which is associated with the object *Tina*, and 'knowingly risk', associated with the object *disaster*. It is the fact that each object corresponds to a different sense of *court* that gives (38) its zeugmatic quality. We can, however, imagine two different contexts in which (38) might be uttered (Riemer 2005: 141). In the first, the speaker means that *in* courting Tina, Hank is courting a disaster. In this case, *Tina* and *disaster* ultimately both refer to the individual Tina. The second context is one in which *Tina* and *disaster* are in no way coreferential: where, for example, at the same time as 'courting' Tina, Hank is also, unrelatedly, contemplating a disastrous career-change. This suggests that it is the referent, not the sense, of the lexeme to which the linguistic test is sensitive. Questions of polysemy and monosemy, which concern sense, not reference, cannot therefore be illuminated by these phenomena.

5.3.3 Polysemy and monosemy as a cline

The fact that none of the proposed tests of polysemy seems to deliver reliable results has led many linguists to dismiss the polysemy/monosemy contrast as a false dichotomy. One of the earliest to do so was Geeraerts, who rejects the idea that we should think of meanings as 'things, prepackaged chunks of information that are contained in and carried about by word bags' (Geeraerts 1993: 259; see also Tuggy 1993, Allwood 2003). This idea is compatible with the 'conduit metaphor' discussed in 1.6.2, and once we abandon it, it is no longer important to know whether a word carries around one prepackaged information chunk (monosemy) or several (polysemy).

One possible alternative to the view of words having a determinate and finite number of senses would be to think of a word's meaning as a continuum of increasingly fine distinctions open to access at different levels of abstraction (cf. Taylor 2003: Chapter 8). Depending on the level of abstraction at which a word's meaning is considered, different elements of its meaning may appear as distinct or not, with the word consequently appearing variously polysemous or monosemous on the different polysemy tests. For example, consider the dialogue in (39), adapted from Tuggy (1993):

(39) A: *What have you two been doing all afternoon?*
    B: *I've been painting and so has Jane.*

If Jane has been painting a portrait and B has been painting stripes on the road, this answer will be misleading since it suggests that they have been engaged in the *same type* of painting; as a result, B's reply could only be uttered facetiously, punningly, or with the intention to mislead. On the linguistic criterion discussed above, *paint* would thus be polysemous between two senses which we could provisionally gloss as 'engage in artistic activity involving the application of paint' and 'engage in a non-artistic activity involving application of paint'. In other contexts, however, the linguistic test does not point to different senses of *paint*, suggesting that it is in fact monosemous (general) between the portrait and road stripe-painting senses. Thus, imagine in (40) that Franz is painting a portrait, and that the speaker is painting stripes on the road:

(40) *When I'm painting I try to get the colour on evenly and so does Franz.*

How can this clash between the test results be resolved? One answer would seem to be that (39) and (40) invoke differing levels of abstraction of the concept of *painting*. The verb *paint* can be used to refer to a broad continuum of different activities (as well as road and portrait painting, there is face-painting, painting of walls, rust-proofing, nail-painting, etc.). Strictly speaking, none of these individual instances of painting is absolutely identical to any other: two acts of wall-painting, for example, will differ in the details of their physical and temporal locations. The function of the verb *paint* is thus to categorize all of these different referents together (Taylor 2003; see 7.1 for further discussion). The relative importance of individual instances of painting is not, however, stable. When, as in (39), an accurate description of the *type of activity* being undertaken is called for, then painting a portrait and painting stripes on the road will be seen as fundamentally different activities: one is an artistic pursuit often associated with the leisure activities of amateurs, while the other takes place in the context of professional employment. Given the differing values of the two types of painting in our society, their common description by the same verb would be misleading. In (40), however, painting is considered not in terms of its wider socio-cultural import, but in terms of its actual mechanics. In this context, the differences between road-stripe painting and portrait painting disappear, since even application of colour is equally relevant to both; consequently, the verb *paint* may be used to refer to both types of situation without any punning, awkwardness or risk of misinformation. It is as though *paint* comprehends a variety of related notions, such as portrait painting, painting road-stripes, painting walls, painting the face, etc., which may be 'zoomed' in on and out from. When what is required is a fine-grained description of the type of activity in question, a 'close-up' view of the notions covered by *paint* makes each one stand out as a distinct unit, in the same way that a photographic close-up will reveal the detailed structure of an object. But when the focus is wider, the differences between the internal constituents become blurred and lose their distinctness. Accordingly, *paint* will appear monosemous or polysemous as a result of the level of abstraction or resolution at which its meanings are accessed. To think of a lexical item like *paint* as *either* monosemous *or* polysemous is therefore to ignore the fact that meanings can be accessed at a variety of levels. Rather than being absolute alternatives, monosemy and polysemy name the end points of a **cline** of semantic separateness.

This type of answer has found a number of recent adherents in discussions of polysemy (see for instance Taylor 2003: Chapter 8). In one sense, however, it does not resolve the problem, and for a similar reason to the one for which we rejected the linguistic test of polysemy: it ignores the distinction between the sense and the reference of *paint*. The cases discussed in (39) and (40) constitute different situations to which *paint* refers. But how do we know when a different situation corresponds to a different *sense* of the verb? Might not all the occurrences of *paint* we have discussed be examples of a single, schematic sense along the lines of 'apply paint to a surface' (which will cover both the portrait and the road-painting cases), even at the most fine-grained level of resolution? Difference of reference does not automatically entail difference of sense; if it did, the very distinction between sense and reference would lose its point. As a result, the mere fact that *paint* can be used to refer to a variety of different situations tells us nothing about the number of senses involved.

By now it will be obvious that this issue involves a number of complex questions. For some investigators, the phenomena discussed in this section problematize the very objectivity of meaning as a linguistic phenomenon (Geeraerts 1993; Riemer 2005).

Summary

As well as knowing a word's definitional meaning, a competent speaker knows how it relates to other words of the language. Five important types of **lexical relation** have been identified.

Antonymy

Antonymy (oppositeness) may be characterized as a relationship of incompatibility between two terms with respect to some given dimension of contrast. The principal distinction to be made in discussion of antonymy is between **gradable** (e.g. *hot–cold*) and **non-gradable** (e.g. *married–unmarried*) antonyms, i.e. antonyms which do and do not admit a midpoint.

Meronymy

Meronymy is the relation of part to whole: *hand* is a meronym of *arm*, *seed* is a *meronym* of *fruit*, *blade* is a meronym of *knife*. Not all languages seem to have an unambiguous means of lexicalizing the concept PART OF, but meronymy is often at the origin of various polysemy patterns in languages.

Hyponymy and taxonomy

Hyponymy and **taxonomy** (*kind of*-ness) define different types of class-inclusion hierarchies; hyponymy is an important structural principle in many languages with classifiers, while taxonomy has been argued to be basic to the classification and naming of biological species.

Synonymy

Synonymy is frequently claimed to exist between different expressions of the same language, but genuine lexical synonyms prove extremely hard to find: once their combinatorial environments have been fully explored, proposed lexical synonyms often prove not to be such.

Componential analysis

The importance of appreciating a lexeme's semantic relations in order to understand its meaning is one of the motivations for a componential approach to semantic analysis. Componential analysis analyses meaning in terms of binary features (i.e. features with only two possible values, + or -), and represents a translation into semantics of the principles of structuralist phonological analysis. As a type of definitional analysis, componential analysis inherits the failings of traditional definitions, and words for which it proves hard to couch definitions are also hard to analyse componentially.

Polysemy and monosemy

Theoretical and ordinary description of meaning would both be impossible without the recognition of separate senses within the same word. Words with several related senses are described as **polysemous**. Polysemy contrasts simultaneously with **monosemy**, the case where a word has a single meaning, and **homonymy**, the case where two unrelated words happen to share the same phonological form. In spite of the intuitive obviousness of these distinctions, there are many instances where it is not clear whether a word should be analysed as polysemous or monosemous, and no absolute criteria have ever been proposed which will successfully discriminate them.

....

Further reading

Cruse (1986) is a standard discussion of lexical relations in general; see Murphy (2003) for another, more theoretical treatment. Jones (2002) is a recent detailed study of antonymy. For two radically different approaches to taxonomy, contrast Berlin (1992) and Ellen (1993). Note however that both these works are primarily aimed at anthropologists, in spite of the importance of linguistic evidence to both. Chapters 2 and 3 of Quine (1961) contain discussion of synonymy from the point of view of a philosopher. Gross and Miller (1990) discuss English antonymy from a computational perspective. On the development of the componential analysis of kin terms, see the opening chapters of D'Andrade (1995). For readers of French, Rastier (1987) and Coseriu (2001 [1983]) contain useful discussions of the status of componential analysis in linguistics. On monosemy, see especially Ruhl (1989), a detailed theoretical and empirical treatment. Polysemy has recently spawned a vast literature, especially in cognitive linguistics. In addition to the sources quoted in the text, see Ravin and Leacock (2002), Nerlich et al. (2003), Cuyckens, Dirven and Taylor (2003) and Riemer (2005) for a selection of different views.

Exercises

Questions for discussion

1. Consider the following statements from Lehrer (2002: 504) on the use of morphology to create antonyms in English:

   Although *un-* is the most productive of these affixes and has been displacing *in-*. . . , there are interesting restrictions on its application. First, it does not attach to simple words that have negative connotations. Words like *uncruel*, *unsick*, and *unstupid* are rejected, whereas *unkind*, *unwell* and *unintelligent* are normal. Secondly, *un-* does not attach to many common positive and neutral adjectives, either, so that words like *ungood*, *unnice*, *unrich* and *untall* are also unacceptable.

   Are Lehrer's generalizations accurate? Can you develop any theory of which adjectives are compatible with *un-*?

2. In certain contexts, non-gradable antonyms also seem open to comparison. For example, we might say of John that he is *more male* than Hamish, or of Beethoven that he is *more dead* than Kurt Cobain. How could these exceptions be explained? Are *male/female* and *dead/alive* accurately described as non-gradable in spite of these examples?

3. Consider the following sentences (from Murphy 2003: 39):

(1) a. *I'd like a {large/ᵎbig/small/ᵎlittle} amount of cash.*
 b. *Here comes a {large/big/small/little} dog.*
 c. *The dog let out a {ᵎlarge/big/ᵎsmall/little} yelp.*
 d. *They made a {ᵎlarge/big/small/little} mistake.*
 e. *What a cute {ᵎlarge/big/ᵎsmall/little} doggie!*
 f. *The twins are {ᵎlarge/big/small/ᵎlittle} for their age.*

Large and *big* and *small* and *little* are characteristically taken as synonymous. The quoted sentences demonstrate, however, that their possibilities of substitution are not equivalent. What factors (semantic or pragmatic) might be proposed to account for the facts in (1)?

4. (*For native speakers of languages other than English*). Assemble a list of antonyms from your native language and investigate their committedness. Do they conform to the generalizations identified in 5.1.1?

5. Consider verbs of liquid motion such as *splash, trickle, spurt, drip, spray, run, spill, flow, leak, stream*, etc. Is it possible to arrange these into a hyponymic hierarchy like those that might be proposed for nouns? What are the problems of doing so?

6. Answer the same question for the verbs *look, stare, watch, see, observe, contemplate, spy on, glimpse*.

7. Murphy 2003: 126: 'In common examples of the hyponymy relation, we also find examples that are not transitive, as in (19), again contradicting the logical definition of hyponymy (Cruse 1994: 174).

(19) a. *A hang-glider is a glider.*
 b. *A glider is an airplane.*
 c. *?A hang-glider is an airplane.*'

Are there many examples like this? Can any general principles be discovered which govern the presence of transitivity in hyponymy chains like those of (19)?

8. Construct a componential analysis for the following verbs: *catch, grab, fumble, take, hold, pick up, put down, throw away, release, drop*. Can the meaning of each verb be adequately captured in such an analysis? What has to be left out? What are the advantages and disadvantages of this analysis in comparison to a definitional description of each verb?

9. Consider the following quotations from Lyons:

As far as the empirical investigation of the structure of language is concerned, the sense of a lexical item may be defined to be, not only dependent on, but identical with, the set of relations which hold between the item in question and the other items in the same lexical system.

(Lyons 1968: 443, quoted by Murphy 2003: 67)

I consider that the theory of meaning will be more solidly based if the meaning of a given linguistic unit is defined to be the set of (paradigmatic) relations that the unit in question contracts with other units of the language (in the context or contexts in which it occurs), without any attempt being made to set up 'contents' for these units. (1963: 59)

Discuss Lyons' identification between sense and meaning relations. Would it be empirically possible to describe the vocabulary of a language simply in terms of relations, without proposing contents for each lexeme? What problems (practical and principled) would such an account face? What are its advantages? Is it possible to conceive of two expressions which are '"merely" different in meaning but not bound by any of the meaning-relations that it is proposed to recognize in the definition of semantic structure'? (Lyons 1968: 60).

10. Section 5.3.2 discussed problems with the definitional criterion of polysemy. The examples given there concern extensional definitions (Chapter 2). Are the issues the same or different for cognitive definitions?

11. At a number of points in this chapter we have found ourselves faced with a clash between our intuitive conception of a theoretical linguistic category and the definition being proposed of it. For example, we noted in 5.1.3 that neither the formal class-inclusion definition of hyponymy nor the metalinguistic definition through *kind of* seems to adequately capture the conception of hyponymy we want to advance, which includes *car* as a hyponym of *vehicle* but excludes *policeman* as a hyponym of *someone's son*. Similarly, one of the main problems we encountered with the various polysemy tests discussed in 5.3.2 was the fact that they often diagnose the presence of polysemy in cases which do not correspond to our pretheoretical notion of what polysemy is. In cases like this, it is often assumed that it is OK to apply labels like 'hyponym' and 'polysemy' in a purely intuitive way, as long as we do so unambiguously. On this view, tests for homonymy and polysemy are unneeded, since we have an intuitive sense of the categories; as a result, the fact that the tests don't work doesn't matter. Is this view satisfactory? Should we be able to provide absolute definitions of theoretical terms, or hard and fast criteria showing where they are applicable?

6 Logic as a representation of meaning

CHAPTER PREVIEW

Logic is the study of the nature of valid inferences and reasoning. The logical tradition constitutes one of the major strands in the study of meaning, and some knowledge of its background is indispensable in linguistic semantics. In this chapter we will study some basic logical tools and concepts. Our aim is twofold:

◆ first, to understand the ways in which some types of meaning can be represented in logical symbolism

◆ second, to appreciate the advantages and disadvantages of this type of representation.

We begin by introducing the ideas of **validity**, **soundness** and **logical form** (6.1): these define the context and aims of a logical approach to language. In 6.2 we present an exposition of the basic principles of **propositional logic**, the logic of basic sentences, including a treatment of the principal logical **operators**: **and**, **not**, **or** and **if …then**. In 6.3 we discuss the extent to which these logical concepts overlap with the meanings of their ordinary language equivalents. Section 6.4 introduces **predicate logic**, the logic of expressions like **some** and **all**. In 6.5 we discuss the ways in which the concept of a **model** allows us to describe reference using logical techniques. Section 6.6 contains a discussion of the sentence relations of **entailment**, **presupposition** and **contradiction**. This leads to a discussion of **meaning postulates** in Section 6.7, which use the sentence relations introduced in 6.6 as part of a non-decompositional approach to meaning. In 6.8 Russell's **theory of descriptions** is discussed. This is a proposal for the analysis of noun phrases containing the definite article, and provides an instructive example of the advantages and problems of applying logical tools to the analysis of natural language.

We end the chapter in 6.9 with a short discussion of the controversies surrounding the use of logic as an aid in the analysis of natural language.

6.1 Validity, soundness and logical form

Logic may be defined as the study of valid reasoning and inference. On this definition, logic investigates the properties of valid chains of reasoning, and specifies the conditions which these chains must meet in order to be valid, in order to work as arguments. Consider the following exchange:

(1) A: Koko is a primate, so she likes daytime television.
     B: What? I don't get it.
     A: *All* primates like daytime television

Initially, B is unable to follow A's line of thought, and as a result A is forced to state the general principle on which her conclusion rests. This allows us to reconstruct A's original train of thought as the following argument or **syllogism**:

(2) 1. All primates like daytime television.
     2. Koko is a primate.
     therefore
     3. Koko likes daytime television.

Argument (2) thus reveals the explicit logical structure of A's comment in (1). As Kneale and Kneale explain (1962: 12), the 'first tentative steps towards logical thinking are taken when men try to generalize about valid arguments and to extract from some particular valid argument a form or principle which is common to a whole class of valid arguments'. Given the meanings of the words *all*, *like* and *is*, the conclusion *Koko likes daytime television* just *has to* be true as long as we accept the truth of the proposition *All primates like daytime television*. It seems likely that it was in domains like mathematics, especially geometry, that the need to make the principles of valid reasoning explicit first arose (Kneale and Kneale 1962: 2); in modern times, the study of logic has been particularly undertaken in the attempt to symbolize the types of reasoning that underlie mathematical arguments.

Logic is important to linguistics for at least three reasons. First, the study of logic is one of the oldest comprehensive treatments of questions of meaning. When people first began to think systematically about the meanings of language and the relations between these meanings, it was logical concepts to which they often appealed for explanations. As a result, the tradition of logical analysis, which we can trace as far back as Aristotle, provides a rich body of reflection on meaning, and most scholars who have studied meaning in the Western tradition have had at least some knowledge of logical principles. The relevance of logic to linguistics is far from simply historical, however. Logical concepts inform a wide range of modern **formal** theories of semantics, and are also crucial in research in computational theories of language and meaning. We will not be exploring formal theories in themselves here, but our exposition of some fundamental logical ideas will provide some background for those wanting to do so. Lastly, logical concepts provide an enlightening point of contrast with natural language. The basic logical concepts are accessible to practically anyone; indeed, many philosophers have seen in logical principles the universal 'laws of thought' which constitute the basic grounds of human rationality: for Immanuel Kant, for example, 'logic is the science that exhaustively presents and strictly proves nothing but the formal rules of all thinking' (1998 [1787]: 106). Yet, as we will see, logical meanings often differ strikingly from the types of meaning found in natural language. Studying logic therefore provides a window onto a body of apparently universal concepts with strikingly *different* behaviour from natural language, which provide a rigorous and enlightening way of disambiguating certain types of natural language expression.

Formal theories

A formal theory is one which offers an analysis of meaning in a technical, usually symbolic, metalanguage, according to principles which can be expressed in mathematical terms. A formal representation of meaning avoids the ambiguities contained in natural language by enforcing a strict correspondence between symbols and meanings: whereas natural languages always contain ambiguous or polysemous terms, in which a single form stands for several meanings (think of English *step*, *match* or *get*), a formal language has a strictly one-to-one relation with its meanings, so that each symbol of the formalism has one and only one interpretation.

As the above quotation from Kant suggests, the principles of valid argument have typically been taken, in the logical tradition, as the very principles governing rational human thought. Logic can be seen, from this perspective, as the science of the laws of rational thought. On this view, logic is the science which tries to specify all the conclusions that can validly be reached from a given set of propositions. It is logical principles which thus describe the process of valid reasoning.

The first two propositions in (2) are called the **premises**. An argument's premise may be defined as its starting-point, one of the propositions from which the **conclusion** follows. In (2), the last proposition is the conclusion. Note that the validity of arguments or of chains of reasoning has a special relationship to the words in which the premises and conclusion may be stated: substitute different words, and the argument may not be valid. None of the following arguments, for instance, is valid:

(3) a. Most primates like daytime television.
     Koko is a primate.
     therefore
     Koko likes daytime television.

b. All primates may like daytime television.
Koko is a primate.
therefore
Koko likes daytime television.

c. All primates used to like daytime television.
Koko is a primate.
therefore
Koko likes daytime television.

d. Some primates like daytime television.
Koko is a primate.
therefore
Koko likes daytime television.

e. All primates like daytime television.
Koko wants to be a primate.
therefore
Koko likes daytime television.

QUESTION   For each of these arguments, explain why it is not valid.

We may therefore say that the validity of this argument type is a function of the *meaning* of the terms in the syllogism, in particular the meanings of the determiner *all*, and of the verbs *like* and *is*. In (4), if we retain the 'logical' words *all* and *are*, but substitute words whose meaning is unknown, the resulting argument is still valid: if the premises are true, the conclusion *must* be true:

(4)   All sclaps are hillories
Steven is a sclap,
therefore
Steven is a hillory.

Any argument which conforms to the pattern of (4) will be valid. All the arguments below contain the same pattern of reasoning as (4):

(5)   a. All primates like daytime television.
Humans are primates.
therefore
Humans like daytime television.

b. All computers will break down.
Laptops are computers.
therefore
Laptops will break down.

c. All gladiators feared defeat.
The Thracian was a gladiator.
therefore
The Thracian feared defeat.

This allows us to see that the pattern of valid inference exemplified in (4) and (5) is systematic and does not depend on the details of the material inserted into the logical formula. The validity of these arguments is a function purely of the *meaning* of the predicates and of the term *all* and of the argument's **logical form**, its underlying logical structure.

The fact, however, that an argument conforms to the pattern of (4) may make it valid, but this does not make its conclusion *true*. Logical validity and truth are quite different properties: validity is a property of arguments, truth a property of sentences. The following argument is valid in logic, but its first premise is not true.

(6)   All people born on a Tuesday are unhappy.
      Bogomil was born on a Tuesday.
      therefore
      Bogomil is unhappy.

This means that (6) is valid in logic, but it is not true. Valid arguments whose premises are true are referred to as **sound**. Arguments like (6) which are valid, but which do not have true premises, are thus **unsound**. We can tell that (6) is valid, since *if* the first premise were true, then the conclusion would also *necessarily* be true. (Note that whether Bogomil is, as a matter of fact, unhappy, has nothing to do with the soundness of (6). Bogomil may well actually be unhappy, but this is not proven by the argument in (6).)

QUESTION   Assess the following arguments, stating whether they are valid and sound, valid but unsound, or invalid.

1. All people need oxygen.
   Harry is a person.
   therefore
   Harry needs oxygen.
   (Assume that Harry is a parrot.)

2. Brazil is a country.
   All countries belong to the UN.
   therefore
   Brazil belongs to the UN.

3. Henry has fallen in the pool.
   If someone has fallen in the pool, then they are wet.
   therefore
   Henry is wet.
   (Assume that the first premise is true.)

4. Gin and tonic is a popular drink.
   Popular drinks are cheap.
   therefore
   Water is cheap.

5. Mirrors reflect things.
   This glass reflects things.
   therefore
   This glass is a mirror.

6. Koko is hairy.
   All primates are hairy.
   therefore
   Koko is a primate.

As we have observed, the properties of sentences which make them true are linguistic properties. This suggests that logic and semantics are closely related. Some scholars, indeed, such as McCawley (1981: 2), have assumed that logic and semantics share an identical subject matter: the meanings of natural language sentences. As we will see, not everyone would agree with this: the degree of correspondence between logic and natural language has often been questioned, and with good reason. Nevertheless, as McCawley (1981: 2) notes, logic requires semantic analysis: the meanings of sentences must be identified before their logical properties can be discussed. If we do not know the meanings of *are* and *all* in (4) we are not in a position to determine the validity of the arguments involving them.

The link between logic and semantics is further revealed by the fact that it is meanings, not sentences, that function as the premises and conclusions of arguments. Thus, assuming (perhaps wrongly) that *unhappy* and *discontented* are synonyms, we can substitute any of the synonymous expressions in (7) for the premise of (6), and the synonymous expression in (8) for the conclusion of (6):

(7)   All humans born on a Tuesday are unhappy.
      All people born on a Tuesday are discontented.
      All people who were, are or will be born on a Tuesday are unhappy.

(8)   Bogomil is discontented.

These variations do not affect the underlying logical form of the argument.

6.2 Propositional logic

Having introduced the basic notions of validity, soundness and logical form, we will begin our exploration of logic by considering the topic of propositional logic, the branch of logic which deals with relations between **propositions**. A proposition is something which serves as the premise or conclusion of an argument. In (2) above, *Koko is a primate*, *All primates like daytime television*, and *Koko likes daytime television* are all propositions. Propositions are either true or false. In English, we may think of propositions as roughly like positive or negative factual sentences. The parallel between sentences and propositions is not absolute, however. A sentence like (9) expresses an infinite number of different propositions, depending on the values of the deictic expressions *I (my)*, *you (your)* and *this afternoon*:

(9)   *I want you to know that your behaviour this afternoon had nothing to do with my decision to drop out.*

For each assignment of referents to the deictic expressions, a different proposition results. Similarly, 'Koko likes daytime television' can only be considered a proposition as long as the referent of the noun 'Koko' has been fixed. Only if we know who 'Koko' refers to can we know whether a proposition in which she is mentioned is true or not.

Strictly, the notion of a proposition belongs to logic. We can, however, see it in mental terms. A series of experiments by psychologists has shown that people are very bad at remembering the actual words of utterances. About twenty seconds after hearing or reading an utterance, all people remember is its content or gist: the actual words used usually can't be remembered accurately. Given this, the propositions discussed here would be one possible representation of this remembered content or gist (see Barsalou *et al.* 1993 for discussion).

Natural language is not a collection of brute propositional statements without any mutual interrelations: a single statement like (10a) or (10b) can serve as the basis for a whole series of additional statements, depending on the additional linguistic elements added to it. Some examples of these additional statements are given in (10c–h):

(10) a. Daryl Tarte grew up to publish a raunchy family saga in 1988.
   b. Patsy Page is telling the truth.
   c. Someone *suspects* that Daryl Tarte grew up to publish a raunchy family saga in 1988.
   d. *It is probable* that Daryl Tarte grew up to publish a raunchy family saga in 1988.
   e. Daryl Tarte did *not* grow up to publish a raunchy family saga in 1988.
   f. Daryl Tarte grew up to publish a raunchy family saga in 1988, *and* Patsy Page is telling the truth.
   g. *Either* Daryl Tarte grew up to publish a raunchy family saga in 1988, *or* Patsy Page is telling the truth.
   h. *If* Daryl Tarte grew up to publish a raunchy family saga in 1988, *then* Patsy Page is telling the truth.

It is the italicized elements in (10c–h) which chiefly serve to insert the original propositions (10a–b) into a new, longer one. Among these elements, propositional logic attaches special importance to the four found in (10 e–h). In English, these four elements are expressed by the words *and*, *or*, *not* and *if…then*. We will refer to these as the **propositional connectives** or **logical operators** (already mentioned in 4.3.1). These four differ from others, such as those in (10c–d), in that they are **truth-functional**. This means that whether the larger propositions they are part of are true or not depends solely on the truth of the original basic propositions to which they have been added: the logical operators do not add anything true or false to the basic propositions themselves; all they do is generate additional propositions from the basic ones.

Let's demonstrate truth-functionality by considering the operator *not*. Let's grant that (10a) 'Daryl Tarte grew up to publish a raunchy family saga in 1988' is true. Then, (10e) 'Daryl Tarte did *not* grow up to publish a raunchy family saga in 1988' cannot be true: the two propositions are contradictory, and we cannot imagine a world in which they could be simultaneously possible. Conversely, if (10e) is true, then (10a) *must* be false. We can deduce the truth or falsity of one proposition from the other: if one is true, the other *can only be* false. Similarly, if (10a–b) are true, then (10f) must also be true. But if one or both of (10a–b) are false, then (10f) as a whole must likewise be false.

As we will see, the other two connectives are also truth-functional. Before showing this, however, we need to abstract away from the English words which express them. Observe that (10e) is not the only way in which negation is expressed in English. The following sentences all involve negations or denials, but unlike (10e), they do not use the grammatical means of *do/did* + *not* to express this:

(11) a. *Neither* the newspaper *nor* the radio gave more details.
      b. She has *not* been an opera enthusiast all her life.
      c. The Post Office had taken *no* notice of her death.
      d. He was *unable* to tell the difference between Schumann and Schubert.
      e. He *failed* the driving test for the third time.

Intuitively, however, it seems obvious that all these sentences contain a denial or a negation, but under different grammatical guises. Examples like these show that language makes differing means available to express what is, intuitively, a single logical operation, negation. Let's further assume that propositions like those in (11a–e) can be expressed in every language. Let's assume, in other words, that there is no reason that the propositions have to be stated in English: speakers of *any* language can negate propositions in a way that is semantically identical to the English negations in (11a–e).

QUESTION   What are some alternative ways in which the other operators could be expressed in English?

Considerations like these mean that we need to find some other way of symbolizing the operators which abstracts away from their translations into any single natural language. To do this, we will adopt a set of symbols for negation and the other operators. Negation, for example, will be symbolized with the symbol ¬. We will introduce the other symbols in the rest of this section. Note that the symbols apply uniquely to entire propositions. If the small letters p, q, r... stand for given propositions, $\neg p$, $\neg q$ and $\neg r$ stand for their negations. We cannot use ¬ to symbolize negations of non-propositional elements like *not tomorrow, not again*, etc.

The values or meanings of the operators can be specified in the form of diagrams called truth tables. Truth tables display the way in which logical operators affect the truth of the propositions to which they are added. (The use of truth tables is a fairly recent innovation in logic: they are implicitly present in Frege, but first overtly used by Wittgenstein.) The truth table for ¬ is very simple, and is given in Table 6.1:

Table 6.1. Truth table for ¬.	
p	**¬p**
T	F
F	T

All this says, reading left to right and top to bottom, is that if p is true, $\neg p$ ('not p') is false, and that if p is false, $\neg p$ is true. Let's say that p is the proposition 'Marie Bashir is governor of New South Wales'. If this is true, then $\neg p$, 'Marie Bashir is not governor of NSW' *must* be false; conversely, if it is false, then $\neg p$ must be true. The truth table can be read in either direction. It is equally true, then, that if $\neg p$ is false, then p is true, and if $\neg p$ is true, then p is false.

The next logical operator is conjunction. As its name implies, this denotes the conjunction or union of two propositions. The conjoined propositions are called **conjuncts**. The symbol for conjunction is the ampersand, &. The lexical realizations of conjunction are quite various. In particular, the logical operator translates English *and* and *but*, as well as other contrastive conjunctions like *in spite of* and *although*. If p stands for the proposition 'The Emperor has no money' and q for 'he has 400 000 soldiers', then p & q can stand for any one of the following complex propositions:

(12) The Emperor has no money, and he has 400 000 soldiers.
     The Emperor has no money, he has 400 000 soldiers.
     The Emperor has no money, but he has 400 000 soldiers.
     The Emperor has no money, although he has 400 000 soldiers.
     The Emperor has no money even though he has 400 000 soldiers.
     The Emperor has no money, in spite of which he has 400 000 soldiers.

The truth-table for & is given in Table 6.2:

Table 6.2. Truth table for &.		
	p q	**p & q**
a.	T T	T
b.	T F	F
c.	F T	F
d.	F F	F

If two propositions are both true, then their conjunction is also true (case (a) in Table 6.2). If the proposition *apricots are fruit* and the proposition *beans are vegetables* are both true (as, indeed, they are), then the compound proposition *apricots are fruit and beans are vegetables* must also be true. But if one of the conjoined propositions (conjuncts) is false, then the entire conjunction is also false (cases (b) and (c)). For example, let's take the two propositions *apricots are fruit* (which is true) and *beans are fruit* (which is false); their conjunction, *apricots are fruit and beans are fruit*, is false since the second conjunct is false. The fact that one of the conjuncts is true makes no difference: we could have a conjunction made up of ninety-nine true propositions and a single false proposition, but as a whole the conjunction would be false (*apricots are fruit, and peaches are fruit, and apples are fruit, and pomegranates are fruit, and tamarinds are fruit…and beans are fruit*). Finally, if both conjuncts are false then the conjunction is clearly also false. If *apricots are vegetables* and *beans are fruit* are individually false, their conjunction *apricots are vegetables and beans are fruit* can only be false.

Note that ordinary language *and* does not always correspond to logical &. As we have seen, & serves purely to join propositions. In natural language, however, *and* frequently links nominals:

(13) *Barb and Philippe had a baby.*

This is not equivalent to (14), in which *and does* correspond to &:

(14) *Barb had a baby and Philippe had a baby.*

Conjunction joins two propositions together. Propositions may also, however, be dissociated. This is accomplished by the operation of **disjunction**. The two propositions in a disjunction are called the **disjuncts**. There are two types of disjunction. **Exclusive disjunction** says that just one of the disjuncts applies, but not both. Exclusive disjunction is not usually given a special symbol; we shall refer to it simply as 'X-OR'. Its truth table is shown in Table 6.3.

Only in cases (b) and (c) is the disjunction true.

In many respects, exclusive disjunction is like English *either…or*, but with one important difference. In English, *either … or* can be used inclusively, that is, even if both disjuncts are affirmed:

(15) *He is either a coward, or he's a liar, or he's both.*

This type of disjunction is known as **inclusive disjunction**. We will symbolize it with the sign $\vee$. Note that inclusive disjunction is an even more likely interpretation of simple English *or* (without *either*), in contexts like the following:

(16) *People were wearing hats or they had put on sunscreen.*

Clearly, (16) leaves open the possibility that some people were wearing both hats and sunscreen: to enforce an exclusive reading, we would have to add the phrase *but not both*.

Table 6.3. Truth table for X-OR.

	p q	p X-or q
a.	T T	F
b.	T F	T
c.	F T	T
d.	F F	F

As Table 6.4 shows, $\lor$ is only false when both disjuncts are false:

Table 6.4. Truth table for $\lor$.		
	p q	*p $\lor$ q*
a.	T T	T
b.	T F	T
c.	F T	T
d.	F F	F

QUESTION Using the abbreviations supplied, symbolize the following propositions in logical notation. In (v), use brackets to enclose the last two propositions.

c Chile produces wine   s Scotland produces whisky
b Barbados grows cane   f France produces exquisite cognac
k Kirsch contains cherries   g German brandies are mediocre

 (i) Either Barbados grows cane or France produces exquisite cognac.
(ii) German brandies are mediocre, but France produces exquisite cognac.
(iii) German brandies are mediocre, or they're not.
(iv) Either Scotland does not produce whisky or Barbados grows cane.
 (v) Kirsch does not contain cherries and either Chile produces wine or
     Scotland produces whisky.

The last operator is also the most interesting. It is called the **material conditional**, and it corresponds (roughly – but *only* roughly) to the meaning of English *if p...then q*. It is symbolized by the operator $\supset$. The proposition to the left of $\supset$ is known as the **antecedent**; the one to the right is called the **consequent**. Thus, in (17), the underlined clauses are the antecedents, and the italicized ones the consequents::

(17) a. If <u>you refuse to stop talking</u>, then *I'll walk out*.
     b. If <u>there's no one at the counter</u> then *the museum is closed*.
     c. If <u>we can't agree</u> then *we have a problem*.
     d. If <u>you are young, rich and educated</u>, then *you are unhappy, neurotic and alone*.

Let's start our exploration of this operator by examining its truth table (Table 6.5):

Table 6.5. Truth table for $\supset$.		
	p q	*p $\supset$ q*
a.	T T	T
b.	T F	F
c.	F F	T
d.	F T	T

Case (a) of the truth table says that if two propositions are true, then the material conditional in which they are antecedent and consequent is also true. Thus, since each antecedent and consequent in (18a–d) is true, the material conditionals are also true:

(18) a. If snow is white, then pigs have curly tails.
      b. If this is a semantics book, then everyone has a birthday.
      c. If France has hosted the Winter Olympics, then there is no prime number between 24 and 29.
      d. If Christian Dior was born in 1905, then Sartre was born in 1905.

The propositions in (18) are, of course, somewhat odd, and we would not normally express them in ordinary language. This is because the *meanings* of antecedent and consequent are completely unrelated. The fact that snow is white does not usually allow us to draw any conclusions about whether pigs have tails, and whether or not this is a semantics book has nothing to do with everyone's having birthdays. Recall, however, that like the other operators, ⊃ is purely truth-functional: all that matters is whether the antecedent and consequent it relates are true, and whether they have anything to do with one another is completely irrelevant. Thus, the fact that the sentences in (18 a–d) would not normally be uttered in language is irrelevant to the calculation of truth-values for ⊃: the truth or falsity of the proposition is the only relevant consideration. And since the antecedents and consequents in (18 a–d) are all true, the material conditionals involving them are also true.

In real language, the material conditional is often found in an argument type traditionally known as **modus ponens** (Latin: 'affirming mode'). In this argument type, an antecedent is affirmed (i.e. said to be true) and the truth of the consequent is deduced from it, as in (19):

(19) 1. If Newton formulated the law of gravitation, then he was hit by an apple.
      2. Newton formulated the law of gravitation.
      therefore
      3. He was hit by an apple.

Note that the order in which the first two propositions are stated makes no difference to the logical form of the argument. Thus, (19) could just as easily be stated as (20):

(20) 1. Newton formulated the law of gravitation.
      2. If Newton formulated the law of gravitation, then he was hit by an apple.
      therefore
      3. He was hit by an apple.

In case (b) of the truth table, where the antecedent is true and the consequent is false, the conditional is also false. Here are some examples:

(21) a. If there is a recession, then interest rates have fallen.
   b. If the 2008 Olympics were in Beijing, then the 2012 ones are in Paris.
   c. If the moon orbits the earth, then *k* is a vowel.
   d. If breakfast is a meal, then our intestinal flora are the reincarnated souls of our dead ancestors.

In (21a), imagine that there is a recession, but that interest rates have not fallen. The proposition as a whole is clearly false. The same is true for (21b): France did not successfully bid for the 2012 Olympics, so (21b) as a whole is false. (21c) and (d) remind us that all the logical operator cares about are truth-values, and that antecedent and consequent do not have to have anything to do with each other.

   Let's now consider case (c) of the truth table, in which antecedent and consequent are false. In this case, we can see from the truth table that the conditional proposition which links them is still true. This is exemplified by the following conditionals.

(22) a. If Tolkien wrote *War and Peace*, then rain falls upwards.
   b. If pigs eat rocks, then Trivial Pursuit is an Olympic sport.
   c. If Christmas is in July, then Pavarotti was mute.

These conditionals are all true, even though antecedents and consequents are false. We will explain the reasoning behind this after introducing the last row of the truth table for the material conditional.

   Case (d) of the truth table for the material conditional says that if the antecedent is false and the consequent is true, the conditional is also true. This means that the following statements must be true:

(23) a. If Tolkien wrote *War and Peace*, then rain falls downwards.
   b. If pigs eat rocks, then Trivial Pursuit is a board game.
   c. If Christmas is in July, then Pavarotti was a tenor.

There is something slightly peculiar about saying that cases like (23) are true. The rationale for this, however, is that one is entitled to deduce *anything* from a false premise: in case (c) of the truth table we deduced a false consequent from a false premise; here, we deduce a true one. (The principle that anything follows from a false premise was first enunciated in the Middle Ages.) If we start out with something that is false, we have a basis for *any* conclusion, whether or not it is true. Given the premise 'Tolkien wrote *War and Peace*', which is false, we can draw true and false conclusions alike: since the initial premise is false, whether or not the consequent is true is simply irrelevant.

QUESTION   Consider the following sentences in light of the truth-table for ⊃. What are their truth-values? Which of these truth-values seem intuitively 'correct'?

a. If diamonds are valuable then water is a gas.
b. If horses are reptiles then the moon is a star.

c. If Australia is a continent then Tasmania is an island.

d. If horses are reptiles then the moon is not a star.

e. If plastic isn't a mineral then phones are only ever made of clay.

f. If bridge is a board game then poker is not a card game.

Question   Using the supplied abbreviations, translate the following propositions into logical symbolism:

d	Dante is the greatest poet	m	Marlowe died in a brawl
o	O'Hara was run over by a dune-buggy	b	The best poets die young
s	Shakespeare is the greatest poet	c	Coleridge died happy

(i) If the best poets die young then Coleridge died happy.

(ii) If Dante is the greatest poet then Shakespeare isn't.

(iii) If Marlowe didn't die in a brawl then O'Hara was run over by a dune-buggy.

(iv) If Coleridge didn't die happy then either Shakespeare or Dante is the greatest poet.

(v) If O'Hara wasn't run over by a dune-buggy then either Dante is not the greatest poet or if Marlowe died in a brawl then the best poets die young.

6.3 Logic as representation and perfection of meaning

Our exposition of the propositional connectives *and*, *or*, *not* and *if…then* has revealed that their truth-functional definitions are quite often counter-intuitive and unnatural, failing to correspond to the norms of ordinary English. None of the operators corresponds perfectly with any English equivalent (see Bach 2002 for further discussion). The discontinuity between natural language *and* and & has already been discussed in Chapter 4 (see 4.3.1); another example of the discontinuity between natural language and logical operators is provided by negation: given principles which we have not made fully explicit here but which are reasonably obvious, two negatives cancel each other out, giving a positive statement. Thus, the proposition $\neg\neg p$ is logically equivalent to p. This logical principle is well understood by educated speakers of English, who regularly avoid the use of double negatives like those in (24):

(24) *He didn't say nothing.*
     Are you going to spend your whole life not trusting nobody?
     Nobody here didn't point no gun at nobody (Huddleston and Pullum 2002: 846, adapted)
     It ain't no way no girl can't wear no platforms to no amusement park (Baugh 1983: 83, cited in Martínez 2003: 480)

Constructions like this were once common in English; their decline only started in the seventeenth century (Martínez 2003: 478). The prescriptive grammatical tradition of English has proscribed the use of such double negatives for hundreds of years; nevertheless, the double negative continues to thrive 'as a regular and widespread feature of non-standard dialects of English across the world' (Huddleston and Pullum 2002: 847). Furthermore, in many languages, such as Spanish (25a), Italian (25b), Portuguese (25c) and Ancient Greek (25d), double negatives regularly perform a reinforcing, rather than a cancelling function:

(25) a. *No   vino   nadie*
     not   came no one
     'No one came' (Martínez 2003: 477)

   b. *Giovanni   non   vide   nessuno*
     Giovanni   not   saw   no one
     'Giovanni didn't see anyone' (Martínez 2003: 477)

   c. *Nâo   viste   nada?*
     not   saw   nothing
     'Didn't you see anything? (Martínez 2003: 477)

   d. *ouk   ara... gignōsketai   tōn   eidōn   ouden*
     not   then   is known   of the   forms   nothing
     'Of the forms then nothing is known' (Plato, *Parmenides* 134b, cited by Horrocks 1997: 274)

Another particularly flagrant example of discontinuity between the operators and natural language is provided by the material conditional; indeed, the correspondence between ⊃ and ordinary language has been a matter of philosophical controversy since the time of Stoic logicians in antiquity. Case (d) of the truth table is the most problematic, since it means that a statement is automatically true where the antecedent is false and the consequent is true. But this seems to fly in the face of our intuitions about ordinary language. To borrow Girle's example (2002: 240), why should it be automatically true that *If Henry VIII was a bachelor then he was King of England*? As Girle comments (2002: 240), many people 'would want to say that it's very difficult to say whether it's true or false. To say it's automatically true is too much.' The truth-functional definition of ⊃ therefore seems not at all accurate as a representation of the meaning of English *if...then*. This is not a peculiarity of English: conditional expressions in other languages seem to be like English, and unlike ⊃, in this respect.

    We will see more examples of discrepancies between logic and ordinary language later in the chapter, and logicians have expended considerable effort to reconcile the two. The theory of conversational implicature developed by Grice, discussed in 4.3, is one such attempt. This theory leaves the truth-functional definitions of the operators intact, but there have been other attempts to amend the truth tables in order to bring the meanings of the operators into line with their natural language equivalents. For reasons that go beyond the scope of this chapter, however, no one satisfactory way of doing this has ever gained wide acceptance: it would seem that we are stuck with the operators in their current state.

The clash between the meanings of the logical operators and their ordinary language equivalents reveals a contrast between two different interpretations of the nature of logic: logic as a representation and logic as a perfection of meaning. The two construals carry very different implications for the relevance of logic to linguistic semantics. According to the first view of logic, the truth-functional definitions of logical operators like ¬, &, $\lor$ and ⊃ represent fundamental categories of human thought, and, as such, underlie the meanings of natural language at a certain degree of abstraction. Even though actual natural languages typically do not contain words whose meanings correspond to those of the logical operators, this does not mean that the logical operators are not representative of the meanings relevant to the analysis of natural language, nor that logic as a whole has nothing to do with the study of natural language. For McCawley (1981), for example, there is no clash between logic and linguistics: the two disciplines share a subject matter: meaning. Many linguists, indeed, would maintain that discontinuities between natural language and logic like those discussed in this section are to be explained by the fact that natural languages possess a pragmatic dimension which prevents the logical operators from finding exact equivalents in ordinary discourse. The fact that logical notions like ¬, &, $\lor$ and ⊃ are not transparently reflected in natural language is in itself no reason to doubt their importance as fundamental primitives of meaning, any more than the fact that people cannot draw freehand circles means that we do not have a concept CIRCLE. 'Formal' semantic theories in linguistics assume precisely that the principles of logic form part of a viable model of natural language meaning.

According to the second view of the relation of logic to natural language, logic does not distil principles already present in natural language, but transcends and perfects natural language. While logical principles may reveal the fundamental workings of thought, their utility lies precisely in that they allow us to escape the inadequacies of ordinary language. For Grice (1989), the fact that discrepancies exist between logical operators and their natural language equivalents 'is to be regarded as an imperfection of natural languages': the natural language expressions corresponding (imperfectly) to the logical operators 'cannot be regarded as finally acceptable, and may turn out to be, finally, not fully intelligible' (1989: 23). Natural language is not, therefore, to be appealed to in logical investigation, and the validity of logic has nothing to do with whether it turns out to be useful as a representation of natural language meaning.

This second view is appealing to logicians who see the principal purpose of logic as being to provide a solid basis for accurate reasoning of the sort required by science. Wittgenstein sums up this point of view when he says that 'the crystalline purity of logic was of course not a result of investigation; it was a requirement' (1953: §107): in other words, the value of logic is precisely that it takes us beyond the imperfections of natural language, allowing us to discern logical structures which the messiness of natural language obscures. As Barwise and Perry comment (1983: 28), the principal concern of the founders of modern logic – Frege, Russell and Whitehead, Gödel, and Tarski – was to provide a sure footing for the study of mathematics, and hence of science. This meant that logical investigation was in fact often oriented away from natural language, embodying assumptions designed to put mathematical notions on a sound footing, which have made it 'increasingly difficult to adapt the ideas of standard model theory to the semantics of natural languages'.

We will take up this question again at the end of the chapter.

6.4 Predicate logic

Consider the following argument:

(26) 1. All primates are hairy.
    2. Koko is a primate.
    therefore
    3. Koko is hairy.

This argument is clearly valid. But notice that using the propositional symbols we have introduced so far, we cannot demonstrate this validity. The two premises and the conclusion of (26) each express different propositions. We have no way, in our existing symbolism, of showing that these propositions involve the recurrent elements *Koko*, *primate* and *hairy*. As things stand, we can only assign a different letter variable to each of the propositions, giving us the following symbolism for the argument:

(27) 1. All primates are hairy.   *p*
    2. Koko is a primate.   *q*
    therefore
    3. Koko is hairy.   *r*

The logical form '*p, q,* therefore *r*' is thus the only way we have in propositional logic to symbolize the structure of the argument. But, in itself, this logical form is invalid. To see this, recall that *p, q,* and *r* can refer to *any* proposition; thus (28) is equally an instance of an argument with the form *p, q,* therefore *r*:

(28) 1. Henry Darger created a beautiful and violent fantasy world.   *p*
    2. India is smaller than Africa.   *q*
    therefore
    3. Thinking is the soul's conversation with itself.   *r*

Clearly, wherever the validity of (27) comes from, it does not derive from its conformity to the logical form *p, q* therefore *r*; as demonstrated by (28), not all arguments of this form are valid. Instead, the validity of (27) springs principally from the meaning of the term *all*. In order to symbolize (27) in a way that makes its validity clear, we will need to go beyond a purely propo-sitional notation so that the idea of 'all' can be captured in a logically rigorous way.

Now consider the argument in (29):

(29) Some things can only be seen when they move;
     therefore
     if nothing moves, there are things which can't be seen. (Ruyer 1998: 101)

Propositionally, this argument has the form p, therefore $(q \supset r)$: again, a clearly invalid argument form. Yet (29) is obviously valid, and its validity derives from the meaning of the term *some*. In order to symbolize the validity of arguments like (29), we therefore also need some way of captur-ing the idea of 'some'.

'Some' and 'all' are the basic notions in the other branch of logic with which we will be concerned in this chapter. This branch is **predicate logic**, also known as **quantificational** or **first-order logic**. What exactly are predicates? Let's examine (27) again. From a logical point of view, (27) contains three basic types of term: terms referring to individuals, such as *Koko*, terms referring to quantities, like *all*, and general terms like *primate* and *hairy*. Terms referring to individuals are called **singular terms** or **individual constants**. We will symbolize them with lower case letters. Koko, for instance, can be symbolized simply by k. Terms referring to quan-tities like 'all' or 'some' are called quantifiers: we will introduce the sym-bols for them presently.

'Primate' and 'hairy' in (27) are predicates. 'Predicate' has rather a dif-ferent meaning in logic from the meaning it typically has in syntax. In syntax, 'predicate' is often roughly synonymous with 'verb'. In logic, how-ever, predicates are terms which represent properties or relations: here, the properties of 'primateness' and 'hairiness'. A logical predicate could thus be a general noun like *primate*, an adjective like *hairy* or a verb like *adore* in *Koko adores the news*. Whereas singular terms refer to specific indi-viduals, predicates refer to general terms, terms which are potentially true of numerous individuals. Being a primate and being hairy are proper-ties which any number of individuals can hold. By contrast, the term *Koko* picks out just a single individual. The properties and relations expressed by predicates can be quite complex and lengthy. For instance, as well as 'is hairy' and 'is a primate', the expressions 'is a good student', 'is taller than the Eiffel tower', 'loves skiing' and 'bought a book on the giant sloth from Amazon' are all predicates. We will discuss these different types of predi-cate below.

Predicates are typically symbolized by single capital letters. The predi-cate 'is a primate', for example, could be symbolized P, and the predicate 'is hairy' by H. When expressions containing predicates and singular terms are translated into logical notation, the capitalized predicate sym-bol is written first, followed by the symbol for the singular term to which the predicate applies. Thus, we can translate the expressions 'Koko is a primate' and 'Koko is hairy' as follows:

(30) Koko is a primate   Pk
       Koko is hairy   Hk

The individual a predicate applies to is called its **argument**: P and H in (30) each have a single argument. But this notation will only get us a certain way. Eventually, we want to be able to translate propositions like 'All primates are hairy'. To do this, we need to examine **quantifiers**. Quantifiers are the logical expressions 'some' and 'all', symbolized by the operators ∃ and ∀ respectively.

Inferences which, like (27) and (29), involve the notions of 'some' and 'all' are very common. Examine the following formula:

(31) (∀x) Px

(31) reads as 'For every x, x is a primate'. What this says is that every individual in the domain in question is a primate. (31) is thus the translation of 'Everything is a primate' (an obviously false statement). Compare this to (32):

(32) (∃x) Px

This reads as 'there exists at least one x, such that x is a primate'. This says that *something* (or someone) is a primate – an obviously true statement.

∀ is known as the **universal quantifier**. Universal quantification is the logical operation which says that a predicate is true of every entity in the domain under discussion. Including ∀ in a formula thus applies the predicate to every entity (argument) in the domain in question. In English, universal quantification can be expressed by the words *all* and *every*, and the phrases *each and every* and *everything*.

∃ is known as the **existential quantifier**. Existential quantification is the logical operation which says that a predicate is true of at least one entity in the domain under discussion. Including ∃ in a formula applies a predicate to at least one entity (argument) in the domain in question. In English, existential quantification can be expressed by the words *some, at least one*, and *something*.

The quantifiers can be combined with the propositional operators. Some examples of this are given below. In (33), the abbreviation S stands for 'is simple', and F stands for 'is fun'.

(33) (∃x) Sx & Fx at least one thing is simple and fun
       (∃x) Sx x-OR Fx at least one thing is either simple or fun, but not
           both
       (∃x) ¬Fx something is not fun
       (∃x) ¬Sx & ¬Fx something is not simple and not fun
       ¬(∃x) Fx it's not the case that there is at least one thing that is fun
           (i.e., nothing is fun)

       (∀x) Sx & Fx everything is simple and fun
       (∀x) Sx x-OR Fx everything is either simple or fun, but not both
       (∀x) ¬Fx everything is not fun (i.e., nothing is fun)
       (∀x) ¬Sx & ¬Fx everything is not simple and not fun

The most interesting combinations, however, result from the use of $\supset$. Consider the following formula in conjunction with the explanations of the symbols:

(34) P 'is a primate'
    H 'is hairy'
    $(\forall x)\ Px \supset Hx$

This says that for all x's, if x is a primate then it is hairy. This allows us to give the following translation of the argument in (27), with the justification for the steps shown at the right (k = Koko)

(35) 1. $(\forall x)\ Px \supset Hx$ premise
    2. Pk   premise
    therefore
    3. Hk   by 1.

'To be hairy' and 'to be a primate' are **one place** predicates: this means that they can only be associated with a single individual constant at a time. (Recall that individual constants, or singular terms, are terms referring to a single individual. Individual constants are sometimes known as **variables**.) For example, the sentence 'Koko and Wilma are primates' can only be expressed logically as (36a), not as (36b).

(36) a. Pk & Pw.
    b. P k, w

The formula in (36b) is ill-formed. Since the property of being a primate only ever involves a single individual at a time, one of the constants in (36b) is left 'floating': it is not attached to any predicate, and nothing (even existence) is asserted of it.

Not all predicates are one-place predicates. The predicate 'admire', for example, is a **two-place** predicate: if admiring is going on, then two participants are necessarily involved, the admirer and the admiree. Using A for 'admire', we can express the sentence 'Dietmar admires Horst' as (37) and 'Horst admires Dietmar' as (38):

(37) Ad, h

(38) Ah, d

A two-place predicate can thus be interpreted as indicating a set of ordered pairs of individuals: here, the pair Dietmar and Horst. It is a set of *ordered* pairs precisely because the order in which the individuals occur is crucial: the first individual is the one who admires, the second the one who is admired.

There is no limit on the number of places a predicate may have. 'Give' is an example of a **three-place** predicate, as in G d, b, h 'Dietmar gave the book to Horst'.

We have been defining 'predicate' as a general term expressing a property or a relation. But we may also think of predicates in terms of the individuals to which they apply. Thus, a one-place predicate may be interpreted as a set of individuals: those individuals to which the predicate applies (these are sometimes referred to as the individuals that 'satisfy' the predicate). A two-place predicate applies to an ordered pair of individuals, a three-place predicate to an ordered triple of individuals, and so on. Accordingly, a predicate can have as many places as the members of the ordered n-tuple of individuals that satisfy it.

We are now in a position to be able to produce translations into logical notation of some reasonably complex propositions. These examples involve one- and two-place predicates, and show how the propositional operators are used with them. We first give the logical formula, then a translation into 'logiceeze', then a translation into idiomatic English.

(39) a. $(\forall x)\ Fx \supset Sx$ (S = is simple; F = is fun)
      For every x, if x is fun then x is simple
      Everything fun is simple.

    b. $\neg(\exists x)\ Sx\ \&\ Fx$ (S = is simple; F = is fun)
      It is not the case that there is at least one x such that x is simple
        and x is fun.
      Nothing is simple and fun.

    c. $(\forall x)\ Tx, 1 \supset Rx, x$ (T = trusts, R = respects; l = Lucy)
      For every x, if x trusts Lucy then x respects x.
      Everyone who trusts Lucy respects themselves.

    d. $(\forall x)\ Fx \supset Fl$ (F = is fun; l = linguistics)
      For every x, if x is fun then linguistics is fun.
      If anything is fun then linguistics is fun

    e. $(\forall x)\ (Sx\ \&\ \neg Bx) \supset Hx$ (S = is a student; B = is bald; H = is hilarious)
      For every x, if x is a student and x is not bald, then x is hilarious.
      All students who are not bald are hilarious.

    f. $(\exists x)\ Sx\ \&\ (Bx \lor Lx)$ (S = is a student; B = is studying ballet; L =is
                                    studying linguistics)
      There is at least one x such that x is a student and x is studying
        ballet or x is studying linguistics.
      There is a student who is studying ballet or studying linguistics,
        or both.

    g. $(\forall x)\ (Vx\ \&\ Ix) \supset Ux$ (V = is a virtue; I = is interesting; U = is useful)
      For every x, if x is a virtue and x is interesting, then x is useful
      All interesting virtues are useful.

    h. $(\forall x)\ (Lx\ \&\ Sx) \supset \neg Gx$ (L = is liquid; S = is a substance; G = is a gas)
      For every x, if x is a liquid and x is a substance then x is not a gas
      Liquid substances are not gases.

    i. $(\forall x)\ Vx \supset \neg(Ix \lor Ux)$ (V = is a virtue; I = is interesting; U = is useful)
      For every x, if x is a virtue, then it is not the case that x is inter-
        esting or x is useful.
      No virtue is interesting or useful.

Note that the last example could also be translated as follows

(40) ¬(∃x) (Vx & (Ix ∨ Ux))
   It is not the case that there is at least one x, such that x is a virtue
      and x is interesting or useful.
   No virtue is interesting or useful.

The examples given so far involve only a single quantifier. But natural language frequently expresses propositions involving multiple quantification, i.e. expressions which refer to two or more quantities. A two-place predicate, for example, may be quantified in various different ways, some of which we will now illustrate with the two-place predicate R 'remember'.

   The simplest case of multiple quantification is where both variables have the same quantifier:

(41) (∀x) (∀y) Rx, y   (R = remembers)
   For every x and for every y it is true that x remembers y.
   Everyone remembers everyone.
   (∃x) (∃y) Rx, y
   There is at least one x and at least one y such that x remembers y.
   Someone remembers someone.

Note that this formula would be valid in the case where someone remembers themselves.

   More complex are cases where one variable receives universal quantification and the other existential. Consider the following example:

(42) (∃x) (∀y) Rx, y
   There is at least one x such that for every y, x remembers y.
   Someone remembers everyone.

Here we will say that ∀y is in the **scope** of ∃x. Let's now consider what happens if we swap the order of the individual variables:

(43) (∃y) (∀x) Rx, y
   There is at least one y such that for every x, x remembers y.
   Someone is remembered by everyone.

Here, ∀x is in the scope of ∃y. The contrast between (42) and (43) is the difference between an active (42) and a passive (43) sentence. Importantly, the order of the variables in (43) is crucial: (43) is *not* logically equivalent to (44), which expresses a quite different proposition:

(44) (∀x) (∃y) Rx, y
   For every x, there is at least one y such that x remembers y.
   Everyone remembers someone.

The difference between (43) and (44) is subtle but real. (43) says that there is at least one single individual whom everyone remembers. It is the *same* individual who is remembered by everyone: in a universe consisting of Nina, Andrew, Tom, Harry and Briony, Tom might be remembered by Nina, Andrew, Harry and Briony. (44), by contrast, says that every person remembers at least one person. This single person remembered by everybody may well differ from person to person: Briony may remember Harry, Nina may remember Andrew, Andrew may remember Tom. In (44), the existential quantifier is said to be in the scope of the universal quantifier.

To take another example of scope differences, consider the two-place predicate F 'is the father of' in the following two propositions (see Allwood *et al.* 1977: 67 for discussion):

(45) (∀y) (∃x) Fx, y
> For every y, there is an x such that x is the father of y.
> Everyone has a father.

(46) (∃x) (∀y) Fx, y.
> There is at least one x, such that for every y, x is the father of y.
> Someone is the father of everyone.

The first proposition, (45), is true, the second, (46), is not. Yet the difference between them consists solely in the order of the existential and universal quantifier, and the consequent scope differences between the two.

Predicate logic notation can be used to precisely represent ambiguities in natural language. Sentence (47a), for example, has, among other readings, (47b) and (47c):

(47) a. Everyone here works for two companies.
    b. Everyone works for the same two companies.
    c. Everyone works for two companies, which may or may not be the same.

We can represent this difference concisely using the constant p for a person and c for a pair of companies, and the predicate W 'work for':

(48) a. (∃c) (∀p) Wp, c
> There is at least one pair of companies c, such that for every
>   person p, p works for c
> Everyone works for the same two companies.

    b. (∀p) (∃c) Wp, c
> For every person p, there is at least one pair of companies c such
>   that p works for c. Everyone works for two companies (which
>   may or may not be the same).

QUESTION Using the abbreviations supplied, (i) translate the following logical formulae into idiomatic English:

P is a poet   N is a novelist
T is talented   W is a prize winner
S is a simpleton

1. (∃x) Px & Tx
2. (∀x) Px ⊃ Sx
3. (∀x)(Px & Wx) ⊃ Tx
4. (∃x) Nx & Px

and (ii) translate the following propositions into logical symbolism:

a. No talented novelist is a simpleton.
b. At least one prize-winner is neither talented nor a simpleton.
c. Simpletons are not prize-winners.
d. No talented simpleton is a prize-winning poet.

6.5 Truth, models and extension

For logical approaches to semantics, reference and truth are the principal semantic facts: the most important thing about the meaning of a word is what it refers to, and the most important thing about a sentence is whether or not it is true – whether or not things are as the sentence says they are. Meaning for a logical approach to semantics is thus principally **truth-conditional** (see 3.2.1). As discussed in Chapter 3, for a truth-conditional theory of meaning, knowing the meaning of a factual sentence is the same as knowing what the world would have to be like for that sentence to be true. This does not mean that truth conditions are all there is to meaning. It just means that, as Chierchia and McConnell-Ginet (2000: 72) put it, 'if we ignore the conditions under which S [a sentence] is true, we cannot claim to know the meaning of S. Thus, knowing the truth conditions for S is at least necessary for knowing the meaning of S.'

Logical approaches to semantics deal with the question of truth and reference by providing a **model** for the sets of logical formulae used to represent meaning. The model of a set of logical formulae is a description of a possible world to which the formulae refer, a set of statements showing what each individual constant and predicate refers to in some possible world. The model relates the logical language to this world, by assigning referents to each logical expression. The aim of this is ultimately to produce, for a given set of referents, a statement of the truth values of the logical formulae in which they are included. In other words, the logical formalism will tell us, given a particular world, which sentences describing this world are false and which are true. Given the assumption of the centrality of truth to meaning, this is an important part of describing the meanings of a language. If the logical formulae are identified with sentences of natural language, we will have obtained a logical characterization of the truth conditions of a subset of natural language. We will see a simple example of such a truth-value assignment below.

The referent of a logical expression is called its **extension**. We will consider the extension of both individual constants (singular terms) and of predicates. The extension of an individual constant is simply the individual entity which the constant picks out or refers to in the world. In a universe consisting simply of Tom, Dick, Harry and Jemima, the individual constants t, d, h and j have the following extensions:

(49) t = Tom
    d = Dick
    h = Harry
    j = Jemima

What is the extension of a predicate? Predicates are interpreted as *sets* of entities: a one-place predicate like 'tall' will have as its extension the entire set of tall entities. Imagine that Tom, Dick and Jemima are all tall, but that Harry isn't. In this possible world the extension of 'tall' will be the set of entities {Tom, Dick, Jemima}. The extension of a two-place predicate like 'respect' will be the set of all *pairs* of individuals such that the first respects the second. Consider for example a universe where Jack respects Jill, Hank respects Mark, Holly respects René, and Adrian respects money. The extension of the predicate 'respect' will thus be the following:

(50) {(Jack, Jill), (Hank, Mark), (Holly, René), (Adrian, money)}

The extension of a three-place predicate will be an ordered *triple* of entities. The predicate 'give', for instance, might have the following extension:

(51) {(Don, wine, David), (Briony, present, Tom), (Judge Judy, fine, Selina)}

This extension describes a universe in which Don gives David wine, Briony gives Tom a present, and Judge Judy gives Selina a fine.

In general, we can say that the extension of an *n*-place predicate is a set of ordered *n*-tuples of entities. It's important to realize how extensions differ from senses. When describing the sense (meaning, definition) of a verb like *respect* or *give*, we would not usually bother specifying the participants involved in different giving or respecting events. Instead, we would try to specify what seems to be essential to the event itself (for *respect*, something like 'esteem', and for *give* something roughly like 'freely transfer to'). In logical approaches to semantics, this sort of definitional information is called the **intension** of a predicate. Its extension, on the other hand, is a purely external matter, the set of ordered *n*-tuples to which the predicate applies. Consequently, it is possible for two predicates to differ in intension but to have identical extensions. Say that in our universe in (50) the things which are respected are also disliked: Jack respects Jill but dislikes her, Hank respects Mark but dislikes him, and so on. In this case, the predicates 'respect' and 'dislike' will have the same extensions, while differing in intension or meaning. In a different universe, of course, there is no reason that the extensions of the two predicates should be identical.

We can now sketch the way in which the truth values of the sentences of the logical formula can be specified. Take a possible world with the following components:

(52) individual constants:
    t 'Tom'   *j* 'Jemima'
    d 'Dick'   *b* 'Briony'

h 'Harry'   *c* 'Cath'
e 'Everest'   *k* 'Kosciuszko'

one-place predicates:
S 'is a ski-instructor' *M* 'is a mountain-climber'

two-place predicates:
T 'is teaching' *C* 'is climbing'

We will now provide a model for these terms, in other words a statement showing their extensions. The individual constants have the following extensions:

(53) t = Tom   j = Jemima
     d = Dick   b = Briony
     h = Harry   c = Cath
     e = Everest   k = Kosciuszko

(Note how (53) differs from (52): (52) shows how the single-letter constant abbreviations are to be translated; (53) shows the actual individuals to which they refer.)

The one-place predicates have the following extensions:

(54) S: {Tom, Briony, Harry}
     M: {Dick, Jemima, Cath}

The extensions of the two-place predicates are as follows:

(55) T: {(Tom, Jemima), (Briony, Dick)}
     C: {(Dick, Everest), (Cath, Kosciuszko)}

Together, these assignments of referents constitute the model of the language in (52).

Our aim here will be to determine the truth or falsity of sentences involving the constants and predicates we have just introduced. In order to do this, we need a statement of what it is for a sentence to be true in a given model. To accomplish this, let's use the following definitions (adapted from Allwood *et al.* 1977: 74):

(56) Truth for one-place predicates
     A sentence *Pt* is true if and only if the object that is assigned to the individual term *t* is a member of the set of objects assigned to *P* in the model.

(57) Truth for two-place predicates
     A sentence Pt_1, t_2 is true if and only if the ordered pair of the objects assigned to the individual terms t_1, t_2 is a member of the set of ordered pairs assigned to *P* in the model.

Let's use (52) to construct some arbitrary sentences, which we will give both in their logical formulation, and in English translation:

(58) a. Tt, j   Tom is teaching Jemima.
     b. S h   Harry is a ski-instructor.
     c. Cd, e   Dick is climbing Everest.
     d. Tc, j   Cath is teaching Jemima.
     e. M b   Briony is a mountain-climber.
     f. Ct, k   Tom is climbing Kosciuszko.
     g. Td, b   Dick is teaching Briony.

The definitions in (54)–(55) give the following truth values:

(59) a. Tt, j   Tom is teaching Jemima.   T
     b. S h   Harry is a ski-instructor.   T
     c. Cd, e   Dick is climbing Everest.   T
     d. Tc, j   Cath is teaching Jemima.   F
     e. M b   Briony is a mountain-climber.   F
     f. Ct, k   Tom is climbing Kosciuszko.   F
     g. Td, b   Dick is teaching Briony.   F

Note especially (59 g). 'Dick' and 'Briony' do, it is true, individually figure among the constants described by the predicate T 'is teaching'. But the ordered pair of constants which constitutes the extension of this predicate in (55) is (b, d), not (d, b). Hence, the formula Td, b is false in this model. Taking these truth assignments, we can now use the truth tables given in 6.1 to read off the truth values of compound sentences. Let's start with (60):

(60) a. Tt, j & Cd, e Tom is teaching Jemima and Dick is climbing Everest.

We can symbolize this propositionally as *p* & *q*, where *p* stands for Tt, j 'Tom is teaching Jemima' and *q* for Cd, e 'Dick is climbing Everest'. The truth table for & (Table 6.2) shows us that this compound proposition is true in the current model: both its conjuncts are true.

     Now consider (61) in light of the truth table for $\lor$ (inclusive disjunction; Table 6.4)

(61) Tt, j $\lor$ Cd, e 'Tom is teaching Jemima or Dick is climbing Everest'

T t, j and C d, e are both true. The truth-table for $\lor$ tells us that complex propositions involving $\lor$ are true when both disjuncts are true. For this reason, (61) is true in the current model.

     In (62), the definitions in (54) tell us that the antecedent Mb is false and the consequent Sh is true:

(62) Mb $\supset$ Sh 'If Briony is a mountain-climber then Harry is a ski-instructor'.

This corresponds to the fourth line of the truth-table in Table 6.5, and is therefore true.

The truth tables allow us to work out the truth-values of some quite complex sentences. Consider the following:

(63) (Tt, j $\lor$ Ct, k) $\supset$ ¬Td, b 'If Tom is teaching Jemima or (Tom is) climbing Kosciuszko, then Dick is not teaching Briony.'

We can determine the truth-value of this proposition by starting from its individual components and working upwards. We start by assigning truth-values to the individual propositions in accordance with the model:

(64) Tt, j   T
     Ct, k   F
     Td, b   F

We then assign truth values to the complex propositions, i.e. the propositions obtained by combining the simple propositions into complex propositions with the propositional operators. Let's start with the proposition ¬Td, b. We always start with the basic proposition without any preceding operator: in this case, Td, b. Td, b is false. The truth-table tells us that the negation of a false proposition is true. ¬Td, b is therefore true. Now for Tt, j $\lor$ Ct, k. The first disjunct, Tt, j, is true, the second, Ct, k, is false. According to the truth table for $\lor$, a proposition with one true and one false disjunct is true. This means that the disjunction Tt, j $\lor$ Ct, k as a whole is true. For ease of memory, let's label the truth values we have determined so far:

(65) (Tt, j $\lor$ Ct, k) $\supset$ ¬Td, b

$$\frac{\underline{T} \quad\quad \underline{F}}{T} \quad\quad \frac{\underline{F}}{T}$$

We have therefore reduced the entire complex proposition to a material conditional in which the antecedent (Tt, j $\lor$ Ct, k) and consequent ¬T d, b are both true. The truth-table given in Table 6.5 tells us that a material conditional is true when its antecedent and consequent are both true; as a result, (63) as a whole is true.

In this way, it is possible to specify the truth-values for arbitrarily long sentences, as long as a model is given showing the extensions of the basic terms.

QUESTION   Determine the truth or falsity of the following propositions using the abbreviations and model given below.

Individual constants:

b	the beer	p	the party
a	Agatha	j	Jose
d	the dip	f	the fridge
r	Rita	m	Max

One-place predicates:
F　{p, d, r} 'is a failure'　　　C　{b, d} 'is cold'
E　{b} 'is enjoyable'　　　　　T　{a, j} 'is tipsy'

Two-place predicates:
D　{(m, a), (j, m)} 'declares love to'　　L　{(r, p)} 'leaves'
The first argument is the declarer of love,　The first argument is the
the second the one to whom love　　　leaver, the second the thing
is declared.　　　　　　　　　　left.

Three-place predicates:
W　{(a, b, m), (j, d, r)} 'throw'　　　G　{(j, f, a)} 'give'
The first argument is the thrower,　　The first argument is the giver,
the second the thing thrown,　　　　the second the thing given,
the third the target.　　　　　　　the third the recipient.

a. If Agatha declares love to Jose then the party is a failure.
b. The party is enjoyable and Jose is tipsy.
c. Either Max throws the beer at Agatha or he throws the dip at Jose.
d. Max declares love to Jose.
e. Either Jose throws the dip at Max or the party is not enjoyable.
f. If the beer isn't cold then the dip is a failure.
g. If the beer is enjoyable then either Max is tipsy or Agatha does not leave the party.
h. Either Jose throws the dip at Rita or he gives the fridge to Max.

6.6 Relations between propositions

In 5.1 we discussed meaning relations between words. We can now discuss relations between entire propositions. Recall that propositions differ from sentences in that whereas sentences may have many different reference-assignments, a single proposition only ever refers to a single defined state of affairs.

6.6.1 Entailment

We will start with the relation of **entailment**. Entailment may be defined in a number of equivalent ways. Here are three:

(66) p entails q
  • whenever p is true, q must be true
  • a situation describable by p must also be a situation describable by q
  • p and not q is contradictory (can't be true in any situation)

Take proposition (67). This entails all the propositions in (68):

(67) The constables drove the fast cars.

(68) The constables drove.
　　The constables drove something.

Some law enforcement officers drove the fast cars.
Someone drove fast cars.
Some fast cars were driven by someone.
The fast cars were driven by someone.
The constables existed.
The constables did something.
The constables drove automobiles.
Some police officers drove automobiles.
Some people did something to automobiles.

These sentences all meet the criteria in (66): they are true whenever 'The constables drove the fast cars' is true; if we can describe a situation with (67), we can also describe it with any of the sentences in (68) (although the informativeness of the different formulations is not equivalent); and the conjunction of (67) and the negation of any of the propositions in (68) is contradictory (e.g. *The constables drove fast cars and the constables did not drive*). Note that entailment has nothing to do with truth in a particular situation: whether or not (67) is true in a given situation, it has the entailments listed in (68).

Sentence (67) does *not* entail any of the sentences in (69):

(69) Not everyone drove fast cars.
Some people drove slow cars.
The constables drove fast.
Fast cars are dangerous.
The constables wanted to drive fast cars.
The constables drove Ferraris.
The probationary constables drove fast cars.
The constables drove fast police cars.
The constables were in uniform.

Any of these additional statements might be true, but none of them is entailed by (67): we could imagine a world where (67) was true but where the sentences in (69) were not.

As demonstrated by (67) and (68), the range of a proposition's entailments is related to the lexical relations of the proposition's elements. Thus, we can substitute a hyperonym of *constable* (police officer, law enforcement officer, person), but we cannot substitute a hyponym (*probationary constable* in (69)).

QUESTION   Propose as many entailments as possible of the following sentences.

a. Michelangelo painted the ceiling of the Sistine Chapel.
b. Switzerland makes no great wines.
c. Grandpa finds love in all the wrong places and Loretta doesn't deal with it well.
d. Someone will be punished.
e. In Antarctica no one deserves to be unhappy.
f. A team of scientists search beneath the waves for shipwrecks.

6.6.2 Presupposition

We have seen that a proposition p entails another proposition q if q must be true whenever p is true. In this light, consider the following two propositions:

(70) The fortieth pope was a German (p)

(71) There was a fortieth pope (q)

(70) and (71) are p and q. On our definition of entailment, p certainly entails q: if it's true that the fortieth pope was German, it must be true that there was a fortieth pope. But notice that q can still be true even if p is negated. Thus, if the fortieth pope was actually Spanish, (71) is still true. Rather than saying that (70) entails (71), we will say that it **presupposes** (71), and that (71) is a **presupposition** of (70). A proposition p presupposes another proposition q if both p and the negation of p entail q. (Another way of thinking about presupposition is that a proposition's presupposition is the precondition of its truth or falsity.)

For ease of reference, let's call the proposition whose presuppositions we're interested in the **trigger**. Thus, (70) is the trigger for (71). Presuppositions differ from entailments in that they are true under negation: a presupposition is true even when its trigger is false. Contrastingly, a trigger whose presupposition is false is neither true nor false. An example would be (72):

(72) The sixth Monday in September is a holiday.

This presupposes (incorrectly) that there is a sixth Monday in September; accordingly, (72) is neither true nor false: if asked whether (72) was true or false, the most natural answer would be that the question of truth simply does not arise, since it presupposes a state of affairs that does not exist. (Another possibility would be to answer that (72) is false, on the same grounds.) The existence of presuppositions therefore leads us to posit a third truth-value, neither true nor false, relevant in examples like (72). Presuppositions arise because speakers assume certain propositions as part of the background of what they are saying, rather than specifically asserting them. Specifying a proposition's presuppositions is thus like specifying the background knowledge a speaker is drawing on, and which the hearer will be expected to share.

As we will see, the existence of presuppositions was originally proposed (by Strawson 1950) in order to deal with cases like (70) above containing a **definite description**: a noun phrase introduced by *the* picking out a unique individual (in (70), *the fortieth pope*; see 6.8 below). More recently, however, the account of presupposition has been extended in order to cover triggers like the following:

(73) Alma regretted that Karin lived on an island.

(74) Alma realized that Karin lived on an island.

Regret and *realize* are said to presuppose the propositions expressed as their clausal object; here, the presupposition is (75).

(75) Karin lived on an island.

Consistent with the definition of presupposition we have given, (75) can still be true when *regret* and *realize* are negated:

(76) Alma did not regret that Karin lived on an island.

(77) Alma did not realize that Karin lived on an island.

However, this need not be the case, as demonstrated by (78) and (79):

(78) Alma did not regret that Karin lived on an island – Karin didn't live on an island.

(79) Alma did not realize that Karin lived on an island –
Karin didn't live on an island.

Examples (78) and (79) call the very existence of presupposition into question. If presuppositions are defined as propositions which are entailed (must be true) when their trigger is both asserted and negated, (78) and (79) suggest that no such propositions may actually exist: alleged presuppositions sometimes turn out to be true, sometimes false. In short, there may be no consistent category of presupposition which can be given a definition comparable to the definition of entailment proposed in (66). Instead, the question of what propositions are assumed as the background of a given trigger is purely a contextual matter determined by particular utterance situations. The discussion here has done no more than outline the beginnings of this problem: the existence of presuppositions has been a topic of lively and continuing debate in linguistics, and many researchers would by no means accept that (78) and (79) are conclusive evidence that no category of presupposition should be recognized in the study of relations between propositions. See Kempson (1977: Chapter 9) for further discussion.

QUESTION   Identify the presuppositions in the following sentences:

a. I recently stopped smoking.
b. Max finally managed to pick the lock.
c. Chirac was not reelected.
d. It was Columbus who discovered America.
e. The president has left the building.
f. She is glad she rejected the offer.
g. Maybe board games will be popular again.
h. Henry didn't criticize every left-handed DJ.

6.6.3 Contradictories, contraries and subcontraries

A **contradiction** is a pair of propositions with opposite truth values. We will distinguish three types of contradictions, **contradictories**, **contraries** and **subcontraries**.

The most basic type of contradiction is formed by a proposition and its negation.

(80) a. The winner of the 1984 Nobel Peace Prize was Desmond Tutu.
     b. The winner of the 1984 Nobel Peace Prize was not Desmond Tutu.

(80a) and (80b) are **contradictories**. It is impossible to conceive of a world in which (80a) and (80b) are both true. Nor can we conceive of a world in which they are both false: if one is true, the other *must* be false, and if one is false, the other *must* be true.

Contradictory pairs of propositions do not always contain negations:

(81) a. Water freezes at exactly zero degrees.
     b. Water freezes at temperatures either greater than zero degrees, or less than zero degrees.

These propositions cannot both be simultaneously true or both simultaneously false: they always must have opposite truth-values. They are therefore contradictory, but they do not contain any negation.

QUESTION Think of ten pairs of propositions which are contradictories.

The contradiction of a proposition is, of course, a denial of that proposition. It is not the only type of denial, however. Some contradictions cannot be simultaneously true, but can be simultaneously false. (82a) and (82b) are cases in point:

(82) a. José Bové is happy.
     b. José Bové is sad.

(82) (a) and (b) cannot be simultaneously true, but they can be simultaneously false. José Bové might be neither happy nor sad: he might, for example, be neutral, or asleep. Pairs of propositions like this, which cannot both be true but can both be false, are called **contraries**.

QUESTION Think of ten pairs of propositions which are contraries.

For completeness, let's finally look at **subcontraries**, pairs of propositions which cannot be simultaneously false, but can be simultaneously true:

(83) a. Some people are happy.
     b. Some people are not happy.

(84) a. The Eiffel tower is over 150 metres high.
     b. The Eiffel tower is less than 200 metres high.

These can be true at the same time: in (83), it is perfectly possible for some people to be happy while others are not, while in (84), (a) and (b) are both true if the Eiffel tower is 175 metres high. They cannot both, however, be false, since the two propositions in each pair exhaust the possibilities. If

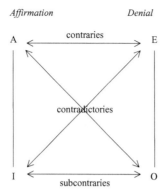

FIGURE 6.1
The square of opposition.

(83a) is false, i.e. if some people are not happy, then (83b) must be true: there is no other possibility. Hence, (83) (a) and (b) cannot be simultaneously false. As for (84), if (a) is false and the Eiffel tower is not over 150 metres high, then (b) must be true: the two propositions do not exclude each other, but they exhaust all the possibilities.

QUESTION   Think of five pairs of propositions which are subcontraries.

We can show the different relations of opposition between propositions using the traditional **square of opposition** (Figure 6.1), which goes back to Aristotle and the mediaeval logical tradition. This diagram allows a concise representation of the relationships between the different quantificational operators ('all' and 'some') and negation.

The letters A E I and O are used to mark the four corners of the square (they are taken from the vowels of the Latin verbs *affirmo* 'I affirm' and *nego* 'I deny'). They represent the fact that the left-hand propositions are positive, and the right-hand ones negative. The square can be used to represent both propositional and quantificational operators, but here we will only discuss the traditional quantificational version (see Girle 2002: 24 for the propositional square of opposition), as shown in Figure 6.2.

Reading B as 'book' and W as 'white', the square represents the following relationships:

- *Every book is white* and *No book is white* are contraries. Both cannot be true, but both may be false: this would be the case if some books are white and some are grey.
- *Every book is white* and *Some book is not white* are contradictories. They always have the opposite truth value.

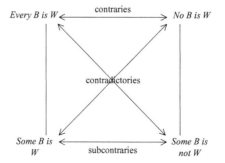

FIGURE 6.2
The square of opposition
and quantification.

- *Some book is white* and *No book is white* are also contradictories. They always have the opposite truth value.
- *Some book is white* and *Some book is not white* are subcontraries. They can both be true (as they are when some books are white and some are grey), but cannot both be false.

QUESTION Give the contradictories of the following propositions:

a. No monarchy is democratic.
b. All horses detest cobblestones.
c. No Italian twilight is not beautiful.
d. All Italian twilights are not beautiful.

QUESTION Label the following pairs of propositions as contrary, contradictory or subcontrary:

a. All magicians are ignorant.
   Some magicians are not ignorant.
b. Some beavers don't build dams.
   Some beavers build dams.
c. Some painters are not surrealists.
   Some painters are surrealists.
d. No mushrooms grow on mountains.
   No mushrooms do not grow on mountains.

The organization of quantified expressions into the square of opposition reveals some interesting facts about the way that natural languages express quantification. English is entirely representative in this respect, in that it has individually lexicalized words for the A, I and E squares, but not for the O square, as shown in Figure 6.3:

$$
\begin{array}{ccc}
\text{A: } \textit{all} & — & \text{E: } \textit{no} \\
| & & | \\
\text{I: } \textit{some} & — & \text{O: \_\_}
\end{array}
$$

FIGURE 6.3
English quantifiers and the square of opposition.

In order to express the O corner of the square, English, like many other languages, must resort to the expression *some... not* or *not all* (these two are logically equivalent, as can be seen by comparing the expressions *Some book is not white* and *Not all books are white*). This is true of many unrelated languages. Furthermore, the pattern extends to a whole range of related negative notions, as shown in Table 6.6 (adapted from Horn 1989: 254):

Table 6.6. Quantification and lexical gaps in English.

	Ordinary quantifiers	Quantificational adverbs	Binary quantifiers
A	*all* [noun], *everybody*	*always*	*both (of them)*
I	*some* [noun], *somebody*	*sometimes*	*one (of them)*
E	*no* [noun], *nobody* (= all ¬ / ¬ some)	*never* (= always ¬)	*neither (of them)* (= both ¬/¬ either)
O	**nall* [noun], **neverybody*	**nalways* (= ¬ always)	**noth (of them)* (¬ both)

Let's examine each column in turn. The first column we have already seen: English has pronouns and pronominal adjectives for each of the quantifiers in the square of opposition except O. There is no hypothetical pronoun *neverybody* with a use like that in (85):

(85) **Neverybody jumped overboard.*
     'Some people didn't jump overboard'/'Not everybody jumped overboard'

Nor is there a pronominal adjective with an equivalent function:

(86) **Nall children had to jump overboard.*
     'Some children didn't have to jump overboard'/ 'Not all children had to jump overboard'

The second column concerns adverbs of time, which can be seen as quantifying over the domain of time. The A corner is occupied by *always*, the I corner by *sometimes* and the E corner by *never*. These represent universal, existential and the negation of universal quantification respectively. But the O corner, again, has no monolexemic expression in English: *not always* has to be used instead.

(87) **The library nalways closes early.*
     'The library does not always close early.'

Lastly, let's turn our attention to the case of 'binary quantifiers', in other words quantifiers which apply to pairs of objects. Once again, it is only the O corner of the square of opposition which cannot be expressed by a single word in English:

(88) **Noth of them jumped overboard.*
     'It's not the case that both of them jumped overboard.'

(Note that (88) would be true where only one, or neither of them, jumped overboard.)

This generalization holds true in many languages. In Hungarian (Finno-Ugric, Hungary), for instance, there is no monolexemic O quantifier. The O corner of the square is expressed as in English by combining the words for *some* and *not*:

FIGURE 6.4
Quantification and lexical
gaps in Hungarian.

A: *mindan* — E: *nincs*

|

I: *némely* — O: ____

This is exemplified by the following sentences:

(89) *Minden   könyv   fehér.*
     every   book   white
     'All books are white'

(90) *Nincs   fehér   könyv.*
    there isn't   white   book
    'No books are white'

(*Nincs* actually means 'there isn't', but is used to translate 'no' in many contexts.)

(91) *Némely   könyv   fehér.*
    some   book   white
    'Some books are white'

(92) *Némely   könyv   nem   fehér.*
    some   book   not   white
    'Some books are not white'

Why should this be the case? Horn (1989) offers the following explanation. The subcontrary I tends to implicate the other subcontrary O: in other words, the use of the I-subcontrary *some* in a sentence like *some Xs are Y* invites the inference that the O subcontrary *some…not* also holds: *some Xs are not Y/not all Xs are Y*. If I say (93a), you will conclude that (93b) is also true.

(93) a. *Some snow is white.*
    b. *Some snow is not white.*

The subcontrary quantifiers I and O are thus informationally equivalent. As a result, Horn argues, languages do not need separate words for both the I and the O quantifiers: given the informational equivalence between them, just lexicalizing one is enough. (This does not explain why it is the I corner and not the O corner that is lexicalized: for some discussion see Horn 1989: 264.)

6.7 Meaning postulates

Since propositions correspond to sentences, the logical formalism we have been developing has practically nothing to tell us about the meanings of individual words. We can, it is true, say something about the meanings of the quantifiers and of the operators ¬, &, $\vee$ and $\supset$: the meanings of the latter are given by their truth tables (Tables 6.1, 6.2, 6.4 and 6.5), and the meanings of the universal and existential quantifiers can be explained as a picking out of all, and at least one of, the entities in the domain of discourse in question, as explained in 6.4 above. Granting that English *all*, *some*, *not*, *and*, *or* and *if…then* mean something similar to their logical counterparts, we at least have a logical analysis of these six expressions. This is all, however: taking the formula $(\forall x)\ Sx \supset Wx$, translated 'all snow is white', we have no way of saying anything about the meanings of either *snow* or *white*.

Obviously, a theory of meaning that can only define the quantifiers and propositional operators is woefully inadequate as a semantic theory of natural language.

The propositional and quantificational operators can, however, be used to explore word meaning. These operators can be used to propose **meaning postulates**, logical statements which specify the relations that obtain between the different lexemes of a language. Originally advanced by Carnap (1947), meaning postulates offer an alternative mode of meaning representation to the approaches we have largely discussed until now. Most of these approaches are **decompositional**: to specify the meaning of a word, in other words, we decompose or break it down into its component parts, envisaged as, for example, bundles of semantic features (see 5.2) or clauses in a paraphrase corresponding to conceptual universals (2.5; for more on decomposition, see 8.1.1). The meaning postulates approach, however, adopts exactly the opposite technique. It does not attempt to break down word meanings into sets of components, but to *describe the relations which a word has with other members of the same vocabulary.* We can get an idea of what this involves by examining some examples of meaning postulates adapted from Murphy (2003: 63). On this picture, the grammar of English can be seen as containing the meaning postulates (94)–(96):

(94) ($\forall$x) (*phone* x $\supset$ *telephone* x)
   For every x, if x is a phone then x is a telephone.
   Phone and *telephone* are synonyms.

(95) ($\forall$x) (*hot* x $\supset$ ¬*cold* x)
   For every x, if x is hot then x is not cold.
   Hot and *cold* are antonyms.

(96) ($\forall$x) (*apple* x $\supset$ *fruit* x)
   For every x, if x is an apple then x is fruit.
   Apple is a hyponym of *fruit*.

Postulates (94)–(96) are all to be taken as rules which speakers of English obey in their use of the words concerned. The import of each meaning postulate is paraphrased in terms of the familiar lexical relations on the last line of each example. The idea behind the meaning postulate approach is that we should be able to specify constraints on the use of any given item of the vocabulary which dictate what relations it may have with other items. Words which are synonyms, for example, may not be used in the following type of context:

(97) *It's a phone, but it's not a telephone.*

Antonyms, on the other hand, will be precluded from contexts like (98):

(98) *It's hot and it's also cold.*

Specification of the entire set of meaning postulates governing the use of a word is thus intended to define the possible range of the word's cooccurrence with other lexemes of the same language. Lyons (1963: 59) echoes the type of thinking behind the meaning postulates approach when he says that 'the meaning of a given linguistic unit is defined to be the set of (paradigmatic) relations that the unit in question contracts with other units of the language (in the context or contexts in which it occurs), without any attempt being made to set up "contents" for these units'.

Meaning postulates are not just limited to the formalization of the specific lexical relations discussed in Chapter 5. They can also be used to express more particular interrelations between particular words. For instance, (99) says that if someone knows something, then that thing must be true:

(99) $(\forall x)\,(\forall y)\,(know\,(x, y) \supset y)$

Postulate (99) allows us to predict, correctly, that sentence (100) will be semantically odd:

(100) ⌐*Jack knows that New York is the capital of the United States.*

Similarly, the verb *marry* entails (except in exceptional cases which pose a problem for any theory of meaning) that both its object and its subject be alive: one cannot, for example, marry Cleopatra; no more, of course, can Cleopatra marry anyone herself. We can represent this constraint on the meaning of *marry* as, once again, a material conditional involving the universal quantifier:

(101) $(\forall x)\,(\forall y)\,(marry\,(x, y) \supset (alive\,(x)\ \&\ alive\,(y)))$

This formulation will predict the bizarreness of sentences like the following:

(102) *Cleopatra married Mark Antony on January 1, 2006.*

The relation between *marry* and *alive* does not form one of the standard lexical relations to which *marry* would usually be considered to belong, but it is very much part of the verb's meaning, and we can represent this fact by proposing a meaning postulate.

The meaning postulates approach treats words as semantically unanalysable. Facts about meaning are not facts about the internal semantic composition of words, but about the relations which words have among themselves. We cannot, on this picture, exhaustively break a word down into its individual meaningful elements, but we can detail the various relations which it contracts with other words of the language. Meaning postulates thus have the advantage of avoiding the many problems confronted by attempts to decompose a word into its constituent parts (see 2.6). But by the same token, they can offer no explanation for the meaning relations into which a word enters. A definition of *marry* would make clear, among other things, that marrying is a particular type of *activity* found in human societies. From this it would follow that only living people can be married. For the meaning postulates approach, however, this is just an arbitrary fact.

A more serious problem for the meaning postulates approach is that relations between words are seldom able to be represented convincingly in logical formalism. Most of the facts about the meaning of a word are more variable and context-dependent, and less absolute, than the types discussed in (94)–(102). For example, we might propose the following meaning postulate to describe the verb *love*:

(103) $(\forall x)\,(\forall y)\,(\text{love } (x, y) \supset \neg\text{hate } (x, y))$
    For every x and for every y, if x loves y, then x does not hate y.

This reflects the idea that loving something is the opposite of hating it – surely a valid description of the meaning of the verb. But it is often the case that we might simultaneously love and hate something at the same time, and sentences like (104) are entirely possible:

(104) *I love and hate it.*

This suggests that the postulate in (103) cannot be maintained. But what other postulates could we advance? We could certainly advance postulates showing that *love*, like *hate,* is a hyponym of *experience an emotion*, but this is very far from giving us the detail we need in order to understand what *love* actually *means*. It would seem that the verb *love* in itself carries a meaning which does not necessarily impose any necessary set of cooccurrence relations on it: *love* can be put into an unlimited number of novel contexts, with new meaning combinations thereby being generated:

(105) a. *Computers really love me.*
     b. *For a split second, he loved skiing – and then he broke his leg.*

Sentence (105a) flies in the face of the usual expectation that the subject of *love* is an animate entity; (105b) counters the expectation that love is an ongoing state. It is, indeed, precisely because of this sort of flexibility that language has the productivity it has: we use a finite set of lexical items to create an infinite set of meanings, and one of the ways we do this is by varying the relations into which we put the items of our vocabulary.

As we have seen, it is possible to formulate a definition of *love* which allows for the fact that someone might simultaneously love and hate something, but it is hard to see how this same information could be couched as meaning postulates. The whole idea of the meaning postulate approach is that it is possible to specify certain propositions which follow *necessarily* from others. The proposition 'I do not hate you', for example, should flow necessarily from 'I love you'. Yet, in language, this is rarely the case. Words can often be used in contexts where they lose many of their expected meaningful properties. This circumstance creates problems for *any* attempt to discern regularity in the lexicon, whether through definitions, semantic features or meaning postulates. The meaning postulates approach, however, is especially vulnerable to it, since it is limited to a logical formalism which seems ill-suited to the representation of the messy, variable and context-dependent relations that words contract with each other. The meaning postulate approach has not, indeed, ever resulted in any comprehensive body of semantic description.

QUESTION   Suggest possible meaning postulates that describe the relationship between the following terms:

Tuesday and *weekday*
couch and *sofa*
dead and *alive*
guess and *not know*
relative and *cousin*
reptile and *mammal*

What are some of the problems encountered in this attempt?

6.8 Definite descriptions

In this section we consider an important application of logical principles to the analysis of natural language, the theory of **definite descriptions** proposed by Bertrand Russell (1905), one of the originators of the logical formalism introduced in this chapter. Definite descriptions are noun phrases like those in (106):

(106) *the President of Iraq*
      the greatest poet
      the Chancellor of Germany

Definite descriptions are singular terms: they refer to a single, specific individual. (In this they contrast to what Russell (1949: 214) called *ambiguous descriptions*, which contain the indefinite article and do not refer to a single specific individual: *a President of Iraq, a Chancellor of Germany*.) Since Frege, the need for a formal logical analysis of definite descriptions had been keenly felt. Frege himself treated definite descriptions as referring expressions, and distinguished between the referent of a definite description and its sense (see Chapter 3). Thus, the definite descriptions in (107) all have a sense, but they do not have any reference, since there is no individual which they pick out:

(107) *The first 12-year-old Prime Minister of Australia*
      The nation of Antarctica
      The largest prime number

Russell proposed a different treatment. According to him, definite descriptions like those in (106) and (107) are not actually understood as referring expressions at all: in fact, their logical structure is quantificational. Russell treated any sentence containing a definite description as equivalent to a quantificational sentence. For example, the sentence *The King of France is bald* is interpreted in the following way:

(108) The King of France is bald =
    There is exactly one King of France,
    and everything that is the King of France is bald.

This can be formalized as in (109):

(109) (∃x) (K(x) & (∀y) (K(y) ⊃ y = x) & B(x))

(109) reads as follows: 'there is an x, such that x is the King of France, and for all ys, if y is the King of France, then y is x, and x is bald'. In the formula, '(∃x) (K(x)...)' asserts the existence of an individual, the King of France. This is what we can call the **existence clause**. '(∀y) (K(y) ⊃ y = x)' says that every individual who is the King of France is x: in other words, there is only one King of France; this is the **uniqueness clause**. The last section, B(x), adds the information that the King of France is bald.

As another example, consider the representation of the proposition *the Chancellor of Germany is a woman*:

(110) (∃x) (C(x) & (∀y) (C(y) ⊃ y = x) & W(x))

Russell's analysis explains how definite descriptions can be understood even when we do not know the identity of their referent. As long as we understand the meaning of the predicates involved, we can understand the definite description, even if, as in (108), there *is not*, in fact, any individual to whom the examples refer.

QUESTION   Give equivalent analyses of the following expressions:

The emperor of China is a child.
The only house in Mosman is for sale.
The law is an ass.

Russell's analysis of definite descriptions has been highly influential and has stimulated wide debate. One of the most influential criticisms is due to P. F. Strawson (1950), who argued against both the existence and uniqueness clauses of Russell's analysis. According to Strawson, a speaker's use of a definite description does not *assert* that anything exists, as it does in Russell's analysis; rather, it *presupposes* (Strawson actually uses the term 'implies') this existence. Thus, if I utter a statement like 'The King of France is angry', I am not *explicitly* committing myself to the existence of an individual, the King of France; I am simply taking his existence for granted, and not putting it forward as a matter of discussion. Strawson also criticized the uniqueness clause: to say 'the table is covered with books', for example, is certainly not to claim that there is one and only one table. (Russell might reply, of course, that the table is in fact unique within the universe of discourse in question: if uttered, for example, in a room with only one table; if it were not, it would be necessary to specify which table was meant.)

6.9 Logic and language

The preceding account is only the most modest sketch of the bases of a logical approach to meaning. Before ending the chapter, we should register some of the advantages and controversies surrounding the use of logic as a tool for the analysis of natural language. As we have shown at a number of points, there seem to be areas of clear incompatibility between logical constructs and the natural language terms which partly translate them. One such area of incompatibility has just been noted in Strawson's critique of Russell's theory of definite descriptions. A more serious incompatibility between logic and natural language, however, is the one discussed in 6.3: it would seem that natural language connectives frequently do not behave in anything like the same way as their logical counterparts. This immediately problematizes any attempt to advance logical constructs as somehow underlying or as basic to natural language meanings. Another problem for the suggestion that logical constructs are relevant to the understanding of natural language relates to the role of truth in the two systems. As discussed in Chapter 3, there are many reasons to doubt the centrality of truth to everyday language. As Halliday and Matthiessen (2004: 117) put it, '[s]emantics has nothing to do with truth; it is concerned with consensus about validity, and consensus is negotiated in dialogue'. A factor which deserves special emphasis in the context of logic is that truth can only be a relevant consideration to factual sentences, i.e. to declarative statements. Questions, requests, commands and apologies, to name only a few, are neither true nor false, and as a result need a different logical formalism from the one introduced here.

Even in the case of declarative sentences, the question of truth is far from straightforward. As we have seen, logically oriented semanticists would claim that knowing the truth conditions for a sentence is at least necessary for knowing that sentence's meaning. For example, the claim would be that one cannot know the meaning of the sentence in (111) unless one knows the kind of situation in which the sentence would be true.

(111) *The door is closed.*

However, this claim seems questionable. One can perfectly well know what (111) means without knowing whether it's *true* in a certain case: the notions of truth and falsity are immensely obscure and complex. For example, is it *true* that the door is open if it is slightly ajar? What if the door has been taken off its hinges and leant against the wall, in exactly the same position it would be in if it had been opened normally? It would seem, in other words, that there are more options than simply true or false. We return to this point in Chapter 7. The incorporation of these considerations into logical accounts of language is a lively area of ongoing research, and a very necessary one for anyone committed to maintaining the relevance of logic to language.

On the positive side, the study of linguistic meaning from a logical point of view brings a number of important advantages. First, in its attention to declarative sentences it promises a formalization of a very important subset of natural language sentences. Declarative sentences are certainly not the only sentence-type in language: far from it. But they are, by any account, an important one (see Givón's remarks in 4.1). In particular, they are a crucial format for the presentation of many culturally important types of knowledge in our society, such as scientific statements, and fictional, journalistic and historical narrative. If a logical approach can help to illuminate the underlying structure of this particular sentence type, then it will have advanced our understanding of an important part of language. Second, the logical approach permits a degree of rigour and formalization which entirely outstrips that of the more descriptive approaches to meaning discussed in most of the rest of this book. As a result, it is eminently amenable to manipulation by computer, and logical principles form the basis of computational approaches to language. As a result, the development of programs that mimic human language behaviour have a vital reliance on logical ways of modelling language and meaning (see 8.2 for discussion). Lastly, the focus of logical analysis on propositions has been seen by some researchers as supported by psychological evidence. As noted in 6.2, experimental evidence suggests that what people remember are not the actual words of utterances, but their content or gist. Propositions can be taken as one way of representing this remembered content (Barsalou *et al.* 1993). In other words, logical symbolism may not always very accurately mirror the apparent *use* of words in natural language, but it may well serve as a valuable way of capturing the underlying structure of certain aspects of their *meaning*.

Summary

The nature and importance of logic

Logic investigates the properties of valid arguments and chains of reasoning, and specifies the conditions which arguments must meet in order to be valid. It is important to linguists for three principal reasons:

- it constitutes one of the oldest and most developed traditions of the study of meaning
- it is at the heart of formal and computational theories of semantics
- certain logical concepts, like ¬ or ⊃, provide an interesting point of contrast with their natural language equivalents.

Logical form, validity and soundness

Logic analyses the underlying logical structure of arguments, known as their **logical form**. This is independent of the way in which the argument happens to be phrased in any given language.

We distinguished between valid and sound arguments:

- Valid arguments are ones in which, if the premises are true, the conclusion must also be true.
- **Sound** arguments are valid arguments which have true premises.

Propositional logic

Propositional logic is the branch of logic that studies relations between **propositions**. A proposition is something which serves as the premise or conclusion of an argument. In propositional logic, special importance is given to the four **propositional connectives** or operators *not*, *and*, *or* and *if…then*. These connectives are **truth-functional**. This means that whether the propositions to which they are added are true or not depends solely on the truth of the original propositions. The values or meanings of the operators can be specified in the form of truth tables, which display the way in which logical connectives affect the truth of the propositions in which they appear.

Logic as representation and as perfection of meaning

The truth-functional definitions of the propositional connectives are quite often counter-intuitive and unnatural. None of the operators corresponds perfectly with any English equivalent. The clash between the meanings of the logical connectives and their ordinary language equivalents reveals a contrast between two different interpretations of the nature of logic: logic as a representation and as a perfection of meaning.

Predicate logic

'Some' and 'all' are the basic notions of **predicate logic**. Predicate logic studies the logical form of propositions involving three kinds of expression:

- **singular terms** or **individual constants**, which refer to individuals (whether things or people). Singular terms are symbolized by lower case letters.
- **predicates**, which represent properties or relations, such as 'primate', 'hairy' or 'adore'. Predicates are symbolized by upper case letters.
- **quantifiers**, like 'some' ($\exists$) and 'all' ($\forall$).

Predicates have a certain number of **arguments**. An argument is the individual or individuals to which the property or relation expressed by the predicate is attributed.

$\exists$ is called the **existential quantifier**. $(\exists x)$ is read as 'there is at least one x, such that'. $\forall$ is called the **universal quantifier**. $(\forall x)$ is read 'for every x, it is the case that'. Quantification may be **single** or **multiple**. A singly quantified proposition contains only a single quantifier. A multiply quantified proposition contains several. Propositions with both

the universal and the existential quantifiers allow for the disambiguation of sentences like *everyone loves someone*.

Reference, truth and models

For logical approaches to semantics, reference and truth are the principal semantic facts: the most important thing about the meaning of
a word is what it refers to, and the most important thing about a sentence is whether or not it is true. The **model** of a set of logical formulae is a set of statements showing what each expression of the formula
refers to in some possible world (6.5). The referent of a logical expression is called its **extension**:

- The extension of an individual constant (singular term) is simply
  the individual entity which the constant picks out.
- The extension of a one-place predicate is the entire set of individuals to which the predicate applies. The predicate 'tall', for instance,
  applies to all tall entities.
- The extension of a two-place predicate like 'respect' will be the set
  of all *pairs* of individuals such that the first respects the second.

In general, we can say that the extension of an n-place predicate is an
ordered n-tuple of entities.

Relations between propositions

Entailment is the relation between propositions where the truth of the
first guarantees the truth of the second. **Presupposition** is the relation
between two propositions p and q, such that both p and $\neg p$ entail q. A
contradictory is a pair of propositions which always have opposite truth
values. Pairs of propositions which cannot both be true but can both be
false are called **contraries**. Pairs of propositions which cannot be simultaneously false, but can be simultaneously true are called **subcontraries**.

Meaning postulates

The theory of **meaning postulates** uses logical notions to describe the
relations which a word has with other members of the same vocabulary, and constitutes a possible alternative to the decompositional
modes of meaning analysis.

Russell on definite descriptions

Russell's theory of **definite descriptions** offers an analysis in logical terms
of the meaning of propositions involving the English determiner *the*,
according to which such propositions contain disguised quantifications.

Is logic relevant to the semantics of natural language?

In the course of the chapter we saw a number of reasons to doubt that
logical tools provide an appropriate model of the meanings involved in
natural language. These include:

- the existence of incompatibilities between logical operators and their natural language equivalents
- the orientation of logic to reference and truth, which are only some of the considerations relevant to natural language.

However, many linguists in favour of logical approaches to semantics would claim that:

- in its attention to declarative sentences a logical approach promises a formalization of an important subset of natural language sentences, and that
- a logical approach permits a degree of rigour and formalization which entirely outstrips that of the more descriptive approaches to meaning.

Further reading

Girle (2002) is an eminently readable introduction to logic, complete with many exercises. For a treatment of logic specifically aimed at linguists, try Allwood, Andersson and Dahl (1977); for a more recent account, Chierchia and McGonnell-Ginet (2000) is a very thorough introduction to the main issues. Bach (1989) is short, untechnical and readable. The most comprehensive introductory work specifically for the linguist of which I am aware is McCawley (1981): note however that this adopts a syntactic approach to proof which has not been touched on here. Carpenter (1997) is an introduction to type-logical semantics, an important approach. Seuren (2009) is a mammoth reconsideration of the place of logic-inspired techniques in language research. For readers of French, Meyer (1982), directed specifically at linguists, contains a useful short history of the modern contribution logic has made to the understanding of language. For the original definition of the syllogism, see Aristotle, *Prior Analytics* I.1 25b. On presupposition, see Chapter 9 of Kempson (1977), Chapter 9 of McCawley (1981) and Strawson's *Introduction to Logical Theory* (1960). Horn (1989: 252–267) is a detailed (and advanced) exploration of the relation between negation and the square of opposition discussed in 6.6. Jackendoff (1990: 39) has some interesting criticism of a meaning-postulate approach to semantics. Kahrel and van den Berg (1994) is a typological study of differences in the expression of negation in the languages of the world. For Russell's theory of descriptions, see his 'On denoting' (1905); for the wider background, see Russell (1949) and Strawson's initial critique, in Strawson (1950).

Exercises

Analytical questions

1. Use bracketing and logical notation to represent the different possible meanings of the following sentences. Use the following abbreviations:

   l   Richard likes Gwynn
   t   Richard tolerates Gwynn
   e   Richard envies Gwynn
   d   Richard detests Gwynn

   Richard likes Gwynn or he tolerates and envies him.
   Richard likes and envies or tolerates Gwynn.
   Richard likes, envies, and tolerates Gwynn.
   Richard likes and envies or tolerates and detests Gwynn.

2. In the following pairs of sentences, which are contradictories, which are contraries and which are neither?

   a. All magicians are deceitful.
     No magicians are deceitful.
   b. No magicians are deceitful.
     Some magicians are deceitful.
   c. All magicians are deceitful.
     Some magicians are deceitful.
   d. All magicians are deceitful.
     There are no deceitful magicians.
   e. No magicians are deceitful.
     At least one magician is deceitful.

3. Is *because* a truth-functional connective? Justify your answer.
4. Translate the following sentences into logical notation, symbolizing each verb, noun phrase and prepositional phrase with a memorable abbreviation.
   Example: The mosquito stung the lion. Sm, l.
     Either the lion or the wasp stung Androcles. Sl, a X-OR Sw, a

   a. The lion was stung by the mosquito.
   b. The lion was in the jungle.
   c. The bite stung.
   d. The mosquito, the wasp and the bee stung the lion, the farmer and the apiarist respectively.
   e. The lion told the lamb the truth.
   f. The lion is Androcles' friend.
   g. Either the lion told Androcles the truth, or the mosquito stung Androcles.
   h. If the mosquito stung the lamb, the lion didn't tell Androcles the truth.

5. Translate the following sentences into logical notation:

   a. Every poet wrote at least one great poem.
   b. All poets are meritorious.
   c. There's at least one poem about spaceships.
   d. All poems about spaceships are unreadable.
   e. There is at least one poet who wrote one great poem.
   f. There's at least one spaceship which has a poem written about it.

Questions for discussion

6. What aspects of meaning are *not* captured by a translation into logical formalism? Do logical formalisms of the type discussed in this chapter seem to miss out on *more* aspects of meaning than other formalisms, e.g. those used in componential analysis?
7. Do you think it would be possible to specify all the presuppositions of a proposition? If so, why? If not, why not?
8. Not just statements have presuppositions. Questions do as well. Identify the presuppositions of the following questions, and any problems you encounter in doing so.

   a. Who killed Sylvia?
   b. Where did you put the cheese?

c. Why is there sadness in the world?
d. Are you coming to the party?
e. Is your new horse better than your old one?

9. What are the arguments for and against the proposition that declarative sentences are basic to natural languages?
10. Discuss Horn's rationale for the lexical gaps discussed in 6.6.3. How plausible is his argument? Are there any problems with it?
11. Pick a language you know other than English and discuss how the logical connectives are represented in it.
12. Both these sentences receive the same logical representation (c), which uses obvious abbreviations:

a. *Anyone enrolled in the course will receive a personalized timetable.*
b. *Everyone enrolled in the course will receive a personalized timetable.*
c. (∀x) (Ex ⊃ Tx)

What, if any, are the differences in meaning between (a) and (b)? Is it reasonable for them to be ignored in the logical representation?

13. What are the principal advantages and disadvantages of a logical analysis of meaning? How suitable, in your judgement, are logical concepts as a means of representing meaning?
14. Discuss the argument that logic is irrelevant to the study of linguistics, since it concerns nothing but semantic principles, whereas language necessarily involves at least semantic *and* grammatical ones.
15. Discuss the discrepancy between the truth-table of ⊃ and the meaning of English *if…then*. What, if anything, does this discrepancy tell us about the place of logic in the semantic analysis of natural language?

7 Meaning and cognition I: categorization and cognitive semantics

CHAPTER PREVIEW

This chapter considers meaning from the perspective of the cognitive operations which the mind can be hypothesized to perform in using language. We begin by introducing the idea that words in natural language can be seen as categories, and discuss two different models of the way categories work, the **classical** view of categorization and the **prototype** view (7.1), exploring the advantages and problems of each. We then discuss **cognitive** approaches to meaning, which developed out of the prototypical model of categorization. These approaches have introduced a rich model of the cognitive architecture underlying language (7.2).

7.1 The semantics of categorization

Categorization is an important topic in semantics because language can be seen as means of categorizing experience. A word like *flower*, for example, categorizes an indefinitely large number of different entities in the world as all examples of a single kind of thing, the category FLOWER. The actual types of flower vary widely – think of the difference between a tulip, a carnation and a sunflower – but these differences in no way affect the categorization of all types as flowers. The same is true of other lexical categories. The types of action I might describe by saying *I am writing*, for example, cover a wide range: filling in a form with a biro, typing on a keyboard, drawing letters in freshly poured concrete with a stick, and sitting in front of a blank sheet of paper with a pen, wondering how to begin a sentence. These outward differences are all glossed over by the verb *write*, which can be used for all of these activities indifferently. For both linguists and psychologists it is a question of considerable interest how such natural language categories arise. What principles govern what may and may not be categorized under a single word like *flower* or *write*? In this section, we explore an answer to this question from the perspective of a conceptualist theory of meaning, which sees the origin of linguistic categories in the nature of human psychology.

7.1.1 Classical categorization

Standard logical approaches to language, like the ones discussed in Chapter 6, are **two-valued** approaches. This means that they only recognize two truth values, true and false. On this approach, any proposition must either be true or false. There is no room for the proposition to be partly true and partly false, or true in some respects but false in others. The two-valued approach goes hand in hand with the classical view of definition (the one assumed throughout Chapter 2). The classical view was summarized as follows by Frege in his 1903 work *Foundations of Arithmetic*:

A definition of a concept… must be complete; it must unambiguously determine, as regards any object, whether or not it falls under the concept… Thus there must not be any object as regards which the definition leaves in doubt whether it falls under the concept; though for us men, with our defective knowledge, the question may not always be decidable. We may express this metaphorically as follows: the concept must have a sharp boundary.

(In Aarts *et al.* 2004: 33)

Another way of describing this view is the idea that definitions are lists of **necessary and sufficient conditions** for particular meanings. Consider as an example the definition of *bird* as a feathered, egg-laying, flying vertebrate. This definition involves the four properties feathered, egg-laying, flying and vertebrate, and on the classical view of definition those four properties constitute necessary and sufficient conditions of birdhood:

- The conditions are **necessary** because something must meet *all* of them if it is to count as a bird – if something only has some of the four properties, for instance, it does not count as a bird. (This might be the case with bats, which are flying and vertebrate, but which are not feathered or egg-laying.)

- The conditions are **sufficient** because *anything* that has *all four* properties counts as a bird: no further conditions need to be met.

The classical view of definition is also a view of the nature of the categories to which the definition applies. To say that the definition of bird consists of the four properties above is, quite clearly, the same thing as saying that the category BIRD is also so constituted. Accordingly, this view is often referred to as the **classical view of categorization**, or, because of the figure credited with its proposal, the **Aristotelian view of categorization**. Classical or Aristotelian categories have the following two important characteristics:

- The conditions on their membership can be made explicit by specifying lists of necessary and sufficient conditions.
- As a result, their membership is determinate: whether or not something is a member of the category can easily be checked by seeing whether it fulfils the conditions.

QUESTION   Try to develop a list of necessary and sufficient conditions for the following categories: *sport, building, planet, book, animal, weapon* and *bodypart.* What problems do you encounter?

7.1.2 Problems with classical categories

The classical view of categorization is open to a number of criticisms. First, there are remarkably few examples of adequate definitions in the classical mould. In fact, as discussed in Chapter 2, some researchers doubt that there are *any*. We noted in 2.6 that many definitions do not seem successful in specifying necessary and sufficient conditions for membership of a given category. This is certainly true of dictionary definitions, but the same problem applies to more technical and detailed definitions like those given in semantics. To pick an example almost at random, the *Concise Oxford*'s definition of *food*, 'substance(s) (to be) taken into the body to maintain life and growth' applies just as much to medicine as it does to food like bread or apples, a circumstance which invalidates that particular definition. Similarly, the same dictionary's definition of *game* as 'contest played according to rules and decided by skill, strength or luck' does not apply to card games like patience (solitaire), which involve a single participant and are thus not contests, nor to a game in which a child throws a ball against a wall. Further, it also applies to wars and exams, which are decidedly *not* examples of games. As discussed in Chapter 2, the history of semantics is full of examples of a proposal for the correct definition of a term being shown to be inaccurate. A famous example is the previously standard definition of *kill* as 'cause to die'. Imagine that someone has tampered with the sheriff's gun in such a way as to cause it not to fire in a shoot-out with an outlaw. As a result, the outlaw is able to shoot the sheriff to death. In a case like this, we would say that the tamperer has caused the sheriff to die, but has not actually killed the sheriff (for further problems with this case, see Fodor 1970). Furthermore, even longer and more detailed definitions like those advanced by Wierzbicka and her colleagues apparently do not resolve these problems. Cases like this occur time and time again in the history of definitional semantics. The problems of definition are discussed at length in Chapter 2 (see especially 2.6).

Rosch and Mervis outline a more influential criticism of the classical view of categorization (1975: 573–574):

> As speakers of our language and members of our culture, we know that a chair is a more reasonable exemplar of the category furniture than a radio, and that some chairs fit our idea or image of a chair better than others. However, when describing categories analytically, most traditions of thought have treated category membership as a digital, all-or-none phenomenon. That is, much work in philosophy, psychology, linguistics, and anthropology assumes that categories are logical bounded entities, membership in which is defined by an item's possession of a simple set of criterial features, in which all instances possessing the criterial attributes have a full and equal degree of membership.

In other words, the classical interpretation of categories (and hence meanings) as sets of necessary and sufficient conditions fails to do justice to the fact that there seem to be **different statuses of category membership**: some members of a category seem to be **better examples** of that category than others.

We can illustrate this with an example which has played an important role in critiques of classical categorization. Consider a colour category like RED. We can think of many shades of red, including the red of a fire-engine, the deep reds found on fruit like plums, which might also be described as purple, and very pale reds which might also be described as pink. It seems impossible to identify any single point along the scale of redness that constitutes the boundary between red and other colours, and as a result it seems clear that the category RED is *not* defined by any necessary and sufficient conditions, or anything else that might provide a clear category boundary for it. Yet there is a clear sense in which the red of a fire engine seems a better example of red than the colour of a ripe plum. In order to give an idea of the type of colour referred to by *red*, we would obviously do much better pointing to a fire-engine or a standard red rose, than to a ripe plum or the orangey-pink of a sunset, even though both of these might also be described as 'red'. RED, then, seems to be a category of which some members are better examples than others.

QUESTION   What are some other categories in which some members are better examples of the category than others?

Colours are by no means the only example of categories with different statuses of category membership. Consider Figure 7.1 below, a series of representations of various cup- and mug-like objects, taken from an influential study by Labov (1973).

FIGURE 7.1
Series of cup- and mug-
like objects (Labov 1973:
354).

It seems obvious that some of these objects, like (1), are very good examples of cups, and that others, like (11), are very good examples of mugs. There also seem to be several intermediate cases, like (7), in which it is not clear whether *cup* or *mug* is the better description, as well as others, like (17) and perhaps (4), where we might hesitate to apply *either* label. (If some of the objects were represented with accompanying saucers this might reduce the ambiguity, of course.) This is, in fact, exactly what Labov found when he asked subjects to decide which was the appropriate label in each case.

We could make similar observations about many other categories in natural language. The category CHAIR is a case in point (Figure 7.2). The chair in the centre of the diagram seems a particularly good example of the category, unlike the high chair on the middle left or the deck chair in the bottom row. The arm chair and the rocking chair also seem clear examples of the category, but somehow less obvious than the original ordinary four-legged chair. That, indeed, is the only one of the pictured chairs which is precisely that: an *ordinary* chair of the sort we might refer to through expressions like *a normal chair, an ordinary chair, a standard chair*, and so on.

There are two important points to draw from these examples:

- There are categories in which some members are better exemplars of the category than others.
- There are categories in which the boundaries of membership are not clear-cut: it is not always possible to say whether or not something is a member of the category.

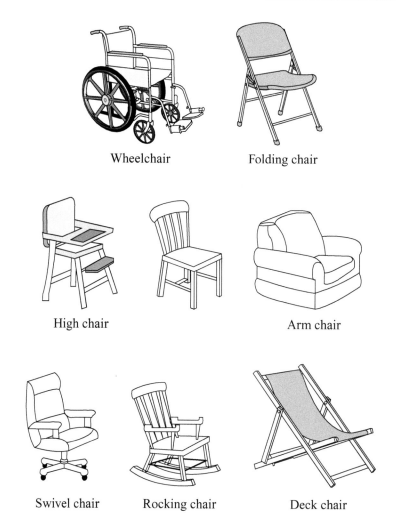

FIGURE 7.2
Chairs and non-chairs.

Wheelchair   Folding chair

High chair   Arm chair

Swivel chair   Rocking chair   Deck chair

If categories are constituted by nothing other than sets of necessary and sufficient conditions, neither of these points is expected. The second one in particular is very unexpected: if there is a finite set of necessary and sufficient conditions for a category, we should be able to state unambiguously what a given category's members are.

What conclusions can we draw about the nature of the categories? One possible answer is that these categories are not structured in terms of necessary and sufficient conditions, but that membership in them is **graded**: a matter of degree.

7.1.3 Prototype categorization

The idea that category membership is graded is at the heart of the **prototype** theory of categorization, most strongly associated with the psychologist Eleanor Rosch and her colleagues (Rosch 1975, 1978; Rosch and Mervis 1975). Rosch was impressed by one of the many observations about meaning made by the philosopher Ludwig Wittgenstein in his *Philosophical Investigations* (1953: §66):

Consider for example the proceedings that we call 'games'. I mean board-games, card-games, ball-games, … and so on. What is common to them all? – Don't say: There *must* be something common, or they would not be called "games" – but *look and see* whether there is anything common to all. – For if you look at them you will not see something that is common to *all*, but similarities, relationships, and a whole series of them at that. To repeat: don't think, but look! – Look for example at board games, with their multifarious relationships. Now pass to card games; here you find many correspondences with the first group, but many common features drop out, and others appear.

The result of comparison between different types of game, Wittgenstein says, is that 'we see a complicated network of similarities overlapping and criss-crossing' (1953: §66), and he compares the relationships between different games to the family resemblances that exist in the outward appearances of members of the same family. Members of a single family might be identifiable by certain characteristic features – prominent cheek bones, a certain hair colour, a certain type of walk or laugh, and so on – without any single member of the family necessarily having all of these attributes. (In fact, it might even be the case that a particular member had none of the characteristic attributes.) In the same way, Wittgenstein suggests, members of the category 'game' might not be defined by any core of shared attributes that we could capture by listing necessary and sufficient conditions, but by a network of 'family resemblances': there is a certain set of possible attributes which tie together the members of the category GAME, but not every member of the set need possess every attribute. This is displayed in Table 7.1.

Table 7.1. Family resemblances among attributes of the category 'game'.

	Patience	Hopscotch	Cat's cradle	Tennis	bouncing a ball	Trivial Pursuit	flipping a coin	'I Spy'
mostly outdoor		×		×	×			
played with others		×	×	×		×		×
has rules	×	×	×	×		×		×
clear winner				×		×		
uses ball				×	×			
uses string			×					
uses cards	×							
uses board						×		
luck mostly determines result							×	

Rosch generalized the family resemblance structure which Wittgenstein saw in GAME to other categories. She and her colleagues conducted experiments in which subjects were asked to consider examples of different natural language categories like FRUIT, BIRD, VEHICLE, and CLOTHING, and rate them on a scale of representativity for each category. These experiments demonstrated convincingly the truth of the initial belief that some members are better examples of their category than others. For the category BIRD, for instance, subjects consistently rated robin and sparrow as better examples than penguin or emu. Rosch described this situation as one in which robin and sparrow are more **prototypical** examples of the category BIRD than emu or penguin. Prototypicality judgements for this type of category proved to be remarkably consistent across different speakers: subjects consistently converged on the same members when asked to say what the best examples of different categories were.

QUESTION   Consider the categories PROFESSION, LADDER and PLANE. What are the best examples of each? Why? What are some marginal examples?

The prototype of a category, for Rosch, is not any one of its members, no matter how good an example of the category this might be. Rather than one of the members, the prototype of a category can be thought of as the **central tendency** of that category's members (see Barsalou *et al.* 1993). Any particular member of the category will be closer to or further from the prototype. What are these degrees of prototypicality based on? According to Rosch, prototypical category members are those which share the most attributes with other members of their category, and the fewest with members of other categories. BIRD, for instance, might be defined through attributes such as 'egg-laying', 'flying', 'small', 'vertebrate', 'pecks food', 'winged', 'high-pitched call', 'builds nests' and so on. Not every member of the category, however, has to possess *all these attributes*: emus, for instance, are neither small nor flying, but they are still birds. But the more attributes an example possesses the better an example of the category it appears.

Categories are not structured, then, by a set of necessary and sufficient conditions; instead, they consist of entities with various shared attributes. We can illustrate this with the category COAT, whose members might include trenchcoats, overcoats, raincoats, duffel coats, parkas, fur coats, labcoats, topcoats and frockcoats. The attributes of this category presumably include the following features:

 (i) covers the body from the shoulders to the thigh/knee
 (ii) worn on top of other clothing
 (iii) has sleeves
 (iv) for both sexes
  (v) can be fastened closed
 (vi) worn for protection from cold or rain

Certain examples of the category, like trenchcoats or overcoats, possess all or most of these attributes: these are the most prototypical. Less prototypical examples have fewer: a labcoat, for example, is not worn for protection from the weather, and a parka does not extend to the thigh. The more attributes a member shares with *other*, different categories, the less typical it is of its *own* category. Think of the difference between the categories COAT and JACKET. These categories share a certain number of attributes, such as being sleeved, being able to be fastened closed, and being worn on top of other clothing. They are distinguished principally in terms of length and purpose; coats extend below the waist and are principally worn for protection from cold or wet weather, whereas jackets typically end around waist level and are not principally worn for protection against the elements. This distinction is clearly true of the most typical examples of each category: for example, it is a correct description of the difference between a woollen overcoat and a suit jacket. But when we consider less representative examples of coats and jackets, we find that they are less distinct. Parkas, for instance, which are less typical examples of coats, have a jacket attribute: they do not extend below the waist. Similarly, a light linen thigh-length jacket is not a typical example of a jacket, because it does extend beyond the waist: this is, of course, a coat-attribute. So as we move away from the central members, the differences between categories become less marked.

QUESTION   Consider the following garments. How many superordinate categories do they belong to? Describe as fully as possible the prototype of each category.

   dinner suit jacket
   hospital gown
   poncho
   cape
   academic gown
   anorak
   cardigan

QUESTION   What are the attributes of the category BOAT? What attributes might the prototype of the category possess? Rank the following examples with respect to their closeness to the prototype. Are all of them members of the category? If not, what other categories might they belong to?

   raft
   sailboard
   buoy
   kayak
   canoe
   airboat
   dragonboat
   barge
   catamaran
   ferry
   cutter
   yacht

dinghy
gondola
hydrofoil
submarine
ocean liner

Prototype theory was originally developed as a theory of how concrete, visual objects, like furniture, colour or fish, are categorized. But several studies have revealed prototype effects in domains involving activities. Thus, Coleman and Kay (1981) discuss the nature of the prototype of the category LIE. Pulman (1983: 113) analysed the members of the categories KILL, SPEAK and WALK with respect to prototypicality (the leftmost verb is the most prototypical member, the rightmost the least):

KILL: *murder, assassinate, execute, massacre, sacrifice, commit suicide*
SPEAK: *recite, mumble, shout, whisper, drone, stutter*
WALK: *stride, pace, saunter, march, stumble, limp*

QUESTION   Consider the structure of the category EAT. What verbs are its members? Assume that the category is arranged around a prototype, and try to specify the appropriate attributes.

The hypothesis that categories are structured in terms of prototypes is consistent with a number of experimental results. In fact, Rosch says that 'the prototypicality of items within a category can be shown to affect virtually all of the major dependent variables used as measures in psychological research' (1978: 38). For instance, Rosch and her colleagues performed experiments in which subjects were asked to verify statements about category membership of the form 'An [exemplar] is a [category name]' (e.g. 'a robin is a bird') as quickly as they could. Response times were shorter when the exemplar was a representative member of the category; subjects took less time, in other words, to confirm that a robin is a bird, than they did to confirm that an emu is. Prototype effects like these are systematic and have been confirmed widely in the experimental literature (Mervis and Rosch 1981: 96). Second, Mervis and Rosch (1981: 96–97) report experiments by Battig and Montague (1969) in which subjects were asked to list exemplars of each of 56 superordinate categories such as furniture, fruit, weapons, sports or parts of the human body. Prototypical members of the categories were found to be mentioned more frequently than non-prototypical ones. Lastly, natural languages possess mechanisms for expressing the extent to which an exemplar of a category is typical. In English, for example, a sentence like *A sparrow is a true bird* is perfectly normal, unlike *A penguin is a true bird*: sparrows, not penguins, are prototypical exemplars of the category BIRD. Conversely, *technically* can only be applied to non-prototypical category members: *A penguin is technically a bird* is acceptable, but *A sparrow is technically a bird* is not (Lakoff 1973).

Many linguists have seen the graded structure of categories discovered by Rosch as an indication of the nature of the meanings of natural language category terms. The idea that categories are structured by attributes and degrees of membership solves some difficult problems in semantic analysis. As commented by Lehrer (1990: 380), 'When we look at some of the detailed lexical descriptions that have been done, the data themselves often have forced the investigator to posit fuzzy boundaries and partial class inclusion, implicitly acknowledging something like prototype theory.' Consider the problems associated with the definition of *game* as 'contest played according to rules and decided by skill, strength or luck'. As noted earlier, this does not apply to card games like patience (solitaire), which involve a single participant and are thus not contests, nor to a game in which a child throws a ball against a wall. Problems like this might constitute a reason to reject the definition as inaccurate, but a prototype interpretation of category membership allows us to save it. On the proto-type approach, the definition can be rephrased as an identification of the *most prototypical attributes* of the category GAME: the most typical, best examples of games are precisely those which can be defined as 'contests played according to rules and decided by skill, strength or luck'. This covers football, hide-and-seek and many other games: the fact that it does not obviously apply to other activities like patience, etc., can be explained by the fact that these are not central members of the category.

7.1.4 Problems with prototype categories
For all its attractions, prototype theory is open to a number of problems, which we consider briefly in this section.

7.1.4.1 Problems identifying the attributes
The first type of problem concerns the nature of the semantic attributes on which judgements of prototypicality are based. In our discussion of categories we have simply isolated the attributes in an intuitive fashion, an apparently unproblematic procedure. For instance, it doesn't seem unreasonable to suggest that people use the attribute 'has a seat' as part of the decision about whether to classify a particular object as a CHAIR. But Rosch herself acknowledges that the ease of identification for many attributes is deceptive (1978: 42). There are essentially three problems, which we deal with in turn:

- attributes can often only be identified after the category has been identified
- attributes are highly context-dependent
- there are many different alternative descriptions of the attributes of a given category

Attribute identification depends on category identification   In the 'has a seat' case, for example, the identification of this attribute seems to para-doxically depend on a prior identification of the CHAIR category itself: how do we know, for instance, that an armchair 'has a seat' unless we have already categorized it as a chair? Why do we not treat the seat of the arm-chair simply as a physical zone of the armchair without any particular func-tional significance, in the same way we treat, for example, the separately stitched piece of material which covers the shoulder section in a shirt? The answer seems to be that we can isolate the seat as a distinctive attribute of an armchair only because we already know that the armchair is designed to be sat on – that it is a chair. This is a paradox for the theory: examples are supposed to be assigned to a category in virtue of their attributes, but at least some attributes seem to depend for their identification on a prior identification of the category in question.

Rosch also points out (1978: 42) that some attributes, like 'large' for the category PIANO, depend on considerable background knowledge: pianos are large for pieces of furniture, but small for buildings. It could therefore be objected that attributes like this are not more basic cognitively than the whole objects to which they belong, and that they cannot be considered the basis for the categorization. As Rosch puts it, 'it appeared that the analysis of objects into attributes was a rather sophisticated activity that our subjects…might well be considered to be able to impose only *after* the development of the category system' (1978: 42; italics original).

Attributes vary with context   In a similar spirit, Khalidi (1995: 404) notes that

the kinds of features that subjects associate with certain concepts vary widely and almost without limit when one varies the experimental context in which they are tested. Rather than accessing a fixed set of features in conjunction with each concept, there is apparently no limit to the features that even a single subject associates with a certain concept depending on the context in question.

For example, members of the category MEAL will have very different attributes if the context is a hospital, a wedding banquet, a camping trip or the family dinner table. What would be a good example in one of these contexts will not be a good example in another, and the attributes on which prototypicality depends will vary similarly. The same remarks apply to the category MUSICAL INSTRUMENT: a plastic recorder is a good example and a bassoon a bad one if the context is an infants' school music class, whereas these values are reversed if the context is a symphony orchestra. Similarly, the concept PIANO will be credited with different features depending on whether the context is taken to be producing music or moving furniture (Barclay *et al.* 1974, cited by Khalidi 1995: 405). Any attempt to specify the prototypical features of a category or the attributes of one of its members will therefore have to deal with the possibility that these features may change significantly from one context to another.

Alternative descriptions of attributes   Another question arises even if we grant that a relatively fixed list of attributes could be constructed for a category: how do we know which descriptions of the attributes are psychologically real? For example, what are the attributes of the category TREE? Langacker (1987: 374) suggests 'tall plant', 'with leaves', 'with branches' and 'with bark'. It is true that these attributes are among those which distinguish trees *as a matter of fact*, but we may not be entitled to assume that they enter into the conceptual representation of the category. It may be, for example, that the relevant attributes of TREE are actually best described as 'made of wood', 'growing in ground', 'with long trunk' and 'sometimes covered in small green objects'. This description of the attributes makes no difference to the rankings of exemplars of trees: an oak will still be a prototypical tree, and a cactus will be an atypical one. But the nature of the attributes on which the prototypicality judgements are claimed to rest will reflect an entirely different understanding of the underlying structure of the category. Indeed, the category TREE might not depend on any underlying abstract features like 'with bark'. Instead, it could be based around a particular *example* of a tree as stored in long-term memory. This, indeed, is precisely the hypothesis made in **exemplar** theories of categorization, which are alternatives to the prototype model in psychology (see Storms *et al.* 2000).

7.1.4.2 Accounting for category boundaries

A second type of problem with the prototype theory of categorization is that it fails to account for category boundaries. The very insight behind prototype theory is that category boundaries are 'fuzzy'. Membership is a graded phenomenon defined through attribute-possession, and there is no hard and fast division between members and non-members of a category. For example, two important attributes of the category BIRD are 'flies' and 'winged'. On the prototype model, *anything* that is winged and flies fulfils two of the attributes of birdhood, and is thus a potential member of the category. For instance, bats have partial membership in the category BIRD on this model of categorization. Yet speakers have strong intuitions that many categories *do* have absolute, unfuzzy boundaries: bats simply are not birds; they are not even atypical birds. These intuitions suggest that there is something more to natural language categories than closeness to a prototype (see Cruse 1990: 388–389 and Wierzbicka 1990: 350–351).

7.1.4.3 Scope of prototype categorization

A third type of question concerns the scope and applicability of prototype theory as a general explanation of natural language semantics. Most of the original work on prototypes concerned visible categories like BIRD or FURNITURE. In spite of prototype theory accounts of categories like LIE, mentioned above, several scholars have questioned whether the theory is equally justified when applied to abstract, non-visual categories. Since there is not the same perceptual basis for the analysis of attributes, it may be that the diagnosis of prototypes is more hazardous. Lehrer (1990) notes that this question is especially acute for the highly abstract categories expressed in language by prepositions and sentence connectives. Another challenge to the scope of prototype categorization is Wierzbicka's (1990) critique of Rosch's assimilation of taxonomic concepts like BIRD to what Wierzbicka calls 'collective' concepts, such as KITCHENWARE or CLOTHING. Taxonomic concepts, according to Wierzbicka, have clear boundaries (recall the bat/bird contrast just discussed) and are not open to a prototype account. (On the other hand, collective concepts, which refer to things of many different kinds, are fuzzy, and prototype approaches may well be able to contribute to their analysis.)

In this context, it is worth noting a change in the way Rosch presented the results of her research. Sometimes Rosch presents prototypes as a theory of 'the nature of the cognitive representation' associated with category terms (Rosch 1975: 192). Often, however, she stressed the opposite, claiming that prototype theory is not a theory of how the mind actually represents semantic content (Rosch 1978: 40–41; see also MacLaury 1991: 57). For example, she said that 'facts about prototypes can only constrain, but do not determine, models of representation' (1978: 40). On this view, prototype theory is a description of the structure of categories which highlights a number of prototype effects – goodness of exemplar ratings, response times, and so on. These effects are, in principle, compatible with a number of different hypotheses on the mental representation of categories, and there is no reason to believe that *all* words in natural language will correspond to concepts with a prototypical structure.

7.1.4.4 Prototypes and formulating definitions

Another objection concerns the effect of prototype theory in semantics. Wierzbicka (1990), for example, complains that the idea that categories have fuzzy boundaries has served as an excuse to avoid the painstaking work of accurate definition. According to prototype theorists, she says,

> …the actual usage of individual words is too messy, too unpredictable, to be accounted for by definitions. But fortunately, semanticists don't have to worry about it any longer: they can now deploy the notion of 'prototype'… Semantic formulae SHOULD NOT 'work'; that's one thing that 'prototypes' have taught us. (1990: 347)

This objection will only have any force if it turns out that traditional definitions are in fact possible for natural language categories – a possibility about which many researchers are sceptical, as discussed in Chapter 2.

7.1.4.5 Prototype experiments and metalinguistic belief

A final objection concerns the contrast between the evidence for a prototype model of semantics versus more traditional ones. At least some of the experimental evidence that motivates the postulation of prototypes can be criticized on the grounds that it is not evidence about how speakers *actually* use words, but evidence about how they *think* words are used or should be used. For instance, one of Rosch's standard sets of instructions to the subjects of her experiments makes it clear that subjects are being asked to assess how far an example 'represents what people mean' when they use particular category terms (1975: 198), and subjects in one of Rosch's classic experiments were asked how far certain words represented their 'idea or image of what the category is' (Rosch and Mervis 1975: 588). The problem here is that the results of these experiments are about subjects' *beliefs about* language and the categories referred to in it, not about their actual language use itself:

they are, in short, **metalinguistic**. As such, they may be the result of an unpredictable range of prescriptive and other considerations which may not be operative in ordinary language use. Just as subjects' ideas about how to define words are notoriously unreliable and unrepresentative of words' actual use, so too their goodness of exemplar ratings may not tell us anything about the underlying meanings of the words concerned. This criticism is avoided to a certain extent by other experiments, such as the reaction time experiments mentioned in the previous section, which show various ways in which goodness of exemplar rating is correlated with actual processing time. But even these apparently less metalinguistic experiments may not be representative of people's real-time categorizing behaviour in ordinary unmonitored discourse. In one type of experiment, for instance, subjects 'typically are required to respond true or false to statements of the form X item is member of Y category' (Rosch 1978: 38), with their speed in doing so correlating to the prototypicality of the exemplar in question. This experiment may reveal various psychological facts about categorization, but it could not be taken to reveal anything about the *meaning* of the words involved without the additional assumption that people's natural language use involves the same principles observed in experimental situations, where subjects are consciously attending to issues of the truth and falsity of category terms. Thus, while prototype theory may be well-founded as a theory of categorization, we should not assume that its results can be transferred immediately to the explanation of language use, since the naming options which people exercise in actual discourse may be affected by many other factors than the prototypicality of the referent.

This criticism does not have to apply to the necessary and sufficient conditions view of categorization. When assembling a list of necessary and sufficient conditions, an investigator can proceed simply by observing how words are actually used, and hypothesizing necessary and sufficient conditions to explain these uses; no-one has to be consulted in order to discover their beliefs about what words mean, as in the prototype approach. The centrality of subjects' judgements about their own language use in prototype theory is a potential problem if there is any chance that subjects may simply be mistaken about the ways in which they use words. I may well say, when asked or tested by a prototype researcher, that tennis is a better example of a game than patience, but what if it turns out that in spite of this judgement I typically refer to tennis as a *sport* in my *actual language use*? The frequency of this sort of mismatch between subjects' self-reports and their actual behaviour is unknown; however, it is clearly an important issue that needs to be settled.

In spite of these problems, prototype models of categorization have been the source of a major reorientation in the practice of much semantic description. In spite of Rosch's unwillingness to elevate prototype theory into a full-blown theory of mental representation, many semantic investigators now take it for granted that the meaning of all or most lexical items consists in a prototype structure. As a result, the semanticist's role is to characterize only the most prototypical aspects of that structure, and a range of meanings outside it is only to be expected.

7.2 Language and conceptualization: cognitive approaches to semantics

As just noted, Rosch did not intend prototype theory as a comprehensive theory of mental representation, the concepts with which we think (see 1.6.2). Many of the insights of prototype research, however, are accounted for in **cognitive** approaches to semantics, which do set out to develop a comprehensive theory of mental representation.

7.2.1 Commitments of cognitive semantics

The label cognitive semantics covers a variety of quite different approaches. In general, however, these approaches are characterized by a **holistic** vision of the place of language within cognition. For many investigators, this involves the following commitments:

- a rejection of a modular approach to language
- an identification of meaning with 'conceptual structure'
- a rejection of the syntax–semantics distinction
- a rejection of the semantics–pragmatics distinction

We will briefly outline each of these commitments in turn.

Rejection of modularity   Many cognitivists share a commitment to understanding language as governed by the same cognitive principles at work in other psychological domains. This holistic approach to language structure contrasts with the strongly **modular** approach promoted by investigators in the tradition of Chomsky (1965) and Fodor (1983). Modular research assumes that language is one of a number of independent **modules** or faculties within cognition, each of which has a structure and principles independent of those at work in other cognitive domains. On a modular vision of the mind, the principles of the language module will be entirely distinct from those of the others, like vision, memory, reasoning or musical cognition. Cognitivists like Langacker (1987), Lakoff and Johnson (1980), and Lakoff (1987) reject the modularist idea that language constitutes an independent cognitive competence governed by its own distinctive principles. Instead, cognitivist research pursues a holistic understanding of language structure, in which linguistic data are explained through psychological mechanisms known to operate elsewhere in cognition.

For instance, Langacker proposes that the general psychological phenomenon of attention, our ability to attend selectively to different aspects of a scene, can be used to understand a wide range of linguistic and grammatical phenomena. One example would be the contrast in the meanings of words like *buy* and *sell*. These words both evoke the same scene, that of a transaction between two parties, but each of them directs attention to, or **profiles**, different aspects of it: *buy* profiles (directs attention to, highlights) the perspective of the buyer, *sell* that of the seller. This selective profiling is interpreted by Langacker as the linguistic analogue of our ability to focus our attention onto a narrow subset of the total visual or auditory stimuli in our perceptual field, ignoring others, such as when we concentrate on a single conversation in a loud restaurant, or follow the position of a ball in a tennis match. The conceptualization underlying *buy* and *sell*, in other words, differs only in what part is profiled.

Meaning as conceptual structure   Most cognitivists share a rejection of the dictionary–encyclopedia distinction (see 3.3): in the words of Jackendoff (2002: 293), 'we must consider the domain of linguistic semantics to be continuous with human conceptualization as a whole'. In other words, studying linguistic meaning is the same thing as studying the nature of human **conceptual structure** – a cover-all term for our 'thoughts, concepts, perceptions, images, and mental experience in general' (Langacker 1987: 98). The meaning of a word like *house* simply *is* the concept we have of houses; as discussed in 3.3, any aspect of the knowledge we have of houses can become linguistically relevant. Cognitive approaches to semantics aim to describe the full knowledge structures that are associated with the words of a language. As a result, conceptualist descriptions of the meanings of words are considerably more rich, complex and open-ended than in other varieties of semantic analysis.

Rejection of the semantics–syntax distinction   Just as language as a whole is not seen as a distinct cognitive capacity in conceptualist frameworks, so too the language-*internal* division between semantics and syntax often recognized in linguistics is typically rejected. Evans and Green (2006) identify a number of fundamental cognitive principles which do not respect any division between these two domains: prototype effects, polysemy (4.3) and metaphor (see below), for example, seem to exist not only in the domain of word meaning, but in morphology and syntax as well. It has even sometimes been suggested that phonological categories are prototypes. This is all taken as a reason not to assume that syntax and semantics constitute different domains, and that linguists will most fruitfully spend their time seeking explanatory principles which apply across them all. (This problematization of the syntax–semantics boundary is not unique to cognitive linguistics: it is also characteristic of, for example, systemic functional grammar; see e.g. Halliday and Matthiessen 2004.)

Rejection of the semantics–pragmatics distinction   Cognitive linguistics also typically rejects the distinction between a purely semantic level of word meaning and a non-semantic level of language use. This means that facts which in other frameworks might be attributed to inferences based on literal meanings (see Chapter 4) are assumed to reflect aspects of the actual, literal meaning of the words concerned. We will see in the sections that follow how this and the other related commitments of cognitive semantics affect the analyses of semantic content proposed in these frameworks.

7.2.2 Idealized cognitive models

The conclusions of prototype research inspired much cognitivist reflection on meaning. Inspired by the work of Fillmore (1982), Lakoff (1987) proposed that prototype effects are by-products of the fact that our knowledge is organized into structures stored in long-term memory that he calls **idealized cognitive models** (ICMs). The notion of ICM is meant to capture the contribution of encyclopaedic knowledge to our understanding of concepts. ICMs can be thought of as theories of particular subjects – the implicit knowledge we have about the objects, relations and processes named in language (Lakoff 1987: 45). Lakoff introduces the notion of ICMs with the example of the English word *Tuesday*. The meaning of *Tuesday*, he says, can only be represented by specifying the underlying knowledge English speakers have of the organization of time into days and weeks, and the place of Tuesday within this organization. This underlying knowledge is the ICM evoked by *Tuesday*, and this ICM is what needs to be made explicit in any explanation of the meaning of the word:

> *Tuesday* can be defined only relative to an idealized cognitive model that includes the natural cycle defined by the movement of the sun, the standard means of characterizing the end of one day and the beginning of the next, and a larger seven-day calendric cycle – the week. In the idealized model, the week is a whole with seven parts organized in a linear sequence; each part is called a day, and the third is *Tuesday*. Similarly, the concept weekend requires a notion of a *work week* of five days followed by a break of two days, superimposed on the seven-day calendar.
>
> (Lakoff 1987: 68–69)

Lakoff refers to this underlying knowledge as 'idealized' since it is a human construct: seven-day weeks are not objectively found in nature, but are the product of human cultural organization. The idealized nature of ICMs is what causes prototype effects. Consider the ICM behind the word *bachelor*. Lakoff says that *bachelor*

> is defined with respect to an ICM in which there is a human society with (typically) monogamous marriage, and a typical marriageable age. The idealized model says nothing about the existence of priests, 'long-term unmarried couplings', homosexuality, Moslems who are permitted four wives and only have three, etc. With respect to this idealized cognitive model, a *bachelor* is simply an unmarried adult man. (1987: 70)

The ICM is out of step with the way the world actually is. As a result, some 'unmarried men' seem less good exemplars of the category BACHELOR than others. But this isn't because the category itself has a prototype structure. It's because the ICM clashes with the way the world actually is – the world *does* contain priests, homosexuals, polygamists and so on. The cases which we might describe as less prototypical bachelors are cases where there is an incomplete correspondence between the world and the ICM.

The background conditions of the *bachelor* ICM rarely make a perfect seamless fit with the world as we know it. Still we can apply the concept with some degree of accuracy to situations where the background conditions don't quite mesh with our knowledge. And the worse the fit between the background conditions of the ICM and our knowledge, the less appropriate it is for us to apply the concept.

(Lakoff 1987: 71)

The result of this looks just like the cases of prototypicality described by Rosch. But in this way of looking at things, categories are not defined in terms of attributes or central tendencies. Categories are broad knowledge structures, and words can be seen as points of access to them.

7.2.3 Embodiment and image schemas

Many cognitive semanticists stress the **embodied** nature of the conceptualizations underlying language. To say that a conceptualization is embodied is to draw attention to its origin in basic physical experience. Johnson (1987) pointed out that much language use reflects patterns in our own bodily experience, particularly our perceptual interactions, movements and manipulations of objects. Particularly basic patterns of repeated experience give rise to the conceptual categories which Johnson called **image schemas**, such as CONTAINMENT, SOURCE-PATH-GOAL, FORCE, BALANCE and others. These 'operate as organizing structures of our experience and understanding at the level of bodily perception and movement' (Johnson 1987: 20), and thus also underlie the conceptual categories deployed in language. For instance, from an early age we frequently experience containment and boundedness, interacting with containers of different sorts. The most important type of container with which we interact is our own body, which functions as a container into which we put things like food, water and air. We also experience physical containment in our surroundings, interacting with receptacles of many sorts. These repeated patterns of spatial and temporal organization give rise to the image schema of CONTAINMENT, which underlies the linguistic representation of many scenes, and which Johnson diagrams, very simply, as follows:

FIGURE 7.3
The CONTAINMENT schema
(Johnson 1987: 23).

Our real-life experience of containers establishes the following pieces of typical knowledge about containment:

- the experience of containment usually involves protection from or resistance to external forces
- containment restricts the movement of whatever is in the container
- as a result, whatever is contained has a relatively fixed location – it is *in* the container

- the object in the container may be either visible or invisible to an observer
- containment is transitive (see 5.1.2.). If A is in B, and C is in A, then C is also in B.

Another important image schema is PATH:

FIGURE 7.4
The PATH schema.

This image schema consists of a source point (A), an end point (B), and a relation between them, which we can think of as a force moving from A to B. Johnson claims that a structure like this underlies the understanding of such diverse events as walking from one place to another, throwing a ball to someone, hitting someone and giving someone a present. All these situations are understood, he claims, as consisting of the same basic parts and relations.

The CONTAINMENT and PATH schemas can be used to understand the behaviour of prepositions like *out*. Typically, Johnson notes, *out* has been taken to show a large variety of unrelated meanings, some of which are exemplified in (1):

(1)   a. *John went out of the room.*
      b. *Pump out the air.*
      c. *Let out your anger.*
      d. *Pick out the best theory.*
      e. *Drown out the music.*

(1a), for example, might be taken to exemplify a 'physical motion' sense, (1b) and (1c) a literal and metaphorical 'expulsion' sense respectively, (1d) a 'choice' sense, and (1e) a 'removal from sensory field' sense. However, following Lindner (1983), Johnson claims that the meaning of *out* in all the examples in (1) can be understood as relating to a combination of the path and containment image schemas. Figure 7.5 is Johnson's diagrammatic representation of the meanings involved in (1):

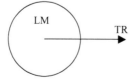

FIGURE 7.5
Trajector-landmark struc-
ture for *out*$_1$.

This scene involves an object labelled TR (**trajector**) moving along a path from a position of containment within a bounded entity marked LM (**landmark**). ('Trajector' and 'landmark' are alternative names for **figure** and **ground** respectively; the trajector/figure is 'a moving or *conceptually movable* object whose path or site is at issue'; the landmark/ground is 'a reference-frame, or a reference-point stationary within a reference-frame, with respect to which the Figure's path or site is characterized' (Talmy 1985: 61).) The claim is that this single structure underlies the diverse uses of *out* in (1). The *out* of (1a), for example, obviously fits this diagram: in (1a), John is the trajector, and the room is the landmark. But it can also, Johnson claimed, be seen as underlying (1d) and (1e), apparently unrelated usages. In (1d) the trajector is 'the best theory', and the landmark is the set of theories from which it is being selected. Notice that this is not represented explicitly in the wording of (1d). But if we understand the meaning of *out* in this context by reference to the image schema of containment, as diagrammed above, a landmark is revealed as an inherent aspect of our understanding of the scene. Sentence (1d) thus represents a metaphorical application of the schemas, in which choice is assimilated to the pattern of containment and motion. Sentence (1e) is also metaphorical, and the landmark is once again implicit: here the trajector is the music, which is made to leave an implicit region of audibility, the landmark. Drowning the music out involves bringing it out of a position of audibility into one of inaudibility.

The cases in (2) relate to the same image schemas of CONTAINMENT and PATH, but are understood in a slightly different way, as diagrammed in Figure 7.6:

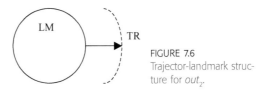

FIGURE 7.6
Trajector-landmark structure for *out₂*.

(2) a. *Pour out the beans.*
     b. *Roll out the red carpet.*
     c. *Send out the troops.*
     d. *Hand out the information.*
     e. *Write out your ideas.*

Here the path and containment schemas relate somewhat differently. Instead of a single entity moving progressively further along a path from a container towards an end point, we have an entity whose outside edge progressively expands outwards from a position of containment. Unlike in the previous case, the area between the container and the edge of the trajector is taken up by a continuous quantity of the moving entity – think of the beans being poured from a tin onto a plate. Once again, a variety of apparently dissimilar forms is argued to correspond to a single image-schematic structure.

QUESTION   Consider the following passage (Johnson 1987: 30–31).

You wake *out* of a deep sleep and peer *out* from beneath the covers *into* your room. You gradually emerge *out* of your stupor, pull yourself *out* from under the covers, climb *into* your robe, stretch *out* your limbs, and walk *in* a daze *out* of the bedroom *into* the bathroom. You look *in* the mirror and see your face staring *out* at you. You reach *into* the medicine cabinet, take *out* the toothpaste, squeeze *out* some toothpaste, put the toothbrush *into* your mouth, brush your teeth *in* a hurry, and rinse *out* your mouth.

Can the uses of *out* here be described in the same way? How might we describe the uses of *in*?

The type of diagrammatic representation seen in the discussion of *out* has proved a popular means of indicating the different meanings of prepositions. This means of representation was developed principally by Langacker (1987) and Lakoff (1987). Here we will briefly give the flavour of an influential analysis of the preposition *over* by Brugman and Lakoff, as presented in Lakoff (1987: 416–461).

Lakoff distinguishes four basic senses of *over*, each of which receives a diagrammatic representation. The first is the one found in clauses like *the plane is flying over the hill* or *the bullet passed over our heads*, which Lakoff represents as in Figure 7.7.

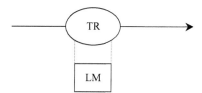

FIGURE 7.7
Over: Schema 1. The *above-across* sense.

The trajector (the plane/bullet) is conceived as on a path which passes above and across the landmark (the hill/heads). The diagram gives a concise abstract representation of the spatial configurations involved.

The second sense of *over* is the stative *above* sense, as found in *the helicopter is hovering over the hill* or *the painting is over the fireplace*. This is identical to schema 1, except that it lacks the path component:

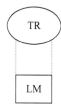

FIGURE 7.8
Over: Schema 2. The *above* sense.

A third sense of *over* is the *covering* sense, as in *the blanket is over the bed*. Here the trajector is at least two-dimensional, and extends across the edges of the landmark, as in Figure 7.9.

TR

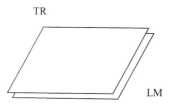

LM

FIGURE 7.9
Over: Schema 3. The *covering* sense.

The final basic schema is the 'reflexive' schema, which occurs in such uses as *turn the paper over* or *roll the log over*. Here we have the object moving above and across *itself*, as illustrated in Figure 7.10.

TR = LM

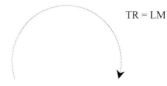

FIGURE 7.10
Over: Schema 4. The *reflexive* sense.

Each of these four basic senses can be specialized to cover a range of subsenses. Consider the use of *over* in *Sam walked over the hill*. This is a specialization of schema 1, except that there is contact between the landmark (the hill) and the trajector (Sam). Similarly, *Sam lives over the hill* can be treated as an instance of schema 1, but with the path as understood, and a focus on the endpoint. Lakoff diagrams the image schema for this as follows:

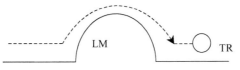

LM   TR

FIGURE 7.11
Variation on schema 1.

To say that *Sam lives over the hill* is to evoke the image of a trajector (Sam) on one side of a landmark (the hill), and an imagined path which the trajector has taken in order to arrive there. This representation accounts for the fact that we use the same preposition for two quite different types of situation, by associating both situations with fundamentally the same trajector–landmark structure. Similarly, Lakoff proposes the image-schema in Figure 7.12 to account for instances like *I walked all over the hill*:

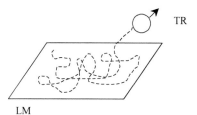

FIGURE 7.12
Variation on schema 3.

This is a variation on the *covering* schema (Figure 7.9). Here, it is the path taken by the trajector which ends up covering the landmark.

QUESTION What are some of the advantages and problems of diagrammatic representations like these?

QUESTION Consider the following uses of *over*:

The ball landed over the wall.
The town is over the next hill.
Sam climbed over the wall.
Someone has stuck some cardboard over the hole in the ceiling.

Which image schematic sense of *over* do they belong to? How easy is it to decide? Could any use ever belong to more than one sense?

7.2.4 Metaphor and metonymy

Some of the sentences discussed in the previous section involved metaphorical appearances of the image schemas of path and containment. Metaphor is stressed in much cognitive semantics as 'an inherent and fundamental aspect of semantic and grammatical structure' (Langacker 1987: 100). This contrasts with the more traditional view of metaphor as a special, additional feature of particular utterances, associated with imaginative or artistic uses of language rather than with everyday speech. On the traditional view of metaphor, metaphors are assumed not to reveal anything fundamental about the nature of meaning. Metaphor was originally a category of literary and rhetorical analysis, not of linguistic description (see e.g. Ricœur 1975). In contrast, a tradition of research inaugurated by Lakoff and Johnson (1980) has demonstrated the ubiquity of metaphor in ordinary, everyday speech and claimed that it has a central importance in language structure.

On the traditional view of metaphor, which goes right back to Aristotle, metaphors are principally seen as a matter of (especially literary) usage. On this understanding, metaphors assert a resemblance between two entities. Thus, the metaphor *the holiday was a nightmare* works because it asserts a resemblance or similarity between the holiday and a nightmare. Understanding the meaning of the metaphorical utterance involves identifying things which holidays and nightmares might hold in common, such as being unpleasant. Metaphors like this are no more than isolated usages which can only be discussed on a case-by-case basis: we should not expect there to be any significant generalizations about metaphorical usages.

Lakoff and Johnson (1980, Lakoff 1993) questioned this traditional view on two grounds. First, they noticed that metaphor is much less exceptional and more widespread than is traditionally claimed. As an example of the widespread nature of metaphor, consider some of the expressions we use to talk about obligations:

(3)   a. *She's **loaded** with responsibilities.*
      b. *She **shouldered** the task with ease.*
      c. *She's **weighed down** with obligations.*
      d. *She's **carrying** a **heavy load** at work.*
      e. *I have to **get out from under** my obligations.*
      f. *I have a **pressing** obligation.*
      g. *She **bears** the responsibility for the success of this mission.*
      h. *We shouldn't **overload** her.*

Lakoff and Johnson noted that far from being unusual or atypical, metaphorical utterances like those in (3) are actually the basic, ordinary way in which obligations would be described in English. They also observed that these expressions all express a common underlying idea, which we could label OBLIGATIONS ARE PHYSICAL BURDENS. The sentences in (3) all express this single underlying idea differently, but this diversity should not obscure the fact that they all essentially make reference to the same similarity between obligations and physical burdens. Lakoff and Johnson observe that this systematicity is entirely characteristic of metaphor crosslinguistically. We typically find a variety of ways in which a single underlying metaphorical correspondence can be expressed.

Second, Lakoff and Johnson propose that it is not simply a random linguistic fact that English has so many expressions along the lines of (3). There is a reason that obligations are described as though they were physical burdens, and not in any other of the innumerable ways we could dream up. This is that the very idea of obligation is *conceptualized* through the idea of a physical burden: we actually think of, or conceptualize, obligations, Lakoff and Johnson claim, through the idea of burdens. The concept of assuming an obligation is structured on the analogy of the simpler concept of carrying a physical burden. We explore this idea in the following paragraphs.

The idea that some concepts can have metaphorical structure is referred to by Lakoff and Johnson as the **conceptual theory of metaphor**. This theory focuses on metaphor as a cognitive device which acts as a model to express the nature of otherwise hard-to-conceptualize ideas. Lakoff and Johnson's claim rests on the idea that certain concepts lack independent structure of their own. Obligations would be one example of this: on the conceptual theory of metaphor, the concept of obligation inherits its structure from the concept of physical burdens. There are three terms which will help us to describe this process. The **target** concept – here, obligations – is the concept which is being understood metaphorically. The **vehicle** concept – here, physical burdens – is the concept which imposes its structure onto the target. On the conceptual metaphor theory, we understand the target through the vehicle: the structure of the vehicle concept shapes the structure of the target concept. This is usually described by saying that the conceptual metaphor OBLIGATIONS ARE PHYSICAL BURDENS **maps** our concept of obligation onto our concept of physical burdens.

We can show the details of this mapping by lining vehicle and target up as follows. The capitalized concepts in the target domain correspond to those in the vehicle domain:

a. CARRYING PHYSICAL BURDENS requires the expenditure of energy and can become tiring.
b. If the burden is too HEAVY, it is impossible to CARRY: if you do not LOWER it, or DROP it, it will CAUSE YOU PHYSICAL DAMAGE.
c. DROPPING the physical burden may damage it.
d. The BURDEN may be TRANSFERRED to someone else.
e. In some cases its WEIGHT MAY BE LESSENED by removing some of its parts.

a. FULFILLING OBLIGATIONS requires the expenditure of energy and can become tiring.
b. If the obligation is too ONEROUS it is impossible to FULFIL: if you do not FREE YOURSELF OF IT, or RELINQUISH IT SUDDENLY, it will CAUSE YOU UNDUE STRESS.
c. SUDDENLY RELINQUISHING THE OBLIGATION may BE HARMFUL TO THOSE TO WHOM THE OBLIGATION IS OWED.
d. The OBLIGATION may BE FULFILLED by someone else.
e. In some cases it may be made LESS ONEROUS by removing some of its parts.

On the conceptual metaphor view, metaphor is a cognitive process which helps us to conceptualize our experience by setting up correspondences between easily understood things like burdens and hard to understand things like obligations. A metaphorical mapping allows knowledge about the metaphor's vehicle domain to be applied to the target in a way that fundamentally determines or influences the conceptualization of the target: metaphor is a cognitive operation first and foremost.

To give another example, Lakoff identifies the connections between a target concept, love, and the metaphorical vehicle used to conceptualize it, the image of a journey. In the following paraphrase, the capitalized concepts in the vehicle domain correspond to those in the target domain:

Two TRAVELLERS are in a VEHICLE, TRAVELLING WITH COMMON DESTINATIONS. The VEHICLE encounters some IMPEDIMENT and gets stuck, that is, becomes nonfunctional. If the travellers do nothing, they will not REACH THEIR DESTINATION.

Two LOVERS are in a LOVE RELATIONSHIP, PURSUING COMMON LIFE GOALS. The RELATIONSHIP encounters some DIFFICULTY, which makes it nonfunctional. If they do nothing, they will not be able to ACHIEVE THEIR LIFE GOALS.

(Lakoff 1993: 208)

In this instantiation, lovers correspond to travellers, the love relationship corresponds to the vehicle, and the lovers' common goals correspond to their common destinations on the journey. The mapping is found in many common English metaphors for love and the situation of lovers, especially in times of difficulty: a relationship is *stalled*, lovers cannot *keep going the way they've been going*, they must *turn back*. Alternatively, the participants in the relationship may say *look how far we've come, we can't turn back now, we're at a cross-roads*, or *we may have to go our separate ways* (Lakoff 1993: 206). Since we actually use the concept of a journey in our reasoning about love, it is not surprising that English has so many different expressions in which journey-language is used to represent love. Treating metaphor as simply a matter of linguistic usage misses this obvious generalization.

QUESTION   What evidence might there be in English for the conceptual metaphor TREATING AN ILLNESS IS FIGHTING A WAR?

On the conceptual theory of metaphor, metaphor is a deep-seated cognitive process which can be used to understand the structural relations between the meanings of lexical items. It is not the only such process, however. Another important structural relation is the relation of **metonymy**. In traditional rhetoric, metonymy is the figure of speech based on an interrelation between closely associated terms – cause and effect, possessor and possessed, and a host of possible others. The common element in metonymy is notion of **contiguity**: the things related by a metonymy can be understood as contiguous to (neighbouring) each other, either conceptually or in the real world. Here are some examples:

(4)   a. ***Moscow*** *has rejected the demands.*
       b. *The **kettle** is boiling.*
       c. *This cinema complex has seven **screens**.*
       d. *I **saw** the doctor today.*
       e. *My **bags** were destroyed by customs.*

In (4a) we understand that *Moscow* refers to the Russian government. In (4b) it isn't the kettle itself, but the water inside it, which is boiling. In (4c) the cinema is not claimed to just have seven screens: the speaker means that it has seven separate auditoriums, each with its own screen. In (4d) the speaker does not mean that they just *saw* the doctor: they mean that they consulted the doctor. In (4e) it was not just the bags, but their contents as well which were destroyed. In all these examples the highlighted word expresses something associated with its literal meaning: in (a), a place stands for one of its salient institutions (the Russian government), in (b) the container stands for the contents, in (e) the container stands for the container *and* the contents, and in (c) an important part of the auditorium stands for the whole auditorium. Example (4d) is the verbal equivalent of (4c): one event, *seeing*, stands for the wider event of which it is part: having a medical appointment.

Notice the difference between metonymies and metaphors: in metaphor, there is a relation of mapping between two concepts, with the structure of one concept (JOURNEYS, PHYSICAL BURDENS) being imposed onto another (LOVE, OBLIGATIONS). Metonymies do not serve to structure one concept in terms of another: it is not possible to articulate the detailed mappings we established in the love and obligation cases. Instead, they draw on the associations *within* a single conceptual 'domain', allowing one part of a concept to convey another. We will see further examples of this in the next section.

7.2.5 Radial categories in word meaning

Recall that cognitive semantics identifies meaning with conceptual structure, the network of stored representations in our memory involved in thought and language (see 1.6.2 for discussion). A word can be seen as an entry point to a certain 'region' of our conceptual structure. Using the ideas discussed in the preceding sections, we can now sketch the way in which cognitive semantics models the conceptual knowledge structures underlying meaning. We will do this with the English noun *head*.

The meaning of *head* depends on a specific aspect of our conceptual structure: the underlying knowledge English speakers have about heads – the ICM of *head*, in Lakoff's terminology. This knowledge is, of course, encyclopaedic, but this does not mean that everything we know about heads is automatically evoked by every use of the noun *head*. Instead, an occurrence of the word allows access to this idealized model, not all of which will necessarily be relevant in any single context. What might some of this knowledge be? Presumably, for most English speakers, the ICM of *head* contains such information as the fact that the head is at the top of the body, that it contains the brain, the fact that ears, eyes, mouth and nose are located on it, the fact that it is mostly made of bone, that thinking happens inside it, and so on (see 3.3 for a discussion of encyclopaedic information). Perhaps, as suggested by some investigators, one aspect of the conceptualization associated with *head* (as with any other non-abstract word) is a visual/spatial element, encoding such features as the referent's typical shape, colour and overall appearance (Jackendoff 2002: 345–350).

The ICM of *head* determines the way in which ordinary sentences involving it are understood. For instance, we know that the expression *shake one's head* refers to a particular back and forth movement of the head, rather than to an action in which one takes one's head in one's hands and shakes it. Similarly, we know that if asked to *turn one's head* we should turn it horizontally from one side to another, not move it in a fixed circular motion without allowing it to come to rest. Facts like these are part of our understanding of *head*, and must therefore be represented in conceptual structure.

Different aspects of this ICM may become relevant in different contexts. For instance, the expressions in (5) call on the knowledge that the head is where thinking occurs.

(5) *to use one's head*
    to lose one's head
    to be a hot head
    to be off one's head
    to get one's head around a problem/question/subject

Relatedly, (6) involves that part of the ICM which states that the head contains ideas:

(6) *He needs his head read.*
    Something has just popped into my head.
    Calculus is over my head.
    It's amazing how you keep all those facts in your head.

The expressions in (7a) and (7b) highlight those parts of the *head* ICM which represent the importance of the head in our understanding of vertigo and alcohol consumption, respectively.

(7) a. *a head for heights*
    b. *a head for alcohol*

That part of the *head* ICM specifying that the head consists of a hard layer of skull enclosing the brains is relevant to the interpretation of (8):

(8) *to have a thick head*

Expression (9) appeals to our knowledge that the head is the location of the main perceptual organs; if the head is buried, these obviously cannot function:

(9) *to bury one's head in the sand*

Expression (10) depends on the knowledge that the head is a highly salient part of the body, and one which often serves to identify people:

(10) *to keep one's head down*

Finally, our knowledge that a typical human head is covered with hair allows us to correctly interpret the following expressions:

(11) *head lice*
    a redhead

It should be clear that different facets of the head ICM may be relevant at different times. On this approach to meaning, we do not need to conclude that the noun *head* has a large variety of distinct, polysemous senses (see 5.3), such as 'location of perceptual organs', 'site of thought', 'part of body from which scalp hair grows', and so on. Instead, we simply posit that *head* evokes a single ICM, and that different aspects of that ICM become relevant or profiled in different contexts. Note also that the ICM is *idealized*. It is modelled on the *human* head. The closer a creature's head is to a human head, the more appropriate it is to describe it as having a head. Thus, there is nothing odd about describing monkeys, dogs, cats and many other types of animal as having heads, whereas it seems more strained so to describe the corresponding bodyparts of worms, whales, spiders, snails and starfish.

We have not exhausted the uses of *head* in English, however. None of the following uses can be explained with reference to the ICM we have just described:

(12) a. *head of the queue*
     b. *head of a comet*
     c. *head of a page*
     d. *head of a hammer/axe*
     e. *head of a department*
     f. *head of a bed*

Since the original ICM does not apply, we will describe these uses as **semantic extensions** from it. These extensions can plausibly be analysed as metaphors. In all of them, aspects of the head ICM are mapped onto other domains. In (12a–d) the structure of the human body, with the head at the top, is exploited metaphorically as a model for objects which do not obviously have this structure. In (12e) we have a metaphorical use in which the head's control of the rest of the body serves as the foundation for a metaphorical mapping onto an organization, while in (12f) the head–foot structure of the human body is mapped onto the structure of a piece of furniture.

Note that while it seems plausible to interpret the uses of *head* in (12 a–f) as metaphorical mappings, this interpretation disguises many of the uncertainties that surround the details of this process. Thus, (12a) may be based on the image not of a human head, but on the head of a snake, or perhaps a worm. Similarly, (12f) is no doubt partly due to the fact that people lie in beds, providing a very obvious way of aligning the dimensions of the two. It may not be simply the case that the structure of the body is mapped onto the structure of the bed metaphorically; instead, we might have a metonymy, in which *head* stands for the place at which the head lies. In (12e), is the use of head motivated by the position of the *head* at the top of the hammer or axe, or is it rather dependent on the separate bulbous nature of heads?

QUESTION What are some possible motivations of the expressions *head of a valley* and *head of state*? What evidence might be appealed to to substantiate one particular analysis of these expressions over another?

Head also shows a number of clearly metonymic uses:

(13) a. *... the Democrats would be well served to follow the advice of the wisest* **heads in** *their caucus* (www.indiancountry.com/content.cfm?
id=1096414018)

b. *The outbreak of the disease among animals has caused the death of 33* **head** *of cattle, including three more today, according to reports reaching here this afternoon.* (www.tribuneindia.com/2005/20050219/
himachal.htm)

c. *Guests at the $70 per* **head** *seminar at Old Parliament House ... were greeted by 50 protesters ...* (www.greenleft.org.au/2006/689/35784)

d. *How long have you been suffering these* **heads**? – *For months now ... they have become more frequent.* (OED *head* 1d)

In (13a–c), *head* refers not simply to that body part alone, but to the whole person or animal. In (13a), for instance, *heads* clearly conveys that the Democrats should follow the advice of the wisest *people* in their caucus (cf. (5) above). What we have here, then, is the use of a word denoting part of a body to stand for the whole person: this part-for-whole relation is a classic metonymy, parallel to the use of *screen* for *auditorium* in (4b) above. Exactly the same metonymy is present in (13c). In (13d), on the other hand, the metonymic extension goes from the standard sense to the sense *illness of the head, headache*, using the bodypart to stand for the pain experienced in it.

Representing the meaning of *head* in English therefore involves a detailed specification of the ICM underlying it, and of the metaphorical and metonymic relations in which this ICM participates. Note that given the ICM of *head*, we cannot predict *what* extended meanings it will take on. However, once we know what these extended meanings are, we are able to account for them economically in terms of metaphor and metonymy. This type of analysis can be applied quite generally to the lexicon. This type of structure, 'where there is a central case and conventionalized variations on it which cannot be predicted by general rules', is called a **radial structure** by Lakoff (1987: 84). For *head*, the central case is represented by uses consistent with the ICM described above, and the variations are the metaphoric and metonymic extensions we have discussed.

Note that some of the expressions involving *head* may be conventionalized or idiomatic: in other words, some of the collocations in which *head* participates may be partly preformed or fossilized. This seems particularly likely for expressions where the use of *head* is not productive, such as *head of cattle* or *redhead* (cf. **head of poultry/fish, *blondehead/brownhead*). Conventionalization could be taken as evidence against the radial categories and metaphorical and metonymic extensions from them postulated in cognitive semantics. The production and interpretation of expressions like *head of cattle*, it might be argued, is not explained by these structures at all; *head of cattle* and other conventionalized expressions are simply listed in the lexicon as separate units. A cognitive semanticist could reply that conventionalization like this in no way invalidates the notion of a radial category with senses being elaborated from the basis of a core ICM; indeed, the gradual 'freezing' of various collocations into fixed expressions and idioms is only to be expected. The analysis given above can be taken to explain the origin of such expressions, as well as the process of interpretation a hearer would have to go through in order to understand the meaning on first exposure to the idiom. The explanatory contribution of the radial category model is thus not committed to the idea that every aspect of the ICM and extensions from it are freshly activated on every occurrence of the noun. Nevertheless, the description we have given allows a compendious and elegant representation of the conceptual links between the different aspects of the word's meaning and the extensions which they undergo.

Question   Consider the English nouns *neck, mouth, eye, nose, arm* and *back*. Are their meanings amenable to a similar treatment to that of *head*?

7.2.6 Problems with cognitive semantics

Cognitivist analyses of meaning focus on metaphor and metonymy, encyclopaedic meaning description and semantic extension, and enable a much more detailed representation of semantic content than is possible in more formal or componential approaches. The radial network models and image-schema diagrams allow a rich description of meaning that seems to make contact with perceptual and cultural aspects of language – aspects which are easily left out in other types of analysis. In spite of these attractions, however, cognitivist analyses of meaning have been criticized for a number of reasons. We will consider three:

- the ambiguity of diagrammatic representations;
- the problem of determining the core meaning; and
- the indeterminate and speculative nature of the analyses.

Diagrams like those in Figures 7.3 and following have often been criticized as inherently ambiguous. If the diagrams are to correctly indicate the meanings of the prepositions, they must not be ambiguous with entirely different concepts. This is exactly the same requirement we would place on a verbal definition: if a definition of *over* is to be accepted, it must correctly distinguish the meaning of *over* from that of other, non-synonymous expressions. The diagrams in Figure 7.3 and following, however, fail to meet this very requirement. For instance, consider Figure 7.8. This is presented as an explanation of the meaning of *over*, but there would seem to be many other ways of taking it. For example, how do we know that it is not intended as a representation of the verb *hover*? Any theory which represented *over* and *hover* as having identical meanings should surely be rejected. In a similar spirit, Figure 7.10 seems just as suited as a representation of the words *round* or *curve* as it does of the reflexive sense of *over*. The problem here is that the highly abstract nature of the diagrams allows them to apply well beyond their intended range. *Over* does not have the same meaning as *hover, round* or *curve*, yet the representations can be interpreted as referring to these concepts. This is clearly an indication that there is more to the meanings than can be captured in a visual format. If image schemas are advanced as underlying the use of terms like *over*, the diagrammatic representations we give of them seem not to go nearly far enough in bringing out the full details of the meanings involved.

Another problem concerns the radial model of category structure discussed in 7.2.5. The main cognitivist model assumes a central meaning which serves as a basis for various metaphorical and metonymic extensions from it. The problem here is that it is often hard to pin down exactly what the nature of this basic core meaning is and, as a result, exactly when we have a metonymic or metaphorical extension from it. For example, consider the metonymies in (13a) and (13d) above. In (13a), for instance, what makes us so sure that we have a metonymic extension from the basic *head* ICM? How do we know that this ICM excludes the interpretation 'thinking people' that seems active in this context? After all, it is part of the broad knowledge we have of heads that they come attached to people. Similarly, in (13d), can we be certain that the interpretation 'headache' results from a metonymic extension? We know that people often suffer from pains in the head; why should this information be considered as an *extension* from the basic *head* ICM, and not part of it?

Lastly, cognitivist theories are often criticized for their arbitrary and speculative character. The model of categorization proposed in cognitive semantics is offered as a psychologically realistic model of conceptualization, but has not yet been subjected to significant psychological experimentation, although this is beginning (Boroditsky 2000; Boroditsky & Ramscar 2002; Matlock *et al.* 2005). The analyses have largely been based on linguistic evidence – a problematic state of affairs for a theory which wants to develop a psychologically realistic model. Kamp and Reyle point to the circularity of any attempt to explain meaning ('content') by way of the mental representations lying behind uses of language:

> it won't do to base whatever one has to say about mental representations of content solely on what can be learned from studying the linguistic expressions through which these contents are publicly expressed, and then to offer mental representation as explaining the content of the corresponding expressions of the public language.
>
> (Kamp and Reyle 1993: 10)

In other words, since the main evidence for the nature of the underlying representations (ICMs, image schemas, etc.) is language itself, we have no independent means of checking that the putative representations are in fact psychologically realistic! If we want to explain the meanings of words in a psychologically realistic way, we need to do more than simply develop a theory which fits the evidence of the words themselves: there is a crucial additional step, which is to look for non-linguistic evidence of conceptualizations, and to conduct and develop experimental ways of testing the models advanced in linguistics. Without this experimental, psychologically grounded work, much about the theory seems unmotivated, and there is little to stop theorists developing models in a psychological vacuum, with nothing other than quite general hunches about what a psychologically realistic model of the mind should look like. Lakoff's analysis of *over*, for instance, has spawned a huge amount of discussion and alternative models (Vandeloise 1990, Dewell 1994, Kreitzer 1997, Tyler and Evans 2001), with, as yet, no clear way of discriminating between them. Clearly, the development of psychological or other means of testing cognitive semantics models would be welcome. In the meantime, many cognitivists would probably acknowledge that these concerns are challenges for the model. But they might also counter that the benefits of the approach – rich meaning description – are more than reason enough to pursue the programme in the hope of resolving any outstanding problems.

Summary

Two views of categorization

Categorization is a fundamental psychological process: the human mind can class different things in the world in the same category, and denote them with a single term. Since words can be seen as the names of categories, categorization has been a major focus of investigations of word meaning. Linguists and psychologists typically contrast two views of categorization:

- the **classical** view, on which membership of a given category is an either-or property, with no in-between cases. For example, on the classical view, something either is or is not a flower, or a lie, or red.
- the **prototype** view, on which a category is structured in terms of a central tendency. On this view, categories like FLOWER, LIE or RED each have more and less central (prototypical) members.

Problems with classical categorization

The classical view of categorization is rejected by many semanticists since it seems unable to account for basic semantic phenomena, such as the following:

- There are categories in which some members are better exemplars of the category than others.
- There are categories in which the boundaries of membership are not clear-cut: it is not always possible to say whether or not something is a member of the category.

Problems with prototype categorization

The prototype view is certainly able to account for these facts, but is open to several questions and problems:

- how do we identify the relevant attributes in a category?
- how can we account for the boundaries of prototype categories?
- how much of the vocabulary is structured according to prototype categories?

- prototype semantics may simply absolve the semanticist from the serious effort of lexical description
- the evidence for prototypes may be metalinguistic in nature

Cognitivist approaches to semantics

Cognitivist approaches to semantics are directly inspired by prototype theory. These approaches have four important commitments:

- an identification between meaning and conceptual structure
- a rejection of the syntax–semantics distinction
- a rejection of the semantics–pragmatics distinction
- a rejection of a modular approach to language

ICMs and image schemas

A central notion in cognitive semantics is that linguistic meaning depends on encyclopaedic knowledge structures stored in long-term memory. Lakoff (1987) calls these **idealized cognitive models** (ICMs), and sees prototype effects as explained by them. ICMs can be thought of as theories of particular subjects – the implicit knowledge we have about the objects, relations and processes named in language. The knowledge structures typically involve **image schemas**, such as CONTAINMENT, SOURCE-PATH-GOAL, FORCE, BALANCE and so on. These are organizing structures of our experience and understanding at the level of bodily perception and movement. They are usually represented diagrammatically. Image schemas are particularly useful as representations of the meanings of prepositions.

Metaphor

Metaphor is stressed in much cognitive semantics as an inherent aspect of language structure. Cognitive semantics shows that metaphor is not the exception in language: metaphorical ways of talking are just as widespread as 'literal' ones. The normal way of referring to many domains of meaning, such as that of obligation in English, is metaphorical. Lakoff and Johnson's **conceptual theory of metaphor** proposes that metaphor is a cognitive process which helps us to conceptualize our experience by setting up correspondences between easily understood things like burdens and hard to understand things like obligations. A metaphorical mapping allows knowledge about the metaphor's source or vehicle domain (burdens) to be applied to the target (obligations) in a way that fundamentally determines or influences the conceptualization of the target.

Metonymy

Another important cognitive process is **metonymy**: the concepts related by a metonymy can be understood as contiguous to (neighbouring) each other, either conceptually or in the real world.

Semantic extension and radial categories

Metaphor and metonymy constitute the principal mechanisms of **semantic extension**, as seen in expressions like *head of a queue, head of cattle* and so on. This type of structure, where there is a central case and conventionalized variations on it which cannot be predicted by general rules, is called a **radial structure**. For *head*, the central case is represented by uses consistent with the ICM described above, and the variations are the metaphoric and metonymic extensions.

Problems with cognitive semantics

Cognitive approaches to semantics have proven very popular, but can be criticized for three main reasons:

- the ambiguity of diagrammatic representations
- the problem of determining a lexical item's core meaning, and
- the indeterminate and speculative nature of the analyses.

Further Reading

Aarts *et al.* (2004) conveniently collect some key texts on linguistic categorization, along with a useful introduction. On problems with classical categorization, see Cruse (1990) and Vandeloise (1990). Rosch (1978) is a very clear summary of prototype research. See Geeraerts (1988) and Bärenfänger (2002; in German) for discussion of some of the ambiguities of prototype theory from the point of view of linguistics. See Prinz (2002: Chapter 3) for more general problems. Ross and Makin (1999) compare prototype and exemplar models of categorization. Taylor (2003) and (2002) are comprehensive outlines of issues in categorization and cognitive linguistics respectively. Lakoff (1993) concisely presents conceptual metaphor theory, as updated since the classic works in Lakoff and Johnson (1980) and Lakoff (1987); see Evans and Green (2006: Chapter 9) for a survey of subsequent developments and a useful discussion of metonymy, as well as Rakova (2003), Haser (2005) and Riemer (2005) for criticisms. There is a vast bibliography on metaphor; Goatly (1997) and Knowles and Moon (2006) are recent works. Rakova (2003) discusses metaphor and polysemy research in cognitive linguistics. The journal *Mind & Language* devoted its volume 21:3 (2006) to pragmatic work on metaphor.

Exercises

Questions for discussion

1. Construct an analysis of the semantics of *under* using image-schematic diagrams like those of 7.2.3. How many different senses need to be posited? What is the justification for doing so? Some of the uses of *under* to consider are

> *The car went under the bridge.*
> *The rug is under the table.*
> *The wall is under the painting.*
> *under a hot sun*
> *He put the box under his arm.*
> *He wore socks under his shoes.*

Run a burn under water.
There are monsters under the sea.

Compare these uses to *beneath* and *underneath.* What are the differences between the prepositions?

2. Consider the sentence *I'd had a bit to drink the previous night … and then I crashed. Crash* seems to be a cardinal example of a metaphor. What is its vehicle domain? How precisely can this be specified?

3. Consider this short example of journalistic prose:

   Rose Shaffer's heart attack taught her a lot of things that, as a nurse, she should have known. She learnt it pays to eat carefully and exercise regularly. And she learnt the hard way that if you cannot afford medical insurance, you better hope you don't get sick. (Julian Borger 'Land where calling an ambulance is first step to bankruptcy' *The Guardian* (UK), Tuesday 4 November 2003.)

   Which words are used metaphorically, and which literally? What are the vehicle domains of the metaphors? What are the target domains? Discuss any problems you encounter in trying to decide.

4. Consider the following use of *ahead of,* which is common in journalistic prose:

   Ahead of results on Monday Barclays Bank shed 5p to 351p. (OED *ahead* 6b. 1982 Times 27 Feb. 13/2)

   Explore the metaphorical aspects of this expression. Can you relate it to other metaphors in English?

5. Look up the French preposition *chez* in a French–English dictionary, and list its principal meanings.

   Propose a radial-category interpretation of the underlying semantics of this term. Are image-schematic diagrams like those in 7.2.3 suitable as a means of representing its meanings?
      What, if any, are the problems involved in doing this if one is not a native speaker of French?

6. English *get* is a highly polysemous verb which appears in many different contexts. Consult the *Oxford English Dictionary* for as many examples of *get* as you can find that date from 1900 on. Is it possible to propose a single core meaning for this word from which other senses are derived by metaphor and metonymy? (Note: there is no single, simple answer to this question. It is designed to get you thinking about the problems and possibilities of semantic analysis in the radial category model.)

7. Consider the difference between Lakoff's 'above' and 'covering' schemas for *over* (Figures 7.8 and 7.9 above). Is there a case for combining these into a single schema? What would be gained by this move? What would be lost? What evidence, if any, could we bring to bear on the question?

8. Ask three people to write down as many examples as they can of the following categories in one minute: *tool, sport, accident, vegetable.*
      How would you determine which members of each category, if any, are the most prototypical? What might the attributes be on which prototypicality is based?

9. Read Searle's 1979 essay on metaphor in Ortony's 1993 anthology, listed in the bibliography. Write a rebuttal of Searle's theory of metaphor from Lakoff's perspective.

10. A recent Australian road-safety campaign used the slogan *if you're hammered, expect to get nailed* (i.e. 'if you're drunk, expect to get arrested'). Do these expressions belong to any wider conceptual metaphors?

11. Consider the following sentences:

    The bookshop holds over 1 million *titles.*
    Upstairs for hotel and *backpackers.* [Sign]
    Since *Beijing,* the Olympics have got even more popular.

    The italicized words would traditionally be considered as examples of metonymy. Explain why, and for each example try to identify other metonymies with similar conceptual bases.

12. How might the adoption of a radial category model of word meaning solve the problem of contextual modulation of meaning discussed in 2.2.4?

8 Meaning and cognition II: formalizing and simulating conceptual representations

CHAPTER PREVIEW

In the previous chapter we looked at some proposals about the types of cognitive operation that underlie semantic ability. In this chapter, we examine some attempts to formalize and model the conceptual representations involved in language. In 8.1 we examine Jackendoff's **conceptual semantics**, a theory about the cognitive structures behind language and the modes of their interaction. This is followed by a discussion of the treatment of meaning in computational linguistics, which uses computer models of language as an aid to understanding the mental processes involved in language production and understanding (8.2). We will concentrate on the aspects of computational linguistics which give insight into the nature of the task of meaning-processing. We specifically look at WordNet, an online lexical database, at the problems of **word-sense disambiguation**, and at Pustejovsky's solution to this in his model of **qualia structure**.

8.1 Conceptual semantics

Jackendoff's **Conceptual Semantics** framework is an important approach to meaning (Jackendoff 1983, 1990, 1991, 2002, 2007). Conceptual Semantics shares a key commitment with the cognitivist approaches we looked at in the last chapter: Jackendoff rejects any distinction between meaning and conceptualization, stating (2002: 282) that 'we must consider the domain of linguistic semantics to be continuous with human conceptualization as a whole'. As a result, Jackendoff aims to situate semantics 'in an overall psychological framework, integrating it not only with linguistic theory but also with theories of perception, cognition, and conscious experience' (1990: 2). Conceptual Semantics differs from Cognitivist approaches, however, in two important ways.

- It is committed to a strict distinction between syntax and semantics. Conceptual Semantics is designed to be compatible with generative grammar, one of whose tenets is an autonomous level of syntactic organization. Consistent with this, Jackendoff sees linguistic ability as involving an interface between conceptualization on the one hand and phonology and syntax on the other.
- It uses a formalism, rather than the somewhat vague diagrams and similar notational conventions deployed in cognitivist semantics. (See Jackendoff 1990: 16 for discussion of more differences between the approaches.)

Both of these features will be discussed more below.

8.1.1 Concepts and decomposition

Like many semantic theories, Jackendoff claims that a **decompositional** method is necessary to explore conceptualization. Just as one of the ways a physical scientist tries to understand matter is by breaking it down into progressively smaller parts, so a scientific study of conceptualization proceeds by breaking down, or decomposing, meanings into smaller parts. Clearly, however, this decomposition cannot go on forever: we must 'reach bottom' at some stage. This is the level of conceptual structure, the level of mental representations which encode the human understanding of the world, containing the primitive conceptual elements out of which meanings are built, plus their rules of combination. Just as generative syntax posits a finite set of syntactic categories and rules for combining them, so Conceptual Semantics posits 'a finite set of mental primitives and a finite set of principles of mental combination' governing their interaction (Jackendoff 1990: 9). Jackendoff refers to this set of primitives and the rules governing them as the 'grammar of sentential concepts' (Jackendoff 1990: 9). His starting point is a close analysis of the meanings of lexemes, dedicated to bringing out parallelisms and contrasts which reveal the nature of the conceptual structures underlying them. What his method shows, he says, is that the psychological organization on which meaning rests 'lies a very short distance below the surface of everyday lexical items – and that progress can be made in exploring it' (1991: 44).

Since the primitives revealed by decomposition are designed to characterize thought, they are universal, not language-specific (Jackendoff 1991: 11). They are also not in themselves meaningful. This is a major point of difference between Jackendoff's approach and many others, including Wierzbicka's NSM (2.5) or those discussed in the previous chapter. Jackendoff draws a parallel between semantic and phonological analysis to explain this aspect of his system. In the analysis of phonology, we start with a level of ordinary words. This level is decomposed into a level of phonemes like English /k/, /iː/, /w/, etc., most of which cannot be words in their own right. This level of phonemes is then decomposed into a further, more abstract level of phonological features ([± voice], [± coronal], etc.). *None* of these features can constitute a word; furthermore, none can even be independently pronounced. Semantic decomposition for Jackendoff shows a similar logic. We start with the actual meanings of whole words. But when we break these meanings down, we soon 'find layers of structure whose units cannot individually serve as possible word meanings' (Jackendoff 2002: 335). This has important methodological consequences: it means that we must instead develop a set of *technical* primitives to analyse word-meanings with. The words of ordinary language are not themselves basic enough.

As a sample of the type of analysis done in Conceptual Semantics, consider the analysis of the sentence *Bill went into the house*. This has the syntactic structure shown in (1), and the underlying conceptual structure given in (2):

(1) [$_S$ [$_{NP}$ Bill] [$_{VP}$ [$_V$ went] [$_{PP}$ [$_P$ into] [$_{NP}$ the house]]]]

(2) [$_{EVENT}$ GO ([$_{THING}$ BILL], [$_{PATH}$ TO ([$_{PLACE}$ IN ([$_{THING}$ HOUSE])])])]

The square brackets in (2) identify the sentence's **conceptual constituents** – the actual 'bits' of meaning or semantic content which the sentence expresses. Each of these constituents can be assigned to a major ontological category, such as Thing, Event, State, Action, Place, Path, Property and Amount, coded in subscript capitals. Jackendoff describes these ontological categories as conceptual 'parts of speech'. Just as parts of speech like Noun, Verb and Adjective constitute a constrained set of categories to which words can be assigned on the basis of distributional criteria (see 9.1.2.1), so the ontological categories constitute the major groupings to which our concepts can be assigned on the basis of what they mean. Each major syntactic category in (1) corresponds to a conceptual constituent: the NPs *Bill* and *the house* correspond to Thing slots in the conceptual structure, the verb *went* corresponds to the Event slot, the prepositional phrase *into the house* corresponds to the Path slot.

Each conceptual category can, like logical predicates (see 6.4), take **arguments** – other elements of conceptual content which have to be inserted into positions in the formalism in order to make them complete. Every argument belongs to one of the major conceptual categories. This is illustrated in (3):

(3)   a. *John is tall.*

$[_{\text{STATE}} \text{BE} ([_{\text{THING}} \text{JOHN}], [_{\text{PROPERTY}} \text{TALL}])]$

b. *John loves Mary.*

$[_{\text{STATE}} \text{LOVE} ([_{\text{THING}} \text{JOHN}], [_{\text{THING}} \text{MARY}])]$

c. *Nina went into the room.*

$[_{\text{EVENT}} \text{GO} ([_{\text{THING}} \text{NINA}], [_{\text{PATH}} \text{TO} ([_{\text{PLACE}} \text{IN} ([_{\text{THING}} \text{ROOM}])])])]$

As these decompositions illustrate, the conceptual structure of a lexical item is an element with zero or more open argument slots, which are filled by the syntactic complements of the lexical item: *is* in (3a) expresses the major conceptual category State, whose arguments are found in the subject (*John*) and predicate adjective position (*tall*); *love* in (3b) also expresses a State-function, with the arguments supplied by the grammatical subject (*John*) and object (*Mary*); *went* in (3c) expresses an Event-function whose arguments are the subject *Nina* and the path phrase *into the room* and so on.

Let's concentrate on (3c). Jackendoff (1991: 13) gives the following explanation of the formalism. The capitalized expressions denote conceptual content. (NINA and ROOM are left unanalysed for the moment, though we assume that each does have a conceptual analysis which will need to be given for the theory to be complete.) The other three elements are the 'functions' IN, TO and GO. IN is a one-argument function: it maps a single object (here, *the room*) into a region or place that encompasses the interior of that object. TO is also a one-argument function: it maps a Thing or Place into a Path that terminates at that Thing or Place. Thus the constituent '$[_{\text{PATH}} \text{TO}$ $([_{\text{PLACE}} \text{IN} ([_{\text{THING}} \text{ROOM}])])]$' in (3c) can be read roughly as 'a trajectory that terminates at the interior of the room'. GO is a two-argument function that maps a Thing and a Path into an Event consisting of the Thing traversing the Path. Thus the entire Event in (3c) can be read roughly as 'Nina traverses a path that terminates at the interior of the room'.

Recall that Jackendoff's framework presupposes a strict division between syntax and semantics. This means that a mechanism is needed in order to associate the conceptual structure in (3c) with its syntactic realization. This is accomplished by the lexical entries of *into* and *go*, given in (4), which each contribute part of the overall conceptual structure (Jackendoff 1991: 14):

(4)   a.

into	(phonological structure)
P	(syntactic structure)
$[_{\text{PATH}} \text{TO} ([_{\text{PLACE}} \text{IN} ([_{\text{THING}}])])]$	(conceptual structure)

b.

go	(phonological structure)
V	(syntactic structure)
$[_{\text{EVENT}} \text{GO} ([_{\text{THING}}], [_{\text{PATH}}])]$	(conceptual structure)

The bottom line gives the LCS (Lexical conceptual structure) associated with each lexical item. The conceptual structure of *go* includes a Path slot as one of its arguments; this allows the Path element of (4a) to be incorporated into it; adding the subject argument into the first Thing position generates the full conceptual structure as given in (3c).

8.1.2 Developing conceptual semantics analyses

How are Conceptual Semantics analyses like these developed? As with any empirical investigation, there are no hard and fast rules. One simply starts with whatever presents itself – interesting questions, hunches, or existing analyses which seem to provide a promising starting point for further investigation. One such existing analysis is provided by the data in (5)–(8). In the spirit of Gruber (1965), Jackendoff points to the fact that there are apparent parallelisms in the use of the verbs *go*, *be* and *keep* and the prepositions *to* and *from* across four different semantic domains: spatial location and motion, possession, property-ascription and activity-scheduling (examples adapted from Jackendoff 1990: 25–26):

(5) *Spatial location and motion*
  a. *The bird **went** from the ground to the tree.*
  b. *The bird **is** in the tree.*

(6) *Possession*
  a. *The inheritance **went to** Philip.*
  b. *The inheritance **is** Philip's.*

(7) *Ascription of properties*
  a. *The light **went from** green **to red**.*
  *Harry **went from** elated **to** depressed.*
  b. *The light **is** red.*
  *Harry **is** depressed.*

(8) *Scheduling of activities*
  a. *The meeting **has gone from** Tuesday **to** Monday.*
  b. *The meeting **is** on Monday.*

These sentences show the same verbs and prepositions operating in intuitively similar ways across the four semantic domains. Concentrating simply on the verbs, the sentences with *go* (the (a) sentences in (5)–(8)) express a change of some sort, with the end points of the change being expressed by sentences using the verb *be* (the (b) sentences).

In order to capture these intuitive similarities, Jackendoff claims that *go* and *be* each realize an identical conceptual meaning across all the sentences in which they appear. He expresses these identical conceptual meanings with the following formalism:

(9) a.
$$\left[_{EVENT} GO ([\quad], \begin{bmatrix} FROM ([\quad]) \\ {}_{PATH} TO ([\quad]) \end{bmatrix})\right]$$

  b. $\left[_{STATE} BE ([\quad], [_{PLACE} \quad])\right]$

Inserting the content from (5), we get the following structure:

(10) a.

$$[_{\text{EVENT}} \text{GO} ([_{\text{THING}} \text{BIRD}], \begin{bmatrix} \text{FROM} ([_{\text{THING}} \text{GROUND}]) \\ _{\text{PATH}} \text{TO} ([_{\text{THING}} \text{GROUND}]) \end{bmatrix})$$

b. $[_{\text{STATE}} \text{BE} ([_{\text{THING}} \text{BIRD}], [_{\text{PLACE}} \text{IN} ([_{\text{THING}} \text{TREE}])])]$

The important claim that Jackendoff makes about this analysis is that it also applies to all the other (a) and (b) sentences. The scheduling examples, for instance, are represented as in (11):

(11) a.

$$[_{\text{EVENT}} \text{GO} ([_{\text{THING}} \text{MEETING}], \begin{bmatrix} \text{FROM} ([_{\text{THING}} \text{TUESDAY}]) \\ _{\text{PATH}} \text{TO} ([_{\text{THING}} \text{MONDAY}]) \end{bmatrix})]$$

b. $[_{\text{STATE}} \text{BE} ([_{\text{THING}} \text{MEETING}], [_{\text{PLACE}} \text{ON} ([_{\text{THING}} \text{MONDAY}])])]$

The other examples can be given similar analyses. All that differentiates them is a semantic field feature that specifies whether the concepts are applying to possession, property-ascription, motion, or whatever. (The change of semantic field also introduces variations in the expression of the Place argument: in (5b) and (8b) it is expressed by a prepositional phrase headed by *in* and *on* respectively; in (6b) by a possessive noun phrase (*Philip's*) and in (7b) by an adjective phrase. These variations have to be explained by other mechanisms, which do not affect the point relevant here.)

What is the advantage of this representation? Here is Jackendoff's own explanation:

> The point is that at this grain of analysis the four semantic fields have a parallel conceptual structure. They differ only in what counts as an entity being in a Place. In the spatial field, a Thing is located spatially; in possessional, a Thing belongs to someone; in ascriptional, a Thing has a property; in scheduling, an Event is located in a time period.
>
> This notation captures the lexical parallelisms in [(5)–(6)] neatly. The different uses of the words *go, … be, …, from,* and *to* in (6) are distinguished only by the semantic field feature, despite the radically different sorts of real-world events and states they pick out. (1990: 26)

BE and GO are core functions in the conceptual organization of events. Two other important ones are INCH and CAUSE. To illustrate them, let's consider the three sentences in (12).

(12) a. *The door was open.*
  b. *The door opened.*
  c. *John opened the door.*

Sentence (12a) is the conceptually simplest, consisting simply of the state function BE with Thing and Property arguments, as diagrammed in (13):

(13) [$_{\text{STATE}}$ BE ([$_{\text{THING}}$ DOOR], [$_{\text{PROPERTY}}$ OPEN])]

To obtain (12b), we add the INCH function. This stands for 'Inchoative' (Latin: 'beginning'), and denotes the coming into being of an event. *The door opened* thus receives the following analysis:

(14) [$_{\text{EVENT}}$ INCH ([$_{\text{STATE}}$ BE ([$_{\text{THING}}$ DOOR], [$_{\text{PROPERTY}}$ OPEN])])]

To get (12c), we can add the CAUS function. This stands for 'causative'. *John opened the door* is analysed as simply involving the addition of this function to the previous structure:

(15) [$_{\text{EVENT}}$ CAUSE ([$_{\text{THING}}$ JOHN], [$_{\text{EVENT}}$ INCH ([$_{\text{STATE}}$ BE ([$_{\text{THING}}$ DOOR], [$_{\text{PROPERTY}}$ OPEN])])])]

As we have seen, this is one of the attractions Jackendoff claims for Conceptual Semantics analysis: the fact that primitives postulated for one area of meaning turn out to have a wide explanatory potential (1991: 42). We will end this short description of the framework by considering two other examples of this.

The first concerns the parallelism between the plural of nouns (*mice, committees, funfairs*), and iterative uses of verbs like those in (16):

(16) The light **flashed** for ten seconds.

Here *flashed* can only be understood as indicating a repeated series of individual flashes. It has often been observed that this 'iterative' meaning can be compared to the meaning of the plural in nouns: in both cases there is a multiplicity of entities – several mice, committees, funfairs; and several separate flashes. Jackendoff therefore proposes that plural and repetitive meanings correspond to the same element in conceptual structure, which he represents as PL. When added to a Thing element, PL creates a multiplicity of things, when added to an Event element, it creates a multiplicity of events (1991: 16).

A more complex example (1991: 31) also concerns a conceptual correspondence between spatial and temporal domains. Jackendoff proposes a 4-place dimensionality feature DIM which represents the conceptual underpinnings of dimensionality. Points are conceptualized as DIM 0D, lines/curves as DIM 1D, surfaces as DIM 2D, and volumes as DIM 3D. Consider line-like entities like roads, rivers, or ribbons. Jackendoff analyses our conceptualization of their spatial qualities as involving two DIM specifications. The most basic specification is DIM 1D: this expresses the conceptualization we have of such entities as single lines. (This conceptualization is reflected in the way rivers are represented on maps, for example.) But there is also a secondary dimension, the lateral cross-section dimension. This is the dimension which we attend to when we cross a road or river, or cut a ribbon. The two dimensions are shown in Figure 8.1.

primary
dimension

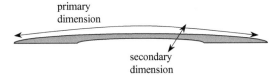

secondary
dimension

FIGURE 8.1
Primary and secondary
dimensions of a line/
curve.

The primary dimension may be conceptualized as bounded, as in a particular length of ribbon, or unbounded, as in a road that we think of as continuing indefinitely. The secondary dimension, by contrast, is always bounded: a ribbon has an edge, a road has a side, and rivers have banks. Boundedness is coded by the feature [±b]. There is also a feature [±i], which refers to 'internal structure' – whether or not the entity consists of a 'multiplicity of distinguishable individuals' (Jackendoff 1991: 19). Aggregates (the entities usually expressed by plural nouns) will be [+i], singular nouns and nouns for substances (entities normally expressed by mass nouns), will be [−i] (1991: 19–20). This gives us the following specification for the conceptual structure underlying the nouns *road*, *river* and *ribbon* in the singular. The inner brackets refer to the secondary dimension:

(17)

$$
\text{road, river, ribbon}
\begin{bmatrix}
\pm b, -i \\
\text{DIM 1D} \\
\begin{bmatrix} +b, -i \\ \text{DIM 1D} \end{bmatrix}
\end{bmatrix}
$$

Adding the [PL] operator has the function of changing the [i] value in the outer bracket to positive.

The dimensionality feature is not limited to space: it can be extended to time. Points in time (*midnight, the moment I realized my mistake*) and point-events (*the light turned on, they blinked, the climber reached the summit*) are [DIM 0D]. Periods of time and states and events with duration are [DIM 1D]. Space and time, on this picture, are thus represented by identical conceptual primitives.

Any one-dimensional entity can also have a direction, which Jackendoff represents with the feature [DIR]. Ordinary lines, for example, which are directionless, lack this feature, but arrows and vectors possess it. The direction feature allows us to generalize between Places and Paths, which we introduced above as two of the major conceptual categories in Jackendoff's system. Paths are conceptualizations like *from the starting line to the finish* or *to the lighthouse*: these are one-dimensional and directional, coded as [DIM 1D DIR]. Places, contrastingly, are non-directional, and can be regions of any dimensionality: *at this point* is zero-dimensional, *along the line* is one-dimensional, *in the circle* two-dimensional and *in the cup* three-dimensional (Jackendoff 1991: 31).

Jackendoff then applies a similar analysis to events and states. Here are his own words:

I would like to extend this, a little speculatively, to the relation between Events and States. States like *X is red* or *X is tall* are conceptualized as 'just sitting there' – they have no inherent temporal structure. … Events, by contrast, do have an inherent temporal structure which proceeds in a definite direction. I would like to suggest therefore that the two categories be combined into a supercategory called Situation, with States as the undirected case and Events as the directed case. (1991: 31)

He summarizes this as follows:

$$[\text{PLACE}] = \begin{bmatrix} \text{SPACE} \\ -\text{DIR} \end{bmatrix}$$

$$[\text{PATH}] = \begin{bmatrix} \text{SPACE} \\ \text{DIM ID DIR} \end{bmatrix}$$

$$[\text{STATE}] = \begin{bmatrix} \text{SITUATION} \\ -\text{DIR} \end{bmatrix}$$

$$[\text{EVENT}] = \begin{bmatrix} \text{SITUATION} \\ \text{DIR} \end{bmatrix}$$

This representation shows the same characteristics as the other examples we have seen – it posits a small number of abstract conceptual constituents which underlie an apparently divergent range of different meanings.

8.1.3 Problems with conceptual semantics

Jackendoff's system could be criticized for precisely this feature: its highly abstract primitives. These may permit interesting connections to be made between apparently unrelated meanings, but how justified are we in believing that these connections are cognitively real? Clearly, the more abstract the conceptual primitives we propose, the greater the number of possible connections between domains we can make. This is a similar criticism to the criticism of arbitrariness earlier made against cognitive semantics (7.2.6). What guarantee do we have, for instance, that a conceptual feature like [PL] really exists? In its current early state, the theory seems somewhat arbitrary and unconstrained: the investigator simply looks for plausible underlying conceptual structures, but there are no clear procedures for determining when a primitive is justified.

Jackendoff has addressed this question in two ways. First, he has stated that it is simply too early to demand that the theory justify its primitives: as in any immature science, all we have to go on are hunches; only when we have a good description of the semantic phenomena can we begin to constrain the theory (1990: 4). Second, he adopts a holistic approach to the justification of his primitives:

In fact, an isolated primitive can never be justified: a primitive makes sense only in the context of the overall system of primitives in which it is embedded. With this proviso, however, I think a particular choice of primitives should be justified on the grounds of its capacity for expressing generalizations and explaining the distribution of the data. That is, a proposed system of primitives is subject to the usual scientific standards of evaluation. (1991: 12)

This reply might not satisfy everyone, since it does not tell us which generalizations are psychologically real and which are merely artefacts of the analysis. One possible way of constraining the generalizations is to look for ones for which there is some independent linguistic evidence. For example,

Jackendoff's proposal that verb iterativity as illustrated in (16) above and nominal plurality are varieties of a single conceptual feature, PL, might be supported by the fact that some languages instantiate this with an identical morphological category. In Siraya, for example (Austronesian, Taiwan; extinct), reduplication had these very functions (Adelaar 2000). Another might be to look for psychological or perhaps neurological evidence to support the analyses developed in Conceptual Semantics.

A different line of criticism would be to question how we know whether the primitives are actually primitive. Perhaps it will turn out that some of them can be decomposed into even smaller conceptual units. Jackendoff is not perturbed by this possibility. He has often stated that there is no way to know exactly how far decomposition will be possible; and, in fact, his own work has suggested further decompositions for what were originally presented as primitives, such as the proposed decomposition of Path and Place into dimensionality and directionality features. Semantics is no different in this way from the decomposition characteristic of physical sciences: particle physicists do not know how far their decomposition of matter will lead, but that does not deprive their current attempts of legitimacy.

8.2 Semantics and computation

One of the obvious differences between Jackendoff's conceptual semantics and the theories examined in the previous chapter is the formal nature of Jackendoff's theory. This formal character means that Jackendoff's system is already in a form which would ideally allow it to be implemented on a computer. Computer technology has taken on great importance in linguistics generally since the 1970s, and semantics is no exception. Computers come closer than any other artificial system to matching the complexity and interconnectedness of the human brain, and it has often been assumed that we can learn important lessons about the way language is processed in real-life minds/brains by trying to simulate this ability computationally.

The mind as a computer

Belief in the similarities between human minds and computers has been crucial for many strands of research into human cognitive abilities. The Chomskyan revolution in linguistics, for one, was just part of a growing tendency to understand human cognition itself, including language, as a series of computational operations performed over mentally represented symbols. On this view, there is not just an analogy between the operation of human cognition and a computer program: the two processes are fundamentally identical, since the human mind *is*, first and foremost, an information processing system that works in the same way as a von Neumann (stored-program) computer, i.e. by performing specific formal operations over strings of symbols. This view of the mind as a computer is at the heart of the classical research programme in artificial intelligence (AI). See 1.6.3.

Computer simulations are not simply of theoretical interest, however. They also contribute to diverse practical applications, such as machine translation, the development of searchable corpora, speech recognition, spell-checking, and so on. Much of the research in computational linguistics is geared precisely towards these practical applications, and is conducted just as much by computer scientists as by linguists. This means that computational linguistics is a highly cross-disciplinary field. Another result is that researchers are often more interested in satisfying practical needs rather than theoretical ones. A software engineer concerned to develop a functional natural-language processing system will have scant regard for the psychological plausibility of the result: what determines its success is simply whether it performs the task at hand, not whether it does this in a way that might mirror human abilities. It is therefore important not to expect to learn too much about the mind/brain from computer simulation. Computer architectures certainly are the closest simulations available for the complexity of the brain, but they still vastly underperform humans in linguistic ability, as anyone who has used such functions as grammar checkers, automatic translation programmes, voice recognition systems and the like will be able to agree. One reason for this may be that there are, in fact, many respects in which the analogy between mind and computer breaks down. (There have been many critiques of attempts to understand and model the mind on the analogy of computers. Searle 1980 and Dreyfus 1992 are two prominent examples.)

Another reason not to attach excessive significance to the mind–computer parallel comes from the history of technology. As has often been pointed out, it frequently proves to be the case that artificial simulations of natural abilities harness *different* underlying principles from those actually found in nature. For example, early attempts to build flying-machines tried to replicate bird flight, in the belief that the movable wing structures found in nature provided the best solution to the engineering problems involved. These attempts, however, never succeeded. The flying technology perfected by humans uses fixed-wing principles, which, of course, are unknown in birds. Fixed-wing flying is ultimately responsible to the same physical principles as bird flight, but makes use of them in a fundamentally different way. There is a cautionary lesson to be learnt here. An artificial system can accomplish similar goals to a natural one through quite different means. It may therefore be mistaken to look to artificial computer simulations of natural language for specific insights into the nature of the human language faculty: the neurological and psychological process of language may be entirely unlike the computational processes of a computer.

But the brain need not resemble a computer for the study of computer simulation of human linguistic ability to be fruitful. Whether or not humans and computers process information in fundamentally similar ways, we can look to computer simulation as a way of appreciating, often in fine detail, the *tasks* which any language-processor, people included, must perform. Computer programs are blind. They cannot rely on humans' general intelligence in solving problems or applying general principles to particular cases. A computer will not fill in gaps using general common-sense knowledge. Instead, every step of a programme must be explicitly spelled out in minute detail if the 'right' result is to be achieved. The process of automating natural linguistic abilities therefore demands a fine-grained attention to the detail of linguistic processes. This requires computational linguistic programmes to be specified in extremely close detail. Only when language is simulated by a machine can we test the explicitness and completeness of a given linguistic theory. In this section, we will therefore concentrate on the aspects of computational linguistics which give insight into the nature of the task of language-processing as it concerns semantics.

8.2.1 The lexicon in computational linguistics

Computers' ability to store and process large amounts of information makes them particularly valuable tools for the modelling of lexical knowledge, easily the aspect of human linguistic ability in which the greatest quantity of information has to be manipulated. Apart from their speed, computer lexical databases have a major advantage over dictionaries, their paper competitors. Whereas dictionaries only allow words to be searched for alphabetically, an electronic database allows for as many different search criteria as there are different data-codes in the entries (Fellbaum 1998: 7). This allows a much more efficient retrieval of information.

The most comprehensive attempt to model lexical knowledge on a computer is the **WordNet** project, which has been running since 1985. WordNet is an online lexical database which sets out to represent and organize lexical semantic information in a psychologically realistic form that facilitates maximally efficient digital manipulation. So far, the creators of WordNet have completed the coding of many thousands of English nouns, verbs, adjectives and adverbs; similar work has also been begun in a range of other languages.

The basic motivation behind WordNet was the 'patterning assumption': the assumption that ' people could not master and have readily available all the lexical knowledge needed to use a natural language unless they could take advantage of systematic patterns and relations among the meanings that words can be used to express' (Miller 1998: xv). WordNet shows words' mutual interrelations within the system (the 'net') of lexical relations such as synonymy, antonymy, hyponymy, entailment, and so on (see Chapter 5). The main organizational unit in WordNet is the **synset**, conventionally marked by curly brackets. Synsets are groupings of near-synonyms, like {*beat, crush, trounce, vanquish*}, which identify a particular lexicalized concept (word sense): here, the 'defeat' sense of *beat*. Each synset is given a short definition or gloss: 'come out better in a competition, race, or conflict' is the WordNet gloss of this synset, and serves as a definition of *all* the words in that synset.

Polysemous words are dealt with by being assigned to multiple synsets, one for each sense. Thus *beat* also belongs to the following synsets (Fellbaum 1990: 279): {*beat, flatten*}, {*beat, throb, pulse*}, {*beat, flog, punish*}, {*beat, shape, do metalwork*}, {*beat, baffle*}, {*beat, stir, whisk*} and so on. Each of these synsets reflects a different sense of the verb – the 'change' sense, the 'pulsate' sense, and so on. Similarly, the polysemous noun *board* belongs to the synsets {*board, plank*} and {*board, committee*}. There is also the sense found in collocations like *full board* and *room and board*, for which a suitable synonym is not available; in cases like these the gloss of the meaning is used to identify the intended sense: {*board*, (a person's meals, provided regularly for money)}.

WordNet's focus on synonyms means that it is just as much a sophisticated thesaurus as a dictionary. In many ways, it privileges a thesaurus-style, relational representation of semantic information over a dictionary-like, definitional one. Originally, WordNet's designers believed that the synsets on their own would be adequate to identify the different senses of terms, and that there would be no need to supply glosses. 'For example,' explains Miller (Miller *et al.* 1990: 240), 'someone who knows that *board* can signify either a piece of lumber or a group of people assembled for some purpose will be able to pick out the intended sense with no more help than *plank* or *committee*. The synonym sets, {*board, plank*} and {*board, committee*} can serve as unambiguous designators of these two meanings of *board*.' But it soon became obvious that glosses were needed to separate different senses of words, and to identify the meanings involved. That itself, of course, is an interesting result. The amount of synonymy in the lexicon is simply not adequate to differentiate the total number of words' senses, since many senses exist for which there simply are no synonyms. The entry for the noun *key* is a good example of this situation. Synsets 1, 2, 3, 5, 6, 7 and 10 have no other members than *key* itself, and the sense is only identified by a gloss (in round brackets).

1. {key (metal device shaped in such a way that when it is inserted into the appropriate lock the lock's mechanism can be rotated)}
2. {key (something crucial for explaining)} 'the key to development is economic integration'
3. {key (pitch of the voice)} 'he spoke in a low key'
4. {key, tonality (any of 24 major or minor diatonic scales that provide the tonal framework for a piece of music)}
5. {key (a list of answers to a test)} 'some students had stolen the key to the final exam'
6. {key (a list of words or phrases that explain symbols or abbreviations)}
7. {key (a generic term for any device whose possession entitles the holder to a means of access)} 'a safe-deposit box usually requires two keys to open it'
8. {winder, key (mechanical device used to wind another device that is driven by a spring (as a clock))}
9. {keystone, key, headstone (the central building block at the top of an arch or vault)}
10. {key (a lever that actuates a mechanism when depressed)}

This is an interesting finding about the extent of synonymy in English. English is known to be a language rich in synonyms, but even so it frequently turns out that words have numerous senses for which no synonyms exist.

Hyponymy/taxonomy is another crucial relation for the organization of WordNet, which displays the entire hyponymic/taxonomic hierarchy for every noun. For example, the nouns *table* and *furniture* would be linked by a hyponym–superordinate relation: the WordNet entry for *table* would include a pointer that labelled *furniture* as the superordinate term, called the **hypernym** (Miller 1998: xvi; in Chapter 5 we call it the *hyperonym*). These hyponymy relations can be followed in both directions. Thus, the following tree of synsets contains *furniture* and *table*:

<table>
<tr><td></td><td>{entity}</td><td></td></tr>
<tr><td></td><td>{physical entity}</td><td></td></tr>
<tr><td></td><td>{object, physical object}</td><td></td></tr>
<tr><td></td><td>{whole, unit}</td><td></td></tr>
<tr><td>**hyponymy**</td><td>{artefact}</td><td>**hypernymy**</td></tr>
<tr><td></td><td>{instrumentality, instrumentation}</td><td></td></tr>
<tr><td></td><td>{furnishing}</td><td></td></tr>
<tr><td></td><td>{furniture, piece of furniture, article of furniture}</td><td></td></tr>
<tr><td></td><td>{bed}, {cabinet}, {chest of drawers}, {table} etc.</td><td></td></tr>
</table>

Several of the hypernyms, such as {instrumentality, instrumentation} and {whole, unit} are probably not typical of natural discourse. Nevertheless, their inclusion in the hierarchy is claimed to reflect the conceptual structure of the vocabulary.

The fact that every noun is linked to its hyponyms and superordinates creates what is normally known in computer science as an **inheritance hierarchy**. Standard dictionary entries rely on readers' general intelligence to supplement definitions with necessary information that is only implicit. For instance, a standard definition of *tree* – say 'a large, woody, perennial plant with a distinct trunk' – does not say anything about trees having roots, or consisting of cells having cellulose walls, or even being living organisms: the reader is expected to assume all of that information by virtue of the fact that trees are plants. But the dictionary itself doesn't make this connection explicit – and, in fact, a reader needs to know which sense of *plant* is the relevant one to the definition of *tree*: the biological one, or the one that means 'place where a product is manufactured'. All of this implicit information 'is omitted on the assumption that the reader is not an idiot, a Martian, or a computer' (Miller 1990: 246). In an inheritance hierarchy, however, each term 'inherits' the information associated with its hypernyms. In WordNet, the user can immediately see the inheritance hierarchy of the term in question, thereby gaining access to all the relevant definitional information. Here, for example, is the inheritance hierarchy for *French horn*, in which each synset is the hyponym of the one above it:

1. {musical instrument, instrument (any of various devices or contrivances that can be used to produce musical tones or sounds)}

2. {wind instrument, wind (a musical instrument in which the sound is produced by an enclosed column of air that is moved by the breath)}
3. {brass, brass instrument (a wind instrument that consists of a brass tube (usually of variable length) that is blown by means of a cup-shaped or funnel-shaped mouthpiece)}
4. {French horn, horn (a brass musical instrument consisting of a conical tube that is coiled into a spiral and played by means of valves)}

By viewing the complete inheritance hierarchy all at once, the WordNet user has access to far more definitional information than would be available for the single term *French horn* alone. The user also has immediate access to a range of other information about the definiendum: for instance, simply by clicking on the 'sister term' link, the user gains access to a list of *other* hyponyms of *brass instrument*, such as *trombone*, *bugle* and *flugelhorn*, which occupy the same level of the hyponymic tree as *French horn*. As Miller (1990: 247) puts it, 'lexicographers make an effort to cover all of the factual information about the meanings of each word, but the organization of the conventional dictionary into discrete, alphabetized entries and the economic pressure to minimize redundancy make the reassembly of this scattered information a formidable chore'. The electronic possibilities of an electronic database greatly reduce the difficulty of the task.

This is not the only advantage of the explicit labelling of the relations between words in WordNet: another is that the user is given great freedom of movement. 'Unlike in a thesaurus, the relations between concepts and words in WordNet are made explicit and labeled; users select the relation that guides them from one concept to the next and choose the direction of their navigation in conceptual space' (Fellbaum 1998: 8). Finally, not the smallest advantage of an inheritance hierarchy is that it saves space: since each piece of information percolates down the hierarchy, it does not need to be reduplicated at several different points.

So far, we have mainly considered the representation of nouns in WordNet. Other parts of speech pose different representational problems. Here we only have space to briefly consider verbs. There are fewer genuine synonyms for verbs than for nouns in English (Fellbaum 1990: 280), a situation which reduces the usefulness of the synset as a means of identifying verb meaning. An inheritance hierarchy arrangement also organizes the representation of verbs. The verbal equivalent of hyponymy/taxonomy is the relation of **troponymy**. A verb *x* is the troponym of a second verb *y* if to *x* is to *y* in some particular way. Thus, *stroll* is a troponym of *walk*, *gobble* a troponym of *eat*, and *punch* a troponym of *hit*. Verb hierarchies are much shallower than noun hierarchies, typically showing no more than four levels (Fellbaum 1990: 287). Furthermore, antonymy is another significant structuring principle.

QUESTION Explore WordNet's representation of verbs further by starting with the entry for *walk*. What are the differences between the information supplied in the *walk* (n.) entry and the *walk* (v.) entry?

We will end this discussion by considering some of the problems of WordNet. First, WordNet does not have a principled means for determining the number of polysemous senses of a word. As a result, its distinction between different senses can often seem arbitrary. For instance, consider the WordNet entry for *trouble*:

1. {trouble, problem (a source of difficulty)} 'one trouble after another delayed the job'; 'what's the problem?'
2. {fuss, trouble, bother, hassle (an angry disturbance)} 'he didn't want to make a fuss'; 'they had labor trouble'; 'a spot of bother'
3. {trouble (an event causing distress or pain)} 'what is the trouble?'; 'heart trouble'
4. {trouble, difficulty (an effort that is inconvenient)} 'I went to a lot of trouble'; 'he won without any trouble'; 'had difficulty walking'; 'finished the test only with great difficulty'
5. {worry, trouble (a strong feeling of anxiety)} 'his worry over the prospect of being fired'; 'it is not work but worry that kills'; 'he wanted to die and end his troubles'
6. {trouble (an unwanted pregnancy)} 'he got several girls in trouble'

This arrangement of senses could be accused of masking the fundamental similarity between these different senses. Indeed, an argument could be mounted that *trouble* only has a single sense in English.

QUESTION   Can you formulate a definition of *trouble* that accounts for all of the sentences quoted in the WordNet entry?

Relatedly, the format of WordNet entries obscures the fundamental difference between homonymy and polysemy. The user who consults the entry for *bank*, for instance, finds no indication that the two senses 'financial institution' and 'sloping land, especially by water' are semantically unrelated. These two meanings simply appear in the list of senses, in exactly the same way as the 'problem' and 'unwanted pregnancy' senses of *trouble*, between which there *is* a clear relation. Most theories of lexical representation would assume, however, that there is a fundamental distinction here that needs to be recognized, expressed by saying that *trouble* exemplifies polysemy, and *bank* homonymy.

Both these problems can be summarized by questioning the extent to which the principles underlying WordNet live up to the psychological realism for which its creators were aiming. WordNet is motivated by the patterning assumption, but there has been very little attempt to reflect the results of psycholinguistic studies of meaning. Indeed, the restriction of the number of semantic relations which WordNet recognizes constitutes a serious limitation. There is no formal way in WordNet to recognize contextual relations between words like *ball, racquet* and *net*. The fact that these all belong to a single semantic domain – that of ball-games – is presumably a fact of some psychological importance, but WordNet has no way of representing it, since the relation does not correspond to any of the semantic relations which the database recognizes. This would seem to significantly compromise the seriousness with which WordNet can be viewed as a complete model of human lexical memory. Murphy (2003: 113) sums this criticism up as follows: 'while WordNet has been claimed to be a psycholinguistic model, its architects have used psycholinguistic evidence selectively and its architecture limits it severely'.

8.2.2 Word sense disambiguation

WordNet may well be criticized for arbitrariness in its division of words into different polysemous senses, but no one doubts that a division of some kind is a practical necessity. Any automatic language processing system will have to be able to 'individuate' (differentiate between/disambiguate) the different senses of polysemous or homonymous word-forms if it is to correctly interpret the meaning of a sentence. For instance, the failure to distinguish between the different senses of the highlighted words in (18) would be disastrous for any automated translation of the sentences:

(18) a. *The **bank** will have more **branches** after the expansion.*
  b. *The **match** really **ignited** after half time.*
  c. *The tailor gave him a **cuff** around his neck.*
  d. *The insider-trading scandal led to the **chair** being kicked off the **board**.*
  e. *I just can't see the **point** of a compass when you've got a GPS system.*

Since in French, for instance, the two senses of *bank* are translated by two different words (*rive* for the 'edge of river' sense and *banque* for 'financial institution'), a necessary first step in any automatic translation is the selection of the appropriate sense for the context. If this is not done, we risk obtaining translations of the following meanings:

(19) a. The financial institution will have more tree-parts after the expansion.
  b. The small wooden shaft with flammable head started spontaneously burning after half time.
  c. The tailor gave him a sleeve-end around his neck.
  d. The insider-trading scandal led to the piece of furniture being kicked off the hard flat rectilinear surface.
  e. I just can't see the tip of a compass when you've got a GPS system.

In natural language, sentences (18a–e) do not typically create confusion. Why not is still a mystery. We do not yet know how humans succeed in picking the right senses of ambiguous words: the relevant psychological processes are simply not at all understood (see Taylor 2003: Chapter 8 for discussion). This is quite a remarkable state of affairs. As discussed in 5.3, polysemy is a universal feature of natural language. If we do not understand how the correct polysemous sense is selected in a particular context, we clearly lack a fundamental part of the explanation of linguistic processes.

  Developing a successful sense-individuation procedure for computers may therefore give us some clues about the relative advantages of different solutions to the problem. It will not, of course, show us what procedures the human mind *does* in fact use, but it may give us some insight into the nature of the task and point us in the direction of likely hypotheses. Given the complexity of the task of developing a sense-individuation procedure, we fortunately do not need to aim for complete accuracy. After all, people do not themselves correctly identify the intended sense one hundred per cent of the time in ambiguous contexts: as an initial goal, we should not expect to develop programs which achieve full accuracy either.

There are currently two main approaches to word-sense disambiguation in computational linguistics. The first, the **selectional restriction** approach (Hirst 1987), generates complete semantic representations for all the words in a sentence, and then eliminates those which violate selectional restrictions coded in the component words. For instance, consider (20), taken from Jurafsky and Martin (2000: 632):

(20) a. *In our house, everybody has a career and none of them includes washing* **dishes***.*

b. *In her tiny kitchen at home, Ms Chen works efficiently, stir-frying several simple* **dishes***, including braised pig's ears and chicken livers with green peppers.*

Dish is ambiguous between the senses 'piece of crockery' and 'course in a meal'. Selection restrictions on the patient argument of the verbs in (20) would be used to exclude the wrong reading of *dish*. The lexical entry for *wash* would include the specification that the verb could only take a physical object as its patient argument, which would guarantee the correct reading in (20a), and the entry for *stir-fry* would specify that the argument had to belong to the category of food in (20b). These selectional restrictions would be encoded reasonably straightforwardly by adopting categories from WordNet: thus, the possible object of *wash* could be limited to any noun which had 'artefact' or 'natural object' as a hypernym, and the possible object of *stir-fry* to nouns with 'food' as a hypernym. In both these cases, selectional restrictions on the verbs eliminate the wrong sense of the nouns.

Similarly, *serve* in the following sentences has three different senses (Jurafsky and Martin 2000: 633):

(21) a. *Well, there was the time they* **served** *green-lipped mussels from New Zealand.*
(*provide* [food] *as a meal sense*)

b. *Which airlines* **serve** *Denver?*
(*include on transport network sense*)

c. *Which ones* **serve** *breakfast?*
(*provide* [meal] *sense*)

Once again, selectional restrictions can be used to ensure the correct interpretation is reached: the sense in (21a) is only found with food objects; the (21b) sense only with place objects, and (21c) only with meal objects. Giving the program access to this information would allow the wrong interpretations to be avoided.

QUESTION   What are some problems and limitations of this procedure?

One major problem with this approach is that selection restrictions will often not be available to resolve ambiguities. 'What kind of dishes would you recommend?' is one such example: either the 'course in meal' or the 'piece of crockery' sense could be intended. While the non-linguistic context would probably resolve the ambiguity, nothing in the linguistic context itself does. Another difficulty is caused by the fact that selection restrictions may often be violated. For instance, the representation of the meaning of *eat* would presumably contain the restriction that only food could be selected as object. Jurafsky and Martin cite (22) as examples of perfectly well-formed sentences which violate this restriction:

(22) *You can't eat gold for lunch if you're hungry.*
In his two championship trials, Mr Kulkarni ate glass on an empty stomach, accompanied only by water and tea.

More generally, the ubiquity of metaphor and metonymy in language poses significant problems for sense-individuation based on selectional restrictions, since these create contexts in which words' typical co-occurrence restrictions do not hold.

A possible solution to these problems might be to take selection restrictions not as absolute criteria which must be met, but as probabilistic preferences (Resnik 1998). There is not time to discuss this development here, beyond noting that this way of thinking is a semantic analogue to the optimality theory approach to syntax and phonology, which describes grammatical phenomena not as the results of absolute rules, but as the most optimal results of the satisfaction of competing constraints. We should also note that Resnik (1998) only reported fairly low success rates with this approach, an average of 44 per cent for verb–object relationships. This is actually an improvement over the average success rate of 28 per cent (Jurafsky and Martin 2000: 633–634). The extreme modesty of these figures highlights the difficulty of the task.

The other approach uses the **immediate context** of the target word as a clue in identifying the intended sense. The computer assesses the words surrounding the target word, and chooses the appropriate sense on the basis of the other words in this immediate context (the size of this 'window' varies from program to program). For instance, if the word to be disambiguated is *pen*, the 'writing implement' sense will be chosen if other words in the environment include *paper, write*, etc., whereas 'sty' will be chosen if the words are 'pig', 'feed', 'farm' and so on. Similarly, Manning and Schütze (1999: 238) give the following contextual clues for sense disambiguation of *drug*:

(23) 'medication' sense: *prices, prescription, patent, increase, consumer, pharmaceutical*
'illegal substance' sense: *abuse, paraphernalia, illicit, alcohol, cocaine, traffickers*

QUESTION   Suggest possible contextual clues for the different senses of *tank*, *match* and *interest*.

There are many contexts, however, which pose a problem for these context-based disambiguation procedures. Wilks *et al.* (1996: 202) discuss the particular problem posed by a sentence like *The young page put the goat in the pen*. This will be a challenge for any disambiguation procedure that chooses the relevant word sense on the basis of the immediate context, since the cooccurrence of *pen* and *page* might lead to the wrong sense of each being chosen. Other sentences which might raise a similar problem are the following:

(24) *A cigarette is no **match** for a pipe.*
      *The **table** displays the location of the **beds** in the Botanic garden.*
      *The censors **screened** all films for unsuitable content.*
      *The painter put on a new **coat**.*

QUESTION   Are there other contextual features of the sentence which would allow these problems to be avoided?

These studies are in their infancy, and we can certainly expect improvements in the efficiency of disambiguation programs. Nevertheless, the fact that most current disambiguation processes have been tested on a very small number of lexical items, or report low success rates, means that the question of polysemy and sense-disambiguation will be the focus of intense theoretical and applied research for some time to come.

8.2.3 Pustejovskian semantics

The problem of word-sense disambiguation was the stimulus for an important approach to the lexicon in computational linguistics developed by Pustejovsky (1991, 1995; Pustejovsky and Boguraev 1994). This approach, dubbed the **generative lexicon** approach, claims to solve many of the types of problem seen in the previous section by adopting an entirely different picture of lexical information. Pustejovsky criticizes the standard view of the lexicon, on which each lexeme is associated with a fixed number of senses. Lexical databases like WordNet are exactly like traditional dictionaries, in that they simply enumerate a static number of fixed senses for every word. Pustejovsky and Boguraev describe the generative lexicon alternative as follows:

In contrast, rather than taking a 'snapshot' of language at any moment of time and freezing it into lists of word-sense specifications, the model of the lexicon proposed here does not preclude extendability; it is open-ended in nature and accounts for the novel, creative uses of words in a variety of contexts by positing procedures for generating semantic expressions for words on the basis of particular contexts.

(Pustejovsky and Boguraev 1994: 297)

This can be exemplified with the adjective *fast*, which traditional descriptions (including WordNet) need to credit with a large number of different senses. For instance, *fast* seems to have rather different senses in the three phrases in (25):

(25) a. *a fast typist* (one who types quickly)
b. *a fast car* (one which can move quickly)
c. *a fast waltz* (one with a fast tempo) (Pustejovsky 1995: 413)

These uses of *fast* seem to involve at least three senses: 'performing an act quickly' (25a), 'moving quickly' (25b) and 'involving a fast tempo' (25c). Any computer needs to keep these senses separate, recognizing, for example, that a 'fast typist' is not one who moves quickly in the way that a fast car does. This is usually achieved simply by listing a number of distinct senses for *fast*. Pustejovsky notes a problem with this strategy: it will not account for 'creative applications' of the adjective in English, like *fast motorway* or *fast garage*. Neither of these fits any of the senses in (25): the former refers to a motorway on which vehicles can travel fast, the latter to a garage which services cars quickly. Pustejovsky claims that the standard sense-listing approach to the lexicon will always fail to cover *all* the possible meanings of an adjective like *fast*; furthermore, it is 'unable to capture interesting generalizations concerning relationships between "senses" of the same word' (Pustejovsky and Boguraev 1994: 302).

In order to avoid these problems, Pustejovsky proposes that lexical analysis needs to recognize different levels or perspectives of lexical meaning. Two of these levels, argument structure and lexical inheritance, are already familiar. Argument structure is the level of lexical representation for verbs which specifies the number and type of noun complements (see Chapter 10). Lexical inheritance structure refers to the conceptual relations between words in the lexicon, as discussed in 8.2.1. In addition, Pustejovsky identifies **event structure** (see 10.2), and **qualia structure** as crucial levels of word meaning. We will concentrate here on qualia structure.

Qualia structure is a system of relations that has a similar importance for the meaning of nouns as argument structure has for verbs. It reflects those aspects of the referent of a noun which 'have long been considered crucial for our common-sense understanding of how things interact in the world' (Pustejovsky and Boguraev 1994: 305). A word's qualia structure has four aspects, its **Constitutive Role**, **Formal Role**, **Telic Role** and **Agentive Role**. These roles constitute the framework for the word's meaning. Pustejovsky describes the type of information expressed by these roles as follows (1995: 426):

1. **Constitutive Role**: the relation between an object and its constituents, or proper parts.
   - Material
   - Weight
   - Parts and component elements

2. **Formal Role**: that which distinguishes the object within a larger domain.
   - Orientation
   - Magnitude

- Shape
- Dimensionality
- Colour
- Position

3. **Telic Role**: purpose and function of the object.
   - Purpose that an agent has in performing an act
   - Built-in function or aim that specifies certain activities

4. **Agentive Role**: factors involved in the origin or 'bringing about' of an object.
   - Creator
   - Artefact
   - Natural Kind
   - Causal Chain

How does this relate to the problem of determining the right meaning of *fast* in the examples above? The essence of Pustejovsky's theory is that the lexical entry for *fast* specifies that it only ever applies to the telic role of nominals. The telic role specifies the purpose and function of the noun. Thus the specification of the telic role of *motorway* tells us that a motorway's purpose is to bring about a certain event, road travel: this is what *fast* is referring to. Similarly, *typist* has a telic role determining the function of performing a different type of event: typing, and it is this which *fast* qualifies. Similarly, a fast waltz is fast with respect to the telic role of that noun, which will refer to dancing. By introducing an additional level of structure into the description of nominals, this approach succeeds in retaining a single meaning for *fast*, which will be defined as something like 'at a rapid rate'; the contextual meanings it takes on in the noun phrases above are a result of the differing telic roles to which this single meaning applies.

Easy and *hard* might be two other adjectives which are specified as referring to a noun's telic role. Thus, *easy books*, *easy loads*, *easy (ski) slopes* and *easy software* are easy with respect to their telic roles: being read, being lifted, being skied down and being used. Similar remarks apply to *hard*. We are not likely to interpret an *easy book* as a book that is easy to lift, since lifting is not part of the event described in the telic role for book.

Another application of qualia structure occurs in the analysis of sentences like (26a) and (26b):

(26) a. *Sam baked a potato.*
     b. *Sam baked a cake.*

The sentences' interpretations are fundamentally different: the potato exists before Sam baked it, whereas the cake is only created by the act of baking. Pustejovsky (1995: 421–423) accounts for this contrast through differing agentive roles in the qualia structure of the two nouns. *Cake* is classified as an artefact; as a result, it is part of our specific lexical knowledge about it that there is an event associated with its coming into being. The verb *bake* is thus interpreted as referring to this aspect of the noun's qualia structure. *Potato*, on the other hand, is classified as a natural kind. It cannot therefore be brought into being by any artificial process. The predicate *bake* is thus understood as denoting an action which takes place on the potato, but which does not bring the potato into being.

The introduction of qualia structure allows us to avoid postulating a large number of polysemous senses for a single lexical item. Systematic ambiguity in words like *fast, easy* and *bake* is not explained by postulating multiple senses for these words, but by recognizing that the underlying structure of their associated nominals is more complex than was originally thought. The increased semantic complexity of lexical entries for nominals is ultimately a saving, since the uniformity of qualia structure allows both a systematic account of polysemy and a reduction in the overall number of senses postulated in the lexicon.

Summary

Jackendoff: Conceptual Semantics

Jackendoff's **Conceptual Semantics** shares with cognitive semantics a commitment to analysing meaning as inherently linked to conceptualization. Its most important difference from cognitive semantics is that it uses a formalism.

Decomposition and conceptual primitives

Jackendoff claims that a **decompositional** method is necessary to explore conceptual structure, in which the concepts underlying word meaning are broken down into their smallest elements: conceptual primitives envisaged as the semantic equivalents of phonological features. Conceptual Semantics posits 'a finite set of mental primitives and a finite set of principles of mental combination' governing their interaction. The conceptual structure of a lexical item is an element with zero or more open argument slots, which are filled by the syntactic complements of the lexical item. Jackendoff's system permits interesting connections to be made between apparently unrelated meanings, but can be criticized for the apparently somewhat arbitrary nature of the conceptual constituents it recognizes.

Modelling meaning computationally

Computers come closer than any other artificial system to matching the complexity and interconnectedness of the human brain, and it has often been assumed that the attempt to simulate human linguistic ability computationally will teach us important lessons about the way language is processed in real-life minds/brains. This is particularly true of studies of words and their meanings, though it is important not to push the mind–computer analogy too far.

WordNet and the lexicon

The most comprehensive attempt to model lexical knowledge on a computer is **WordNet**, an online lexical database which sets out to represent and organize lexical semantic information in a psychologically realistic form that facilitates maximally efficient digital manipulation. The main organizational unit in WordNet is the **synset**. Synsets are groupings of near-synonyms, arranged into hyponymic/taxonomic trees called **inheritance hierarchies**. Each term in an inheritance hierarchy 'inherits' the information associated with its hypernyms: this gives the user immediate access to the full range of information associated with a lexical item.

Word sense disambiguation

One of the hardest problems in computer simulations of natural language processing is the problem of word-sense disambiguation. Computers must know how to distinguish between the different senses of ambiguous words like *bank* if they are to be able to process language correctly. We discussed two main approaches to this task:

- **selectional restriction** approaches, which use selectional restrictions to weed out improperly formed semantic representations; and
- the **contextual** approach, in which the computer assesses the words surrounding the target word, and chooses the appropriate sense on the basis of the other words in this immediate context.

Both approaches are in their infancy and programs using them significantly underperform humans.

Pustejovsky and qualia structure

Pustejovsky attempts to solve a number of problems in word-sense disambiguation by proposing a richer structure for nominal entries in the lexicon. He claims that the meaning of nouns is best modelled by the notion of **qualia structure**. A noun's qualia structure consists of four roles, the **constitutive**, **formal**, **telic** and **agentive roles**. The key element of Pustejovsky's theory is that each of these roles can operate independently within the semantics of a clause. For example, we know that a *fast car* is one that moves quickly, and a *fast motorway* is one on which cars can move quickly, since *fast* applies to the telic role of the noun: the role that refers to the function or purpose which the referent fulfils.

Further reading

For an exposition of conceptual semantics, Jackendoff (2002) is a convenient summary, and situates the theory within a wider approach to language. Jackendoff (1989) explains the background to the theory. WordNet can be used online at http://wordnet. princeton.edu/. See www.globalwordnet.org/ for links to non-English WordNets. For discussion of WordNet, see the special issue of the *International Journal of Lexicography* 3 (4) 1990, updated in Fellbaum (1998). Jackendoff (2002: 369ff) is a discussion of Pustejovsky. Blackburn and Bos (2005) is an introduction to computational semantics which assumes minimal background in logic.

Exercises

Analytical questions

1. Look up WordNet at http://wordnet.princeton.edu/perl/webwn. Find the definitions for the synsets containing the following words: *dream* (n.), *chief, dramatic, manage.* How adequate are these definitions? Do they apply equally to every word in the synset?

2. What factors could be used by a natural language processing system to distinguish correctly between the two readings of *relish* in *I ate the meat with relish*? What clues might *people* use to infer the correct reading in natural conversation?

Questions for discussion

3. Both Jackendoff's proposals about conceptual structure and the image schemas discussed in Chapter 7 propose to uncover an identical meaning structure underlying apparently unrelated expressions. To what extent are the proposals similar? How explanatory are they?

4. How many of the ambiguities in 8.2.2 could be solved by adopting a qualia-structure approach to the semantics of nominals?

5. Consider the following nouns: *day, computer, haircut, meal, mail, news-day, thinker, book, beginning* and *oven.* How many different senses of *slow* would it be necessary to posit to account for the following noun phrases: *a slow day, a slow computer, a slow haircut, a slow meal, the slow mail, a slow news-day, a slow thinker, a slow book, a slow beginning, a slow oven*? Can you give a description of these nouns' telic or other roles which would explain the different senses of *slow*?

9 Meaning and morphosyntax I: the semantics of grammatical categories

CHAPTER PREVIEW

This chapter and the next investigate a range of semantic phenomena which are relevant to morphosyntax. This chapter focuses on morphosyntactic categories such as noun and verb and tense and aspect. The major questions are these:

◆ Does a word's meaning determine its grammatical category?
◆ How can we describe the meanings of major verbal categories like tense and aspect?

We begin with a discussion of the meaning of lexical categories (parts of speech), exploring the possible semantic contribution made by a word's categorization as noun, verb, adjective, and so on (9.1). Section 9.2 focuses on the verb, investigating the semantics of tense and aspect: two central dimensions of verb meaning with major consequences on the verbal and clausal levels.

9.1 The semantics of parts of speech

Analysing a language grammatically involves analysing it into a variety of elements and structures: phonemes, morphemes and words, and, within the words, syntactic categories of various sorts. Among these categories are the **parts of speech** (also known as **lexical** or **grammatical categories**): noun, verb, adjective, determiner and so on. We usually think of these classifications as inherent properties of words. We imagine, in other words, that the lexicon of English is arranged with each word specified as belonging to a particular part of speech, or sometimes to several parts of speech. A word's membership in a particular part of speech category is thus one of its inherent properties. As a result, we say that *quickly* is an adverb; *woman* a noun and *capsize* a verb; on the other hand, *catch* is both noun and verb (*a catch; to catch*), and *green* is noun, verb and adjective (*They are on the green; the council is greening the city; I like green asparagus*).

QUESTION   Find as many English words as possible which can be used as a noun, a verb and an adjective, without any alteration. What semantic changes follow from the change of syntactic category?

Parts of speech are indispensable in stating grammatical generalizations, since they allow us to capture the classes of words to which different morphological and syntactic operations apply. For example, we need the categories noun and verb in order to describe the role of the English nominalizing suffix *-er*. Given a set of forms *think/thinker, glide/glider, race/racer, bind/binder* and so on, we can describe the suffix *-er* as converting a verb into a noun. If those two categories were not part of the grammar, stating the role of *-er* would be greatly complicated. Similarly, one of the rules for the English noun phrase, NP → (Det) N, makes crucial reference to the categories determiner and noun.

Not all of the categories we use in linguistic analysis can be given semantic definitions. Phonemes like /n/ and /i/ or distinctive features like [± coronal], [± back] are good examples of linguistic units which in themselves just don't have any meaning. The same is true of phrasal and higher constituents: it makes no sense to ask what the meaning of the category Verb Phrase or Sentence is, since the role of these categories is in the analysis of syntactic arrangement, and they simply lack any independent meaning. Other categories that we use in grammatical analysis, however, *do* have their own meanings. Individual words are the best example, but other elements, like clause-patterns (declarative, interrogative, imperative), as well as utterances and even whole texts, can also informally be said to have their own meanings: the typical meaning of the interrogative-pattern in English, for instance, is that the clause is a question (see 4.1 for problems and discussion). It also often makes sense to ask for the meaning of elements below the word level, such as some bound morphemes like the English plural marker *-s* or the tense suffix *-ed* (see 2.2).

What about the parts of speech? Are they like phonemes or phrasal constituents in simply not having any meaning of their own? Or are they like words and clause-patterns in having an identifiable semantic content? In this section, we will explore just how far it is possible to give a semantic definition of the parts of speech, and what the alternatives to semantic definition might be.

9.1.1 Variation in parts of speech systems

The languages of the world show some variation in what parts of speech their grammars contain. In a typical sentence of any language, we can identify constituents which are translated by, and seem to function in a similar way to, nouns and verbs in English or other familiar languages. But whether we want to call these words 'nouns' and verbs' depends on a number of considerations; some researchers deny that there is any meaningful sense in which those two parts of speech can be said to exist universally (Foley in print; see also Croft 2003: 183, and Evans and Osada 2005). We will say more about nouns and verbs shortly. Once we move away from these categories, however, there is greater variation. Adjectives and adverbs are frequently missing from the inventory of grammatical categories found in the languages of the world. In Warao (isolate; Venezuela), for example, the single form *yakera* can be used without any modification both referentially, as a name of the abstract thing 'beauty' (1a), and as a modifier of both a referential object (1b), and a predicate (1c):

(1) a. *yakera*
        beauty
        'beauty'

     b. *Hiaka   yakera   auka   saba   tai   nisa-n-a-e.*
        garment   beauty   daughter   for   she   buy-SG-PUNCT-PAST
        'She bought a beautiful dress for her daughter.'

     c. *Oko   kuana   yaota-te   arone   yakera   nahoro-te...*
        we   hardness   work-NPAST   although   beauty   eat-NPAST
        'Although we work hard and eat well, ...' (Romero-Figeroa 1997,
        quoted by Hengeveld *et al.* 2004: 531–532)

These uses would call for three quite formally distinct categories in English and many other languages: noun (1a), adjective (1b) and adverb (1c). In Ancient Greek (Indo-European, Greece and Mediterranean; extinct), for example, the translations of *yakera* in (2a–c) are as follows:

(2) a. *to kallos* ('(the) beauty'; noun)
     b. *kalos* ('beautiful'; adjective)
     c. *eu, kalōs* ('well'; adverb)

In contrast, Warao shows no morphological distinction between the three uses.

Differences in part of speech systems are not limited to the presence or absence of adjectives/adverbs. We can see this by comparing some rough part-of-speech inventories from four languages: Chickasaw (Muskogean; Oklahoma, USA), Wolof (Niger-Kordofanian; Senegal and Gambia), San Lucas Quiavini Zapotec (Zapotec, Mexico), and Warlpiri (Pama-Nyungan, Australia) as laid out in Table 9.1 (Munro 2006; Nash 1986):

Table 9.1. Part of speech categories in four languages.

Wolof	Chickasaw	Zapotec	Warlpiri
nouns	nouns	nouns	nouns
pronouns	pronouns	pronouns	pronouns
determiners[a]	–	–	determiners
–	demonstratives	demonstratives	–
verbs	verbs	verbs	verbs
–	–	adjectives	–
adverbs	–	adverbs	–
prepositions	–	prepositions	–
quantifiers	–	quantifiers	–
–	–	–	preverbs
–	–	–	auxiliaries
interjections	interjections	interjections	interjections
particles	particles	particles	particles

[a](demonstratives and articles)

9.1.2 How are parts of speech delimited?

The world's languages differ, therefore, in the parts of speech recognized in their grammars. In order to understand this variation fully, we need to understand how we decide what parts of speech a language has. This is not a simple question. Modern European languages have inherited a ready-made classification of grammatical categories from traditional grammar, as developed since ancient times (see text box p. 295). We simply take it for granted that it is appropriate to think of our languages as having nouns, pronouns, verbs, adverbs, adjectives, determiners/articles, prepositions, as well as a few additional minor categories like interjections and conjunctions. For the purposes of teaching grammar at school these categories are certainly adequate. But when we turn to languages without any indigenous tradition of part of speech distinctions, or when we examine a familiar language like English objectively, we discover that determining exactly what the parts of speech are is a complicated question: there are often several different ways of analysing the facts of any one language, and the question of how the parts of speech should be identified seems open to answering in a variety of different ways.

QUESTION   Over the past few decades, grammarians have proposed several different parts-of-speech lists for English and other languages, ranging from eight categories to as many as a dozen or so. Before we discuss this in the text, think about what the major reasons for these differences might be.

Let's illustrate this with English. One of the main descriptive grammarians of modern English, Rodney Huddleston, states in his 1984 grammar of

English that 'It is inconceivable… that one might write a viable grammar of English that failed to distinguish classes of nouns, verbs and adjectives with very much the same coverage as in traditional grammar…' (1984: 98). As we'll see, this is largely true. But notwithstanding that hard core of central categories, different modern descriptive theories of grammar have made quite different divisions. Let's look, then, at three different catalogues of English parts of speech, Huddleston and Pullum (2002), Radford (2004/1988) and Hockett (1958), before going on to consider the criteria on which we might base a classification.

Leaving aside interjections, which we're going to ignore in what follows, Huddleston and Pullum's classification recognizes eight categories:

Huddleston and Pullum (2002)

Noun	*tree pig sugar hatred union Picasso London I you me it*
Verb	*do fly melt think damage give have be must*
Adjective	*good nice big easy ugly helpful reddish fond*
Adverb	*obviously easily helpfully frankly soon so too*
Preposition	*of to by into between over since towards*
Determinative	*the this that a(n) some all every each*
Subordinator	*that for to whether if*
Coordinator	*and or but not*

Radford, by contrast, has eleven. One difference is largely terminological: Radford's complementiser is equivalent to Huddleston and Pullum's subordinator. Some of Radford's categories are unfamiliar: quantifier includes words which fall into Huddleston and Pullum's determinative category, and prepositions include conjunctions; the tensemarker category contains forms which Huddleston and Pullum class as verbs (*can, could, might, may, must, shall, should, will, would*) – and includes infinitival *to* (as in *I want to go home*).

Radford (2004/1988)

Noun
Verb
Adjective
Adverb
Preposition (including particles and conjunctions: Radford 1988: 137)
Determiner
Quantifier
Pronoun
Auxiliary
Tensemarker (= finite auxiliaries and infinitival *to*)
Complementiser

Finally, let's look at Hockett's (1958) classification, focusing purely on his treatment of nouns, verbs and adjectives. In fact, Hockett divides those three parts of speech into no fewer than seven separate categories, depending on the syntactic possibilities of their members. The seven categories are N, A, V, NA, NV, AV and NAV. A word is an N if, like *cat*, it can *only* occur in the syntactic positions traditionally associated with nouns (e.g. following a determiner). It is NA if it can occur as both a traditional noun and a traditional adjective: an example would be *good*, as in *the good soldier* (adjectival use) and *the government is concerned for both the public and the private good* (nominal use). In its adjectival use, *good* displays the grammatical possibilities characteristic of adjectives (notably comparison: *good, better, best*), whereas in its nominal use it can follow a determiner and may take plural marking (*no goods may be left in storage*). A word is NV if it can be used as both a traditional noun and verb: an obvious example is *cook* (*The cook* (N) *is too drunk*; *now let's cook* (V) *the duck*). Finally, NAVs, such as *green*, display all three uses (*This green* (N) *is darker than that one; the green* (A) *grass; the council wants to green* (V) *the city*). In Hockett's scheme, then, the 'pure' categories N, V and A are just the kernel of a more elaborate system.

QUESTION   In some classifications, pronouns are considered as a subcategory of nouns and auxiliaries are considered a subcategory of verbs. What might some advantages and disadvantages of these categorizations be? Consider both the consequences for assigning a meaning to the category, and the consequences for describing grammatical structure.

It's clear just from a cursory examination of the three interpretations of English that quite a lot of variation is possible in parts of speech systems, especially in the less central categories. This variability in modern classificatory schemes shows that there's no sense in which the division of the entire vocabulary into parts of speech is natural. Terms like 'noun', 'verb', 'conjunction' and so on are ones which many of us feel entirely familiar with, and which we apply unhesitatingly. It's tempting to feel that there's no more doubt about whether something is a noun or a verb than there is about whether a rabbit is a plant or an animal. Yet the variety of classifications which have been advanced shows that the opposite is the case. What the parts of speech are is a matter for discussion, not an obvious and straightforward *fact* about language. Whether or not *she* is a noun or pronoun depends on what your criteria for nounhood and pronounhood are. And, as we're about to see, different criteria are possible, and it may well be that some criteria are better than others.

QUESTION   Suggest some criteria for determining parts of speech in English.

QUESTION   What part of speech is *say* in *Say we come tomorrow…*? What about *come* in *Come Tuesday, we'll know the answer*?

QUESTION   There are a few items whose function is to introduce an utterance in discourse, such as *well* (as in *Well, are you coming this Sunday?*) and *now* (as in *Now, we can do one of two things*). What are the arguments for and against these constituting a separate part of speech category?

9.1.2.1 Morpho-distributional criteria

The languages for which the earliest parts of speech classifications were developed were strongly inflectional in nature. In both Latin and Greek, nouns and verbs took two entirely different sets of suffixes. As a result, the inflections provided a very obvious way of dividing the vocabulary up into different word classes: nouns can be defined as the words which take a certain set of inflectional suffixes; and verbs as words which take a certain different set. The classification into noun and verb, in other words, can unproblematically be read off the morphology, and if we ever had a doubt about what part of speech a given word belongs to, we can quickly resolve it by checking which set of inflections it took. At an earlier stage of its linguistic history, English itself used to be much more like Latin and Greek, as we can see from the paradigms of the Old English nouns *stān* 'stone', *giefu* 'gift' and *hunta* 'hunter', and of the verb *fremman* 'do' (note the character *þ*, pronounced [θ] and called 'thorn'):

Singular:	Nom	*stān*	*gief-u*	*hunt-a*
	Acc	*stān*	*gief-e*	*hunt-an*
	Gen	*stān-es*	*gief-e*	*hunt-an*
	Dat	*stān-e*	*gief-e*	*hunt-an*
Plural:	Nom	*stān-as*	*gief-a*	*hunt-an*
	Acc	*stān-as*	*gief-a*	*hunt-an*
	Gen	*stān-a*	*gief-a*	*hunt-ena*
	Dat	*stān-um*	*gief-um*	*hunt-um*

SG	1	*fremm-e*	'I do'
	2	*frem-est*	'you do'
	3	*frem-eþ*	'he/she/it does'
PL		*fremm-aþ*	'we/you (pl.)/they do'

In order to discover whether *hunta* is a noun or verb, then, we simply ask what set of inflectional endings it can take.

In Modern English, where the morphology has greatly decayed, we cannot determine word class from inflections: there just isn't enough inflectional morphology, and what there is isn't regular enough through any one word class. For example, we couldn't define nouns as the class of words which take plural markers, since some words which we clearly want to recognize as nouns, like *equipment, worth, emptiness, suffrage, marketing* or *music*, typically do not have this possibility. The English category 'adjective' is similar. We might suggest that adjectives can be defined as those words which can accept comparative/superlative morphology: think of *fast–faster–fastest, hot–hotter–hottest, black–blacker–blackest* and *kind–kinder–kindest*. The problem is that while this criterion applies to some basic adjectives, it will end up excluding many words we accept as adjectives, like *prior* (**priorer/*more prior*), *former* (**formerer/*more former*), *total* (**totaler/*more total*), *future* (**futurer/*more future*) and many others.

QUESTION   Is it possible to identify a morphological criterion for verbs in English? What prevents us giving a simple answer to this question?

The difficulty of coming up with satisfactory definitions of these basic parts of speech is somewhat embarrassing, since it is precisely the traditional categorization of verb, noun and adjective that we need if we are to describe English in the way that most syntacticians believe is required.

Another criterion often used to define parts of speech is a **distributional** one. A distributional approach to parts of speech classifies parts of speech on the basis of the way they pattern in sentences. One way of defining these patterns is to advance sample contexts which can serve as test-frames. For example, Radford (2004: 30) suggests that (3) can serve as a test for nouns, since it is only by a noun that it can be completed:

(3)   *They have no _____.*

Thus, cardinal nouns like *house, dog, patience, recognition* and many others can be substituted into the sentence, whereas adjectives/adverbs (*sad(ly), correct(ly), canine*), verbs (*eaten, dwell, conceal*) and prepositions (*to, with, by*) cannot. More examples are given in (4).

(4)   (a)   *They have no **car**/**conscience**/**friends**/**ideas** [nouns]*
       (b)   **They have no **went** [verb]/**for** [preposition]/**older**
              [adjective]/**conscientiously** [adverb] (Radford 2004: 31)

However, further reflection soon reveals that not all words which we usually count as nouns can be appropriately put in the frame, as shown in (5):

(5)   *⁇They have no instance.*
       ⁇They have no possibility.
       ⁇They have no inconvenience.

These sentences might be improved by adding further material after the noun (*'They have no possibility of improvement*). However, a better test-frame for nouns might be the following one:

(6)   *There is/are no _____.*

This works for all the nouns we have seen so far. But it is not free of problems, since it also admits the following, as any quick search of the Internet will show:

(7)   a.   *There is no **I**/**me** [pronouns].*
       b.   *There is no **why**/**if** [conjunctions].*
       c.   *There is no **then** [adverb]/**after**/**before** [adverbs/prepositions].*
       e.   *Do Or Do Not. There Is No **Try** [verb?].*

None of the highlighted words is usually considered a noun in the senses which they exemplify here. Consistently, none of these words should be able felicitously to appear in the test-frame in (7).

QUESTION   Consider the following test-frame for adverbs (Radford 2004: 31):

(a) *He treats her _____.*
(b) *She behaved _____.*
(b) *He worded the statement _____.*

Does this test work for all and only those words which we traditionally classify adverbs?

Even if we were able to devise appropriate test-frames which did isolate the categories in a way that matched our traditional classifications, there is still a problem: the morphological and distributional tests only work if the membership of the different parts of speech categories is already known. That is why we can say that the words in (7a–e) are not nouns in spite of their compatibility with the test-frame, and why we know that the words in (5) are nouns even though they do not fit into the test context in (3). In neither case are we using the test sentences to *establish* the part of speech classification of a given noun; we are using it to *justify* a traditional classification which we consider as self-evident. The traditional part of speech categories seem simply to be so entrenched in the way we think of our own language that we cannot avoid using them, even if we have a hard time specifying exactly what criteria govern their application. It seems as though we have to look elsewhere for some insight into this question.

The origin of parts of speech systems

The parts of speech categories used in modern linguistic theory go back to the classical grammarians of Greek and Latin. Both Plato and Aristotle include embryonic classifications of words into parts of speech; the expression 'parts of speech', indeed, is first recorded in Aristotle. But the first systematic classification of parts of speech is due to the Stoics – philosophers who belonged to the school of Zeno of Citium, who was active round 300 BC. The early Stoic classification recognized just four parts of speech: nouns, verbs, articles (including pronouns) and conjunctive particles (including prepositions; Michael 1970: 48). **Dionysius Thrax**, the grammarian responsible for the first surviving work of Western grammar (see Kemp 1986), recognized twice the number, distinguishing nouns, verbs, participles (which roughly correspond to the -*ing* form of English verbs), articles, pronouns, preposition, adverbs and conjunctions.

This eight-fold classification persisted in the influential system of the Latin grammarian **Donatus** (mid-fourth century AD), the teacher of St Jerome (the translator of the Bible into Latin). Donatus' list of categories was the following: noun, pronoun, verb, adverb, participle, conjunction, preposition and interjection. Note that this list substitutes interjections for articles. This reflects a significant difference between Greek, the language for which Thrax's grammar was designed, and Latin, Donatus' concern. Unlike Greek, Latin lacks a word meaning 'the', making the 'article' category completely redundant for this language (neither Greek nor Latin has a word for 'a(n)'). This difference aside, however, the two languages are sufficiently similar for the rest of the Greek word classes still to play a plausible role in the description of Latin. Donatus' system forms the basis for the whole grammatical tradition of the Middle Ages, and, consequently, for the classification which we're familiar with ourselves. That's not to say that the system didn't go unchallenged. Various scholars throughout the medieval period tinkered with the basic eight-way division found in Donatus (details in Michael 1970). But it was Donatus' system that held sway. Smaragdus (a celebrated theologian active towards the start of the ninth century AD) followed Donatus' view that there were only eight parts of speech, adding that 'the whole church ... holds that there are only eight, and I have no doubt that this view is divinely inspired' (quoted in Michael 1970: 51). When grammarians first began to describe the grammar of European vernaculars, they based their classifications closely on these Latin systems, regardless of how appropriate they were to the language being described. It is as though principles from cricket were automatically used to describe *any* ball game, with terms like *stumps*, *wicket*, *run*, *fielder* and *innings* being applied indifferently to football, hockey, lawn bowls and tennis.

9.1.2.2 Semantic criteria

One particularly obvious way of delimiting the categories is on the basis of semantic criteria; in other words, on the basis of commonalities in the meanings of words in any given class. This may well have been the way you yourself were first taught to think of major parts of speech like noun, verb and adjective/adverb. The following set of traditional definitions are representative of semantic interpretations of the parts of speech (adapted from Huddleston 1983, following Curme 1935):

> Noun (substantive): word used as the name of a living being or lifeless thing.
> Verb: word which denotes action or a state of being.
> Adjective: word which denotes a property or characteristic of some object, person or thing.

QUESTION   What might some problems be with these definitions?

Semantic criteria for the parts of speech are very entrenched in our grammatical thought. One of the earliest English grammarians to write in the vernacular, William Lily (c. 1468–1522), defined *noun* in his Latin grammar as 'the name of a thing that is and may be seen, felt, heard, or understood'; the connection with Curme's definition is obvious. In (7) above, one of the reasons that we're likely to reject *why/if, then, after/before* and *try* as nouns is that we feel they're not 'thingy' enough: their referents are not abstract or concrete objects, unlike the referents of prototypical nouns.

   Semantic definitions, however, prove to be hopelessly inadequate as definitions of the parts of speech. On the semantic definition, verbs are supposed to 'denote action or a state of being' or, in an alternative formulation (COBUILD grammar, p. 137), 'indicate what sort of action, process or state you are talking about'. If that definition is to be accurate, it must mean that anything which does that is a verb; otherwise, the definition won't work. But we find that there are countless *nouns* which 'denote action or a state of being' or 'indicate what sort of action, process or state you are talking about':

Action/process: *riot, ceremony, election, conference, sport, genocide, trick, celebration, party, war, conversation, meal, punishment, sleep, bloodshed ...*

State of being: *ability, old age, youth, maturity, arrogance, ignorance, stupidity, preference, sickness, health, trouble ...*

You'll be able to think of many more examples for yourself (see Hopper 1997 for interesting discussion). Some scholars have developed more sophisticated descriptions of the claimed underlying semantics of nouns and verbs. Thus, Givón (1979) claims that noun meanings and verb meanings occur at opposite ends of a 'time-stability' continuum: nouns prototypically denote percepts which possess 'time-stability' – they refer, in other words, to things or objects, which persist over time. Verbs, by contrast, prototypically denote percepts which lack time-stability – actions and events, which evolve through time and cannot be fixed (on prototypicality, see 7.1.3). This is an attractive idea, but it does not prove to be a viable definition of noun and verb meanings. For every noun referring to a time-stable thing or object, we can produce one which refers to a fleeting 'object' which lacks time-stability: think of the nouns *spark, glint, flash, splash, wince, cry, blink, shiver.* Many verbs, by contrast, denote stable situations: *to exist, remain, soak, rest, belong* and many others. These seem just as 'prototypical' as any others. These facts challenge Givón's claim of prototypicality. The grammatical difference between nouns and verbs simply does not seem to be reducible to a semantic one.

Attempts to discover a semantic commonality to the class of adjectives fare no better. The traditional semantic definition of adjective, 'word which denotes a property or characteristic of some object, person or thing', is far from an adequate way of delimiting the category. There are many nouns and, to a lesser extent, verbs which perform exactly that function:

Nouns: *happiness, sadness, freedom, slavery, winner, loser, age, youth...*
Verbs: *differ, resemble, contrast...*

For instance, if I say that her *sadness increased, sadness* refers quite unambiguously to a 'property or characteristic' of the person, just as much as it does to 'a lifeless thing', the definition of noun. Similarly, to say that something *differs* from something else, is certainly not to say anything about an action or event in which it's involved; we could say that it denotes a *state* of the referent, but there's no reason not to also say that it denotes a property or characteristic. Indeed, whenever something is in a particular state it can be described as possessing the property characteristic of that state: if, for example, I *know French*, then I am in a particular state of being (knowing French), and I possess the property of knowing French. Or again, if you *live in Sydney*, the living can be described both as a state of being you're in, and as a property you possess – the property of living in a certain place. That crossover between states and properties introduces a total indeterminacy into the semantic definitions of adjective and verb, rendering them useless as definitions of the categories.

But these sorts of indeterminacy aren't even the main problem with a meaning-based classification. The real problem is that such classifications are circular. As pointed out by Lyons (1968: 318), the 'only reason we have for saying that truth, beauty and electricity are things is that the words which refer to them in English are nouns'. In other words, what counts as a 'thing' in English seems not to be independently established, but depends on whether the word for it is a noun: *possibility*, *fraud* and *implication* are nouns and therefore can all be thought of as the names of things, whereas *if*, *then*, *try* are not nouns and cannot. Lexical category, in other words, seems to determine thingness, not the other way around. If we had some independent way of saying what counts as a thing in English, we would be in a better position. As it is, however, it seems that virtually the only evidence we have on the thingness of a concept is, precisely, what part of speech it belongs to. Why is *to operate* an action, but *an operation* a thing? For Lyons, the only reason is that the former is a verb, the latter a noun. This means that we cannot appeal to thingness, eventhood and so on as criteria for grammatical category, since they are not known independently of the very grammatical features which they are supposed to establish.

But perhaps there are some more general definitions we can find. What about the *function* of verbs and nouns? Could we say that verbs are the part of speech which predicate (i.e. attribute a property to a referent), and nouns are the part of speech which refer? In a sentence like *Sarkozy has resigned*, for instance, the proper noun *Sarkozy* refers to an individual, while the verb *has resigned* attributes the property of having resigned to him. Unfortunately, neither predication nor reference will work as definitions of 'verb' and 'noun'. Predication can't be an adequate definition of verb, since the notion of 'predicate' is usually understood in terms of the notion 'verb'. Any attempt to define verbs as predicates would therefore be circular. (See the box 'Verbs and predication' for discussion.) As for defining nouns through reference, there are two problems. First, nouns don't always refer. In a sentence like *Charles will not be king*, the subject noun *Charles* refers to an individual, but the complement noun *king* is non-referring (see 3.2.2.2 for discussion). Thus, we cannot identify the function of the noun as always being referential: many nouns and noun phrases will be non-referential.

Maybe we could get around this by saying that nouns are that part of speech which *can* refer, but which *need not* do so. This might prove to be an effective strategy, if it weren't for our second problem: once we look closely at the question, we find that it isn't *nouns* that refer, but *noun phrases*. Consider the following sentences:

(8) a. <u>Ice</u> *melts in the sun.*
     b. <u>Civilization</u> *is headed for the scrap-heap.*
     c. <u>Books</u> *annoy me.*

(9) a. <u>Ice that has not been chemically modified</u> *melts in the sun.*
     b. <u>Your tawdry little human civilization</u> *is headed for the scrap heap.*
     c. <u>Those books we borrowed from the library</u> *annoy me.*

The underlined phrases in (8a–c) are noun phrases, not just nouns, for well-known syntactic reasons which I'm assuming are familiar. (If they're not, you'll find clear explanations in standard syntax texts like Carnie 2007, Radford 2004, or Bloor and Bloor 2004.) Sentences (8a–c) show that noun phrases can *sometimes* consist of a sole noun (*ice*, *civilization* and *books* respectively). Often, however, there needs to be more than just this single 'head' noun in order to convey the intended reference. In (9a–c), the underlined noun phrases contain many other parts of speech than the head noun. Yet only the full underlined noun phrase contains the information we need in order to identify the referent. Clearly, then, reference is achieved at the level of the entire phrase, not at that of the part of speech itself (see 3.2.2.2). So our suggestion that nouns might be defined as the part of speech that refers won't turn out to be right: noun *phrases*, not nouns, are the bearers of referential force.

Maybe we can save the situation. Maybe if we start from a different point we can still use the connection between noun phrases and reference as a way to define nouns. What if, instead of defining nouns through reference, we defined nouns through noun phrases, and then NPs through reference? In other words, maybe we could say that nouns are the heads of NPs, and that NPs are constituents which can refer. If we were able to do that, we'd have discovered a way to account for the membership of the noun category syntactically (by defining it as the head of an NP), and we'd have defined NP functionally (as a potentially referring constituent). Unfortunately, there are two problems with this. First, the very definition of NP makes reference to the category noun. Let's assume the rule NP → (Det) (Adj) N. Since this contains the category Noun in its definition, we need to know what the nouns are in a sentence before we can identify what the noun phrase is. That's obviously going to be a problem if we want to use the NP category as a way of defining nouns. Second, not just Ns are the heads of NPs. Any pronoun can constitute an NP on its own:

(10) *I/you/he/she/we/they stole the diamonds.*

Furthermore, if sentences like *There is no after* and the others in (7) contain NPs, then these are arguably headed by parts of speech other than Ns. As a result, the suggestion that we could define noun as the head of an NP will not isolate those parts of speech which we want to count as nouns in the first place. It looks as though we just won't be able to ground the category of noun in reference after all.

Verbs and predication

Verbs can be described as 'predicators', and the role of the verb in the clause can be described as 'predicating'. Could we use these notions to give a foundation to the category of verb? Can we say that verbs are defined by their role as predicators? Unfortunately, the answer to this has to be 'no'. Let's see why.

The predicate is the part of the sentence which attributes a property to a referent (see Rothstein 2006). The term 'property' is a bit misleading: it covers not just adjectival properties, but verbal ones too. So in (1), the referent in question is Stephen, and the properties attributed to him are all properties which consist of performing a certain action: walking home, shooting Nazis and accepting the glass. Because these actions all involve other entities (home, Nazis and the glass) the sentences include the NPs *home*, *seventeen Nazis* and *the glass*, which specify additional information about the action.

(1)   a.   *Stephen walked home.*
       b.   *Stephen shot seventeen Nazis.*
       c.   *Stephen accepted the glass.*

These NP objects aren't necessary for a predication, since we can remove them and still succeed in attributing properties to Stephen: the properties of walking (2a), shooting (2b) and accepting (2c):

(2)   a.   *Stephen walked.*
       b.   *Stephen shot.*
       c.   *Stephen accepted.*

As a result, it's conventional in linguistics to say that it's the *verb* which is the predicator in a sentence: in a well-formed English sentence, there must be a verb, but there need not be anything other than a verb. The verb can bring associated NPs along as objects or complements, as in (1), but these associated NPs don't themselves predicate, as we can see if we remove the verb from the sentences of (1):

(3)   a.   **Stephen home.*
       b.   **Stephen seventeen Nazis.*
       c.   **Stephen the glass.*

These sentences are ill-formed: in the absence of a verb, the non-subject NPs can't contribute to specifying the property attributed to Stephen. For this reason the verb is thought of as the necessary part of the predicate, and the verb is known as the predicator.

That, then, explains what predicates and predicators are. Back to the question of whether we could define verbs in terms of predication, thereby providing a semantic basis for the category. Unfortunately, it turns out there are also *other* parts of speech than the verb which can be considered as predicates. Look at (4):

(4)   a.   *Stephen walked home* **ecstatic/ten feet tall/ravenous.**
       b.   *Stephen shot seventeen Nazis* **dead.**
       c.   *Stephen accepted the glass* **empty.**
       d.   *Stephen accepted the prize* **delighted.**

Here we find additional properties being attributed to the referents of the sentence. In (4a) and (4d), the property of being ecstatic/ten feet tall/ravenous or delighted is attributed to the sentence's subject (Stephen), while in (4b) and (4c) properties are attributed to the sentence's objects: in (4b) the property of being dead is attributed to the Nazis, and in (4c) the property of being empty is attributed to the glass.

This creates a serious problem if we want to define verbs as predicators, since what the sentences in (4) show is that not all predicators are verbs. If we're planning to identify verbs with the class of predicators, the (4) examples show that this will also include *ecstatic*, *ten feet tall*, *ravenous*, *dead* and *empty* as verbs – a consequence we must avoid, since these words aren't verbs on anyone's criterion!

Can we do anything about this? Perhaps we could introduce a contrast between 'primary' and 'secondary' predicators, and say that primary predicators like those in (2) are verbs, but that secondary predicators like the highlighted words in (4) are not. But how do we define primary predicator? It seems the only obvious way is to say that the primary predicator is the main *verb*. But this would be circular: since we want to use 'primary predicator' as a definition of verb, we can't use 'verb' to define 'primary predicator'. To do so would be uninformative: it would leave us with no way of identifying either the verbs or the primary predicator in a clause, since we would have to be able to identify each before we could identify the other. (Someone might suggest here that we define primary predicator as something like 'the only obligatory predicator in a clause'. The problem with this is that the idea of a clause itself depends on the notion 'verb', which means that a circularity will once again be introduced.)

There's one other compelling reason not to identify the notions of 'verb' and primary predicator: in some languages, like Warlpiri, nouns can be the primary predicators:

(5) *Ngaju*   *mata*
    I   tired
    'I am tired' (Hale, Laughren and Simpson 1995: 1430)

On morphological criteria, *mata* 'tired'(which can also mean 'lame') is a noun in Warlpiri (as seen in Table 9.1 above, there is no separate adjective category), yet in this sentence it is the only possible primary predicator.

The upshot of this dispiriting situation is this. We have to conclude that verbs can't be usefully defined as the class of (primary) predicators in a language: to define them in this way only gives the appearance of a definition, and does not actually get us anywhere.

QUESTION   In Somali (Afro-Asiatic; Somalia), the words for 'black', 'white' and 'red' are intransitive verbs, those for 'yellow' and 'green' are denominal adjectives and the word for 'blue' is a noun: something can't be said to *be blue*; instead, it 'has blue' (Kay 2001: 2251). How serious a problem does this pose for a semantic definition of parts of speech? Is there any way a supporter of semantic definitions could respond?

9.1.2.3 Multicategoriality

Another factor which creates problems when we try to theorize about grammatical categories is that in some languages, including English, there are many words which are *both* nouns *and* verbs:

(11) *catch, run, fish, clasp, head, ride, go, move, hit, break, fall, slip, drink, smoke, risk, box, saddle, read...*

Even words which are typically members of just one category *can* be used in the other. (12) (a–b) show verbs appearing as nouns:

(12) a. *As your road speed increases in the Commodore, the **dwell** of the intermittent windscreen wipers reduces.* (Jones 2001: 18).
   b. *We can see a real **disconnect** here.*

In contrast, contexts like (13) show nouns being used as verbs:

(13) *Don't **baby** me; just **Google** it.*

These possibilities are not limited to nouns and verbs. Contexts like (14a–b) allow the titles *sir* and *madam*, which are certainly not verbs, to be inserted into verb slots:

(14) a. *'Madam,' I began, very conscious of the evil glitter of her knife, 'if you will permit me to–' 'Don't "madame" me, young man! I don't like it...'* (http://infomotions.com/etexts/gutenberg/dirs/etext04/pereg10.htm)

   b. Colonel: *Don't sir me!* Clevinger: *Yes, sir.* (www.geocities.com/stuartthiel/clevingerscript.html)

Many types of word can be inserted into a pre-nominal position, and hence interpreted as an adjective, as happens with *badge of honour* in (15):

(15) *Another army of women is bandaged and bruised.... they wear their wounds with much the same badge-of-honour determination.*

Badge of honour is typically a noun; but when it takes on the grammatical position associated with adjectives, it assumes a qualifying role. Examples like these are widespread, and they suggest that there is a high degree of fluidity to the English part-of-speech system.

QUESTION   Traditionally the first noun in cases like (15) is labelled 'a noun used as an adjective'. What are the advantages and problems with this? Think of other noun–noun combinations, such as *snail mail, weekend warrior*, etc.

Some languages have even more far-reaching possibilities of multicategoriality. In some languages of the Pacific Northwest of America and Canada, there is a widespread cross-over between noun and verb categories. The following examples are from St'át'imcets (Salishan; British Columbia; Davis and Matthewson 1999: 38):

(16) a. *t'ak*   *ti=nk'yáp=a*
     go.along   DET=coyote=EXIS
     'The/a coyote goes along'

    b. *nk'yap*   *ti=t'ák=a*
     coyote   DET=go.along=EXIS
     'The one going along is a coyote'

In (16a) we find the root *nk'yáp* 'coyote' performing a function typically associated with nouns – reference – and supplied with a determiner. The root *t'ak* 'go along' functions as a verb. In (16b) these functions are completely reversed. Now it is *nk'yap* 'coyote' which has the verbal function, and *t'ák* 'go along' the nominal morphology. This possibility for roots to appear in either nominal or verbal contexts is widely found in the Pacific North West of North America, such as Nuu-chah-nulth (Wakashan; British Columbia; often referred to as 'Nootka'), as well as in other languages of the world, including Tagalog (Austronesian; Philippines): (17) gives some Tagalog examples (Evans and Osada 2005: 368):

(17) a. *nag.ta.trabaho*   *ang*   *lalaki*
     work.AT.IMPF   TOP   man
     'The man will be working.'

    b. *lalaki*   *ang*   *nag.ta.trabaho*
     man   TOP   work.AT.IMPF
     'The one who is working is a man.'

The predicate in Tagalog is signalled by clause-initial position; (17) gives a sense of the freedom with which roots can be inserted into this position.

Sign languages also often have words which are able to function equally as nouns or verbs. In DGS (*Deutsche Gebärdensprache*, German Sign Language), for instance, both the signs in (18) can be translated as both nouns and verbs:

(18) a. ARBEIT   'the work, to work'
    b. DENKEN 'to think, a thought' (Schwager and Zeshan n.d.: 1)

(The handsigns are represented here by their approximate German translation equivalents, given in capital letters.)

Facts like these give us a different way of thinking about the nature of verbhood and nounhood. We began this section by saying that nounhood and verbhood are usually thought of as inherent properties of lexical roots: a word 'brings' its status as a noun or verb with it to the sentence. The thoroughgoing multicategoriality found in languages like St'át'imcets, Tagalog and Nuu-chah-nulth, as well as the more limited, but still frequent multicategoriality of a language like English, give us good reason not to talk in this way. Instead, we can think of nouns and verbs as 'slots' or contexts available in each clause, each of which comes associated with typical grammatical machinery (TMA markers for verbs/events; plurality/definiteness etc. markers for nouns). In English, these slots are the phrase-level categories of NP and VP, each of which prototypically has its distinctive grammatical markers. In other languages, the marking of the slot may be purely morphological. But in both cases we can see the grammatical slots themselves as the carriers of the nounhood or verbhood which the word ends up acquiring. These slots display the typical structure of a prototype category: prototypically, a noun slot is filled with words denoting perceptible, time-stable referents, and a verb slot is filled with words denoting concrete actions. In some languages, there are roots which are uniquely licensed to appear in either noun or verb slots. In others, a given root may appear in both. But in both cases, the categoriality comes from the slot in the clause, not from the root itself.

9.1.3 Grammatical category and discourse function

In a well-known article, Hopper and Thompson (1984) suggested an alternative to semantically or grammatically oriented approaches to the parts of speech like those discussed above. Hopper and Thompson claim that nounhood and verbhood should be defined in terms of discourse-functional factors: factors which are not primarily about meaning or grammatical rules, but about the *informational roles* which words play in actual discourse, the particular function of different words in organizing the information conveyed by the utterance.

We'll mainly concentrate on Hopper and Thompson's proposals about nouns. They begin by observing that the grammatical properties associated with nouns are not constant across all the contexts in which nouns appear. They compare three uses of the noun *fox*:

(19) a. *Early in the chase the hounds started up **an old red fox**, and we hunted him all morning.*
 b. ***Foxes** are cunning.*
 c. *We went **fox**-hunting in the Berkshires.*

In all three cases *fox* is, of course, a noun. But Hopper and Thompson note that the grammatical 'nouniness' of fox is manifested in rather different ways in the three cases. In English, nouns are often distinguished grammatically by the ability to take plural suffixes, and appear in NPs introduced by determiners. Ability to host number markers and compatibility with determiners are therefore among the cardinal grammatical possibilities that an English noun has. Most common nouns have these possibilities. But even though *fox* is an entirely typical English noun in terms of these abstract grammatical possibilities, whether or not the possibilities are available depends on the particular grammatical context in which the noun occurs. In (19) above, the full possibilities of number-hosting and determiner acceptance are, in fact, only both available in (19a). Case (19a) already contains the determiner *an*, and we could pluralize it to *foxes* (an alteration which would necessitate substituting the determiner *some* for *an*). In order to express the generic meaning of (19b), we either use the plural *foxes*, or we can use a singular noun with determiner: *the fox is cunning*. But we don't have both options. We can't say *Fox is cunning* (singular noun; no determiner) or *the foxes are cunning* (plural noun; determiner) and preserve the same meaning: *the foxes are cunning* doesn't mean that foxes *in general* are cunning, just that *these particular* foxes, which we're already talking about, are cunning. In (19c) *fox* can have *neither* plural marking nor a preceding determiner. In (19a) *fox* identifies a concrete, perceptible entity which is introduced as a participant into the discourse. In (19b) and (19c) *fox(es)* does not refer to any single, concrete set of foxes, but to the class of foxes in general.

What accounts for these differences? Hopper and Thompson suggest that nouns can be understood as prototype categories defined by their discourse functions. The difference in the grammatical options available to a given occurrence of a noun correlates with the discourse function that that noun is playing in any given context – the closer the noun is to playing its prototypical discourse role, the closer it comes to exhibiting the full range of grammatical possibilities of its class. Nouns' prototypical function, Hopper and Thompson claim, is to introduce 'participants' and 'props' into the discourse, and to deploy them, as in (19a). We use nouns to bring participants into the discourse, and then to manipulate them through the course of the text. It is only in grammatical contexts which can fulfil this discourse role that nouns display their full range of grammatical options. That is the reason that the possibilities of pluralization and determiner selection are greatest in (19a). In (19b) and (19c), the grammatical context is not one which allows *fox* to be deployed as a participant/prop in the discourse; as a result, fewer of the grammatical options associated with nounhood are available (see Table 9.2).

Hopper and Thomspon detail a large amount of cross-linguistic evidence designed to 'show that the extent to which prototypical nounhood is achieved is a function of the degree to which the form in question serves to introduce a participant into the discourse' (1984: 708). Not all occurrences of a given noun, in other words, are equally 'nouny'. Even though *fox* is a typical English noun in having the full range of grammatical characteristics we associate with nouns – compatibility with number markers and determiners – these characteristics can only be manifested in some contexts. The context where the full range of these grammatical characteristics can be manifested is when the noun is fulfilling its prototypical

Table 9.2. Discourse function and grammatical nounhood.

Discourse function	Can show a singular/plural contrast	Can take a determiner	*Both* singular/plural *and* determiner
Introduces or deploys participants/props	✓	✓	✓
Generic reference	✓	✓	✗
Non-referential	✗	✗	✗

discourse function: introducing or deploying a participant or prop, as in (19a). When a noun isn't doing this, the range of grammatical possibilities shrinks (19b–c). 'From the discourse viewpoint', Hopper and Thompson explain,

nouns function to introduce participants and 'props' and to deploy them. To the extent that a linguistic form is carrying out this prototypical function, it will be coded as N, and will manifest the full possible range of nominal trappings conventional in the language. Forms which fail in some way to refer to concrete, deployable entities will typically lack some or all of these trappings (1984: 710–711).

One obvious type of noun which does not introduce a participant into the discourse are those nouns which are complements of verbs of being. This type of nominal, Hopper and Thompson show, often loses many of the grammatical characteristics associated with full nounhood. In Mokilese (Austronesian, Micronesia) and Hungarian (Finno-Ugric, Hungary) (optionally), and in French and Ancient Greek (obligatorily), nouns which are the complements of verbs of being do not take determiners, even though appearance with determiners is one of the grammatical hallmarks of nounhood in these languages:

(20) a. Mokilese (Harrison 1976: 74)
     Johnpadahkk-o   doaktoa
     teacher-DEF   doctor
     'The teacher is a doctor' (*not* 'the doctor is a teacher') (Hopper and Thompson 1984: 716)

   b. Hungarian (Károly 1972: 86)
     A   báty-ám   katona
     DEF   brother-my   soldier
     'My brother is a soldier' (*not* 'the soldier is my brother') (Hopper and Thompson 1984: 717)

   c. French
     Il   est   médecin.
     He   is   doctor
     'He is a doctor' (*not* 'the doctor is him')

   d. Ancient Greek
     nuks   hē   hēmerē   egeneto.
     night   the.FEM.SG.NOM   day.FEM.SG.NOM   become.IMPF
     'The day became night' (*not* 'the night became day') (Goodwin 1894: 208)

In all these languages, however, when the noun phrases serve their prototypical function of introducing or deploying a participant or prop, they regain the possibility of taking a determiner. The loss of this grammatical possibility in the above examples

correlates with an absence of intention to refer to an extant entity: the thing named is not used as a participant or prop in the discourse. In other words, there are no discourse contexts in which such a predicate nominal serves to introduce a participant into the discourse for further deployability (Hopper and Thompson 1984: 716).

Another context in which participants are clearly *not* introduced or deployed is that of negation. Nouns under the scope of negation (e.g. nouns which are the objects of verbs in negative clauses) often cannot take the same range of determiners as nouns which are not under the scope of negation:

(21) a. Modern Hebrew

    lo   *kaniti*   *sefer(*-exad)*

    NEG   bought.I   book one/a

    'I didn't buy a book' (Hopper and Thompson 1984: 717, quoting Givón 1977: 304)

   b. Hungarian

    Jancsi   *nem*   *olvasott*   *(*egy)*   *könyvet*

    John   NEG   read   a   book

    'John didn't read any books' (Hopper and Thompson 1984: 717, quoting Givón 1979: 98)

Since a noun under the scope of negation cannot have the function of deploying a participant or prop, its grammatical possibilities are much more restricted.

We will not go into the details of Hopper and Thompson's discussion of verbhood, which sees assertion of the occurrence of an event as the proto-typical discourse function of a verb. When verbs assert the occurrence of events, they characteristically can take the full range of tense–mood–aspect markers available in the language, as well as the other hallmarks of verbhood, like syntactic agreement with associated noun phrases. In contexts where verbs do not assert the occurrence of an event, many of these possibilities disappear. This accounts for the difference between (22a) and (22b):

(22) a. *After the break, McTavish* **threw** *the log.*

   b. *To* **throw** *a log that size takes a great deal of strength.*

The verb in (22a) asserts the occurrence of an event and, as a result, can occur with a wide range of tense, aspect and modality inflections (*McTavish threw/is throwing/will throw/might throw*, etc.), and may, depending on the language, show agreement with its associated NPs. In (22b), on the other hand, no event is asserted to have occurred and these possibilities are lacking (*to throw/*will throw/*may throw/*can throw/*should throw*, etc.).

Hopper and Thompson's conclusion is that 'linguistic forms are in principle to be considered as LACKING CATEGORIALITY completely unless nounhood or verbhood is forced on them by their discourse functions … In other words, far from being given aprioristically for us to build sentences out of, the categories of N and V actually manifest themselves only when the discourse requires it' (1984: 747; emphasis original). This conclusion is similar to the one we reached at the end of the previous section, where we argued that nounhood and verbhood need to be considered not as properties of given roots, but of grammatical 'slots' or 'contexts' in the sentence. Hopper and Thompson's analysis suggests that this is an oversimplification: there is no such thing as a 'noun' slot or a 'verb' slot, each of which is defined by a fixed range of grammatical properties. Rather, the slots into which nouns and verbs can be inserted are structured around a central, most prototypical member, which most completely manifests the available grammatical properties for the category in question. Hopper and Thompson's innovation was to explain the origin of this prototype structure: the most grammatically prototypical nouns or verbs are those which fulfil the most prototypical discourse function – introducing/naming a participant in the case of nouns, and asserting the occurrence of an event in the case of verbs. When nouns introduce props and participants, they can appear in the most elaborated versions of their own slots – versions where the full range of grammatical possibilities is available. When they do not, the grammatical slots show a correspondingly reduced set of grammatical options.

Hopper and Thompson's analysis has certainly not gone unchallenged (see Francis 1998). In particular, critics might well wonder whether the notions of introducing a participant and asserting an event are any less slippery than the semantic notions of reference and predication they replace. But it is extremely suggestive, and in its refusal to ground categoriality in semantics alone, it opens up the interesting question of how many grammatical facts can be explained by discourse-functional principles rather than semantic ones.

9.2 The semantics of tense and aspect

Exploration of semantic aspects of grammar has not come to an end once we have a satisfactory theory of the parts of speech: we still have to understand the meanings of the many morphosyntactic categories to which grammatical principles apply, principally number and case for nouns, and tense, mood and aspect for verbs. In this section, we will focus on the semantics of the verbal categories of tense and aspect. These are categories with interesting and complex semantics, which show close relations with other grammatical properties of the clause.

9.2.1 Tense

A famous comment about the difficulty of thinking about time is usually attributed to Saint Augustine (354–430 AD): 'What then is time? If no one asks me, I know what it is. If I wish to explain it to him who asks, I do not know.' We could make a similar observation about the two linguistic categories in which information about time is presented, tense and aspect. The first of these categories, tense, is a familiar part of the way we talk about English grammar: one does not need to have studied very much grammar to know that *Jane runs* is usually described as present tense, *Jane ran* as past, and *Jane will run* as future. It also seems to make perfect sense for a language to mark differences in the temporal location of different events.

But the picture gets more complicated when we look at the details of the way these different verb forms actually work in English. Tenses are very good examples of prototype categories: their meanings can be defined by specifying the central tendency of their members, but we find many peripheral instantiations of the category which lack the prototypical features. These central tendencies are often the meanings suggested by the grammatical label for the tense-marker in question. But it soon becomes apparent that the labels 'past', 'present' and 'future' can be quite misleading as descriptions of the time-reference of some uses of English verb forms. For example, take the English present tense, as exemplified by forms like *Jane runs* or *Jane is running*. These are both examples of the present tense; *runs* is traditionally known as the 'simple present' tense, and *is running* as the 'present continuous'. What's odd about these labels is that the simple present tense – *runs* – actually *can't* be used to refer to an action that's happening at the moment of speaking. To see this, imagine that you and Jane are in a room. You are speaking on the phone to Michael. While you're still talking Jane gets up, waves, and moves towards the door. You shout out 'goodbye' and Michael asks what's happening. Your reply could only be (23a), and not (23b)

(23) a. *Jane's leaving.*
　　 b. *Jane leaves.*

The 'simple' present is unavailable as an option for actions happening at the moment of speaking; only the present continuous can be used. That's far from being the end of the story, however. Note that we can use the simple present to describe an action that someone habitually takes, even if they're not performing it *now*. For instance, *She flies* is a good reply to the question 'how does Jane get to Canberra?' regardless of whether Jane is currently in the air. As long as flying is her regular mode of transport the simple present tense is appropriate.

　　Both varieties of the present can be used to describe future events:

(24) Q: *When are you flying/do you fly out?*
　　 A: *I'm leaving/leave next week.*

QUESTION　Can you discern any regular semantic difference between the simple present and the continuous on the basis of this reply?

And it even works the other way round: there are situations where the *future* tense can be used to refer to a situation unfolding at the present moment. For example, (25) often has present time reference:

(25) *I'll look forward to seeing you tomorrow.*

The speaker who says this doesn't mean to imply that they're not *already* looking forward to it *now*. Instead, the future *will look forward* seems equivalent in its temporal reference to the present continuous, *I'm looking forward*: both refer to the present time.

The future tense, then, can sometimes be used to refer to presently occurring actions. To make matters worse, we can sometimes use the present tense to refer to past actions. This is especially common in narrative:

(26) *You'll never believe what happened.* I'm **hanging round** *waiting to go home when he* **bursts** *into the room,* **pulls** *out a packet of cigarettes,* **lights** *one and then* **swallows** *it ...*

The events being related occurred in the past, but the speaker chooses the present tense to refer to them.

Clearly, there is a lot more to the use of the 'past', 'present' and 'future' tenses in English than those simple labels imply. We will return to the description of English at the end of this section.

9.2.1.1 Tense and time

Tense is the name of the class of grammatical markers used to signal the location of situations in time, such as English *sing–sang–had sung–will sing*. A language's tense system isn't its only means for signifying temporal relations, of course: as well as grammatical markers, languages have *lexical* means of referring to temporal distinctions – words like English *now, then, yesterday, formerly* and so on. Usually a much greater range of temporal distinctions can be expressed lexically than by the grammatical markers: languages have lexical expressions which mean *the week before my mother's birthday*, but there is no tense that can express this meaning. Some languages, indeed, lack a system of grammatical tense anything like the one familiar from languages like English or German.

Tense markers are typically found on verbs. (See Nordlinger and Sadler 2004 for a survey of tense in nominals.) The moment of speaking typically provides the point around which temporal reference is 'anchored', in the same way that the speaker and their location constitute the 'deictic centre' for person and place deixis (see 3.2.3). Just as the speaker's own person is the 'I' and their spatial location is the 'here', so the time of utterance is the 'now'. This 'now' is what serves to locate the other temporal categories of the language. In tense systems which distinguish past, present and future tenses, the timeframe evoked by present tense verbs will typically include the 'now' of utterance, but it will by no means be limited to it. The events and states expressed by verbs usually last longer than the actual moment of speaking. Really only in explicitly performative uses of verbs (4.1) such as 'I promise' or 'I apologise' can the time of the event and the time of utterance be said to overlap. The activity or state referred to by a present tense form will usually also have been true in the immediate past and may also extend into the future; use of the present tense, however, simply asserts that the action or state in question obtains *now*.

QUESTION   Can habitual uses of the present tense, like *Jane flies to Canberra* be reconciled with this last statement? If so, how?

QUESTION   Sometimes the present tense is used for past time situations: *I **hear** you're getting married; Glen **tells** me you've been sacked.* Are there other examples like this? Can you explain this use of the present?

Three basic temporal divisions are relevant to the representation of time in language: what is happening now, what will happen afterwards, and what has already happened. These three distinct temporal zones can be treated in a number of different ways. Some languages display a three-way division between past, present and future, with each tense marked separately on the verb, as in (27). Others have a two-way distinction; either between past and non-past, as in (28), or (more rarely) future and non-future as in (29) (examples (27) and (29) are from Chung and Timberlake 1985: 204–205):

(27) Past–present–future distinguished: Lithuanian (Indo-European; Lithuania)
    a. *dirb-au*
       work-ISG (PAST)
       'I worked/was working.'

    b. *dirb-u*
       work-ISG (PRES)
       'I work/am working.'

    c. *dirb-s-iu*
       work-FUT-ISG
       'I will work/will be working.'

(28) Past and non-past distinguished: Guugu-Yimidhirr (Pama-Nyungan, Australia)
    a. *Ngayu*   *mayi*   *budaara-l*   *ngayu*   *yi-way*
       1SG.NOM   food.ABS   eat-NONPAST   1SG.NOM   here-LOC
       nhinga-l
       sit-NONPAST
       'I'm eating food [and] I'll stay here' (Haviland 1979: 92)

    b. *Badhibay*   *ngarraa*   *yarra guwa*   *dhamba-rrin*
       bone.ABS   skin.ABS   yonder west.ALL   throw-PST
       '[She] threw the skin and bone[s] off to the West yonder.' (Haviland 1979: 92)

(29) Future–non-future distinguished: Takelma (Penutian; Oregon; extinct)
    a. *yaná-t'eʔ*
       go(IRR)-ISG(FUT)
       'I will go.

    b. *yan-t'eʔ*
       go (REAL)-I SG(NONFUT)
       'I went/am going/am about to go.'

Languages with bipartite systems will, of course, have other means of indicating distinctions within the non-past or non-future categories. Adverbs with meanings like 'tomorrow', 'now', 'at some point in the future', 'formerly' are obvious examples. However, no language is recorded as having a single tense covering *both* past and future: it would seem that the regions of temporal reference covered by a single tense have to be continuous (Comrie 1985: 15).

One reason for the lack of any grammatical categories which merge past and future meanings may be that the future has rather a different status from the past (and, for that matter, from the present). Whereas past and present events are usually knowable, at least in principle, what is going to happen in the future is unknown. This means that a much greater deal of uncertainty attaches to future meanings; as a result, the grammatical category of future is often mixed up with **modal** categories – categories which register the speaker's attitude to and degree of confidence in the events reported. We can see this in the following examples from Lakota, which show the same morpheme that expresses futurity also being used in modal contexts:

(30) Lakota (Siouan; Dakota, USA; Chung and Timberlake 1985: 206)
  a. *Ma-khúžį*
     I-sick
     'I was sick/am sick.'

  b. *Ma-khúžįkte*
     I-sick FUT
     'I will be sick.'

  c. *Yį-kta   iyéčheča*
     go-FUT   perhaps
     'He ought to go.'

This added modal coloration of future meanings may be what blocks the assimilation of past and future into a single category.

Many languages express gradations within the past or future. In Cocama (Tupi, Peru; Fabricius-Hansen 2006: 568), there are three past tenses, each of which indicates a different depth of temporal distance from the moment of utterance:

(31) a. *ritama-ca   tuts-ui*
        town-to   go-PAST$_1$
        'I went to town today'

  b. *ritama-ca   tutsu-icuá*
        town-to   go-PAST$_2$
        'I went to town yesterday/a few days ago'

  c. *ritama-ca   tutsu-tsuri*
        town-to   go-PAST$_3$
        'I went to town a long time ago'

The tense system of some languages, like Tiwi (isolate; Australia), Yandruwandha (Pama-Nyungan; Australia; extinct) or Kom (Niger-Congo; West Africa), includes morphemes indicating the time of day (e.g. morning, evening) at which the situation denoted by the verb occurs. Yet others, like Haya (Niger-Congo; Tanzania), have past tenses which encode a contrast between 'earlier today', 'yesterday' and 'before yesterday'.

9.2.1.2 Perfect tenses

An obvious characteristic of the English tense system is the availability of a contrast between the simple past or preterite tense (32a), and the present perfect (32b):

(32) a. *We saw the Queen.*
     b. *We have seen the Queen.*

Both sentences locate the event of seeing the Queen in the past; however, the choice between preterite and present perfect construes the implications of the event in different ways. Meanings like that of the English present perfect (32b) are common in the world's languages, yet prove remarkably hard to describe in a satisfying way. The perfect is often explained as conveying the *continuing relevance of the past action* (Comrie 1985; Fabricius-Hansen 2006). Intuitively, there seems something right about this. But how to be precise about the exact meaning conveyed here? Imagine that B is in the room, and A comes in and initiates an exchange with the words 'What's going on?'. Three possible replies are given in (33) and (34):

(33) A: *What's going on?*
     B: a. *Well, I've been a bit naughty...*
         b. *Well, I've written the email...*
         c. *Well, I've broken your Ming vase...*

(34) A: *What's going on?*
     B: a. *Well, I was a bit naughty ...*
         b. *Well, I wrote the email ...*
         c. *Well, I broke your Ming vase ...*

The (33) sentences use the present perfect; the (34) the preterite. Presumably B's answer is just as relevant in both cases; the difference must be that in (33) B is *specifically representing* their answer as relevant, whereas in (34) they are not. The problem here is that in the absence of any way of knowing whether something is or isn't being 'specifically represented' as relevant, we don't really know whether our description of the semantics of the present perfect is on the right track. 'Relevant' is a slippery label: without an independent way of showing what is and isn't perceived as relevant, we arguably lack any way of testing it (Klein 1992).

     We can also point to some cases where the present perfect seems to be *less* likely a choice than the preterite, even though the situation referred to is clearly relevant:

(35) a. ?*What **have you said**?*
     b. ?*You've **frowned**. Is something wrong?*
     c. ?*Why **have you laughed**?*

(36) a. *What did you say?*

    b. *You frowned. Is something wrong?*

    c. *Why did you laugh?*

In all three cases the present perfect in (35) is less idiomatic than the simple past equivalent in (36).

QUESTION   Can you account for this situation? How restricted is it to a certain class of verbs?

QUESTION   Can you account for the varying acceptability of the following sentences and ones like them? Sentences (i) and (ii) may appeal to different explanations. What do they contribute to our understanding of the meaning of the English perfect?

(i)   a. *I have read fifty novels since Christmas.*

     b. **I have read fifty novels last year.*

(ii) a. *I have eaten kangaroo many times before.*

     b. **/?I have eaten some kangaroo many times before.*

     c. *I have eaten some kangaroo.*

9.2.2 Aspect and Aktionsart

Our discussion of English in the previous section has a glaring omission: we haven't yet discussed the progressive forms, i.e. forms like *I am eating, I was eating, I have been eating, I will be eating* and so on. These forms have a fundamental difference from tenses: they're not, like tenses, about the *event* in *time*, i.e. about whether the event is located in the past, present or future; instead, they're about whether time is seen as moving through the event: they're about *time* in the *event*.

    What do I mean by this? Think about the contrasts in (37).

(37) a. *John laughed.*

    b. *John was laughing.*

John laughed is in the simple past or preterite tense: it tells us that at some point before the time of utterance, John was expressing his amusement. How does that contrast with (37b), *John was laughing*? With respect to the event's location in time, it doesn't contrast at all: just like (37a), (37b) tells us that the laugh occurred some time before the moment of speaking. From the point of view of how they locate the event in time, (37a) and (37b) are identical.

    So how do they differ? Think about the different ways each presents what John was doing. *John was laughing* seems to emphasise the progress or unfolding of the event over a period of time (several seconds, presumably): *John laughed*, on the other hand, seems to treat the event as a single moment in time, and not to focus any attention on the existence of different stages within the laughing event itself. Another way of putting this contrast would be to say that *John was laughing* 'zooms in' on the event so that we become aware of its internal temporal duration; *John laughed*, on the other hand, 'zooms out' to a distance at which the event just appears as a single, undifferentiated whole.

The difference between (37a) and (37b) is a difference of **aspect**. Aspect is the name of the grammatical category which expresses differences in the way time is presented in events. Different tenses show different locations of the event in time; different aspects show different ways of presenting time within the event itself: as flowing, or as stationary. The aspectual system, then, is about how the internal temporal constituency of an event is viewed; about whether the event is viewed from the distance, as a single unanalysable whole, with its beginning, middle and end foreshortened into one, or from close-up, so that the distinct stages of the event can be seen individually.

The principal aspectual distinction is between **perfective** and **imperfective** aspect. Perfective aspect is the one found in (37a); imperfective in (37b). In English, perfective aspect is expressed by the 'simple' forms of the verb, and imperfective by the 'progressive' or 'continuous' ones – those that are formed by the BE + -*ing* construction. (The English term 'progressive' or 'continuous', which we used above to describe forms like (37b), are language particular labels for imperfective aspect: in what follows, we will mainly use them as labels for the *formal* grammatical category marked by BE + -*ing*. To mark the semantic values that these categories express, we will use the terms *perfective* and *imperfective*.) We find the same perfective/imperfective contrast in the following forms:

perfective	imperfective
Briony read the paper	*Briony was reading the paper*
Briony will do the crossword	*Briony will be doing the crossword*
Briony's practised	*Briony has been practising.*

Note that the distinction has nothing to do with the actual nature of the event: exactly the same event can be expressed using imperfective or perfective aspect, without this entailing any difference in what actually happened. The same event of reading the paper, doing the crossword or practising is described in the two columns above. The shift between perfective and imperfective aspect reflects no difference in the event itself, but simply a difference in the way the speaker chooses to present (or 'construe') the event. It's especially important to realize that the contrast between perfective and imperfective is independent of the *actual duration* of the event in question. Events that lasted a long time can often be described in perfective aspect, as in (38a), whereas instantaneous ('punctual') events may also be presented imperfectively, although this is somewhat rarer (38b):

(38) a. *Evolution created the eye over many millennia.*
   b. *I was turning the key in the lock when I heard a funny noise in the room*
      (Larreya and Rivière 1999: 44)

Similarly, the choice between perfective and imperfective aspect is also independent of the question of whether the event is completed:

(39) a. *We climbed the mountain all day yesterday and still didn't reach the top.*

    b. *We were climbing the mountain all day yesterday and eventually reached the top.*

Sentence (39a) uses perfective aspect (*climbed*) but signifies an incomplete action; (39b) uses imperfective (*were climbing*) but refers to an event which was completed.

The aspectual contrast between perfective and imperfective therefore can't be reduced either to a contrast of duration or of completion. The default correlation is for verbs in the perfective to refer to complete actions, and for verbs in the imperfective to refer to ones with a temporal duration, but the above examples show that these default specifications can easily be overridden. Aspect refers to a quite distinct semantic category from completion or duration, and languages have different morpho-syntactic means of conveying these notions. In Warlpiri (Pama-Nyungan, Australia), for example, duration of an event can be registered through reduplication of the verb stem.

Aspectual contrasts play an important role in discourse, especially in narrative. The choice of an imperfective or perfective form influences the interpretation of the chronological relations between the different actions reported in a text. For example, consider the short narrative in (40):

(40) *Kewell runs across the field and passes the ball. Cahill scores.*

These verbs are all perfective. This indicates a *sequence* of events. We can only understand the different actions as following each other: first Kewell runs, then he passes, then Cahill scores. Varying the order of the verbs also varies the temporal order in which we understand the events occurred:

(41) *Cahill scores. Kewell passes the ball and runs across the field.*

By contrast, a string of imperfective verbs denotes a set of *simultaneous* actions:

(42) *Cahill was scoring, Kewell was running and Kennedy was fixing his boot.*

Lastly, the combination in (43) shows a foregrounded perfective event cutting into a background imperfective event:

(43) *Cahill scored. Kewell was running and Kennedy was fixing his boot.*

This time, we can vary the order of the verbs without any change to the temporal relations: whatever the order of the clauses, the default interpretation is that Cahill scored *during the period* in which Kewell was running and Kennedy fixing his boot. For more discussion of the role of aspect in discourse, see Hopper (1982) and Thelin (1990).

A major difference between tense and aspect is that tense is deictic (3.2.3) and aspect isn't. The time of utterance forms the point of reference which structures a language's tense system; since the time of utterance changes from one utterance to the next, the actual values of past, present and future themselves change, future becoming present becoming past as time moves on. The particular time reference of any tense therefore has to be anchored deictically in the moment of utterance, just as the reference of spatial deictics like *here* and *there* has to be anchored by considerations of the speaker's location. Aspect, by contrast, doesn't depend like tense on any external, deictic connection to the speech situation; it only makes reference to the internal temporal properties of the event, regardless of its location with respect to the continually shifting present moment. But despite this important difference, aspect and tense categories are typically merged in the grammatical categories of a particular language. Two well-known examples are the Spanish 'imperfect' tense, which combines imperfective aspect and past time, and the 'perfective' in Arabic (perfective aspect and past time).

QUESTION   Aspectual considerations give us a way to explain the impossibility of using the English simple present (*I read, I run, I fly*) to refer to presently occurring events. Can you see what the explanation is?

9.2.2.1 A rich aspectual system: Mandarin

As an example of a fairly rich system of aspectual markers, let's consider Mandarin Chinese (Smith 1997). Aspectual markers are optional in Mandarin, and they are frequently omitted. When this happens, the aspectual interpretation of the sentence is flexible. Thus, (44) can receive either perfective or imperfective interpretation:

(44) *Zhangsan   xiuli   yitai   luyinji.*
　　　Zhangsan   repair   oneCL   tape recorder
　　　'Zhangsan repaired/is repairing a tape recorder.' (Smith 1997: 277)

Since Chinese has no grammatical marking of tense, (44) can reasonably prompt the questions 'is he still repairing it?' and 'did he finish repairing it?'.

　　If a speaker chooses to introduce aspectual meaning, Mandarin offers two perfective and two imperfective markers, each with a differing meaning. The perfective markers are *le* and *guo*. As perfectives, they present the situation as simple and closed – lacking any of the internal complexity associated with imperfectives. The following sentences show some typical uses of -*le*:

(45) a. *Tamen   shang   ge   yue   qu-le   Xiang Gang*
　　　　they   last   CL   month go-LE   Hong Kong
　　　　'Last month they went to Hong Kong.' (Smith 1997: 266)

　　b. *Wo   shuaiduan-le   tui*
　　　　I   break-LE   leg
　　　　'I broke my leg.' (Smith 1997: 267)

We said a moment ago that perfectivity is not the same as completion, and Chinese illustrates this very nicely. Thus, the perfective form in (46a) does not entail that the action be completed, as we can see in (46b); (46c) gives another example of the perfective used without the implication of completion:

(46) a. *Wo zuotian xie-le yifeng xin*
         I   yesterday   write-LE   oneCL   letter
         'I wrote a letter yesterday.' (Smith 1997: 68)

     b. *Wo zuotian xie-le yifeng xin, keshi mei*
         I   yesterday   write-LE   oneCL   letter   but   not
         xie-wan.
         write-finish
         'I wrote a letter yesterday but didn't finish it.' (Smith 1997: 68)

     c. *Wo gangcai xie-le yifeng xin yinwei shijian*
         I   just   write-LE   oneCL   letter   because   time
         guanxi mei.you xie-wan
         issue   not.have   write-finish
         'I was just writing a letter and because of issues with time I didn't finish writing it.'

Completion is signalled by an entirely different morpheme, *wan*, in (46b) and (46c).

Like *-le*, the second perfective marker, *-guo*, also presents a closed, simple situation. Unlike *-le*, however, it indicates that the final state of the situation no longer holds. In contrast to (45a), compare (47):

(47) *Tamen shang ge yue qu-guo Xiang Gang*
      they   last   CL   month   go-GUO   Hong Kong
      'Last month they went to Hong Kong (and they are no longer there)' (Smith 1997: 267)

(45a) gave no information about whether the people referred to are still in Hong Kong; (47), on the other hand, tells us through *-guo* that the final part of the situation referred to by the verb no longer holds. The final part of the situation denoted by *qu* 'go' is being in Hong Kong: they must, therefore, no longer be in Hong Kong.

Here is another example of *-guo*, to be contrasted with (45b) above:

(48) *Wo shuaiduan-guo tui*
      I   break-GUO   leg
      'I have broken my leg (it has healed since)' (Smith 1997: 267)

The final part of the event of breaking one's leg is having a broken leg. *-guo* tells us that this situation no longer obtains: the leg must have subsequently healed.

The two Mandarin imperfective markers present the situation from an internal point of view. One of them, *-zhe*, has a resultative stative meaning which we will not discuss (for details, see Smith 1997: 273ff). The other, *zai*, is a typical imperfective with a meaning similar to the English progressive:

(49) a. *Tamen*   *zai*   *da*   *qiu.*
         they   ZAI   play   ball
         'They are playing ball' (Smith 1997: 272)

   b. *Zhangsan*   *zai*   *xie*   *yifeng*   *xin.*
       Zhangsan   ZAI   write   oneCL   letter
       'Zhangsan is writing a letter.' (Smith 1997: 272)

There are some differences between the English progressive and Mandarin *zai*, however. In English, verbs which denote instantaneous events can be compatible with progressive markers. It is possible to say *he is winning the race* or *he is dying*, even though winning a race and dying are strictly events which occur instantaneously. With both these verbs, the progressive means that the subject is in the lead-up to the occurrence itself. Mandarin *zai* does not allow this interpretation: instantaneous events are incompatible with *zai*, as the following examples show:

(50) a. **Ta*   *zai*   *ying*   *sai*   *pao.*
          He   ZAI   win   race   run
          'He is winning the race.' (Smith 1997: 272)

   b. **Lao*   *Wang*   *zai*   *si.*
       Old   Wang   ZAI   die
       'Old Wang is dying.' (Smith 1997: 272)

The impossibility of these sentences in Mandarin raises another set of important considerations. As we have just seen, what rules these sentences out is the incompatibility of imperfectivity with the inherent nature of the events concerned – winning a race, or dying. These events are, as we've seen, instantaneous; they just can't be 'stretched out' in order to accommodate a progressive meaning. We might say that 'win' and 'die' are *inherently perfective* events. But, in this case, what about the English translations of (50)? How can *win* and *die* receive imperfective treatment in English if the verbs refer to inherently perfective events? We will consider the answer below.

QUESTION   In the meantime, can you account for the acceptability of the English translations of (50a) and (50b)?

9.2.2.2 States and occurrences

The idea that events have certain inherent aspectual properties goes back to Aristotle. In the twentieth century, the philosopher Zeno Vendler (1957) put forward an influential framework for the study of these properties, claiming that events could be classified into four basic classes: states, activities, accomplishments and achievements. The term for an event's inherent aspectual classification is **Aktionsart** (German: 'action kind'). These classes show significant interaction effects with perfective and imperfective meanings, as we will see below. The four basic Aktionsart classes do not reflect properties of individual verbs: as we will see in a moment, *I am drawing* is an activity, whereas *I am drawing a picture* is an

accomplishment. A single verb can thus have different Aktionsart properties in different contexts.

The most basic Aktionsart distinction is between **states** and **occurrences**.
States are, unsurprisingly, static; they involve an unchanging situation.
Occurrences, by contrast, are dynamic, and involve something happening.
States don't involve anything happening; they just exist or obtain, without
any sequence of internal phases. Because of this lack of any internal,
dynamic phases, they are associated cross-linguistically with perfective
aspect, as can be shown in English, for instance, by the following grammatical properties, both of which distinguish them from occurrences:

States vs. occurrences

- states can't appear, or can only appear exceptionally, with the progressive (imperfective): *I am/was knowing Greek; *I am understanding
  what you're telling me; *[?]They are liking tomatoes.* Occurrences can take
  the progressive.
- states can take the simple present in reference to the present moment,
  whereas occurrences can't: *I know Greek* (= I know Greek now); *I teach the
  class French* (≠ I am teaching the class French now)

Another grammatical feature separating states and occurrences is the following:

- states can't appear in the frame *What she did next was_____.* E.g.
  *What she did next was like tomatoes/know German/believe in a supreme
  being.*

Not all occurrences are alike. Based on considerations of inherent differences between the events involved, Vendler distinguished three different types of occurrence, **achievements**, **activities** and **accomplishments**.

Achievements are **punctual** occurrences; this means that they are
instantaneous, occurring at a point in time. Examples of achievements
would be *realizing the truth, buying the paper, dying, recognizing/spotting/
identifying something, losing/finding something, reaching the summit, crossing
the border, starting/stopping/resuming something* ... These verbs essentially
refer to an instantaneous or near-instantaneous transition between two
states: not knowing and knowing the truth; not owning and owning the
paper, being alive and being dead, etc. Because the transition is conceptualized as instantaneous, achievements often resist imperfective aspect,
as is reflected by their frequent incompatibility with the English progressive:

(51) *[?/*]I was noticing a problem*
     [?/]I was losing my keys*
     [?/]I was finding the keys* (= in the process of finding them; the sentence is
     acceptable if taken to mean 'I was meant to find the keys'/'I was the
     one in charge of finding the keys')

In addition to their incompatibility with imperfective aspect, achievements in English are distinguished from activities and accomplishments by the following grammatical features:

Achievements vs activities/accomplishments

- Achievement expressions are not compatible with *begin* or *stop/finish*:

  ?He began to reach the summit.
  ?She stopped noticing a sudden dimming of the lights.
  ?He stopped buying the apple.
  Cf. *she began/stopped/finished building the wall* [accomplishment]

- Achievement expressions can't appear in the 'middle alternation':
  They found the keys > **The keys find easily.* [= *the keys are easy to find*]
  They noticed the difference > **The difference notices easily.* [= *the*
      difference is easy to notice]
  They bought the book > **The book buys easily* [= *the book is easy to buy*]
  They solved the problem > *?The problem solves easily* [= *the problem*
      is easy to solve]
  Cf. *They read the book* [accomplishment] > *The book reads easily*

QUESTION   What other achievements can you think of?

Unlike achievements, accomplishments and activities are durative: they occur over a period of time. This means that they can freely appear with imperfective aspect. Accomplishments are **bounded** or **telic** (Greek *telos* 'goal'): they have an inherent final point beyond which they cannot continue. Delivering a speech is a good example of an accomplishment: this is an event that *cannot* continue beyond a certain point: the point where the speech is finished. The speaker can make the speech as long as they like, of course, but once they have reached the end of the speech, the action of delivering the speech is obviously over (although the speaker may continue to stay on the podium, answer questions, shuffle their notes, and so on: none of this counts as *delivering a speech*). Other accomplishments are painting a picture, making a chair, building a house, writing/reading a novel, giving/attending a class, playing a game of chess ...

Activities differ from accomplishments in being **unbounded** or **atelic**: they don't have any inherent terminal point. Running, walking, swimming, pushing or pulling something, watching and doodling are all examples of activities. These occurrences can continue indefinitely: one can go on running, walking and so on without any limit.

QUESTION   Name the following occurrences as activity, accomplishment, or achievement.

They watched the TV.
He found his pen.
She walked to the museum.
You were talking.
I'll take the bus.

The difference between an activity and an accomplishment (or an achievement) will often be correlated with the presence of other grammatical structures in the clause, in particular, the presence of certain types of direct object or certain types of adverbial modification. Activities, as we've seen, are unbounded processes. But they can be transformed into achievements/accomplishments by altering these other grammatical variables. For instance, consider (52):

(52) a. *I'm reading* [activity]
    b. *I'm reading books* [activity]
    c. *I'm reading a book* [accomplishment]
    d. *I'm reading three books* [accomplishment]

Reading in (52a) is an activity: it denotes an ongoing process with no inherent temporal boundary. The same is true in (52b): since the clause doesn't tell us how many books are being read, we assume that the process of reading can continue indefinitely. But if the verb's object is precisely quantified, as in (52c–d), the verb phrase is an accomplishment: the object serves to identify the end-point of the event. We know that the event will have reached its inherent end-point once one or three books have been finished.

Since mass nouns are not, by definition, precisely quantified, the verb phrases they appear in will typically count as activities:

(53) a. *I ate pasta* [activity]
    b. *I maintained machinery* [activity]

What about other types of modification than NP objects? Think about the contrast between (54a) and (54b):

(54) a. *I fell.*
    b. *I fell down.*

Fall in (54a) is an activity; it can continue indefinitely (in space, say); *fall down*, however, imposes an end-point, transforming the event into an achievement.

The difference between activities and accomplishments can also be captured by thinking about how we would describe what is happening within the event itself. Activities like *running* are homogeneous: they consist of themselves; the sub-events they are composed of can be described in exactly the same way as the entire activity itself. As Vendler explains 'If it is true that someone has been running for half an hour, then it must be true that he has been running for *every period within that half hour*' (Vendler 1957: 145–146; emphasis added). The activity of pulling something – let's say, a cart – is similarly homogeneous: it consists of itself; any period within the timeframe of the complete event can also be described as pulling a cart. A donkey that is pulling a cart for half an hour is also pulling a cart during any smaller interval within that half hour.

Unlike activities, accomplishments aren't homogeneous: they don't consist of themselves; the sub-events they are composed of *cannot* themselves be described in the same way as the complete event itself. Unlike *running*, *running a mile* is an accomplishment: the addition of the noun phrase *a mile* imposes an inherent limit on the event, transforming it from an activity to an accomplishment. To take Vendler's example, if an athlete has run a mile in four minutes, they haven't *run a mile* [accomplishment] in any sub-part of that four minutes, even though they have *been running* [activity] (Vendler 1957: 146). Vendler summarizes the difference between activities and accomplishments as follows:

It appears, then, that running and its kind [*activities*] go on in time in a homogeneous way; any part of the process is of the same nature as the whole. Not so running a mile or writing a letter [*accomplishments*]; they also go on in time, but proceed towards a terminus which is logically necessary to their being what they are. Somehow this climax casts its shadow backward, giving a new color to all that went before. (1957: 146)

The principal linguistic test to distinguish activities from accomplishments in English is the following:

Activities vs. accomplishments
Activity predicates

- can't be modified by time-frame adverbials like *in an hour*:

  *?/*I watched television in an hour*
  *?/*They walked in an hour*

- resist appearing as the complement of *finish*
  *?/*I finished daydreaming*

Accomplishment predicates can appear in both type of structure:

  He cooked the meal in three hours.
  She finished writing her novel.

QUESTION   Consider the effect of *almost* in the following sentences:

(a) *I almost washed the car.*
(b) *I almost sang.*
(c) *I almost ran a mile.*
(d) *I almost rang.*
(e) *I almost reached the top.*
(f) *I almost took the blame.*

Sentences with *almost* are sometimes ambiguous. Identify and describe the ambiguity. Is it correlated with any Aktionsart class(es)?

Focusing on what is happening inside the event itself gives us a way to think about the difference between the first class, achievements, and the other two. Achievements are usually described as punctual or instantaneous; we followed this description a few paragraphs ago. An alternative, and in fact better way of thinking of achievements is the following, due to Dowty, which we will quote at length:

> It is often suggested that accomplishments differ from achievements in that achievements are 'punctual' in some sense, whereas accomplishments have duration: dying, an achievement, happens all at once, while building a house, an accomplishment, takes time. However, many events usually classed as achievements do in fact have some duration. [... For example,] a physician may [...] view dying as a process with multiple stages happening in sequence. [...] Rather, I think the distinction as Vendler and others must have intuitively understood it is something like the following: achievements are those kinesis predicates which are not only typically of shorter duration than accomplishments, but also those which we do not normally understand as entailing a sequence of sub-events, given our usual every-day criteria for identifying the events named by the predicate. Dying, or reaching the finish line, take place, according to every-day criteria, when one state – being alive or being not yet at the finish line – is recognized as being replaced by another: being dead, or being at the finish line, respectively.
>
> (Dowty 1986: 42–43)

On Dowty's view, the difference between accomplishments and achievements is not a contrast between events which do and don't have duration. The idea of a durationless event is, in any case, paradoxical. Instead, the contrast is between events (accomplishments) which are normally thought of as containing a series of subevents, and those (achievements) which are not. Another way of expressing this distinction, inspired by Bache (1997: 219), would be to say that achievements are events which are 'conceived of as taking up an absolute minimum of time'.

Bearing in mind how we are now interpreting 'punctual', we can diagram the four Aktionsart classes in the following way:

State	[+static], [−telic], [−punctual]
Activity	[−static], [−telic], [−punctual]
Achievement	[−static], [+telic], [+punctual]
Accomplishment	[−static], [+telic], [−punctual]

Following Smith (1997), many discussions of aspect now recognize a fifth Aktionsart class, the **semelfactives** (Latin *semel* 'once'; *fact-* 'done'). Semelfactives are single-instance events like *cough, knock, blink, flap (a wing)*, etc. They are punctual, since we conceive of them as occupying a bare minimum of time. Somewhat less obviously, Smith classifies them as atelic, since they have no result or outcome (Smith 1997: 29). Atelicity, indeed, is the only feature distinguishing semelfactives from achievements, the class to which these verbs had previously belonged. The feature specifications for semelfactives are therefore

Semelfactive	[−static], [−telic], [+punctual]

When semelfactives combine with progressive or durative constructions, they take on an **iterative** interpretation, i.e. one where we understand that several instances of the event took place:

(55) a. *I was knocking* (several individual knocks)
     b. *I was blinking* (several individual blinks)

As a result, they are compatible with expressions for durations of time:

(56) a. *The bird flapped its wings for half an hour* (numerous individual flaps)
     b. *I was coughing all day yesterday*

9.2.2.3 Variation within a single class: achievements

The traditional account of Aktionsart classes assumes that the four classes are homogeneous cross-linguistically. On this account, verbs which have similar meanings should have similar aspectual properties from one language to another, since they will belong to the same Aktionsart class. In this section we will see that the picture is not as simple as this: cross-linguistic investigation reveals some fairly significant differences in the temporal properties associated with verbs of the same Aktionsart class in different languages.

In order to show this, we'll explore a classic achievement verb, *die*, discussed by Botne (2003). Recall that achievements are instantaneous or minimally lasting occurrences, in which the actor passes from one state to another: *realizing the truth, losing/finding something, noticing something,* and so on. Dying is just about as instantaneous an event as they come. One moment we're alive, the next moment we're dead: blink and you might miss it. Dying is thus something that happens in an absolute minimum of time. Of course, the lead-up to the moment of death might be protracted, but someone who's near to death is still, quite clearly, alive. The instantaneous nature of *die* in English is reflected by its incompatibility with *in the midst of*: one cannot, in English, be *in the midst of dying*. Other classic achievement verbs show the same restriction: **I'm in the midst of realizing the truth/losing my wallet/noticing a problem.*

Botne proposes that achievement verbs can, in fact, potentially encode durative temporal phases. This doesn't mean that their traditional classification as punctual is wrong; just that we need to adopt a more detailed view of their meaning. According to Botne, achievement verbs aren't limited to simply expressing a single punctual culmination point. Instead, some achievement verbs may have a more complex temporal structure, in which the central point is surrounded by one or two subsidiary phases, a preliminary ('onset') phase and a 'coda' phase ... It is this tripartite structure which constitutes 'the underlying fabric of the event' (Botne 2003: 236).

Botne claims that all languages have a verb which expresses the instantaneous transition from life to death. Where languages differ is in the temporal phases *surrounding* this central nucleus. Let's begin our cross-linguistic survey by looking at English *die*. Botne claims that *die* in English consists of two phases: the punctual nucleus, and a durative onset phase.

His main evidence for this claim is that, unlike some other achievement verbs, *die* can appear in the progressive, as in (57):

(57) *The old man is dying.*

Given that achievements are described as punctual or instantaneous, this is a somewhat unexpected situation. Some other achievement verbs, like *buy*, can appear in the progressive. Many, however, resist progressive contexts:

(58) *?/*She is losing her wallet.*
     *?/*She was recognizing her brother.*

Consider the force of the progressive *be dying*. This refers not to the transition moment between life and death itself, but to the lead-up to this moment; *to be dying* typically means to be in the last stages of life. Someone who is dying is still alive. (This explains the occurrence of *die* with the present continuous that we noted in (50b) above. *Win*, as exemplified in (50a), has exactly the same explanation.)

Unlike achievements, activities and accomplishments are durative and, as a result, freely appear in the progressive. But there is an important difference in the effect of the progressive on achievements and activities/accomplishments. Consider the entailment structure of the activity *weep* and the accomplishment *recover* (as in *recover from an illness*):

(59) a. ACTIVITY   *The old woman is weeping.*
      entails   *The old woman has wept.*
   b. ACCOMPLISHMENT   *The old man is recovering (from an illness).*
      does not entail   *The old man has recovered.*
      does entail   *The old man has recovered somewhat.* (Botne 2003: 240)

Compare this to the facts for *die*:

(60) ACHIEVEMENT   *The old man is dying.*
      does not entail   *The old man has died.*
      does not entail   *The old man has died somewhat.*

QUESTION   Compare the entailments of *is buying the paper, is opening the door* and *is realizing the truth*. Do they pattern like *die*?

With *die*, the progressive does not entail that *any* amount of dying has already occurred – the opposite of the case with activities and accomplishments. Botne concludes from this that our conceptualization of *dying* consists of two phases, a durative onset phase, which is what the progressive targets, and a punctual nucleus.

Botne (2003: 240) states that Arabic, Hausa (Afro-Asiatic; Nigeria) and French are like English in that their *die* verbs consist of a durative onset phase preceding the nucleus. He calls this **inceptive type coding**. In Egyptian Arabic, for example, the root *mwt* 'die' takes the progressive prefix *bi-*, as do non-achievement verbs:

(61) a. *Bi-y-muut.*
PROG-3SG.M.PRES-die
'He is dying.' [Achievement] (Botne 2003: 243)

b. *Bi-yi-qra*   *(it-taqriir).*
PROG-3SG.M.PRES-read   (DEF-report)
'He is reading (the report).' [Activity] (Botne 2003: 243)

Further, the progressive can be used even when the nucleus itself did not eventuate, as in (62):

(62) *Kaan*   *bi-y-muut*   *bas*   *il-amaliyya*
3SG.M.was   PROG-3SG.M.PRES-die   but   DEF-operation
ʔanqaz-it-u.
save-3SG.F-3SG.M
'He was dying, but the operation saved him.' (Botne 2003: 244)

The possibility of the progressive here is explained by the hypothesis that *mwt* is not simply an instantaneous state-transition event; the verb's temporal structure also includes an anterior phase which can have durative structure.

Another type of temporal structure found in *die* verbs is what Botne calls **resultative-type encoding**. We will illustrate this from Japanese. The Japanese counterpart to the English progressive is the so-called *-te iru* construction, illustrated in (63):

(63) a. *Warat-te*   *i-ru.*
laugh.3-GER   be-IMPF
'S/he/they is/are laughing.' (Botne 2003: 250)

b. *Tanaka-wa*   *muse-te*   *i-ru.*
Tanaka-TOP   choke-GER   be-IMPF
'Tanaka is choking.' (Botne 2003: 250)

This construction consists of a gerundive form of the verb (glossed GER) and the auxiliary *iru*, an imperfective form of 'be'. When applied to *sinu*, 'die', the *-te iru* construction does not produce a 'progressive' meaning. Instead, it refers to the *state* of death that results from the instantaneous transitional moment:

(64) a. *Tanaka-wa*   *sin-de*   *i-ru.*
Tanaka-TOP   die-GER   be-IMPF
'Tanaka is dead/*is dying.' (Botne 2003: 250)

Botne claims that Japanese has no way to refer to the onset phase of dying. Rather, all one can say is that someone is 'about to die', or 'appears about to die', as in (65).

(65) a. *Tanaka-wa*   *sini-soo-da.*
Tanaka-TOP   die-appear/about.to-be
'Tanaka is about to die.' (Botne 2003: 249)

　　b. *Tanaka-wa*　　*sini-kake-te*　　　　*i-ru.*
　　　 Tanaka-TOP　 die-about.to-GER　 be-IMPF
　　　 'Tanaka is about to die.' (Botne 2003: 249)

All this says is that the moment of death is imminent – not that it is already 'in progress'.

Lastly, we will discuss the purest type of temporal structure for *die*, in which the verb only expresses the instantaneous nucleus. An example of this structure is Assiniboine (Siouan; Dakota, USA). Assiniboine *t'a* can only have a punctual reading, referring to a non-extended point of time (66a). This contrasts with other verbs, such as activity verbs, which also have a progressive reading without any modification to the root (66b).

(66)　a.　*T'a.*
　　　　 die
　　　　 'He dies/(has) died/*is dying.' (Botne 2003: 269)

　　　b.　*Mani.*
　　　　 walk
　　　　 'He walks/(has) walked/is walking.' (Botne 2003: 269)

Assiniboine does have both a progressive (-*hã*) and a continuative (-*ga*) suffix, as seen in (67):

(67)　a.　*Mani-hã.*
　　　　 walk-PROG
　　　　 'He is [in the midst of] walking.' (Botne 2003: 270)

　　　b.　*Manii-ga.*
　　　　 walk-CONT
　　　　 'He is continuing to walk.' (Botne 2003: 270)

However, *t'a* is compatible with neither of these suffixes.

How, then, does one express the inceptive meaning encoded in the English progressive? To convey this meaning, Assiniboine uses the auxiliary verb *aya* 'become', as in (68):

(68)　*T'a*　　*aya.*
　　　 die　　 become
　　　 'He is becoming dead.' (Botne 2003: 269)

This construction cannot, however, be used with activity verbs:

(69)　**Mani　aya.*
　　　 walk　 become (Botne 2003: 270)

Botne concludes from these facts that *t'a* is best thought of as only encoding the nucleus transition.

QUESTION　Can you think of any other ways of analysing the facts?

What is the upshot of this survey? Botne's discussion shows that the verb meanings typically classed as achievements have a more complex temporality than was originally assumed. We cannot simply describe achievements as instantaneous transition points and leave it at that. What is punctual about achievement verbs like *find*, *die*, *notice*, or *recognize* is their *nucleus*; in addition to this nucleus, they may well express a durative onset or coda.

9.2.3 Typology of tense–aspect interactions

Some languages lack any grammatical means of expressing tense–aspect contrasts. In such languages, the relevant contrasts will be achieved through non-grammatical (lexical and pragmatic) means; see Dahl (2001) for details. The complete absence of grammatical coding of tense and aspect is not uncommon in the languages of the world. On the other hand, it is relatively uncommon for languages to show a fully elaborated set of tense and aspect markers in which a past/non-past contrast is available in both perfective and imperfective aspect. Russian is a well-known language which does have just such a full contrast. The range of cross-linguistically attested tense–aspect systems is shown in Figure 9.1.

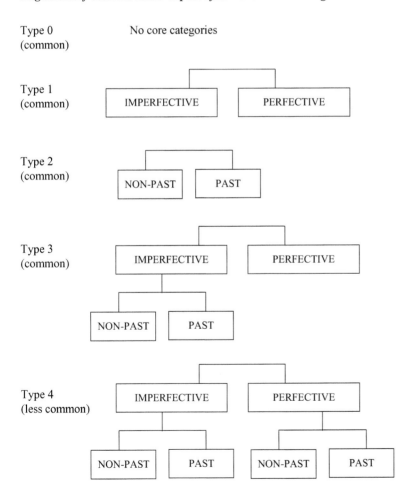

Type 0 (common)   No core categories

Type 1 (common)

Type 2 (common)

Type 3 (common)

Type 4 (less common)

FIGURE 9.1
Cross-linguistic frequency of tense-aspect marker combinations (Dahl 2000: 17).

Summary

What parts of speech a language has is a matter of interpretation

There are usually several different plausible interpretations of the **part of speech categories** (**lexical categories**, **grammatical categories**) of any language.

Morphological and distributional criteria for parts of speech

Some languages have clear **morphological** criteria for assigning words to parts of speech: we can divide up the classes on the basis of what affixes they appear with. In languages without clear morphology, a **distributional** approach to parts of speech can sometimes be used to classify parts of speech on the basis of the way they pattern in sentences. Both morphological and distributional methods for part of speech classification are unreliable. In any case, both presuppose a pre-existing decision about how the parts of speech are to be defined.

Semantic definitions of parts of speech

The same problem affects **semantic definitions** of parts of speech: we cannot appeal to thingness, eventhood and so on as criteria for grammatical category, since they are not known independently of the very grammatical features which they are supposed to establish.

Multicategoriality

Many languages show widespread **multicategoriality** (roots which may appear as different parts of speech). We can think of nouns and verbs as 'slots' or contexts available in each clause, each of which comes associated with the appropriate grammatical machinery. The grammatical slots themselves can be seen as the carriers of the nounhood or verbhood which the word ends up acquiring.

Hopper and Thompson: parts of speech and discourse function

Hopper and Thompson suggest that parts of speech can be understood as **prototype categories** defined by their **discourse functions**. The difference in the grammatical options available to a given occurrence of a noun or verb correlates with its discourse function in a given context – the closer the noun or verb is to playing its prototypical discourse role, the closer it comes to exhibiting the full range of grammatical possibilities of its class. It is open to question whether the discourse function definition of parts of speech is any less problematic than the semantic definitions it replaces.

Tense

Tense is the name of the class of grammatical markers used to signal the location of situations in time. Three basic temporal divisions are relevant to the representation of time in language: what is happening now, what will happen afterwards, and what has already happened. Some languages display a three-way division between past, present and future, with each tense marked separately on the verb. Others have a two-way distinction; either between past and non-past, or (more rarely) future and non-future. **Perfect** tenses are often described in terms of relevance to the speech situation, but this definition is problematic.

Aspect

Aspect is the grammatical category which expresses differences in the way time is presented in events. Aspectual categories express the **internal temporal constituency** of an event; whether the event is viewed from the distance, as a single unanalysable whole (**perfective aspect**), or from close-up, so that the distinct stages of the event can be seen individually (**imperfective aspect**). The perfective/imperfective distinction has nothing to do with the actual nature of the event, but is all about how the event is construed by the speaker. In particular, it is independent of the actual duration of the event in question.

Tense is deictic, aspect isn't

A major difference between tense and aspect is that tense is **deictic** and aspect isn't.

The particular time reference of any tense therefore has to be anchored deictically in the moment of utterance.

Aktionsart

Aktionsart is the term for an event's inherent aspectual classification. Many researchers claim that events can be classified into five basic Aktionsart classes:

- states
- activities
- accomplishments
- achievements, and
- semelfactives

These classes show significant interaction effects with perfective and imperfective meanings. The five Aktionsart classes can be summarized along the dimensions of whether they are **static** (whether they refer to unchanging states or to occurrences), **telicity** (whether they have an inherent end-point) and **punctuality** (whether they are conceived of as consisting of internal temporal parts):

State	[+static], [−telic], [−punctual]
Activity	[−static], [−telic], [−punctual]
Achievement	[−static], [+telic], [+punctual]
Accomplishment	[−static], [+telic], [−punctual]
Semelfactive	[−static], [−telic], [+punctual]

The internal structure of achievements

Botne showed that achievement verbs have a more complex temporality than was originally assumed. What is punctual about achievement verbs like *find*, *die*, *notice*, or *recognize* is their **nucleus**; in addition to this nucleus, a verb may contain a preceding **onset** phase or a subsequent **coda** phase. Languages differ in the temporal phases surrounding the central nucleus.

Tense and aspect-less languages

Some languages lack any grammatical means of expressing tense–aspect contrasts. In such languages, the relevant contrasts will be achieved through non-grammatical (lexical and pragmatic) means. The complete absence of grammatical coding of tense and aspect is not uncommon in the languages of the world.

Further reading

On parts of speech, see Croft (1991; 2001), Baker (2003) and Evans and Osada (2005) and the other articles in the same issue of *Linguistic Typology*. Kinkade (1983) is a classic paper on the absence of the N/V contrast in Salish. Dixon and Aikhenvald (2004) is a cross-linguistic survey of adjectives. On parts of speech in general, and adjectives in particular, see Beck (2002). On tense and aspect, see Comrie (1985) and (1976) respectively. Reichenbach (1947) sets out an influential theory of tense. Klein (1992) is an interesting discussion of the English present perfect. Binnick (1991) is a compendious treatment of tense and aspect. Ter Meulen (1995) and Hopper (1982) relate aspect and discourse. Van Valin (2005) has a useful discussion of Aktionsart classes. An online bibliography of literature on tense, mood and aspect can be found at www.utsc.utoronto.ca/~binnick/TENSE/index.html. *Lingua* 117:2 (2007) is devoted to tense, while volume 118:11 (2008) is devoted to perfectivity.

Exercises

Questions for discussion

1. Morphological criteria for lexical category require that we already know which inflectional endings are the ones that identify nouns, and which are the ones that identify verbs. This seems to render them circular. Discuss whether the circularity is a problem. What are its implications?

2. Think of thirty English adjectives which do not permit comparison. Are there any obvious generalizations you can make explaining why comparison is not a possibility?

3. On the traditional definition, adjectives are defined as qualifying nouns. But in *she smoked an occasional cigarette, occasional* doesn't qualify the noun but the event/act of smoking. Are there other adjectives like this? Can you reformulate the traditional definition in a way that avoids this problem?

4. Consider the following observation:

   … human characteristics tend to be designated by nouns rather than adjectives if they are seen as permanent and/or conspicuous and/or important. The common denominator is, I think, this: a noun indicates a categorization; an adjective, on the other hand, indicates a mere description.' clever/genius; blonde/redhead; *greyhead, *blackhead.

(Wierzbicka 1988: 468)

Another example of this phenomenon is that 'Max is fat' doesn't, according to Wierzbicka (p. 469) imply that Max is the kind of person who is fat; it just mentions fatness as one of the many things that can be said about Max. Do you think this is right? Can you give some other examples of the same contrast in adjective/noun pairs? Does it apply beyond the domain of human characteristics?

5. What are the virtues and disadvantages of a coarse-grained or fine-grained part of speech system?

6. Discuss Hopper and Thompson's claim that nouns function in discourse to introduce participants and 'props' and to deploy them. Assemble and examine samples from a variety of different text types (newspaper articles, blog entries, novels). To what extent is Hopper and Thompson's claim reasonable?

7. Gather a corpus of examples of the English perfect tense from the Internet and elsewhere. Can you improve on 'relevance' as a characterization of its semantics?

8. Tenses in English can often be used to convey other distinctions than those of time. What are some of these?

9. Phrases like *reach the summit* are usually classed as achievements. How then can the possibility of 'it took three hours to reach the summit' be explained?

10. The following sentences seem to be exceptions to the principle that states do not occur in the progressive Can we explain them in some way?

   (a) *You're looking well today.*
   (b) *I'm living in Australia now.*
   (c) *I was feeling good that morning.*
   (d) *Jones is sitting on his horse right in front of her.*
   (e) *Another week passed and even the missionaries were enjoying the voyage.*
   (f) *I'm hoping you'll be able to join us for dinner tonight.*
   (g) *I'm wondering what to do about the twins.*

10 Meaning and morphosyntax II: verb meaning and argument structure

CHAPTER PREVIEW

This chapter discusses the semantics of the clause, particularly the relationship between a verb and its noun participants. This relationship is called the verb's **argument structure**. There are three basic questions:

◆ What principles determine which of the noun phrases associated with a transitive verb will be expressed as subject and which as object?

◆ Can verbs be grouped into classes about which argument structure generalizations can be made?

◆ Can constructions have meanings on their own?

We begin by looking at the semantics of argument structure, a central topic in investigation of the way semantics and syntax are connected. We introduce and motivate the notion of **thematic role**, and go on to consider the modifications this notion has undergone in research into argument structure (10.1). We then consider argument structure **alternations** (10.2), the name for situations where a single verb can take several different argument structures. Lastly, we consider construction grammar, which attributes many apparently lexical meanings to the grammatical constructions in which they occur (10.3).

10.1 Verbs and participants

As the core of the clause, verbs play an important role in the interaction between meaning and syntax. This is because verbs are typically accompanied by nouns which refer to the participants in the event or state the verb describes. These participants receive a range of morphosyntactic markers – case suffixes, subject or object markers, etc. – specifying which participant is the 'actor' or instigator of the action, which the undergoer of the action, as well as other possible roles. In English, these distinctions are made clear by grammatical relations: the noun's coding (or, better, the noun-*phrase*'s coding) as subject, object or indirect object of the verb. In some other languages the job of indicating who acted on whom is done by affixes or particles, without any system of grammatical relations. We will see examples of both types of arrangement in this section.

There's an obvious question we can ask here: what principles govern the morphosyntactic relationship between a verb and its arguments? In English, for example, how do we know which noun phrase to code as subject and which to code as object? Given a situation in which a car hit a tree, why is it that we must describe this as *the car hit the tree*, and not as *the tree hit the car*? Or again, why can we convert (1a) into (1b) and (1c), and (2a) into (2b), but not (2a) into (2c)?

(1)   a. *I gave the bone to the dog.*
      b. *I gave the dog the bone.*
      c. *The dog was given the bone (by me).*

(2)   a. *I sent the chimp to the cage.*
      b. *I sent the chimp.*
      c. **The cage was sent the chimp by me.*

Similarly, why is the last sentence in (3) ungrammatical?

(3)   a. *John opened the door with a key.*
      b. *The key opened the door.*
      c. *The door was opened by John with a key.*
      d. **The key opened the door by John.*

These questions all concern the ways noun phrases relate morphosyntactically to verbs. More generally, we can ask what semantic distinctions are operative in case-systems like the ones illustrated in (4) from Finnish (Finno-Ugric; Finland):

(4)   a. *ammu-i-n*   *karhu-a*
         shoot-PST-1SG   bear-PART
         'I shot at the (a) bear' (Kiparsky 1998: 276)

      b. *Ammu-i-n*   *karhu-n*
         shoot-PST-1SG   bear-ACC
         'I shot the (a) bear' (Kiparsky 1998: 276)

The choice between different case-endings for *karhu* 'bear' has implications for the overall interpretation of the sentence. An obvious general answer to these questions is that the morphosyntactic facts somehow depend on the meaning being conveyed. In English, whether a noun is subject or object depends on what its role is in the meaning of the clause to which it belongs: if a car hits a tree, we have to say that *the car hit the tree*, with *car* as subject and *tree* as object, because that is, in some sense, part of the *meaning* of subject and object position in an active clause. The semantic basis of these choices is made very clear in the Finnish example: when the noun for 'bear' is in the accusative case, the clause means 'shoot the/a bear'; when it's in the partitive case, it means 'shoot *at* the/a bear'. In this section, we will be exploring the ways in which meaning affects the clause-level relation between a verb and its participants.

10.1.1 The traditional picture: thematic roles

The problem of understanding the relations between a verb and its arguments is often talked about as a problem of the syntax–semantics interface. This is a term used mainly in generative grammar (Chomsky 1965, Carnie 2007), the theoretical tradition in linguistics in which these questions have mostly been explored. Generative grammar postulates a strict division between different components of the grammar: syntax, phonology, semantics, and so on, each of which is assumed to have its own explanatory principles and structure (cf. 7.2.1). The interfaces between each of the components are the areas where these different explanatory principles interact: in the present case, there is an interaction between semantic principles concerning the meaning conveyed by the clause, and the morphosyntactic principles governing such phenomena as case-marking and grammatical relations. For reasons that will become apparent, the questions we asked above are referred to in the generative tradition as the **linking** problem, the **argument mapping**, **argument selection** or **argument realization** problem, or the **theta-role** problem. We'll explore this mainly in relation to English, specifically concentrating on the question of the principles determining subject and object choice in the clause.

Complements and adjuncts

A verb's **complements** (in bold below) are the non-subject NPs which must obligatorily be expressed in order for the clause in which the verb figures to be grammatical *in that meaning*. A verb's adjuncts (italicized) are any optional arguments:

(1) The eunuchs had **many ways of augmenting their incomes**.
(2) The eunuchs always kept **a complete range of court clothing** *for officials*.
(3) Most of the eunuchs fled *after the 1911 revolution*.
(4) The terror-struck Dowager summoned **the imperial council** *to an emergency meeting*.

> (5) I would accuse **the eunuchs** *of disloyalty to me for trifling*
> *reasons.*
> (6) My English interpreter explained *things to me.*
>
> QUESTION   Mark the subjects, complements and adjuncts in the following clauses:
>
> (1) Bismarck coveted power in the 1870s.
> (2) Bismarck waged war against Denmark in 1864.
> (3) Prussia has been compared by Bismarck to ancient Rome.
> (4) Lieutenant-General Graf Fink von Finkenstein is Head Tutor.
> (5) The boy's mind was opened by his tutor to a lively perception of things round him.

The standard explanation of the linking problem in generative syntax is due to Gruber (1965) and Fillmore (1968), later developed and extended by a host of investigators. This approach has two parts. First, the lexical entries (the representations of linguistic information associated with a lexeme) for verbs are assumed to include a specification of the types of argument they have associated with them. It was assumed that the possible arguments of all verbs could be classified into a small number of classes, called **thematic roles**, **participant roles**, **semantic roles**, or **theta roles**. The following list (based on the one in Carnie 2007) shows a commonly assumed set of roles:

Agent: the initiator of the action
Experiencer: the entity that feels or perceives something
Theme/Patient: entity that undergoes an action, undergoes motion, is experienced or perceived
Goal: entity towards which motion takes place
Recipient: subclass of goal for verbs involving a change of possession
Source: entity from which motion takes place
Location: place where the action occurs
Instrument: object with which an action is performed
Beneficiary: one for whose benefit an event took place

In the words of Fillmore (1968: 24–25), these roles 'comprise a set of universal, presumably innate, concepts which identify certain types of judgments human beings are capable of making about the events that are going on around them, judgments about such matters as who did it, who it happened to, and what got changed'. It was assumed that the arguments of all verbs could be assigned to one of these roles.

Take *kill*, for example. Killing involves someone who kills (the 'killer'), and someone who is killed (the 'killee'). Obviously, the killer is 'the initiator or doer of the action', and the killee is the 'entity that undergoes the action'. This means that *kill* is associated with agent and theme participants. This information about *kill* is stored in long-term memory as a distinct part of the verb's lexical entry:

kill <agent, theme>

We will talk of this situation as *kill* **subcategorizing** agent and theme roles. Other verbs that subcategorize these roles are *hit*, *drive* as in *Wotan drove the chariot*, and *hug*.

Now consider *fear*. The 'fearer' isn't considered to be 'initiating' or 'doing' the action of fearing, since this implies a greater degree of agency and control than actually exists. We're not really in control of whether we fear something or not. The first participant of *fear* therefore isn't an agent, but an 'experiencer'. The thing feared, however, is still a theme:

fear <experiencer, theme>

In *receive* we have a recipient and a theme as participants. The 'receiver' doesn't 'initiate' the action of receiving, which isn't under their control:

receive <recipient, theme>

Put, as in *put the book on the table*, subcategorizes three roles, since it is characteristically ditransitive. The *putter* is an agent, the thing that is put is the theme, and the place where it is put is the goal.

put <agent, theme, goal>

Die, by contrast is intransitive, and consequently subcategorizes only a theme:

die <theme>

The idea here is that by matching up the specific semantics of the arguments of individual verbs with the wider classes of 'agent', 'theme', 'experiencer' and so on, it would be possible to classify the entire verbal lexicon using a finite set of participant roles. The list of the subcategorized arguments of each verb was assumed to constitute a separate aspect of the verb's lexical entry, its **theta-grid** or **subcategorization frame**. Such grids or frames are shown for five verbs in (5).

(5) *break* <agent, theme>
  donate <agent, theme, recipient>
  send <agent, theme, goal>
  google <agent, theme>
  get <recipient, theme>

These grids were taken to be a distinct part of a verb's lexical entry, separate from all other aspects of its semantic representation.

  The identification of verbs' theta-grids constitutes the first part of the standard generativist explanation of the linking problem. The second part explains how the various labelled participant roles are linked or mapped onto morphosyntactic positions like subject and object. As the examples we've looked at show, subjects aren't always agents, and objects aren't always themes. This means that it's not possible to propose any invariant linking rules associating a particular thematic role or (set of thematic roles) with either subject or object position. Instead, the basic insight behind the proposed solution is that *the different thematic roles are not equivalent*: some are more likely to be coded as subject, and others as object. It was suggested that it is possible to rank the different roles in an order which shows their relative accessibility to subject position.

Many versions of this ranking have been suggested. For English, an appropriate ranking might be something like this, with '>' read as 'outranks for subject':

Possible thematic hierarchy for English:
Agent > Beneficiary/Experiencer > Instrument > Theme/Patient > Goal/Source/Location

This ranking says that if there is an Agent in the situation being referred to, it will automatically be coded as subject. In the absence of an agent, any Beneficiary or Experiencer will be given subject status, and so on. In a transitive clause, the other participant will be coded as object, and any other participants as adjuncts (obliques). We won't attempt to give evidence for the whole of the hierarchy here. Instead, we will illustrate various parts of it. In each case, the subject of the clause is the participant that is ranked higher. We will start with evidence showing that Agent outranks all other roles.

(6) a. Agent > Beneficiary
         Bismarck helped the King.

     b. Agent > Experiencer
         Bismarck informed the King.

     c. Agent > Instrument
         Bismarck used a faked telegram.

     d. Agent > Theme
         Bismarck hoarded bullion.

     e. Agent > Goal/Source/Location
         Bismarck entered/left/occupied the Palace.

If there is no Agent, the Beneficiary is the next highest-ranked participant:

(7) Beneficiary > Theme
     a. *Bismarck received the King's support.*
     b. *Bismarck inherited an estate.*

If there is an Experiencer and a Theme, the Experiencer is ranked higher:

(8) Experiencer > Theme
     Bismarck heard the news.

If there is an Instrument and a Theme, Instrument is ranked higher:

(9) Instrument > Theme
     The hammer shattered the rock.

If the arguments are a Theme and a Location, Theme outranks Location:

(10) Theme > Location
     The gas was filling the room.

Facts like these lead to the postulation of the hierarchy. Researchers initially assumed that it would be possible to discover a single, cross-linguistically valid hierarchy of participant roles, specified by Universal Grammar. This allowed evidence from *other* languages to be used to fill in the gaps left in a single language.

QUESTION   How would you categorize the arguments of the following clauses? Is Carnie's list sufficient?

(a) *The trip cost us two months' pay.*
(b) *She owns three racehorses.*
(c) *The fence surrounds the field.*
(d) *The CD contains twenty-five tracks.*
(e) *The trip lasted four days.*
(f) *Clouds mean rain.*
(g) *Henry needs help.*
(h) *Their slavishness matches their intelligence.*
(i) *The luggage weighs twenty kilos.*
(j) *Fred realized the truth.*

QUESTION   Propose subcategorization frames for the following verbs, inventing clauses which exemplify them. Some verbs may take more than one frame, and not all verbs may be easy to classify. Note any of these difficult cases, and keep them in mind in the discussion that follows:

bend, throw, show, get, apologize, yawn, roll, open, fall down, stroll, collide, see, watch, offend, cry, touch, applaud, like, bother, rent

QUESTION   Can you think of any other examples of verbs which (a) have more than a single subcategorization frame; (b) have arguments which can be assigned to more than one thematic role; and (c) have arguments which it is not easy to classify using the list given above? Keep these verbs in mind in the discussion that follows.

10.1.2 Problems with thematic roles

Doing the above questions may have given you an insight into some of the problems involved in assuming a fixed inventory of thematic roles. The motivation for postulating a thematic hierarchy was the existence of cases where it's fairly easy to decide what role to assign arguments to. In *John* [Agent] *kills Mary* [Theme], for instance, the identity of the roles couldn't be more obvious. But there are many occasions where things are much less clear cut, and where we could assign an argument to several thematic roles. In (11), for example, the subject could be analysed as both Agent (initiator of the action) and Theme (entity undergoing motion):

(11) *John rolled down the hill.*

In response to data like these, some researchers have suggested that nouns may instantiate two thematic roles simultaneously (see Jackendoff 1990).

The arguments of many verbs seem hard to assign to any of the conventional thematic roles. For example, it's not obvious how we should label the roles associated with the following clauses:

(12) a. *The shirt fits me.*
     b. *The caravan sleeps a whole family.*
     c. *Ten cents will buy you thirty seconds.*
     d. *Clouds mean rain.*
     e. *The book weighs half a kilo.*
     f. *The committee confirmed the appointment.*
     g. *This job requires skill.*

In none of these cases is it obvious that the arguments can be assimilated into any of the basic roles. One could, of course, invent new roles for each of the verbs individually, but this tactic would threaten the strength of the original proposal: if our aim is to account economically for the observed general patterns of argument structure, we can't just invent new roles every time the system breaks down – this would risk exploding the number of roles beyond what investigators have assumed to be reasonable boundaries. Dowty (1991: 561) puts the problem like this:

[t]he variety of semantic distinctions that correlate with syntactic and lexical patterns in one way or another is surely enormous. To postulate thematic role types for each of them is, quite possibly, to dilute the notion beyond its usefulness, but what we lack is a principled way to decide what kind of data motivates a thematic role type.

Even if these problems are resolved, the difficulties are not over. Not only has it not been possible to unambiguously assign arguments to thematic roles, but the thematic hierarchy ranking these roles has proven extraordinarily elusive. Cross-linguistic investigation over a long period has failed to produce any version of the hierarchy on which investigators can agree, since the rankings between different arguments seem to vary considerably from one language to the next. This in itself is reason to be sceptical of the very idea that Universal Grammar (UG) specifies a thematic hierarchy. As Newmeyer says, '[t]here is reason for strong doubt that there exists a Thematic Hierarchy provided by UG. That seems to be the best explanation for the fact that after over three decades of investigation, nobody has proposed a hierarchy of theta-roles that comes close to working' (Newmeyer 2002: 65). This has certainly not been helped by the fact that different investigators have applied thematic role terms inconsistently. But the problems of reconciling conflicting theta hierarchies is more than simply terminological. Two authoritative investigators, in fact, go so far as to claim that it is simply 'impossible to formulate a thematic hierarchy which will capture all generalizations involving the realization of arguments in terms of their semantic roles' (Levin and Hovav 2005: 183).

But even if there were a cross-linguistically accepted thematic hierarchy, cases still exist which call into question its ability to explain argument structure. So-called **symmetrical predicates** – *equal, be similar to, be near, resemble, weigh as much as* – show that the thematic hierarchy isn't the only determinant of argument selection, since the two arguments of these verbs, by definition, share an identical thematic role (see Dowty 1991: 556 for discussion). *Something* determines the choice between subject and object – just not thematic role. But if thematic role doesn't determine subject-selection in these cases, perhaps it *never* does.

Now consider the following pair:

(13) *Mary owns the book/The book belongs to Mary*

The book presumably instantiates the role of theme; *Mary* is less clear, but perhaps beneficiary is the most appropriate label. In any case, *own* and *belong* show a contradictory ranking of arguments. In cases like this, the thematic hierarchy predicts the correct subject–object choice for only one of the verbs. For the other, there must be some other explanation.

Examples like (14), from Italian, pose a similar problem. Here we find experiencer and theme roles being differentially assigned to subject and object position:

(14) a. *Questo*   *preoccupa*   *Gianni.*
       this   worries   Gianni
       'This worries Gianni.'

    b. *Gianni*   *teme*   *questo.*
       Gianni   fears   this
       'Gianni fears this.' (Levin and Hovav 2005:23)

This sort of phenomenon is widespread cross-linguistically. English is actually rather lacking here, but the pairs in (15) show the same flipping of thematic roles:

(15) **Experiencer subject; theme**   **Theme subject; experiencer**
     object   **object**
     I like this   *This pleases/appeals to me*
     I fear this   *This frightens me*
     I think that   *It strikes me that*
     I missed what he was saying   *What he was saying escaped me*

These sentences represent different linguistic construals of the same (or at least a highly similar) situation, one of which is in accordance with the thematic hierarchy, and one not. The verbs in the left column, whose arguments obey the hierarchy, are unproblematic: the grammar does not need to include any special information about how these verbs' arguments are linked to subject and object, since this is explained by general principles. But the badly behaved cases on the right are different: since *frighten*, *please*, and their ilk all violate the thematic hierarchy, the learner has to learn the appropriate argument linking patterns for each verb. This means that there are two types of verb in the lexicon: those whose argument-linking properties conform to the thematic hierarchy and don't need to be separately learned; and those whose arguments don't observe the hierarchy and so do need to be learned. Given this situation, it might be a simpler solution to say that the verb *always* individually specifies what arguments are linked to subject and object, and dispense with the thematic hierarchy altogether as a component of the grammar.

Supporters of the hierarchy could answer here that doing this would ignore a significant generalization: the arguments of most verbs *are* assigned to subject and object position in accordance with the hierarchy. It's only exceptional ones like those in (15) which show an option. Furthermore, these verbs are a coherent cross-linguistic class. It's not just *any* verb and argument combinations which exist in the pairs like those above. Instead, the choice between two alternants seems mainly to be available for **psych-verbs**, i.e precisely those verbs which subcategorize experiencer and theme. Other verbs mostly don't show alternants in which the arguments are flipped: as observed by Carter, there is no English verb *benter which has the same meaning as *enter*, except that the agent and goal arguments are swapped (*The room bentered John.) The fact that alternants which violate the thematic hierarchy are the exception rather than the rule means that the best policy is to allow the exceptions' argument linking to be part of the information included in each verb's lexical entry, leaving the thematic hierarchy to determine all the rest. Proponents of the hierarchy could also point to the fact that its usefulness in the grammar is not confined to solving the linking problem: as noted by Newmeyer (2002), thematic role hierarchies have also been appealed to as the explanation of a range of other grammatical phenomena (e.g. antecedence for reflexivization (Jackendoff 1972) and the choice of controller in embedded infinitivals (Culicover and Jackendoff 2001)). If we need the hierarchy to do other work in the grammar anyway, the motivation for dispensing with it is reduced.

Whether thematic hierarchies should be retained as part of the explanation of linking depends on a number of tricky metatheoretical issues – in other words, issues about the circumstances in which one theoretical explanation should be preferred to another. It's fair to say that there is rather little consensus on these issues. At the moment, it is simply unclear whether thematic hierarchies are an appropriate device in the grammar.

10.1.3 Proto-roles

Dowty (1991) proposed a solution to some of the problems with thematic roles. The first component of Dowty's solution was the suggestion that the different participant roles 'are simply not discrete categories at all, but rather are cluster concepts, like the prototypes of Rosch and her followers' (1991: 571; on prototypes, see 7.1.3). What this means is that the boundaries between different roles are fuzzy: an argument isn't classified as *either* an Agent *or*, say, an Instrument; instead, it's classified as more or less Agent-*like*. The prototypical nature of the thematic role types explains why it is hard to assign each argument neatly to a single role: a single argument, like the subject of *roll* in (11) above, can have both Agent-like and Theme-like aspects at the same time. Because the boundaries between roles are fuzzy, it's expected that there should be these sorts of effects.

The second aspect of Dowty's proposal was that thematic roles are based on entailments of verb-meanings. A verb's entailments are those propositions that must necessarily be true whenever the verb itself is true (see 6.6.1). For example, consider the subject argument, *Gavrilo*, and the verbs *murder*, *nominate* and *interrogate*, in (16):

(16) *Gavrilo murders/nominates/interrogates the Archduke.*

These verbs share the following entailments:

- VOLITION: Gavrilo acted volitionally;
- INTENTION TO PERFORM THE ACT NAMED BY THE VERB: Gavrilo intended to murder, *nominate* or *interrogate* the Archduke; these weren't things that just happened as a side-effect of what he was doing;
- CAUSATION: Gavrilo caused some event to take place that involved the Archduke; and
- MOTION OR EXTERNAL CHANGE: Gavrilo either moved or changed in some external (i.e. not just mental) way in performing the action.

Note the affinity of these entailments with our definition of Agent, the 'initiator of the action'. In standard accounts of linking, *Gavrilo* would be classified as an Agent in all three contexts. Not all subject arguments, however, share these entailments. Dowty gives the following verbs as examples:

- volitional action isn't an entailment of *kill* (traffic accidents kill without being volitional)
- intending to perform the act named by the verb isn't shared by *convince* (I can convince you without intending to convince you, even though I am intending to *speak*)
- causation isn't shared by *look at*
- motion or external change isn't shared by *understand*

These arguments lack some of the Agent entailments, but they are still treated as subject. Dowty proposed that only two role-types are needed to account for linking. He called these role-types **Proto-Agent** and **Proto-Patient**. Each proto-role is identified by a number of properties. The more of these properties a verb's argument entails, the more it belongs to the appropriate proto-role. The properties for the two roles are as follows:

Contributing properties for the Agent Proto-Role:
a. volitional involvement in the event or state
b. sentience (and/or perception)
c. causing an event or change of state in another participant
d. movement (relative to the position of another participant)
e. exists (independently of the event named by the verb)

Contributing properties for the Patient Proto-Role:
a. undergoes change of state
b. incremental theme
c. causally affected by another participant
d. stationary relative to movement of another participant
e. does not exist (independently of the event named by the verb) (Dowty 1991: 572)

Incremental theme is a new term due to Dowty (1991) and Krifka (1987). The object NPs in (17) are examples:

(17)   *build a house, write a letter, play a sonata*
      eat a sandwich, polish a shoe, proofread an essay

The key to the idea of Incremental theme is that the verb's object is progressively – 'incrementally' – affected by the action of the verb as the event unfolds. Building a house, for example, happens over a certain period of time, with the house getting more and more built with each passing day. Similarly, a letter gets more and more written as I write it, the sandwich more and more eaten as the eating progresses, and so on. To see how much has been built, written, or eaten we need only compare the house, the letter or the sandwich at two different points in time during the event. The verb, in other words, affects the theme 'incrementally'. Examples of nonincremental themes would be the objects of achievement predicates like *reach the top*, *shoot the target*, and so on (see 9.2.2.2).

QUESTION   Can you think of any examples in which the subject (instead of the object) is the incremental theme?

As we have seen, the entailments are independent of each other – not every verb has every one. Dowty (1991: 572) gives the following examples of the independence of the Proto-Agent entailments:

Volition alone: *John is being polite to/is ignoring Mary, What he did was not eat for two days.*
Sentience/perception alone: *John sees/fears Mary.*
Causation alone: *Teenage unemployment causes delinquency.*
Movement alone: *Water filled the boat. He accidentally fell.*

Dowty points out, however, that *build* has all subject and all object entailments.

QUESTION   Can you find equivalent sentences showing the independence of the Proto-Patient entailments?

The full solution to the linking problem may already be clear to you. Dowty suggests that the argument with the most Proto-Agent entailments will be coded as subject, and the one with the most Proto-Patient entailments as object. This principle has two related corollaries. First, it's possible for some arguments to share the same role, have neither role, or qualify partially but equally for both proto-roles. Second, if two arguments satisfy roughly the same number of Proto-Agent and Proto-Patient entailments, then either may be coded as subject or object. This is the case for psych-verbs such as *Joe likes sausages/Sausages please Joe*: in this situation, regardless of how it is described, both participants have just a single entailment each: *Joe* has the proto-agent entailment of sentience, and *sausages* has the proto-agent entailment of causation. Dowty says that neither argument has any other entailments. This means that each argument has equal likelihood to surface as subject.

The same explanation accounts for other doublets like *Fabienne lent Briony a book/Briony borrowed a book from Fabienne*. We can see this in the following table:

Table 10.1. Proto-agent and proto-patient entailments for *lend/borrow*.		
Lend/borrow: Proto-agent entailments	Briony (borrower)	Fabienne (lender)
Volition	✓	✓
Sentience	✓	✓
Causation	✓	✓
Movement	✗	✗
Lend/borrow: Proto-patient entailments	Briony (borrower)	Fabienne (lender)
Changes state	✗	✗
Incremental theme	✗	✗
Causally affected	✓	✓
Stationary	✓	✓

QUESTION Dowty (1991: 576) makes the following statement about three place predicates like *give*:

COROLLARY 2: With a three-place predicate, the non subject argument having the greatest number of entailed Proto-Patient properties will be lexicalized as the direct object and the nonsubject argument having fewer entailed Proto-Patient properties will be lexicalized as an oblique or prepositional object (and if two nonsubject arguments have approximately equal numbers of entailed P-Patient properties, either or both may be lexicalized as direct objects).

Does this work for the following clauses?

x made y a meal/x made a meal for y
x brought the package to y/brought y the package

10.1.4 Thematic relations and conceptual structure

So far, none of the theories we have discussed uses verb meaning to determine argument selection directly. In the traditional theta-role system, verbs
are associated in the lexicon with theta-grids, and it is the hierarchy that
determines how arguments get into a verb's subject and object positions. As
a result, even though the *investigator* uses the verb's meaning to work out its
theta-roles, and then uses the thematic hierarchy to work out its argument
structure, the crucial dependence of argument structure on meaning isn't
explicitly formalized: argument structure cannot be read directly off the
verb's meaning, but proceeds via the intermediate stage of theta-roles.

This type of theoretical arrangement is somewhat redundant: looking
at a verb's meaning provided the justification for the theorist's decision
about what theta-roles a verb was given, but the precoded roles still constituted a separate aspect of the verb's lexical representation, independent of its meaning. The precoded roles only exist for the syntactic purpose of getting the 'right' arguments as subject and object. In Dowty's
system, something similar is true: the theorist has to examine the verb's
meaning and decide in each case how many of the proto-role entailments
are satisfied. There is no way in which argument structure can follow
automatically from the verb's meaning: since neither traditional theta-role
theories nor Dowty's proto-role system offers any way to represent verb
meaning explicitly, a direct mapping from verb meaning to argument
structure is impossible.

Explicit representation of verb meaning is therefore a prerequisite for a
more unified theory of linking. Jackendoff (1987, 2002) offers just such a
theory. As discussed in 8.1, Jackendoff's theory of semantic representation
involves a decomposition of meanings into primitive elements – BE, GO,
CAUSE and so on. As we will see, according to Jackendoff it is the nature of
the primitive elements within the semantic decompositions of verbs which
directly determines argument structure. This allows Jackendoff to dispense
completely with theta-roles or proto-roles, and to derive argument structure
directly from semantics. Jackendoff explains the virtue of this as follows:

> What is at stake is the issue of language acquisition. If a word's syntactic
> behavior (including its syntactic argument structure) were always tightly
> linked to its meaning (including semantic argument structure), there
> would be far less lexical idiosyncrasy for the child to learn, always a
> desideratum …
>
> (Jackendoff 2002: 138)

The primitives of Jackendoff's system provide a new way of thinking about
the nature of theta-roles. Consider Jackendoff's representation of the conceptual structure underlying the following three sentences (also discussed
in 8.1.2);

(18) a. *The door was open.*

    b. *The door opened.*

    c. *John opened the door.*

Sentence (18a) is the conceptually simplest, consisting simply of the state function BE with two semantic arguments: Thing (which refers to the door) and Property (which refers to openness), as diagrammed in (19):

(19) $[_{STATE}$ BE $([_{THING}$ DOOR], $[_{PROPERTY}$ OPEN])]

(To say that Thing and Property are 'semantic arguments' is to say that they are necessary complements of the function BE – concepts unavoidably bound up with its meaning in this use: see 8.1.1 for explanation.)

Jackendoff defines the thematic role of 'Theme' as 'the first argument of the functions GO, STAY, BE and ORIENT' (1987: 378). The conceptual representation of (18a) contains the element 'BE', with two arguments, DOOR and OPEN. This means that the first argument in (18a), DOOR, which is realized by the lexeme *door*, is interpreted as Theme.

Now consider (18b). This has the same conceptual structure as (18a), except that it has added the 'INCHoative' function (Latin: 'start'), which denotes the coming into being of an event. *The door opened* thus receives the following analysis:

(20) $[_{EVENT}$ INCH $([_{STATE}$ BE $([_{THING}$ DOOR], $[_{PROPERTY}$ OPEN])])]

The addition of INCH makes no difference to the thematic roles in the sentence: DOOR/*door* still satisfies the definition of 'theme'.

Sentence (18c) adds the 'CAUSative' function to the previous structure:

(21) $[_{EVENT}$ CAUSE $([_{THING}$ JOHN], $([_{EVENT}$ INCH $([_{STATE}$ BE $([_{THING}$ DOOR], $[_{PROPERTY}$ OPEN])])])]

CAUSE is a two-argument function: the first argument is a Thing (here, John), the second an Event (here, the door becoming open). Jackendoff defines Agent as the first argument of the Event-function CAUSE. This makes *John* Agent in (18c).

The other thematic roles are dealt with in exactly the same way. Source, described above as 'the entity from which motion takes place', is analysed as the argument of the Path-function FROM. Goal, the 'entity towards which motion takes place' is the argument of the Path-function TO. The experiencer argument, Jackendoff says, 'presumably is an argument of an as yet unexplored State-function having to do with mental states' (1987: 378).

This approach has an important consequence: 'Agent', 'Theme' and the other roles can be eliminated from the theory. Since Jackendoff defines the theta-roles in terms of underlying conceptual structure, it's the underlying conceptual elements, not the theta-roles themselves, which do all the explanatory work. As Jackendoff puts it, the names of theta-roles 'are just convenient mnemonics for particularly prominent configurations' of underlying conceptual primitives. This means that we can restate the thematic hierarchy in terms of underlying conceptual configurations. Instead of Agent, for example, we substitute the first argument of the predicate CAUSE; instead of Theme, we substitute the single argument of GO, STAY, BE or ORIENT. Jackendoff is claiming, in other words, 'that the terms *Theme, Agent*, and so on, are not primitives of semantic theory. Rather, they are relational notions defined structurally over conceptual structure' (2002: 378–379). He compares this to the way 'subject' and 'object' are not primitive notions of generative syntax, but structural positions in the classical tree structure: subject is the NP immediately dominated by S, and object the NP immediately dominated by the VP.

The types of semantic distinction conveyed by the different theta-roles or, for Jackendoff, underlying conceptual configurations, are not the only semantic connections between a verb and its arguments. Verbs also place selectional restrictions on their arguments: the object of *eat* must be a solid, that of *drink* a liquid, that of *read* something visible, that of *pay* (in one of its uses) an amount of money. In Jackendoff's theory of conceptual structure, these selectional restrictions are, like theta-roles, specified directly by the conceptual structure: they are not *extra* information which needs to be learnt in addition to the meaning of the verbs themselves. Jackendoff observes that a sentence like *Bill paid* inherently entails the information that what Bill paid was an amount of money; similarly, *Harry drank* contains the information that what Harry drank was something liquid. This shows that if an argument isn't expressed lexically, information about its nature is still available. As a result, the selectional restrictions on the objects of *drink* and *pay* are 'essentially explicit information that the verb supplies about its arguments' (1987: 385). Selectional restrictions are 'part of the verb's meaning and should be fully integrated into the verb's argument structure' (1987: 385).

The lexical entry for *drink*, for example, is something like this (Jackendoff 1987: 386):

$$(22) \begin{bmatrix} \text{drink} \\ [-N, +V] \\ \underline{\quad}(NP_j) \\ [_{\text{EVENT}}\, \text{CAUSE}\, ([_{\text{THING}}]_i,\, [_{\text{EVENT}}\, \text{GO}\, ([_{\text{THING}}\, \text{LIQUID}]_j, \\ [_{\text{PATH}}\, \text{TO}\, (_{\text{PLACE}}\, \text{IN}\, ([_{\text{THING}}\, \text{MOUTH OF}\, ([_{\text{THING}}]_i\,)])])])] \end{bmatrix}$$

The Thing arguments which can be subcategorized by the verb are marked by the indices *i* and *j*. The first of these, indexed *i*, is the first argument of the CAUSE predicate: this makes it an Agent. The second, indexed *j*, is the first argument of the GO predicate: this makes it a theme. But the parentheses around 'NP$_j$' in the third line of the representation indicate that *drink* doesn't have to have a fully expressed direct object – the verb can be intransitive. But whether it does or not, the verb's meaning itself contains the information that the thing being drunk is a liquid.

We can see another illustration of this approach to argument structure by considering the difference in meaning between the verbs *butter* and *bottle*, as in *Harry buttered the bread* and *Joe bottled the wine*. The meanings of these verbs are quite different: *butter* means 'to put butter on something'; *bottle* means 'put wine in a bottle'. Jackendoff represents the conceptual structures as follows (1987: 387):

(23) a. *butter*

$[_{\text{EVENT}}$ CAUSE $([_{\text{THING}}]_i, [_{\text{EVENT}}$ GO $([_{\text{THING}}$ BUTTER$], [_{\text{PATH}}$ TO $([_{\text{PLACE}}$ ON $([_{\text{THING}}]_j)])])])]$

b. *bottle*

$[_{\text{EVENT}}$ CAUSE $([_{\text{THING}}]_i, [_{\text{EVENT}}$ GO $([_{\text{THING}}]_j, [_{\text{PATH}}$ TO $([_{\text{PLACE}}$ IN $([_{\text{THING}}$ BOTTLE$])])])])]$

In (23a) the subject argument (*Harry* in our example) is indexed with the letter *i*. As the first argument of CAUSE, this identifies the verb's Agent. (Recall that terms like 'Agent' are just convenient shorthand here; what we mean is 'first argument of a CAUSE predicate'.) The verb's object – the bread – is also indexed, showing that it is subcategorized. As the argument of a TO function, *bread* would traditionally be called a Goal. Unlike the other two semantic arguments, the Theme argument, BUTTER, does not have an index linking it with an argument. This means that it is not connected to a subcategorized position. Jackendoff explains that, as a result, 'this argument is totally filled in with information from the verb and is understood as "nonspecific butter" (1987: 387) – when we are told that *Harry buttered the bread* we don't know anything about the identity of the butter involved. This contrasts with (23b). Here it is the Goal argument – the argument of the TO function – that doesn't have an index. This means that it gets its interpretation entirely from the verb: all we know is that Joe bottled some specific wine, but we know nothing about the identity of the bottle into which the wine was put. Jackendoff notes that comparing these examples shows us that 'the similarities and differences between *butter* and *drink* fall out directly from the notation adopted here. There is no need to interpose a level of argument structure to encode them' (1987: 387). Argument structure and selectional restrictions are not separately coded pieces of information that have to be learnt *as well as* the meaning of the verb; they are part of the meaning of the verb itself. As a result, the learner's task is simpler.

Theories and simplicity

Proposals to streamline the number of theta-roles, à la Dowty, or to derive thematic relations from conceptual structure, à la Jackendoff, are often well received, for reasons of theoretical simplicity: it's thought that the fewer components or levels of structure a theory has, the simpler and hence more desirable it is. But how cogent this reasoning is depends on the position you take on some methodological questions often discussed by philosophers of science. As we've seen, the virtue of deriving grammatical relations from conceptual structure is that it cuts down on the theoretical machinery, hence observing the principle of **Ockham's Razor** – don't posit more entities than you need to. Some critics, however, might point out that since both ways of doing things make exactly the same predictions, they're equivalent in every way that matters, and we shouldn't worry about which we adopt. Furthermore, the question of simplicity isn't as simple as it seems. How can you tell which out of two rival theories is simpler? It's surely not the case that the theory with the fewer bits of mechanism is the simpler one: a theory which used three counterintuitive bits of machinery doesn't seem simpler than one which uses four intuitive bits. Jackendoff's conceptual representations eliminate theta-roles, but involve a complex decomposition of verb meanings which introduce many extra components. Is this a gain in simplicity or not? Also, how do you tell what counts as a single piece of theoretical machinery? Ludlow (1999) concludes that there's no objective way to tell a simpler theory from a less simple one – it's just a question of what the community of linguists find simpler.

10.2 Verb classes and alternations

We saw in the previous section how many psych-verb meanings (the meanings of verbs for mental states) can be realized by two variants, each of which selects different subject and object arguments: *fear* vs. *frighten*, *like* vs. *please/appeal to*, *think* vs. *strike*, and so on. Doublets like these, widespread cross-linguistically, pose a problem for linking rules, since they allow quite different mappings from meaning to argument structure, only one of which is consistent with the thematic hierarchy. Because of these verbs, Culicover and Jackendoff (2005: 184) suggest that the thematic hierarchy 'does not apply to all combinations of thematic roles'.

In this section we will consider another problem-case for the standard account of argument structure and the thematic hierarchy: **argument structure alternations**. Many verbs show not just one argument structure, but several. Consider the verbs in (24). They can all appear in an <agent patient> array:

(24) *Ben ripped the ricepaper.*
     Emily broke the laptop.
     Ron shattered the walnut.
     Mill cut the fabric.
     The camper slashed the tarpaulin.
     The carpenter sawed the wood

But, along with many other verbs, they can also appear in a so-called **middle alternation**, with <theme> as the only subcategorized argument:

(25) *Ricepaper rips easily.*
     Laptops break often.

Walnuts will only shatter along the seam.
The fabric cuts from both ends.
The tarpaulin slashes really easily.
This wood saws easily.

Not all verbs allow the middle alternation. The verbs in (26), for instance, are impossible in the middle:

(26) *Mill pats Macintosh/*Macintosh pats easily.*
     They stroked its back/*Its back strokes easily.
     They touched the surface/*The surface touches easily.
     They hit the ball/*The ball hits easily.
     They kicked the ball/*The ball kicks easily.
     I bashed the nail/*The nail bashes easily.

Are there any general principles governing which verbs allow the middle alternation and which don't? Hale and Keyser (1987) use an archaic English verb, *gally*, to suggest an answer. If you're like me, *gally* isn't always on the tip of your tongue; in fact, this may well be the first time you've come across the word. Imagine two English speakers hearing the sentence *The sailors gallied the whales* for the first time (*gally* is a word particularly used in whaling jargon). One speaker might assume that *gally* means 'see', while the other might think it means 'frighten'. Hale and Keyser point out that each assumption has certain consequences for what the two speakers will consider as possible alternations for the verb. If *gally* is assumed to mean *frighten*, then the middle alternation – *the whales gallied easily* – will be acceptable, whereas if it is thought to mean *see*, the middle alternation will not. This suggests that whether the middle alternation is possible depends on the verb's meaning. (*Gally* means 'frighten', by the way, not 'see'.)

What is the factor in the meaning that makes the difference? Hale and Keyser suggest that verbs which do allow the middle alternation all express the bringing about of a change of state in the verb's object. This meaning is absent from the ones that don't allow the middle, like *see, consider, believe* and *notice*.

We have, then, two hunches about the relation between semantics and argument structure:

- a verb's meaning determines what syntactic alternations it participates in;
- verbs fall into semantically defined classes, which all show similar syntactic behaviour with respect to their alternations.

These ideas have been especially pursued by Levin and Hovav (Levin 1993; Levin and Hovav 1995, 2005).

Let's continue our exploration of this by considering a couple of other alternations. The **conative** alternation is exemplified by each of the second sentences in (27):

(27) a. *The zombies slashed my face/The zombies slashed at my face.*
  b. *They cut the root with the blade/They cut at the root with the blade.*
  c. *They sawed the rafters that pinned my legs/They sawed at the rafters that pinned my legs.*
  d. *They hit me fiercely/They hit at me fiercely.*
  e. *They kicked the pile of wood/They kicked at the pile of wood.*
  f. *I bashed the nail/I bashed at the nail.*

As the term 'conative' (Latin 'attempt') suggests, this alternation conveys a reduced degree of effectiveness: (27a) suggests that the zombies directed the slashes at my face, but that their slashing didn't succeed in putting me out of action completely – I could still slash back at them, perhaps. The reduced effectiveness is also true for the verbs in (27b–f).

As with the middle alternation, not all verbs allow the conative alternation:

(28) a. *They touched its paw/*They touched at its paw.*
  b. *They stroked its back/*They stroked at its back.*
  c. *They patted its head/*They patted at its head.*
  d. *They broke the screen/*They broke at the screen.*
  e. *They ripped the cloth/*They ripped at the cloth.*
  f. *They shattered the vase/*They shattered at the vase.*

Now consider the **body-part possessor ascension alternation**. Many verbs can appear in this alternation:

(29) a. *Terry touched Bill's shoulder/Terry touched Bill on the shoulder.*
  b. *James kicked Margo's shin/James kicked Margo on the shin.*
  c. *The door bashed Grahame's elbow/The door bashed Grahame on the elbow.*
  d. *Margaret cut Bill's arm/Margaret cut Bill on the arm.*
  e. *The blade slashed my finger/The blade slashed me on the finger.*
  f. *The drill scratched my hand/The drill scratched me on the hand.*

With some verbs, though, this alternation is impossible:

(30) a. *Janet broke Bill's finger/*Janet broke Bill on the finger.*
  b. *Janet ripped Bill's palm/*Janet ripped Bill on the palm.*
  c. *Janet shattered Bill's knee/*Janet shattered Bill on the knee.*

QUESTION   Can you find any regular meaning difference in the sentence pairs in (29a–f)?

QUESTION   What other types of verb alternation can you think of?

If we examine (24) – (30) we can see a pattern. The verbs in these examples seem to cluster together in a way that allows us to predict what alternations they will appear in. *Shatter* and *rip* always behave the same as *break*: if *break* allows an alternation, so will the other two; if it doesn't, *rip* and *shatter* won't either.

Table 10.2. English verb classes and three alternations.				
	touch verbs	*hit* verbs	*cut* verbs	*break* verbs
Middle	No	No	Yes	Yes
Conative	No	Yes	Yes	No
B-p p ascension	Yes	Yes	Yes	No

On the basis of these regularities, Levin (1993) identified the following classes of verbs, each one named after its most general member:

(31) a. *Break* verbs: *break, crack, rip, shatter, snap,* ...
   b. *Cut* verbs: *cut, hack, saw, scratch, slash,* ...
   c. *Touch* verbs: *pat, stroke, tickle, touch,* ...
   d. *Hit* verbs: *bash, hit, kick, pound, tap, whack,* ...

The verbs in each class, Levin claimed, pattern in exactly the same way with respect to the middle, conative and body-part possessor ascension alternations (subject, of course, to dialectal differences). The patterns can be summed up in Table 10.2 (Levin 1993: 7).

   In the spirit of Hale and Keyser's discussion of *gally*, Levin suggested that the differences between these classes are basically semantic: what alternations a verb participates in is explained by its underlying semantic structure. These differences can be revealed by decomposing the verb's meaning into a set of basic sub-events, involving primitives such as CAUSE, ACT, BECOME, like the Jackendoffian decompositions already discussed in 10.1.4. The particular way in which these subevents are present in the meaning of any given verb is known as that verb's **event structure**.

   We have already seen the meaning difference hypothesized to explain the middle alternation: *cut* and *break* verbs, which do manifest the alternation, include the idea of a change of state being brought about. We could represent their event structure as follows:

(32) x cuts/breaks y = [[x ACT] CAUSE [y BECOME <cut/broken>]]

Hit and *touch*, on the other hand, do not decompose into an underlying change of state structure.

   In the middle alternation, the *cut* and *break* verbs lose the idea of causing anything to happen, and jettison the 'Agent' argument as a result. This just leaves the 'change of state' idea intact:

(33) [y BECOME <cut/broken>]

Can we apply similar reasoning to the conative alternation, manifested by *hit* and *cut* verbs? Following a suggestion by Guerssel *et al.* (1985), Levin proposes that verbs of these classes involve two ideas: contact, and motion preceding the contact. *Break* verbs, on the other hand, lack both components: one can break something without coming into contact with it, and without the presence of any preceding motion. For instance, I can break an appliance by not turning it off, and a glass can be shattered by a high pitched sound. *Touch* verbs *do* include a contact component, but they lack a motion one. Levin suggests that *both* motion *and* contact are necessary for the conative alternation to be possible. Confirmation for this idea comes from the fact that verbs involving motion alone don't allow the alternation either:

(34) a. *Jean moved/shifted the table.*
     b. **Jean moved/shifted at the table.*

If *both* motion *and* contact are required to qualify a verb for the conative alternation, the incompatibility of pure motion verbs with this alternation is exactly what we would expect.

What about a possible semantic basis for the body-part possessor ascension alternation?

This alternation is available to all the verb classes except the *break* verbs. Again, contact is the relevant component: *hit*, *cut* and *touch* classes all involve a notion of contact, but *break* verbs, as we just saw, don't.

Confirmation of this analysis of the semantics of the four verb classes comes from another alternation, the **causative/inchoative** alternation. As we have seen, the meanings of both *cut* and *break* involve a change of state. *Cut* verbs, however, also involve notions of contact and motion. This semantic difference is correlated with a syntactic difference; only *break* verbs participate in the causative/inchoative alternation:

(35) a. *The child broke the screen* (causative)
     b. *The screen broke* (inchoative)
     c. *The child cut the ribbon* (causative)
     d. **The ribbon cut* (inchoative)

Similar behaviour is found with the other verbs of each class:

(36) *Jeff cracked/ripped/shattered/snapped his credit card* (causative)
     The credit card cracked/ripped/shattered/snapped (inchoative)
     Jeff sawed/scratched/slashed the plank (causative)
     *The plank sawed/scratched/slashed (inchoative)

The causative/inchoative alternation appears to be confined to pure change of state verbs. Since *hit* and *touch* aren't change of state verbs, they don't display the alternation:

(37) *Jeff touched/hit his credit card.*
     *The credit card touched/hit.

Another important alternation is the **locative alternation**:

(38) *Seth loaded hay onto the cart* (locative variant)
     Seth loaded the cart with hay (with variant)
     Ruth sprayed water on the wall (locative variant)
     Ruth sprayed the wall with water (with variant)

The key to the understanding of this is that the *with* variant entails the locative variant, but not vice versa. That is, (39a) entails (39b), but (39b) doesn't entail (39a):

(39) a. *Seth loaded the cart with hay*   *Ruth sprayed the wall with paint*

              entails   entails

    b. *Seth loaded hay onto the cart*   *Ruth sprayed paint onto the wall*

The reason that the entailments hold in one direction only is that the two variants differ in the extent to which the object of the verb is affected. If Seth *loaded the cart with hay*, the default interpretation is that the cart is fully loaded, whether or not all the hay has been transferred. But if Seth *loaded hay onto the cart*, no such implication holds. Similarly, if Ruth *sprayed the wall with paint*, we understand that the wall was entirely covered, whether or not all of the paint was used up. But if Ruth *sprayed paint onto the wall*, we have no information either about whether the paint was used up, or whether the entire wall was covered.

    The core of the lexical semantic representations proposed by Rappaport and Levin (1988) for the locative alternation are shown in (40a) and (b), corresponding to (39a) and (b). The 'x' variable refers to the subject, the 'y' to the hay, and 'z' to the cart:

(40) a. *With* variant: *load the cart with hay*

        load: [x CAUSE [z TO COME TO BE IN STATE]

        BY MEANS OF [x CAUSE [y TO COME TO BE AT z]]]

    b. Locative variant: *load hay onto the cart*

        load: [x CAUSE [y TO COME TO BE AT z]]

The differing degrees of affectedness are correlated with the linking of arguments to the direct object position: whichever argument is direct object is understood as wholly affected by the verb. Assuming a general principle like that of Jackendoff, according to which the first argument of a BE function is coded as direct object, the differing object assignments fall out from the representations in (40): in (40a) the cart is the first argument of the main (COME TO) BE function; in (40b) the hay is.

    Levin and Hovav (2005: 206) observe that this analysis is supported by some other facts about English. There are some verbs – *putting* verbs – which only appear in locative-type structures, and some – *filling* and *covering* verbs – which only allow structures like the *with* variant:

(41) *Putting* verbs

    *Seth put the hay on the cart/*Seth put the cart with hay*

    *Nigella poured/dripped the oil into the frying pan/*Nigella poured/dripped*

        the frying pan with oil

(42) *Filling* and *covering* verbs

    *Seth filled the cart with hay/*Seth filled hay onto the cart*

    *Seth covered the cart with hay/*Seth covered hay onto the cart.*

We have, then, a situation where verbs' syntactic behaviour seems to divide them into a small number of semantically differentiated classes. Levin and Hovav (2005: 18) observe that

verb classes are similar in status to natural classes of sounds in phonology and the elements of meaning which serve to distinguish among the classes of verbs are similar in status to phonology's distinctive features. Furthermore, since these grammatically relevant facets of meaning are viewed as constituting the interface between a full-fledged representation of meaning and the syntax, most researchers have assumed that, like the set of distinctive features, the set of such meaning elements is both universal and relatively small in size.

This approach to alternations shares with Jackendoff the idea that a verb's syntactic possibilities are derived from the nature of its underlying semantic representation. This allows a far more economical description of the grammatical facts: instead of coding each verb separately with a list of the possible syntactic alternations in which it can appear, the analysis simply derives these possibilities directly from the details of the verbs' meanings.

Getting the verb classes right

Levin and Hovav (2005: 13) note that 'there is more than one way of semantically characterizing most verbs, and it is not always a priori obvious which characterization is appropriate for argument realization'. How do we know, for example, that *cut*, *hack*, *bash* and *hit* contain a motion component, whereas *pat* and *touch* don't? It's not at all clear. The fact that the classifications are often indeterminate in this way might seem to undermine the very idea of semantically based verb classes, and hence undo the attempt to derive argument-structure alternations from semantics. As a result, a critic could make the following objection to Levin and Hovav: if several different descriptions of the meaning of the same verb can be validly given, isn't it arbitrary to claim that just one drives argument alternation? What about all the incompatible semantic descriptions that also fit the verb?

This objection raises an interesting issue about the process of empirical research in a domain like linguistics. We normally think of theories being based on some sort of solid evidence: we start out with an unambiguous set of observed facts, and then try to come up with a theory that explains them. The theory matches the facts, which are therefore evidence for the truth of the theory. For example, the facts on which Copernicus based his theory of the solar system are ultimately observations made of the sky. Because the Copernican theory fits these observations, we have a reason to think the theory is true.

This is only part of the story, however. Often, the facts aren't solid and unambiguous. It's frequently the case that we're not exactly sure what all the observational facts actually are: maybe our measurements aren't always precise enough, maybe there's disagreement about whether a phenomenon is relevant, maybe there are conflicting observations about the same phenomenon. In the case of astronomy, maybe there weren't good enough instruments to check the details of the heliocentric theory directly. In this sort of situation, it's often argued to be appropriate to *let the theory tell you what the facts are*. As long as we have enough clear cases, it's OK to allow the unclear ones to be interpreted in whatever way is most favourable to the theory. Just as we adjust the theory to reflect the facts, so we can sometimes adjust our idea of what the facts are in order to fit the theory. Applied to verb-classes, if we follow this approach we could accept that the semantic classification of some verbs isn't obvious. But we wouldn't see this as a threat to the broader theory. Instead, we could just say that considerations from the theory as a whole allow us to resolve the uncertainties of verb meaning. Independent of the theory, there are arguments both for and against including motion in the semantic representation of *pat* and *touch*. But since the theory only works if we say that this component is absent, that in itself is all the justification we need.

QUESTION   Psych-verbs do not allow the middle alternation, as the following sentences show. Can you suggest why not?
   *Amber considers the problem/*The problem considers easily.*
   *Sophie believes Sam/*Sam believes easily* [this can only mean that Sam believes other people easily, not that he is easy to believe, the meaning required for the middle].

10.3 The meaning of constructions

The accounts of argument structure and alternations that we have looked at so far are sometimes described as **projectionist**. This means that they are ultimately based in the verb's semantic representation, which 'projects' (determines) its syntactic behaviour (either directly, or via theta-roles). Projectionist accounts give the individual lexeme a central role in the explanation of the clause: the argument structure and the alternations associated with a verb are always the product of its semantic representation.

Projectionist accounts seem plausible as long as the verb only participates in a limited number of alternations. The locative alternation, discussed above for the verbs *spray* and *load*, is a good example of an alternation plausibly handled in a projectionist account. There is a basic variant, the locative variant, whose underlying representation forms part of the *with* variant, as in (43):

(43) a. Locative variant: *load hay onto the cart*
       load: [x CAUSE [y TO COME TO BE AT z]]

   b. *With* variant: *load the cart with hay*
       load: [x CAUSE [z TO COME TO BE IN STATE]
               BY MEANS OF [x CAUSE [y TO COME TO BE AT z]]]

On this account, *load* has two separate lexical entries, one for each variant. *Load* is, in other words, polysemous (5.3).

Let's now think about the verb *siren*. This can appear with a number of quite distinct argument structures:

(44) a. *The factory horns sirened through the raid.*
    b. *The factory horns sirened midday and everybody broke for lunch.*
    c. *The police car sirened the Porsche to a stop.*
    d. *The police car sirened up to the accident site.* (adapted from Levin and Hovav 2005: 190)

In (44a) the verb is intransitive and denotes the emission of a sound. In (44b) it still denotes sound-emission, but has an object, which denotes not the sound emitted, but the time of day which the siren marks. In (44c) the verb's object denotes the entity caused to stop by the sirening. In (44d) *siren* is again intransitive, but this time seems to be primarily a verb of motion, and only secondarily one of sound-emission.

Different syntactic complement structures like these are usually taken to reflect differences in the verb's semantic representation: *siren* has to have a number of polysemous senses to account for the different structures in (44). But Goldberg (1995) points out that this approach leads to a blow-out in the number of senses which we attribute to verbs. Take *sneeze*. We usually think of this as an intransitive verb. But Goldberg notes that it's ditransitive in the phrase *sneeze the napkin off the table*, suggesting an entirely separate, polysemous sense.

For Goldberg, this analysis is undesirable. *Siren* and *sneeze* should not be credited with a large number of senses, one for each different argument structure pattern they display. In order to avoid this, Goldberg develops a different conception of the nature of grammar. On this conception, words are not the only meaning-bearing units in grammar. Semantic representations are also associated with **constructions**. In the most general terms, constructions are form–meaning pairs, just like words. The difference is that the forms involved in constructions are on a higher level than individual lexemes: they are particular grammatical *patterns*, which individual lexemes instantiate. Some examples of constructions are given in Table 10.3 (Goldberg 1995: 3–4).

Each construction can be instantiated by a large number of lexical items. This is most obvious with the intransitive motion construction. As well as appearing with verbs of motion (*go*, *come*) and manner of motion (*run*, *limp*, *hobble*, *slide*, *fall*, *drop*), the construction can be instantiated by verbs of sound emission (*buzz*, *siren*), by verbs of bursting (*burst*, *pop*) and even by verbs such as *sweat* (*the runners sweated up the hill*). The construction is thus a broad general pattern in the grammar.

QUESTION   Consider the following examples. Which constructions might they instantiate?

Fred watered the plants flat.
Jack licked the platter clean.

Table 10.3. Four constructions		
Name	Meaning	Syntactic structure
Caused motion	X CAUSES Y TO MOVE Z	SUB V OBJ OBLique *Pat sneezed the napkin off the table.*
Resultative	X CAUSES Y TO BECOME Z	SUBJ V OBJ X-COMP *She kissed him unconscious.*
Intransitive motion	X MOVES Y	SUBJ V OBL *The fly buzzed into the room.*
Conative	X DIRECTS ACTION AT Y	SUBJ V OBL$_{at}$ *Sam kicked at Bill.*

Note: In the 'Meaning' column, the Z after the 'move' predicate in the caused motion construction, and the Y after the 'move' predicate in the intransitive motion construction do not stand for the object of the verb 'move', but for a specification of the path along which the movement takes place, corresponding to 'off the table' for the first, and 'into the room' for the second.

He pried it apart/open/loose/free. (Goldberg and Jackendoff 2004: 559)
It came apart/open/loose/free. (Goldberg and Jackendoff 2004: 559)
Pat sliced the carrots into the salad. (Goldberg 2006: 7)
Pat sliced the box open. (Goldberg 2006: 7)

The descriptions of the syntax of each construction are essentially specifications of argument structure. An important feature of a constructional account of the syntax–semantics interface is that arguments can be subcategorized by the construction itself. In (45), for example, the highlighted phrases are all brought into the structure of the clause by the construction: they are not subcategorized by the verb:

(45) a. *She sneezed **the napkin off the table**.*
    b. *The fly buzzed **into the room**.*
    c. *She kissed him **unconscious**.*
    d. *Sam kicked **at Bill**.*

Note that all the sentences are grammatical *without* the highlighted phrases. This means that the highlighted phrases are adjuncts: the verbs do not obligatorily select them as part of their argument structure. It is important to see that adding the highlighted phrases doesn't simply add an argument to the verb; it also changes the basic meaning of the sentence. On its own, *sneeze* is simply an intransitive verb denoting a bodily emission. But when it is plugged into the caused motion construction, the construction supplies two extra argument slots, filled in (45a) by *the napkin* and *off the table*, and is paraphrased 'she caused the napkin to move off the table'. Complementation patterns are therefore the joint product of verbs and the constructions in which they are placed.

In this respect, constructions are like idioms. Consider an idiom like *take (someone) to task* or the *let alone* idiom, as in *I wouldn't do X, let alone (do) Y*. These idioms are listed in the lexicon with a syntactic structure, a meaning, and a partially filled phonology. For example, the lexical entry for *take to task* would specify the structure [*take* NP *to task*], and include the information that the NP must be human. The *let alone* idiom could be described as [V NP, *let alone* (V) NP], with the specification that the first V NP component must have a negative interpretation. (For discussion of *let alone*, see Fillmore *et al.* 1988; for comparison of idioms and constructions, Goldberg and Jackendoff 2004.) Constructions are like this too, except that they are even less specified lexically. The intransitive motion construction, for instance, just specifies the structure V PP, and imposes certain constraints on what types of verb and prepositional phrase may instantiate it (more on this below). The conative construction, again, just specifies the structure V *at* NP. Constructions are thus clausal/phrasal shells, waiting to be filled with lexical material.

As we have already seen, the important difference between a constructional and a traditional account of argument structure is that the constructional account reduces the proliferation of verb-senses. *Sneeze* has exactly the same semantic structure in (45a) as it does in its ordinary intransitive use (*someone sneezed loudly*, say). We do not have to list *sneeze* as polysemous between the basic sense *sneeze₁* 'involuntarily emit burst of air as result of nasal irritation' and a *sneeze₂* sense ('cause to move by sneezing₁'). Instead, the extra meaning, 'x causes y to move z', comes from the caused motion construction itself, which we only need to state once. Similarly, we do not have to postulate a different polysemous sense of *slice* in order to account for the different complement configurations in which it figures. Rather, exactly the same lexical entry of *slice* is operative in each of the contexts below; it is different constructions which contribute the different arguments, and the particular semantic interpretations:

(46) *He sliced the bread.* (transitive construction)
  Pat sliced the carrots into the salad. (caused motion construction)
  Pat sliced Chris a piece of pie. (ditransitive construction)
  Emeril sliced and diced his way to stardom. (way construction)
  Pat sliced the box open. (resultative construction) (Goldberg 2006: 7)

Not all verbs can appear in all constructions. Take the caused-motion construction. We can *sneeze a napkin off the table*, but we cannot *use* or *waste a napkin off the table*: *use* and *waste* are not compatible with the caused-motion construction. In the same way, the intransitive-motion construction cannot be used with verbs of sense-perception (**Ann smelled/noticed/listened into the room*) or some verbs of striking (**She hit/knocked into the room*), among others.

QUESTION   What restrictions are there on the resultative construction? Consider the following sentences, which are all ungrammatical in the resultative reading (though they may be grammatical in some other reading):

*He pried it flat/straight.
*He opened the letter flat.
*She held the plastic cup crumpled.
*They played the tape broken.
*They cleaned the room sparkling.
*She taught the children tired.

How can we account for these constraints? As Goldberg (1995: 24) puts it, constructions don't just impose their meaning on 'unsuspecting' verbs; a verb's meaning determines whether it is compatible with a given construction. She gives two general conditions governing which verbs can appear in which construction. The conditions turn on the question of what Goldberg calls the 'event type' of the verb and construction – whether the verb/construction concerns motion, change of state, causation, and so on. Here are the conditions, with e_c standing for the event type designated by the construction, and e_v for the event type designated by the verb.

I. e_v must be related to e_c in one of the following ways:

A. e_v may be a subtype of e_c
B. e_v may designate the means of e_c
C. e_v may designate the result of e_c
D. e_v may designate a precondition of e_c
E. To a very limited extent, e_v may designate the manner of e_c, the means of identifying e_c, or the intended result of e_c

II. e_c and e_v must share at least one participant (Goldberg 1995: 65)

Let's see how these conditions apply to the examples in (47):

(47) a. *She sneezed **the napkin off the table**.*
     b. *The fly buzzed **into the room**.*
     c. *She kissed him **unconscious**.*
     d. *Sam kicked **at Bill**.*

In (47a) and (47c) the verb denotes the means by which the construction's event type arises. ((47a) is a caused-motion event type, (47c) resultative.) (47b) denotes the manner, or perhaps the means, in which the fly entered the room – *buzzing* – and (47d) denotes a subtype of the category 'directed action' – here, obviously, kicking. Constraints like these, Goldberg claims, determine the range of constructions in which a verb can appear.

QUESTION The following sentences are ungrammatical. State which constructions they exemplify. Does the ungrammaticality result from a failure to meet the event-type conditions, or must we look for some other reason?

a. *The car honked down the road.
b. *The dog barked out of the room.
c. *Bill whistled past the house. (Goldberg and Jackendoff 2004: 540)
d. *Someone coughed into the room.

The constructional approach to language has a wide application. Goldberg states that '[e]ven basic sentence patterns of a language can be understood to involve constructions. That is, the main verb can be understood to combine with an argument structure construction (e.g. transitive, intransitive, ditransitive, etc.)' (2006: 6). We will illustrate this with the ditransitive construction, which we have not yet discussed. The ditransitive construction is the following:

(48) X CAUSES Y TO RECEIVE Z   SUbject Verb OBJect OBJect$_2$
                                Pat faxed Bill the letter

This covers *any* situation in which the verb appears with a double object:

(49) *Nigella baked me a cake.*
     They showed me the problem.
     Just read me the letter.
     He asked her a question.
     The travel agent booked me a ticket.
     I chose myself a new suit.

These sentences don't, of course, satisfy the semantic description 'x causes y to receive z' since the object doesn't receive anything. Nevertheless, they count as instances of the construction. The justification for this is that Goldberg sees constructions as basically polysemous: they do not have a single sense, but a family of closely related senses, arranged according to the same principles of prototypicality as other radial sense networks (on polysemy and radial networks, see 7.2). In the ditransitive construction, the core sense is 'actual transfer' (Goldberg 1995: 32). But many instances of the construction, such as all of those in (49), don't entail that the recipient actually receives the theme. Further, the 'transfer' involved may not be literal, but metaphorical, as in *Claude taught the class French*.

Thinking of the ditransitive as a construction with its own polysemous set of meanings is a radical departure from projectionist accounts of grammar, in which different argument options are interpreted as reflecting differences in the lexical entries of verbs themselves. For Goldberg, *everything* in language can be seen as a construction – a form–meaning pairing in which the phonology may be more or less fully specified. From this point of view, individual lexemes are themselves a type of construction. For Goldberg, an uttered expression 'typically involves the combination of at least half a dozen different constructions' (2006: 10). The centrality of constructions to grammar is not, of course, limited to English. As an example of an obvious construction in another language, Goldberg (2006: 7–8; examples from Chidambaram 2004) discusses the Russian data in (50):

(50) a. *Kirill   v   magazin*
        Kirill-NOM   to   store-ACC
        'Kirill goes/will go to the store.'

     b. *Kirill   iz   magazina*
        Kirill-NOM   from   store-GEN
        'Kirill just got back from the store.'

The constructions express the meaning that motion occurred, without the presence of any verb whatsoever. Cases like these provide clear evidence that certain form–meaning pairs need to be credited with meaning in their own right, and that it should not be the verb which is automatically assumed to be the kernel of the meaning of the rest of the clause.

Summary

The linking problem

The **linking problem** is the problem of accounting for the relations between a verb and its associated noun phrases. According to the traditional generative understanding, the lexical entries for verbs include a specification of the types of **argument** they have associated with them. It was assumed that the possible arguments of all verbs could be classified into a small number of classes, called **thematic roles, theta-roles, participant roles** or **semantic roles**. Typical roles include **agent, patient/ theme, goal, source, location, instrument, beneficiary** and **experiencer**. Some roles are more likely to be coded as subject, and others as object. It was suggested that it is possible to rank the different roles in an order which shows their relative accessibility to subject position.

Problems with thematic roles

There are three main problems with thematic roles:

- The arguments of many verbs seem hard to assign to any of the conventional thematic roles.
- There are also many occasions where an argument could be assigned to several thematic roles.
- It has not proven possible to formulate a universal thematic hierarchy ranking these roles.

Proto-roles

Dowty (1991) suggested that the different participant roles are cluster concepts, like Roschean prototypes, and that thematic roles are based on entailments of verb-meanings. The argument with the most Proto-Agent entailments will be coded as subject, and the one with the most Proto-Patient entailments as object.

Thematic roles and conceptual structure

Jackendoff's theory of semantic representation dispenses completely with theta-roles, and derives argument structure directly from the semantics of the verb. This means that the thematic hierarchy can be completely restated in terms of underlying conceptual configurations. In Jackendoff's theory of conceptual structure, **selectional restrictions** are also specified directly by the conceptual structure: they are not extra information which needs to be learnt in addition to the meaning of the verbs themselves.

Verb classes and alternations

Many verbs show several different argument structures. These different types of argument structure are known as **alternations**. They include the **causative**, **middle**, **resultative**, **conative** and others. Levin and Hovav proposed that which alternations a verb participates in is explained by its underlying semantic structure. On their theory, verbs fall into semantically defined classes, which all show similar syntactic behaviour with respect to their alternations.

The meaning of constructions

Words are not the only meaning-bearing units in grammar. Semantic representations are also associated with **constructions**. Goldberg put forward a constructional account of the syntax–semantics interface, in which arguments can be subcategorized by the construction itself. Not all verbs can appear in all constructions. A verb's meaning determines whether it is compatible with a given construction. The constructional account reduces the proliferation of verb-senses.

Further reading

On the semantics of verbal arguments, see Van Valin (2005) and Levin and Hovav (2005), which surveys the main theories of argument realization. Levin (1993) is a comprehensive discussion of English verb classes and alternations. On construction grammar, see Goldberg (2006). Newmeyer (2002) justifies scepticism about the existence of a thematic hierarchy.

Exercises

Questions for discussion

1. The discussion of verb complementation in this chapter has assumed that single verbs with fairly stable patterns of complementation are of central importance to the structure of grammar. However, an examination of texts reveals that constructions involving a single verb are far from being in the majority for the purposes of expressing the occurrence of events (Hopper 1997). What other means does English present of lexicalizing events?

2. Consider the *with/against* alternation (*hit the wall with a stick* vs. *hit the stick against the wall*). Is there any consistent meaning difference between the different members of the alternation? Answer the same question for alternations such as *water leaked from the tank/the tank leaked water* and *the tank filled with water/water filled the tank* (Levin and Hovav 2005: 195).

3. It is often pointed out that not all semantic distinctions are syntactically relevant. For example, verbs of colouring like *paint, colour, bleach, whiten, stain,* etc. do not constitute a single class for the purposes of alternations or argument structure generalizations. Similarly, there seem to be no syntactically relevant distinctions between verbs of loud and soft speech (*shout* vs.

whisper). Is it possible to generalize about what types of meanings are syntactically relevant in English? In another language you know?

4. Would it make sense to extend the term 'incremental theme' to the patient argument of change-of-state verbs, such as *open, close, break,* etc.? Why (not)?

5. Goldberg (1995: 11) claims that standard accounts of argument structure are circular: 'it is claimed that *kick* has an *n*-argument sense on the basis of the fact that *kick* occurs with *n* complements; it is simultaneously argued that *kick* occurs with *n* complements because it has an *n*-argument sense'. Is Goldberg's criticism justified? Does a constructional account avoid the problem?

6. Think about the sentence *The Romans defeated Hannibal's army at Zama* from the point of view of the linking problem. The two arguments we need roles for are *Hannibal's army* and *The Romans*. Which is theme? Theme is usually defined as the participant affected by the action; or, sometimes, as the participant which undergoes a change of state as a result of the action. Well, weren't both sides here affected? Didn't both undergo a change of state? Hannibal's army went from the state of non-defeated to the state of defeated; the Romans from the state of not-victors to the state of victors. How do we know which is the right state for the purpose of argument selection?

7. Consider the ditransitive construction, described by Goldberg as follows (cf. (48) above).

Semantics	CAUSE-RECEIVE	(agent	recipient	theme)
	|	|	|	|
Syntax	V	Subj	Object	Object$_2$)

Are the following verbs compatible with the description offered by Goldberg?

 arrange me a table; book me a ticket; take me 50 kilometres; choose me a jacket; charge me fifty euros; cost me fifty euros; show me a room; ask me a question; give them prominence.

8. Other factors than semantic ones can determine the distribution of arguments in actual discourse. Two such factors are the 'heaviness' of the NP, and its information status (whether it refers to given or new information). Read Levin and Hovav (2005: 216–218) and Arnold *et al.* (2000) and discuss the implications of their results for the linking theories we have discussed in this chapter.

11 Semantic variation and change

CHAPTER PREVIEW

Variation is one of the most immediately obvious facts about meaning. Everyone is aware of how the meaning of identical expressions can differ from one person to another, sometimes significantly. There are two aspects of meaning variation: a synchronic and a diachronic (historical) one; we examine each in turn in this chapter. After a quick tour of some important preliminary questions (11.1), we begin diachronically by illustrating the traditional categories with which meaning change has been described, and we consider some of the shortcomings of this approach (11.2.1). We then move on to more recent studies of the pathways and mechanisms of semantic change (11.2.2) and a brief discussion of **grammaticalization**, the process by which full lexical words are converted into grammatical morphemes (11.2.3). The second half of the chapter discusses synchronic meaning variation. We start by examining the subtle types of semantic variation which exist within a single language community at any one time. Powerful new tools developed within corpus linguistics allow this kind of variation to be studied in a way that was not previously available: these are illustrated in 11.3. We then look at the field of **semantic typology**, which studies possible constraints on meaning variation and seeks out possible semantic universals in various semantic fields such as the body, colour, space and motion (11.4). Lastly, we consider the implications of these studies for the question of the influences between language and cognition, discussing the famous **Sapir–Whorf** or **linguistic relativity** hypothesis (11.5).

11.1 Sense, reference and metalanguage in semantic comparisons

Since meanings are unobservable, we cannot examine their historical variation or cross-linguistic universality directly in the way that we might, for instance, explore the history or distribution of a particular sound. In principle, it is a fairly straightforward matter to answer the question of whether the nasal [n], for instance, is found universally, and of what diachronic developments it is likely to undergo. To do this, one examines every language in turn, or at least a large sample of languages, to see whether they all have sounds which meet the criteria for [n] – criteria established by the discipline of phonetics – and uses this as the basis for exploration of its historical developments. In semantics, things are not so simple. In this section, we will discuss two particular points:

- the difference between universality/variation of sense and universality/variation of reference, and
- the problems of the appropriate metalanguage in undertaking cross-linguistic or historical semantic study.

Sense and reference are both crucial aspects of meaning (see Chapter 3). But there is a big difference between them when we study meaning cross-linguistically or historically: it is much easier to establish cross-linguistic identity of reference than of sense. To see why, imagine that we are conducting an investigation into body-part terminology in the languages of the world. As part of this study, we want to test the hypothesis that all languages have at least one expression which has the meaning 'skin' (perhaps among other, polysemous meanings). Questions like this are the stock-in-trade of the study of semantic typology, which we discuss in 11.4. In the course of this investigation, we discover an interesting situation in Warlpiri (Pama-Nyungan, Central Australia). In Warlpiri, the word for 'skin', *pinti*, is also used to refer to bark and peel, and these two other uses are just as literal as the 'skin' use itself. What conclusions should we draw from this about the sense of *pinti*? *Pinti* clearly *refers to* skin, but does it contain 'skin' as one of its senses? Perhaps Warlpiri doesn't actually express the distinct meaning 'skin', but contains instead a single *general* meaning applying to all three types of referent simultaneously, along the lines of 'outer layer of person, animal, tree or fruit'. In this case, we would have to claim that 'skin' isn't a semantic universal, since it doesn't independently exist in Warlpiri: *pinti refers to* skin, but 'skin' isn't a separate *sense* of the word.

QUESTION   Would this seem a reasonable conclusion? What are its advantages and problems?

The conclusion that *pinti* is general in meaning would also have consequences for historical study. For example, it would mean that there would be no point in asking questions about the diachronic origin of the 'skin' meaning, such as whether it developed from the 'bark' or 'peel' meanings, or vice versa. If *pinti* is general between these senses, these questions cannot be asked.

Another possibility, though, is that *pinti* is polysemous, with the three distinct meanings {skin, bark, peel}. In this situation, *pinti* not only *refers* to skin, it also contains 'skin' as one of its three separate *senses*. If this was the case, the status of 'skin' as a semantic universal wouldn't be threatened: we could claim that the meaning 'skin' *is* found in Warlpiri, but that it is not individually **lexicalized**. This means that there is not a word which just expresses the meaning 'skin' on its own; 'skin' always comes along in a 'package' with other meanings included, even though each of the meanings is conceptually separate. Speakers of Warlpiri can obviously distinguish skin, bark and peel, as shown by the fact that they treat each in different ways. They can also distinguish between them linguistically at a phrasal level (e.g. a phrase like '*pinti* of animal' can only mean 'skin'). It's just that in *pinti*, they're all combined together. (See 5.3 for discussion of the problems that affect attempts to tell whether an expression is general or polysemous.)

Whether *pinti* is general or polysemous, its reference is determined by its sense. Determining its reference is, at least for practical purposes, easy enough: we can get a Warlpiri speaker to point, draw pictures, and so on. These activities have their own subtle ambiguities (see 2.3.2), but, at least for concrete nouns like *pinti*, they are usually straightforward enough for the purposes of practical linguistic description. As a result, we can talk with some certainty about cross-linguistic differences of reference for this kind of noun. But what this discussion has shown is that questions of cross-linguistic differences of sense are more complicated, and conclusions based on them accordingly harder to reach.

An associated problem is the question of the correct or optimal metalanguage for the description of meanings. Claims about the universality of given meanings necessitate a particular metalanguage in which the meanings can be described. Similarly, studying meaning change implies that we have a reliable metalanguage which can be used to represent historical sense developments accurately. But this immediately introduces complications since there is not yet any agreement about what the correct metalanguage for semantic description is. Semantic theories like those of Jackendoff, Wierzbicka and many others presuppose a universal set of primitive concepts lexicalized in all languages. In claiming that the meanings of all languages can be translated into a unique, universal metalanguage, these types of theory constitute strong hypotheses of semantic universalism. As illustrated elsewhere, however, these hypotheses are also highly controversial (2.5; 8.1.3). There is no agreement that a single universal metalanguage for semantic description is even possible, let alone agreement on what it should be like. The absence of an agreed standard for description complicates the process of achieving consensus in comparative or historical studies of meaning. Two investigators can always disagree about the details of a word's meaning. But the prospects for agreement are obviously improved if they are at least working with the same descriptive metalanguage: if they are not, it may not be even clear whether they agree or not. We will see some examples of this sort of problem in 11.4.2 and 11.4.4 below.

The idea that the variation among languages conceals an identity of meaning at some deeper level has a lot to be said for it. Humans share the same perceptual and cognitive organs, and we regularly succeed in making ourselves understood, even across breathtaking cultural and linguistic divides. We also inhabit the same shared world to which we refer. Surely, one might ask, this means that the meanings we express are also the same, deep down? If they weren't, we couldn't accurately translate from one language to another, and we would have no guarantee that understanding was possible across linguistic divides (see Chapter 1).

Linguistics in general, and semantic theory in particular, certainly assume that languages are mutually translatable in a way that preserves important meaning components. If we abandoned this assumption, any cross-linguistic work involving meaning would be impossible. But it is one thing to presuppose a rough and ready translatability, and quite another to suppose that exactly the same meaning or concept can be captured by the words of different languages. Just as it seems obvious that we can convey the essence or gist of our thoughts in another language, so it is a commonplace that no two languages ever convey *exactly* the same ideas. The cross-linguistic and historical study of meaning has to weave a course between these two equally obvious positions.

11.2 Semantic change

Meaning change is everywhere, and no words are immune from it. A striking example of this is the English conjunction *and*. At face value, it seems that this is such a simple and basic word that we would be safe in assuming that its meaning has been the same throughout the history of English. But this isn't at all the case. In premodern English, *and* was polysemous with 'if', as exemplified in (1):

(1)   *And I had but one penny in the world, thou shouldst have it to buy gingerbread.* (Shakespeare, *Love's Labours Lost*, Vi 71–2)

The only possible reading of this sentence is '*If* I had just one penny in the world…'. This polysemy has been lost in modern English. But it shows that even elements of the vocabulary that one would think are conceptually the most basic, and hence the least likely to shift, can change their meaning.

QUESTION   Before we begin exploring semantic change, ask yourself what semantic change could consist in. How might we know when a change has occurred? What evidence could we draw on?

Like many other branches of linguistics, the modern study of semantics began with a largely diachronic focus, investigating meaning change. Knowledge of the history of Indo-European languages had sensitized scholars to the extreme fluidity of words' meanings through time. Traditional scholarly study of ancient languages in the nineteenth century (**philology**) meant that the details of meaning change in European languages were well known. The availability of a long written tradition, going back in the case of Greek to well before the sixth century BC, supplied an enormous quantity of texts through which changes in words' meaning could be traced. Because of this history, Indo-European languages have had an overwhelming importance in the study of semantic change. The rich textual tradition of European languages and its associated history of scholarship mean that studies of semantic change have traditionally relied on Indo-European evidence much more than have other domains of modern linguistics. In contrast, we are largely in the dark about long-term sense developments in the languages of oral societies, which lack the written evidence on which historical study needs to be based.

Unlike sound change, which seems to be governed by regular laws of great generality which were open to 'scientific' study, meaning change has often struck investigators as chaotic and particularistic. Since changes in words' meaning are often determined by socio-cultural factors, much meaning change is not even linguistically motivated. For instance, since the advent of modern air transport, the verb *fly* can refer to travelling as a passenger in an aeroplane. This is a meaning that was obviously unavailable before the twentieth century. But it does not necessarily correspond to any change in the sense of *fly* itself: this is still arguably 'travel through the air'. What has caused the change of meaning is arguably not anything to do with language, but simply a change in the word's denotation.

An important characteristic of semantic change is that it crucially involves polysemy (see 5.3). A word does not suddenly change from meaning A to meaning B in a single move; instead, the change happens via an intermediate stage in which the word has *both* A and B among its meanings. Consider the French noun *glace* 'ice'. In the course of the seventeenth century, it acquired the additional sense 'ice cream/iced drink', but this did not replace the original sense. Instead, *glace* had simply acquired an extra polysemous sense in addition to its original one. This is the usual case in semantic change. Meaning change most often takes the form of an addition of polysemous senses. The *loss* of the original sense is less common. In all of the changes discussed in this chapter, we will assume the presence of an intermediate polysemous stage, though we won't always mention it specifically.

11.2.1 The traditional categories

Early studies of semantic change like those in Bréal (1897) did little more than set up broad categories of change, described with very general, and often vague, labels like 'weakening', 'strengthening' and so on. In the first instance, we will consider four of these traditional categories of semantic change: **specialization**, **generalization**, **ameliorization** and **pejorization**. These categories were not part of an effort to explain *why* meaning change happens, but were meant to contribute to a typology of semantic changes – a precondition of any further explanatory progress.

One common type of change is **specialization (narrowing)**, in which a word narrows its range of reference:

- English *liquor* used to refer to liquid of any kind: the reference to alcohol was a subsequent specialization.
- English *pavement* originally referred to any paved surface, but specialized to simply cover the footpath on the edge of a street (called *sidewalk* in American English).
- The proto-Romance word for ointment, *unctu*, specialized in Romanian so as only to refer to a single type of 'ointment', butter (as well as undergoing some phonological changes to become *unt*; Posner 1996: 319).

The opposite tendency is **generalization (broadening)**, in which a word's meaning changes to encompass a wider class of referents.

- *zealot* first referred to members of a Jewish resistance movement against the occupying Romans in the first century AD; its contemporary meaning 'fanatical enthusiast' is a later generalization.
- French *panier* 'basket' originally meant just a bread-basket; it was subsequently generalized to baskets of any kind.
- The Latin noun *passer* means 'sparrow', but in a number of Romance languages it has generalized to the meaning 'bird': this is the case, for example, with Spanish *pájaro* and Romanian *pasăre*.
- The most common verb for 'work' in Romance languages, like French *travailler* and Spanish *trabajar*, is a result of a generalization from the Latin **tripaliare* 'torture with a tripalium', a three-spiked torture instrument (Posner 1996: 322).
- The German adverb *sehr* 'very' originally meant 'cruelly' or 'painfully' (Kluge 1989; a trace of this meaning survives in the verb *versehren* 'injure, hurt'). The shift to 'very' is an example of an extreme generalization that has lost almost all connection with the original sense. A similar change is found in many English intensifier terms, like *terribly* and *awfully*.

QUESTION Classify each of the following semantic changes as either generalization or specialization. Are there any cases where it is hard to decide?

- Latin *curtus* 'short (in space)' > 'short (in space and time)': French *court*, Spanish *corto*, Portuguese *curto*, Italian *corto*.
- Midde Japanese *ake-sita*, 'dawning time, dawn' > *asita* 'tomorrow' (Traugott and Dasher 2002: 56).
- Dutch *drukken* 'to press, to push hard' > 'to print (books)'.
- French *arriver* 'arrive at the shore' > 'arrive (anywhere)'.

Two other traditional categories in the analysis of meaning change are **pejorization** (Latin *pejor* 'worse') and **amelioration** (Latin *melior* 'better'). These refer to change in words' evaluative force. In pejorization, a word takes on a derogatory meaning. This is frequently seen with words for animals, which can be used to refer to people negatively or insultingly, as when someone is called a *monkey*, *parasite*, *pig*, *sow*, and so on. Another example of pejorization is the adjective *silly*. This originally meant 'blessed, happy, fortunate'; its contemporary meaning 'foolish' is a later development – and one which, this time, has entirely displaced the original sense. Similarly, *boor*'s original meaning was 'farmer'; 'crude person' was a later pejorization. *Accident* originally meant simply 'chance event', but took on the meaning 'unfavourable chance event'.

Ameliorization is the opposite process, in which a word's meaning changes to become more positively valued. The normalization of previously proscribed taboo words is a good example. *Bum*, for example, appears to be gaining somewhat in social acceptability, at least in Australian English. It has thus started on the path to what could be full ameliorization: this would be attained if it eventually became fully synonymous with *bottom*. Another example of ameliorization is provided by English *nice*. The earliest meaning of this adjective, found in Middle English, is 'simple, foolish, silly, ignorant'; the basic modern sense, 'agreeable, pleasant, satisfactory, attractive' is not attested until the eighteenth century.

These four categories on their own are not at all adequate to describe the complexities and diversity of the types of meaning change encountered in the history of languages. How do we explain, for instance, the shift of Latin *ver* 'spring' to the meaning 'summer' in many Romance languages (Romanian *vara*, Spanish *verano*, Portuguese *verão*; Bourciez 1967: 207)? This seems to fit none of the four categories we have mentioned. The same could be said for the development from Latin *sensus* 'sensation, consciousness, sense' to the meaning 'brains' in Spanish *seso*. Similarly, how to account for the shift from 'count' to 'read' in Tolai *luk* (Austronesian, Papua New Guinea; Tryon 1995 IV: 509)?

A solution to this sort of problem comes from recognizing specialization and generalization as just two types of **metonymic change**. Metonymy (see 7.2.4) is the process of sense development in which a word shifts to a contiguous meaning. 'Contiguous' has a number of meanings (Peirsman and Geeraerts 2006), but the essential idea is that two senses are contiguous if their referents are actually next to each other (either spatially or temporally), or if the senses underlying the words are closely related conceptually. The Spanish 'consciousness' > 'brains' shift exemplifies conceptual contiguity (brains and consciousness have a close conceptual association), while the 'spring' > 'summer' shift exemplifies both temporal and conceptual contiguity: summer is next to spring in time, and also a closely related notion conceptually. Some instances of pejorization and ameliorization can also be considered metonymic: the shift of *boor* from 'farmer' to 'crude person' could be considered to be based on the close association of these two notions.

Metonymy is a powerful category: it can describe many types of change which can't otherwise be accommodated. The English noun *bead* originally meant 'prayer' in Old English. Its present meaning can be explained through the widespread use of the 'Rosary', a chain of beads which Christians used to keep track of prayer sequences. This association established a conceptual link between the notions 'prayer' and 'bead', explaining the metonymic transfer of *bead* to the latter meaning in the Middle English period. This is neither generalization/specialization, nor ameliorization/pejorization, so a new category is clearly needed to describe it.

Metonymic changes are common. A particularly colourful one underlies the word *pupil*, which in English refers both to a student and to the opening in the eye through which light passes. This puzzling polysemy goes back to Latin, where *pupilla* means both 'small girl, doll' and 'pupil'. This can be explained by metonymy. Our eyes have 'pupils' because of the small doll-like image that can be observed there: spatial contiguity, in other words, underlies the shift. Greek *khōrē* has exactly the same metonymically related meanings. Another example of a metonymic meaning shift is the Romanian word *bărbat* 'husband', which derives from the Latin *barbatus* 'bearded'. If husbands often have beards, the ideas will be conceptually associated.

Metonymy was a notion adopted into linguistics from rhetoric, the traditional study of figurative, literary and persuasive language. Another originally rhetorical concept with linguistic application is **metaphor**, discussed from the synchronic point of view in 7.2.4. Metaphors are based not on contiguity, but similarity or analogy. English *germ* is a good example of a metaphor-based meaning change. The earlier meaning of this word was 'seed', clearly visible in a sentence like (2), from 1802:

(2) *The germ grows up in the spring, upon a fruit stalk, accompanied with leaves* (OED *germ* 1a).

The word's application to the microscopic 'seeds' of disease is a metaphorical transfer: ailments are likened to plants, giving them 'seeds' from which they develop. The Old French word for 'head', *test*, is another example of metaphorical development. Originally, *test* meant 'pot' or 'piece of broken pot': the semantic extension to 'head' is said to be the result of a metaphor current among soldiers, in which battle was colourfully described as 'smashing pots' (Hock 1991: 229). Exactly the same metaphor explains the sense development of German *Kopf* 'head', which used to mean 'cup'. The use of *monkey*, *pig*, *sow*, etc. in pejorative reference to people can also be seen as the result of a metaphor based on perceived similarity with the animals concerned. Another, very common, metaphor relates space and time. It is seen in the use of verbs with spatial meanings in temporal ones, as when English conveys the 'immediate' future tense using *go* (*I'm **going** to stop now*), or French uses *venir* 'come' to express events in the recent past (*je viens de terminer* 'I have just finished', literally 'I come from finishing'). In these expressions temporal events are expressed in language on the analogy of spatial ones. Many investigators have commented on the deep-seated nature of this transfer, which is widely attested cross-linguistically (Bybee, Perkins and Pagliucca 1994).

The centrality of metaphor and metonymy in semantic change is due to the fact that they jointly exhaust the possibilities of innovative word use and thus subsume all the other descriptive categories. If you want to express yourself innovatively *and* be understood, then 'there are only two ways of going about that: using words for the near neighbours of the things you mean (metonymy) or using words for the look-alikes (resemblars) of what you mean (metaphor)' Nerlich and Clarke (1992: 137).

QUESTION   Consider the following changes, and decide in which of the six categories of change discussed in this section they are best classified. Note any changes which belong to more than one category, and any which do not seem to fit into any.

- Old English *steofan* 'die' > Modern English *starve.*
- *broadcast* 'sow seeds' > 'transmit'
- *fair* 'beautiful' > 'unbiased'
- *nasty* 'filthy, dirty' > 'ill-natured, unpleasant, objectionable'
- *naughty* 'having or possessing naught; poor, needy' > 'morally bad, disobedient'
- Greek *eksupnos* 'awakened from sleep' > 'clever'

QUESTION   Motu (Austronesian, PNG), shows a semantic development from 'tree house' to 'tower' in the word *kohoro* (Tryon 1995 IV: 619). Adzera (Austronesian, PNG) uses the word for 'bamboo' for 'pipe', as does Tawala (also Austronesian, PNG; Tryon 1995 III: 238). How could these semantic changes be classified? Is there any way of distinguishing between different possible analyses?

11.2.2 Mechanisms and pathways of semantic change

The descriptive approach to semantic change described in the previous section is far from ideal. The categories are vague and purely taxonomic, and offer no explanatory insight into the conditions under which meaning change happens. They are also highly informal, and lack clear criteria for their application. This is particularly true for ameliorization and pejorization: whether a meaning change is in a positive or negative direction will often depend on little more than the subjective judgement of the investigator. For example, the change of English *knight* from the meaning 'boy, servant' to the meaning referring to the aristocrat is often described as ameliorization. But this is only the case if the latter meaning is evaluatively superior to the former, a judgement that not everyone would share. Another problem with the traditional categories is that they are also either too powerful or not powerful enough: in the case of generalization/specialization and ameliorization/pejorization, there are many meaning changes which do not seem to fit, and in the case of metonymy/metaphor, the categories seem to be able to explain *any* change, since we can always find some connection of similarity or contiguity between two meanings to justify their treatment as one or the other category. The traditional analysis of semantic change seems worlds away from the kinds of precise explanations that were possible in the study of sound change. Work in the second half of the twentieth century, still continuing, has tried to remedy some of these defects.

One of the features of this more recent work is the attempt to go beyond the mere description of changes, and search for causal explanations. For some scholars, the categories of metonymy and metaphor themselves are cognitively real and hence explanatory: as discussed in Chapter 7, cognitive linguists take metonymy and metaphor as basic cognitive operations which are at work throughout language. From this point of view, it is not surprising that metaphor and metonymy are prominent in meaning change, since they are also the principles behind much synchronic semantics. For someone committed to understanding language in terms of metaphor and metonymy, the contrast between explaining semantic change and just describing or classifying it collapses: the shift from *germ* 'seed' to *germ* 'microbe' is *explained*, not just classified, simply in virtue of being identified as a metaphor.

For others, however, this type of explanation is not satisfactory. Much modern work on semantic change stresses the role of the **conventionalization of implicature** as a source of semantic change. Consider the pejorization of English *accident*, discussed above. The original sense of 'chance event' would often have been used in discourse circumstances where the unfavourable nature of the event was strongly implied, as in (3):

(3)   1702: *The wisest councils may be discomposed by the smallest accidents.*
      (OED *accident*, 1)

The description 'chance event' would seem perfectly appropriate to the sense of *accident* present here. The context, however, strongly implies that the chance event is unfortunate or regrettable, since it 'discomposes the wisest councils'. According to the conventionalization of implicature theory of semantic change, *accident* would have become increasingly associated with contexts like (3), and the implication that the event was unfavourable or regrettable would have been progressively strengthened. On encountering *accident*, speakers would increasingly associate it with contexts like (3), and assume that the event was an unfavourable one. With time, this process of strengthening would change the status of the reading 'unfortunate/unfavourable chance event' from an implication to part of the word's literal meaning. The pejorization of *accident* is thus the result of the conventionalization of an implicature. This explanation does not deny that there is a relation of 'contiguity' between the notions 'chance event' and 'unfavourable chance event', and is not incompatible with an explanation based on metonymy. But it goes further, by showing the actual discourse mechanisms which allow the contiguity to become relevant.

Another instance where a conventionalization of implicature explanation is persuasive is the transfer of spatial to temporal meanings, as in the case of English *go* or French *venir* 'come', mentioned in the previous section. Bybee, Pagliucca and Perkins (1991) argue that description of this change as a metaphor is misleading: the transfer of 'go' and 'come' meanings to temporal uses does not spring from any general *analogy* or *resemblance* that speakers exploit between the domains of time and space. They point out that the semantic change only affects the verbs in specific grammatical contexts – not what one would expect for a metaphorical change grounded in a large-scale analogy between the temporal and spatial domains. Instead, the meaning change should be seen as the conventionalization of implicatures generated in *particular* uses of the spatial verbs. For *go*, the uses that give rise to the future meaning are those which specifically refer to an agent on a path moving toward a goal. In other words, *go* on its own is not enough to trigger an implicature of futurity; instead, it must be in an imperfective or progressive construction (see 9.2.2), with an **allative** (goal-directed) component. The future meaning will then arise as a conversational implicature of the verb under those discourse conditions. As Bybee *et al.* explain

The temporal meaning that comes to dominate the semantics of the construction is already present as an inference from the spatial meaning. When one moves along a path towards a goal in space, one also moves in time. The major change that takes place is the loss of the spatial meaning. Here ... the function of expressing intention comes into play. When a speaker announces that s/he is going somewhere to do something, s/he is also announcing the intention to do that thing. Thus intention is part of the meaning from the beginning, and the only change necessary is the generalization to contexts in which an intention is expressed, but the subject is not moving spatially to fulfill that intention.

(Bybee, Perkins and Pagliucca 1994: 268).

In other words, *go* only takes on a future reference in contexts like (4a), which could be used by someone leaving one room to go into another in order to watch television. This context is both imperfective/progressive, describing an action currently unfolding, and allative, in that it involves a specific goal. In contrast, contexts like (4b) (neither imperfective nor allative), (4c) (imperfective but not allative), and (4d) (allative but not imperfective) do not give rise to an implication of futurity:

(4)   a. *I am going to watch some TV.*
    b. *I usually watch TV for a while and then just go.*
    c. *I'm going now.*
    d. *I go there every Tuesday to watch some TV.*

For Bybee *et al.*, any explanation of the semantics of *go* based on metaphor cannot explain these constraints. Only by attending to pragmatic, discourse-based factors can we understand the circumstances in which the change from spatial to temporal meaning takes place.

    This explanation, then, puts pragmatic considerations at the heart of the understanding of semantic change: to understand why meaning changes, we should not be thinking in terms of broad cognitive operations like metaphor and metonymy, but should look instead at how inferences generated in discourse become part of lexicalized word meaning. The conventionalization of implicature theory of semantic change allows us to add a stage to our earlier generalization about the role of polysemy in semantic change. In light of the role of implicature, we can now describe the process of semantic change of a form between meanings A and B as in Figure 11.1:

FIGURE 11.1
The conventionalization of
implicature theory of
semantic change.

$$A \quad > \quad A + B_{\text{implicated}} \quad > \quad A + B_{\text{polysemous}} \quad (> \quad B)$$

The pragmatic origin of semantic change in conventionalized implicatures is now widely accepted. But what about the actual meanings themselves? Figure 11.1 tells us *how* a change from A > A (+ B) happens. But is it possible to generalize about the meanings A and B themselves? Can *any* meaning change into any other via a conventionalization of implicature, or are there regularities of semantic change which make some meanings more likely than others to appear as the As and Bs in the figure? Traugott has proposed several general tendencies of semantic change (1987, 1989; Traugott and Dasher 2002), of which we will discuss two.

The first is that '[m]eanings based in the external described situation' shift to 'meanings based in the internal (evaluative/perceptual/cognitive) described situation' (1989: 34). We might call this **semantic internalization**. This category takes in many changes from the concrete to the abstract, particularly the common change whereby words for physical properties are extended to also denote mental ones. Many languages show evidence of this type of change. The change in the Old English verb *felan* from the meaning 'touch' to the meaning 'feel' is a case in point: the earlier meaning makes no reference to the internal psychological domain, while the later one does. The history of Greek (Indo-European; Greece) gives many other examples:

(5) a. *dexios* 'on the right hand' > 'clever'
    b. *pikros* 'pointed, sharp, bitter' > 'embittered, angry, spiteful, mean'
    c. *skaios* 'left' > 'stupid'
    d. *isos* 'equal in size' > 'fair, impartial'
    e. *elaphros* 'light in weight/movement' > 'flighty, frivolous, wanton'
    f. *eksupnos* 'awake' > 'clever'

QUESTION   Can you think of any analogies for these changes in your own native language?

The second tendency is also the more important. This is the tendency of **subjectification**, which Traugott sees as the 'dominant tendency' in semantic change (Traugott and Dasher 2002: 96). This is the tendency for meanings to 'become increasingly based in the speaker's subjective belief state/attitude toward the proposition' (Traugott 1989: 96). Ameliorization and pejorization are prime examples of subjectification: the shift of *boor* from meaning 'farmer' to 'crude person' involves the speaker's subjective attitude being imported into the meaning of the noun, displacing the previously non-evaluative sense 'farmer'. The ground of the meaning thus shifts from the realm of public observable facts to the subjective opinion and assessment of the speaker. Another common example of this tendency is the development of **epistemic modality**. Epistemic modality is manifested by *may* and *must* in (6):

(6) a. *Alfred must be guilty* (= the evidence suggests/I conclude that Alfred is guilty)

    b. *Alfred may be guilty* (= I think it is possible that Alfred is guilty)

The speaker uses epistemic modality to indicate that they suspect (6b), or have concluded (6a), that Alfred is guilty: they assert that Alfred's guilt is possible or likely, rather than an accepted fact. Epistemic modal meanings are thus firmly based in the speaker's subjective belief state towards the proposition. But an examination of the history of epistemic modal verbs shows that they have not always expressed epistemic meanings. *Must*, for example, goes back to Old English *motan*, which meant 'be able/ obliged to', not an epistemic meaning, since it concerns the subject's ability or obligation to do something, not the speaker's opinion about the likelihood of their doing it. In Middle English, this quite often occurred with the adverb *nedes* 'necessarily'; the following sentence, from a mid-fifteenth century text (the end of the Middle English period), illustrates this:

(7) | *ho-so* | *hath* | *with* | *him* | *godes* | *grace:* | *is* | *dede* | *mot* |
|---|---|---|---|---|---|---|---|---|
| who-so-ever | has | with | him | god's | grace | his | deed | must |
| *nede* | | *beo* | *guod* | | | | | |
| necessarily | | be | good | | | | | |

    'He who has God's grace necessarily is required to be/we can conclude is good' (Traugott and Dasher 2002: 128)

The contribution of *nede* 'necessarily' in this sentence makes an epistemic reading possible as an implicature: not only is a possessor of God's grace *obliged* to be good (the original sense of *motan* 'must'), but we have good reason to *conclude* that they are, in fact, good – an epistemic meaning. It would have been this sort of context that encouraged the development of the epistemic meaning of the modal through the conventionalization of the implicature. In sentences like (8) *only* the epistemic reading is available:

(8) *For yf that schrewednesse makith wrecches, than mot he nedes ben moost wrecchide that lengest is a schrewe.*

    'For if wickedness makes men wretched, then he must necessarily be most wretched that is wicked longest' (Traugott and Dasher 2002: 129).

There is no question here of any obligation to be wretched; the speaker/ writer simply *concludes* that, as a matter of fact, the person who is 'wicked longest' will also be the most wretched.

We will end our discussion of semantic change by considering investigation into some more specific pathways of meaning change, specifically those involving verbs of perception and cognition. These types of verb seem particularly likely to feature in semantic change. In an influential study, Viberg (1984) found that the following strong cross-linguistic hierarchy (in a slightly more complicated version) governed the polysemies of perception verbs.

$$\text{sight} > \text{hearing} > \text{touch} > \left\{ \begin{array}{c} \text{smell} \\ \text{taste} \end{array} \right\}$$

The visual modality of perception, in other words, is always the source, but never the target of processes of polysemy involving other perceptual meanings. Since, as we have seen, semantic change always proceeds via an intermediate polysemous stage, Viberg's hierarchy can also be interpreted diachronically and taken to express constraints on the possible direction of meaning development. The hierarchy expresses the relative strengths of perception verbs cross-linguistically. A verb whose prototypical meaning belongs to a sense modality further to the left in the hierarchy can get a polysemous meaning referring to some (or all) of the modalities to the right. Verbs principally referring to sight, for instance, can have polysemies of 'hear', 'touch', 'smell' and 'taste', but verbs whose prototypical sense is in these other domains don't take on polysemies referring to vision. Hearing verbs can develop polysemous meanings in the domains of touch, taste and smell, but verbs prototypically from these latter three domains never develop the additional meanings 'hear' (or 'see').

QUESTION   What tests do you think could be used to work out what the prototypical sense of a perception verb is?

Polysemies in numerous languages conform to Viberg's hierarchy. In Swahili (Niger-Congo; Tanzania), the basic sense of *ona* is 'see', but it can polysemously convey 'taste' when followed by the noun *ladha* 'taste' in the phrase *ona ladha*, literally 'see taste'. The verb *sikia* basically means 'hear', but can also be used for 'touch'. In Kurdish (Indo-European; Turkey and Middle East) *dîtin* 'see' also means 'touch', and can mean 'smell' and 'taste' when paired with nouns for these words in the same way as Swahili *ona ladha*. In Luo (Nilo-Saharan, Kenya) *winjo* basically means 'hear', and has polysemies of 'touch', and 'taste' and 'smell' when combined with the appropriate NPs. As discussed by Evans and Wilkins (2000), Australian Aboriginal languages also conform to Viberg's hierarchy: to give just two of many possible examples, Mayali *bekkan* 'hear' also means 'touch,' and Guugu Yimidhirr *nhaamaa* 'see/look' also means 'hear', with an additional polysemy to 'think'.

This Guugu Yimidhirr polysemy shows an extension out of the domain of perception proper into that of cognition. This looks rather like a pattern of semantic extension familiar in Indo-European languages, in which verbs of cognition like 'know'/ 'think'/ 'understand' are often derived from verbs of seeing. This is seen again and again in Indo-European. For example, Proto-Indo-European *weid-* 'see' not only gives many IE daughter languages their word for 'see' (Latin *video*, Russian *videt* 'see', etc.), but also becomes the verb for 'know' in many languages (Ancient Greek *oida*, Dutch *weten*, German *wissen*), and gives other parts of speech related to cognition in other languages (English *wise, wit*; Irish *fios* 'knowledge').

Sweetser (1990) explained this pattern of extension as an instance of what she termed the **mind-as-body-metaphor**: the persistent equation of the physical and the inner self. The world of concrete physical experience serves as an analogical model for talking about abstract mental phenomena like knowing and understanding. For example, many Indo-European languages recruit their vocabulary of intellection (understanding) from that of physical holding. English *grasp* is a perfect illustration of this polysemy. Other examples include Latin *comprehendere* 'seize', which gives French *comprendre* 'understand' and Ancient Greek *katalambanō* 'seize', which had the metaphorical sense of 'grasp, understand', and is the source of Modern Greek *katalabaino* 'understand'.

For Sweetser, the mind-as-body metaphor is what lies behind the extension of 'see' verbs to 'know/understand'. Vision is a concrete phenomenon which serves as the metaphorical model for knowing, conceived of as inner 'vision'. Sweetser says that this metaphor is based in the primary status vision has as a source of information about the world: since vision gives us our most certain knowledge of what is outside us, physical seeing is a natural model for inner, mental understanding. Sweetser points out that the use of physical, vision-based vocabulary for abstract domains of intellection is by no means limited to verbs. Thus, we speak in English of 'a *clear* presentation', '*opaque* statements' and '*transparent* ploys', in all cases appropriating the vocabulary of visual experience to describe more abstract mental domains. Sweetser's conclusion (1990: 45) is that the vocabulary of physical perception

> shows systematic metaphorical connections with the vocabulary of internal self and internal sensations. These connections are ... highly motivated links between parallel or *analogous* areas of physical and internal sensation . ... The internal self is pervasively understood in terms of the bodily external self, and is hence described by means of vocabulary drawn (either synchronically or diachronically) from the physical domain.

A natural question to ask is how widespread the mind-as-body metaphor is as a source of polysemies and semantic changes. In this light, the Guugu Yimidhirr 'see, hear, think' polysemy mentioned above suggests that the same vision > intellection shift may be observed in an entirely different language family. However, Evans and Wilkins (2000) found that it is in fact the meaning 'hear', not 'see', which leads to inner, cognitive meanings in Australian Aboriginal languages. A representative survey of 'see' words in Australian languages reveals that the extension to 'understand' is only found when the verb also means 'hear'. 'Understand' is typically associated with the verb for 'hear', as in this example from Pitjantjatjara (Pama-Nyungan, central Australia):

(9) *Mutuka/   computer   ngayulu   puṯu   kulini*
     car   computer   I   in vain   hear/understand
     'I don't understand cars/computers.'

The link between hearing and cognition is a frequent polysemy pattern in Australian languages, not restricted to verbs alone. Evans and Wilkins give the following list of reflexes of the Proto-Pama-Nyungan word for 'ear', *pina*:

(10) Yidiny *pina* 'ear'; *pina*-N 'hear, listen to, think about, remember'
     Guugu Yimidhirr *pinaal* (adj.) 'smart, clever, know'
     Gugu Yalanji *pinal* 'to know'
     Warlpiri *pina* 'wise, knowing, experienced', *pinarri* 'wise, knowledgeable, smart', *pina-wangu* [ear-without] 'ignorant'; *pina(pina)(ri)-jarrimi* [ear-INCH] 'to learn', *pina(pina)-mani* [ear-put] 'to teach'
     Jaru *pina yungan* [lit. ear put] 'to learn', *pinarri* 'knowing'
     Gooniyandi *pinarri* 'know, knowledgeable'

Vanhove (2008) shows that the link between audition and cognition is a widespread polysemy in the languages of the world.

11.2.3 Grammaticalization

One particular context for semantic change is **grammaticalization**, the process of semantic bleaching and category change by which grammatical forms develop in a language. Grammaticalization is a complex subject, and we will only touch on it briefly here. Grammaticalization can be defined as the process by which open-class content words (nouns, verbs, adjectives) turn into closed-class function forms like adpositions, conjunctions, pronouns, particles and demonstratives, as well as case- and tense-markers, by losing elements of their meaning, and by a restriction in their possible grammatical contexts. Study of these processes has revealed a number of regular pathways which recur again and again in the world's languages, linking particular open-class lexemes with particular grammaticalized functions (see Heine and Kuteva 2002). A simple example is the grammaticalization of the word meaning 'circle' into a preposition in many European languages. In Icelandic, German and Latin, for instance, the noun meaning 'ring, circle' (*kring, Ring* and *circus* respectively) is the source of the preposition 'around' (*kring, rings* and *circum*). The shift involves a change in both meaning ('circle' > 'around') and grammatical category (noun > preposition: see Heine and Kuteva 2002: 68 for details). Another example, this time from outside Europe, is that perfect/completive markers are often derived from lexical roots meaning 'throw'. Examples are Korean *pelita*, a perfect aspect marker, and Japanese *sutsu (utsu, tsu)*, a completive marker, both of which developed out of the lexical verbs meaning 'throw away' (Heine and Kuteva 2002: 297).

   The following example from Ewe (Niger-Congo; Ghana) shows different stages in a common grammaticalization process. We start with a content word, the body-part noun 'back' (11a), which is grammaticalized into a marker of spatial and other relations:

(11) a. *épé*   *megbé*   *fá*
      3sg.POSS   back   be cold
      'His back is cold.'

  b. *é-le*   *xɔ*   *á*   *megbé*
      3sg-be   house   DEF   behind
      'He is behind the house.'

  c. *é-nɔ*   *megbé*
      3sg-stay   behind
      'He stays back.'

  d. *é-kú*   *le*   *é-megbé*
      3sg-die   be   3sg.POSS-behind
      'He died after him.' (Heine, Claudi and Hünnemeyer 1991:65–66)

Here, just as in English, the word for 'back', *megbé*, is used to cover a variety of notions. In (11a) it simply refers to an object, the body part. In (11b) it expresses a spatial relation which we can see as the application of a metaphor: just as in English, the subject is said to be at the house's 'back'. In (11c) no obvious metaphorical motivation is any longer present, and *megbé* conveys the fact that the subject stayed while the others left, while in (11d) it refers to time. Categorial development runs from ordinary noun in (11a), to adverb in (11c), to postposition in (11b) and (11d). This change of syntactic category goes hand in hand with a progressive shifting of the form's meaning from concrete to abstract.

    The history of French negation provides a well-known example of grammaticalization. In Old French, negation could simply be achieved through a negative particle, *ne* (*n'* before a vowel):

(12) *Don*   *ne*   *porroit*   *ce*   *estre?*
    Then not   could   this be
    'Couldn't this happen?' (Einhorn 1974: 78)

But the negation was often strengthened by the addition of a further noun, determined by the context. Some of these nouns were *mot* 'word', *mie* 'crumb', *gote* 'drop', *grain* 'grain' and *point* 'point'. Originally, as in (13a), the additional noun has its full lexical value and was only used when semantically appropriate – in contexts of speaking or thinking for *mot*, eating for *mie*, drinking for *gote* and so on: (13a) is an example of this for *mot*. Often, however, this original value is bleached away and it does no more than reinforce the negation, as in (13b):

(13) a. *Mot*   *n'*   *en*   *sait*
      Word not   about it   knows
      'He doesn't know (a word) about it.' (Einhorn 1974: 95)

  b. *Morir* *ne*   *voldroie*   *je*   *mie*
      to die not would want I   crumb
      'I wouldn't like to die.' (Einhorn 1974: 95)

Verbs of motion typically formed their negative with *ne … pas*, the noun *pas* meaning 'step':

(14) *Vos   n'   irez   pas   uan   de   mei   si   luign.*
     you   not   will go   step   one   from   me   so   far
     'You will not go one step away from me.' (*Song of Roland* 250; Segre 1989: 105)

This was subject to exactly the same sort of bleaching as the other nouns, and often occurs in contexts where no motion is relevant:

(15) *n'   est   pas   mervelle,   se   vous   estes   lassés*
     not   is   step   marvel   if   you   are   tired
     'It is not a marvel if you are tired.' (Winters 2002: 627)

In contemporary non-formal French, *pas* on its own has assumed the role of principal negative (Ashby 1981), as in (16):

(16) *Moi,   j'   aime   pas   ça*
     Me   I   like   not   that
     'I don't like that.' (Bourciez 1967: 704)

In these contexts, *pas* is no longer a noun, but has been grammaticalized into a negative particle by losing its original sense 'step'. This coalition of semantic bleaching and change of grammatical category is typical of grammaticalization.

QUESTION   Could this grammaticalization chain be described through any of the traditional notions discussed in 11.2.1 (generalization, metaphor, etc.)? If so, how?

11.3 Meaning through corpora

The seeds of semantic change are found in synchronic meaning variation in everyday discourse. Although many differences in meaning and usage between different people are obvious, still more of this variation occurs below the threshold of our awareness, and we fail to notice the ways in which language is changing all around us. Only in exceptional circumstances do we become aware of the extent of the variation in meaning and usage. Stubbs (2001) reports the story of Monica Baldwin, who entered a strict convent shut off from the outside world in 1913. She spent the next 28 years in complete isolation, without access even to newspapers or radio, the other members of the convent providing her only company. In her autobiography, Baldwin records the words and expressions she did not understand after she left the convent in 1941. These included *cocktail*, *hard boiled*, *have a hunch*, *nosey parker*, *it's your funeral*, *jazz*, *close-up*, *streamlining*, *plus fours*, *cutie*, *robot*, *parking*, *Hollywood*, *believe it or not* and *striptease*. Some of these expressions may, of course, now be unfamiliar to contemporary readers.

Because of the vast amount of data involved, studying this language-wide variation in depth is not feasible without the use of computers. The field of **corpus linguistics** uses computers to store and analyse **corpora** (Latin: 'bodies'; singular *corpus*), collections of large amounts of text. There are several large corpora of written and spoken English, such as the British National Corpus, the Cobuild corpus, the London–Lund corpus of British English (LLC), the Lancaster-Oslo/Bergen corpus (LOB) and the Australian Corpus of English. Corpora of various kinds are also available for many other languages, including Japanese, Chinese and most European languages. The wide availability of these corpora means that the methods of corpus linguistics are replicable: a statistical analysis of a corpus can be repeated and confirmed by any number of researchers.

Corpora are useful for semantic analysis because they can reveal unsuspected patterns of **collocation**, or regular word combination. The extent to which discourse consists of predictable word-sequences is easy to underestimate. In general, corpus study has shown that many words (called **nodes** in corpus linguistics) have fairly predictable patterns of collocation within a given **span** (the number of words taken into account before and after the node). Take *brightly* as an example. Stubbs (2001: 81) reports that a search of the Cobuild corpus shows that *brightly* occurs 1,467 times. In 26% of these occurrences, it occurs within four words of *coloured*. This is conventionally represented in the following way:

> *brightly* 1,467 <*coloured* 26%>

Such a high degree of collocational predictability isn't uncommon. Roughly four per cent of a sample of the headwords in the Cobuild corpus fell into a category in which the most frequent collocate occurred with the node in at least twenty per cent of cases (Stubbs 2001: 81). Here are some examples:

> *calorie* 846 <*low* 29%>; *classical* 5,471 <*music* 22%>; *profile* 5,584 <*high* 28%>; *shuttle* 3,453 <*space* 33%>; *tricks* 2,202 <*dirty* 25%>

For another twenty per cent of all nodes, the top collocate was found with the node in between ten and twenty per cent of the node's occurrences, while for forty per cent of nodes, the top collocate was recorded in between five and ten per cent of cases.

If one considers variant forms of the collocates, these scores often go up impressively. Stubbs (2001: 83) gives the following examples, in which the combined proportion of the collocates' occurrences, given as the final percentage, accounts for a significant proportion of the nodes' occurrences:

> *cheering* 1,226 <*crowd* 13%, *crowds* 6%> 19%
> *resemblance* 1,085 <*bears* 18%, *bear* 11%, *bore* 11%, *bearing* 4%> 44%

Thus, almost one in five occurrences of *cheering* is collocated with *crowd(s)*, while more than two in five occurrences of *resemblance* occurs with a form of the verb *bear*. And once one takes into account semantically related words (synonyms, hyponyms, hyperonyms, etc.), the figures skyrocket (Stubbs 2001: 83):

> breakaway 1,379 <republic(s) 35%, group, faction, party> 45%
> cheering 1,226 <crowd(s) 19%, people, supporters, fans, audience> 30%
> doses 1,687 <large 13%, high, small, low, higher, lower, massive, heavy, larger> 48%
> humanitarian 3,933 <aid 23%, relief, assistance, help> 39%
> warring 1, 586 <factions 49%, parties, sides> 73%

Findings like these, according to Stubbs, 'show that there is a level of organization beyond lexis and syntax, which is only starting to be systematically studied, and which is not reducible to any other level of organization' (2001: 97).

Studies of collocation can give surprising results. In an earlier study, Stubbs found that nearly 80% of the 38,000 occurrences of *cause* (both the noun and the verb) in a million-word corpus were paired with clearly negative collocates in the span of three words before or after. The most frequent collocates are the following:

> cause <problem(s) 1806, damage 1519, death(s) 1109, disease 591, concern 598, cancer 572, pain 514, trouble 471>

(Stubbs 2001: 46)

On the evidence of this corpus, *cause* is not used neutrally, as most speakers would probably guess, but has a strong tendency to be associated with negative events. This tendency is not yet strong enough to count as a connotation of *cause*, but it constitutes a striking regularity which would come as a surprise to most speakers. Simply introspecting about the meaning of *cause* would be unlikely to reveal the collocational tendencies uncovered by the corpus search.

The situation with *cause* is not unusual. Stubbs comments that '[a]ll of the most frequent content words in the language are involved in [collocational] patterning. This is not a peripheral phenomenon (collocations are not an idiosyncratic feature of just a few words), but a central part of communicative competence' (2001: 96). Another example of this situation comes from Channell (2000). Consider *regime*. Intuitively, one would say that it simply refers to a ruling political administration. Channell discovered, however, that the most frequent collocates of the word in the British Cobuild corpus were *military, communist, ancien, Nazi, Soviet, Vichy, fascist, present* and *Iraqi*. Channell comments that these are words 'which from a British perspective represent those types of government which are generally disapproved of' (2000: 46). *Regime*, in other words, seems to have a tendency to occur in unfavourable contexts. Native English speakers would not necessarily have predicted this result through merely introspecting about the word's meaning. Channell also investigated the phrase *roam the streets*. There are 113 occurrences of this in the Bank of English corpus, with the subjects *prostitutes, vagrant children, armed men, mobs, looters, right-wing youth gangs and neo-Nazis, vandals, wild dogs* and *bigots* (Channell 2000: 53). The activities associated in the corpus with *roam the streets* included *searching for food, attacking people, stoning cars, randomly beating people, burning and looting* and *rioting*. This collocation is, then, typically associated with activities that are dangerous, threatening and censured. Again, this is not a result that is available through mere introspection. Channell predicts on the basis of these data that the negative evaluation associated with *roam* in these collocations will extend to all uses of the verb, and become one of its regular connotations.

Partington (2004) examined the English adverbs *completely, entirely, totally* and *utterly*. These share a large number of collocates with each other, and, as a group, share very *few* collocates with apparently broadly synonymous adverbs like *perfectly* or *absolutely*. Partington reports some interesting patterns. *Utterly*, for instance, modifies items that 'almost invariably express either the general sense of "absence of a quality" or some kind of "change of state"' (2004: 147), such as *helpless, useless, unable, forgotten; changed, different; failed, ruined* and *destroyed*. Only two of the collocates of *utterly* had positive connotations: *pleasant* and *clear*. *Totally* also had many 'absence' or 'lack of' collocates, such as *bald, exempt, incapable, irrelevant, lost, oblivious, uneducated, unemployed, unexpected, unknown, unpredictable, unsuited, ignored, excluded, unfamiliar, blind, ignorant, meaningless, unaware, unable, vanished, naked* and *without*. Similar patterns of collocation were found for *completely* and *entirely*.

Speakers are mostly unaware of these sorts of patterns. As Channell observes (2000: 54), 'it is disturbing to discover that important aspects of the use of lexical items are not open to conscious reflection'. The regularities of use demonstrated by Stubbs, Partington and Channell are clearly robust enough to warrant linguists' attention, but they are hard to come to grips with theoretically. Specifically, the regularities of use revealed by corpus study seem not to appropriately fit into the categories of either an expression's literal meaning or its connotation (see 1.4.2). The differences between synonymous adverb intensifiers demonstrated by Partington operate among words with near-identical literal meanings. Perhaps, you might think, that shows they are connotational: perhaps *utterly*, for example, has a connotation 'absence of a quality' or 'change of state'. But this suggestion is clearly not plausible: most connotations are fairly stable aspects of an expression's meaning which are hard to cancel. The correlations we have seen in this section are mostly not like this. It isn't a connotation of *utterly* that it refer to absences of a quality: we can say things like *the meal was utterly perfect* without the slightest feeling of clash. Similarly, it is not a connotation of *cause* that it be associated with negative occurrences. Nevertheless, corpus data demonstrate that these words show these associations in a significant proportion of cases. This raises the questions of just what, on the speaker level, causes these patterns, and of how they are to be described linguistically. As Channell points out, to talk of the collocational facts discussed here as facts about 'meaning' is to use that term in a non-standard sense.

11.4 Semantic typology

Semantic typology is a fairly recent development in linguistics. Because of the problems of determining universals of sense discussed above, it often concentrates on the question of cross-linguistic regularities in *denotation* or *extension*. What is the range of possible variation shown by the world's languages in the references of words for colours, body parts and basic actions? Are there any universal or widespread similarities in the boundaries between different words in each of these domains? Since serious cross-linguistic investigation of these questions has only begun recently, there is still only a small range of evidence available, and we will often be forced to exemplify points from the same handful of languages. Nevertheless, even the preliminary work done so far can disabuse us of any simplistic assumption of universalism: cross-linguistic variation in meaning is at least as great as variation in form. We will begin our survey of this question by looking at the way different languages refer to the human body.

11.4.1 Body parts

Because of our common physiology, the body is an obvious place to look for universally shared aspects of meaning. But cross-linguistic investigation reveals that there is actually huge variety in the extensions of human body-part terms. Languages certainly do not all divide the body up in the same way for the purposes of reference. This is a significant finding. If languages don't treat something as basic and universal as the body identically, what is the likelihood that there will be semantic universals in less basic domains?

A first surprising fact is that not all languages even have a term for 'body'. Tidore (Papuan, Indonesia) has a word for 'flesh', but this does not cover the body as a whole, and no other word in the language does either. In order to refer to the body as a whole, Tidore speakers must either use the Indonesian word *badan* 'body', or speak non-literally using a Tidore word, *mansia* which literally means 'person, human' (van Staden 2006: 330). Absence of a word referring to the body is not confined to Tidore. In Thaayoore (Pama-Nyungan, Australia), the word with the closest extensional range to English *body* is *pam-minj*. This doesn't just cover the physical body, however. It also denotes many other related ideas, such as people's tracks, their voice, and their shadow, none of which can be referred to with *body* in English (Gaby 2006). *Pam-minj* in Thaayoore thus spills over the familiar boundaries of the physical body to encompass entirely non-corporeal referents. The same phenomenon can be repeated at the level of body parts. Thus, the word for 'bottom' in Thaayoore is also the word for 'excreta', and in Jahai (Mon-Khmer, Malaysia/Southern Thailand; Burenhult 2006: 168), 'belly' and 'excreta' are expressed by the same word. To Western ears, this is a highly unfamiliar polysemy, that strikingly suggests that the divisions of the world presupposed in familiar languages are by no means universal.

The world's languages display, then, remarkable variety in their treatment of the different parts of the body. Sometimes, for example, there simply are no words for (to our minds) important body parts. Jahai has no word for 'mouth', 'face' or 'leg' (Burenhult 2006). Instead, there are many morphologically simple terms for more detailed body parts: *wɛ̃s* 'frontal tuber', *nus* 'upper lip' and *mŋkaʔ* 'molar tooth' (Burenhult 2006: 167). Jahai also lacks terms for 'arm' and 'leg', and the word for 'head', *kuy*, only refers to the part of the head covered by head-hair (Burenhult 2006: 169). These facts disprove the assumption that languages always favour lexicalization of body-part categories at the level of the limb or other major 'whole' body part (head, trunk).

Let's now consider how different languages segment the parts of the body. The body is obviously a continuous whole, but is made of perceptually discontinuous parts: the trunk, limbs and head, at the highest level of structure, with each of these parts presenting easily distinguishable subparts (chest, back; fingers, elbows; mouth, ears). Since these divisions are so perceptually salient, a natural hypothesis is that all languages exploit them for the purpose of body-part labelling. This hypothesis has been tested through the use of a body-colouring task, in which consultants are given an image of a body and asked to shade in the region that corresponds to a given body-part term. Experiments using this kind of method have partly confirmed the hypothesis that visual discontinuities like those of the limb-joints guide the referential range of body-part terms. For example, no languages are known in which perceptual discontinuities play *no* role in the segmentation of body-part terminology. Most languages respect the discontinuity of the joints of the arm and leg in the extensions of at least some of their terms for these regions of the body (Enfield *et al.* 2006: 141). In other words, there are always some words in a language which divide the body at the shoulder/elbow/wrist or hip/knee/ankle, even if not all the language's body-part terms do. For example, many languages, like Punjabi (Indo-European, India) and American Sign Language (signed; USA), distinguish upper and lower leg (Enfield *et al.* 2006: 141), with the knee constituting the point of division. Yélî Dnye (isolate; Papua New Guinea) is an example of a language which does *not* observe the joint-division below the knee: a single term covers the lower leg and the foot, ignoring the discontinuity of the ankle. A single term for leg/foot and another for arm/hand is a common situation in Austronesian and Papuan languages (van Staden 2006: 327).

QUESTION Use a line drawing outline of a human body to colour in the boundaries between the different body-part terms in your own language. How easy is it to designate clear boundaries? Are there any cases where the boundaries are unclear?

Two interesting exceptions to the relevance of visual discontinuity in body-part naming have been noted in the recent literature. The first comes from Tidore. Here, the word *yohu*, translated as 'leg', does not actually correspond fully to that English body part, since it does not include the upper thigh. According to van Staden (2006: 327), this is explained by the fact that exposure of the upper part of the thigh is considered indecent, and it must be covered in public. It is therefore not a perceptual, but a cultural discontinuity that determines the limits of this body-part term. The second exception is the Jahai word cɲĩŋ, which refers to a spectacle-shaped area around both eyes (Burenhult 2006: 167) – again, not an extension with any obvious visual determinant, although there may well be socio-cultural factors behind the salience of this region of the face which explain its lexicalization.

Finally, many investigators of cross-linguistic body-part terminology report widespread inconsistency among speakers of the same language about the extension of body-part terms. For example, speakers of Lavukaleve (East Papuan; Solomon Islands) were divided over whether the word *vatu* 'head' also includes the meaning 'face' (Terrill 2006: 3070). This uncertainty may partly be a product of the body-colouring task, the unfamiliarity of which may induce a higher level of self-consciousness and hence hesitation than spontaneous, unmonitored language use. But it might also indicate that it is wrong in many cases to imagine that body-part terms have a single fixed, circumscribed meaning in a language community: both within and between speakers, there may be considerable variation in the extensions of terms in this semantic domain. It would be a mistake here, as in most other areas in semantics, to imagine that everything is cut and dried.

11.4.2 Colour vocabulary

At first blush, the domain of colour seems a prime example of language introducing distinctions within the continuous flux of our experience. It has been known for a long time that different languages divide up the visible spectrum in various and incompatible ways, and the consequent difficulty of translating colour terms from one language to another has often been commented on. There often is no simple equivalent for one language's colour words in another: Ancient Greek *khlōros* is not really *green*, its typical English translation, but a green-yellow colour combination which can refer to the colours of young grass/leaves, sand and honey (Liddell and Scott 1940: 890). Since we all see the same wavelengths of light, this cross-linguistic variation cannot be the result of differences in colour perception, but must be language-internal: we see the same colours, but different languages name them differently. For this reason, colour-naming was often taken as the crucial example of the **linguistic relativity hypothesis** (see 11.5). The cross-linguistic variation in colour naming strategies suggests that speakers do not simply label pre-existing categories, which are objectively out there, 'staring them in the face'. Instead, languages *create* the colour categories for themselves and, once created, speakers categorize colours in the terms particular to their language. Colour categories, in other words, are not universal, but language-relative.

However, a tradition of research inaugurated by Berlin and Kay (1969) and still continuing has led to some important revisions of this relativist picture. Berlin and Kay hypothesized that each language has a set of **basic colour terms** (BCTs). In English, *black, white, red, yellow, green, blue, purple,* and *grey* are BCTs, whereas *violet, ochre, eggshell blue, turquoise,* etc. are not. To be counted as a BCT, a colour term has to meet the following criteria:

- it must be psychologically salient, i.e. one of the commonly remembered and used terms. This excludes English *russet, cyan, jade, sepia, magenta,* etc.;
- it must not be included in the range of another colour term; this excludes *crimson* (a type of red), *indigo* (a type of purple), *tan* (a type of brown) and *light green* (a type of green);
- it must be morphologically simple. This excludes *grey-green* and *reddish*;
- it must be applicable in all contexts, i.e. able to refer to a colour regardless of the object which has it. This excludes English *sorrel* and *blonde*, which primarily refer to colours of horses and hair/furniture/ beer respectively.

The number of BCTs can vary widely from language to language. The smallest number recorded is just two; on the other side, very few languages have more than eleven. Berlin and Kay and their colleagues have now explored the typical range of reference of BCTs in a wide range of different languages. They did this using 330 colours from the **Munsell colour system**, a standardized set of samples showing fine gradations between colours, rather like the colour sample cards available in paint shops. They particularly concentrated on what they termed the **focus** of colour terms. This meant the best example of a particular colour. For instance, the focus of English *red*, 'focal red', is that particular shade of red (say London bus red) which speakers would indicate as the 'reddest' red possible.

QUESTION   What is the full set of 'basic colour terms' of English, according to the criteria listed above?

The general findings of work in the Berlin and Kay tradition challenges relativist beliefs about colour terms. Berlin and Kay discovered that even though languages differed in the number of their colour terms, and in the boundaries of any one of their terms, speakers show remarkable convergence, both between and within languages, in the particular shades they nominate as the focal colours of each category. Out of the 330 Munsell colours Berlin and Kay presented to speakers, only a pool of thirty closely similar colours were chosen as examples of focal hues. These thirty were concentrated on the most typical examples of black, white, red, green, yellow, blue, grey, brown, orange, purple and pink. Take as an example those languages with a term for 'red'. There is, in general, wide variation in the range of colours which speakers of these languages will count as examples of this category: sometimes it includes pale, pinkish reds, sometimes oranges, sometimes even whites. But in spite of this wide range of reference, there is consistent agreement between speakers of different languages about what counts as the *best example* of red: speakers consistently choose a very narrow range of Munsell chips, regardless of how many other shades the term also covers. Similarly, some languages have a term for 'blue/green', but speakers always chose either a single shade of blue (**focal blue**) or a single green (**focal green**) as the best example of this colour, not any of the large range of other blue and green shades to which the term can refer. A similar situation exists with other BCTs: their boundaries vary widely, but their focal hues show clear cross-linguistic convergence. This is a remarkable finding. It suggests that colour terminology is not an unconstrained free-for-all. Basic colour terms in all languages target a restricted range of colours.

The restriction of focal hues to a small set was not Berlin and Kay's only discovery. They also found that the number of BCTs in a language makes it possible to predict exactly *what* the basic colour terms would be. For example, consider those languages with only two colour terms. Berlin and Kay claimed that such languages have one term for white, red and yellow, and another for black, green and blue. No languages with only two BCTs have any different combinations: for example, no language has as its two BCTs one referring to white, green and blue, and the other to red, yellow and black. Similar generalizations were also made for larger BCT systems as well. In general, Berlin and Kay's findings were that the range of colour term references in the languages of the world represents a tiny selection out of the myriad theoretically possible options. Languages don't just choose their colour terms arbitrarily, but observe quite strict constraints in the range of possible focal colours to which their BCTs refer. Berlin and Kay interpreted these findings as an evolutionary sequence. Colour vocabularies started with just two terms, and developed diachronically into more ramified, complex systems, with different hues splitting off to create independent colour categories. Table 11.1 sets out these findings, showing the five different evolutionary 'stages' into which colour-naming systems can be arranged. The colour names (given in obvious abbreviations) refer to the best examples of the colours.

Terms for brown, purple, pink, orange and grey are added in two later stages, giving the maximal system of eleven colour terms observed cross-linguistically, arranged in a seven-stage system.

It is important to be clear about what these stages mean. First, note that it is *not* the case that a language cannot refer to any colour incompatible with its typological stage. Just because a language belongs to stage V, for example, does not mean that speakers do not acknowledge brown, orange, purple or pink hues as genuine colours. All it means is that these colours are treated as variants or types of one of the named colours in the language, and thus fail to count as *basic* colour terms. Second, note that the focal colours for some of these categories vary by both language and speaker. We can illustrate this with the different focal colours for the Green/Blue category found at Stages III and IV. Speakers of some languages

Table 11.1. Five stages of BCT vocabulary in Berlin and Kay.

		Stage I		
		W/R/Y		
		Bk/G/Bu		
		Stage II		
		W		
		R/Y		
		Bk/G/Bu		
		Stage III		
W		W		W
R/Y	*or*	R/Y	*or*	R
G/Bu		G		Y
Bk		Bk/Bu		Bk/G/Bu
		Stage IV		
	W		W	
	R		R	
	Y	*or*	Y	
	G/Bu		G	
	Bk		Bk/Bu	
		Stage V		
		W		
		R		
		Y		
		G		
		Bu		
		Bk		

choose blue as the focus, speakers of some choose green, speakers of some choose both, and speakers of others chose either one, but not both (MacLaury 1999: 5). Categories like this with more than one focal colour are called **composite categories**.

We don't have to go along with Berlin and Kay's evolutionary interpretation of their own findings. The five stages can be interpreted simply as typological generalizations stating the references of colour term systems of different sizes. Here are some examples of the stages (from Kay *et al.* 1997):

Stage II

Ejagham (Niger-Congo; Nigeria, Cameroon: Kay *et al.* 1997: 37):

ényàgà 'black/green/blue'

ébáré 'white'

ébí 'red/yellow'

Stage III$_{Bk/G/Bu}$

Kwerba (Trans-New Guinea; Irian Jaya; Kay *et al.* 1997: 44)

icəm 'black/green/blue'

əsiram (əhɛrɛm, ərɛm) 'white'

nokonim 'red'

kainanesɛnum 'yellow'

Stage IV$^{G/Bu}$

Sirionó (Tupí; Bolivia: Kay *et al.* 1997: 46):

erondeɨ 'black'

eshī 'white'

eirẽ́ɨ 'red'

echo 'yellow'

eruba 'green/blue'

Stage V

Kalam (Trans-New Guinea; Papua New Guinea: Kay *et al.* 1997: 51)

mosimb 'black'

tund 'white'

likañ 'red'

walin 'yellow'

minj-kimemb 'green'

muk 'blue'

The seven-stage typology revealed by Berlin and Kay's research has been broadly confirmed (MacLaury 1999: 30). This doesn't mean, however, that it's always *easy to tell* what stage of colour vocabulary a language instantiates. Since languages are in a continual state of change, there will often be transitional cases which complicate the analysis. For example, a language will accomplish the transition from one colour stage to another by introducing a new, special term which only gradually becomes a BCT, and it may well be hard to decide exactly when the transition is complete. But this is no more than a typical problem encountered in any attempt to distinguish typologically significant generalizations in the flux of language variation and change. On the other hand, there are some significant counterexamples to Berlin and Kay's typology, as well as fundamental criticisms of their methodology. We will explore each in turn.

As acknowledged by Kay and Regier (2003: 9085), some exceptions to the Berlin and Kay findings have come to light, and the original typology cannot any longer be claimed as universal. Some of the exceptions necessitate only minor adjustments. Thus, Russian (Indo-European; Russia) has 12 BCTs, one more than the maximal number originally recognized, including *goluboj* 'light, pale blue' and *sinij* 'dark, bright blue.' Hungarian (Finno-Ugric;

Hungary) has both *piros* 'light red' and *vörös* 'dark red' BCTs (MacLaury 2002: 499), not a possibility accommodated in the original system.

More seriously, the Salishan languages of the Pacific North West of North America include a yellow-with-green BCT, which does not fit any of the predicted types (MacLaury 1999: 20–21). Further, parameters not considered in Berlin and Kay's original investigation, such as brightness, seem to form the basis of basic colour terms in some languages (see MacLaury 1999 for discussion), a possibility which challenges the original decision to exclude this parameter from the investigation. Another serious challenge to Berlin and Kay's findings comes from investigation of Yélî Dnye (isolate; Papua-New Guinea). This language appears not to *have* any colour terms which would count as basic on Berlin and Kay's criteria. This is because Yélî Dnye colour terms are often simply the reduplicated names of objects; for instance, the word glossable as 'red', *mtyemtye*, comes from *mtye*, 'red parrot species', and *kpêdêkpêdê*, glossable as 'black', is a reduplication of *kpêdê* 'tree species'. Furthermore, large zones of the Munsell colour space are simply unnamed, lacking any distinct term (Levinson 2001). This poses a major challenge to the premises of the Berlin and Kay investigation.

Counterexamples like those above have led to the Berlin and Kay typology being restated not as a universal of colour semantics, but as merely a particularly strong cross-linguistic tendency, to any part of which exceptions will exist. This does not remove its value: there are very few, if any, areas in language where iron-clad generalizations are possible. A more serious type of challenge is one which questions the very basis of Berlin and Kay's colour survey. A number of such challenges have been made. For example, MacLaury (1999: 19) notes that Berlin and Kay's findings may have been skewed by the nature of the Munsell colour system itself, which does not allow representation of a psychologically important dimension of colour perception, *luminosity*. Luminosity is non-reflective brightness originating within the source of the colour itself, for example the sun, or a hot, glowing object. It contrasts with *lightness*, which is reflected illumination. Since the Munsell chips are only reflective, 'they may not adequately reveal the meanings of certain color terms that principally name luminosity' or involve luminosity as a crucial factor. Similarly, Lucy (1997) criticizes the Berlin and Kay tradition on the grounds that it usually omits consideration of the colour term's characteristic referential range, simply assuming that the BCTs elicited are in fact primarily used for the coding of colour (see Lucy 1997: 322–333). Lucy claims that this ignores the way 'colour' terms are actually used in a language. The set of Munsell chips used in the study is not at all representative of the everyday contexts in which colour vocabulary is used. We rarely use colour terms in the context of an abstract exercise in hue-naming. Typically, a colour term will be predicated of a real object, which necessarily introduces many other considerations as possible determinants of its use. But all these other components are factored out by the use of the Munsell array. 'In a sense', Lucy says, use of the set of Munsell chips

dictated in advance the possible meanings the terms could have since no other meanings were embodied in the samples. Although restricted in this way, the stimulus array was also very complex, and the labeling task performed with it forced informants to make referential microcomparisons and judgements of a sort rarely encountered in daily life. The task assumed that speech is about labeling accuracy rather than situational intelligibility...

(Lucy 1997: 333)

Lucy's criticism, in other words, is that Berlin and Kay's methodology artificially constituted 'colour' as a meaningful category in the languages they tested, without any attention to the contextual values of colour terms, or consideration of non-colour uses – uses which might, after all, be extremely revealing about the semantics of the terms.

QUESTION   Does this seem a fair criticism? Why (not)?

One obvious example of the selectivity of the Berlin and Kay scheme is discussed by Payne (2006: 605). Some languages' colour words also include reference to factors which fall outside the domain of colour pure and simple. For example, in Maasai (Nilo-Saharan, Kenya/Tanzania), there are colour-plus-design terms for 'spotted black and white', 'thinly striped, typically with tan and white'. These would presumably not count as basic colour terms for Berlin and Kay, but this raises exactly the point in question: how far does 'colour' reflect a psychologically or culturally real category?

This point can be most clearly seen in work done by Conklin (1964) on colour terms in Hanunóo (Austronesian; Philippines). In Berlin and Kay's terms, Hanunóo has a stage III colour system, with categories translated 'black', 'red', 'white' and 'light green'. But Conklin's account shows that translation simply with English colour adjectives makes the wrong predictions about what the terms will be used to refer to, since the words in question have other semantic values which it is crucial to take into account. In fact, Conklin shows, Hanunóo 'colour' terms refer to three other parameters as well as hue: a light/dark opposition; a dryness/wetness (freshness) one, and a deep versus pale distinction. The reason that these other values matter is that they are just as important as the hue dimensions in governing what Hanunóo colour terms refer to. For example, a shiny section of newly cut bamboo, which English speakers would describe as brown, is described in Hanunóo as *malatuy* 'green' (Conklin (1964 [1955]: 191). This is extremely surprising, if we assume that *malatuy* and related terms have hue as their basic reference. But if we include the three other dimensions in our description of the terms' meanings, we have a way of understanding what is going on. Instead of *malatuy* meaning 'green', it really means something like 'wetness', a description which explains its application to the newly cut bamboo – and also to many green things as well. As Lucy puts it (1997: 326), '[w]hat is crucial to recognize here is that an "adequate knowledge" of the system would never have been produced *by restricting the stimuli to color chips and the task to labeling*' (italics original). Berlin and Kay's colour elicitation methodology simply presupposes that words which can be used to refer to Munsell chip categories are basically colour terms; Conklin's research suggests that this may seriously misrepresent the semantics of an individual language. Only investigation of actual, natural discourse will reveal the semantics of 'colour' terms in a language, and any attempt to erect universals of colour vocabulary that does not include such investigation risks prejudging the data.

11.4.3 Deictic motion

We have seen that although the body is a basic and universal aspect of our experience, there are remarkably few cross-linguistic generalizations that hold about the semantics of body-part terms. The basic actions expressed in English as 'coming' and 'going' present a similar situation, at least on the evidence of a smaller-scale study undertaken by Wilkins and Hill (1995). 'Come' and 'go' are deictic motion verbs, expressing movement to and away from an anchoring point (the **deictic centre**). These meanings have often been assumed to be universally lexicalized.

QUESTION   Does *go* show any non-deictic motion senses in English?

Wilkins and Hill examined the verbs translating *come* and *go* in Arrernte (Pama-Nyungan, Australia) and Longgu (Austronesian, Solomon Islands). They found that the basic types of scene which the verbs express in the two languages do not coincide. The languages differ in both the scope of application of the terms – how broad a range of situations the *come* and *go* verbs can refer to – and in what counts as the most typical example of each category. In our discussion we will only consider the expressions translating 'come', the Longgu verb phrase *la mai* and the Arrernte verb root *petye-*. Wilkins and Hill used diagrams like those in Figure 11.2 to capture the essential parts of these verbs' meaning.

'O' represents the deictic centre, understood as 'the place where both speaker and hearer are located, and where the speaker is reporting the whole motion event to the addressee' (Wilkins and Hill 1995: 217). The arrows are the path along which the motion proceeds, and the dots represent the place from which it originates: notice that this is missing in scene 3, which corresponds to a situation in which the origin of the motion is not specifically represented (when someone approaches from over the horizon, for example).

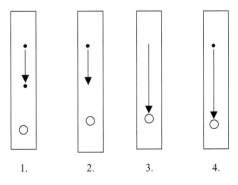

FIGURE 11.2
Motion scenes for *come* verbs. *Key*: Arrow = 'oriented motion path'. Dot = place. 'O' = deictic centre.

The differences between *la mai* and *petye-* can be seen through these examples. The four scenes in the diagram can all be described in Arrernte with the verb *petye-*. This is appropriate whether or not the thing in movement reaches the deictic centre: all that is required is that the thing in motion move *towards* the deictic centre. Indeed, some Arrernte speakers feel that the verb is most appropriate precisely in scenes 1 and 2, when the deictic centre is *not* reached. By contrast, Longgu *la mai* can only be used when the deictic centre is actually reached, which rules out scenes 1 and 2, the very ones sometimes judged as central by Arrernte speakers.

This simple case reveals how much semantic detail is obscured by the identical English translations of the two verbs. Translation into the same English word is no guarantee of semantic identity. Only a more fine-grained metalanguage, in this case using diagrams, can show the cross-linguistic differences in meaning.

11.4.4 Lexicalization patterns in motion verbs

Come and *go* differ in the type of **path** they express: in *come,* the path is oriented towards the deictic centre, whereas in *go* it need not be. Path, the route traversed by the object in motion, is one of the major elements of a motion situation. In English, motion verbs often do not express path in the verb root, as *come* and *go* do. Mostly, the path element is expressed in a preposition or 'particle', like *in, out, away, along, down, through* etc., with the verb root expressing the manner of the motion. Thus, English has a wide range of verb roots indicating different manners of motion: *crawl, run, roll, walk, skip, fly, float, stroll, tumble* and so on. In themselves, these verbs do not convey anything about the path along which the motion takes place: to express this, it is necessary to specify the path using a directional expression:

(17) *crawl **off**, run **out of the room**, fly **over the Alps***

In an influential study, Talmy (1985) compared how different languages lexicalize the four elements of motion, path, manner and figure (the moving object), which he took to be the essential components described by motion verbs. He was particularly concerned to see how the manner and path components are shared between the verb root itself and elements like prepositions and particles. Talmy coined the term **satellite** to refer to this latter type of structure. Satellites are 'certain immediate constituents of a verb root other than inflections, auxiliaries or nominal arguments' (1985: 102). *Off, out of the room* and *over the Alps* in (17) are all satellites.

Talmy hypothesized the existence of three basic combinations of the possible components of the motion event, depending on whether the basic motion element is paired with manner, path or figure. Languages differ in which of these three options predominates. As we will see, English is biased towards the first, but also illustrates the second:

Motion + manner   *run, slide, bounce, waddle, spin, totter, hop, stroll, amble…*
Motion + path   *enter, exit, come, go, leave, skirt …*

The third lexicalization pattern, motion + figure, is the least represented in English. A language that exemplifies it generously is Atsugewi (Hokan; northern California):

(18) -*lup*- 'for a small shiny spherical object (e.g.a round candy, an eye-
     ball, a hailstone) to move/be located'
    -*caq*- 'for a slimy lumpish object (e.g. a toad, a cowdropping) to
     move/be located'
    -*qput*- 'for loose, dry dirt to move/be located' (Talmy 1985: 73)

QUESTION Talmy proposes that *rain* and *snow* exemplify this third
pattern in English. Can you think of any other examples?

Talmy proposed a major typological division between what he called **verb-framed** and **satellite-framed** languages. This division concerns whether the path component is lexicalized in the verb root itself or in a satellite element.

Germanic languages like English and German are principally satellite-framed: most verbs of motion are not like *enter* or *exit* (both of them loan words in English). Instead, most Germanic motion verbs express the manner in which the motion occurred, and any specification about the path has to be introduced in a separate locative expression. Consider, for example, the German sentences (from Brecht 1967: 81) and their English translations in (19)–(20):

(19) a. *Als*   *Martin Gair* *eines* *Nachmittags* *bei* *guter* *September-*
        while   Martin Gair   one   afternoon   in   fine   September

        sonne   *in*   *einer* *vornehmen* *Straße* *promenierte...*
        sun   in   a   exclusive   street   was walking

    b. *While Martin Gair was walking one sunny September afternoon in an*
       exclusive street...

(20) a. *die*   *Witwe*   *Marie Pfaff...*   *an*   *den*   *Auslagefenstern entlang*
        the   widow   Marie Pfaff   at   the   display windows along

        schritt
        walked

    b. *The widow Marie Pfaff was walking beside the shop windows.*

English *walk* denotes a particular manner of motion and does not say anything about the path the motion took: this is conveyed in the satellite prepositional phrases *in an exclusive street* (19b) and *beside the shop windows* (20b). The German original has exactly the same structure. The verbs *promenieren* and *schreiten* (past tense *schritt*) both mean 'walk', expressing both the fact and manner of motion in a single form. Like English, German encodes the path in a satellite, consisting of a prepositional phrase (*in einer vornehmen Straße/ an den Auslagefenstern*). Slavic, Celtic and Finno-Ugric languages are also satellite-framed.

Romance languages, however, are characteristically verb-framed: the path is specified in the verb root itself. Here is an example from Spanish:

(21) Y   todas   las   abejas   salen   volando   de   la   colmena
     and   all   the   bees   exit   flying   of   the   hive
     'All the bees fly out of the hive.' (literally 'All the bees exit the hive
     flying'; Ibarretxe-Antuñano 2004: 485)

As the literal translation 'exit' makes clear, the verb *salen* inherently
expresses the path element 'out of'. Greek, Semitic, Turkic, Basque, Korean
and Japanese are all verb-framed languages like Romance. Here is the same
sentence as (21) in Basque (isolate; Spain and south-west France):

(22) *Eta   erlauntzatik   erle   guztiak   irten   ziren   hegaka*
     and   hive.FROM   bee   all.ABS.DET.PL   depart.PERF   AUX   flying
     'All the bees fly out of the hive.' (literally 'All the bees exit the hive
     flying'; Ibarretxe-Antuñano 2004: 485)

Notice how the most natural English translation – 'all the bees fly out of
the hive' – doesn't reflect the literal structure of the original.

It is worth emphasizing that statements about such and such a language
being verb or satellite framed do not mean that *every* motion verb in the language is of the appropriate type; it is a question of which type is most characteristic of the motion expressions in the language. Talmy defines 'characteristic' as meaning (i) that the verb-type is the one found in colloquial, not literary, language; (ii) that it occurs frequently, and (iii) that it is pervasive, meaning that a wide range of different types of motion are expressed by it.

QUESTION   Assemble as long a list as possible of English motion verbs,
and note whether they include a Path component. Are there any where
it is hard to decide? Is Talmy's classification of English as a satellite-
framed language justified?

Talmy illustrated this with the following selection of Spanish motion
expressions, all of which show the verb-framing characteristic of the language. Comparison with the English translations shows how systematically the two languages diverge: English always expresses manner in the
verb, and path in a satellite, while Spanish expresses path in the verb, and
manner in a satellite (*flotando*).

(23) a. *La   botella   entró   a   la   cueva   (flotando)*
        The   bottle   moved-in   to   the   cave   (floating)
        'The bottle floated into the cave.'

     b. *La   botella   salió   de   la   cueva   (flotando)*
        The   bottle   moved-out   from   the   cave   (floating)
        'The bottle floated out of the cave.'

     c. *La   botella   pasó   por   la   piedra   (flotando)*
        The   bottle   moved-by   past   the   rock   (floating)
        'The bottle floated past the rock.'

     d. *La   botella   pasó   por   el   tubo   (flotando)*
        The   bottle   moved-through   through   the   tube   (floating)
        'The bottle floated through the tube.'

e. *El*   *globo*   *subió*   *por*   *la*   *chimenea*   *(flotando)*
   The   balloon   moved-up   through   the   chimney   (floating)
   'The balloon floated up the chimney.'

f. *El*   *globo*   *bajó*   *por*   *la*   *chimenea*   *(flotando)*
   The   balloon   moved-down   through   the   chimney   (floating)
   'The balloon floated down the chimney.'

g. *La*   *botella*   *se fue*   *de*   *la*   *orilla*   *(flotando)*
   The   bottle   moved-away   from   the   bank   (floating)
   'The bottle floated away from the bank.'

h. *Las*   *dos*   *botella*   *se juntaron*   *(flotando)*
   The   two   bottles   moved-together   (floating)
   'The two bottles floated together.' (Talmy 1985: 69–70)

Note that the indication of the path isn't limited to the verb in Spanish: all the sentences contain satellites which convey additional path-related information. So in (23a) the verb *entró* supplies the information that the path is an inwards one, whereas the satellite *a la cueva* tells us that it had the cave as its goal. In the right context it would also be possible to say *La botella entró desde la cueva (flotando)* 'the bottle floated in *from* the cave'. This shows that the verb itself expresses a different path element from the one mentioned in the prepositional phrase. This is also clear from (23e) and (23f), where the difference between the verbs corresponds to a difference in path, in spite of the identical prepositional phrase.

As well as verb- and satellite-framed languages, some linguists claim that there is a third type, **equipollent** languages. This is a type in which both path and manner are treated in the same way by the language's morphosyntax (see Slobin 2004, 2006). Most equipollent languages are ones with serial verbs, i.e. verb complexes consisting of several independent verbs, each making a separate semantic contribution, as in the following sentence from Papiamentu (Afro-Iberian creole; Netherlands Antilles):

(24) *e-l*   *a*   *bula*   *bai*
     3-SING   ASP   fly   go
     'he flew away' (Muysken and Veenstra 1995: 289)

The verb phrase contains a sequence of equally central and morphosyntactically equivalent verb morphemes 'fly, go', which does not admit any sort of verb–satellite distinction on Talmy's criteria.

Talmy's typology has been widely discussed, and the distinction between verb- and satellite-framing is often invoked as a way of characterizing how different languages distribute motion information in the clause. It has not gone unchallenged, however. We will consider two types of criticism.

The first typically hinges on Talmy's notion of *characteristic* motion expression, mentioned above. As we have seen, languages usually contain other types of lexicalization pattern than the one reflected by their classification as verb- or satellite-framed. These categories are idealizations which capture what Talmy takes as the predominant, most basic type of lexicalization pattern in the language. This leaves it open to other scholars to probe whether, and how far, the idealization is justified. Kopecka (2006: 97), for example, claims that French 'does not correspond to a consistent type within Talmy's typology and furthermore exhibits a greater variety of lexicalization patterns than had previously been recognized'. This is because there is a large number of basic motion expressions in which the path is expressed by a prefix, a satellite element. This conflicts with the status of French as a verb-framed language in Talmy's scheme. Some of the many possible examples are *accourir* 'run to' and *atterir* 'land, touch down', formed with the prefix *a(d)*, *s'envoler* 'fly away' and *s'enfuir* 'run away', formed with the prefix *en-* and *parcourir* 'run all over', formed with the prefix *par* (see Kopecka 2006: 86 for more examples). A similar criticism is made for Spanish by Cuartero Otal (2006). This type of criticism does not undo the distinction between verb- and satellite-framing, but simply questions its status as a language-wide phenomenon. If many languages initially taken as exemplars of one type prove to be mixed, Talmy's principal typological conclusion – that languages typically display a single lexicalization pattern – will be disproven.

The second criticism questions the legitimacy of the very category 'motion verb'. Talmy-style analyses take this as a basic semantic class and as the site of the major typological distinction between verb- and satellite-framing languages. Concentrating on French, Cadiot *et al.* (2006) argue that it is a mistake to see 'displacement' – physical motion in space – as the basic component of the meaning of many of the verbs relevant to Talmy's analysis. This suggests that Talmy's typology overemphasizes a single aspect of what is actually an intricate and multifaceted array of meanings. Cadiot *et al.* claim that the traditional way in which we describe the meaning of French motion verbs is basically flawed. It is a mistake, they suggest, to see displacement as the most central aspect of the *sense* of motion verbs, even if they are obviously often used to *refer* to motion events. They claim that the assumption that motion in space is semantically basic is untrue to the experiential grounding of language. Talmy's distinction of path, manner and figure as fundamental components of the motion scenario ignores the fact that human beings do not experience motion in abstracted, 'geometrized' terms; as they put it, the abstract framework of space in the Talmy tradition 'is neutral with respect to any practical engagement' (2006: 187). We do not simply move from point A to B in a particular manner, but do so with aims and intentions, in a way that involves many types of subjective, perceptual and qualitative factors which are ignored by Talmy's analysis. Cadiot *et al.* argue that these additional factors reveal themselves in the numerous non-spatial, non-physical uses of motion verbs, which have to be taken as metaphorical or otherwise non-literal in Talmy-style approaches. For Cadiot *et al.*, a unified analysis of these various uses is possible which does not privilege displacement as the key notion. This unified analysis avoids postulating a literal, basic motion use and a set of non-literal semantic extensions from it. Instead, they claim it is possible to discern aspects of meaning common to the so-called 'literal' and 'metaphorical' uses alike which reflect the distinctive subjective character of the experience of motion expressed by the verbs.

The French verb *tomber* 'fall' is an example. For Talmy, *tomber* would count fundamentally as a verb of manner of motion. But Cadiot *et al.* propose that other aspects are equally important, specifically the aspects of verticality, suddenness, non-control and surprise. These elements are all features of the human experience of things that fall. For Cadiot *et al.*, it is illegitimate to treat these as secondary. Indeed, their presence is revealed in uses of the verb usually considered as metaphorical, such as the following (among others):

(25) *la nouvelle tombe* 'the news has just come through' (literally 'is falling')
     ça tombe bien 'it comes at the right moment' (literally 'it falls well')
     tomber amoureux 'fall in love'

Uses like these do not involve displacement. Instead, they foreground aspects of the meaning of *tomber* which Cadiot *et al.* claim are always present even in 'literal' uses referring to motion. Ignoring them in a way that treats motion as the principal 'core' of the verb's meaning is, they suggest, an important distortion of the semantics of *tomber*. One can, indeed, use *tomber* in a way exactly parallel to the English 's/he fell down/ over', and this is a use which need not encode any motion in the sense of displacement in space: one can fall without changing one's spatial position in any significant sense. Instead, what has changed when a subject falls over is the degree of their *control* over their own body. In this instance, motion of the type privileged by Talmy, displacement on a path between distinct points, is not an important aspect of the verb's meaning. To make displacement central to the semantic analysis of *tomber* is to 'ignore dimensions bound to the subject, which are not necessarily associated with an actual displacement, but rather with a change that is perceived from inside and outside the subject, and that cannot be reduced to an external trajectory in a topological space' (Cadiot *et al.* 2006: 182). Again, these 'subject-bound' dimensions of meaning are revealed in a use of the verb usually treated as metaphorical or extended, and thus as derived from some more basic meaning. The expression *tu tombes bien*, literally 'you fall well', expresses the idea 'you're just in time': a meaning in which abstract motion is significantly less important than the more subjective dimensions of suddenness or surprise.

QUESTION   Consider English *fall*, assembling as many representative examples as possible. How far is abstract, Talmy-style motion a central part of its meaning? Is an analysis in Cadiot's terms attractive?

The verb *monter*, glossed as 'go up', is exactly analogous. Here too it would be a mistake to treat motion as *the* central aspect of the verb's meaning. Indeed, the gloss 'go up' obscures the fact that *monter* can have transitive uses which have little to do with spatial verticality, as Cadiot *et al.* explain (2006: 194):

It is essential to notice the dimension of intentional programming or the anticipation of a terminal point, which is more readable in the 'assembly/put together' uses (*monter un kit* 'to assemble/put together a kit', or even *monter une maison* 'to build a house', where the construction process is considered to be inherently programmed) or in the constitution uses (*monter un projet* 'to set up a project'). We therefore see an inherent telicity or programmed aiming at the center of the meaning of *monter*...

Verbs like *tomber* and *monter*, then, are semantically more complex than their simple treatment as motion verbs implies. Cadiot *et al.* criticize investigators in the wake of Talmy for their privileging of motion, which leads them to artificially introduce it as a component of the meaning of these verbs in many cases where it is not in fact relevant. A particular case is the metaphorical expression *la route monte*, an exact French equivalent of the English 'the road goes up'. This is usually explained as involving metaphorical motion based on the personification of the road, or as representing the mobile point of view of a subject following the road uphill. Yet this use is better understood, Cadiot *et al.* claim, as instantiating the semantic feature of 'anticipation of a terminal point' referred to in the passage just quoted. The road does not in any sense move: indeed, precisely the point of a road as opposed, say, to an escalator, is that it is not itself in motion. To introduce motion into the semantic analysis of *la route monte* is therefore unreasonable. The use of *monter* is explained by what Cadiot *et al.* see as a permanent feature of its semantics, the notion of 'anticipation of a terminal point'. To say that the road 'goes up' is to register the difference in verticality between its initial and terminal points, not to attribute motion to it in any way. A similar case would be the verb *sortir* 'come out', which, in French just as in English, applies to many cases where there's no actual physical motion, like *la photo est bien sortie* 'the photo came out well'.

Cadiot *et al.* do not *deny* that real, physical motion between spatial points is often a part of the meanings of verbs like *monter*, *tomber* and *sortir*. But they do not believe that it should be privileged as the unique or determinative aspect of their semantics. In their opinion, analysis in terms of the motion of a figure on a path is insufficiently focused on the embodied, subjective qualities of our experience of these actions, and reflects an overly abstract, conceptual approach to meaning. This analysis springs from a very different understanding of meaning from Talmy's. Talmy's approach involves abstracting from the multiplicity of uses of motion verbs and concentrating on just one aspect of their meaning. By contrast, Cadiot *et al.* resist the instinct to abstract, believing that there is a basic mistake involved in taking displacement as the central aspect of the semantics of verbs like *monter*, *tomber* and *sortir*. Instead, they emphasize how the meanings of these verbs reflect subjective, qualitative dimensions of experience which are not easily reduced to configurations of paths and figures. In doing so, they offer a more holistic, but considerably more complicated analysis.

The two styles of analysis can coexist. Talmy can always claim that his analysis does not have to be taken as the end of the story about motion verbs' meaning. The verb/satellite distinction only targets those aspects of the verbs' meaning which are relevant to displacement between points, and nothing in it precludes the more subjective, qualitative approach advocated by Cadiot *et al.* If displacement is not an important part of the meaning of many motion verbs, this in itself does not challenge the typological division between verb- and satellite-framing; it simply deepens our appreciation of the semantic complexity of the verbs in question.

11.4.5 Spatial reference

All languages have some means of indicating the spatial position of objects. In English, this is achieved through terms like *left* and *right,* and *front* and *back*: these words, which have counterparts in a wide range of European and other languages, use the planes of the body itself to identify different regions of space (*it's on the left/at the front*). In fact, this type of spatial reference seems so basic that it is hard to conceive of any serious alternatives. As a result, the systems of spatial reference involved in terms like *left, right, front* and *back* have often been assumed to be innate, and hence universal. For the great Enlightenment philosopher Immanuel Kant (1724–1804), for instance, the concept of space is not derived empirically from any experiences, but is one of the innate mental 'intuitions' which the mind brings to the understanding of the world (see Kant 1998).

Cross-linguistic study does not bear out this expectation of universality. Instead, it turns out that there are other systems of spatial reference employed in the languages of the world than the one familiar from English and other European languages. The large-scale investigation undertaken by researchers from the Max Planck Institute for Psycholinguistics, reported by Pederson *et al.* (1998) and Levinson (2003), tested how speakers of different languages describe the spatial relations between simple objects.

Pairs of speakers sitting out of view of each other were each presented with an identical set of twelve photographs like those in Figure 11.3, as part of an experiment known as the 'Men and Tree Game'. One speaker, the 'director', described a particular photograph, and the other, the 'matcher', had to guess, on the basis of the director's description alone, which picture was meant. The photographs were of a sort which necessitated the use of the language's spatial vocabulary; because director and matcher could not see each other or each other's pictures, the matcher only had the director's verbal descriptions to go on. Because of this arrangement, games of this type are an efficient way of eliciting spatial reference terms.

Experiments like these were conducted around the world on speakers of a broad range of mostly small-scale, traditional languages, but also in languages of non-traditional, largely urban societies, like Dutch and Japanese. These experiments explored the varying **frames of reference** used in languages for spatial location. A frame of reference is 'the internally

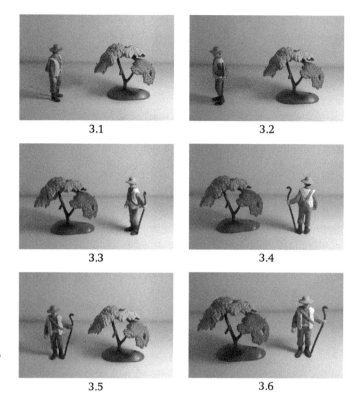

FIGURE 11.3
Six 'Men and Tree game'
photographs, showing
left–right relations.

consistent system of projecting regions of space onto a figure-ground relationship in order to establish specification of location' (Pederson *et al.* 1998:
571). English, for instance, uses left/right and front/back to divide space
into different regions which can then be used to locate an object (the **figure**) with respect to a reference point (the **ground**): the man (figure) is to
the left of the tree (ground), the tree (figure) is to the right of the man
(ground), and so on. We will concentrate here on the frame of reference
used for **transverse** (left–right) relations.

European languages including English, Japanese, and other languages
have a **relative** frame of reference. This is a system of spatial identification which uses information about the bodily arrangement of a speech
participant, often the speaker. Languages with relative frames of reference use spatial expressions with meanings like 'in front of me/behind
me' and 'to (my) left/right'. For instance, in describing picture 3.6 in
Figure 11.3, a Japanese player of the Men and Tree game produced the
following sentence:

(26) *de*   *ki*   *no*   *migi-gawa ni*   *hito*   *ga*   *i-te*
       then   tree   GEN   right-side at   man   NOM   exist-CONN
       kocchi   *o*   *mi-te*   *i-ru*   *shashin*
       this.way   ACC   look-CONN   PROG-PRES   photo
       'Then the photo where the man is at the right side of the tree and
       looking this way' (Pederson *et al.* 1998: 573)

Just as in English, the Japanese terms for 'left' and 'right' designate spatial regions which project out from the speaker's own body. As a result, if the speaker changes position, the description of an object as on the left or right may also change: the frame of reference is 'relative' to the speaker's location.

The relative reference frame is highly familiar and intuitive to an English or Japanese speaker. But it is not the only one. Some languages also contain an **absolute** frame of reference. This is a system of spatial location which does not depend on the position of a speech participant, but which is anchored instead in unchanging features of the geography, like uphill/downhill distinctions, or in the cardinal directions (north, south, east, west). In absolute frame of reference languages that use the cardinal directions, one does not say 'the man is on the left'; instead, one says 'the man is at the eastern/western/ northern/southern side'. Arrernte (Pama-Nyungan, Australia) is an example of a language with an absolute frame of reference, as exemplified in (27), also a description of picture 3.6:

(27) *Ikngerre-thayte-le* *warlpele*   *re*   *tne-me*   *ularre-theke*
    east-side-LOC   whitefella   3SGS   stand-NPP   face.towards-WARDS
    are-me   *arne-arle*   *kenhe* *itere-le.*
    look-NPP   tree-FOC   but   side-LOC
    'The whitefella is standing on the east side and looking towards us, but the tree is at (his) side.' (Pederson *et al.* 1998: 565)

As speakers of a relative frame of reference language like English, it is easy to mistake what is going on in a sentence like (27). English speakers can superimpose the four cardinal directions onto a figure like 3.6 as conventional markers of the top ('north'), bottom ('south'), left ('west') and right ('east') sides. To say 'the man is on the east side' can, for us, simply be equivalent to 'the man is on the right-hand side'. As a result, 'the man is on the east side' could be an appropriate description of picture 3.6, with 'east' functioning simply as an alternative for 'right'. In Arrernte, however, the cardinal direction terms are not used like this. Instead, *east really means* East, the direction of sunrise. For Arrernte speakers, the words for 'north', 'south', 'east' and 'west' aren't able to be used as conventional substitutes for top, bottom, right and left; they are *literal descriptions* relating figures to absolute coordinates of the external world. The speaker of (27) describes the man-figure as 'on the east side' because it really was on the Eastern (sunrise) side of the picture, *given the way the picture had been placed on the table during the experiment, and the table's orientation in actual space.* The ability of an Arrernte participant in the Men and Tree game to identify the correct image thus depends on their ability to orient themselves in space with respect to the cardinal directions. The fact that Arrernte speakers are typically able to do this is, to Westerners, a surprising ability. Given that both players in the Men and Tree game were seated facing the same way, cardinal points can be appealed to in order to precisely identify position.

The relative and absolute frames of reference often combine. About half of the languages investigated in the Men and Tree experiments use both frames of reference. English speakers, for example, occasionally use absolute frames of reference, as when they say that someone lives *to the west of the bridge*, or when they describe themselves as going *further inland*, or *towards the coast*. Some languages, however, only use one of the two: this is the case with Arrernte.

Apparently the least common frame of reference in the languages of the world is the **intrinsic** frame of reference. This system only makes reference to intrinsic features of figure and ground: 'the man is at the side of the tree, the tree is at the chest/face/back of the man' and so on. In the intrinsic frame of reference, there is no way of dividing space which is independent of the objects in it. In languages with other frames of reference, by contrast, it is possible to refer to regions of space without making any reference to objects: we can talk about the left side of the picture, or the eastern side of the picture, for example. These possibilities are not available in a language with only an intrinsic frame of reference. In the Men and Tree game, the only way of conveying the pictured spatial relations is by anchoring the descriptions in the man or the tree themselves: descriptors which are independent of these objects, like 'left/right' or 'north/south', are unavailable.

A language using an intrinsic frame of reference is Mopan (Mayan; Belize). Here is a typical example:

(28) *Ka'*   *a-ka'-käx-t-e'*   *a*   *nene'* *tz'ub'*
     CONJ   2ACTOR-again-seek-TR-SUBJ_3UNDERGOER   ART little child
     a...   *t-u-ta'an*   *ke'en-∅*   *top'-o*
     ART   at-3POSSESSOR -chest be_located-3UNDERGOER bush-ECHO
     'You should find the little child again who ... has the bush at his chest.' (Pederson *et al.* 1998: 570)

This was the instruction given by the director in the Men and tree game as a way of identifying photograph 3.3 in Figure 11.3 above. Notice that, as a matter of fact, there are actually two pictures which meet the description of the tree being at the man's chest: 3.1 and 3.3. These pictures are mirror-reflections of each other, differing only in their transverse (left–right) orientation: precisely the distinction that is not made in intrinsic frame of reference languages. As a result, speakers of this language consistently failed to differentiate pictures 3.1 and 3.3 in the Men and Tree game: when prompted to identify 3.3, they chose 3.1, and vice versa. Mopan provides no means for conveying this distinction.

What about the other pictures involving a left–right contrast, specifically 3.5 and 3.6? Given our description of Mopan as an intrinsic frame of reference language, it may come as a surprise to learn that it contains spatial terms corresponding in form to *left* and *right*, *lef* and *rait*. But these terms have a crucial difference in meaning from their English analogues. In English, *left* and *right* project regions of space relative to the speaker. Looking at picture 3.6, for instance, we would say 'the bush is on the left [of the man]' or 'the man is on the right [of the bush]'. This left–right division is anchored in the speaker: our left is, of course, the man's right. This English form of spatial reference is non-intrinsic: it depends on more than the inherent features of the reference objects, but invokes a set of coordinates which originate in a speaker external to the scene.

With this in mind, consider the Mopan description of picture 3.6:

(29) *Ich*   *rait*   *ke'en-∅*   *a*   *top'= -o*
    in   right   be_located-3UNDERGOER   ART   bush-ECHO
    'The bush is to the [the man's] right':

What the speaker means is that the bush is *on the man's right*: a correct description. This strikingly illustrates the difference between an intrinsic and a relative frame of reference. In a relative reference frame, left/right divisions are based on a participant in the speech situation, often the speaker. On their own, 'the left' and 'the right' of a picture refer to *the speaker's* left and right, and if this is different from the hearer's, further specification is necessary. In Mopan, by contrast, *lef* and *rait* refer to parts of the object, here, the man's right side. The bush is on the right-hand side *of the man*, and this form of spatial identification is exactly parallel to the one quoted in (28) above. *Rait* is just like 'chest': it refers not to a generalized spatial region, but to an intrinsic part of one of the objects in the scene. 'Man's right-hand side' would thus be a more accurate translation in this context.

These Mopan results serve as a reminder that notions like the left/right contrast which we take to be experientially basic and therefore likely to be present in all languages may not prove to be universal. Claims about what is and isn't conceptually or semantically basic should not therefore be made without close cross-linguistic comparison.

11.5 Language and thought

An age-old philosophical tradition emphasizes the close links between language and thought. In the *Theaetetus* (189e–190a) Plato said that thought is 'the conversation [*logos*] the soul has with herself'. (In Ancient Greek, in fact, *logos* means both 'sentence, word, conversation, discourse, language' and 'thought, reason'.) In a clear echo of Plato, the German philosopher Johann Gottfried von Herder (1744–1803) claimed that language is the 'common understanding of the soul with itself' (Herder 2002 [1771]: 90). For Herder, language and reason (we would say 'cognition') are intimately connected, perhaps the same thing.

This understanding of the connection between language and thought had its most influential recent advocate in the linguist Benjamin Lee Whorf (1897–1941). Whorf believed that the grammatical and lexical categories of one's language determine the categories in which we think:

We dissect nature along lines laid down by our native languages. The categories and types that we isolate from the world of phenomena we do not find there because they stare every observer in the face; on the contrary, the world is presented in a kaleidoscopic flux of impressions which has to be organized by our minds – and this means largely by the linguistic system in our minds. We cut nature up, organize it into concepts, and ascribe significances as we do, largely because we are parties to an agreement to organize it in this way – an agreement that holds throughout our speech community and is codified in the patterns of our language.

(Whorf 1956: 213)

For Whorf, in other words, language itself shapes the categories we use to reason about the world. Our conceptual categories are derived from the semantic categories of our native language. This idea is known as **linguistic determinism** or the **linguistic relativity hypothesis**, and is often paraphrased as the proposal that language determines thought, which thus varies from one language to another. Obviously, this proposal could mean many different things. 'Thought' is an extremely vague expression: it covers conscious and subconscious mental processes, reasoning, the holding of beliefs and desires, and so on. No investigator would be willing to claim that *everything* we call 'thought' is determined by language. In particular, we need to distinguish thinking in general from **thinking for speaking**. This latter term refers to the particular types of cognitive process involved in preparing and uttering language. Slobin (1996, 2001) and Levelt (1989) emphasize the extent to which the types of semantic distinctions encoded in language may direct the speaker to explicitly engage in certain thoughts. For example, a language which obligatorily encodes a perfective/imperfective contrast on the verb will require the speaker to subconsciously determine the relevant aspectual construal of the event being referred to in the lead-up to the utterance. Similarly, a language with a definite/indefinite contrast on NPs requires the correct definiteness value to be chosen for every NP, which means that speakers have no choice but to subconsciously attend to this contrast. This process of thinking for speaking means that the grammatical categories of a language *must* determine thinking *for speaking*.

It is during first language acquisition that the effects of thinking for speaking are most noticeable. In learning their native language, the child gradually learns what kind of conceptual distinctions are relevant in framing messages:

In learning the language, the speaker (the child) must surely have realized that the language requires him to attend to certain perceptual or conceptual features when he encodes a message. And ... the child makes characteristic errors that reveal his successive hypotheses about the conceptual properties required for the assignment of his language's morphology.

(Levelt 1989: 104–105)

Each native language, in other words, 'has trained its speakers to pay different kinds of attention to events and experiences when talking about them' (Slobin 1996: 89). Languages without an explicit perfective/imperfective contrast, for example, do not require speakers to attend to this dimension of an event, whereas languages with an explicitly coded definite/indefinite contrast will require speakers to determine the definiteness values of the NPs they mention. Building on Levelt's and Slobin's proposals, Gentner and Boroditsky (2001) qualify the extent to which language exerts an influence on conceptualization in child learning. Based on evidence from language acquisition, they suggest that the conceptualizations referred to by verbs, prepositions, and other relational predicates are linguistically influenced, 'whereas concrete nouns are in many cases simply names for preexisting cognitively natural referents' (2001: 241). According to Gentner and Boroditsky, the denotations of concrete nouns tend to follow natural partitions – naturally preindividuated perceptual groupings. Nouns like *rock*, *apple* and *box* denote entities which are highly demarcated from their environment. Acquisition of grammatical distinctions relevant to these nouns, like number, does not require learners to attend to aspects of the objects which are not already salient perceptually: it is obvious from just looking whether there is one apple, or more than one. Relational terms, however, like concrete verbs and prepositions, are more linguistically influenced. In order to learn them, speakers have to enter the system of semantic distinctions that their language uses. Learners are forced to go beyond the most perceptually salient aspects of the referents, and have to actively attend to those specific aspects of the event relevant to their subsequent linguistic coding.

As a result, acquisition of relational terms is hypothesized to only come later, after the child has had more exposure to the language. In the same study, Gentner and Boroditsky show evidence that the hypothesized acquisition sequence is indeed the one that occurs – concrete nouns are acquired earlier than verbs. This is true even if the nouns are morphologically more complex, a feature which could be expected to disfavour their early adoption. Gentner and Boroditsky describe the process as follows:

Consider the child's initial task in its simplest terms, as one of attaching words in the stream of speech to their referents in the stream of experience...Concrete objects and entities have already been individuated prelinguistically...Given a salient potential referent, part of the child's task of finding word-referent connections is already solved; it remains only to find the correct linguistic label. In contrast, for verbs and other relational terms, isolating the word is only part of the job. The child must also discover which conflation of the available conceptual elements serves as the verb's referent in her language.

(2001: 219)

If language plausibly influences conceptual development through the demands of thinking for speaking, what happens later? By adulthood, Levelt suggests that thinking for speaking no longer actively happens:

although conceptualizing and grammatical encoding *are* interacting for the language-acquiring child, the mature speaker has learnt what to encode when preparing a message for expression. He knows by experience whether his language requires a category of medial proximity, number, tense, object shape, or whatever is needed, and he will select the appropriate information in building his preverbal messages.

(Levelt 1989: 105)

This would explain some of the difficulties of second language acquisition. The process of learning our first language 'sets' the mind in a particular way that sensitizes it to certain distinctions while accustoming it to ignoring others. Mastery of a second language therefore requires sensitization to unfamiliar categories, and is correspondingly difficult.

What about cognition that is not purely geared towards speaking? Can we discern any wider influence of language on non-linguistic thinking ('thinking for action', such as planning sequences of events, or navigating on a map)? The idea that our thinking in general is influenced by the language we speak seems both plausible and implausible. Its plausibility comes from the following fact: the thought processes of which we are most consciously aware are precisely the explicitly linguistic ones. The experiences we call 'thinking' usually take place subconsciously. If you read a sentence that you don't understand, for example, and stop to think about it, you usually aren't aware of any explicit thoughts unfolding in your mind as you try to work out what it means. Instead, what happens is that you reread it, or go over it mentally until, suddenly, you understand. This sudden understanding usually just happens: the pieces just fall together all at once. We're not aware of any of the mental processing that must be going on in the background: it is all below the level of consciousness. Sometimes, though, our thought surfaces in an explicitly conscious form. Examples of conscious thought include visualizing scenes in the imagination, performing thought experiments like rotating geometrical figures, or doing mental arithmetic. One of the most obvious forms of this self-aware thought is **inner speech**. Thinking quite often takes the form of silent talk to oneself. For me, this is often the case for planning sequences of events. When thinking about what order to do things in, I will often mentally construct sentences: *if I go to the library first, it will be too late to buy bread, but if there's no bread there'll be nothing for lunch tomorrow, so I should go and get bread first.* Experiences like these are apparently common. Because of them, the idea that thinking actually *is* linguistic in form seems to make a lot of sense.

From another point of view, however, the idea that thought is in language, and hence determined by whatever language we speak, is most implausible. We're frequently aware of how inadequate language is to the ideas we want to express. Often, for example, words are ambiguous, and only one of the possible interpretations corresponds to the meaning we want to convey. Cases like this seem clear evidence of the non-identity of language and thought: we have a particular intention or meaning that we want to express, and it just so happens that our language expresses this meaning ambiguously. Surely this shows that the categories of language and thought are separate. More evidence of language–thought separability comes from coinages and borrowings. We resort to coinages and borrowings because it seems that the resources of our native language aren't adequate on their own to the ideas we want to express.

The variations in meaning discussed in the previous section provide a good test case for the linguistic relativity hypothesis. If general cognition really is determined by the semantics of natural languages, there ought to be experimental evidence of a correlation between a speaker's native language and their performance in non-linguistic tasks in the relevant domain. If this correlation was found to exist, it would not be direct evidence that language influences cognition, but would establish a correlation between the two. Further studies would be required to show whether the correlation was the result of cognition influencing language, or language influencing cognition. But if no correlation between language and thought is found, then that will be a clear refutation of linguistic determinism.

As part of the same study into spatial reference discussed in the previous section, a team of investigators from the Max Planck Institute for Psycholinguistics set out to test the linguistic relativity hypothesis. This research is discussed in a string of books and papers (see the further reading section at the end of the chapter); here, we will rely mainly on the account in Pederson *et al.* (1998). After establishing the features of spatial reference in the languages concerned, Pederson *et al.* conducted an experiment designed to reveal how speakers of different languages behave in spatial reasoning tasks. Subjects were presented with three different toy animals arranged in a row. They were asked to memorize the order of the animals 'just as they are', then turned around 180 degrees and after a thirty second delay asked to rearrange the animals in the 'same' order. This task thus required subjects to store the order of the animals in memory, and to draw on these stored memory representations in order to reproduce the original array. The hypothesis was that the type of spatial frame of reference characteristic of the language would influence the way subjects behaved in non-linguistic spatial reasoning tasks.

In principle, two types of result in these non-linguistic tasks are possible, corresponding to the relative and non-relative (intrinsic/absolute) frames of reference described in 11.4.5. A subject observing a relative frame of reference will reconstruct the row of animals in the same left–right order as the original. If the original array was in the order pig on the left, horse in the middle and cow on the right, a subject observing a relative frame of reference will reconstruct the array as pig–horse–cow from left to right, mirroring the original scheme. This preserves the animals' orientation with respect to the subject's own body. On the other hand, a subject observing an absolute frame of reference will keep the order of the animals fixed with respect to external anchoring points like the cardinal points or landmarks. Because of the 180 degree rotation, the order will be inverted on the transverse (left-right) axis, but fixed with respect to the external bearings. For such a subject, the animals will be rearranged in the order cow left, horse middle and pig right.

Pederson *et al.* found a statistically very highly reliable correlation between the type of response in the non-linguistic animals-in-a-row task and the prevailing frame of reference used in the subject's native language. Speakers of Arrernte, Tzeltal and Longgu, which all have absolute frames of reference, were likely to reconstruct the animals in an inverted order which preserved their orientation with respect to the external bearings. In contrast, speakers of Dutch and Japanese, languages with relative frames of reference, were likely to preserve the left–right order of the animals, inverting their order with respect to fixed external bearings. These differences of behaviour were independent of other variables such as literacy, schooling, sex or age (Levinson *et al.* 2002: 161). These results do not mean that speakers are locked into any one form of reasoning. Anyone is able to reason in any of the three ways at different times, and context may play a large role in determining which style of reasoning will be adopted at any one time. The original Max Planck Institute findings are still controversial, but have stood up to challenge (by, for example, Li and Gleitman 2002: see Levinson *et al.* 2002).

This experiment therefore provides evidence of a correlation between language type and non-linguistic cognition. The frame of reference used in a language is correlated with the way people conceptualize spatial relations in non-linguistic reasoning. This is enough to keep the linguistic relativity hypothesis in the game, but it is not yet enough to confirm it. The experiment tells us nothing about the *direction* of any influence between language and thought. Do speakers behave as they do in the memory task because their language has moulded the concepts they use to reason spatially? Or does the frame of spatial reference characteristic of a particular language derive from patterns in the way its speakers think? Many researchers think the former conclusion is the more likely. Levinson *et al.* (2002: 161–162) construct the argument that language moulds thought like this. Neighbouring, closely related cultures can use an entirely different mix of reference frames: Mopan, for example, uses intrinsic only, while the neighbouring Tzeltal, another Mayan language, has absolute and intrinsic frames. In a case like this, there simply is no other source for the observed differences in spatial reasoning techniques than the individual's native language. As Levinson (2003: 214) puts it, 'linguistic determinism seems the most likely explanation for the correlation … it would seem to take a communicative system to induce cognitive uniformity throughout a community in such an abstract psychological domain'. In the same vein, for Pederson *et al.* the language structure manifested in language use provides individuals with a system of spatial representation:

use of the linguistic system, we suggest, actually forces the speaker to make computations he or she might otherwise not make. Any particular experience might need to be later described, and many are. Accordingly many experiences must be remembered in such a way as to facilitate this. Since it seems, based on our findings, that the different frames of reference cannot be readily translated, we must represent our spatial memories in a manner specific to the socially normal means of expression. That is, the linguistic system is far more than just an AVAILABLE pattern for creating internal representations: to learn to speak a language successfully REQUIRES speakers to develop an appropriate mental representation which is then available for nonlinguistic purposes.

> (Pederson *et al.* 1998: 586; emphasis original)

Pederson *et al.* express confidence that similar effects will be observed in other areas of language:

> We do, however, feel optimistic that these correlations between language and thought will generalize to some other domains as well – when these are investigated in the manner described here. The domain of these spatial relations seems especially basic to human experience and is quite directly linked to universally shared perceptual mechanisms. Since linguistic relativity effects are found here, it seems reasonable that minimally they could be found in other, less basic domains as well. Finally, there must be a mechanism at work that creates mental representations consistent with social language use. It seems improbable that such a mechanism would be specific only to this one domain. Rather, such a mechanism would potentially operate across many areas of human cognition.
>
> (1998: 586)

Even if Pederson *et al.* are right that similar effects of language on cognition exist elsewhere, there is still a substantial body of evidence from other domains suggesting that Whorfian effects are not *pervasive*. Papafragou (2002), for example, investigated path and manner distinctions of the type studied by Talmy (11.4.4). She showed that the differences between English and Greek in the lexicalization of motion don't correlate with any differences in the behaviour of Greek and English speakers in memory and classification tasks based on these variables. Subjects don't differ in their memory or classification for path and manner distinctions, in spite of the differences between their languages. Malt *et al.* (1999) studied perceptions of container similarity for bottle and jar-like objects among speakers of languages which draw the boundaries between these categories in very different ways. Speakers of Argentinian Spanish, Chinese and American English were asked to undertake sorting tasks in which they had to sort photos of objects into piles that were physically similar, functionally similar, and similar overall. Here again, no significant linguistic relativity effect was found. Malt *et al.* conclude as follows:

> our correlations suggest that linguistic categories are not even the primary determinant of perceived similarity. Our data, if anything, suggest that perception of the similarity among objects remains relatively constant despite wide variation in linguistic category boundaries.
>
> (1999: 258)

Perceptions of similarity among objects are thus not influenced by striking cross-linguistic differences in the way objects are categorized. This is consistent with the results of Gentner and Boroditsky mentioned earlier. The challenge for linguistic research is to clarify exactly which domains seem to involve Whorfian effects like those uncovered in the spatial domain.

Summary

Diachronic and cross-linguistic meaning comparison presupposes a correct metalanguage

Claims about the variation or change of given meanings necessitate a particular metalanguage in which the meanings can be described, a situation which immediately introduces complications since there is not yet any agreement about what the correct metalanguage for semantic description is. Linguistics in general, and semantic theory in particular, assume that languages are mutually translatable in a way that preserves important meaning components.

Importance of polysemy in meaning change

Meaning change crucially involves **polysemy**. A word does not suddenly change from meaning A to meaning B in a single move; instead, the change happens via an intermediate stage in which the word has *both* A and B among its meanings.

The traditional classification of semantic change

The traditional classification of semantic change recognized the following six types:

- **Specialization (narrowing)**, in which a word narrows its range of reference
- **Generalization (broadening)**, in which a word's meaning changes to encompass a wider class of referents
- **Pejorization**, in which a word takes on a meaning with a less favourable evaluative force
- **Amelioration**, in which a word takes on a meaning with a more favourable evaluative force
- **Metonymy**, the process of sense-extension in which a word shifts to a contiguous meaning
- **Metaphor**, changes based on similarity or analogy

Conventionalization of implicature

Much modern work on semantic change examines pathways and regularities of semantic change, stressing the role of the **conventionalization of implicature**. This is the theory that semantic change occurs through the progressive strengthening of the implicatures of expressions in particular contexts, until the implicated meaning becomes part of the expression's literal meaning. These explanations can supersede ones based on the traditional categories.

Subjectification

An important tendency in semantic change is **subjectification**. This is the tendency for meanings to 'become increasingly based in the speaker's subjective belief state/attitude toward the proposition'.

Perception verbs and the mind-as-body metaphor
Viberg (1984) found a strong cross-linguistic hierarchy governed the polysemies of **perception verbs**. The visual modality of perception is always
the source but never the target of processes of polysemy. The **mind-as-
body metaphor** is a possible explanation of the extension of 'see' verbs
to 'know/understand' in Indo-European languages, but is not universal:
many languages draw their 'know' verb from verbs for hearing.

Grammaticalization
One particular context for semantic change is **grammaticalization**,
the process by which open-class content words turn into closed-class
function forms. They do this by losing elements of their meaning, and
by a restriction in their possible grammatical contexts. Study of these
processes has revealed a number of regular pathways which recur
again and again in the world's languages linking particular open-class
lexemes with particular grammaticalized functions.

Corpus studies of meaning variation
The seeds of semantic change are found in synchronic meaning variation in everyday discourse. **Corpora** are useful for semantic analysis
because they can reveal unsuspected patterns of **collocation** (regular
word combination). Many words cluster in predictable collocational
patterns. Studies of collocation can give surprising results: for example, corpus investigation reveals that *cause* is not used neutrally, but
has a strong tendency to be associated with negative events.

Semantic typology
Because of the problems of determining universals of sense, **semantic
typology** concentrates on the question of cross-linguistic regularities
in *denotation* or *extension* (11.4).

Typology of body-part reference
The **human body** is a basic and universal aspect of our experience,
but there are remarkably few cross-linguistic generalizations that hold
about the semantics of body-part terms.

Typology of colour-reference
Colour terms have been an important site of cross-linguistic investigation. Berlin and Kay hypothesized that each language has a set of
basic colour terms (BCTs). Basic colour terms in all languages target a
restricted range of colours, but the boundaries between these targets
vary widely. The number of BCTs in a language makes it possible to
predict exactly *what* the basic colour terms are, and Berlin and Kay
proposed seven types of language, classified according to the number
of BCTs. Berlin and Kay's findings have been broadly confirmed, but

there are some significant counterexamples to their typology, as well as fundamental criticisms of their methodology which cast doubt on the significance of their approach.

Deictic motion typology

Meanings in the domain of **deictic motion**, the actions expressed in English as 'coming' and 'going', also vary widely cross-linguistically.

Typology of motion, path and manner lexicalization

Talmy (1985) compared how different languages lexicalize the four elements of **motion, path, figure** and **manner** in motion verbs. Talmy proposed a major typological division between **verb-framed** and **satellite-framed** languages. In verb-framed languages the path component is lexicalized in the verb root itself. In satellite-framed languages it is lexicalized in a satellite element. As well as verb- and satellite-framed languages, some linguists claim that there is a third type, **equipollent** languages, in which both path and manner are treated in the same way. Talmy's typology has been widely discussed, and the distinction between verb- and satellite-framing is often invoked as a way of characterizing how different languages distribute motion information in the clause. It has been challenged, however, on the grounds that it artificially targets an abstract motion component in verbs whose meaning is actually much less abstract.

The typology of spatial reference

A **frame of reference** is 'the internally consistent system of projecting regions of space onto a figure-ground relationship in order to establish specification of location' (Pederson *et al.* 1998: 571). Languages with a **relative** frame of reference use spatial expressions with meanings like 'in front of me/behind me' and 'to my left/right'. Other languages contain an **absolute** frame of reference. This is a system of spatial location which does not depend on the position of a speech participant, but is anchored instead in unchanging features of the geography, like uphill/downhill distinctions, or in the cardinal directions (north, south, east, west). The least common frame of reference in the languages of the world is the **intrinsic** frame of reference. This system only makes reference to intrinsic features of figure and ground: 'the man is at the side of the tree, the tree is at the chest/face/back of the man' and so on.

The relation of language and thought

Differences in semantic typology raise the question of the influence between language and thought. **Whorf** believed that the grammatical categories of one's language determine the categories of broader cognition. This idea is known as **linguistic determinism** or the **linguistic relativity hypothesis**. Thinking in general must be distinguished from **thinking for speaking**. The grammatical categories of a language must determine thinking for speaking. The interesting question is whether they also determine general cognition. Research has found a statistically very highly reliable correlation between the prevailing frame of spatial reference used in a language and the types of response in non-linguistic cognitive tasks. These suggest a limited influence of language on general cognition. There are many other domains, however, where such an effect is not observed.

....

Further reading

The *Oxford English Dictionary* copiously documents the history and etymology of English words. Rey *et al.* (ed.) (2000) and Kluge (ed.) (1989) are etymological dictionaries of (and in) French and German, respectively. Buck (1949) is a fascinating thesaurus of semantic changes in Indo-European languages. Tryon (ed.) (1995) is a mammoth equivalent for Austronesian languages. Traugott and Dasher (2002) is a major synthesis on work in semantic change. Williams (1976) is an early attempt to uncover regularity in semantic change. Wilkins (1996) discusses some interesting changes in Australian languages. On grammaticalization, see Heine *et al.* (1991) and Hopper and Traugott (2003). Stubbs (2001) and Jones and Jackson (forthcoming) survey the field of corpus semantics. Free access to the British National Corpus is available for anyone who signs up at http://bncweb.lancs.ac.uk/bncwebSignup/. For surveys of work on semantic typology, see Koptjevskaja-Tamm *et al.* (2007) and Evans (forthcoming). Volume 28 of *Language Sciences* (2006) contains a comprehensive study of body-part terminology. There is a voluminous literature on colour: Berlin and Kay (1969), and Hardin and Maffi (eds.) (1997) are good places to start. See Talmy (1985) for the original presentation of lexicalization patterns. Much of the large literature on spatial reference is referenced in Levinson (2003). For the relation between language and thought more generally, see Lucy (1992), the chapters in Bowerman and Levinson (2001) and Gumperz and Levinson (1996).

Exercises

Questions for discussion

1. Many types of semantic change seem to involve a shift from concrete to abstract meanings. Can you find counterexamples to this from the history of English? What might explain them?
2. Browse through Buck (1949) in search of interesting meaning developments. Are there any which can't be described in any of the terms we have used in this chapter?
3. The examples of ameliorization and pejorization discussed in this chapter seem different from other processes of semantic change in that the later meaning has often displaced the earlier one completely. Can you suggest why this might be the case?
4. Sweetser's mind-as-body metaphor is meant to explain the origin of intellectual vocabulary in the vocabulary of vision. But what about the sources of vision verbs? Look up the etymology of *see, discern, examine, scrutinize, perceive* and *behold* in the *Oxford English Dictionary*. Is it possible to generalize about the sources of these verbs?
5. Lucy (1997: 331) says that the Berlin and Kay colour typology provides a 'view of the world's languages through the lens of our own category, namely, a systematic sorting of each language's vocabulary by reference

to how, and how well, it matches our own'. To what extent, if at all, is this an inevitable feature of cross-linguistic semantic research? What are the problems it might involve? Is it necessarily problematic?

6. Discuss the problem posed by language change for the attempts to do semantic typology discussed in this chapter.

7. Consult the entries for the following adjectives in the full version of the *Oxford English Dictionary*: *smart, stern, kind, decent, coarse, base, merry, sad, fair, silly, gentle, clever, nasty, mean, honest, poor, happy, naughty*. Which of the mechanisms of semantic change discussed in this chapter are best able to describe, and account for, these changes? What problems are there in answering this question?

8. Visit www.doubletongued.org, an online slang and new-word dictionary. Gather twenty-five single word entries. How far can the categories introduced in 11.2.1 account for the meaning developments documented there? Are there any types of new meaning which cannot be accommodated? Are there any points where a different description can be given of the new meaning, allowing it to fit into one of the categories?

9. In the context of their discussion of Australian 'hear/know' verbs, Evans and Wilkins (2000: 581) comment that

it remains possible that there is no one-to-one semantic correspondence between the English verbs and those in Australian languages. For some Australian languages one might venture to argue that 'know' could be defined, for example, along lines like 'because of what I have heard, I say: X; because I heard it from the right people, I can say: X is true'. Mutatis mutandis, one might seek to define 'know' for Indo-European languages through the verb 'see'.

They say that this is a real possibility, but one which needs to be 'subjected ...to the testing of careful paraphrasing with native speakers'. What types of tests could be developed to explore this hypothesis?

10. Compare Cadiot *et al.*'s critique of Talmy with Lucy's critique of the Berlin and Kay colour tradition. Are the two critiques motivated by similar considerations? How valid are they?

11. Read Pederson *et al.* (1998), followed by Li and Gleitman (2002) and Levinson *et al.* (2002). What aspects of the Li and Gleitman critique survive Levinson *et al.*'s (2002) rejoinder? How strong is the case for Whorfian effects in spatial reasoning?

12. Meaning changes often accompany lexical borrowings. For example, in Atayal (Austronesian, Taiwan), [taŋ] 'coin' is borrowed from a word meaning 'copper, brass'. In Murut (Austronesian, Malaysia), the word for 'coin' [usin], is borrowed from Dutch *cent* 'cent'. Is it legitimate to treat borrowings like these as instances of semantic change, or are they fundamentally different?

13. Is there any sense in which the collocational tendencies described in 11.3 can be considered part of the words' *meanings*? What are the implications for semantics of corpus studies like those described there?

Glossary

&:	Logical symbol for conjunction ('and'; 6.2).
⊃:	Logical symbol for material conditional ('if … then'; 6.2).
∨:	Logical symbol for inclusive disjunction ('or'; 6.2).
¬:	Logical symbol for negation ('not'; 6.2).
Accomplishment:	Aktionsart category referring to durative processes with an inherent end point beyond which the process cannot continue, e.g. *walk to school*, *draw a picture*, etc. (9.2.2.2).
Achievement:	Aktionsart category referring to an instantaneous occurrence occurring at a point in time, e.g. *recognize*, *find*, etc. (9.2.2.2).
Activity:	Aktionsart category referring to a durative process which does not have an inherent endpoint, e.g. *run*, *swim*, etc. (9.2.2.2).
Agent:	Theta-role referring to the initiator of an action (10.1.1).
Aktionsart:	An event's inherent aspectual classification, irrespective of the aspectual coding of the verb which expresses it. The four basic Aktionsart classes are states, achievements, accomplishments and activities. Semelfactives were added to this list later (9.2.2).
Amelioriration:	Meaning change in which a word takes on a meaning with a more favourable evaluative force. Cf. **pejorization** (11.2.1).
Antonymy:	The semantic relation of oppositeness (5.1.1).
Argument structure alternation:	Cases where a single verb can appear with different complementation patterns. E.g. *load* can either appear with the goal argument as direct object and the theme argument in a *with* phrase (*George loaded the truck with hay*), or with theme as direct object and goal in an *onto* phrase (*George loaded hay onto the truck*). If a verb shows an argument structure alternation, it is associated with several theta-grids (10.2).
Argument:	In **logic**, the thing of which a predicate is predicated (6.4). A one-place predicate takes one argument, a two-place predicate two arguments, etc. (6.4). In **syntax**, a verb's arguments are the noun phrases referring to the participants in the event or state the verb describes, coded as subject, object, etc. of the verb (10.1).
Aspect:	The grammatical category which expresses the **internal temporal constituency** of an event: whether the event is viewed as a single unanalysable whole (**perfective aspect**), or so that the distinct stages of the event are foregrounded (**imperfective aspect**) (9.2.2).
Atelic:	Aktionsart category referring to processes which do not have any inherent end point, like *wander* or *sweat* (9.2.2.2).
Autoantonymy:	The situation in which a single word has two antonymous meanings (5.1.1).
Beneficiary:	Theta-role referring to the participant for whose benefit an event took place (10.1.1).
Binary features:	Features with only two possible values, + or − (5.2).

Body-part possessor ascension alternation:
The **argument structure alternation** seen in pairs like *Terry touched Bill's shoulder/Terry touched Bill on the shoulder* (10.2).

Broadening:
See **generalization**.

Causative-inchoative alternation:
The argument structure alternation exemplified by the pair *Jeff cracked/ripped/shattered/snapped his credit card* (causative) and *The credit card cracked/ripped/shattered/snapped* (inchoative) (10.2).

Circular definition:
A definition or series of definitions is circular if the words of the definition contain the word they are meant to define (1.5).

Citation form:
The particular morphological variant of a lexeme used to refer to the lexeme as a whole, e.g. in dictionaries (1.4.1).

Classical category:
A category whose membership can be defined with a list of necessary and sufficient conditions (7.1).

Cognitive definition:
A type of definition which brings about an understanding of the meaning of a word (2.3.1).

Collocation:
Regular word combinations (11.3); the immediate context of words and morphemes in which a word occurs (2.2.4).

Committedness:
The fact that, in many antonym pairs, one antonym is typically 'uncommitted', i.e. neutral or unmarked, simply serving to invoke the dimension of contrast as a whole, without attributing either of the properties to the noun it qualifies. In the antonym pair *hot/cold*, *hot* is the uncommitted member, as seen by its use in questions like *how hot is it?* (5.1.1).

Communicative intention:
The intention to communicate a meaning. Talking to oneself, for example, does not involve any communicative intention (1.1).

Componential analysis:
A type of definitional analysis which breaks meanings down into (usually) binary features (5.2).

Composite category:
In colour research, a colour category with more than one focus (11.4.2).

Compositionality:
An expression is compositional when its meaning is made up, or 'composed', of the meanings of its constituent parts (1.4.3).

Compound:
Two or more lexemes conjoined into a single conventionalized semantic unit, such as *lunchbox* (2.2.1).

Conative alternation:
The argument structure alternation exemplified by *James hit the fence* (non-conative)/*James hit at the fence* (conative) (10.2).

Conceptual theory of meaning:
The theory that the meanings of linguistic expressions are concepts (1.6.2).

Conclusion:
In logic, a proposition deduced from premises by an argument (6.1).

Conjuncts:
Conjoined propositions. 'Julie likes cheese and Xavier likes chips' has two conjuncts: 'Julie likes cheese' and 'Xavier likes chips' (6.2).

Connotation:
An expression's connotation is those aspects of its meaning which do not affect its sense or denotation, but which have to do with secondary factors such as its emotional force, its level of formality, its character as a euphemism, etc. (1.4.2).

Constative:
In Austin's theory of speech acts, an utterance is constative if it describes or states facts about a situation (4.1.1).

Construction:
Any form–meaning pair. In construction grammar, constructions are the conventionalized 'patterns' with which semantic representations are associated. The caused motion construction, the resultative construction and the intransitive motion construction are all examples of constructions (10.3).

Contextual modulation:	The way in which the meaning of a lexeme varies slightly depending on the other lexemes with which it cooccurs (2.2.4).
Contradiction:	A pair of propositions with opposite truth values. There are three types of contradictions, contradictories, subcontraries and contraries (6.6.3).
Contradictories:	Contradiction whose two members always have opposite truth values to each other: if one is true, the other must be false, and if one is false, the other must be true (6.6.3).
Contraries:	Contradiction whose two members can both be false at the same time but cannot both be true (6.6.3).
Conventional implicature:	In Grice's theory of communication, an implicature based on the conventional meaning or typical force of the word (4.3.2).
Conventionalization of implicature:	Mechanism of semantic change in which pragmatically generated implications become part of the expression's meaning (11.2.2).
Conversational implicature:	In Grice's theory of communication, conversational implicatures are those that arise in particular contexts of use, without forming part of the expression's characteristic or conventional force (4.3.2).
Conversational maxims:	In Grice's theory of communication, the principles which speakers mainly observe, and expect others to observe, in conversation. There are four general maxims: quality, quantity, relevance and manner (4.4).
Cooperative principle:	In Grice's theory of communication, the principle that the participants in a conversation recognize a common purpose or direction for the conversation, and work together to achieve it (4.4).
Corpus (plural: *corpora*):	Any collection of texts which serves as an empirical basis for linguistic research (11.3).
Decomposition:	Applied to meaning, the process of analysis which consists of breaking an expression's meaning down into a number of separate parts (6.7).
Definiendum (plural: *definienda*):	The object language word whose meaning is being or has been defined (2.3.3).
Definiens (plural: *definientia* or *definientes*):	The metalanguage word(s) proposed as an expression's definition (2.3.3).
Definite descriptions:	Singular terms like *the President of Iraq* referring to a single, specific individual. In English, definite descriptions are usually expressed by noun phrases starting with *the*. Definite descriptions contrast with *ambiguous descriptions*, which contain the indefinite article and do not refer to a single specific individual: *a President of Iraq* (6.8).
Definition by context:	Defining a word by describing the context in which its referent typically occurs (e.g. defining *glass* with 'what you usually drink water out of') (2.3.4).
Definition by genus and differentia (GD definition):	Defining a word by specifying the broader class (the *genus*) to which the definiendum belongs, and then showing the distinguishing feature of the definiendum (the *differentia*) which distinguishes it from the other members of this broader class (2.3.5).
Definition by typical exemplar:	Defining a word by specifying a typical example (e.g. specifying 'robin' for *bird*) (2.3.4).
Definitional test for polysemy:	A type of polysemy test which identifies the number of senses of a word with the number of separate definitions needed to convey its meaning accurately (5.3.2).

Deictic:	Expression whose interpretation always depends on reference to the personal, spatial, or temporal context of the utterance. The referents of deictic expressions vary with the situation in which they are used. Examples of deictics in English are *this*, *here*, *there* and *now* (3.2.3).
Deictic centre:	The anchoring point from which the meaning of a deictic expression is determined. The deictic centre of *here* and *there* is the spatial location of the speaker (11.4.3).
Deictic motion:	A class of motion event expressed with reference to a **deictic centre**, such as 'coming' and 'going' in English (11.4.3).
Demonstrative:	A deictic pronoun or adjective like English *this* or *that* (3.2.3).
Denotation, denotatum (plural: *denotata*):	The entire class of objects to which a linguistic expression correctly refers (1.4.2; 3.3.2).
Dictionary meaning:	A word's inherent, linguistic meaning (3.3).
Disjunctive definition:	A definition that contains two clauses linked by 'or' (5.3.2).
Distal:	A class of demonstratives, equivalent to *that* in English, which is used to refer to objects not in the immediate vicinity of the deictic centre. Cf. **proximal** (3.2.3).
Distributional criterion:	A criterion for part of speech classification, which assigns words to part of speech categories on the basis of their morphosyntactic properties and/or distribution (9.1.2.1).
Durative	Event which occurs over a period of time, e.g. *sleep*. Contrasts with **punctual** (9.2.2.2).
Embodied conceptualization:	A conceptualization which originates in basic physical experience (7.2.3).
Encyclopaedic meaning:	Factual information about a word's denotation (3.3).
Entailment:	The relation between propositions where the truth of the first guarantees the truth of the second. *P* entails *Q* if whenever *P* is true, *Q* must be true (6.6.1).
Epistemic modality:	A type of modality expressing the speaker's subjective belief state towards the proposition. *Might* in *it might already be raining* is an example of epistemic modality, since it shows that the speaker is uncertain about whether it is raining or not (11.2.2).
Equipollent antonyms:	A class of gradable antonyms: they are symmetrical in their distribution and interpretation, with neither member of the pair having an uncommitted use (5.1.1).
Event structure:	The arrangement of subevents like CAUSE, ACT or BECOME within the semantic representation of a verb (10.2).
Exemplar theory of categorization:	A theory of categorization in which categories are structured around a particular example of the category as stored in long-term memory (7.1.4.1).
Existential quantification:	In logic, the operation which says that a predicate is true of at least one entity in a domain. The symbol for existential quantification is ∃, the existential quantifier. ∃(x) is read as 'there is at least one x, such that …' (6.4).
Experiencer:	Theta-role referring to the entity that feels or perceives something (10.1.1).
Extension:	The items to which a predicate applies. The extension of an *n*-place predicate is a set of ordered *n*-tuples of entities. Cf. **intension** (6.5).

Extensional definition:	A definition which precisely identifies the denotation of the definiendum (2.3.1).
Felicity conditions:	The conditions under which performative utterances are appropriate (3.4.2).
Figure:	Any object which is distinguished from a background (the **ground**). A word on a page is an example of a figure (7.2.3; 11.4.5).
Focus:	The focus of a colour term is the best example of the colour to which the term refers (11.4.2).
Frame of reference:	An internally consistent system of spatial reference. Different frames of reference are the absolute frame of reference, the intrinsic frame of reference and the relative frame of reference (11.4.5).
Generalization:	A type of semantic change in which a word's meaning changes to encompass a wider class of referents. Contrasts with **specialization** (11.2.1).
Goal:	Theta-role referring to the entity towards which motion takes place (10.1.1).
Gradable antonyms:	A gradable pair of antonyms names points on a scale which contains a midpoint (e.g. *hot* and *cold*). Gradable antonyms are open to comparison (*hotter, colder*) (5.1.1).
Grammatical categories:	The traditional part of speech categories like Noun, Verb, Determiner, etc. Also known as **lexical categories** (9.1.1).
Grammaticalization:	The process of semantic bleaching and grammatical category change by which lexical forms develop into grammatical ones (11.2.3).
Ground:	The background against which an object (the figure) stands out. The page on which a word is written is an example of a ground (7.2.3; 11.4.5).
Holonym:	A word *x* is the holonym of another word *y* if *y* is part of *x*. *Arm* is the holonym of *hand* (5.1.2).
Homonymy:	The situation where two unrelated meanings happen to be expressed by the same phonological form (e.g. *bank*, which means both 'edge of river' and 'financial institution') (5.3.1).
Hypernym:	see **hyperonym**.
Hyperonym:	A higher term in a hyponymic hierarchy. *Musical instrument* and *stringed instrument* are both hyperonyms of *violin* (5.1.3).
Hyponym:	A lower term in a hyponymic hierarchy. *Violin* is a hyponym of *musical instrument* and *stringed instrument* (5.1.3).
Idiom:	A non-compositional expression, e.g. 'throw in the towel' (1.4.3).
Illocutionary force:	In Austin's theory of speech acts, the status of an utterance as a warning, request, statement, etc. (3.4.1).
Image Schemas:	In cognitive semantics, conceptual categories such as CONTAINMENT, SOURCE-PATH-GOAL, FORCE, BALANCE and others, arising from basic patterns of repeated experience (7.2.3).
Imperfective aspect:	An aspectual category emphasizing the internal temporal constituency or duration of the situation or event, so that the distinct stages of the event are foregrounded. Often expressed by 'progressive' or 'continuous' forms of the verb (9.2.2).
Implicature:	In Grice's theory of communication, an utterance's implicatures are what it is necessary to believe the speaker is thinking, and intending the hearer to think, in order to account for what they are saying. Often equivalent to 'implied meaning' (4.3).
Inchoative alternation:	See **causative/inchoative alternation.**
Indexical:	See **deictic**.

Indirect speech act:	A speech act whose illocutionary force does not match the overt form of words used. For example, a statement used as a request (4.2).
Individual constants:	See **singular terms**.
Inheritance hierarchy:	A structure of hyponymically related words in which each word inherits the information associated with its hyperonyms (8.2.1).
Instrument:	Theta-role referring to the object with which an action is performed (10.1.1).
Intension:	A predicate's intension is its meaning or definition. The intension of the predicate *eat*, for example, could be described as 'ingest solid', or any other appropriate definition. A predicate's intension can be seen as the criteria that something has to meet in order to qualify as a member of the set denoted by the predicate. Anything that meets the criterion of 'ingesting solid' fulfils the intension of *eat*. Cf. **extension** (6.5).
Intentional-inferential theory of communication:	View of communication as a process in which hearers try to infer speakers' intentions on the basis of the 'clues' provided by their utterances (4.2).
Intentionality:	The property a thought has of being directed to, or about, something other than itself (3.2).
Landmark:	See **trajector**.
Lexeme:	The abstract unit which unites all the morphological variants of a single word and which is the unit whose meaning is principally described in lexical semantics (1.4.1).
Lexical categories:	See **grammatical categories**.
Lexical semantics:	The study of the meaning of individual words as opposed to that of phrases, grammatical constructions and sentences (1.4.3).
Lexical synonymy:	Synonymy between individual lexemes (5.1.5).
Lexicalization:	A meaning is lexicalized when it is expressed by a single form in a language (11.1).
Linguistic ideology:	The set of ideas, values and attitudes that speakers have about language (2.1).
Linguistic relativity hypothesis:	In Whorf and neo-Whorfian approaches, the proposal that our conceptual categories are derived from the semantic or grammatical categories of our native language. Also called **linguistic determinism** (11.5).
Location:	Theta-role referring to place where the action occurs (10.1.1).
Locative alternation:	The **argument structure alternation** exemplified by pairs like *Seth loaded the cart with hay* (*with* variant) and *Seth loaded hay onto the cart* (locative variant) (10.2).
Locutionary act:	In Austin's theory of speech acts, the act of expressing the basic, literal meanings of the words chosen (3.4.1).
Logical form:	The underlying logical structure of propositions and arguments (6.1).
Logical operators:	The elements &, $\vee$ (inclusive *or*), x-OR (exclusive *or*), ¬ (*not*) and ⊃ (*if … then*). Also called **propositional connectives** (6.2).
Logical test for polysemy:	A type of polysemy test, according to which an expression is polysemous if it can be simultaneously true and false of the same referent (5.3.2).
Material conditional:	A logical operator symbolized by ⊃ and roughly corresponding to the meaning of English *if … then* (6.2).
Maxim-flouting:	In Grice's theory of communication, the situation where the speaker exploits an obvious infringement of one of the conversational maxims in order to generate an implicature (4.4.1).

Meaning postulate: Logical statements which specify the relations that obtain between the different lexemes of a language. For example, the synonymy between *phone* and *telephone* can be captured in a meaning postulate that states that 'For every x, if x is a phone then x is a telephone' (6.7).

Mental lexicon: The stock of words and associated meanings that are stored in long-term memory (2.1.1).

Mental representation: Fixed mental content which is instantiated in our minds in some stable, finite medium and manipulated in the process of thought (1.6.2).

Meronym: A term x denoting a part of another term y. *Finger* is a meronym of *hand* (5.1.2).

Metalanguage: The language in which meanings are described (1.5).

Metalinguistic: Metalinguistic knowledge is the explicit, conscious knowledge we have about language. It contrasts with linguistic knowledge, which is the inexplicit, unconscious knowledge we have of our native language (7.1.4.5).

Metaphor: An important variety of figurative language traditionally defined as the use of an expression in a sense which resembles its literal meaning. In the expression *he is loaded down with responsibilities*, *loaded down* is used metaphorically, since it does not refer to actual physical burdens, but to things (responsibilities) resembling them. Metaphor is also a type of meaning change based on analogy or similarity between two objects or concepts (7.2.4; 11.2.1).

Metonymy: An important variety of figurative language traditionally defined as the use of an expression in a sense contiguous to its literal meaning (e.g. in *the kettle is boiling*, *kettle* is metonymic for 'the water in the kettle'). Metonymy is also a process of meaning change in which a word shifts to a contiguous meaning (7.2.4; 11.2.1).

Middle alternation: The argument structure alternation which involves theme as the only subcategorized argument of an otherwise transitive verb, e.g. *the bread cuts easily* (10.2).

Model: In logic, the model of a set of formulae is a set of statements which assigns referents or extensions to each expression of the formulae (6.5).

Monosemy: The situation where a word has a single meaning (5.3.1).

Morpheme: The minimal meaning-bearing unit (2.2.1).

Multicategoriality: The situation in which roots may appear as different parts of speech (9.1.2.3).

Narrowing: See **specialization**.

Necessary and sufficient conditions: Conditions on definition or category membership. The necessary and sufficient conditions of category membership are the minimum conditions an entity must meet if it is to be counted as a member of that category (7.1.1).

Node: In corpus linguistics, the term for word (11.3).

Nominal definition: A description of the meaning of a word. Cf. **real definition** (2.3.1).

Non-natural meaning (meaning$_{NN}$): Term introduced by Grice to describe the type of intention-dependent meaning characteristic of human language (3.5).

Object language: The language whose meanings are described. Cf. **metalanguage** (1.5).

Occurrence: Aktionsart category (opposed to state) referring to dynamic events in which something happens (9.2.2.2).

Onomatopoeia: The situation in which an expression bears a phonological resemblance to its meaning/referent (1.3).

Ostension: A means of definition which consists simply of pointing to the referent of the word whose meaning is to be defined (1.6.1).

Ostensive-inferential communication: View of communication in which the communicator provides a symbolic stimulus which, combined with the context, enables the hearer to infer their meaning (3.9).

Paradigmatic relations: The relations between expressions which determine the choice of one expression over another in any given context. All lexical relations (synonymy, antonymy, etc.) are paradigmatic relations (5.1.1).

Participant roles: See **thematic roles**.

Path: In Talmy's theory of motion lexicalization, Path is the route traversed by a moving object (11.4.4).

Patient: See **theme**.

Pejorization: A meaning change in which a word takes on a derogatory or less favourable evaluative meaning (11.2.1).

Perfect tense: Tense usually described as denoting a past action which has some relevance to the current situation. In English, formed with HAVE and the past participle (9.2.1.2).

Perfective aspect: Aspectual category which presents the situation as an undivided whole, without foregrounding any internal structure (9.2.2).

Performative: In Austin's theory of speech acts, a performative utterance is one which does not describe or state any facts, but which itself constitutes the performing of an action. Typical examples are the acts of warning, promising, and guaranteeing, etc. Explicit performatives are introduced by the words 'I warn …', 'I promise …', 'I guarantee …' and so on. The same utterances without these introductions are implicit performatives (4.1.1).

Perlocutionary act: In Austin's theory of speech acts, the act of producing an effect in the hearer by means of the utterance (4.1.1).

Phonological word: A unit which bears only a single primary stress (2.2.1).

Phrasal semantics: The study of the principles which govern the construction of phrase and sentence meaning out of combinations of individual lexemes (1.4.3).

Phrasal synonymy: Synonymy between expressions consisting of more than one lexeme (5.1.5).

Phrasal verb: A combination, functioning as a single unit, of one 'full' verb and one or more particles, often with an idiomatic meaning. *Make up* ('invent') is a phrasal verb (2.2.1).

Polysemy: The situation where a word has two or more related senses (5.3.1).

Pragmatics: The branch of linguistics which studies utterance meaning and the principles of contextual language use (1.4.4; 3.1; 4.7).

Predicate: In logic, terms which represent properties or relations, such as 'primate', 'hairy' or 'adore'. Predicates are symbolized by upper case letters (6.4). In grammar more generally, predicate is an alternative term for 'verb', or for any part of speech which attributes a property to a referent.

Predicate logic (also quantificational/ first-order logic): A branch of logic that studies the logical form of propositions involving expressions of individual constants, predicates and quantifiers. Predicate logic contrasts with **propositional logic** (6.4).

Predicative function:	When an expression has a predicative function, it is non-referring and its role is to give information about an entity which has already been identified (3.2.2.2).
Premise:	An argument's premise is its starting-point, one of the propositions from which the conclusion follows (6.1).
Presupposition:	A proposition p presupposes another proposition q if both p and the negation of p entail q (6.6.2).
Principle of relevance:	In Relevance Theory, the principle that every utterance 'communicates a presumption of its own optimal relevance' (Sperber and Wilson 1995: 158). By the very act of saying something to a hearer, a speaker implies that the utterance is the most relevant that they could have produced under the circumstances, and that it is *at least relevant enough* to warrant the hearer's attention (4.6).
Productivity:	The fact that the vocabulary of any given language can be used to construct a theoretically infinite number of sentences, by varying the way in which the words are combined (1.4.3).
Projected referents:	Referents as they are subjectively present to the mind of the language user, as distinct from how they actually are in the objective world (1.6.1).
Projectionist accounts:	Theories of argument structure and alternations based on the verb's semantic representation, which 'projects' (determines) its syntactic behaviour (10.3).
Proposition:	A premise or conclusion of an argument, capable of being true or false (6.2).
Propositional connectives:	See **logical operators**.
Propositional logic:	A branch of logic that studies relations between propositions (6.2).
Proto-roles:	Two categories of theta-role, Proto-Agent and Proto-Patient, proposed in Dowty's theory of thematic structure. Each is characterized by a set of verbal entailments (10.1.3).
Prototype:	The prototype of a category is the central tendency of the category's members. Prototypical category members are those which share the most attributes with other members of their category, and the fewest with members of other categories. A sparrow is a more prototypical example of the category BIRD than a penguin (7.1.3).
Proximal:	A class of demonstratives, equivalent to *this* in English, used to refer to objects in the immediate vicinity of the deictic centre. Cf. **distal** (3.2.3).
Psych-verbs:	Verbs signifying mental states (*remember, know, regret*, etc.) (10.1.2).
Punctual:	A punctual event is a virtually instantaneous one that involves almost no time, e.g. *blink*. Contrasts with **durative** (9.2.2.2).
Qualia structure:	In Pustejovsky's approach to semantics, an aspect of the semantics of nouns that reflects those aspects of the referent of a noun which are crucial for our common-sense understanding of how things interact in the world. A noun's qualia structure has four aspects, its **Constitutive Role, Formal Role, Telic Role** and **Agentive Role**, which together constitute the framework for the word's meaning (8.2.3).
Quantifiers:	The logical expressions 'some' and 'all', symbolized by the operators ∃ and ∀ respectively (6.4).

Radial category: Type of lexical category in which the expression's central meaning is associated with a number of extended (metaphorical/metonymic) meanings which cannot be predicted by general rules (7.2.5).

Real definition: A summation of the essence or inherent nature of a thing. Cf. **nominal definition** (2.3.1).

Reductive paraphrase: Form of definition in which the meaning of an expression is exhaustively described through paraphrase into a finite set of semantic primitives (2.5).

Reference: (i) The objects to which a expression refers. In this use it is a synonym of 'referent'; (ii) the act by which a speaker refers to a referent (1.4.2; 3.2).

Register: A particular style of language used for a certain social function or situation (2.4).

Resultative construction: Construction realizing the meaning X CAUSES Y TO BECOME Z, e.g in *Sam bent the wire straight* (10.3).

Satellite: In Talmy's approach to motion lexicalization, an element (other than inflections, auxiliaries or nominal arguments) which combines immediately with a verb to form a verbal complex. In *Helen ran away*, *away* is a satellite (11.4.4).

Satellite-framed languages: Languages (like English) in which the **path** component of motion expressions is expressed in a **satellite** element (11.4.4).

Scalar implicature: A class of implicature which depends on the existence of a scale or ordered set of increasingly stronger meanings with relations of entailment between them. For example, *some* and *all* are members of a scale of quantity, in which *some* is weaker than *all* and *all* entails *some*. Thus use of *some* typically gives rise to the scalar implicature *not all* (4.3.1).

Semantic primitives: Hypothesized fundamental units of meaning which cannot be broken down into anything conceptually simpler (2.5).

Semantic roles: See **thematic roles**.

Semelfactive: Aktionsart category referring to punctual, single-instance events like *cough, knock, blink, flap (a wing)* (9.2.2.2).

Sense: For Frege, the way in which we grasp/understand the object denoted by a linguistic expression. One way of thinking of an expression's sense is as the *mode of presentation* of its referent: the way in which the referent is presented to our understanding (3.2.1). More generally, a lexeme's sense is its *general meaning* which would be translated from one language to another; the *concept* or essential idea underlying the word (1.4.2).

Sentence meaning: The compositional meaning of the sentence as constructed out of the meanings of its individual component lexemes (1.4.3).

Singular terms (also individual constants): In logic, terms referring to individuals, usually symbolized as lower case letters (6.4).

Sound arguments: Valid arguments which have true premises (6.1).

Source: Theta-role expressing the entity from which motion takes place (10.1).

Span: In corpus linguistics, the number of words taken into account before and after the **node** (11.3).

Specialization: A type of meaning change in which a word narrows its range of reference. Opposite of **generalization** (11.2.1).

State: Aktionsart category (opposed to **occurrence**) referring to situations viewed as steady and unchanging, without any sequence of internal phases/changes. States exist or obtain, whereas events happen (9.2.2.2).

Subcategorization: The relationship between a verb and its (obligatory) arguments, usually described in theta-role terms. *Hug* subcategorizes an agent and a theme; *put* subcategorizes an agent, theme and goal (10.1.1).

Subcontraries: Pair of propositions whose two members cannot be simultaneously false, but can be simultaneously true. *Some people are happy* and *some people are not happy* are subcontraries (6.6.3).

Subjectification: The tendency for meanings to 'become increasingly based in the speaker's subjective belief state/attitude toward the proposition' (Traugott) (11.2.2).

Syllogism: In logic, an argument in which a conclusion is deduced from premises. *All men are mortal. Socrates is a man. Therefore Socrates is mortal* is an example of a syllogism (6.1).

Synonymy: The situation where two expressions have the same meaning (5.1.5; 2.3.3).

Target: A metaphor's target is the concept which is being understood metaphorically. In the metaphor LOVE IS A JOURNEY the target concept is love (7.2.4).

Taxonymy: A type of hyponymy, relevant to biological classification, in which each hyponym is understood as a strict biological subclass of the hyperonym (5.1.4).

Telic: Telic events have an inherent final point beyond which they cannot continue. Reading a novel, shaving one's head, and changing a light bulb are all telic events (9.2.2.2).

Tense: The name of the morphological category used to signal the location of situations in time (9.2.1).

Thematic roles (theta-roles): Categories such as agent, experiencer, goal, theme, etc., used to describe the underlying semantics and argument structure of verbs (10.1).

Theme: Theta-role referring to the entity that undergoes an action, undergoes motion, is experienced or perceived (10.1).

Trajector: A moving or conceptually movable object whose path or site is at issue. Its location is specified with respect to a landmark (7.2.3).

Transitivity: (i) The verbal property of taking both subject and object arguments; (ii) A transitive relation is one such that if it holds between A and B, and between B and C, it also holds between A and C. Some examples of transitive relations are identity and meronymy: If A is B, and B is C, then A is C; if A is a meronym of B, and B is a meronym of C, then A is also a meronym of C (5.1.2).

Transverse relations: Left–right relations (11.4.5).

Trigger: The sentence whose presuppositions are in question. *The fourth Monday in September is a holiday* is the trigger for the presupposition 'there is a fourth Monday in September' (6.6.2).

Truth-functional view of meaning: The view that knowing the meaning of an expression consists in knowing the conditions under which it is true (4.3.1).

Truth-functionality: A logical operator is truth-functional if the truth of the complex proposition of which it forms part depends solely on the truth of the original simple proposition to which the operator was added. The logical operators &, $\vee$ (inclusive *or*), X-OR (exclusive *or*), ¬ (*not*) and ⊃ (*if . . . then*) are all truth-functional (6.2).

Truth-table:	A table which displays the way in which logical operators affect the truth of the propositions to which they attach (6.2).
Truth-value:	A proposition's status as true or false (3.2.1).
Underspecification:	The idea that an expression's sense is vague over values which are specified contextually (3.3.1).
Universal quantification:	The logical operation which applies a predicate to every entity in the domain in question. Universal quantification is symbolized by $\forall$ and conveyed in English by such expressions as *all*, *every*, *everything*, and *each and every* (6.4).
Utterance meaning:	The meaning which an expression has on a particular occasion of use in the particular context in which it occurs. Sometimes called **speaker meaning**. Contrasts with **sentence meaning** (1.4.4).
Validity:	A valid argument is one in which, if the premises are true, the conclusion must necessarily also be true (6.1).
Vehicle:	A metaphor's vehicle is the concept which is used to conceptualize the metaphor's **target**. In the metaphor LOVE IS A JOURNEY the vehicle concept is journey (7.2.4).
Verb-framed languages:	Languages (like Spanish) in which the **path** component is lexicalized in the verb root itself (11.4.4).
x-or:	Exclusive disjunction (6.2).

References

Aarts, B., Denison, D., Keizer, E. and Popova, G., (eds.) 2004. *Fuzzy grammar. A reader*. Oxford: Oxford University Press.

Adelaar, K. A. 2000. Siraya reduplication, *Oceanic Linguistics* 39: 33–52.

Aikhenvald, Alexandra A. 1996. Words, phrases pauses and boundaries: Evidence from South American Indian languages, *Studies in Language* 20: 487–517.

Aikhenvald, A. Y. 2000. *Classifiers: A typology of noun classification devices*. New York: Oxford University Press.

Aitchison, Jean. 1994. *Words in the mind: an introduction to the mental lexicon*. Oxford: Blackwell.

Allan, Keith. 1977. Classifiers. *Language*, 53: 285–310.

Allan, Keith. 1986. *Linguistic meaning*. London: Routledge and Kegan Paul.

Allan, Keith. 2001. *Natural Language Semantics*. Oxford: Blackwell.

Allwood, J., Andersson, L. G. and Dahl, Ö. 1977. *Logic in linguistics*. Cambridge: Cambridge University Press.

Allwood, Jens. 2003. Meaning potentials and context: some consequences for the analysis of variation in meaning, in Cuyckens, Hubert, Dirven, René and Taylor, John R. (eds.) *Cognitive approaches to lexical semantics*. Berlin: Mouton de Gruyter, 29–65.

Alpher, Barry and Nash, David. 1999. Lexical replacement and cognate equilibrium in Australia, *Australian Journal of Linguistics*, 19: 5–55.

Apresjan, Juri. 2000. *Systematic lexicography*. Oxford: Oxford University Press.

Ariel, Mira. 2008. *Pragmatics and grammar*. Cambridge: Cambridge University Press.

Arnold, Jennifer E., Losongco, Anthony, Wasow, Thomas, and Ginstrom, Ryan. 2000. Heaviness vs. newness: the effects of structural complexity and discourse status on constituent ordering, *Language* 76: 28–55.

Ashby, W. 1981. The loss of the negative particle *ne* in French. *Language* 57: 674–687.

Atran, Scott. 1990. *Cognitive foundations of natural history*. Cambridge/Paris: Cambridge University Press/ Editions de la Maison des Sciences de l'Homme.

Atran, Scott. 1999. Itzaj Maya folkbiological taxonomy: cognitive universals and cultural particulars, in Medin and Atran, 1999, 119–203.

Auroux, Sylvain. 1994. *La révolution technologique de la grammatisation*. Liège: Mardaga.

Austin, John. 1962. *How to do things with words*. Oxford: Clarendon Press.

Bach, Emmon. 1989. *Informal lectures on formal semantics*. Albany: State University of New York Press.

Bach, Kent. 2002. Language, logic and form, in Jacquette, Dale (ed.) *A companion to philosophical logic*. Malden, MA: Blackwell, 51–72.

Bach, Kent and Harnish, Robert M. 1979. *Linguistic communication and speech acts*. Cambridge, MA: MIT. Excerpt reprinted in Kasher, 1998, vol. II, 65–68.

Bache, C. 1997. *The study of aspect, tense and action*, 2nd edn. Frankfurt: Peter Lang.

Baker, Mark. 2003. *Lexical categories: verbs, nouns and adjectives*. Cambridge: Cambridge University Press.

Bakhtin, M. M. 1986 [1953]. The problem of speech genres, in *Speech genres and other late essays*. Austin: University of Texas Press, 60–102.

Baldinger, Kurt. 1980. *Semantic theory*. Oxford: Blackwell.

Baldinger, Kurt. 1984. *Vers une sémantique moderne*. Paris: Klincksieck.

Barclay, J. R., Bransford, J. D., Franks, J. J., McCarrell, N. S. and Netsch, K. 1974. Comprehension and semantic flexibility, *Journal of Verbal Learning and Verbal Behavior* 15: 667–669.

Bärenfänger, Olaf. 2002. Merkmals- und Prototypensemantik. Einige grundsätzliche Überlegungen 13, *Linguistik Online* 12. 3 [np]. www.linguistik-online.de/

Bar-Hillel, Yehoshua. 1954. Indexical expressions, *Mind* 63: 359–379. Reprinted in Kasher, 1998, vol. I, 23–40.

Barsalou, L. W., Yeh, W., Luka, B. J., Olseth, K. L., Mix, K. S. and Wu, L. 1993. Concepts and meaning, in Beals, K., Cooke, G., Kathman, D., McCullough, K. E., Kita, S. and Testen, D. (eds.), *Papers from the parasession on conceptual representations.* Chicago: Chicago Linguistic Society, 23–61.

Barwise, J. and Perry, J. 1983. *Situations and attitudes.* Cambridge, MA: MIT.

Battig, W. F. and Montague, W. E. 1969. Category norms for verbal items in 56 categories: A replication and extension of the Connecticut category norms, *Journal of Experimental Psychology Monograph* 80: 1–46.

Bauer, Laurie. 1998. When is a sequence of two nouns a compound in English? *English Language and Linguistics* 2: 65–86.

Baugh, John. 1983. *Black Street Speech.* Austin: University of Texas Press.

Beck, David. 2002. *The typology of parts of speech systems: the markedness of adjectives.* New York: Routledge.

Bekkum, Wout Jacques van *et al.* 1997. *The emergence of semantics in four linguistic traditions: Hebrew, Sanskrit, Greek, Arabic.* Amsterdam: John Benjamins.

Berlin, B. 1972. Speculations on the growth of ethnobotanical nomenclature, *Language in Society* 1, 51–86.

Berlin, B. 1992. *Ethnobiological classification.* Princeton: Princeton University Press.

Berlin, B. and Kay, P. 1969. *Basic colour terms: their universality and evolution.* Berkeley: University of California Press.

Berlin, B., Breedlove, D. and Raven, P. 1973. General principles of classifications and nomenclature in folk biology, *American Anthropologist* 75: 214–242.

Binnick, Robert I. 1991. *Time and the verb: a guide to tense and aspect.* New York: Oxford University Press.

Blackburn, Patrick and Bos, Johan. 2005. *Representation and inference for natural language: a first course in computational semantics.* Stanford, CA: Center for the Study of Language and Information.

Blakemore, Diane. 1992. *Understanding utterances.* Oxford: Blackwell.

Bloomfield, Leonard. 1933. *Language.* New York: Holt.

Bloor, T. and Bloor, M. 2004. *The functional analysis of English: a Hallidayan approach,* 2nd edn. London: Arnold.

Bohnemeyer, Jürgen. 1998. Temporal reference from a Radical Pragmatics perspective. Why Yucatec does not need to express 'after' and 'before', *Cognitive Linguistics* 9: 239–282.

Bohnemeyer, Jürgen. 2002. *The grammar of time reference in Yucatec Maya.* Munich: LINCOM.

Bohnemeyer, Jürgen. 2003. NSM without the Strong Lexicalization Hypothesis, *Theoretical Linguistics* 29: 211–222.

Bolinger, Dwight. 1976. The in-group: *one* and its compounds, in Reich, P. A. (ed.), *The second LACUS forum, 1975.* Columbia, SC: Hornbeam, 229–237.

Boroditsky, L. 2000. Metaphoric structuring: Understanding time through spatial metaphors, *Cognition* 75: 1–28.

Boroditsky, L. and Ramscar, M. 2002. The roles of body and mind in abstract thought, *Psychological Science* 13: 185–188.

Botne, Robert 2003. To die across languages: toward a typology of achievement verbs, *Linguistic Typology* 7: 233–278.

Bourciez, E. 1967. *Eléments de linguistique romane.* Paris: Klincksieck.

Bowerman, Melissa and Levinson, Stephen C. 2001. *Language acquisition and conceptual development.* Cambridge: Cambridge University Press.

Bréal, Michel. 1897. *Essai de sémantique.* Paris: Hachette.

Brecht, Bertolt. 1967. *Gesammelte Werke in acht Bänden,* vol. V. Frankfurt: Suhrkamp Verlag.

Breheny, Richard. 2002. The current state of (radical) pragmatics in the cognitive sciences, *Mind and Language* 17: 169–187.

Bright, J. O and Bright, W. 1965. Semantic structures in northwestern California and the Sapir-Whorf hypothesis, *American Anthropologist* 67: 249–258.

Brown, C. H. 1986. The growth of ethnobiological nomenclature, *Current Anthropology* 27: 1–19.

Brown, C. H. 2002. Paradigmatic relations of inclusion and identity I: Hyponymy, in Cruse, D., Hundsnurscher, F., Job, M. *et al.*, *Lexikologie. Ein internationales Handbuch zur Natur und Struktur von Wörtern und Wortschätzen*. Berlin: Mouton, 472–480.

Brown, C. H. and Witkowski, Stanley R. 1981. Figurative language in a universalist perspective, *American Ethnologist* 8: 596–615.

Brown, C. H. and Witkowski, Stanley R. 1983. Polysemy, lexical change and cultural importance, *Man* 18: 72–89.

Buck, C. 1949. *A dictionary of selected synonyms in the principal Indo-European languages*. Chicago: University of Chicago Press.

Burenhult, Niclas. 2006. Body part terms in Jahai, *Language Sciences* 28: 162–180.

Bybee, Joan, Perkins, Revere and Pagliucca, William. 1991. Back to the future, in Traugott, Elizabeth and Heine, Bernd (eds.) *Approaches to grammaticalization: focus on types of grammatical markers*, vol II. Amsterdam: John Benjamins, 17–58.

Bybee, Joan, Perkins, Revere and Pagliucca, William. 1994. *The evolution of grammar: tense, aspect, and modality in the languages of the world*. Chicago: University of Chicago Press.

Cadiot, Pierre, Lebas, Franck and Visetti, Yves-Marie. 2006. The semantics of motion verbs: action, space, and qualia, in Hickmann, Maya and Robert, Stéphane (eds.) *Space in languages*. Amsterdam: Benjamins, 175–206.

Carnap, R. 1942. *Introduction to semantics*, Cambridge, MA. Excerpt reprinted in Kasher, 1998, vol. I, 3–14.

Carnap, R. 1947. *Meaning and necessity*. Chicago: University of Chicago Press.

Carnie, Andrew. 2007. *Syntax: a generative introduction*. Malden, MA: Blackwell Publishing.

Carpenter, Bob. 1997. *Type-logical semantics*. Cambridge, MA: MIT.

Carston, Robyn. 1988. Implicature, explicature and truth-theoretic semantics, in Kempson, Ruth M. (ed.) *Mental representations*. Cambridge: Cambridge University Press, 155–181. Reprinted in Kasher, 1998, vol. IV, 436–464.

Channell, Joanna. 2000. Corpus-based analysis of evaluative lexis, in Hunston, S. and Thompson, G. (eds.) *Evaluation in text*. Oxford: Oxford University Press, 38–55.

Chaurand, Jacques and Mazière, Francine (eds.) 1990. *La définition*. Paris: Larousse.

Chidambaram, V. 2004. Verb of motion ellipsis in Russian. Unpublished MS, Princeton University.

Chierchia, Gennaro and McConnell-Ginet, Sally. 2000. *Meaning and grammar: an introduction to semantics*. Cambridge, MA: MIT.

Chomsky, N. 1959. Verbal behavior, *Language* 35: 26–58.

Chomsky, N. 1965. *Aspects of the theory of syntax*. Cambridge, MA: MIT.

Chomsky, N. 1986. *Knowledge of language: its nature, origin, and use*. Westport, CT; London: Praeger.

Chomsky, N. 1995. Language and nature. *Mind* 104: 1–61.

Chomsky, N. 2000. *New horizons in the study of language and mind*. Cambridge: Cambridge University Press.

Chomsky, N. and Halle, Morris. 1968. *The sound pattern of English*. New York: Harper and Row.

Chung, Sandra and Timberlake, Alan. 1985. Tense, aspect, and mood, in Shopen, Timothy (ed.) *Language typology and syntactic description: Grammatical categories and the lexicon*, vol. III. Cambridge: Cambridge University Press, 202–258.

Clark, Eve V. and Clark, Herbert H. 1979. When nouns surface as verbs, *Language* 55: 767–811.

Cobley, Paul (ed.) 2001. *The Routledge companion to semiotics and linguistics*. London: Routledge.

Coleman, Linda and Kay, Paul. 1981. Prototype semantics: The English word Lie, *Language* 57: 26–44.

Collinot, André and Mazière, Francine. 1997. *Un prêt à parler : le dictionnaire*. Paris: Presses Universitaires de France.

Comrie, Bernard. 1976. *Aspect: an introduction to the study of verbal aspect and related problems*. Cambridge: Cambridge University Press.

Comrie, Bernard. 1985. *Tense*. Cambridge: Cambridge University Press.

Concise Oxford English Dictionary (2004). Oxford: Oxford University Press.

Conklin, H. C. 1954. The relation of Hanunóo culture to the plant world. PhD thesis, Yale University.

Conklin, H. C. 1964 [1955]. Hanunoo color categories, in Hymes, D. (ed.) *Language in culture and society: a reader in linguistics and anthropology*. New York: Harper and Row, 189–192. Reprint from *Southwestern Journal of Anthropology* 11. 4: 339–344.

Coseriu, E. 1971. Zur Vorgeschichte der strukturellen Semantik: Heyses Analyse des Wortfeldes 'Schall', in *Sprache. Strukturen und Funktionen. XII Aufsätze*. 2ed. Tübingen: Tübinger Beiträge zur Linguistik, 179–190.

Coseriu, E. 2001 [1983]. Pour et contre l'analyse sémique, in *L'homme et son langage*. Louvain: Peeters, 355–369. Originally in Hattori, S. *et al.* (eds.) 1983, *Proceedings of the XIIIth International Congress of Linguists*, Tokyo, 137–148.

Croft, William. 1991. *Syntactic categories and grammatical relations*. Chicago: University of Chicago Press.

Croft, William. 2001. *Radical construction grammar: syntactic theory in typological perspective*. Oxford: Oxford University Press.

Croft, William. 2003. *Typology and universals*, 2nd edn. Cambridge: Cambridge University Press.

Cruse, D. Alan. 1986. *Lexical semantics*. Cambridge: Cambridge University Press.

Cruse, D. A. 1990. Prototype theory and lexical semantics, in Tsohatzidis, S. L. (ed.) *Meaning and prototypes: studies in linguistic categorization*. London: Routledge, 382–402.

Cruse, D. Alan. 1992. Antonymy revisited: Some thoughts on the relationship between words and concepts, in Lehrer, A and Kittay, E. F. (eds.) *Frames, fields and contrasts: new essays in semantic and lexical organization*. Hillsdale, NJ: Erlbaum, 289–306.

Cruse, D. Alan. 1994. Prototype theory and lexical relations, *Rivista di linguistica* 6: 167–188.

Cruse, D. Alan. 2002a. Paradigmatic relations of inclusion and identity III: Synonymy, in Cruse, D. Alan, Hundsnurscher, Franz, Job, Michael, *et al.* (eds.) *Lexikologie : ein internationales Handbuch zur Natur und Struktur von Wörtern und Wortschätzen*. Berlin: Mouton, 485–497.

Cruse, D. Alan. 2002b. Paradigmatic relations of exclusion and opposition II: Reversivity, in Cruse, D. Alan, Hundsnurscher, Franz, Job, Michael, *et al.* (eds.) *Lexikologie : ein internationales Handbuch zur Natur und Struktur von Wörtern und Wortschätzen*. Berlin: Mouton, 507–510.

Cuartero Otal, Juan, 2006. How many types of motion verbs can be distinguished in Spanish? *Revista de Filologia Hispanica* 22: 13–36.

Culicover, Peter W. and Jackendoff, Ray. 2001. Control is not movement, *Linguistic Inquiry* 32: 493–512.

Culicover, Peter W. and Jackendoff, Ray. 2005. *Simpler syntax*. Oxford: Oxford University Press.

Cummins, R. 1989. *Meaning and mental representation*. Cambridge, MA: MIT.

Curme, G. O. 1935. *Parts of speech and accidence*. Boston: Heath.

Cuyckens, Hubert, Dirven, René and Taylor, John R. (eds.) 2003. *Cognitive approaches to lexical semantics*. Berlin; New York: Mouton de Gruyter.

D'Andrade, Roy. 1995. *The development of cognitive anthropology*. Cambridge: Cambridge University Press.

Dahl, Östen. 2000. The grammar of future time reference in European languages, in Dahl, Östen (ed.) *Tense and aspect in the languages of Europe*. Berlin: Mouton, 309–328.

Dahl, Östen. 2001. Languages without tense and aspect, in Elbert, Karen H. and Zúñiga, Fernando (eds.) *Aktionsart and aspectotemporality in Non-European languages*. Arbeiten des Seminars für Allgemeine Sprachwissenschaft [ASAS], 16. Zürich: Seminar für Allgemeine Sprachwissenschaft, 159–173.

Davidson, Donald. 1979. Moods and performatives, in Margalit, A. (ed.) *Meaning and use*. Dordrecht: Reidel, 9–20. Reprint in Kasher (ed.), vol. II, 69–80.

Davis, H. and Matthewson, L. 1999. On the functional determination of lexical categories, *Revue québécoise de linguistique* 27: 27–67.

Denny, J. Peter 1982. Semantics of the Inuktitut (Eskimo) spatial deictics, *International Journal of American Linguistics* 48: 359–384.

Devitt, Michael and Sterelny, Kim. 1999. *Language and reality: an introduction to the philosophy of language*, 2nd edn. Cambridge, MA: MIT.

Dewell, Robert. 1994. Over again. Image-schema transformations in semantic analysis. *Cognitive Linguistics* 5: 351–380.

Diessel, Holger. 1999. *Demonstratives. Form, function and grammaticalization*. Amsterdam: Benjamins.

Diller, Anthony. 1994. Thai, in Goddard, Cliff and Wierzbicka, Anna (eds.) *Semantic and lexical universals. Theory and empirical findings*. Amsterdam: Benjamins, 149–170.

Dixon, R. M. W. and Aikhenvald, A. Y. (eds.) 2002. *Word. A cross-linguistic typology*. Cambridge: Cambridge University Press.

Dixon, R. M. W., and Aikhenvald, Alexandra Y. (eds.) 2004. *Adjective classes: a cross-linguistic typology*. Oxford: Oxford University Press.

Donnellan K, S. (1972). Proper names and identifying descriptions, in Davidson, D. and Harman, G. (eds.) *The semantics of natural language*. Dordrecht: Reidel.

Dowty, David. 1986. The effects of aspectual class on the temporal structure of discourse: semantics or pragmatics, *Linguistics and Philosophy* 9: 37–61.

Dowty, David. 1991. Thematic proto-roles and argument selection, *Language* 67: 547–619.

Dreyfus, Hubert. 1992. *What computers still can't do*. Cambridge, MA: MIT.

Dummett, Michael. 2001. Gottlob Frege (1848–1925), in Martinich, A. P. and Sosa, David (eds.) *A companion to analytic philosophy*. Cambridge, MA: Blackwell.

Dunbar, George. 2001. Towards a cognitive analysis of polysemy, ambiguity, and vagueness, *Cognitive Linguistics* 12: 1–14.

Duranti, Alessandro. 1997. *Linguistic anthropology*. Cambridge: Cambridge University Press.

Dwyer, P. 1984. Other people's animals: two examples from New Guinea, *Search* 2: 321–327.

Egbokhare, Francis O. 2001. Phonosemantic correspondences in Emai attributive ideophones, in Voeltz and Kilian-Hatz, 87–96.

Einhorn, E. 1974. *Old French: a concise handbook*. Cambridge: Cambridge University Press.

Ellen, R. 1979. Introductory essay, in Ellen, R. F. and Reason, D. A. *Classifications in their social context*. London: Academic, 1–32.

Ellen, R. 1993. *The cultural relations of classification*. Cambridge: Cambridge University Press.

Enfield, N. J., Asifa, Majid and van Staden, Miriam. 2006. Cross-linguistic categorisation of the body: Introduction, *Language Sciences* 28: 162–180.

Evans, N. and Osada, T. 2005. Mundari: the myth of a language without word classes, *Linguistic Typology* 1: 351–390.

Evans, Nicholas. In print. Semantic Typology, in Song, Jae Jung (ed.) *The Oxford handbook of linguistic typology*. Oxford: Oxford University Press.

Evans, Nicholas and David Wilkins. 2000. In the mind's ear: the semantic extensions of perception verbs in Australian languages, *Language* 76: 546–592.

Evans, Vyvyan and Green, Melanie. 2006. *Cognitive linguistics: an introduction*. Edinburgh: Edinburgh University Press.

Fabricius-Hansen, Catherine. 2006. Tense, in Brown, K. (ed.) *Encyclopedia of language and linguistics*, vol. 12. Oxford: Elsevier, 566–573.

Fellbaum, C. 1990. English verbs as a semantic net, *International Journal of Lexicography* 3: 278–301.

Fellbaum, C. (ed.) 1998. *WordNet: an electronic lexical database*. Cambridge, MA: MIT.

Fillmore, Charles J. 1968. The case for case, in Bach, E. and Harms, R. T. (eds.) *Universals in linguistic theory*. London: Holt, Rinehart, and Winston, 1–88.

Fillmore, Charles J. 1971. Verbs of judging: an exercise in semantic description, in Fillmore, C. J. and Langendoen, D. T. *Studies in linguistic semantics*. New York: Holt, Rinehart and Winston, 272–289.

Fillmore, Charles J. 1982. Frame semantics, in Linguistic Society of Korea (ed.) *Linguistics in the morning calm*. Seoul: Hanshin, 111–137.

Fillmore, Charles J., Kay, Paul, O'Connor, Mary Catherine. 1988. Regularity and idiomaticity in grammatical constructions: the case of 'let alone', *Language* 64: 501–538.

Floyd, Rick. 2003. Completion, comas and other 'downers': Observations on the semantics of the Wanca Quechua directional suffix *–lpu*, in Cassad, Eugene H. and Palmer, Gary B. (eds.) *Cognitive linguistics and non-Indo-European languages*. Berlin: Mouton, 39–64.

Fodor, J. A. 1970. Three reasons for not deriving 'kill' from 'cause to die', *Linguistic Inquiry* 1: 429–438.

Fodor, J. A. 1983. *Modularity of mind*. Cambridge, MA: MIT.

Fodor, J. A. 1998. *Concepts. Where cognitive science went wrong*. Oxford: Clarendon.

Foley, W. A. (In print). *Typology without universals*.

Francis, E. 1998. Some semantic reasons why iconicity between lexical categories and their discourse functions isn't perfect, *Language Sciences* 20: 399–414.

Frawley, William. 1992. *Linguistic semantics*. Hillsdale, NJ: Lawrence Erlbaum.

Frege, Gottlob. 1986 [1892]. On sense and nominatum, reprinted in Martinich, A. P. (ed.) *The philosophy of language*. New York: Oxford University Press, 186–198.

Friedberg, Claudine. 1979. Socially significant plant species and their taxonomic position among the Bunaq of Central Timor, in Ellen, Roy F. and Reason, David (eds.) *Classifications in their social contexts*. London: Academic, 81–101.

Gaby, Alice R. 2006. The Thaayorre 'true man': lexicon of the human body in an Australian language, *Language Sciences* 28: 137–147.

Garman, M. 1990. *Psycholinguistics*. Cambridge: Cambridge University Press.

Geeraerts, Dirk. 1993. Vagueness's puzzles, polysemy's vagaries, *Cognitive Linguistics* 4: 223–272.

Geeraerts, Dirk. 1997. *Diachronic prototype semantics*. Oxford: Clarendon Press.

Geeraerts, Dirk. 1998. Prototypicality as a prototypical notion, *Communication and Cognition* 21: 343–355.

Gentner, Dedre and Boroditsky, Lera. 2001. Individuation, relativity, and early word learning, in Bowerman and Levinson, 215–256.

Gibbs, Raymond W, Jr. 2002. A new look at literal meaning in understanding what is said and implicated, *Journal of Pragmatics* 34: 457–486.

Girle, Roderick A. 2002. *Introduction to logic*. Auckland: Prentice Hall.

Givón, T. 1977. Definiteness and referentiality, in Greenberg, J. *et al.* (eds.) *Universals of human language*. Stanford: Stanford University Press, 291–330.

Givón, T. 1979. *On understanding grammar*. New York: Academic Press.

Givón, T. 1984, *Syntax*, vol. I. Amsterdam: Benjamins.

Glucksberg, Sam. 2004. On the automaticity of pragmatic processes: a modular proposal, in Noveck, I. and Sperber, D. (eds.) *Experimental pragmatics*. Houndmills: Palgrave, 72–93.

Goatly, A. 1997. *The language of metaphors*. London: Routledge.

Goddard, Cliff. 1996. *Pitjantjatjara/Yankunytjatjara to English dictionary*. Alice Springs: IAD Press.

Goddard, Cliff. 1998. Bad arguments against semantic primitives, *Theoretical Linguistics* 24: 129–156.

Goddard, Cliff. 2002. The search for the shared semantic core of all languages, in Goddard, Cliff and Wierzbicka, Anna (eds.) *Meaning and Universal Grammar – theory and empirical findings*, vol. 1. Amsterdam; Philadelphia: John Benjamins, 5–40.

Goldberg, Adele E. 1995. *Constructions: a construction grammar approach to argument structure*. Chicago: University of Chicago Press.

Goldberg, Adele E. 2006. *Constructions at work: the nature of generalization in language*. Oxford: Oxford University Press.

Goldberg, Adele E. and Jackendoff, Ray. 2004. The English resultative as a family of constructions, *Language* 80: 532–568.

Goodenough, W. H. 1956. Componential analysis and the study of meaning, *Language* 32: 195–216.

Goodwin, W. 1894. *Greek grammar*. London: Macmillan.

Gordon, W. Terrence. 1982. *A history of semantics*. Amsterdam: Benjamins.

Greimas, Algirdas Julien. 2002. *Sémantique structurale*, 3rd edn. Paris: Presses Universitaires de France.

Gribbin, John. 2002. *Science. A history*. London: Allen Lane.

Grice, Paul H. 1989. *Studies in the way of words*. Cambridge, MA: Harvard University Press.

Gross, D. and Miller, K. 1990. Adjectives in WordNet, *International Journal of Lexicography* 3: 265–277.

Gruber, J. S. 1965. Studies in lexical relations. PhD Dissertation, MIT.

Guerssel, M., Hale, K., Laughren, M., Levin, B. and White Eagle, J. 1985. A cross-linguistic study of transitivity alternations, in *Papers from the parasession on causatives and agentivity*. Chicago: Chicago Linguistic Society, 48–63.

Gumperz, John and Levinson, Stephen. 1996. *Rethinking linguistic relativity*. Cambridge: Cambridge University Press.

Haiman, John. 1980. Dictionaries and encyclopedias, *Lingua*, 50: 329–357.

Hale, K. L. 1971. A note on a Walpiri tradition of antonymy, in Steinberg, D. and Jakobovits, L. (eds.) *Semantics. An interdisciplinary reader in philosophy, linguistics and psychology*. Cambridge: Cambridge University Press, 472–482.

Hale, K. L. and Keyser, S. J. 1987. *A view from the middle*, Lexicon Project Working Papers 10. Cambridge, MA: Centre for Cognitive Science, MIT.

Hale, Ken L., Laughren, Mary and Simpson, Jane. 1995. Warlpiri syntax, in Jacobs, J., von Stechow, A., Sternefeld, W. and Vennemann, T. (eds.) *Syntax. Ein internationales Handbuch zeitgenössischer Forschung/An international handbook of contemporary research*. Berlin: Walter de Gruyter, 1430–1451.

Halliday, M. A. K. 1978. *Language as social semiotic*. Baltimore: University Park Press.

Halliday, M. A. K. and Hasan, Ruqaiya. 1985. *Language, context and text. Aspects of language in a social-semiotic perspective*. Waurn Ponds: Deakin University Press.

Halliday, M. A. K. and Matthiessen, C. M. I. M. 2004. *An introduction to functional grammar*, 3rd edn. London: Arnold.

Hardin, C. L. and Maffi, Luisa (eds.) 1997. *Color categories in thought and language*. Cambridge: Cambridge University Press.

Harris, Alice. 2002. The word in Georgian, in Dixon and Aikhenvald, 2002, 227–242.

Harrison, Sheldon. 1976. *Mokilese reference grammar*. Honolulu: The University Press of Hawaii.

Haser, Verena. 2005. *Metaphor, metonymy, and experientialist philosophy : challenging cognitive semantics*. Berlin: Mouton de Gruyter.

Haviland, John. 1979. Guugu-Yimidhirr, in Dixon, R. and Blake, B. (eds.) *Handbook of Australian languages*,

vol. 1. Canberra: Australian National University Press, 27–180.

Hawkes, Terence. 1983. *Structuralism and semiotics*. London: Methuen.

Heine, Bernd, Claudi, Ulrike and Hünnemeyer, Friederike. 1991. *Grammaticalization: a conceptual framework*. Chicago: University of Chicago Press.

Heine, Bernd and Kuteva, Tania. 2002. *World lexicon of grammaticalization*. Cambridge: Cambridge University Press.

Henderson, J. and Dobson, V. 1994. *Eastern and Central Arrernte to English dictionary*. Alice Springs: Institute for Aboriginal Development.

Hengeveld, Kees, Rijkhoff, Jan, and Siewierska, Anna 2004. Parts-of-speech systems and word order, *Journal of Linguistics* 40: 527–570.

Herder, J. G. 2002 [1771]. Treatise on the origin of language, in Forster, M. N. (ed.) *Herder: Philosophical writings*. Cambridge: Cambridge University Press, 65–166.

Hirst, Graeme. 1987. *Semantic interpretation and the resolution of ambiguity*. Cambridge: Cambridge University Press.

Hock, H. H. 1991. *Principles of historical linguistics*. Berlin: Mouton.

Hockett, Charles F. 1958. *A course in modern linguistics*. New York: Macmillan.

Hockett, Charles F. (ed.) 1970. *A Leonard Bloomfield anthology*. Bloomington; London: Indiana University Press.

Hopper, P. and Thompson, S. 1984. The discourse basis of lexical categories in universal grammar, *Language* 60: 703–752.

Hopper, Paul J. 1982. *Tense–Aspect: between semantics and pragmatics*. Amsterdam: Benjamins.

Hopper, Paul J. 1997. Discourse and the category 'verb' in English, *Language and Communication* 17: 93–102.

Hopper, Paul J. and Traugott, Elizabeth C. 2003. *Grammaticalization*, 2nd edn. Cambridge: Cambridge University Press.

Horn, Laurence R. 1984. Toward a new taxonomy for pragmatic inference: Q-based and R-based implicature, in Schiffrin, Deborah (ed.) *Meaning, form and use in context: Linguistic applications.* Washington DC: Georgetown University Press, 11–42.

Horn, Laurence R. 1989. *A natural history of negation.* Chicago: University of Chicago Press.

Horrocks, Geoffrey C. 1997. *Greek: a history of the language and its speakers.* London; New York: Longman.

Huddleston, Rodney. 1984. *Introduction to the grammar of English.* Cambridge: Cambridge University Press.

Huddleston, Rodney and Pullum, Geoffrey. 2002. *The Cambridge grammar of the English language.* Cambridge: Cambridge University Press.

Hudson, Richard, Rosta, Andrew, Holmes, Jasper and Gisborne, Nikolas. 1996. Synonyms and syntax, *Journal of Linguistics* 32: 439–446.

Hunn, E. 1982. The utilitarian factor in folk biological classification, *American Anthropologist* 84: 830–847.

Hurford, James R. and Heasley, Brendan. 1983. *Semantics: a coursebook.* Cambridge: Cambridge University Press.

Ibarretxe-Antuñano, Iraide. 2004. Dictomías frente a continuos en la lexicalización de los eventos del movimento, *Revista Española de Lingüística* 34: 481–510.

Iris, Madelyn Anne, Litowitz, Bonnie E. and Evens, Martha. 1988. Problems of the part-whole relation, in Evens, Martha Walton (ed.) *Relational models of the lexicon*, Cambridge: Cambridge University Press, 261–288.

Jackendoff, Ray. 1972. *Semantic interpretation in generative grammar.* Cambridge, MA: MIT.

Jackendoff, Ray. 1983. *Semantics and cognition.* Cambridge, MA: MIT.

Jackendoff, Ray. 1987. The status of thematic relations in linguistic theory, *Linguistic Inquiry* 18: 369–411.

Jackendoff, Ray. 1989. What is a concept, that a person may grasp it?, *Mind and Language* 4: 68–102.

Jackendoff, Ray. 1990. *Semantic structures.* Cambridge, MA: MIT.

Jackendoff, Ray. 1991. Parts and boundaries. *Cognition* 41: 9–45.

Jackendoff, Ray. 2002. *Foundations of language: brain, meaning, grammar, evolution.* Oxford: Oxford University Press.

Jackendoff, Ray. 2007. *Language, consciousness, culture: essays on mental structure.* Cambridge, MA: MIT.

Johnson, Mark. 1987. *The body in the mind: the bodily basis of meaning, imagination, and reason.* Chicago: University of Chicago Press.

Jones, Alex. 2001. *Australian English grammar.* Watsons Bay: Bookhouse.

Jones, S. and Jackson, H. (forthcoming). *Corpora and meaning.* London: Equinox.

Jones, Steven. 2002. *Antonymy. A corpus-based perspective.* London: Routledge.

Jung-Beeman, Mark. 2005. Bilateral brain processes for comprehending natural language, *Trends in Cognitive Sciences* 9: 512–518.

Jurafsky, D. and Martin, J.H. 2000. *Speech and language processing.* Upper Saddle River, NJ: Prentice Hall.

Kahrel, Peter and van den Berg, René (eds.) 1994. *Typological studies in negation.* Amsterdam: Benjamins.

Kamp, Hans and Reyle, Uwe. 1993. *From discourse to Logic.* Dordrecht, Kluwer.

Kant, Immanuel. 1998. *Critique of pure reason*, Guyer, Paul and Wood, Allen W. (eds and trans.). Cambridge: Cambridge University Press.

Károly, Sándor. 1972. The grammatical system of Hungarian, in Benkó, Loránd and Samu, Imre (eds.) *The Hungarian language.* The Hague: Mouton.

Kasher, Asa. 1982. Gricean inference revisited, *Philosophica* 29: 25–42. Reprinted in Kasher, 1998. Vol. IV, pp. 199–214.

Kasher, Asa (ed.) 1998. *Pragmatics. Critical concepts.* Multiple volumes. London: Routledge.

Katz, Jerrold J. and Fodor, Jerry A. 1963. The structure of a semantic theory, *Language* 39: 170–210.

Kay, Paul. 2001. The linguistics of color terms, in Smelser, Neil J. and Baltes, Paul B. *International encyclopedia of the social and behavioral sciences*, vol. IV. Amsterdam: Elsevier, 2248–2252.

Kay, Paul and Regier, Terry. 2003. Resolving the question of color naming universals, *Proceedings of the National Academy of Sciences* 100: 9085–9089.

Kay, Paul, Berlin, Brent, Maffi, Luisa and Merrifield, William. 1997. Color naming across languages, in Hardin and Maffi, 21–56.

Keenan, Elinor Ochs. 1976. The universality of conversational postulates, *Language in Society* 5: 67–80. Reprinted in Kasher, 1998. Vol. IV, 215–229.

Kemp, Alan. 1986. The Tekhne Grammatike of Dionysius Thrax. Translated into English, *Historiographica Linguistica* 13: 343–363.

Kempson, Ruth. 1977. *Semantic theory*. Cambridge: Cambridge University Press.

Khalidi, Muhammad Ali. 1995. Two concepts of concept, *Mind and Language* 10: 402–422.

Kilgarriff, Adam. 1993. Dictionary word sense distinctions: an enquiry into their nature, *Computers and the Humanities* 26: 365–387.

Kinkade, Dale. 1983. Salish evidence against the universality of 'noun' and 'verb', *Lingua* 60: 25–40.

Kiparsky, P. 1998. Partitive case and aspect, in Butt, Miriam and Geuder, Wilhelm (eds.) *The projection of arguments: lexical and compositional factors*. Stanford, CA: CSLI Publications, 275–307.

Klein, W. 1992. The present perfect puzzle, *Language* 68: 525–552.

Kluge, F. 1989. *Etymologisches Wörterbuch der deutschen Sprache*. 22nd edn. Berlin: de Gruyter.

Kneale, William and Kneale, Martha. 1962. *The development of logic*. Oxford: Clarendon.

Knowles, Murray and Moon, Rosamund. 2006. *Introducing metaphor*. London: Routledge.

Kopecka, Anna. 2006. The semantic structure of motion verbs in French: typological perspectives, in Hickmann, Maya and Robert, Stéphane (eds.) *Space in languages*. Amsterdam: Benjamins, 83–101.

Koptjevskaja-Tamm, Maria, Vanhove, Martine and Koch, Peter. 2007. Typological approaches to lexical semantics, *Linguistics Typology* 11: 159–186.

Kreitzer, A. 1997. Multiple levels of schematization: a study in the conceptualization of space, *Cognitive Linguistics* 8: 291–325.

Krifka, M. 1987. Nominal reference and temporal constitution: towards a semantics of quantity. (FNS-Bericht 17.) Tübingen: Forschungsstelle für natürliche Systeme. Universität Tübingen.

Kripke, Saul. 1980. *Naming and necessity*, rev. edn. Oxford: Blackwell.

Labov, W. 1973. The boundaries of words and their meanings, in Bailey, C. J. N. and Shuy, R. W. (eds.) *New ways of analyzing variation in English*. Washington DC: Georgetown University Press, 340–373.

Lakoff, George. 1973. Hedges: A study in meaning criteria and the logic of fuzzy concepts. *Journal of Philosophical Logic*, 1973: 458–508.

Lakoff, George. 1970. A note on vagueness and ambiguity, *Linguistic Inquiry* 1: 357–359.

Lakoff, George. 1987. *Women, fire and dangerous things: what categories reveal about the mind*. Chicago: University of Chicago Press.

Lakoff, George. 1993. The contemporary theory of metaphor, in Ortony, Andrew (ed.), *Metaphor and thought*, 2nd edn. Cambridge: Cambridge University Press, 202–251.

Lakoff, G. and Johnson, M. 1980. *Metaphors we live by*. Chicago: University of Chicago Press.

Lambrecht, Knud. 1994. *Information structure and sentence form: topic, focus, and the mental representations of discourse referents*. Cambridge: Cambridge University Press.

Landau, Sidney I. 1984. *Dictionaries. The art and craft of lexicography*. New York: Scribner's.

Langacker, Ronald. 1987. *Foundations of cognitive grammar*, vol. I. Stanford: Stanford University Press.

Larreya, P. and Rivière, C. 1999. *Grammaire explicative de l'anglais*. Harlow: Longman.

Law, Vivien. 2003. *The history of linguistics in Europe*. Cambridge: Cambridge University Press.

Lehrer, Adrienne. 1990. Prototype theory and its implications for lexical analysis, in Tsohatzidis, S. L. (ed.) *Meaning and prototypes: studies in linguistic categorization*. London: Routledge, 368–381.

Lehrer, Adrienne J. 2002. Paradigmatic relations of exclusion and opposition I: Gradable antonymy and complementarity, in Cruse, D. Alan, Hundsnurscher, Franz, Job, Michael et al. (eds.): *Lexikologie: ein internationales Handbuch zur Natur und Struktur von Wörtern und Wortschätzen*. Berlin; New York: Mouton de Gruyter, 498–507.

Levelt, W. J. M. 1989. *Speaking: from intention to articulation*. Cambridge, MA: MIT.

Levin, Beth. 1993. *English verb classes and alternations*. Chicago: University of Chicago Press.

Levin, Beth and Rappaport Hovav, Malka. 1995. *Unaccusativity: at the syntax-lexical semantics interface.* Cambridge, MA: MIT.

Levin, Beth and Rappaport Hovav, Malka. 2005. *Argument realization.* Cambridge, MA: MIT.

Levinson, S., Kita, S., Haun, D. and Rasch, B. 2002. Returning the tables: language affects spatial reasoning, *Cognition* 84. 2: 155–188.

Levinson, Stephen. 1983. *Pragmatics.* Cambridge: Cambridge University Press.

Levinson, Stephen C. 2000. *Presumptive meanings: the theory of generalized conversational implicature.* Cambridge, MA: MIT.

Levinson, Stephen C. 2001. Yélî Dnye and the theory of basic colour terms, *Journal of Linguistic Anthropology* 10: 3–55.

Levinson, Stephen C. 2003. *Space in language and cognition: explorations in cognitive diversity.* Cambridge: Cambridge University Press.

Li, Peggy and Gleitman, Lila. 2002. Turning the tables: language and spatial reasoning, *Cognition* 83: 265–294.

Liddell, H. G. and Scott, R. 1940. *Greek-English lexicon,* 9th edn. Oxford: Clarendon Press.

Lindner, Susan. 1983. *A lexico-semantic analysis of English verb particle constructions with out and up.* Indiana: Indiana University Linguistics Club.

Lounsbury, F. G. 1956. A semantic analysis of Pawnee kinship usage, *Language* 32: 158–194.

Lucy, John. 1992. *Language diversity and thought: a reformulation of the linguistic relativity hypothesis.* Cambridge: Cambridge University Press.

Lucy, John. 1997. The linguistics of color, in Hardin and Maffi (eds.), pp. 320–346.

Ludlow, Peter. 1999. Simplicity and generative linguistics, in Murasugi, K. and Stainton, R. (eds.) *Philosophy and linguistics.* Boulder: Westview Press, 191–205.

Lyons, John. 1963. *Structural semantics.* Oxford: Blackwell.

Lyons, John. 1968. *Introduction to theoretical linguistics.* Cambridge: Cambridge University Press.

Lyons, John. 1977. *Semantics,* vol. I. Cambridge: Cambridge University Press.

MacLaury, Robert E. 1991. Prototypes revisited, *Annual Review of Anthropology* 20: 55–74.

MacLaury, Robert E. 1999. Basic color terms: twenty-five years after, in Borg, Alexander (ed.) *The language of color in the Mediterranean: an anthology of linguistic and ethnographic aspects of color terms.* Stockholm: Almqvist and Wiksell, 1–37.

MacLaury, Robert E. 2002. Introducing vantage theory, *Language Sciences* 24: 493–536.

Malmqvist, Goran. 1994. Chinese linguistics, in Lepschy, Giulio (ed.) *History of linguistics, Vol. 1: the eastern traditions of linguistics.* England: Longman, 1–24.

Malt, Barbara C., Sloman, Steven A., Gennari, Silvia, Shi, Meiyi and Wang, Yuan. 1999. Knowing versus naming: similarity and the linguistic categorization of artifacts, *Journal of Memory and Language* 40: 230–262.

Manning, C. and Schütze, H. 1999. *Foundations of statistical natural language processing.* Cambridge, MA: MIT.

Marr, D. 1982. *Vision.* New York: Freeman.

Martin, Robert M. 1987. *The meaning of language.* Cambridge, MA: MIT.

Martínez, Ignacio M, Palacios. 2003. Multiple negation in modern English. A preliminary corpus-based study, *Neuphilologische Mitteilungen* 104: 477–498.

Mates, B. 1952 [1950]. Synonymity. Reprint in Linsky, Leonard (ed.) *Semantics and philosophy of language.* Urbana: University of Illinois Press, 111–138.

Matlock, Teenie, Ramscar, Michael and Boroditsky, Lera. 2005. On the experiential link between spatial and temporal language, *Cognitive Science* 29: 655–664.

Matoré, G. 1968. *Histoire des dictionnaires français.* Paris: Larousse.

McCawley, James D. 1981. *Everything that linguists have always wanted to know about logic but were ashamed to ask.* Oxford: Blackwell.

Medin, Douglas L. and Atran, Scott. 1999. *Folkbiology.* Cambridge, MA: MIT.

Mervis, C. B. and Rosch, E. 1981. Categorization of natural objects, *Annual Review of Psychology* 32: 89–115.

Meschonic, Henri. 1991. *Des mots et des mondes: dictionnaires, encyclopédies, grammaires, nomenclatures.* Paris: Hatier.

Mey, Jacob L. and Talbot, Mary. 1988. Computation and the soul, *Journal of Pragmatics* 12: 743–789.

Mey, Jacob L. 1988. Computation and the soul, *Semiotica* 72: 291–339.

Mey, Jacob L. 2001. *Pragmatics: an introduction*, 2nd ed. rev. Malden, MA: Blackwell.

Mey, Jacob L. 2002. Polysemy and pragmatics : a pragmatic view on the indeterminacy of meaning, *Revue de sémantique et pragmatique* 12: 111–128.

Meyer, Michel. 1982. *Logique, langage, argumentation*. Paris: Classiques Hachette.

Michael, I. 1970. *English grammatical categories and the tradition to 1800*. Cambridge: Cambridge University Press.

Miller, G. 1990. Nouns in WordNet: a lexical inheritance system, *International Journal of Lexicography* 3: 245–264.

Miller, G. 1998. Foreword, in Fellbaum (ed.), xv–xxii.

Miller, G., Beckwith, R., Fellbaum, C., Gross, D., Miller, K. 1990. Introduction to WordNet: an online lexical database, *International Journal of Lexicography* 3: 235–244.

Mithun, M. 1984. The evolution of noun incorporation, *Language* 60: 847–894.

Morel, Mary-Annick and Laurent Danon-Boileau (1992). *La deixis*. Paris: PUF.

Munro, Pamela. 2006. From parts of speech to the grammar, *Studies in Language* 30: 307–349.

Murphy, G. 2002. *The big book of concepts*. Cambridge, MA: MIT.

Murphy, M. Lynne. 2003. *Semantic relations and the lexicon. Antonymy, synonymy and other paradigms*. Cambridge: Cambridge University Press.

Muysken, P. and Veenstra, T. 1995. Serial verbs, in Arends, P., Muysken, P., and Smith, N. (eds.) *Pidgins and creoles*. Amsterdam: John Benjamins, 289–302.

Nash, David. 1986. *Topics in Warlpiri grammar*. New York: Garland Publishing.

Nerlich, Brigitte and Clarke, David. 1992. Outline for a model of semantic change, in Kellermann, G. and Morrissey, M. (eds.) *Diachrony within synchrony: language history and cognition*, Duisburger Arbeiten zur Sprach- und Kulturwissenchaft 14. Frankfurt: Peter Lang, 125–141.

Nerlich, Brigitte, Todd, Zazie, Herman, Vimala and Clarke, David D. (eds.) 2003. *Polysemy: flexible patterns of meaning in mind and language*. Berlin: Mouton de Gruyter.

Newmeyer, F. 2002. Optimality and functionality: a critique of functionally-based optimality-theoretic syntax, *Natural Language and Linguistic Theory* 20: 42–80.

Nordlinger, Rachel and Sadler, Louise. 2004. Nominal tense in cross-linguistic perspective, *Language* 80: 776–806.

Noveck, Ira A. and Sperber, Dan (eds.) 2004. *Experimental pragmatics*. Houndmills: Palgrave.

Nyckees, V. 1998. *La sémantique*. Paris: Belin.

Ogden, C. and Richards, I. 1949. *The meaning of meaning*, 2nd edn. London: Routledge and Kegan Paul.

Olawsky, Knut. 2002. What is a word in Dagbani? in Dixon and Aikhenvald, 205–226.

Papafragou, A., Massey, C. and Gleitman, L. 2002. Shake, rattle, 'n' roll: the representation of motion in language and cognition, *Cognition* 84: 189–219.

Parkinson, G. (ed.) 1973. *Leibniz: philosophical writings*. London: Dent.

Partington, A. 2004. 'Utterly content in each other's company': semantic prosody and semantic preference, *International Journal of Corpus Linguistics* 9: 131–156.

Payne, D. L. 2006. Color terms, in Brown, K. (ed.) *Encyclopedia of language and linguistics*, vol. 20. Oxford: Elsevier, 605–610.

Pederson, Eric, Danziger, Eve, Wilkins, David, Levinson, Stephen, Kita, Sotaro and Senft, Gunter. 1998. Semantic typology and spatial configuration, *Language* 74: 557–589.

Peirsman, Yves and Geeraerts, Dirk, 2006. Metonymy as a prototypical category, *Cognitive Linguistics* 17: 269–316.

Posner, Rebecca. 1996. *The Romance languages*. Cambridge: Cambridge University Press.

Pottier, B. 1964. Vers une sémantique moderne, *Travaux de linguistique et de litterature* 2: 107–137.

Pottier, B. 1965. La définition sémantique dans les dictionnaires, *Travaux de linguistique et de litterature* 3: 33–39.

Prinz, Jesse. 2002. *Furnishing the mind: concepts and their perceptual basis*. Cambridge, MA: MIT.

Pulman, S. 1983. *Word meaning and belief*. London: Croom Helm.

Pustejovsky, James. 1991. The generative lexicon, *Computational Linguistics* 17: 409–441.

Pustejovsky, James. 1995. *The generative lexicon*. Cambridge, MA: MIT Press.

Pustejovsky, James and Boguraev, Branimir. 1994. A richer characterization of dictionary entries: the role of knowledge representation, in Atkins, B. T. S. and Zampolli, A. (eds.) *Computational approaches to the lexicon*. Oxford: Oxford University Press, 295–311.

Quine, W. V. O. 1960. *Word and object*. Cambridge, MA: MIT.

Quine, W. V. O. 1961. *From a logical point of view*, 2nd edn. Cambridge, MA: Harvard University Press.

Radford, Andrew. 1988. *Transformational grammar: a first course*. Cambridge: Cambridge University Press.

Radford, Andrew. 2004. *English syntax: an introduction*. Cambridge: Cambridge University Press.

Rakova, Marina. 2003. *The extent of the literal: metaphor, polysemy, and theories of concepts*. Houndmills: Palgrave.

Rankin, Robert, Boyle, J., Graczyk, R., and Koontz, J. 2002. Synchronic and diachronic perspective on 'word' in Siouan, in Dixon and Aikhenvald (eds.) 180–204.

Rappaport, M. and Levin, Beth. 1988. What to do with theta-roles, in Wilkins, W. (ed) *Thematic relations*. San Diego: Academic Press, 7–36.

Rastier, François. 1987. *Sémantique interprétative*. Paris: Presses Universitaires de France.

Ravin, Yael and Leacock, Claudia (eds.) 2002. *Polysemy: theoretical and computational approaches*. Oxford: Oxford University Press.

Recanati, François. 1987. Introduction, in *Meaning and force*. Cambridge: Cambridge University Press, 1–20. Reprinted in Kasher, 1998, 126–143.

Reddy, Michael. 1993. The conduit metaphor: A case of frame conflict in our language about language, in Ortony, Andrew (ed.) *Metaphor and thought*, 2nd edn. Cambridge: Cambridge University Press, 284–324.

Reichenbach, H. 1947. *Elements of symbolic logic*. New York: Free Press.

Resnik, P. 1998. Wordnet and class-based probabilities. In Fellbaum, C. (ed.), 239–264.

Rey, Alain. 1990. Polysémie du terme *définition*, in Chaurand and Mazière (eds.), 13–22.

Rey, Alain. (ed.) 1998. *Le Robert. Dictionnaire historique de la langue française*, vol. II. Paris: Le Robert.

Rey, Alain. (ed.) 2000. *Dictionnaire historique de la langue française*, 3rd edn. Paris: Dictionnaires Le Robert.

Ricœur, P. 1975. *La métaphore vive*. Paris: Seuil.

Riegel, M. 1990. La Définition, acte du langage ordinaire. De la forme aux interprétations, in Chaurand, J. and Mazière, F. (eds.), 97–109.

Riemer, N. 2005. *The semantics of polysemy. Reading meaning in English and Warlpiri*. Berlin: Mouton.

Riemer, N. 2006. Reductive paraphrase and meaning. A critique of Wierzbickian semantics, *Linguistics and Philosophy* 29: 347–379.

Robinson, Richard. 1950. *Definition*. Oxford: Clarendon Press.

Romero-Figeroa, Andrés. 1997. *A reference grammar of Warao*. München: Lincom Europa.

Rosaldo, Michelle Z. 1980. *Knowledge and passion. Ilongot notions of self and social life*. Cambridge: Cambridge University Press.

Rosch, E. 1975. Cognitive representations of semantic categories, *Journal of Experimental Psychology: General* 104: 192–233.

Rosch, E. 1978. Principles of categorization, in Rosch, E., and Lloyd, B. (eds.) *Cognition and categorization*. Hillsdale: Erlbaum, 27–48.

Rosch, E. and Mervis, C. 1975. Family resemblances: studies in the internal structure of Categories, *Cognitive Psychology* 7: 573–605.

Ross, B. H., and Makin, V. S. 1999. Prototype versus exemplar models, in Sternberg, R. J. (ed.) *The nature of cognition*. Cambridge, Mass: MIT Press, 205–241.

Rothstein, Susan. 2006. Predication, in Brown, Keith (ed.) *Encyclopedia of language and linguistics*, 2nd edn, vol. 10. Oxford: Elsevier, 73–76.

Rubino, Carl. 2001. Iconic morphology and word formation in Ilocano, in Voeltz and Kilian-Hatz, 303–320.

Ruhl, Charles. 1989. *On monosemy. A study in linguistic semantics*. Albany: SUNY.

Rumsey, Alan. 1990. Wording, meaning and linguistic ideology, *American Anthropologist* 92: 33–361.

Russell, Bertrand. 1905. On denoting, *Mind* 14: 479–493.

Russell, Bertrand. 1949. *Mysticism and logic and other essays*. London: George Allen and Unwin.

Ruyer, Bernard. 1998. *Logique*, 3rd edn. Paris: Presses Universitaires de France.

Saussure, Ferdinand de. 1967. *Cours de linguistique générale*. Engler, Rudolf (ed.). Wiesbaden: Otto Harrassowitz.

Saussure, Ferdinand de. 1983. *Course in general linguistics*. London: Duckworth.

Schaefer, Ronald P. 2001. Ideophonic adverbs and manner gaps in Emai, in Voeltz and Kilian-Hatz, 339–354.

Schiffer, Stephen. 1987. *Remnants of meaning*. Cambridge, MA: MIT.

Schütze, Hinrich. 1997. *Ambiguity resolution in language learning: computational and cognitive models*. Stanford, CA: CSLI Publications.

Schwager, Waldemar and Zeshan, Ulrike. n.d. Word classes in sign languages: criteria and classifications. Unpublished MS.

Searle, J. 1969. *Speech acts: an essay in the philosophy of language*. London: Cambridge University Press.

Searle, J. 1980. Minds, brains, and programs, *Behavioral and Brain Sciences* 3: 417–457.

Searle, J. 1993 [1979]. Metaphor, in Ortony, A. (ed.) *Metaphor and thought*. 2nd edn. Oxford: Oxford University Press, 83–111.

Sebeok, Thomas. 1994. *An introduction to semiotics*. London: Pinter.

Segre, C. (ed.). 1989. *La chanson de Roland*. Vol. I. Tyssens, M. (trans.). Genève: Droz.

Seuren, P. 2009. *Language in cognition*. Oxford: Oxford University Press.

Skinner, Burrhus Frederic. 1957. *Verbal behavior*. New York: Appleton-Century-Crofts.

Slobin, Dan I. 1996. From 'thought and language' to thinking for speaking, in Gumperz and Levinson, 70–96.

Slobin, Dan I. 2001. Form-function relations: how do children find out what they are? in Bowerman and Levinson, 406–449.

Slobin, Dan I. 2004. How people move: discourse effects of linguistic typology, in Moder, Carol L. and Martinovic-Zic, Aida (eds.) *Discourse across languages and cultures*. Amsterdam: Benjamins, 195–210.

Slobin, Dan I. 2006. What makes manner of motion salient?: Explorations in linguistic typology, discourse, and cognition, in Hickmann, Maya and Robert, Stéphane (eds.) *Space in languages*. Amsterdam: Benjamins, 59–81.

Smith, Carlota. 1997. *The parameter of aspect*, 2nd edn. Dordrecht: Kluwer.

Sperber, Dan and Noveck, Ira. 2004. Introduction, in Noveck, I. and Sperber, D. (eds.) *Experimental pragmatics*. Houndmills: Palgrave, 1–22.

Sperber, Dan and Wilson, Deirdre. 1987. Précis of *Relevance. Communication and Cognition, Behavioral and Brain Sciences* 10: 697–754.

Sperber, Dan and Wilson, Deirdre. 1995. *Relevance. Communication and cognition*. 2nd edn. Oxford: Blackwell.

Sperber, Dan and Wilson, Deirdre. 2002. Pragmatics, modularity and mind reading, *Mind and Language* 17: 3–23.

Storms, Gert, De Boeck, Paul, and Ruts, Wim. 2000. Prototype and exemplar-based information in natural language categories, *Journal of Memory and Language* 42: 51–73.

Strawson, P. F. 1971. Intention and convention in speech acts, *Logico-linguistic papers*. London, Methuen, 149–169.

Strawson, P. F. 1960. *Introduction to logical theory*. London: Methuen.

Strawson, P. F. 1950. On referring, *Mind* 59: 320–344.

Stubbs, Michael. 2001. *Words and phrases: corpus studies of lexical semantics*. Oxford: Blackwell.

Sweetser, Eve. 1990. *From etymology to pragmatics: metaphorical and cultural aspects of semantic change*. Cambridge: Cambridge University Press.

Talmy, Leonard. 1985. Lexicalization patterns: semantic structure in lexical forms, in Shopen, Timothy (ed.) *Language typology and syntactic description. Volume*

III. Grammatical categories and the lexicon. Cambridge: Cambridge University Press, 57–149.

Taylor, John. 2002. *Cognitive grammar.* Oxford: Oxford University Press.

Taylor, John. 2003. *Linguistic categorization*, 3rd edn. Oxford: Oxford University Press.

Ter Meulen, A. 1995. *Representing time in natural language: the dynamic interpretation of tense and aspect.* Cambridge, MA: MIT Press.

Terrill, Angela. 2006. Body part terms in Lavukaleve, a Papuan language of the Solomon Islands, *Language Sciences* 28: 304–322.

Thelin, Nils B. (ed.) 1990. *Verbal aspect in discourse.* Amsterdam: Benjamins.

Traugott, Elizabeth C. 1987. Literacy and language change: the special case of speech act verbs, in Langer, Judith (ed.) *Language, literacy, and culture: issues of society and schooling.* Norwood, NJ: Ablex, 11–27.

Traugott, Elizabeth C. 1989. On the rise of epistemic meanings in English: an example of subjectification in semantic change, *Language* 57: 33–65.

Traugott, Elizabeth C. and Dasher, Richard B. 2002. *Regularity in semantic change.* Cambridge: Cambridge University Press.

Tredennick, Hugh. 1960. *Posterior analytics/Aristotle.* Cambridge, MA: Harvard University Press.

Tryon, Darrell T. (ed.) 1995. *Comparative Austronesian dictionary: an introduction to Austronesian studies.* Berlin: Mouton de Gruyter.

Tsohatzidis, Savas L. 1994. *Foundations of speech act theory. Philosophical and linguistic perspectives.* London: Routledge.

Tuggy, David. 1993. Ambiguity, polysemy, and vagueness, *Cognitive Linguistics* 4: 273–290.

Tyler, Andrea and Evans, Vyvyan. 2001. Reconsidering prepositional polysemy networks: the case of *over, Language* 77: 724–765.

Ullmann, Stephen. 1972. *Semantics: an introduction to the science of meaning.* Oxford: Blackwell.

Valiquette, H. (ed.) 1993. *A basic Kukatja to English dictionary.* Wirrimanu (Balgo): Luurnpa Catholic School.

Van der Henst, Jean-Baptiste and Sperber, Dan. 2004. Testing the cognitive and communicative principles of relevance, in Noveck, I. and Sperber, D. (eds.) *Experimental pragmatics*, Houndmills: Palgrave, 141–171.

Van Staden, Miriam. 2006. The body and its parts in Tidore: a Papuan language of Eastern Indonesia, *Language Sciences* 28: 323–343.

Van Valin, Robert D. 2005. *Exploring the syntax-semantics interface.* New York: Cambridge University Press.

Van Wyk, E. B. 1967. Northern Sotho, *Lingua*, 17: 230–261.

Vandeloise, Claude. 1990. Representation, prototypes and centrality, in Tsohatzidis, S. (ed.) *Meanings and prototypes.* London: Routledge, 403–437.

Vandeloise, Claude. 2003. Containment, support, and linguistic relativity, in Cuyckens, Dirven and Taylor, 393–426.

Vanhove, Martine. 2008. Semantic associations between sensory modalities, prehension and mental perceptions: A cross-linguistic perspective, in Vanhove, M. (ed) *Towards a typology of semantic associations.* Berlin: Mouton de Gruyter, 341–370.

Vendler, Zeno. 1957. Verbs and times, *Philosophical Review* 66: 143–160.

Vendler, Zeno. 1967. *Linguistics in philosophy.* Ithaca; NY: Cornell University Press.

Verschueren, Jef. 1999. *Understanding pragmatics.* London: Arnold.

Viberg, Ake. 1984. The verbs of perception: a typological study, in Butterworth, B., Comrie, B. and Dahl, Ö. (eds.) *Explanations for language universals.* Berlin: Mouton de Gruyter, 123–162.

Voeltz, Erhard and Kilian-Hatz, Christa (eds.) 2001. *Ideophones.* Amsterdam: John Benjamins.

Whorf, Benjamin Lee. 1956. *Language, thought and reality: selected writings of Benjamin Lee Whorf.* Carroll, John B. (ed.) Cambridge, MA: MIT.

Wierzbicka, Anna. 1984. Apples are not a kind of fruit: the semantics of human categorization, *American Ethnologist* 11: 287–313.

Wierzbicka, Anna. 1988. *The semantics of grammar.* Amsterdam: Benjamins.

Wierzbicka, Anna. 1990. 'Prototypes save': On the uses and abuses of the notion of 'prototype' in linguistics and related fields, in Tsohatzidis, Savas L. (ed.), *Meanings and prototypes: studies in linguistic categorization*. London: Routledge & Kegan Paul, 347–367.

Wierzbicka, Anna. 1994. Semantic primitives across languages: A critical review, in Goddard, Cliff and Wierzbicka, Anna (eds.) *Semantic and lexical universals: theory and empirical findings*. Amsterdam: John Benjamins, 445–500.

Wierzbicka, Anna. 1996. *Semantics. Primes and universals*. Oxford: Oxford University Press.

Wilkins, D. 1996. Natural tendencies of semantic change and the search for cognates, in Durie, Mark and Ross, Malcolms (eds.) *The comparative method reviewed: regularity and irregularity in language change*. New York: Oxford University Press, 264–304.

Wilkins, D. and Hills, D. 1995. When 'go' means come: questioning the basicness of basic motion verbs, *Cognitive Linguistics* 6: 209–259.

Wilks, Yorick A., Slator, Brian M. and Guthrie, Louise M. 1996. *Electric words : dictionaries, computers, and meanings*. Cambridge, MA: MIT.

Williams, J. 1976. Synaesthetic adjectives: a possible law of semantic change, *Language* 52: 461–478.

Winston, Morton E., Chaffin, Roger and Herrmann, Douglas. 1987. A taxonomy of part-whole relations, *Cognitive Science* 11: 417–444.

Winters, Margaret E. 2002. Vantage theory and diachronic semantics, *Language Sciences* 24: 625–637.

Witkowski, Stanley R. and Brown, Cecil H. 1985. Climate, clothing and body-part nomenclature, *Ethnology* 24: 197–214.

Wittgenstein, Ludwig. 1953. *Philosophical investigations*. Oxford: Blackwell.

Woodbury, Anthony. 2002. The word in Cup'ik, in Dixon and Aikhenvald, 79–99.

Zwicky, Arnold and Sadock, Jerry. 1975. Ambiguity tests and how to fail them, in Kimball, John (ed.) *Syntax and semantics* 4. New York: Academic Press, 1–36.

Index